Springer

Berlin
Heidelberg
New York
Barcelona
Budapest
Hong Kong
London
Milan
Paris
Santa Clara
Singapore
Tokyo

Lecture Notes in Computer Science 1223

Edited by G. Goos, J. Hartmanis and J. van Leeuwen

Advisory Board: W. Brauer   D. Gries   J. Stoer

Marcello Pelillo   Edwin R. Hancock (Eds.)

Energy Minimization Methods in Computer Vision and Pattern Recognition

International Workshop EMMCVPR'97
Venice, Italy, May 21-23, 1997
Proceedings

 Springer

Series Editors

Gerhard Goos, Karlsruhe University, Germany

Juris Hartmanis, Cornell University, NY, USA

Jan van Leeuwen, Utrecht University, The Netherlands

Volume Editors

Marcello Pelillo
Università "Cá Foscari" di Venezia
Dipartimento di Matematica Applicata e Informatica
Via Torino 155, I-30173 Venezia Mestre, Italy
E-mail: pellilo@dsi.unive.it

Edwin R. Hancock
University of York, Department of Computer Science
Heslington, York YO1 5DD, UK
E-mail: erh@minster.york.ac.uk

Cataloging-in-Publication data applied for

Die Deutsche Bibliothek - CIP-Einheitsaufnahme

Energy minimization methods in computer vision and pattern recognition : international workshop ; proceedings / EMMCVPR '97, Venice, Italy, May 21 - 23, 1997. Marcello Pelillo ; Edwin R. Hancock (ed.). - Berlin ; Heidelberg ; New York ; Barcelona ; Budapest ; Hong Kong ; London ; Milan ; Paris ; Santa Clara ; Singapore ; Tokyo : Springer, 1997
    (Lecture notes in computer science ; Vol. 1223)
    ISBN 3-540-62909-2 brosch.

CR Subject Classification (1991): I.5, I.2.10, I.3.5, F.2.2, F.1.1

ISSN 0302-9743
ISBN 3-540-62909-2 Springer-Verlag Berlin Heidelberg New York

© Springer-Verlag Berlin Heidelberg 1997
Printed in Germany

Typesetting: Camera-ready by author
SPIN 10549585   06/3142 – 5 4 3 2 1 0   Printed on acid-free paper

Preface

Energy minimization methods represent a fundamental methodology in computer vision and pattern recognition, with roots in such diverse disciplines as physics, psychology, and statistics. Recent manifestations of the idea include Markov random fields, deformable models and templates, relaxation labelling, various types of neural networks, etc. These techniques are now finding application in almost every area of computer vision from early to high-level processing. Although the subject is well represented in major international conferences in the fields of computer vision, pattern recognition, and neural networks, there has been no attempt to organize a specialized meeting on energy minimization methods. Collected in this volume are the papers presented at the International Workshop on Energy Minimization Methods in Computer Vision and Pattern Recognition (EMMCVPR'97) held at the University of Venice, Italy, from May 21-23, 1997. Our primary motivation in organizing this workshop was to offer researchers the chance to report their work in a forum that allowed for both consolidation of efforts and intensive informal discussion.

The idea of holding this meeting was originally conceived in York during the summer of 1995. Early in 1996 we issued a call for papers. This resulted in 62 submissions from 19 countries. Each paper was reviewed by three committee members who were asked to comment on the technical quality of the submissions and provide suggestions for possible improvement. In December 1996 we met in Venice to make the selection of papers for the workshop program. Based on the comments of the reviewers as well as on time and space constraints we selected 18 papers for oral presentation and 11 papers to be delivered as posters. We make no distinction between these two types of papers in this book.

An important aspect of this workshop are the keynote and invited talks. The keynote paper which opened the workshop was given by Shimon Ullman whose ideas have exerted a great influence over this subject for almost twenty years. The four invited speakers, Josef Kittler, Anil Jain, Alan Yuille, and Steve Zucker, have all played pivotal roles in the development of key areas in the field.

Finally, we must offer thanks to those who have helped us in bringing reality to the idea of holding this workshop. Firstly, we thank the program committee for reviewing the papers and providing insightful comments to their authors. We also gratefully acknowledge the work of Laure Blanc-Feraud and Mario Figueiredo who provided additional reviews. Although the workshop was intended to be small we hope that this book will reach a larger audience. In this respect we are extremely grateful to Alfred Hofmann at Springer who responded positively to our proposal to publish this volume in the Lecture Notes in Computer Science series. At York most of the hard work of assembling the proceedings volume has been very professionally executed by Philip Worthington. Last, but by no means least, we thank the various organizations who have provided support for this workshop. The International Association for Pattern Recognition provided us with publicity. The University of Venice "Cá Foscari" provided us with a wonderful lecture hall in the "Cá Dolfin" building, right in the historical centre of Venice. The Department of Applied Mathematics and Computer Science of the University of Venice and the SAF s.r.l. company provided administrative support.

In closing, one of us (MP) would like to heartily thank his wife, Rosanna, not only for the invaluable contribution and help given during the various stages of the workshop organization, but also for providing the inspiration to conceive this event.

February 1997   Marcello Pelillo and Edwin Hancock

Program Co-Chairs

Marcello Pelillo   *University of Venice, Italy*
Edwin R. Hancock   *University of York, UK*

Program Committee

Davi Geiger   *New York University, USA*
Anil K. Jain   *Michigan State University, USA*
Josef Kittler   *University of Surrey, UK*
Stan Z. Li   *Nanyang Technological University, Singapore*
Jean-Michel Morel   *University of Paris Dauphine, France*
Maria Petrou   *University of Surrey, UK*
Anand Rangarajan   *Yale University, USA*
Sergio Solimini   *Polytechnic of Bari, Italy*
Alan L. Yuille   *Smith-Kettlewell Eye Research Institute, USA*
Josiane Zerubia   *INRIA, France*
Steven W. Zucker   *Yale University, USA*

Contents

Contours and Deformable Models

Markov Random Fields

Deterministic Methods

Object Recognition

Applications

Contours and
Deformable Models

Reliable Computation and Related Games

Douglas A. Miller* and Steven W. Zucker**

Center for Computational Vision and Control
Yale University
P. O. Box 208285, New Haven, CT U.S.A.
zucker-steven@cs.yale.edu

Abstract. We describe a theory of line and edge detection in layers 2/3 of primary visual cortex. Our analysis shows that, although pyramidal cells can be individually unreliable as processing units, they can nevertheless be extremely reliable as moderate-sized groups. We base our analysis on a dynamic analog model of computation in which the primary visual cortex stores visual contour information in the form of a very large number of small tightly interconnected groups or *cliques* of (excitatory S-type pyramidal) cells.

1 Introduction

Consider a region of our visual field innervating a patch of primary visual cortex a few mm on a side, containing, say, 10^6 mostly mutually excitatory neurons. Does it make sense to talk about this small patch of cortex as a basic unit of our visual system, and, if so, how crude is it? For example, how many distinct lines could *just this one patch of cortex* reliably represent? We suggest that knowing whether the biggest possible number is 10, 10^4 or 10^7 is critical to the understanding of our visual system, because to determine this number we must address how this unit of cortex is functioning. Thus our main goal in this paper is to develop a model of computation sufficiently biological to apply to this patch of cortex, but which can also be viewed as an abstract model of computational vision which can represent lines. To reduce this goal to manageable proportions, we focus on the representation of orientation for short line segments.

Our analysis supports several calculations. First, by developing the model mathematically, we are able to analyze its limits. Just as numerical analysis deals with the precision of computations as a function of the number of bits used in representing numbers, we analyze how orientation acuity is limited by the number of neurons and synaptic connections available. For line orientation

---

* Douglas A. Miller, formerly of the Center for Intelligent Machines, McGill University, Montreal, Canada, passed away in 1994. This article is excerpted from "A Model of Hyperacuity-scale Computation in Visual Cortex by Self-excitatory Cliques of Pyramidal Cells", TR-CIM-93-12, August 1993. Portions were also presented at the Workshop on Computational Neuroscience, Marine Biological Laboratories, Woods Hole, MA, in August, 1993.

** Research supported by AFOSR, NSERC, and Yale University.

this limit is *hyperacuity* (Westheimer 1990), and in Miller and Zucker (1993) we show that this limit agrees with cortical cell counts. However, the computational process of the visual system must not only be accurate, but must be reliable, even though individual neurons are not, and capable of an efficient use of the cortex (cf. Barlow 1983). The second major result, and that on which we shall concentrate in this article, is to describe an explicit network architecture and mode of computation in primary visual cortex which would achieve this reliability and efficiency. Thirdly, we can show that, by modeling the current-spike relations of a system of cortical cells as an *analog* dynamical system, each cortical computation can take place within about 25 msec, which is the kind of time scale which would be required for an early stage of visual processing, given that *total* processing can occur within 200 msec (inter-saccade interval in reading) or even 80 msec (cf. Miller et al. 1993).

Any consistent theory of primary visual cortex must account for the following phenomena (references in Miller and Zucker, 1993):

1. Most connections are local and between spiny excitatory cells (Douglas and Martin 1990).
2. Most, if not all, direct afferents from the lateral geniculate nucleus (LGN) are excitatory. (Bishop et al. 1973, Ferster and Lindström 1983, Douglas and Martin 1992).
3. Inhibition is much less specific than excitation, both temporally and spatially, and is additive, not multiplicative (Bishop et al. 1973, Douglas et al. 1988, Berman et al. 1991).
4. Most, if not all, connections in visual cortex undergoing long-term potentiation and depression ("Hebbian learning") are between spiny excitatory cells (Artola et al. 1990, Douglas and Martin 1990).
5. Most postsynaptic targets of layer 2/3 pyramidal cells are other layer 2/3 pyramidal cells (McGuire et al. 1991, Kisvarday et al. 1986).
6. Intrinsic horizontal connections among layer 2/3 pyramidal cells connect cells with about the same orientation specificity, even though they may be in different iso-orientation areas separated by several mm (Rockland and Lund 1982, 1983; Rockland et al. 1982; Gilbert and Wiesel 1983, 1989; Callaway and Katz 1990).
7. Most excitatory cortical cells exhibit a typical "regular spiking" behavior (McCormick et al. 1985, Agmon and Conners 1989, Douglas and Martin 1990), which adapts within a 25 msec period from an initial high spiking rate (e.g. 300 Hz) to a much lower sustained rate.
8. Most cortical neurons are orientation selective, but crudely (± 7.5 deg in monkeys before significant falloff; see discussion, Section 2.5). Also, even the smallest receptive fields are ≥ 12 arc min^2 on average in monkeys and humans (Hubel and Wiesel 1968, Wilson et al. 1990), in comparison to widths of about 1 arc min for the contours typically used in demonstrations of hyperacuity.
9. Whereas orientation sensitivity is crude, spatio-temporal precision in response to *moving edges* is high for cortical cells S cells, which are found

in abundance in layers 2/3 in both cats and monkeys (Bishop et al. 1971, 1972, 1973; Schiller et al. 1976a,b,c; Henry 1977).

Viewed simply as biological constraints imposed on a model of vision, these characteristics of cortical cells may seem at best unrelated and at worst bizarre and useless. However if we combine these "constraints" with the idea of trying to store enough information in the form of subsets of cortical neurons to account for hyperacuity-scale visual abilities, and doing so in a fast, reliable fashion with components (neurons) which are inherently *unreliable*, [3] then our analysis implies that each of the above features becomes a critical asset. Indeed, in constructing the primary visual cortex as it has, nature appears to have provided exactly the right tools for accurately and reliably representing lines and edges.

2 Cortical Cliques

A major aspect of our model is that it raises the question of how to view a patch of cortical tissue as a computational device. Are individual neurons the natural basis for expressing visual computations, or are visual computations most naturally expressed at the circuit level? In fact we derive the surprising result that a circuit structure can take processing elements (neurons) which by themselves are both extremely crude and highly unreliable, and create aggregate units which are *both* extremely precise and highly reliable. This result is in important contrast to previous attempts to construct reliable systems from unreliable discrete components such as relays (Moore and Shannon 1956), where highly redundant recursive systems were employed. In our parallel analog model of computation the extra number of processors needed to achieve reliability *at the same time* increases the information content of the system (cf. Winograd and Cowan 1963, Wilson and Cowan 1973, Barlow 1983). In the context of the visual cortex this "information" provides an analytical basis for understanding why it can be possible to train humans to exhibit orientation hyperacuity (Westheimer and McKee 1977; Westheimer 1982, 1990). The model also has major implications for development and learning (cf. discussion, Section 4).

The key ideas behind this system model and the corresponding mode of computation, are, first, the idea of groups of tightly interconnected excitatory neurons capable of bringing themselves to saturation feedback response following a modest initial afferent current, rather like a match igniting a conflagration, to borrow a simile from Douglas and Martin (1992). We call these groups *cliques*. [4] Secondly these cliques of neurons, although there may be an extremely large

---

[3] For example, in comparison to digital VLSI components. Also, neuronal unreliability, in the sense used here, refers to any imperfect functioning of the cell, whether due to intrinsic behavior or corrupted lower-level input.

[4] *Clique* in directed graph theory refers to a subset of nodes (neurons, in this case) which is completely interconnected, that is, having an arc (synapse) from each node to each other node. We note that such a perfect arrangement is unlikely in biology, and indeed subsets of neurons which are merely interconnected to a sufficiently high

number of them, are themselves relatively small, consisting of perhaps a few dozen excitatory S cells. On the other hand an individual S cell may simultaneously belong to hundreds of different cliques, and therein lies the system's ability to reliably store and retrieve large quantities of information with highly unreliable processing elements.

3 The Model

Our cortical computational model supposes that we start from a stable reference state in which all or most neurons are quiescent, and then activate a relatively small number of them. Thus our model stores states as highly interconnected self-excitatory cliques of neurons (represented by voltage amplifiers), where activation of some proportion greater than half of the clique members beyond a certain moderate level fully activates the entire clique. There are two phases to this procedure, corresponding to two computations by the network. In the first phase, each amplifier receiving input has its capacitive voltage (membrane potential) raised to some moderate level by a fixed bias or brief pulse current. Those amplifiers undergoing self-excitatory feedback then drive to their saturation values. In the second phase, the input currents are removed and all amplifier responses not undergoing feedback excitation decay out. [5]

This two-phase computational model becomes relevant to the visual cortex by considering a 25 msec computational time frame, and the phenomenon of regular adaptive spiking to constant input current (McCormick et al. 1985, Agmon and Conners 1989, Douglas and Martin 1990), which can be understood in terms of cell membrane properties (e.g. McCormick 1990). Thus a moderately stimulated cell would be likely to produce no more than a single spike in a 25 msec interval (responses for .3 to .6 nA), but one that is fully excited (1.5 nA) could produce about five (cf. also McCormick et al. 1985, Fig. 1).

We presume that under either direct or indirect afferent stimulation from the LGN there is sufficient input current arriving at a given target cell to produce a single spike. For members of a clique this will produce a large number of additional excitatory post-synaptic potentials within a few msec, thus producing more spikes in these same cells, and any others in the clique, and bringing current input to these cells to saturation levels. This chain of events will happen if and only if the initial proportion of activated clique members is sufficiently large. We model this dynamic ensemble feedback process among excitatory neurons with piecewise-linear voltage amplifiers.

During this 25 msec computation, the mild additive feedback inhibition which appears to be an intrinsic part of the visual cortex (Douglas et al. 1988, 1989; Berman et a. 1991) could suppress any tendency of a nonclique cell receiving

---

degree are sufficient for our analysis (cf. Section 3.1). Thus we will use *clique* to refer to either kind of set, and assume that the exact meaning will be made clear from context.

[5] Cf. Wilson and Cowan 1972, 1973, who analyse related kinds of hysteresis behavior among aggregate cell populations.

little or no excitatory feedback to respond more than once in the interval, but would be ineffective against clique cells undergoing short-term feedback excitation. In effect the inhibition would sharpen the distinction between the two classes of cells and reduce noise. The first class of cells could be regarded as undergoing an imprecise decaying input current, the second a highly precise, mutually activating response. In addition (or alternately) inhibition could serve to deactivate the system following a given computation, thus setting the stage for the next.

As we show elsewhere (Miller and Zucker 1993), the end results of both phases can be computed in a number of computational steps which is polynomial in the number of bits needed to specify the problem (as defined in Section 3). This can be done by a type of algorithm which we have described previously (Miller and Zucker 1991, 1992), and which is closely related to the well known simplex method for linear programming. What this analysis shows is that the problem of retrieving information within our cortical model is not in the class of computationally hard problems such as the traveling salesman (Hopfield and Tank 1985) for which no such algorithm is likely to exist (Garey and Johnson 1979). Knowing that a fundamental computation is performable in polynomial time would appear to be a distinct advantage in modeling systems on the scale of the visual cortex.

4 A Mathematical Description of the Model

4.1 Self-Excitatory Sets

We have described in a previous paper (Miller and Zucker 1992) a version of the well-known recurrent analog network discussed in Hopfield (1984) (cf. Cowan 1970, Sejnowski 1981, Cohen and Grossberg 1983) with continuous piecewise-linear amplifiers rather than smooth sigmoids. We showed that the relative simplicity of this version can be useful in computational analysis, while not reducing the plausibility of the model with respect to real neurons. In fact as we have already implied, piecewise-linear amplifiers are in general much *more* realistic than smooth sigmoids for empirically-based input-output relations at the neuronal level (cf. also McCormick et al. 1985, Calvin 1978). This is hardly surprising since for all practical purposes they are a much more general class of functions (cf. Miller and Zucker 1992, Fig. 6).

We shall continue using this kind of analog network here, and in particular shall assume each amplifier i described by a monotonically increasing piecewise-linear function $g_i(u_i) : [\alpha_i, \beta_i] \rightarrow \mathbf{R}$ given by

$$g_i(u_i) = \begin{cases} 0 & u_i < \alpha_{i,1} \\ \gamma_{i,1} u_i + \delta_{i,1} & \alpha_{i,1} \leq u_i \leq \beta_{i,1} \\ \quad \vdots & \\ \gamma_{i,\omega(i)} u_i + \delta_{i,\omega(i)} & \alpha_{i,\omega(i)} \leq u_i \leq \beta_{i,\omega(i)} \\ 1 & u_i > \beta_{i,\omega(i)} \end{cases} \tag{1}$$

where

$$\alpha_i < \alpha_{i,1} < \beta_{i,1} = \alpha_{i,2} < \cdots < \alpha_{i,\omega(i)} < \beta_{i,\omega(i)} < \beta_i$$

and

$$\gamma_{i,k} = [g_i(\beta_{i,k}) - g_i(\alpha_{i,k})]/[\beta_{i,k} - \alpha_{i,k}]$$
$$\delta_{i,k} = g_i(\alpha_{i,k}) - \gamma_{i,k}\alpha_{i,k}$$

for all integers k, $1 \leq k \leq \omega(i)$ In general we will choose the bounds α_i and β_i small and large enough so that they will not enter into the evolution of the system, so that we get the same form Hopfield (1984) gave for his equations:

$$c_i\frac{du_i}{dt} = \sum_{j \neq i} T_{ij}V_j - u_i/R_i + I_i \tag{2}$$
$$V_i = g(u_i)$$

where c_i is the input capacitance to amplifier i, T_{ij} is the conductance between the output of amplifier j and the input of amplifier i, and $1/R_i = \sum_{j \neq i} T_{ij} + 1/\rho_i$, where ρ_i is the "membrane resistance" across c_i. [6]

As with our previous paper we do not assume the connections T_{ij} to be symmetric. However, consistent with the assumption stated in the introduction, we shall assume all $T_{ij} \geq 0$. For convenience but without loss of generality we will also assume $\alpha_{i,1} > 0$ for all i. This implies that the zero state, in which for all i, $u_i = 0$, is asymptotically stable (cf. Hirsch and Smale 1974) whenever the bias terms I_i are zero.

Let S be a nonempty set of amplifiers. Suppose there is an asymptotically stable unbiased equilibrium of (2) in which the amplifiers S have output 1, and all other amplifiers have output 0. We shall call such an S a *self-excitatory set*. Observe that this definition of self-excitatory set makes no statement about the particular form of the amplifier functions g_i, since it is based on the assumption that all amplifiers are at full or zero output. The following proposition gives simple conditions on the g_i for the self-excitatory set to be able to evolve to its excited state from an initial state in which all outputs are zero. In particular, the proposition states that this evolution will occur if the g_i are bounded below by a ramp function, and the initial input voltages are in the ramp portion or higher. This criterion will be extremely useful in view of the definition of cliques given below, and the modeling of real cortical cells by voltage amplifiers. In particular if we know that a clique of model neurons with the dotted-line amplifier functon in Fig. 7 of Miller and Zucker, 1993, *bottom*, would evolve to an excited state, then so would *any* collection of amplifiers whose response curves lay above the ramp function. Thus if we consider that, following the activation of those cells which

---

[6] In general we shall assume the scale of input to output is on the order of mvolts to volts, so that we can assume $R_i \approx \rho_i$, and hence the time constant of each cell is independent of the connection strengths.

spike initially,[7] *all* cells in the clique will be activated, and further consider the appreciable 15 msec time constant of each cell, this propostion, together with these other factors, implies that a clique could sustain its cells' maximum firing rate even as their response curves became substantially reduced.

We now state the proposition. Assuming nonsingularity of the system and nondegeneracy of solutions, we can make the following statement about S:

Proposition 1. Let S be a self-excitatory set for the system (2), and suppose that for all amplifiers i, and u_i such that $\alpha_{i,1} \leq u_i \leq \beta_{i,\omega(i)}$

$$g_i(u_i) \geq \gamma_i u_i + \delta_i \tag{3}$$

where $\gamma_i = 1/(\beta_{i,\omega(i)} - \alpha_{i,1})$ and $\delta_i = -\alpha_{i,1}/(\beta_{i,\omega(i)} - \alpha_{i,1})$. Suppose a bias $I_i > \alpha_{i,1}/R_i$, or alternately, a pulse current I_i in time Δt such that $I_i \Delta t/c_i > \alpha_i$, where $\Delta t \ll R_i c_i$, is applied to each amplifier $i \in S$, and a zero current is applied to all other amplifiers. Then the system will evolve from the zero state to an asymptotically stable state such that $V_i = 1$ for all $i \in S$, and $V_i = 0$ for all $i \notin S$.

The proof is in Miller and Zucker, 1993.

For each amplifier i (not necessarily in S) let $S(i)$ be the set of all $j \in S$ such that $T_{ij} > 0$. Also let T_{max} (T_{min}) be the maximum (minimum) over all T_{ij}. It follows that for each $i \in S$

$$c_i \frac{du_i}{dt} = \sum_{j \in S(i)} T_{ij} V_j - \beta_{i,\omega(i)}/R_i \geq 0 \tag{4}$$

hence

$$|S(i)| T_{max} \geq \beta_{i,\omega(i)}/R_i$$

hence

$$|S(i)| \geq \lceil \beta_{i,\omega(i)}/T_{max} R_i \rceil \equiv \xi_i^l \tag{5}$$

Conversely if

$$|S(i)| \geq \lceil \beta_{i,\omega(i)}/T_{min} R_i \rceil \equiv \xi_i^u$$

then we must have $i \in S$.

Similarly, for each $i \notin S$ we must have

$$c_i \frac{du_i}{dt} = \sum_{j \in S(i)} T_{ij} V_j - \alpha_{i,1}/R_i \leq 0$$

---

[7] In the context of our model neurons an "initial spike" would correspond to the raising of the input capacitance voltage beyond $\alpha_{i,1}$.

hence

$$|S(i)| \leq \lfloor \alpha_{i,1}/T_{\min} R_i \rfloor \equiv \eta_i^u$$

and conversely if

$$|S(i)| \leq \lfloor \alpha_{i,1}/T_{\max} R_i \rfloor \equiv \eta_i^l \tag{6}$$

then we must have $i \notin S$. We state these results as a proposition:

Proposition 2. Let S be a self-excitatory set. Then $i \in S$ implies $|S(i)| \geq \xi_i^l$, and $|S(i)| \geq \xi_i^u$ implies $i \in S$. Also $i \notin S$ implies $|S(i)| \leq \eta_i^u$, and $|S(i)| \leq \eta_i^l$ implies $i \notin S$.

A self-excitatory set will be called *minimal* if no proper subset is also a self-excitatory set. For a simple example of a nonminimal self-excitatory set, note that the union of two distinct self-excitatory sets is necessarily contained in such a set. On the other hand, Proposition 2 immediately gives us an important class of minimal self-excitatory sets. This corresponds to the case where, in terms of its nonzero connectivity, S is a complete graph or *clique* on at least $\xi^u + 1$ amplifiers, such that for all $i \notin S$, $|S(i)| < \eta^l$, where ξ^u is the maximum over all ξ_i^u, and η^l is the minimum over all η_i^l. More generally we can let $S = \bigcap_{i=1}^{k} S^i$, where each set of amplifiers S^i is completely connected, and for certain of the pairs (S^i, S^j) such that $i, j \in \{1, \ldots, k\}$, $S^i \bigcap S^j$ is completely connected as well. The latter type of self-excitatory set could be distributed over a larger cortical surface than perfect cliques since it would not be necessary to connect the most distant cells corresponding to the most distant pairs (S^i, S^j). However we shall base our analysis for the remainder of this paper on pure cliques.

With respect to a clique of actual neurons it of course seems unlikely that a perfectly symmetric arrangement could arise in cortical development, and in fact the connectivity does not have to be perfectly symmetric for our analysis to hold. For example, with the clique sizes discussed in the next section, ten percent of connections could be randomly omitted with the primary negative effect on performance being to raise the self-sustaining activation level ξ_i^u by about that percentage.

4.2 Storage and Input Bounds for Random Data

Suppose we wish to store some collection C of randomly chosen self-excitatory cliques of amplifiers, each of size $M \geq \xi^u + 1$. The question we wish to address is how large we can reliably allow $|C|$ to be, and how many extraneous amplifiers we can allow to be biased in the process of retrieving a member of C. This amounts to evaluating the probabilities of two types of error events, following an attempt to activate a given clique $C^p \in C$ by biasing a set of amplifiers E sufficient to saturate C^p. While E will of course not be independent of C^p, we shall assume that $E \setminus C^p$ is independent of the other $C^q \in C - C^p$. Also we shall assume that formation of a clique that connects amplifiers j to i does not change the value of an existing connection $T_{ij} > 0$.

Error type 1 occurs when there exists an amplifier $i \notin C^p$ with an input bias from C^p that causes it to have a significant nonzero output. A necessary condition is thus

$$\sum_{j \in C^p} T_{ij} V_j > \alpha_{i,1}/R_i$$

However observe that for a typical response curve, such as the dashed line in Fig. 7, Miller and Zucker, 1993, with a large initial slope, requiring

$$\sum_{j \in C^p} T_{ij} V_j \leq \alpha_{i,1}/R_i$$

is unnecessarily stringent, since the response has the same nonsaturated level for a bias considerably larger than $\alpha_{p,1}/R_p$. For more relaxed graphs we get just a single spike in a 25 msec time interval for any bias between .3 and .6 nA. Thus the level of bias which we shall view as a type 1 error can be more reasonably taken as

$$\sum_{j \in C^p} T_{ij} V_j \geq \beta_{i,\omega(i)}/2R_i \tag{7}$$

Similarly to (6) we define

$$\eta_i \equiv \left\lceil \beta_{i,\omega(i)}/2T_{\max} R_i \right\rceil \tag{8}$$

which is the least number of nonzero connections that could cause amplifier i to have an input $\geq \beta_{i,\omega(i)}/2$, and let η be the minimum over all η_i.

Error type 2 occurs when at least one of the cliques $C^q \in C - C^p$ can be saturated by $E \bigcup C^p$.

Observe that errors type 1 and 2 produce unwanted effects that persist after the bias E which saturates C^p is removed. It is only these persistent effects that we shall be interested in, since the state of the system during the biasing by E is not otherwise relevant to the final computation.

Of course the connections that form the cliques in C can inadvertently form new self-excitatory sets, either by extending members of C or creating entirely new self-excitatory sets that contain no member of C as a subset. However we shall arrange for the expected number of type 1 errors to be sufficiently small, so that the probable number of amplifiers involved in either of these scenarios will be small, and thus may be neglected. Thus we shall assume that with C^p saturated, the only remaining self-excitatory sets that $E \setminus C^p$ could activate are those in C.

To estimate the probability of a type 1 error, note that, with respect to (7), this event can only occur if i and at least η' such j are in the same clique. That i and any other random amplifier j are in the same clique has probability

$$\rho = 1 - \left(1 - \frac{M(M-1)}{N(N-1)}\right)^{|C|-1} \tag{9}$$

If M is small relative to $|C|$, the probability of obtaining at least $\hat{\eta}$ such matches for $j \in C^p$ will be given approximately by the binomial distribution, that is

$$\sum_{k=\eta}^{M} C(M, k)\rho^k (1 - \rho)^{M-k} \tag{10}$$

Let X_i be the indicator (0 or 1) random variable for amplifier $i \notin C^p$ receiving the input (7) from C^p, and let $E()$ denote expectation. Then since expectations add the total expected number of such amplifiers is

$$E\left(\sum_{i \notin C^p} X_i\right) = \sum_{i \notin C^p} E(X_i) = \sum_{i \notin C^p} \text{Prob}\{X_i = 1\} \tag{11}$$

Thus since $\text{Prob}\{X_i = 1\}$ is approximately (10), requiring (11) to be $\leq \epsilon$ is approximately equivalent to

$$(N - M)\sum_{k=\eta}^{M} C(M, k)\rho^k (1 - \rho)^{M-k} \leq \epsilon \tag{12}$$

which, solving as an equality for ρ, gives us an upper bound $\rho_\epsilon \leq \rho$. Alternatively we can use the Poisson approximation

$$(N - M)\left(1 - e^{-\rho M} \sum_{k=0}^{\eta-1} \frac{(\rho M)^k}{k!}\right) \leq \epsilon$$

¿From (9) we observe

$$|C| \leq \frac{\ln(1 - \rho_\epsilon)}{\ln\left(1 - \frac{M(M-1)}{N(N-1)}\right)} + 1$$

where ρ_ϵ is the solution to (12).

If we choose ϵ sufficiently small, say ≤ 1 (cf. Willshaw et al., P. 961), the binomial distribution with a large number of trials and small success probability per trial becomes a reasonable approximation, and we may in turn approximate the latter with the Poisson distribution, so that the probability of k type 1 events is $\exp(-\epsilon)\epsilon^k/k!$ and in particular the probability of no type 1 events is $\exp(-\epsilon)$.

Now let us consider the probability of a type 2 error, assuming $\epsilon \leq 1$ as above. Since the probable number of type 1 errors is being kept small, we shall neglect them, and simply assume, using as an upper bound the binomial distribution in (10), that each of the $N - M$ amplifiers outside C^p receives a bias from C^p and the other biased amplifiers E which is

$$\leq T_{\max}\left(\rho_\epsilon(M + |E|/2)\right) \equiv \hat{I}$$

Adding the bias $\hat{I}$ to the left-hand-side of (4) we derive a new version of (5), namely

$$|S(i)| \geq \left\lceil \left(\frac{\beta_{i,\omega(i)}}{R_i} - \hat{I} \right) / T_{\max} \right\rceil = \left\lceil \frac{\beta_{i,\omega(i)}}{T_{\max} R_i} - \rho_\epsilon(M + |E|/2) \right\rceil \equiv \xi_i$$

or in other words, neglecting ceilings,

$$\xi_i = \xi_i^l - \rho(M + |E|/2)$$

Let ξ be the minimum over all ξ_i. Then the probability of a type 2 error for arbitrary $C^q \in C - C^p$, using the hypergeometric distribution, is

$$\leq \sum_{k=\xi}^{M} \frac{C(|E| + M, k)C(N - |E| - M, M - k)}{C(N, M)}$$

Thus if $\hat{\epsilon}$ is a desired bound on the probability of a type 2 error, we can set

$$1 - \left[1 - \sum_{k=\xi}^{M} \frac{C(|E| + M, k)C(N - |E| - M, M - k)}{C(N, M)} \right]^{|C|-1} = \hat{\epsilon} \qquad (13)$$

and solve numerically for $|E|$.

As opposed to ϵ, which was an expected value which we could plausibly leave at about 1, $\hat{\epsilon}$ is a probability which should be small, since setting off the wrong clique ruins the computation. Exactly how small $\hat{\epsilon}$ should be would depend on how sensitive higher level mechanisms would be to an error. Biologically one would expect some tolerance, so we will take $\hat{\epsilon}$ as 10^{-4}. In fact the specific choice of $\hat{\epsilon}$ is not very critical, since the probability of a type 2 error goes effectively from zero to one within a relatively narrow range of $|E|$.

In order to give some computed examples, we need to specify or provide ranges for the additional parameters. We shall assume in all our examples that the T_{ij} are independently distributed around a mean T_μ such that $(M/2)T_\mu = \beta_{i,\omega(i)}/R_i$ for all i, with standard deviation $\sigma = T_\mu/2$. Thus biasing above threshold $M/2$ members of a clique, all of whose members have connections T_μ, will be just sufficient to activate the clique. Since the average output of n random amplifiers will then be T_μ with standard deviation $\sigma/\sqrt{n}$, we can, in order to get a reasonably tight lower bound on the maximum values of $|C|$ and $|E|$, take $T_{\max}$ as $T_\mu + \sigma/\sqrt{n}$. Then substituting in (5) gives us

$$\beta_{i,\omega(i)} / \left[R_i \left(\frac{\beta_{i,\omega(i)}}{R_i} \frac{2}{M} + \frac{\beta_{i,\omega(i)}}{R_i} \frac{1}{M} / \sqrt{\xi_i^l} \right) \right] = \xi_i^l$$

which solving as a quadratic gives us

$$\sqrt{\xi_i^l} = \frac{-1 + \sqrt{1 + 8M}}{4}$$

Similarly from (8) we have

$$\sqrt{\eta_i} = \frac{-1 + \sqrt{1 + 4M}}{4}$$

With regard to the size of N, we provide a range of 10k to 400k.

Note that each clique takes M^2 connections, and with our choice of ϵ each connection will generally belong to just one clique, so we must have $M^2|C| \leq Nf$, where f is the average dendritic fan-in, and hence

$$|C| \leq Nf/M^2 \tag{14}$$

Taking the dendritic fan-in for a pyramidal cortical cell of 6,000 (Douglas and Martin 1990, Douglas 1993) as a value for f, we can obtain graphs for $|C|$ and $|E|$ (Miller and Zucker, 1993).

4.3 Calculation of Cortical Packing Density from Hyperacuity Data

We shall now calculate both the clique size M and the cortical packing density of S-type pyramidal cells necessary for a sufficient number of cliques to perform hyperacuity-scale discriminations of straight line orientations. We shall assume that all available synapses are being efficiently utilized in the formation of cliques, which would correspond in the above random storage model to the assumption that the appropriate curve in Fig. 8, *top*, has reached its linear bound of Nf/M^2. Otherwise all parameter assumptions are based on empirical observation.

We assume the network of S-type cells is storing the cliques efficiently, that is, near its capacity of $|C|$ cliques, each of size M, where C is the total set of cliques. Then each S cell must, on average, belong to

$$|C|M/N$$

cliques. (To consider a totally *inefficient* arrangement imagine each cell belonging to just one clique, so that the number of cliques is $N/M \ll |C|$.)

Now let us consider an S cell which belongs primarily to straight line cliques of the kind indicated in Fig. 6.

We assume (Bishop et al. 1971, 1972, 1973; Schiller et al. 1976 a,b,c) that an S cell responds to a slit of light or a bar by responding to its edges. In general this response is direction dependent, and may strongly depend on variable and relatively nonspecific inhibition (Bishop et al. 1973). For this analysis we shall make the simplifying assumption that each cell responds to both light and dark edges, but only in one direction. [8] Thus the distinctly shaded regions in each receptive field in Fig. 6 are not to be taken as separate ON/OFF regions, but rather their borders are to be taken as the points on the axis perpendicular to orientation of maximum probability of initial spike response to a particular edge, in a particular direction of motion.

---

[8] This was the most common class of S cells found by both Bishop et al. (1971) and Schiller et al. (1976a).

For the network to be efficient there must be $|C|M/N$ distinct contours passing through its receptive field, skirting either of its side regions.

From geometry it is clear that the only way this can happen is for the contours to have varying orientations. In fact for each orientation there are just two contour positions that would put the cell at the appropriate place on its response tuning curve, one corresponding to each inhibitory flank.

We therefore shall assume that each S cell belongs to exactly two cliques for each discriminable orientation of a contour within its tuning range, which in monkeys will be about 15 deg before a steep falloff of over ten percent in average response occurs (Hubel and Wiesel 1968; De Valois et al. 1982, Fig. 1C; Schiller et al. 1976b, Fig. 2). If h is the number of cliques (hence lines) per degree, this means

$$|C|M/N = 2 \times 15 \text{ deg} \times h \tag{15}$$

We assume that storage is at its limiting value of

$$|C| = Nf/M^2 \tag{16}$$

Martin (1984) has found that S cells in cats may be both layer 2/3 pyramidal and spiny stellate, so it is not clear a priori whether to take these cells' respective fan-in values f of 4000-4500 or 6000 (Douglas and Martin 1990, Douglas 1993). However since it is primarily between layer 2/3 pyramidal cells that the intrinsic horizontal inter-iso-orientation area connections have been observed (Rockland and Lund 1982, 1983; Rockland et al. 1982; and Gilbert and Wiesel 1983, 1989) it is the pyramidal fan-in figure of $f = 6000$ which appears most justified. [9] Furthermore the data from orientation hyperacuity (Westheimer 1990) implies a value of h in (15) of 6 lines/deg. Therefore (15) and (16) imply

$$h = \frac{(Nf/M^2)(M/N)}{2 \times 15 \text{ deg}} = 6 \text{ lines/deg}$$

which implies

$$M \approx 33$$

Observe this clique size is about optimal for the random model if we give equal weight to both clique capacity and noise tolerance.

References

1. Abeles, M. 1982. *Studies of Brain Function: Vol. 6. Local Cortical Circuits.* Springer-Verlag, New York.
2. Agmon, A. and B. W. Connors. 1989. Repetitive burst-firing neurons in the deep layers of mouse somatosensory cortex. *Neuroscience Letters*, **99**, 137-141.

---

[9] Rockland and Lund (1983) have also observed less prominent intrinsic horizontal connections in layer 4B in macaque and, particularly, squirrel monkeys.

3. Amari, S. 1989. Characteristics of sparsely encoded associative memory. *Neural Networks,* **2**, 45-457.

4. Amit, D. J., H. Gutfreund, and H. Sompolinsky. 1987. Information storage in neural networks with low levels of activity. *Physical Review A,* **35**, 2293-2303.

5. Amit, D. J. 1989. *Modeling Brain Function: the World of Attractor Neural Networks,* Cambridge University Press, Cambridge, England.

6. Barlow, H. B. 1979. Reconstructing the visual image in space and time. *Nature,* **279**, 189-190.

7. Berkley, M. A. and J. M. Sprague. 1979. Striate cortex and visual acuity functions in the cat. *J. Comp. Neur.,* **187**, 679-702.

8. Bishop, P. O., J. S. Coombs, and H. Henry. 1971. Responses to visual contours: spatio-temporal aspects of excitation in the receptive fields of simple striate neurones. *J. Physiol.,* **219**, 625-657.

9. Bishop, P. O., J. S. Coombs, and H. Henry. 1973. Receptive fields of simple cells in the cat striate cortex. *J. Physiol.,* **231**, 31-60.

10. Bishop, P. O., B. Dreher, and H. Henry. 1972. Simple striate cells: comparison of responses to stationary and moving stimuli. *J. Physiol.,* **227**, 15-17P.

11. Bullier, J., M. J. Mustari, and G. H. Henry. 1982. Receptive-field transformations between LGN neurons and S-cells of cat striate cortex. *J. Neurophysiology,* **47**, 417-438.

12. Callaway, E. M. and L. C. Katz. 1990. Emergence and refinement of clustered horizontal connections in cat striate cortex. *J. Neurosci.,* **10**, 1134-1153.

13. Calvin, W. H. 1978. Setting the pace and pattern of discharge: do CNS neurons vary their sensitivity to external inputs via their repetitive firing processes? *Federation Proceedings,* **37**, 2165-2170.

14. Cohen, M. A. and S. Grossberg. 1983. Absolute stability of global pattern formation and parallel memory storage by competitive neural networks. *IEEE Trans. Sys. Man Cyber.,* **13**, 815-826.

15. Cowan, J. D. 1970. A statistical mechanics of nervous activity. In: *Lectures on Mathematics in the Life Sciences, Vol. 2* (ed. M. Gerstenhaber), 1-58. American Mathematical Society, Providence, RI.

16. Douglas, R. J., K. A. C. Martin, and D. Whitteridge. 1988. Selective responses of visual cortical cells do not depend on shunting inhibition. *Nature (London),* **332**, 642-644.

17. Douglas, R. J., K. A. C. Martin, and D. Whitteridge. 1989. A canonical microcircuit for neocortex. *Neural Computation,* **1**, 480-488.

18. Douglas, R. J. and K. A. C. Martin. 1990. Neocortex. In: *The Synaptic Organization of the Brain, Third Edition* (ed. G. M. Shepherd), 389-438. Oxford University Press, New York.

19. Douglas, R. J. and K. A. C. Martin. 1991. Opening the grey box. *Trends in Neuroscience,* **14**, 286-293.

20. Douglas, R. J. and K. A. C. Martin. 1992. Exploring cortical microcircuits: a combined physiological and computational approach. In: *Single Neuron Computation, Neural Nets: Foundations to Applications (Ser.),* (T. McKenna, J. Davis, and S. F. Zornetzer, eds.), 381-412, Academic Press, New York.

21. Douglas, R. J. 1993. Talk given at the 9th Annual Woods Hole Workshop on Computational Neuroscience, Marine Biological Laboratory, Woods Hole, Mass.

22. Eckhorn, R., R. Bauer, W. Jordan, M. Brosch, W. Kruse, M. Munk, and H. J. Reitboeck. 1988. Coherent Oscillations: A mechanism of feature finking in the visual cortex? *Biol. Cybern.,* **60**, 121-130.

23. Ferster, D. and S. Linström. 1983. An intracellular analysis of geniculo-cortical connectivity in area 17 of the cat. *J. Physiol, 342*, 181-215.

24. Garey, M. R. and Johnson, D. S. 1979. *Computers and Intractability.* W. H. Freeman, San Francisco.

25. Gilbert, C. D. and Wiesel, T. N. 1979. Morphology and intracortical projections of functionally characterized neurones in cat visual cortex. *Nature.* **280**, 120-125.

26. Gilbert, C. D. and Wiesel, T. N. 1983. Clustered intrinsic connections in cat visual cortex. *J. Neurosci..* **3**, 1116-1133.

27. Gilbert, C. D. and Wiesel, T. N. 1990. The influence of contextual stimuli on the orientation selectivity of cells in primary visual cortex of the cat. *Vision Res.*, **30**, 1689-1701.

28. Gray, C. M. and W. Singer. 1989. Stimulus-specific neuronal oscillations in orientation columns of cat visual cortex. *Proc. Natl. Acad. Sci. USA*, **86**, 1698-1702.

29. Gray, C. M., P. König, A. K. Engel, and W. Singer. 1989 Oscillatory responses in cat visual cortex exhibit inter-columnar synchronization which reflects global stimulus properties. *Nature*, **338**, 334-337.

30. Hirsch, M. W. and S. Smale. 1974. *Differential Equations, Dynamical Systems, and Linear Algebra*, Academic Press, New York.

31. Hopfield, J. J. 1984. Neurons with graded response have collective computational properties like those of two-state neurons. *Proc. Natl. Acad. Sci. USA*, **81**, 3088-3092.

32. Hopfield, J. J. and D. W. Tank. 1985. "Neural" computation of decisions in optimization problems. *Biol. Cybern.*, **52**, 141-152.

33. Horton, J. C., L. R. Dagi, E. P. McCrane, and F. M. de Monasterio. 1990. Arrangement of ocular dominance columns in human visual cortex. *Arch Ophthalmol*, **108**, 1025-1031.

34. Hubel, D. H. and T. N. Wiesel. 1977. Ferrier Lecture. Functional architecture of macaque monkey visual cortex. *Proc. R. Soc. Lond. B.*, **198**, 1-59.

35. Krüger, J. and J. D. Becker. 1991. Recognizing the visual stimulus from neuronal discharges. *Trends in Neuroscience*, **14**. 282-286.

36. Martin, K. A. C. 1984. Neuronal circuits in cat striate cortex. In: *Cerebral Cortex, Vol. 2: Functional Properties of Cortical Cells*, (E. G. Jones and A. Peters, eds.), 241-284, Plenum Press, New York.

37. McCormick, D. A., B. W. Connors, J. W. Lighthall, and D. A. Prince. 1985. Comparative electrophysiology of pyramidal and sparsely spiny stellate neurons of the neocortex. *J. Neurophysiol.*, **54**, 782-806.

38. McCormick, D. A. 1990. Membrane properties and neurotransmitter actions. In: *The Synaptic Organization of the Brain*, (G. M. Shepherd, ed.), 32-66. Oxford University Press, New York.

39. McGuire, B. A., C. D. Gilbert, P. K. Rivlin, and T. N. Wiesel. 1991. Targets of horizontal connections in macaque primary visual cortex. *J. Comp. Neurol.*, **305**, 370-392.

40. Miller, D. A. and S. W. Zucker. 1991. Copositive-plus Lemke algorithm solves polymatrix games. *Operations Research Letters*, **10**, 285-290.

41. Miller, D. A. and S. W. Zucker. 1992. Efficient simplex-like methods for equilibria of nonsymmetric analog networks. *Neural Computation*, **4**, 167-190.

42. Miller, D. A. and S. W. Zucker. 1993. In preparation.

43. Moore, E. F. and C. E. Shannon. 1956. Reliable circuits using less reliable relays. *J. Franklin Inst.*, **262**, 191-208, 281-297.

44. Palm, G. 1981. On the storage capacity of associative memory with randomly distributed storage elements. *Biol. Cybern.*, **39**, 125-127.

45. Peters, A. 1987. Number of neurons and synapses in the primary visual cortex. In: *Cerebral Cortex, Vol. 6: Further Aspects of Cortical Functions Including Hippocampus*, (E. G. Jones and A. Peters, eds.), 267-294, Plenum Press, New York.

46. Peters, A. and C. Sethares. 1991. Organization of pyramidal neurons in area 17 of monkey visual cortex. *J. Comp. Neurol.*, **306**, 1-23.

47. Rockland, K. S. and J. S. Lund. 1983. Intrinsic laminar lattice connections in primate visual cortex. *J. Comp. Neurol.*, **216**, 303-318.

48. Schiller, P. H., B. L. Finlay, and S. F. Volman. 1976a. Quantitative studies of single-cell properties of monkey striate cortex. I. Spatio-temporal organization of receptive fields. *J. Neurophysiology*, **6**, 1288-1319; 1320-1333; 1334-1351.

49. Segev, I., J. W. Fleshman, and R. E. Burke. 1989. Compartmental models of complex neurons. In: *Methods in Neuronal Modeling: From Synapses to Networks*, C. Koch and I. Segev, eds. MIT Press, Cambridge, Mass.

50. Sejnowski, T. J. 1981. Skeleton filters in the brain. In: *Parallel Models of Associative Memory* (G. E. Hinton and J. A. Anderson, eds.), Lawrence Erlbaum Assoc., Hillsdale, N. J.

51. Singer, W. 1990. The formation of cooperative cell assemblies in the visual cortex. *J. exp. Biol.*, **153**, 177-197.

52. Westheimer, G. 1990. The grain of visual space. *Cold Spring Harbor Symposia on Quantitative Biology, Vol. LV*, 759-763.

53. Westheimer, G. and S. P. McKee. 1975. Visual acuity in the presence of retinal-image motion. *J. Opt. Soc. Am.*, **65**, 847-850.

54. Willshaw, D. J., O. P. Buneman, and H. C. Longuet-Higgins. 1969. Non-holographic associative memory. *Nature*, **222**, 960-962.

55. Willshaw, D. J. and H. C. Longuet-Higgins. 1970. Associative memory models. In *Machine Intelligence, Vol. 5* (B. Meltzer and D. Michie, eds.), 351-359, Edinburgh U. Press, Edinburgh, U.K.

56. Wilson, H. R. and J. D. Cowan. 1972. Excitatory and inhibitory interactions in localized populations of model neurons. *Biophysical J.*, **12**, 1-24.

57. Wilson, H. R. and J. D. Cowan. 1973. A mathematical theory of the functional dynamics of cortical and thalamic nervous tissue. *Kybernetik*, **13**, 55-80.

58. Winograd, S. and J. D. Cowan. 1963. *Reliable Computation in the Presence of Noise*, MIT Press, Cambridge, Mass.

59. Zucker, S. W., A. Dobbins, and L. Iverson. 1989. Two stages of curve detection suggest two styles of visual computation. *Neural Comp.*, **1**, 68-81.

Characterizing the Distribution of Completion Shapes with Corners Using a Mixture of Random Processes

K. K. Thornber   L. R. Williams

NEC Research Institute
4 Independence Way
Princeton, NJ 08540, USA

Abstract. We derive an analytic expression for the distribution of contours $\mathbf{x}(t)$ generated by fluctuations in $\dot{\mathbf{x}}(t) = \partial \mathbf{x}(t)/\partial t$ due to stochastic impulses of two limiting types. The first type are frequent but weak while the second are infrequent but strong. The result has applications in computational theories of figural completion and illusory contours because it can be used to model the prior probability distribution of short, smooth completion shapes punctuated by occasional discontinuities in orientation (i.e., corners). This work extends our previous work on characterizing the distribution of completion shapes which dealt only with the case of frequently acting weak impulses.

1   Introduction

In a previous paper[19] we derived an analytic expression characterizing a distribution of short, smooth contours. This result has applications in ongoing work on figural completion and perceptual saliency. The idea that the prior probability distribution of boundary completion shapes can be characterized by a directional random walk is first described by Mumford[13]. A similiar idea is implicit in Cox *et al.*'s use of the Kalman filter in their work on grouping of contour fragments[4]. More recently, Williams and Jacobs[20] introduced a representation they called a *stochastic completion field*—the probability that a particle undergoing a directional random walk will pass through any given position and orientation in the image plane on a path bridging a pair of boundary fragments. They argued that the mode, magnitude and variance of the stochastic completion field are related to the perceived shape, salience and sharpness of illusory contours.

Both Mumford[13] and Williams and Jacobs[20] show that the maximum likelihood path taken by a particle following a directional random walk between two position/orientation pairs is a curve of least energy (see Horn[9]). This is the curve that is commonly assumed to model the shape of illusory contours, and is widely used for semi-automatic region segmentation in many computer vision applications (see Kass *et al.*[11]).

The distribution of shapes considered by [4, 13, 19, 20] basically consists of smooth, short contours. Yet there are many examples in human vision where completion shapes perceived by humans contain discontinuities in orientation

(a)

(b)

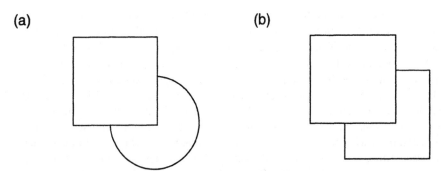

Fig. 1. Amodal completion of a partially occluded circle and square (redrawn from Kanizsa[10]). In both cases, completion is accomplished in a manner which preserves tangent and curvature continuity at the ends of the occluded boundaries.

(i.e., corners). Figure 1 shows a display by Kanizsa[10]. This display illustrates the completion of a circle and square under a square occluder. The completion of the square is significant because it includes a discontinuity in orientation. Figure 2 shows a pair of "Koffka Crosses." When the width of the arms of the Koffka Cross is increased, observers generally report that the percept changes from an illusory circle to an illusory square.

(a)

(b)

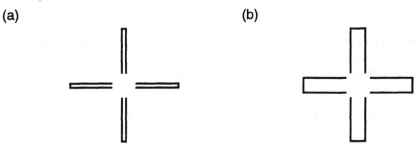

Fig. 2. When the width of the arms of the Koffka Cross is increased, observers generally report that the percept changes from an illusory circle to an illusory square.

Although the distribution of completion shapes with corners has not previously been characterized analytically, the idea of including corners in completion shapes is not new. For example, the functionals of Kass *et al.*[11] and Mumford and Shah[13] permit orientation discontinuities accompanied by large (but fixed size) penalties. This follows work by Blake[2] and others[6, 7, 12, 15] on interpolation of smooth surfaces with creases from sparse depth (or brightness) measurements. More recently, Belheumer[1] (working with stereo pairs) used a similiar functional for interpolation of disparity along epipolar lines. Belheumer's approach is especially related because he derives his functional by considering a distribution of surface cross-section shapes characterized by a mixture of random processes—smoothly varying disparity is modeled by a one-dimensional Brownian motion while depth discontinuities are modeled by a Poisson process.

In this paper, we derive a very general integral-differential equation underlying a family of contour shape distributions. This family is based on shapes traced by particles following any of several default paths modified by random impulses drawn from a mixture of distributions (e.g., different magnitudes, directions, rates). For our figural completion application, we are especially interested in a shape distribution based upon straight line base-trajectories in two-dimensions modified by random impulses drawn from a mixture of two limiting distributions. The first distribution consists of weak but frequently acting impulses (we call this the Gaussian-limit). The magnitude of the random impulses is Gaussian distributed with zero mean and variance equal to σ_g^2. The weak impulses act at Poisson times with rate R_g. The second consists of strong but infrequently acting impulses (we call this the Poisson-limit). Again, the magnitude of the random impulses is Gaussian distributed with zero mean. However, the variance is equal to σ_p^2 (where $\sigma_p^2 >> \sigma_g^2$). The strong impulses act at Poisson times with rate $R_p << R_g$. As in our previous work, particles decay with half-life equal to a parameter τ. The distribution can be summarized by four parameters (of constant value for a given application). The effect is that particles tend to travel in smooth, short paths punctuated by occasional orientation discontinuities.

2 Approach

Suppose we are given a collection of contour segments, for example, as would be present in an image of objects occluded by other objects. Our goal is to predict all reasonably likely completions of these contours and their relative likelihoods. If x_1 is the location of the end of one contour segment, and x_2 is the beginning of another, then one candidate for the most general prior between x_1 and x_2 would be given by:

$$\mathbf{x}(t) = \mathbf{x}_1 + \sum_\ell \Delta\mathbf{x}_\ell u(t - t_\ell), \quad t_1 < t_i < t_2, \quad \mathbf{x}(t_2) = \mathbf{x}_2$$

where $u(\cdot)$ is the unit step function, i.e., $u(t) = 0$ when $t < 0$ and $u(t) = 1$ when $t > 0$ and the displacements $\Delta\mathbf{x}_\ell$ are stochastic with some zero-mean distribution. The times t_ℓ would also be stochastic, e.g., Poisson with some (possibly time varying) rate $\mathbf{R}(t)$. Such curves would resemble the tracks of classical Brownian particles connecting x_1 and x_2. While this represents the most general prior for a continuous curve, lacking any bias, the expected contour will be simply

$$< \mathbf{x}(t) > = \mathbf{x}_1 + \mathbf{x}_2(t - t_1)/(t_2 - t_1) \quad t_1 \leq t \leq t_2$$

which in space is independent of t_1 and t_2, and the details of the distribution of the $(\Delta x_\ell, t_\ell)$. The likelihood that any two points are connected depends on the distribution of the $(\Delta x_\ell, t_\ell)$, and decreases with increasing separation. For ordinary diffusion in one and two dimensions, all points can be reached with probability one. For this reason, such completions are both degenerate and sterile, and will not be considered further.

Except at isolated points (corners, vertices), most boundaries are continuous in position and orientation. Thus, if in the above example, γ_1 and γ_2 are the direction cosines of their respective curves at $\mathbf{x}_1$ and $\mathbf{x}_2$, then two additional boundary conditions enter:

$$d\mathbf{x}/ds = \gamma_1 \text{ at } \mathbf{x}_1 \text{ and } d\mathbf{x}/ds = \gamma_2 \text{ at } \mathbf{x}_2$$

where s is the distance along the curve $\mathbf{x}(s)$ as in differential geometry. Between $\mathbf{x}_1$ and $\mathbf{x}_2$ one would like to write $d\mathbf{x}/ds = \gamma$ where γ is now a random variable (see Mumford[13] and Williams and Jacobs[20]). However, in addition to not being projectively covariant, the constraint that $\mid \gamma \mid = 1$ permits at most $d - 1$ of the d components of γ to vary independently. To avoid this constraint, we consider contours $\mathbf{x}(t)$ with arbitrary parameterization (t), and for each component q, set

$$dx_q(t)/dt = \dot{x}_q(t), \quad q = 1, ..., d$$

where the $\dot{x}_q(t)$ are independent, identically distributed (to ensure the covariance property) stochastic variables. Each $\dot{x}_q$ changes by $\Delta \dot{x}_{q\ell}$ at $t_{q\ell}$ according to a zero-mean distribution on $\Delta \dot{x}_q$, while the $t_{q\ell}$ occur at a mean rate of $R_q(t)$, for example, according to Poisson statistics. This results in what is probably the least constrained, simple prior which captures the essential properties of the missing contour and its relative likelihood:

$$\mathbf{x}(t) = \mathbf{x}_1 + \dot{\mathbf{x}}_1(t - t_1) + \int_{t_1}^{t} dt' \sum_{\ell} \Delta \dot{\mathbf{x}}_{\ell} u(t' - t_{\ell}), \quad t_1 \leq t' \leq t$$

where $\mathbf{x}(t_2) = \mathbf{x}_2, \dot{\mathbf{x}}(t_2) = \dot{\mathbf{x}}_2$. Clearly $\dot{\mathbf{x}}_1$ and $\dot{\mathbf{x}}_2$ will have directions γ_1 and γ_2.

3 Prior Distribution of Smooth Completion Shapes

We define $P(2 \mid 1)$ to be the likelihood that a contour, $\mathbf{x}(t)$, is at $\mathbf{x}_2$ with $\dot{\mathbf{x}}_2$ for $t = t_2$ given that it was at $\mathbf{x}_1$ with $\dot{\mathbf{x}}_1$ for $t = t_1$, averaged over all $\mathbf{x}(t)$ subjected to random impulses. While we calculate $P(2 \mid 1)$ directly in the next section (for a mixture of frequent-weak impulses and infrequent-strong impulses), it is of value to derive an integral-differential equation for $P(2 \mid 1)$ which includes all types of impulses.

The transition probability $P(2 \mid 1)$ embodies three aspects of contour distributions: 1) boundary conditions; 2) base-trajectories (i.e., impulse-free contours); and 3) impulse statistics. Boundary conditions constrain possible contours at keypoints[1] by specifying at least one of $\mathbf{x}_i, \dot{\mathbf{x}}_i, \ddot{\mathbf{x}}_i$, etc. We find the choice of $(\mathbf{x}_i, \dot{\mathbf{x}}_i)$ to be most useful, but other applications may require other combinations. A variety of base-trajectories can represent the contour at times between the arrival of stochastic impulses. As elemental Green's functions, $\mathbf{G}_{tt'}$, nearly any convenient function of $(t - t')$ (or even of (t, t')) can be used, but polynominals and real and imaginary exponentials (especially harmonics) are the most common. Clearly there must be sufficient degrees of freedom to match the boundary conditions given at the keypoint. We have found straight lines,

---

[1] We use this term (adopted from [8]) as a generic term to denote position-velocity constraints derived from the image.

$\mathbf{G}_{t,t'} = (t^+ - t')u(t^+ - t')\mathbf{I}$, to be the most useful in our application. In addition to boundary conditions and base-trajectories, the contour distributions are defined by impulse statistics. Stochastic impulses have the form and distribution, $\dot{\hat{\mathbf{x}}}(t) = \sum_{k\ell} \Delta\dot{\mathbf{x}}_k u(t - t_{k\ell})$, which includes process k with impulses $\Delta\dot{\mathbf{x}}_k$ occuring at times, $t_{k\ell}$, with rate R_k. While we focus here on only two limiting distributions, frequent-weak (Gaussian) and infrequent-strong (Poisson), an entire spectrum between these limits is also available.

We now turn to the calculation of an integral-differential equation for $P(2 \mid 1)$ expressed in terms of the parameters underlying the stochastic processes characterizing the distribution. Recall that $P(2 \mid 1)$ is the probability that given $\mathbf{x}(t_1) = \mathbf{x}_1$ and $\dot{\mathbf{x}}(t_1) = \dot{\mathbf{x}}_1$, then $\mathbf{x}(t_2) = \mathbf{x}_2$ and $\dot{\mathbf{x}}(t_2) = \dot{\mathbf{x}}_2$ for $t_2 > t_1$:

$$P(2 \mid 1) = P(\mathbf{x}_2, \dot{\mathbf{x}}_2, t_2 \mid \mathbf{x}_1, \dot{\mathbf{x}}_1, t_1) = < \delta(\mathbf{x}(t_2) - \mathbf{x}_2)\delta(\dot{\mathbf{x}}(t_2) - \dot{\mathbf{x}}_2) >_1$$

where $< \cdot >_1$ is an average over all contours matching the boundary condition $\mathbf{x}_1, \dot{\mathbf{x}}_1$ at t_1. For simplicity let us write $P(\mathbf{x}, \dot{\mathbf{x}}, t)$ for $P(2 \mid 1)$. Then we find (using $\delta'(t) = \partial\delta(t)/\partial t$):

$$\partial_t P(\mathbf{x}, \dot{\mathbf{x}}, t) = < \dot{\mathbf{x}}_t \delta'(\mathbf{x}_t - \mathbf{x})\delta(\dot{\mathbf{x}}_t - \dot{\mathbf{x}}) >_1 + < \ddot{\mathbf{x}}_t \delta(\mathbf{x}_t - \mathbf{x})\delta'(\dot{\mathbf{x}}_t - \dot{\mathbf{x}}) >_1$$

$$= -\dot{\mathbf{x}} \cdot \partial_{\mathbf{x}} < \delta(\mathbf{x}_t - \mathbf{x})\delta(\dot{\mathbf{x}}_t - \dot{\mathbf{x}}) >_1 - \partial_{\dot{\mathbf{x}}} < \ddot{\mathbf{x}}_t \delta(\mathbf{x}_t - \mathbf{x})\delta(\dot{\mathbf{x}}_t - \dot{\mathbf{x}}) >_1$$

While $\delta(\dot{\mathbf{x}}_t - \dot{\mathbf{x}})$ forces $\dot{\mathbf{x}}_t$ to be $\dot{\mathbf{x}}$ and the first expectation value is simply $P(\mathbf{x}, \dot{\mathbf{x}}, t)$, $\ddot{\mathbf{x}}_t$ is less readily specifiable. According to our prior, $\ddot{\mathbf{x}}_t = \sum_\ell \Delta\dot{\mathbf{x}}_\ell \delta(t - t_\ell)$. However, unless we are careful, the second expectation value will become needlessly complex. We will opt for simplicity but retain sufficient generality to deal with all problems of interest. In Appendix A we calculate the second expectation value in terms of the probability distribution of the number of times in a given interval of time the elementary "force" $\mathbf{f}_k$ acts (assuming these times to be independent). Though exact, for our present purposes, the expression is unnecessarily complicated. As the occurrences of the fluctuations are independent, it is reasonable to take their average instantaneous rate $R_k(t)$ to be independent of the number of fluctuations N_k of type k in the interval of interest. This leads us to the standard Poisson distribution for the probability of N_k independent fluctuations, and simplifies the resulting equation. Should this be an over-simplification, we could still work out $P(2 \mid 1)$ as discussed in [19]. These considerations result in the following integral-differential equation for $P(\mathbf{x}, \dot{\mathbf{x}}, t)$:

$$\partial_t P(\mathbf{x}, \dot{\mathbf{x}}, t) = -\dot{\mathbf{x}} \cdot \partial_{\mathbf{x}} P(\mathbf{x}, \dot{\mathbf{x}}, t) - \ddot{\mathbf{x}}_{1t} \cdot \partial_{\dot{\mathbf{x}}} P(\mathbf{x}, \dot{\mathbf{x}}, t) - P(\mathbf{x}, \dot{\mathbf{x}}, t)/\tau$$

$$- \sum_k \int d\xi R_k(\xi)\mathbf{f}_k(t - \xi) \cdot \partial_{\dot{\mathbf{x}}} P(\mathbf{x} - \int dt' \mathbf{G}_{t,t'} \mathbf{f}_k(t' - \xi), \dot{\mathbf{x}} - \int dt' \dot{\mathbf{G}}_{t,t'} \mathbf{f}_k(t' - \xi), t)$$

where $\mathbf{x}_{1t}$ is $\mathbf{x}(t)$ for impulse-free conditions, $\mathbf{x}(t_1) = \mathbf{x}_1$ and $\dot{\mathbf{x}}(t_1) = \dot{\mathbf{x}}_1$. Since the details of the $\mathbf{f}_k$ are unlikely to matter, letting $\mathbf{v}_k = \int dt \mathbf{f}_k(t)$, we obtain, for $\mathbf{G}_{t,t'} = (t^+ - t')u(t^+ - t')\,\mathbf{I}$ and hence $\ddot{\mathbf{x}}_1 = 0$:

$$\partial_t P(\mathbf{x}, \dot{\mathbf{x}}, t) = -\dot{\mathbf{x}} \cdot \partial_{\mathbf{x}} P(\mathbf{x}, \dot{\mathbf{x}}, t) - P(\mathbf{x}, \dot{\mathbf{x}}, t)/\tau - \sum_k R_k(t)\mathbf{v}_k \cdot \partial_{\dot{\mathbf{x}}} P(\mathbf{x}, \dot{\mathbf{x}} - \mathbf{v}_k/2, t)$$

Equations for specifications of position, velocity, and curvature, etc., can be obtained by analogous reasoning.

These integral-differential equations have the following significance. The (conditional) probability at $(\mathbf{x}, \dot{\mathbf{x}})$ changes in time according to 1) a spatial drift in its gradient (i.e., *advection*); and 2) various terms in its velocity gradient (i.e., *diffusion*). The first of the terms in the velocity gradient is local and is driven by any "acceleration" in the initial, impulse-free contour $\mathbf{x}_1(t)$, $t \geq t_1$. It is the last term which is most significant. It expresses the fact that the stochastic impulses drive the distribution through its velocity gradient averaged over the duration of the impulse. In the limit of impulses of short duration, this average can be approximated by the velocity-gradient evaluated at $\dot{\mathbf{x}} - \mathbf{v}_k/2$ (i.e., the average velocity before and after the fluctuation). In the Gaussian limit of small impulses $\mathbf{v}_k$ and stationary processes R_k, we obtain the simple differential:

$$\partial_t P_0 = -\dot{\mathbf{x}} \cdot \partial_{\mathbf{x}} P_0 + \mathbf{T} \partial_{\dot{\mathbf{x}}}^2 P_0/2 - P_0/\tau, \quad \mathbf{T} = \sum_k R_k \mathbf{v}_k \mathbf{v}_k$$

which for isotropic environments in $(R_k, \mathbf{v}_k)$, that is, isotropic impulses, becomes:

$$\partial_t P_0 = -\dot{\mathbf{x}} \cdot \partial_{\mathbf{x}} P_0 + T \partial_{\dot{\mathbf{x}}}^2 P_0/2 - P_0/\tau$$

Here T is the velocity-variance-rate parameter, analogous to the position-variance-rate parameter (diffusion coefficient) of transport theories.[2] This *Fokker-Planck equation* is similiar to the equation described by Mumford[13]. The only difference is that the diffusion term in our equation involves velocity rather than orientation. One consequence of this difference is that our equation separates, so that $P_0(2 \mid 1) = \exp(-t/\tau) P_{0x}(2 \mid 1) P_{0y}(2 \mid 1)...$, the product extending to as many dimensions as are of interest. Solving, we find for $P_{0x}(2 \mid 1)$:

$$P_{0x}(2 \mid 1; t) = (2\pi T_x t)^{-\frac{1}{2}} \exp[-(\dot{x}_2 - \dot{x}_1)^2/2T_x t]$$

$$\cdot (\pi T_x t^3/6)^{-\frac{1}{2}} \exp[-6((x_2 - x_1) - (\dot{x}_2 + \dot{x}_1)t/2)^2/T_x t^3]$$

and similarly for y, z, ..., etc. Here $t = t_2 - t_1$, and T_x arises from setting $T_{ij} = T_i \delta_{ij}$ rather than taking $T_{ij} = T \delta_{ij}$ (which we will eventually do to ensure rotational invariance). The expression shows clearly the contribution of velocity diffusion, and the persistence of the initial velocity and anticipation of the final velocity in the position dependence.

4 Inclusion of Corners in Prior Distribution

This formulation is clearly not just limited to frequent-weak impulses—it contains the full spectrum of stochastic contributions to $\dot{\mathbf{x}}_t$. While some problems may call for this flexibility in full, it turns out that corners (discontinuities in

---

[2] In these expressions, the zero subscript denotes the fact that the probability, P_0, is averaged over trajectories modified by zero impulses of the large-infrequent type (i.e., the pure Gaussian case). In the next section, we will consider probabilities averaged over trajectories modified by a mixture of weak, frequent impulses and a single impulse of the large, infrequent type. This mixed probability will be denoted, P_1.

orientation) can be included by using a mixture of frequent-weak and infrequent-strong impulses. In fact, for our purposes, it will suffice to include only zero or one large impulse per contour.

Previously[19] we showed how $P(2 \mid 1) \; =< \delta(\mathbf{x}(t_2) - \mathbf{x}_2)\delta(\dot{\mathbf{x}}(t_2) - \dot{\mathbf{x}}_2) >_1$ could be obtained from an evaluation of the characteristic functional $\Phi(\mathbf{k}_t) =< \exp i \int dt \mathbf{k}_t \cdot \mathbf{x}_t >_1$ which since

$$\mathbf{x}(t) = \mathbf{x}_1 + \mathbf{G}(t, t_1)\dot{\mathbf{x}}_1 + \int_{t_1}^t dt' \mathbf{G}(t, t')\mathbf{F}(t')$$

in which $\mathbf{F}(t')$ is the stochastic force, it sufficed to determine

$$\phi(\mathbf{p}_t) =< \exp(i \int dt' \mathbf{p}_{t'} \mathbf{F}_{t'}) >$$

with $\mathbf{p}_{t'} = \int dt \mathbf{k}_t \mathbf{G}(t, t')$ where $\mathbf{G}(t, t') = 0$ for $t \leq t'$. This results in the following expression:

$$< \exp(i \int dt \mathbf{p}_t \cdot \mathbf{F}_t) >= \exp[\int d\xi \sum_k R_k(\xi)(\exp(i \int dt \; \mathbf{p}_t \cdot \mathbf{f}_k(t - \xi)) - 1)]$$

where we used $\mathbf{F}_t = \sum_k R_k(t) \sum_\ell \mathbf{f}_k(t - t_{k\ell})$, the $t_{k\ell}$'s being governed by a Poisson process of rate $R_k(t)$. Although one can use this expression as given (as we do in Appendix A) several limiting cases provide significant and useful simplifications. The most common is the Gaussian limit of small, frequent impulses, which we have already developed, and in which case

$$< \exp(i \int dt \; \mathbf{p}_t \cdot \mathbf{F}_t) >= \exp(-\tfrac{1}{2} \int dt \; \mathbf{p}_t \cdot \mathbf{T} \cdot \mathbf{p}_t)$$

with $\mathbf{T} = \sum_k R_k \mathbf{f}_k \mathbf{f}_k$ and $\mathbf{f}_k(t) = \mathbf{f}_k \delta(t)$.[3] The opposite limit is large-infrequent impulses. These are necessary if we are to include discontinuities in $dx(t)/dt$ (i.e., corners). For the case in which a single, large impulse event can be present in addition to the numerous, small impulses of the Gaussian case, we proceed as follows. Returning to the first expression above for $< \exp(i \int dt \mathbf{p}_t \cdot \mathbf{F}_t) >$ we expand the exponential in $\sum_k R_k(\xi)$ to first order in those elements of k which represent infrequent impulses, i.e., $\sum_s R_s(\xi)$ for small $R_s(\xi)$. In this way, we include only zero and one rare impulse events, obtaining the factor:

$$\frac{1 + \sum_s \int d\xi R_s(\xi) \exp[i \int dt \mathbf{p}_t \cdot \mathbf{f}_s(t - \xi)]}{1 + \sum_s \int d\xi R_s(\xi)}$$

Again taking the impulses $\mathbf{f}_s$ to be of relatively short duration and including an average over a Gaussian distribution of variance σ_p^2 (i.e., the least constrained zero-mean distribution of a given variance) we obtain the factor:

$$\frac{1 + \int d\xi R_p(\xi) \exp(-\tfrac{1}{2}\mathbf{p}_\xi \cdot \sigma_p^2 \cdot \mathbf{p}_\xi)}{1 + \int d\xi R_p(\xi)}$$

---

[3] Since the $\mathbf{f}_k$ are small, the exponential in which they occur can be expanded to second order: the zero order term cancels the "−1," and the first order term is zero since the total force has zero mean.

normalized to unity for $\mathbf{p}_\xi = 0$ and where $R_p(\xi)$ is the mean rate of this process, i.e., $R_p(\xi) = \sum_s R_s(\xi)$. Here σ_p^2 has the dimensions of (velocity)^2 while $\mathbf{T}$ has the dimensions of (velocity)^2/(time). So finally we find that

$$< \exp(i \int dt \mathbf{p}_t \cdot \mathbf{F}_t) > = \frac{\exp(-\frac{1}{2} \int dt \mathbf{p}_t \cdot \mathbf{T} \cdot \mathbf{p}_t)[1 + \int d\xi R_p(\xi) \exp(-\frac{1}{2} \mathbf{p}_\xi \cdot \sigma_p^2 \cdot \mathbf{p}_\xi)]}{1 + \int d\xi R_p(\xi)}$$

So that the probability of two or more impulses is negligible, it is necessary that $\int d\xi R_p(\xi) << 1$. Using the corresponding result in Appendix A for the Poisson case, we find for $P(2 \mid 1)$ in two dimensions, the expression:

$$P(2|1;t) = \frac{P_{0x}(2|1;t)P_{0y}(2|1;t) + \int_0^t d\xi R_p(\xi)P_{1x}(2|1;t,\xi)P_{1y}(2|1;t,\xi)}{1 + \int_0^t d\xi R_p(\xi)} \cdot \exp(\frac{-t}{\tau})$$

$$P_{1x}(2 \mid 1;t,\xi) = (2\pi T_x (D_x H_x)^{\frac{1}{2}})^{-1} \exp[-(A_x^2/D_x + B_x^2/H_x)/2T_x]$$

$$A_x = x_{21} - \frac{(\dot{x}_2 + \dot{x}_1)(t^2/2) + \xi_{px}(\dot{x}_2(t-\xi) + \dot{x}_1\xi)}{t + \xi_{px}}, \qquad B_x = \dot{x}_{21}$$

$$D_x = \frac{(t^4/12) + \xi_{px}(t^3/3 - t^2\xi + \xi^2 t)}{t + \xi_{px}}, \qquad H_x = t + \xi_{px}$$

where $\xi_{px} = \sigma_{px}^2/T_x$ and with analogous expressions for P_{1y}. Note that σ_p^2 is taken to be diagonal. The time ξ is the time of the single, large, scattering event. We observe that the Poisson process will dominate for $\xi_{px}, \xi_{py} >> t$.

The above result for zero and one rare event exhibits several important dependencies. First, recall that the velocity diffusion coefficient T is the velocity-fluctuation rate. Thus, for $Tt < \sigma_p^2$ or $t < \xi_p$ the frequent-weak process will be less effective than a single strong but rare event. This will be the case for higher velocities (i.e., smaller time intervals). Second, if $R_p(\xi)$ is taken to be a constant, R_p, then $R_p t$ will control the number of rare events (preferably $R_p t << 1$). However, P_1 will exceed P_0 when (and only when) two direct, relatively straight contours intersect. We note that it would be possible to derive the distribution for one rare event by appropriate joining of two Gaussian processes, but integrals over all intermediate positions *and* velocities would be required.

Although the expression for $P(2 \mid 1)$ above involves a number of symbols, there are in fact only four basic parameters: T, τ, ξ_p and R_p. The values of these four parameters determine the shape distribution and remain constant for a given application. First, the only parameter in P_0 is $T = T_x = T_y$, the velocity diffusion coefficient: $T = R_g \sigma_g^2$, where R_g is the mean rate of frequent-weak impulses and σ_g^2 is the variance of these impulses.[4] The smaller that T becomes, the greater the degree to which alternative, smooth contours can be discriminated (i.e., the more the most likely completion will dominate the distribution). As noted in Thornber and Williams[19], a factor $\exp(-t/\tau)$ can be included in $P(2 \mid 1)$ to reduce the role of long contours.

---

[4] The "g" reminds us of the Gaussian nature of this limit. Note that only the product of R_g and σ_g^2 appears in the equations.

Turning to P_1 the only parameters (other than T) are R_p and $\xi_p = \xi_{px} = \xi_{py}$. As discussed above, if the time t associated with the most probable contours is significantly less than ξ_p, then there is not enough time for the frequent-weak impulses to bend the contour from the first keypoint to the second. Since this factor is in the exponent of the probability expression, infrequent-strong impulses become favored (with rate proportional to R_p). Having set T to obtain the desired discrimination among smooth contours,[5] and ξ_p to sharpen the corners (suppressing the Gaussian component in P_1), R_p can be adjusted to achieve the desired balance of smooth completions and corners. We should also note at this juncture that $R_g \gg R_p$ and $\sigma_{px}^2 = \sigma_{py}^2 = \sigma_p^2 \gg \sigma_g^2 = \sigma_{gx}^2 = \sigma_{gy}^2$, and recall that $T = R_g \sigma_g^2$ and $\xi_p = \sigma_p^2/T$. Hence $R_g \xi_p = \sigma_p^2/\sigma_g^2$ is the number of weak fluctuations occuring during a time interval of ξ_p.

5   Scale Invariance

It is useful to identify invariants in order to check that results satisfy the proper scaling relations and to ensure that all degrees of freedom are appropriately exploited. Consider the following equation:

$$\frac{\partial Q(\mathbf{x}, \dot{\mathbf{x}}, t)}{\partial t} = -\dot{\mathbf{x}} \cdot \frac{\partial Q(\mathbf{x}, \dot{\mathbf{x}}, t)}{\partial \mathbf{x}} - \Gamma \frac{Q(\mathbf{x}, \dot{\mathbf{x}}, t)}{\tau} - \Gamma \sum_k R_k (\mathbf{A} \mathbf{v}_k) \cdot \frac{\partial Q}{\partial \dot{\mathbf{x}}}(\mathbf{x}, \dot{\mathbf{x}} - \mathbf{A} \mathbf{v}_k/2, t)$$

Here the impulse and decay rates have been increased by the factor Γ and the impulses have been deformed (e.g., scaled and rotated) by the non-singular matrix $\mathbf{A}$. Now it happens that

$$Q(\mathbf{x}, \dot{\mathbf{x}}, t) = cP(\mathbf{A}^{-1}\mathbf{x}, \mathbf{A}^{-1}\dot{\mathbf{x}}/\Gamma, \Gamma t)$$

where $P(\mathbf{x}', \dot{\mathbf{x}}', t')$ solves

$$\frac{\partial P(\mathbf{x}', \dot{\mathbf{x}}', t')}{\partial t'} = -\dot{\mathbf{x}}' \cdot \frac{\partial P(\mathbf{x}', \dot{\mathbf{x}}', t')}{\partial \mathbf{x}'} - \frac{P(\mathbf{x}', \dot{\mathbf{x}}', t')}{\tau} - \sum_k R_k \mathbf{v}_k \cdot \frac{\partial P(\mathbf{x}', \dot{\mathbf{x}}' - \mathbf{v}_k/2, t')}{\partial \dot{\mathbf{x}}'}$$

and c adjusts the normalization, e.g., $c = (\det A^2)^{-1}$. Written out fully, we have

$$Pr_{\Gamma, \mathbf{A}}(\mathbf{x}_2, \dot{\mathbf{x}}_2, t_2 \mid \mathbf{x}_1, \dot{\mathbf{x}}_1, t_1) = cP(\mathbf{A}^{-1}\mathbf{x}_2, \mathbf{A}^{-1}\dot{\mathbf{x}}_2/\Gamma, \Gamma t_2 \mid \mathbf{A}^{-1}\mathbf{x}_1, \mathbf{A}^{-1}\dot{\mathbf{x}}_1/\Gamma, \Gamma t_1)$$

which simply says that the solution to the modified problem is related to that of the unmodified problem by the above indicated transform[18]. While this provides a good sense for the full invariance of our expressions, what is most important is that they scale with the size of objects in the scene. Although this can be achieved in several ways, the most natural is to keep time-like quantities invariant ($\Gamma = 1$) and let velocities change one-to-one with size through $\mathbf{A}$ (which becomes a simple dilation $\gamma \mathbf{I}$). This amounts to keeping the parameters R, ξ_p, and τ fixed (since these are time-like) and scaling T with γ^2 (since T includes

---

[5] Actually, we set $T_{ref} = T/\gamma^2$. See next section.

(a)   (b)

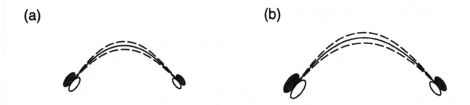

Fig. 3. Two completion fields related through a scale transformation. For a scene magnified γ times, T must be increased by a factor of γ^2 to achieve scale-invariance. Ideally, this would be accomplished without *a priori* knowledge of γ, e.g., by computing the completion field for all combinations of spatial scales within some fixed range and setting γ equal to $(|\dot{\mathbf{x}}_1| + |\dot{\mathbf{x}}_2|)/2$.

a velocity-variance factor). Ideally, this would be accomplished without *a priori* knowledge of γ, e.g., by computing the completion field for all combinations of spatial scales within some fixed range and setting γ equal to $(|\dot{\mathbf{x}}_1| + |\dot{\mathbf{x}}_2|)/2$ (see Figure 3).[6] Using our above relation for $P_{\Gamma,\mathbf{A}}$ and cP, our previous expression for $P_0(2 \mid 1)$, and setting $T_x = T_y = \gamma^2 T_{ref}$ we obtain for scale-invariant transition probabilities in two-dimensions:

$$P_0(2 \mid 1) = (2\pi T_{ref}t)^{-1} \exp[-(\dot{\mathbf{x}}_2 - \dot{\mathbf{x}}_1)^2/2\gamma^2 T_{ref}t]$$

$$\cdot(\pi T_{ref}t^3/6)^{-1} \exp[-6((\mathbf{x}_2 - \mathbf{x}_1) - (\dot{\mathbf{x}}_2 + \dot{\mathbf{x}}_1)t/2)^2/\gamma^2 T_{ref}t^3] \cdot \exp(-t/\tau)$$

The Poisson term $P_1(2 \mid 1)$ changes analogously: T_x in the prefactor becomes T_{ref} and T_x in the exponent becomes $\gamma^2 T_{ref}$. The characteristic time, ξ_{px}, remains invariant. Combining $P_0(2 \mid 1)$ and $P_1(2 \mid 1)$ to form $P(2 \mid 1)$ yields the desired scale-invariant transition probability, which is also translation and rotation invariant.

The careful reader will note that by setting γ equal to a speed, we no longer have the correct normalization for the conditional probability $P(2 \mid 1)$—the probabilities are now relative. Since this is just an overall factor, its value is of lesser importance. However, because $P(2 \mid 1)$ is a function of t, some care is required. For simplicity we have chosen to work with transition probabilities between states of equal speed. For this case, the normalization is only over position (x, y) and orientation θ, and can be closely approximated by replacing the factor $3(\pi T_{ref}t^2)^2$ in $P_0(2 \mid 1; t)$ by $3\sqrt{2}(\pi^3 T_{ref}^3 t^7)^{-1/2}$ and the factor $(2\pi T_{ref})^{-2}(D_x D_y H_x H_y)^{-1}$ in $P_1(2 \mid 1; t, \xi)$ by $(2\pi T_{ref})^{-3/2}(D_x D_y \sqrt{H_x H_y})^{-1}$. Finally, referring to Appendix B, t_{opt} now solves

$$-\frac{7}{4}t^3 + 3(g_a t^2 - 2g_b t + g_c) = 0$$

---

[6] A more practical proposal is to only compute completion fields due to pairs of keypoints of the same spatial scale, i.e., $|\dot{\mathbf{x}}_1| = |\dot{\mathbf{x}}_2|$. Alternatively, we could set γ and speed proportional to the distance between the two keypoints. This would be similiar to the scale-invariant energy of Bruckstein and Netravali[3].

6 Stochastic Completion Fields

The magnitude of the *stochastic completion field* at $(\mathbf{x}, \dot{\mathbf{x}})$ is defined as the probability that a completion, with a distribution of shapes given by $P(2 \mid 1)$, will connect two keypoints via a path through $(\mathbf{x}, \dot{\mathbf{x}})$. The stochastic completion field originating in an arbitrary set of n keypoints can (in turn) be expressed as the sum of n^2 pairwise fields. In this section, we describe the problem of computing the completion field for a pair of keypoints, and give example completion fields for a range of speeds.

To accomplish this, we first consider the distribution of contours which begin at the first keypoint, $(\mathbf{x}_1, \dot{\mathbf{x}}_1)$ at time t_1. We then consider the fraction of those contours which pass through the fieldpoint, $(\mathbf{x}, \dot{\mathbf{x}})$ at t and then through the second keypoint, $(\mathbf{x}_2, \dot{\mathbf{x}}_2)$ at time t_2 (where $t_2 > t > t_1$). Integrating over all t_1 ($-\infty < t_1 < t$) and t_2 ($t < t_2 < \infty$), we find the relative probability that a completion from $(\mathbf{x}_1, \dot{\mathbf{x}}_1)$ to $(\mathbf{x}_2, \dot{\mathbf{x}}_2)$ includes $(\mathbf{x}, \dot{\mathbf{x}})$, giving the value of the stochastic completion field, $C(\mathbf{x}, \dot{\mathbf{x}})$. Since the entire history of the contour at t is summarized by $(\mathbf{x}, \dot{\mathbf{x}})$ (the velocity fluctuations being independent), the probability of $(\mathbf{x}_1, \dot{\mathbf{x}}_1) \rightarrow (\mathbf{x}, \dot{\mathbf{x}}) \rightarrow (\mathbf{x}_2, \dot{\mathbf{x}}_2)$ factors into a product of probabilities for $(\mathbf{x}_1, \dot{\mathbf{x}}_1) \rightarrow (\mathbf{x}, \dot{\mathbf{x}})$ and for $(\mathbf{x}, \dot{\mathbf{x}}) \rightarrow (\mathbf{x}_2, \dot{\mathbf{x}}_2)$:

$$P((\mathbf{x}_2, \dot{\mathbf{x}}_2, t_2), (\mathbf{x}, \dot{\mathbf{x}}, t) \mid (\mathbf{x}_1, \dot{\mathbf{x}}_1, t_1)) =$$

$$P((\mathbf{x}_2, \dot{\mathbf{x}}_2, t_2) \mid (\mathbf{x}, \dot{\mathbf{x}}, t)) \cdot P((\mathbf{x}, \dot{\mathbf{x}}, t) \mid (\mathbf{x}_1, \dot{\mathbf{x}}_1, t_1))$$

Figure 4 (a-d) shows four completion fields due to a pair of keypoints positioned on a horizontal line and separated by a distance of 80 pixels. In each subfigure, the orientation of the right keypoint is $130°$ and the orientation of the left keypoint is $50°$. The speeds in Figure 4 (a-d) are 1,2,4 and 8 respectively. The values of the four parameters defining the contour shape distribution are: $T_{ref} = 0.0005, \tau = 9.5, \xi_p = 100$ and $R_p = 1.0 \times 10^{-6}$. The completion fields were computed using the expression for $P(2 \mid 1)$ given in Section 4 and using the integral approximations for $P'(2 \mid 1)$ described in Appendix B. Figure 4 (a-d) displays images of size 256×256 where brightness codes the logarithm of the sum of the completion field magnitude evaluated at 36 discrete orientations (i.e., at $10°$ increments). As the speed is increased, the relative contribution of P_0 and P_1 reverses. This results in a transition from a distribution dominated by smooth contours to a distribution consisting predominantly of straight (or nearly straight) contours containing a single orientation discontinuity. When the distribution is dominated by P_1, the effect of aliasing in orientation becomes evident.

7 Conclusion

In our previous paper[19], we assumed that the statistics of occluded shapes could be modeled by minimally-constrained distributions over all paths. We derived an analytic expression for the shape, salience and sharpness of illusory contours in terms of the characteristic function of the simplest of these distributions (i.e., Gaussian) and applied this expression to well known examples from the visual psychology literature. In this paper, we extended our work in several important directions. First, we have derived a general integral-differential equation including the full spectrum of stochastic impulses and which we believe will be useful for modeling a broad family of shape distributions. We have also derived an analytic expression characterizing the distribution of completion shapes with corners using a mixture of Gaussian and Poisson limiting cases. Finally, we have presented scale-invariant forms for these expressions.

Appendix A: Expected Distributions

For $\mathbf{x}_t = \mathbf{x}_{1t} + \int dt' \mathbf{G}_{t,t'} \mathbf{F}_{t'}$, $\mathbf{F}_{t'}$ stochastic, $\mathbf{F}_t = \sum_{k\ell} \mathbf{f}_k(t - t_{k\ell})$, and $\mathbf{x}_{1t} = \mathbf{x}_1 + \mathbf{G}_{t,t1} \dot{\mathbf{x}}_1$ we desire

$$\varPhi(\mathbf{k}_t) = < \exp(i \int dt \mathbf{k}_t \cdot \mathbf{x}_t) >_1 = \exp(i \int dt \mathbf{k}_t \cdot \mathbf{x}_{1t}) < \exp(i \int dt' \mathbf{p}_{t'} \cdot \mathbf{F}_{t'}) >$$

with $\mathbf{p}_{t'} = \int dt \mathbf{k}_t \mathbf{G}_{tt'}$. So long as the $t_{k\ell}$'s are independent, we can write

$$\phi(\mathbf{p}_t) = < \exp(i \int dt \mathbf{p}_t \cdot \mathbf{F}_t) >=$$

$$\prod_k \sum_{N_k=0}^{\infty} P_{N_k} (\int dt_k R_k(t_k) \exp(i \int dt \mathbf{p}_t \mathbf{f}_k(t - t_k))/\lambda_k)^{N_k}$$

where $\lambda_k = \int dt_k R_k(t_k)$ (see [5, 16, 17]). Here P_{N_k} is the probability of N_k events in the time interval of interest, and R_k the average rate of these events. To derive $< \ddot{\mathbf{x}}_{t_2} \delta(\mathbf{x}(t_2) - \mathbf{x}_2) \delta(\dot{\mathbf{x}}(t_2) - \dot{\mathbf{x}}_2) >$, for the integral-differential equation in the text, we must calculate at $\eta = 0$:

$$-i \frac{\partial}{\partial \eta} \int \frac{d\boldsymbol{\kappa}}{(2\pi)^3} e^{-i\boldsymbol{\kappa} \cdot \mathbf{x}_2} \int \frac{d\boldsymbol{\lambda}}{(2\pi)^3} e^{-i\boldsymbol{\lambda} \cdot \mathbf{x}_2} \varPhi(\mathbf{k}_t)$$

for $\mathbf{k}_t = \mathbf{k}_r(t) + \eta \delta''(t - t_2)$ and $\mathbf{k}_r(t) = \boldsymbol{\kappa} \delta(t - t_2) - \boldsymbol{\lambda} \delta'(t - t_2)$. Alternatively, $\mathbf{p}_t = \mathbf{p}_r(t) + \eta \delta(t_2 - t)$. Setting $\mathbf{p}(t) = \mathbf{p}_r(t) = \boldsymbol{\kappa} \mathbf{G}_{t_2,t} + \boldsymbol{\lambda} \partial_{t_2} \mathbf{G}_{t_2,t}$ and $\mathbf{k}(t) = \mathbf{k}_r(t)$ results in $P(\mathbf{x}_2, \dot{\mathbf{x}}_2, t_2 \mid \mathbf{x}_1, \dot{\mathbf{x}}_1, t_1)$. Inserting these $\mathbf{p}(t)$ and $\mathbf{k}(t)$ in the expressions for $\varPhi$ and ϕ above and working out the η items, we find for the case that the P_N are Poisson:

$$< \ddot{\mathbf{x}}_{t2} \delta(\mathbf{x}(t_2) - x_2) \delta(\dot{\mathbf{x}}(t_2) - \dot{\mathbf{x}}_2) >=$$

$$\ddot{\mathbf{x}}_{1t} P(\mathbf{x}_2, \dot{\mathbf{x}}_2, t_2 \mid \mathbf{x}_1, \dot{\mathbf{x}}_1, t_1) + \sum_k \int d\xi R_k(\xi) \mathbf{f}_k(t - \xi)$$

$$\cdot P(\mathbf{x}_2 - \int dt' \mathbf{G}_{t,t'} \mathbf{f}_k(t' - \xi), \dot{\mathbf{x}}_2 - \int dt' \partial_t \mathbf{G}_{t,t'} \mathbf{f}_k(t' - \xi), t_2 \mid \mathbf{x}_1, \dot{\mathbf{x}}_1, t_1)$$

We need not take the Poisson limit of P_{N_k}, for we could work directly with $\varPhi$ and ϕ above, but their representation in an integral-differential equation is unnecessarily complex. We note that the above is valid for general Poisson processes—weak/strong, frequent/infrequent and anything in between. To evaluate $P(2 \mid 1)$ for the Poisson case one simply calculates the above without the $(-i\partial/\partial\eta)$ and for $\eta = 0$, proceeding in a manner analogous to [19].

Appendix B: Integral Approximations

The expressions we have derived (thus far) depend on time, i.e., they give the probability that a particle will be at some position and velocity, $(\mathbf{x}_2, \dot{\mathbf{x}}_2)$, at time t given that the particle was observed at some other position and velocity, $(\mathbf{x}_1, \dot{\mathbf{x}}_1)$, at time 0. We refer to this quantity as $P(2 \mid 1; t)$. However, if we are really interested in computing the probability that two boundary fragments are part of the same object, then we are more interested in the integral of $P(2 \mid 1; t)$ over all future times. We refer to this quantity as $P'(2 \mid 1) = \int_0^\infty dt P(2 \mid 1; t)$. To derive an expression for $P'(2 \mid 1)$, we must not only approximate this integral analytically, we must also approximate the integral over the time of the single large impulse, ξ, in the expression for $P(2 \mid 1; t)$.

To begin, we divide the expression for $P(2 \mid 1)$ into two terms, I_0 and I_1, and use the method of steepest descent separately on each part. This requires one steepest descent approximation for I_0 and two steepest descent approximations for I_1 (which contains the additional dependency on ξ):

$$
\begin{aligned}
P'(2 \mid 1) &= \int_0^{t_{max}} dt \, P(2 \mid 1; t) \\
&= \int_0^{t_{max}} dt \, \frac{P_0(2 \mid 1; t) + R_p \int_0^t d\xi P_1(2 \mid 1; t, \xi)}{1 + R_p t} \\
&= \int_0^{t_{max}} dt \, \frac{1}{1 + R_p t} P_0(2 \mid 1; t) + \int_0^{t_{max}} dt' \, \frac{R_p}{1 + R_p t'} \int_0^{t'} d\xi P_1(2 \mid 1; t', \xi) \\
&= I_0 + I_1
\end{aligned}
$$

The first integral to be dealt with is that over the time of the single large impulse:

$$
I_R(t') = R_p \int_0^{t'} d\xi P_{1x}(2 \mid 1; t', \xi) P_{1y}(2 \mid 1; t', \xi)
$$

Here ξ enters the integrand only through the D and A. A more accurate, steepest-decents approximation would include the ξ-dependence in both. However, since the dependence in the A dominates the behavior of the integral, we ignore the dependence in the D in determining the local maximum. We find

$$
\xi_{opt} = -\left(\frac{a_x a'_x}{D_x T_x} + \frac{a_y a'_y}{D_y T_y}\right) / \left(\frac{a'_x{}^2}{D_x T_x} + \frac{a'_y{}^2}{D_y T_y}\right)
$$

$$
a_x = x_{21} - \frac{(\dot{x}_2 + \dot{x}_1)(t'^2/2) + \xi_{px}\dot{x}_2 t'}{t' + \xi_{px}}
$$

$$
a'_x = \frac{\xi_{px}\dot{x}_{21}}{t' + \xi_{px}}
$$

and similarly for a_y and a'_y.[7] The approximate result for the integral is then

$$
I_R(t') \approx F_R(\xi_{opt}) R_p P_{1x}(2 \mid 1; t', \xi_{opt}) P_{1y}(2 \mid 1; t', \xi_{opt})
$$

---

[7] The ξ_{opt} is needed for D_x and D_y, but letting $\xi_{opt} = t'/2$ in the expression for D and then iterating gives quick convergence. Since usually $D_x = D_y$ and $T_x = T_y$, this implicit dependence cancels out.

$$F_R(\xi) = \sqrt{2\pi/(a_x'^2/T_x D_x + a_y'^2/T_y D_y)}, \quad 0 < \xi < t'$$

When $\xi < 0$ or $\xi > t'$ then we set $F_R = 0$. Of course, I_R is never actually zero. If its behavior for $\xi_{opt} < 0$ or $\xi_{opt} > t'$ is important, we must simply approximate more carefully. We also note that at $\xi = \xi_{opt}$, we have the simplification that

$$(A_x^2/D_x T_x + A_y^2/D_y T_y) = (a_x a_y' - a_y a_x')^2/(a_x'^2 D_y T_y + a_y'^2 D_x T_x)$$

which somewhat simplifies the calculation of I_R.

We now face $\int_0^{t_{max}} dt P(2 \mid 1; t)$ where t_{max} is so large that $P(2 \mid 1; t)$ for $t > t_{max}$ is comparatively negligible. Again for the single-event term, we use a poor-man's steepest descent approximation focusing only on the most sensitive dependencies. There are two integrals with different local optima (i.e., t_{opt} and t_{opt}'). The first (lacking single-scattering events) is

$$I_0 = \int_0^{t_{max}} dt \, P_{0x}(2 \mid 1; t) \, P_{0y}(2 \mid 1; t)/(1 + R_p t)$$

Here the dependence on t is the argument of the exponentials:

$$-6(g_a/t - g_b/t^2 + g_c/3t^3) - 4\ln t$$

$$g_a = (v_x^2 + \dot{x}_{21}^2/12)/T_x + (v_y^2 + \dot{y}_{21}^2/12)/T_y$$
$$g_b = 2(x_{21}v_x/T_x + y_{21}v_y/T_y)$$
$$g_c = 3(x_{21}^2/T_x + y_{21}^2/T_y)$$
$$v_x = (\dot{x}_1 + \dot{x}_2)/2, \quad v_y = (\dot{y}_1 + \dot{y}_2)/2$$

This argument has a local maximum at $t_{opt} > 0$, where t_{opt} satisfies

$$-2t^3 + 3(g_a t^2 - 2g_b t + g_c) = 0$$

yielding the approximate value for I_0 of

$$I_0 \approx F_0 P_{0x}(2 \mid 1; t_{opt}) \, P_{0y}(2 \mid 1; t_{opt})/(1 + R_p t_{opt})$$
$$F_0 = \sqrt{2\pi t_{opt}^5/(12(g_c - g_b t_{opt}) + 4t_{opt}^3)}$$

If more than one real $t_{opt} > 0$ exists, the one yielding the largest $P_0(2 \mid 1)$ is chosen. The second term, involving a single, large-scattering event, is

$$I_1 = \int_{t_1}^{t_{max}} dt' I_R(t')/(1 + R_p t')$$

If this term is to be important then $\xi_p = (\sigma_v^2/T) >> t'$, in which case the argument of the exponent in I_1 will be maximum for t' close to

$$t_{opt}' = (x_{21}\dot{y}_{21} - y_{21}\dot{x}_{21})/(\dot{x}_1\dot{y}_2 - \dot{x}_2\dot{y}_1)$$

so that

$$I_1 \approx F_1(t_{opt}')I_R(t_{opt}')/(1 + R_p t_{opt}')$$
$$F_1(t) = \sqrt{2\pi(\dot{x}_{21}^2 D_y T_y + \dot{y}_{21}^2 D_x T_x)/(\dot{x}_1\dot{y}_2 - \dot{y}_1\dot{x}_2)^2}$$

for $0 < t_{opt}' < t_{max}$, and $F_1 = 0$ for $t_{opt}' \leq 0$ or $t_{opt}' \geq t_{max}$. As before, F_1 is never really zero. If $0 \leq t_{opt} \leq t_{max}$ and $t_{opt}' < 0$ or $t_{opt}' > t_{max}$, then $I_0 >> I_1$, and I_1 can be ignored. However, if both t_{opt} and t_{opt}' are greater than t_{max}, then t_{max} is too small and should be increased.

References

1. Belheumer, P.N., Bayesian Models for Reconstructing the Scene Geometry in a Pair of Stereo Images, *Proc. Conf. Information Sciences and Systems*, Johns Hopkins University, Baltimore, MD, 1993.

2. Blake, A., The Least Disturbance Principle and Weak Constraints, *Pattern Recognition Letters* 1, pp. 393-399, 1983.

3. Bruckstein, A.M. and Netravali, A.N., On Minimal Energy Trajectories, *Computer Vision, Graphics and Image Processing* 49, pp. 283-296, 1990.

4. Cox, I.J., Rehg, J.M. and Hingorani, S., A Bayesian Multiple Hypothesis Approach to Edge Grouping and Contour Segmentation, *Intl. Journal of Computer Vision* 11, pp. 5-24, 1993.

5. Feynman, R.P. and A.R. Hibbs, *Quantum Mechanics and Path Integrals*, New York, McGraw Hill, 1965.

6. Geman, S. and D. Geman, Stochastic Relaxation, Gibbs Distributions, and Bayesian Restoration of Images, *IEEE Trans. Pattern Analysis and Machine Intelligence* 6, pp. 721-741, 1984.

7. Grimson, W.E.L., and Pavlidis, T., Discontinuity Detection for Visual Surface Reconstruction, *Computer Vision, Graphics and Image Processing* 30, pp. 316-330, 1985.

8. Heitger, R. and von der Heydt, R., A Computational Model of Neural Contour Processing, Figure-ground and Illusory Contours, *Proc. of 4th Intl. Conf. on Computer Vision*, Berlin, Germany, 1993.

9. Horn, B.K.P., The Curve of Least Energy, MIT AI Lab Memo No. 612, MIT, Cambridge, Mass., 1981.

10. Kanizsa, G., *Organization in Vision*, Praeger, New York, 1979.

11. Kass, M., Witkin, A. and Terzopolous, D., Snakes: Active Minimum Energy Seeking Contours, *Proc. of the First Intl. Conf. on Computer Vision (ICCV)*, London, England, pp. 259-268, 1987.

12. Marroquin, J., Surface Reconstruction Preserving Discontinuities, MIT AI Lab Memo No. 792, MIT, Cambridge, MA, 1984.

13. Mumford, D., Elastica and Computer Vision, *Algebraic Geometry and Its Applications*, Chandrajit Bajaj (ed.), Springer-Verlag, New York, 1994.

14. Mumford, D. and Shah, J., Boundary Detection by Minimizing Functionals, *Proc. IEEE Conf. on Comp. Vision and Pattern Recognition (CVPR)*, 1985.

15. Terzopolous, D., Computing Visible Surface Representations, MIT AI Lab Memo No. 612, MIT, Cambridge, MA, 1985.

16. Thornber, K.K., Treatment of Microscopic Fluctuations in Noise Theory, *BSTJ* 53, pp. 1041-1078, 1974.

17. Thornber, K.K., A New Approach for Treating Fluctuations in Noise Theory, *J. Appl. Phys.* 46, pp. 2781-2787, 1975.

18. Thornber, K.K., Application of Scaling to Problems in High Field Electronic Transport, *J. Appl. Phys.* 52, pp. 279-290, 1981.

19. Thornber, K.K. and L.R. Williams, Analytic Solution of Stochastic Completion Fields, *Biological Cybernetics* 75, pp. 141-151, 1996.

20. Williams, L.R., and D.W. Jacobs, Stochastic Completion Fields: A Neural Model of Illusory Contour Shape and Salience, *Neural Computation* 9 (in press).

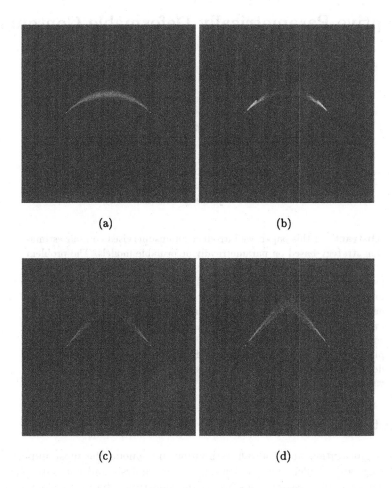

(a)   (b)

(c)   (d)

Fig. 4. Stochastic completion fields (logarithm of magnitude) due to a pair of keypoints positioned on a horizontal line and separated by a distance of 80 pixels. In each subfigure, the orientation of the left keypoint is 130° and the orientation of the right keypoint is 50°. The speeds in Figure 4 (a-d) are 1,2,4 and 8 respectively. The values of the four parameters defining the contour shape distribution are: $T_{ref} = 0.0005, \tau = 9.5, \xi_p = 100$ and $R_p = 1.0 \times 10^{-6}$.

Adaptive Parametrically Deformable Contours

Mário A. T. Figueiredo[1], José M. N. Leitão[1], and Anil K. Jain[2]

[1] Instituto de Telecomunicações, and
Departamento de Engenharia Electrotécnica e de Computadores.
Instituto Superior Técnico, 1096 Lisboa Codex, PORTUGAL
(e-mails addresses: mtf@lx.it.pt and jleitao@red.lx.it.pt)

[2] Department of Computer Science.
Michigan State University, East Lansing, MI 48824, U.S.A.
(e-mail address: jain@cpswells.msu.edu)

Abstract. In this paper, we introduce an unsupervised contour estimation strategy based on parametrically deformable models. The problem is formulated in a (statistical) parameter estimation framework with the parameters of both the contour the and observation model (the likelihood function) being considered unknown. Although other choices could fit in our formulation, we focus on Fourier and B-spline contour descriptors. To estimate the optimal parametrization order (e.g., the number of Fourier coefficients) we adopt the *minimum description length* (MDL) principle. The result is a parametrically deformable contour with an adaptive degree of smoothness and which also autonomously estimates the observation model parameters.

1   Introduction and Previous Work

Image segmentation and contour estimation are among the most important, interesting, and challenging problems in image analysis and computer vision. When no particular assumptions are made concerning the morphology of the objects/regions to be estimated. we are in the presence of an *image segmentation* problem. in the common meaning of the term. When the problem is confined to that of finding the boundary of an individual image region. it is commonly referred to as *contour estimation*; a typical example is organ boundary location in medical images.

1.1   *Snakes* and Related Approaches

Rooted in the seminal work of Kass, Witkin, and Terzopoulos [22], *snake*-type models constitute one of the most successful class of approaches to contour estimation. In its original version [22], snakes work by minimizing an *energy* function composed of an (internal) elastic-type term which penalizes the contour deformations. and an (external) attraction potential linking it with image features

---

The work described in this paper was partially supported by the NATO Collaborative Research Grant #CRG 960010.

of interest. The minimization of this energy function yields a desired compromise between contour *smoothness*, on one hand, and adequacy to the observed data, on the other hand. The major drawbacks of conventional *snakes* are: lack of adaptiveness (parameters have to be set a priori); inability to reparametrize during the deformation process; use of information strictly along the boundary, making it highly "myopic" and sensitive to initialization. Recently, several improvements, modifications, and reformulations have been proposed to overcome these limitations; see [5], [6], [7], [8], [18], [28], [31], and further references therein. Active contours with the ability to grow (or shrink) to accommodate larger (smaller) objects, or even change their topology, have been proposed [26]. A particularly elegant and successful topology-independent formulation was recently proposed in [4] and [25].

1.2 Deformable Templates/Models

Deformable templates and models constitute another important approach to contour and object estimation. Here, global models generally described by a small number of parameters are used (in contrast with snakes, which use explicit contour descriptions). These models may directly describe (contour/object) shapes or, alternatively, deformations suffered by a basic template; in the presence of the observed data/image, these model parameters are somehow estimated. Fundamental work on deformable templates is that of Grenander and his collaborators; see [2], [16], and [17] and references therein. Further recent work adopting this type of approach can be found in (this is by no means an exhaustive list): [20], [21], [33], [36], [37], and other references therein. As in snake-type approaches, one of the main difficulties when using deformable templates is their lack of adaptiveness, with parameters having to be set a priori.

1.3 The Bayesian Estimation Viewpoint

From a Bayesian view-point, active contours are interpretable as *maximum a posteriori* (MAP) estimators; the internal and external energies are associated with the *a priori* probability function and the likelihood function, respectively [15], [34].

Deformable templates may not include a deformation energy (i.e., a Bayesian prior) when the parametrization itself guarantees regularity of the represented shape; in this case, a *maximum likelihood* (ML) interpretation is still possible. In several cases, a prior biasing the estimate towards some preferred shape is included [20], [21], [33], [36], [37]; then a MAP estimation formulation (or interpretation) is adequate.

The Bayesian estimation perspective has the advantage of giving meaning to all the involved entities; e.g., the form of the energy term that links the contour with the image contents (i.e., the likelihood function, in Bayesian terms) can be derived from knowledge about the observation model rather than simply from common sense arguments [12], [15]. The main difficulty in this approach is still the choice of the parameters involved in the definition of the *a priori* probability function and of the observation model. In [15], we have proposed an adaptive Bayesian approach for a ventricular contour estimation problem. A technique which adaptively estimates the observation model parameters (also for ventricular contour estimation) was recently proposed in [12]. Recent work in [38] also presents an adaptive *snake*-related scheme and contributes to the unification of the energy-minimizing and Bayesian approaches.

1.4 Solving the Minimization Problem

Regardless of their theoretical/conceptual setting, both classical *snake*-type approaches and deformable templates/models lead to difficult optimization problems which have stimulated a considerable amount of research. A diverse set of approaches has been proposed to solve them: deterministic iterative energy minimization schemes [15] (see the many references in [7]); dynamic programming [1], [12]; multiresolution algorithms [12], [20]; and stochastic methods including *simulated annealing* [34], the Metropolis algorithm [21], and pure diffusion (Langevin) or jump-diffusion processes [2], [16], [17].

1.5 Proposed Approach

In this paper, we propose a fully adaptive contour estimation strategy based on parametrically deformable models. The problem is formulated in a statistical estimation framework where both the contour parameters and the observation model parameters are considered unknown. Although other choices fit in our formulation, we focus on Fourier and B-spline representations. An issue arising in this type of parametric descriptions of deformable contours is the choice of the parametrization order (i.e., the number of Fourier coefficients or B-spline control points): by interpreting the contour estimation problem as a parameter estimation problem, we open the door to the adoption of Rissanen's *minimum description length* (MDL) principle [29], [30]. The resulting criterion defines a parametrically deformable contour with adaptive smoothness and which autonomously estimates the observation model parameters. Another aspect stressed in this paper is that care should be put in deriving the observation model (the likelihood function): e.g., for certain image models, gradient-based external energies may be completely useless.

2 Proposed Technique

2.1 Parametrically Deformable Contours

General Formulation. Deformable contours are (regular) shapes defined by a small number of parameters. Classical examples include Fourier and spline descriptors. Since the search space is already confined by the fact that the shapes are described by a small number of parameters, the elastic energy which penalizes deformations (as in *snake*-type models) is not needed. For example, a curve described by a small number of Fourier coefficients is automatically smooth.

Let $\boldsymbol{\theta}_{(K)}$ denote the set of parameters (parameter vector) defining the shape of a continuous closed contour. This parameter vector belongs to $\Theta_{(K)}$, the set of allowable configurations. The subscript $\cdot_{(K)}$ is used to indicate a K-order parametrization, e.g., a Fourier description with K terms or a spline with K control points. The closed contour (on the image plane) represented by $\boldsymbol{\theta}_{(K)}$ is a continuous periodic vector function $\mathbf{v}(t) = [x(t)\ y(t)]$, of period 2π, i.e., of unit fundamental angular frequency[3]; its N-points discrete version is a $(N \times 2)$ vector

$$
\mathbf{v} = \begin{bmatrix} \mathbf{v}_0 \\ \mathbf{v}_1 \\ \vdots \\ \mathbf{v}_{N-1} \end{bmatrix} = \begin{bmatrix} x_0 & y_0 \\ x_1 & y_1 \\ \vdots & \vdots \\ x_{N-1} & y_{N-1} \end{bmatrix},
$$

where $\mathbf{v}_i \equiv \mathbf{v}(i2\pi/(N-1))$, for $i = 0, 1, ..., N-1$. Given $\boldsymbol{\theta}_{(K)}$, the explicit contour representation $\mathbf{v}$ is obtained by some deterministic operator $\mathcal{V}_{(K)}$ defined on $\Theta_{(K)}$, i.e., we write $\mathbf{v} = \mathcal{V}_{(K)}\boldsymbol{\theta}_{(K)}$.

Fourier Descriptors. The complex Fourier series description of a continuous closed curve $\mathbf{v}(t) = [x(t)\ y(t)]^T$ (of unit fundamental angular frequency[3]) is

$$
\mathbf{v}(t) = [x(t)\ y(t)] = \sum_{k=-\infty}^{\infty} [c_k\ d_k] e^{jkt}, \quad t \in [0,\ 2\pi], \tag{1}
$$

where the complex Fourier coefficients are

$$
[c_k\ d_k] = \frac{1}{2\pi} \int_0^{2\pi} [x(t)\ y(t)] e^{-jkt} dt \tag{2}
$$

(see [19], [33]). The discrete complex Fourier series representation is

$$
\mathbf{v}_i = [x_i\ y_i] = \sum_{k=0}^{N-1} [e_k\ f_k] e^{jki2\pi/N} \tag{3}
$$

with

$$
[e_k\ f_k] \equiv \mathbf{g}_k = \frac{1}{N} \sum_{i=0}^{N-1} [x_i\ y_i] e^{-jki2\pi/N}. \tag{4}
$$

By truncating the series in Eq. (3) (or in Eq. (1)) to K terms ($K < N$), a smoothed version of the curve is obtained. The above defined parameter vector $\boldsymbol{\theta}_{(K)}$ contains, in this case, $2K$ complex coefficients (i.e., $4K$ real parameters)

$$
\boldsymbol{\theta}_{(K)} = [\mathbf{g}_0^T\ \mathbf{g}_1^T\ \cdots\ \mathbf{g}_{K-1}^T]^T = \begin{bmatrix} e_0 & e_1 & \cdots & e_{K-1} \\ f_0 & f_1 & \cdots & f_{K-1} \end{bmatrix}^T. \tag{5}
$$

---

[3] If t is understood as the arc length of the contour, it can be normalized such that the total length equals 2π.

Thus, the order of the parametrization defines the degree of smoothness of the contours. Operator $\mathcal{V}_{(K)}$ is, in this case, simply a matrix product

$$\mathbf{v} = \mathcal{V}_{(K)} \, \boldsymbol{\theta}_{(K)} = \mathbf{F}_{(K)} \boldsymbol{\theta}_{(K)},$$

where $\mathbf{F}_{(K)}$ is the $(N \times K)$ matrix representing the K-term truncated Fourier series, i.e., $\left[\mathbf{F}_{(K)}\right]_{ik} = e^{jki2\pi/N}$, for $i = 0, 1, ..., N-1$ and $k = 0, 1, ..., K-1$. It is worth noticing that, if there are no further constraints, i.e. $\Theta_{(K)}$ is the Euclidean space $\mathbb{R}^{4K}$, then the set of all contours (described by the elements of $\Theta_{(K)}$) is itself a linear space; it is the range $\mathcal{R}(\mathcal{V}_{(K)})$ of the linear operator $\mathcal{V}_{(K)}$.

Spline Descriptors. We consider cubic B-splines, widely used to represent contours with a small number of parameters [10], [14], [19]. Spline representations in *snake*-type models have been explored by several authors (see [7] and references therein); the key idea has been that since splines minimize a deformation-like energy, the search can be confined to a set of such functions under the action of the image potential. B-splines constitute a set of basis functions based on which a parametric representation for a spline curve takes the form

$$\mathbf{v}(t) = [x(t) \ y(t)] = \sum_{k=0}^{K-1} [\alpha_k^x \ \alpha_k^y] \, B_k(t) \tag{6}$$

where $[\alpha_k^x, \ \alpha_k^y] = \boldsymbol{\alpha}_k \in \mathbb{R}^2$ are the *control points* and the $B_k(t)$ are the (cubic B-spline) *basis functions* (for details on splines and B-splines see [10], [14]). Discretization is obtained by taking N equispaced samples of $\mathbf{v}(t)$; here, we assume that $N > K$. Accordingly, and interpreting the set of K control points as the parameter vector

$$\boldsymbol{\theta}_{(K)} = [\boldsymbol{\alpha}_0^T, \boldsymbol{\alpha}_1^T, ..., \boldsymbol{\alpha}_{K-1}^T]^T = \begin{bmatrix} \alpha_0^x & \alpha_1^x & \cdots & \alpha_{K-1}^x \\ \alpha_0^y & \alpha_1^y & \cdots & \alpha_{K-1}^y \end{bmatrix}^T, \tag{7}$$

the operator $\mathcal{V}_{(K)}$ is, in this case, also a matrix product

$$\mathbf{v} = \mathcal{V}_{(K)} \, \boldsymbol{\theta}_{(K)} = \mathbf{B}_{(K)} \boldsymbol{\theta}_{(K)} \tag{8}$$

where the elements of $(N \times K)$ matrix $\mathbf{B}_{(K)}$ are given by $\left[B_{(K)}\right]_{ik} = B_k(2\pi i/(N-1))$. Note that, again, in the absence of constraints on the control points ($\Theta_{(K)} = \mathbb{R}^{2K}$) the set of all splines with K control points and a given set of basis functions is itself a linear space, the range of matrix $\mathbf{B}_{(K)}$.

2.2 The Observation Model

Although this is an often overlooked aspect, great care should be taken in defining the observation model. For specific applications (e.g., finding organ boundaries in medical images), all the available knowledge about the image acquisition process should be included [12], [15]. Not doing so may result in very poor results.

The observed image $\mathbf{I}$ is an indirect, imperfect, and random function of the parameter vector $\theta_{(K)}$, from which it has to be estimated. This observation model has a set of specific parameters ϕ, i.e., we write $\mathbf{I} = \mathcal{S}\left(\theta_{(K)}, \phi\right)$. The complete observation model is split into two parts as follows:

$$\theta_{(K)} \xrightarrow{\mathcal{V}_{(K)}} \mathcal{V}_{(K)}\,\theta_{(K)} \equiv \mathbf{v} \quad \text{(the ideal contour)} \tag{9}$$

$$\mathbf{v} \xrightarrow{\text{image model}} \mathbf{I} \quad \text{(the observed image)} \tag{10}$$

where the first step depends on the type of parametrization chosen, and the second step captures the image generation/acquisition model. We now make the following assumptions concerning the observed image model, i.e. Eq. (10):

Conditional independence: given the contour $\mathbf{v} = \mathcal{V}_{(K)}\theta_{(K)}$, the image pixels are independently distributed.

Region homogeneity: The conditional probability function of each pixel depends only on whether it belongs to the inside or outside region of the contour; i.e., all pixels inside (resp. outside) have a common distribution characterized by a parameter vector ϕ_{in} (resp. by ϕ_{out}), with $\phi = [\phi_{\text{in}}, \phi_{\text{out}}]$.

From these assumptions, the likelihood function is written as

$$p(\mathbf{I}|\theta_{(K)}, \phi) = \left(\prod_{(i,j) \in \mathcal{I}(\mathbf{v})} p\left(I_{(i,j)}|\phi_{\text{in}}\right)\right)\left(\prod_{(i,j) \in \mathcal{O}(\mathbf{v})} p\left(I_{(i,j)}|\phi_{\text{out}}\right)\right) \tag{11}$$

where $I_{(i,j)}$ denotes pixel (i,j) of image $\mathbf{I}$, while $\mathcal{I}(\mathbf{v})$ and $\mathcal{O}(\mathbf{v})$ are the inside and outside regions of this contour, respectively; likewise, $p(I_{(i,j)}|\phi_{\text{in}})$ and $p(I_{(i,j)}|\phi_{\text{out}})$ are the pixel-wise conditional probabilities, of the inner and outer regions, respectively. This is a region-based model [12], [15], [18], [31] which uses all the data in the image, and not only a narrow stripe along the contour; moreover, it makes sense in situations where gradients do not characterize a region (e.g., two regions with the same mean). This model can be extended to non-independently distributed pixels, e.g., two different Markov random fields; however, this extension raises computational difficulties and will not be considered here.

2.3   The Estimation Criterion

The goal of an unsupervised scheme is clearly to estimate $\theta_{(K)}$ and ϕ from the observed image $\mathbf{I}$ based on the observation model (the likelihood function). A natural choice would be the maximum likelihood (ML) estimate

$$\left(\widehat{\theta}_{(K)}, \widehat{\phi}\right)_{\text{ML}} = \arg\max_{\theta_{(K)}, \phi} p(\mathbf{I}|\theta_{(K)}, \phi). \tag{12}$$

However, since K is unknown, this maximization suffers from a model order problem which can be stated as follows (assuming, for simplicity, known ϕ):

- In the Fourier parametrization, the parameter spaces $\Theta_{(K)}$, $K = 1, 2, \ldots$ are *nested* in the following sense: for each $\boldsymbol{\theta}_{(K)} \in \Theta_{(K)}$, there is some $\boldsymbol{\theta}'_{(K+1)} \in \Theta_{(K+1)}$ such that

$$p(\mathbf{I}|\boldsymbol{\theta}_{(K)}, \boldsymbol{\phi}) = p(\mathbf{I}|\boldsymbol{\theta}'_{(K+1)}, \boldsymbol{\phi}). \tag{13}$$

  In fact, it is clear that both $\boldsymbol{\theta}_{(K)} = [\mathbf{g}_0^T, \mathbf{g}_1^T, \ldots, \mathbf{g}_{K-1}^T]^T \in \Theta_{(K)}$ and $\boldsymbol{\theta}'_{(K+1)} = [\mathbf{g}_0^T, \mathbf{g}_1^T, \ldots, \mathbf{g}_{K-1}^T, [0, 0]^T]^T \in \Theta_{(K+1)}$ describe the same contour.
- Consequently, K can not be estimated directly by maximizing the likelihood function: in fact, $p(\mathbf{I}|\widehat{\boldsymbol{\theta}}_{(K)}, \boldsymbol{\phi})$, where $\widehat{\boldsymbol{\theta}}_{(K)}$ is the ML estimate of $\boldsymbol{\theta}_{(K)}$ given K, is a non-decreasing function of K [27].
- In the B-spline case, this nested space property only occurs in certain ways of building the basis functions. The reason for this is that these basis functions may not be (in generalk they are not) orthogonal. However, the same general tendency of increasing likelihood function with increasing parametrization order is still clearly verified.

To overcome this difficulty, we adopt Rissanen's *minimum description length* (MDL) criterion [29], [30]. MDL is an information-theoretical principle which, simply put, states that the best model is the one allowing the shortest joint description of the observed data and the model itself. Formally,

$$\left(\widehat{\boldsymbol{\theta}_{(K)}}, \widehat{\boldsymbol{\phi}}\right)_{\text{MDL}} = \arg\min\left\{-\log p(\mathbf{I}|\boldsymbol{\theta}_{(K)}, \boldsymbol{\phi}) + L(\boldsymbol{\theta}_{(K)}, \boldsymbol{\phi})\right\}, \tag{14}$$

with $\widehat{\boldsymbol{\theta}_{(K)}}$ standing for the joint estimates of K and $\boldsymbol{\theta}_{(K)}$, i.e., $\widehat{\boldsymbol{\theta}_{(K)}} \equiv \widehat{\boldsymbol{\theta}}_{(\widehat{K})}$. The first term in the right-hand side of Eq. (14) is simply the Shannon codelength[4] obtained when coding $\mathbf{I}$ based on the probabilistic model $p(\mathbf{I}|\boldsymbol{\theta}_{(K)}, \boldsymbol{\phi})$ [9]. The second term is the codelength of the parameters which can be split as $L(\boldsymbol{\theta}_{(K)}, \boldsymbol{\phi}) = L(\boldsymbol{\theta}_{(K)}) + L(\boldsymbol{\phi})$. Being independent of K, $L(\boldsymbol{\phi})$ can be omitted from the objective function. It is shown in [29] and [30] that the optimal codelength for each real-valued parameter is $\frac{1}{2}\log M$, where M is the number of data points to be encoded, i.e., the number of pixels in $\mathbf{I}$; although this is an asymptotic (in M) expression which may not be completely adequate to our situation, its adoption is validated by the good experimental results obtained. In future work we plan to use recent results concerning MDL estimation with small sample sizes [13]. Finally,

$$L(\boldsymbol{\theta}_{(K)}, \boldsymbol{\phi}) = \begin{cases} 2K\log M, & \text{for the Fourier parametrization,} \\ K\log M. & \text{for the spline parametrization,} \end{cases} \tag{15}$$

because a K-order Fourier parametrization involves $2K$ complex parameters, i.e. $4K$ real ones, while a spline with K control point involves $2K$ real parameters. Notice that, if K is known, the MDL and ML estimates coincide; this is an important feature of the MDL principle.

---

[4] In bits or *nats* for binary or natural logarithms, respectively [9].

2.4 A Bayesian Perspective

The MDL principle was not proposed by Rissanen with a Bayesian interpretation in mind [30]. However, Eq. (14) has a clear Bayesian interpretation as a *maximum a posteriori* (MAP) estimator,

$$
\left(\widehat{\boldsymbol{\theta}_{(K)}}, \hat{\phi}\right)_{\mathrm{MAP}} = \arg\max\left\{p\left(\boldsymbol{\theta}_{(K)}, \phi \,|\, I\right)\right\} = \arg\max\left\{p\left(\mathbf{I}|\boldsymbol{\theta}_{(K)}, \phi\right) p\left(\boldsymbol{\theta}_{(K)}, \phi\right)\right\}
$$
$$
= \arg\min\left\{-\log p(\mathbf{I}|\boldsymbol{\theta}_{(K)}, \phi) - \log p\left(\boldsymbol{\theta}_{(K)}, \phi\right)\right\},
$$

with the prior

$$
p\left(\boldsymbol{\theta}_{(K)}, \phi\right) \propto \begin{cases} \exp\left\{-2K\log M\right\}, & \text{for the Fourier parametrization,} \\ \exp\left\{-K\log M\right\}, & \text{for the spline parametrization.} \end{cases} \tag{16}
$$

Since K is the number of terms in the Fourier description of the contour, or the number of control points in the spline model, these are basically implicit smoothing priors. The smaller K is, the simpler (smoother) the contours will be. These priors have the advantage of avoiding the shrinkage associated with smoothing priors explicitly expressed on the contour coordinates [33]. Finally, we stress that the criterion in Eq. (14) does not require the previous specification of parameters, thus constituting a fully unsupervised estimator.

3 Solving the Optimization Problem

3.1 Introduction

We are now left with the difficult task of solving

$$
\left(\widehat{\boldsymbol{\theta}_{(K)}}, \hat{\phi}\right)_{\mathrm{MDL}} = \arg\min E\left(\boldsymbol{\theta}_{(K)}, \phi\right) \tag{17}
$$

where the objective (energy) function is given by

$$
E\left(\boldsymbol{\theta}_{(K)}, \phi\right) = -\sum_{(i,j)\in\mathcal{I}(\mathbf{V})}\log p\left(I_{(i,j)}|\phi_{\mathrm{in}}\right) - \sum_{(i,j)\in\mathcal{O}(\mathbf{V})}\log p\left(I_{(i,j)}|\phi_{\mathrm{out}}\right) + K\beta \tag{18}
$$

with $\mathbf{v} = \mathcal{V}_{(K)}\boldsymbol{\theta}_{(K)}$, while $\beta = 2\log M$, or $\beta = \log M$, for the Fourier or spline descriptors, respectively. Eq. (17) will be dealt with hierarchically: at the lower (inner) level, we minimize with respect to $\boldsymbol{\theta}_{(K)}$ and ϕ, with K constant; in the higher (outer) level, the resulting function is minimized with respect to K, i.e.,

$$
\min_{K, \boldsymbol{\theta}_{(K)}, \phi} E\left(\boldsymbol{\theta}_{(K)}, \phi\right) = \min_{K}\left\{\min_{\boldsymbol{\theta}_{(K)}, \phi} E\left(\boldsymbol{\theta}_{(K)}, \phi\right)\right\}. \tag{19}
$$

3.2 Minimizing the Energy for Fixed K

Introduction. If K is known, the problem stated in Eqs. (17)-(18) is closely related to classical deformable (known order) template matching, which can still only be achieved by iterative schemes. Several two-alternating-steps schemes have been proposed for this kind of objective functions; see [7] for a comprehensive and lucid review. Our particular problem, however, has two important specificities: (i) the observation parameters ϕ are unknown; (ii) the region based formulation does not allow the energy to be written as a sum (or integral) of elementary energies, one for each template point, as is required in [7].

An equivalent constrained problem. To rewrite the problem in terms of the explicit contour $\mathbf{v}$, we have to constrain the solution to the space of those that can be obtained as $\mathbf{v} = \mathcal{V}_{(K)} \, \boldsymbol{\theta}_{(K)}$. This space, which is the range of operator $\mathcal{V}_{(K)}$) will be denoted as $\Omega_{(K)} = \mathcal{R}\left(\mathcal{V}_{(K)}\right)$. Then, a constrained problem equivalent to the unconstrained original one is

$$\left(\widehat{\mathbf{v}}, \widehat{\boldsymbol{\phi}}\right)_{\mathrm{MDL}} = \text{solution of} \left(\begin{array}{l} \text{minimize: } E'(\mathbf{v}, \boldsymbol{\phi}) \\ \text{subject to: } \mathbf{v} \in \Omega_{(K)} \end{array} \right) \tag{20}$$

where $E'(\mathbf{v}, \boldsymbol{\phi})$ is given by Eq. (18) without the βK term. From $\widehat{\mathbf{v}} \in \Omega_{(K)}$, the parameter estimate is obtained as $\widehat{\boldsymbol{\theta}}_{(K)} = \mathcal{V}_{(K)}^{\dagger} \widehat{\mathbf{v}}$, where the *pseudo-inverse* $\mathcal{V}_{(K)}^{\dagger}$ is well defined in $\Omega_{(K)}$ because (in both the Fourier and spline cases) $\mathcal{V}_{(K)}$ is linear and its null space only contains the null vector [23], [3]. This is related to the *invariance property* of ML estimation [27]. Concerning ϕ, there are no constraints and we assume that the energy can be exactly minimized with respect to it (see comments below).

The Algorithm. To solve the constrained minimization in Eq. (20), we use a form of the *gradient projection method* [24], [32]; this is a modification of classical gradient descent, where the (negative) gradient is projected onto the constraint space thus assuring that the updated solutions stay inside it [24]. Of course this is a descent algorithm which may be stuck in local minima of the (non-convex) objective function; however, the esperimental results showed that this is seldom a problem. Formally, the proposed algorithm works as follows:

Fixed-K Algorithm

Step 0: Initialization: assume some initial estimate $\widehat{\mathbf{v}}^0 \in \Omega_{(K)}$. Let $n = 0$.
Step 1 Update the estimate of ϕ

$$\widehat{\phi}^{n+1} = \arg \min_{\phi} E'(\widehat{\mathbf{v}}^n, \phi). \tag{21}$$

Step 2 Compute a small step in the direction opposed to the gradient of the energy with respect to the contour (at its present location)

$$\delta\mathbf{v} = -\varepsilon\,\mathrm{sgn}\left(\nabla E'\left(\mathbf{v}, \widehat{\phi}^{n+1}\right)\Big|_{\mathbf{v}=\widehat{\mathbf{v}}^n}\right) \tag{22}$$

where sgn($\cdot$) denotes a coordinate-wise sign function.

Step 3 Compute the projection of $\delta\mathbf{v}$ onto $\Omega_{(K)}$, denoted $\mathcal{P}_{(K)}\delta\mathbf{v}$, and update the contour estimate as

$$\widehat{\mathbf{v}}^{n+1} = \widehat{\mathbf{v}}^n + \mathcal{P}_{(K)}\delta\mathbf{v}. \tag{23}$$

Step 4 If some stopping criterion is met, stop, otherwise go back to **Step 1**.

Relation to other schemes. The projection operation guarantees that $\widehat{\mathbf{v}}^{n+1} \in \Omega_{(K)}$ since $\widehat{\mathbf{v}}^n \in \Omega_{(K)}$ and $\Omega_{(K)}$ is a linear space. Moreover, since $\mathcal{P}_{(K)}\widehat{\mathbf{v}}^n = \widehat{\mathbf{v}}^n$, and the projection operator is linear, Eq. (23) can be rewritten as

$$\widehat{\mathbf{v}}^{n+1} = \mathcal{P}_{(K)}\left(\widehat{\mathbf{v}}^n + \delta\mathbf{v}\right); \tag{24}$$

this reveals the similarity of this algorithm with the two-step schemes described in [7] (leaving aside the parameter estimation performed in **Step 1**). Our **Step 2** corresponds to what is termed *deformation*, in [7], while our projection step (**Step 3**) corresponds to what is there called *model fitting*. Since a linear space is a convex set, this algorithm also has some relation with the *projection onto convex sets* (POCS) technique [35]. Finally, some resemblance with the *expectation-maximization* (EM) scheme [11] may also be noticed; our **Step 1** plays the role of the M-step, while **Step 2** and **Step 3** represent the E-step.

3.3 Some comments.

Concerning Step 1. Implementing **Step 1** consists in obtaining the ML estimate of $\phi = [\phi_{\mathrm{in}}\ \phi_{\mathrm{out}}]$, considering a fixed contour $\widehat{\mathbf{v}}^n$, from the likelihood function in Eq. (11). This depends on the particular image model assumed which, in the experiments presented ahead, will be:

Gaussian. All pixels are independent and Gaussian distributed with means μ_{in} and μ_{out} and variances σ_{in}^2 and σ_{out}^2, for the inside and outside regions, respectively. In this case, $\phi_{\mathrm{in}} = [\mu_{\mathrm{in}}\ \sigma_{\mathrm{in}}^2]$, $\phi_{\mathrm{out}} = [\mu_{\mathrm{out}}\ \sigma_{\mathrm{out}}^2]$, and **Step 1** consists simply in computing the (inside and outside) sample mean and variance (which are the ML estimates given independent samples).

Rayleigh. In this case, which adequately models echographic images [12], the pixels are Rayleigh distributed. For the inside pixels, we have

$$p(I_{(i,j)}|\sigma_{\mathrm{in}}^2) = \frac{I_{(i,j)}}{\sigma_{\mathrm{in}}^2}\exp\left\{-\frac{I_{(i,j)}^2}{2\sigma_{\mathrm{in}}^2}\right\} \tag{25}$$

and a similar expression (with σ_{out}^2) for the outside ones. The parameter vector is now $\phi = [\sigma_{\mathrm{in}}^2\ \sigma_{\mathrm{out}}^2]$ and the respective ML estimates are (see [12]) simply one half of the sample means of squares.

Concerning Step 2. Here, we have to compute the gradient of the energy $E'(\mathbf{v}, \phi)$ with respect to each coordinate of the explicit contour representation $\mathbf{v}$. Since the coordinates represent pixel locations on a digital image, they are discrete (in fact integer) and the gradient is approximated by discrete differences relative to each contour coordinate. It is possible to show that this gradient is always normal to the contour: this is exactly true for a continuous representation and a good approximation for a fine enough discretization. Parameter ε should be kept small to avoid instabilities near the minima of the objective function.

Concerning Step 3. We have to find the point in $\Omega_{(K)}$ closest to $\widehat{\mathbf{v}}^n + \delta\mathbf{v}$,

$$
\mathcal{P}_{(K)}\left(\widehat{\mathbf{v}}^n + \delta\mathbf{v}\right) = \mathcal{V}_{(K)}\left(\arg\min_{\boldsymbol{\theta}_{(K)}} \| \mathcal{V}_{(K)}\boldsymbol{\theta}_{(K)} - (\widehat{\mathbf{v}}^n + \delta\mathbf{v}) \|^2 \right) \tag{26}
$$

where $\| \cdot \|$ denotes Euclidean norm; in other words, we have to look for the $\boldsymbol{\theta}_{(K)}$ which best fits $\widehat{\mathbf{v}}^n + \delta\mathbf{v}$ in a mean squared error sense. The two parameterizations considered have to be studied separately:

Fourier. In this case, the elements of $\boldsymbol{\theta}_{(K)}$ represent coordinates in an orthogonal basis: so, we have to compute the Fourier series (according to (3)) and truncate it to the first K terms.

Splines. In this case, we have to solve the least squares fit expressed in Eq. (26), with $\mathcal{V}_{(K)} = \mathbf{B}_{(K)}$, which involves the pseudo-inverse of matrix $\mathbf{B}_{(K)}$,

$$
\mathcal{P}_{(K)}\left(\widehat{\mathbf{v}}^n + \delta\mathbf{v}\right) = \mathbf{B}_{(K)}\left(\mathbf{B}_{(K)}^T\mathbf{B}_{(K)}\right)^{-1}\mathbf{B}_{(K)}^T\left(\widehat{\mathbf{v}}^n + \delta\mathbf{v}\right). \tag{27}
$$

Of course, for each K, this matrix is computed before running the algorithm.

3.4 Solving with respect to K

When K is unknown, which is the general case, the algorithm described above is inserted into an outer loop sweeping a range of values $\{K_{\max}, ..., 2, 1\}$, i.e.,

Step A: Let $K = K_{\max}$ and take some initial contour estimate $\widehat{\mathbf{v}}^0 \in \Omega_{(K)}$.

Step B: Run the **Fixed-K Algorithm** with the current value of K, and taking $\widehat{\mathbf{v}}^0 \in \Omega_{(K)}$ as initial contour estimate. Store the final values of $\widehat{\boldsymbol{\theta}}_{(K)} = \mathcal{V}_{(K)}^{-1}\widehat{\mathbf{v}}$ and $E\left(\boldsymbol{\theta}_{(K)}, \phi\right)$.

Step C: If $K > 1$, let $K = K - 1$, let $\widehat{\mathbf{v}}^0 \in \Omega_{(K)} = \mathcal{V}_{(K+1)}\boldsymbol{\theta}_{(K+1)}$, and go back to **Step B** (i.e. take the result of the previous **Fixed-K Algorithm** as the initial estimate for the next one).

Step D: Find the minimum of all stored values of $E\left(\boldsymbol{\theta}_{(K)}, \phi\right)$ and take the corresponding estimates as the final ones.

4 Experimental Results

We present two types of experiments: on synthetic images and on real medical images. The first set of experiments is reported on Fis. 1, 2, and 3; these images were generated artificially with contours having 3, 4, and 5 Fourier coefficients, respectivelly, and with Gaussian image models with parameter values summarized in Table 1. The estimated image model parameters are also presented in Table 1. The estimated contours are superimposed on the images, while the plots show the evolution of the description length as a function of the Fourier parametrization order K. In these tests, the locations of the minima of these curves always coincides with the true order.

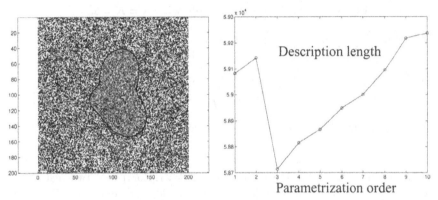

Fig. 1. Synthetic image example with $K = \widehat{K} = 3$.

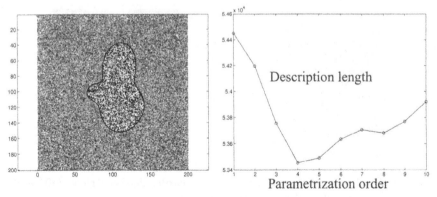

Fig. 2. Synthetic image example with $K = \widehat{K} = 4$.

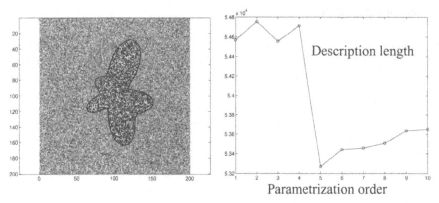

Fig. 3. Synthetic image example with $K = \widehat{K} = 5$.

Fig. 1 ($K = 3$)		Fig. 2 ($K = 4$)		Fig. 3 ($K = 5$)	
$\mu_{in} = 150$	$\widehat{\mu_{in}} = 151.8$	$\mu_{in} = 150$	$\widehat{\mu_{in}} = 150.2$	$\mu_{in} = 120$	$\widehat{\mu_{in}} = 120.8$
$\mu_{out} = 150$	$\widehat{\mu_{out}} = 146.0$	$\mu_{out} = 150$	$\widehat{\mu_{out}} = 148.5$	$\mu_{out} = 170$	$\widehat{\mu_{out}} = 167.7$
$\sigma_{in} = 60$	$\widehat{\sigma_{in}} = 63.8$	$\sigma_{in} = 120$	$\widehat{\sigma_{in}} = 123.1$	$\sigma_{in} = 120$	$\widehat{\sigma_{in}} = 116.6$
$\sigma_{out} = 140$	$\widehat{\sigma_{out}} = 139.1$	$\sigma_{out} = 40$	$\widehat{\sigma_{out}} = 43.6$	$\sigma_{out} = 40$	$\widehat{\sigma_{out}} = 43.4$

Table 1. Summary of parameters and parameter estimates.

The second set of tests (also with Fourier descriptors) uses two real echo-graphical left ventricle images (diastole and systole) and assumes a Rayleigh image model. The images on the left side of Figs. 4 and 5 show the original images, while the images on the right exhibit the estimated contours. Finally, Fig. 6 shows the evolution of the description length for these two examples.

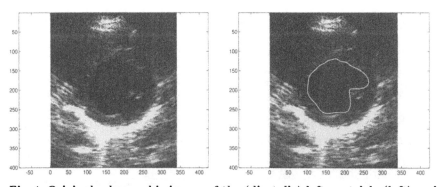

Fig. 4. Original echographic image of the (diastolic) left ventricle (left) and image with superimposed estimated contour (right).

Similar tests with the spline parametrization (not shown here due to lack of

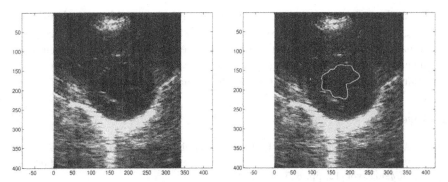

Fig. 5. Original echographic image of the (systolic) left ventricle (left) and image with superimposed estimated contour (right).

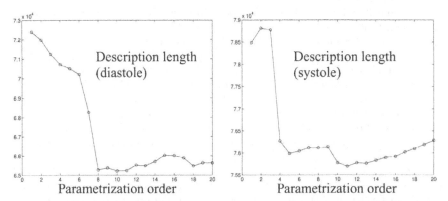

Fig. 6. Description length as a function of the Fourier parametrization order for the two previous examples; the minima are at 10 and 11, respectively.

space) yielded comparable results. For example, for the same pair of echographic images, the optimal numbers of control points were found to be 15 and 16; the estimated contours were visually very similar.

5 Concluding Remarks

We introduced a new approach to unsupervised deformable contour estimation. The problem is formulated as a statistical parameter estimation problem; with the number of parameters (order of the contour parametrization) being unknown, the MDL principle was invoked. The observation model parameters are also taken as unknown and estimated simultaneously with the contour. After showing that, for a given order, the resulting optimization problem can be stated as a constrained one, we used a form of the gradient projection algorithm. This, in turn, was inserted into an outer loop which takes care of the order estimation part.

Examples were presented, using synthetic and medical ultrasound images, showing the ability of the proposed method to estimate contours in an unsupervised manner, i.e. adapting to unknown smoothness and observation parameters. In the case of the synthetic images, the good match between the estimated and true parameters testified to the good performance of our approach.

References

1. A. Amini, T. Weymouth, and R. Jain. "Using dynamic programming for solving variational problems in vision". *IEEE Trans. on Pattern Analysis and Machine Intelligence*, vol. 12, pp. 855–867, 1990.
2. Y. Amit, U. Grenander, and M. Piccioni. "Structural image restoration through deformable templates". *Jour. of the American Statistical Association*, vol. 86, pp. 376–387, 1991.
3. S. Campbell and Jr. C. Meyer. *Generalized Inverses of Linear Transformations.* Pitman, London, 1979.
4. V. Caselles, R. Kimmel, and G. Sapiro. "Geodesic active contours". *in Intern. Conference on Computer Vision – ICCV'95*, pp. 694–699, Cambridge (MA), 1995.
5. A. Chakraborty, L. Staib, and J. Duncan. "Deformable boundary finding influenced by region homogeneity". *in IEEE Conference on Computer Vision and Pattern Recognition – CVPR'94*, pp. 624–627, Seattle, 1994.
6. L. Cohen. "On active contour models and baloons". *Computer Vision, Graphics, and Image Processing (CVGIP): Image Understanding*, vol. 53, pp. 211–218, 1991.
7. L. Cohen. "Auxiliary variables and two-step iterative algorithms in computer vision problems". *Jour. of Mathematical Imaging and Vision*, vol. 6, pp. 59–83, 1996.
8. L. Cohen and I. Cohen. "Finite-element methods for active contour models and baloons for 2D and 3D images". *IEEE Trans. on Pattern Analysis and Machine Intelligence*, vol. 15, pp. 1131–1147, 1993.
9. T. Cover and J. Thomas. *Elements of Information Theory.* John Wiley & Sons, New York, 1991.
10. C. deBoor. *A Practical Guide to Splines.* Springer Verlag, N. York, 1978.
11. A. Dempster, N. Laird, and D. Rubin. "Maximum likelihood estimation from incomplete data via the EM algorithm". *Jour. of the Royal Statistical Society B*, vol. 39, pp. 1–38, 1977.
12. J. Dias and J. Leitão. "Wall position and thickness estimation from sequences of echocardiographic images". *IEEE Trans. on Medical Imaging*, vol. 15, pp. 25-38, 1996.
13. B. Dom. *MDL Estimation for Small Sample Sizes and Its Application to Linear Regression.* IBM Research Report RJ 10030, Almaden Research Center, San Jose (CA), 1996.
14. G. Farin. *Curves and Surfaces for Computer Aided Geometrical Design.* Academic Press, Boston, 1990.
15. M. Figueiredo and J. Leitão. "Bayesian estimation of ventricular contours in angiographic images". *IEEE Trans. on Medical Imaging*, vol. 11, pp. 416–429, 1992.
16. U. Grenander. *General Pattern Theory: A Mathematical Study of Regular Structures.* Oxford University Press, Oxford, 1993.
17. U. Grenander and M. Miller. "Representation of knowledge in complex systems". *Jour. of the Royal Statistical Society B*, vol. 56, pp. 1–33, 1994.

18. J. Ivins and J. Porrill. "Active region models for segmenting medical images". *in IEEE Intern. Conference on Image Processing - ICIP'94*, pp. 227–231, Austin, 1995.
19. A. Jain. *Fundamentals of Digital Image Processing*. Prentice Hall, Englewood Cliffs, 1989.
20. A. Jain, Y. Zhong, and S. Lakshmanan. "Object matching using deformable templates". *IEEE Trans. on Pattern Analysis and Machine Intelligence*, vol. 18, pp. 267–277, 1996.
21. M. Dubuisson Jolly, S. Lakshmanan, and A. Jain. "Vehicle segmentation and classification using deformable templates". *IEEE Trans. on Pattern Analysis and Machine Intelligence*, vol. 18, pp. 293–308, 1996.
22. M. Kass, A. Witkin, and D. Terzopoulos. "Snakes: Active contour models". *Intern. Journal of Computer Vision*, vol. 1, pp. 259–268, 1987.
23. E. Kreyszig. *Introductory Functional Analysis with Applications*. John Wiley & Sons, New York, 1978.
24. D. Luenberger. *Linear and Nonlinear Programming*. Addison Wesley Publishing Company, Reading, Massachusetts, 1984. 2nd Edition.
25. R. Malladi, J. Sethian, and B. Vemuri. "Shape modeling with front propagation". *IEEE Trans. on Pattern Analysis and Machine Intelligence*, vol. 17, pp. 158–175, 1995.
26. T. McInerney and D. Terzopoulos. "Topologically adaptable snakes". *in Intern. Conference on Computer Vision - ICCV'95*, pp. 840–845, Cambridge, 1995.
27. B. Porat. *Digital Processing of Random Signals*. Prentice Hall, New Jersey, 1994.
28. P. Radeva, J. Serrat, and E. Martí. "A snake for model-based segmentation". *in Intern. Conference on Computer Vision - ICCV'95*, pp. 816–821, Cambridge, 1995.
29. J. Rissanen. "A universal prior for integers and estimation by minimum description length". *Annals of Statistics*, vol. 11, pp. 416–431, 1983.
30. J. Rissanen. *Stochastic Complexity in Stastistical Inquiry*. World Scientific, Singapore, 1989.
31. R. Ronfard. "Region-based strategies for active contour models". *Intern. Journal of Computer Vision*, vol. 13, pp. 229–251, 1994.
32. J. Rosen. "The gradient projection method of nonlinear programming. Part I, linear constraints ". *SIAM Journal*, vol. 8, pp. 181-217, 1960.
33. L. Staib and J. Duncan. "Boundary finding with parametrically deformable models". *IEEE Trans. on Pattern Analysis and Machine Intelligence*, vol. 14, pp. 1061–1075, 1992.
34. G. Storvik. "A Bayesian approach to dynamic contours through stochastic sampling and simulated annealing". *IEEE Trans. on Pattern Analysis and Machine Intelligence*, vol. 16, pp. 976–986, 1994.
35. D. Youla. "Generalized image restoration by the method of alternating projections". *IEEE Trans. on Circuits and Systems*, vol. 25, pp. 694–702, 1978.
36. A. Yuille. "Generalized deformable models, statistical physics, and the matching problem". *Neural Computation*, vol. 2, pp. 1–24, 1990.
37. A. Yuille and P. Hallinan. "Deformable templates". in A. Blake and A. Yuille, editors, *Active Vision*, pp. 21–38. MIT Press, 1992.
38. S. Zhu, and A. Yuille. "Region competition: unifying snakes, region growing, and Bayes/MDL for multi-band image segmentation". *IEEE Trans. on Pattern Analysis and Machine Intelligence*, vol. 18, pp. 884-900, 1996.

Kona: A Multi-junction Detector Using Minimum Description Length Principle

Laxmi Parida, Davi Geiger, Robert Hummel

parida@cs.nyu.edu, geiger@cs.nyu.edu, hummel@cs.nyu.edu.

Courant Institute of Mathematical Sciences, New York University, New York, NY 10012, U.S.A.

Abstract. Corners, T-, Y-, X-junctions give vital depth cues which is a critical aspect of image understanding tasks like object recognition: junctions form an important class of features invaluable in most vision systems. The three main issues in a junction (or any feature) detector are: scale, location, and, the junction (feature) parameters. The junction parameters are (1) the radius, or size, of the junction, (2) the kind of junction: lines, corners, 3-junctions such as T or Y, or, 4-junction such as X-junction, etcetera, (3) angles of the wedges, and, (4) intensity in each of the wedges. Our main contribution in this paper is a modeling of the junction (using the minimum description length principle), which is complex enough to handle all the three issues and simple enough to admit an effective dynamic programming solution. Kona is an implementation of this model. A similar approach can be used to model other features like thick edges, blobs and end-points.

1 Introduction

A critical component of most recognition systems is stable, representative, feature extraction from images. One of the key features used in recognition is junctions: T-junctions, Y-junctions, X-junctions and so on. These junctions are also critical for stereo vision modules or motion modules, since these are places where occlusions can be identified. Such points, for example, coincide with the images of trihedral vertices of an object. These are critical features for recognition as suggested by [2], [3], [5]. We use the template deformation framework to develop a "junction detector," to finds corners (two-junctions), tri-corners (tri-junctions), quad-corners (quad-junctions), etc., defined as points where two or more homogeneous surface patches are located within an arbitrarily small neighborhood of the point.

There have been basically two different paradigms for detecting junctions: edge detection followed by grouping of edges to form junctions [13, 12, 1, 16], and, treating junction as a template matching phenomenon [4], In the former, it is assumed that the presence (or absence) of a junction is determined by "grouping" the intensity gradient near a hypothesized junction. Usually one is interested in examining large gradients in the direction perpendicular to the hypothesized radial line. Experiments in this framework are limited and even the richest ones shown in [13] are interesting but not exhaustive. In the latter it is assumed that a (suitably small) local neighborhood is sufficient to detect a junction. The basic idea is to fit a junction-model to the input signal in a neighborhood. This involves minimizing an energy function which gives a measure of the "distance" of the junction-model from the input signal.

The idea of performing local feature detection by projecting image data onto a subspace is fundamental in [4, 7]. Basically, the input is orthogonally projected onto a finite dimensional subspace of the Hilbert space of functions. An energy function (which is the L^2 norm of the the difference of the input and the fitted function) is minimized in this finite dimensional space. The two main issues are finding an orthonormal basis that spans a good finite dimensional subspace and minimizing the energy function. This approach can give closed form solutions for edges [4, 7], and lines [6]. But, the generalization to junctions is complex and the solution is not apparent.

In [9], corners and junctions (which are modeled as two adjacent corners) are represented by functions (models) that are blurred with a Gaussian (or an exponential filter) where the authors use a closed form solution. In general, numerical methods are used to obtain parameters that minimize the distance to the input data using an L^2 norm. This is also the case in [10].

Our approach is to use a combination of the two paradigms: grouping of edges and fitting templates. We use a template deformation framework, using the minimum description length (MDL) principle, that includes the gradient information in order to detect the radial partitions of the template as a grouping mechanism. In other words, the task is to find the minimum number of wedges that best describes the junction. Note that as we increase the number of wedges, the junction description gets more accurate, hence the task is to use the MDL principle to obtain an optimal number of such wedges.

2 The Junction Model

We model a junction as a region of an image where the values are piecewise constant in wedge-shaped regions emanating radially from a central point, covering a small disk centered at the point and omitting a (much) smaller disk centered at this point (see figure1). The parameters of a junction consist of (i) the radius of the junction-disk, (ii) the center location, (iii) the number of radial line boundaries, (iv) the angular direction of each such boundary, and (v) the intensity within each wedge. The radius of the disk addresses the "scale" issue, and the location of the center is a kind of "interest operator" [8] that determines the position where the feature is located in a region, possibly pre-defined.

We can formulate the junction detection problem as one of finding the parameter values that yield a junction that best approximates the local data, and declaring local minima of the error as junctions. The best-fit parameter values provide attributes of the detected junction.

Let T denote the piecewise constant function/template. It has N angles and N intensities if N is the number of constant pieces. The interested reader may

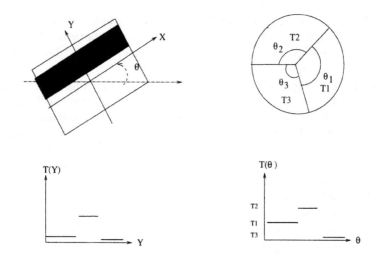

Fig. 1. Piecewise constant features. A bar detector and a junction detector.

look at [14] for a more rigorous definition of the template as a smooth function of two variables. Further, let I denote the input signal.

Define the energy function, at a point (i, j) on the image as follows

$$E = \mathcal{D} + \lambda^2 \mathcal{G}. \tag{1}$$

The first term, $\mathcal{D}$, is a measure of the distance of the fitted function from the *data* using the L^2 norm:

$$\mathcal{D} = \int_0^\infty \int_0^{2\pi} [I(r, \theta) - T(\theta)]^2 g(r) r dr d\theta; \tag{2}$$

where $g(r)$ is an appropriate modulating function that goes to zero for large r, thus defining the template size.

The second term, $\mathcal{G}$, is a measure of the distance of the *gradient* using the L^2 norm. Why is $\mathcal{G}$ required? We show an example, in Figure 2, where considerable improvement is achieved by the use of this term.

$$\mathcal{G} = \int_0^\infty \int_0^{2\pi} |\nabla I(r, \theta) - \nabla T(\theta)|^2 g^*(r) r dr d\theta. \tag{3}$$

where $g^*(r)$ is an appropriate modulating function, not necessarily the same as $g(r)$.

It may be pointed out that this form is different from the Mumford-Shah functional [11] particularly because of the presence of the term $\nabla I(r, \theta)$ in our model. As we explain in the next section, this term is critical in obtaining the portion of the image, or window, to which we fit a multi-junction template.

Note that

$$\nabla I = \frac{\partial I(r, \theta)}{\partial r} \mathbf{e_r} + \frac{1}{r} \frac{\partial I(r, \theta)}{\partial \theta} \mathbf{e_\theta}$$

54

(a) Point on the original image.

(b) Original data.   (c) Projection of (b) to 1D signal.

(d) Gradient is not used.   (e) Gradient is used.

Fig. 2. The use of gradient information in (e) gives a more accurate corner than in (d) where it is not used.

$$\nabla T(\theta) = \frac{1}{r} \frac{\partial T(\theta)}{\partial \theta} \mathbf{e}_\theta$$

where $\mathbf{e_r}$ and $\mathbf{e}_\theta$ are the orthonormal vectors in the r and θ direction respectively, evaluated at (r, θ).

Separating the angular and the radial terms, $\mathcal{G}$ can be written as,

$$\mathcal{G} = \mathcal{A} + \mathcal{R}, \tag{4}$$

where,

$$\mathcal{A} = \int_0^\infty \int_0^{2\pi} \frac{1}{r^2} \left(\frac{\partial I}{\partial \theta} - \frac{\partial T}{\partial \theta} \right)^2 g^*(r) r dr d\theta, \tag{5}$$

$$\mathcal{R} = \int_0^\infty \int_0^{2\pi} \left(\frac{\partial I}{\partial r} \right)^2 g^*(r) r dr d\theta. \tag{6}$$

3 Energy Minimization

This section deals with minimization of the engery function 1. Using equations 1 and 4, the energy equation can be written as: $E = \lambda^2 \mathcal{R} + \overline{E} = \lambda^2 \mathcal{R} + (\mathcal{D} + \lambda^2 \mathcal{A})$. $\mathcal{R}$ is independent of the junction feature and handles the scale and the location issue. $\overline{E}$ is minimized to obtain the most appropriate junction template.

3.1 Scale & Location

Consider a convenient and meaningful definition of $g(r)$ as follows:

$$g(r) = \begin{cases} 0 & r < R_0 \\ \frac{1}{r} & R_0 \leq r \leq R_1 \\ 0 & r > R_1 \end{cases}.$$

A user-defined threshold bounds $\lambda^2 \mathcal{R}$: this defines R_1. R_0 is often a user-defined fraction of R_1: this allows a small hole in the center. A significant observation, from the series of experiments, has been the use of non-zero R_0.

We do the following to obtain the location in a window: $\lambda^2 \mathcal{R}$, (with not necessarily the same R_1), is evaluated for the points and the one with the minimum value defines the location. We illustrate this in Figure 3.

3.2 Junction Parameters

We can carry out an appropriate numerical integration to obtain the value of the first term $\lambda^2 \mathcal{R}$. The second factor, $\overline{E}$, is used to estimate the junction template. The unknown factors are: N, the number of intersecting lines (or wedges) at the junction [1], $\{\theta_p\}, \{T_p\}, p = 1 \ldots N$, where N is the number of wedges, θ_p's are the angles where the partitions occurs, T_p's are the intensity values.

We can write down $\overline{E}$ as

$$\overline{E} = \mathcal{F} + \mathcal{V},$$

where, $\mathcal{F}$ is fixed, that is, it does not depend on the unknown parameters, where as, $\mathcal{V}$ does. Setting $g^*(r) = r^2 g(r)$, and, with some simple manipulations we obtain

$$\mathcal{F} = \int_0^\infty \int_0^{2\pi} \left[I^2(r, \theta) + \lambda^2 \left(\frac{\partial I(r, \theta)}{\partial \theta} \right)^2 \right] g(r) r \, dr \, d\theta.$$

$\mathcal{F}$ can be approximated numerically. Also, $\mathcal{V}$ can be approximated as,

$$\mathcal{V} = \sum_{p=1}^{N} \left[(\theta_{p+1} - \theta_p)(-2T_p \bar{I}_{\theta_p, \theta_{p+1}} + T_p^2 C) + \lambda^2 (-2T_p' (\partial_\theta \tilde{I})_{\theta_p} + C T_p'^2) \right],$$

---

[1] N for homogeneous region is 1, for line and corner is 2, for junctions like T-, Y-junction is 3, 4 for X-junction and so on.

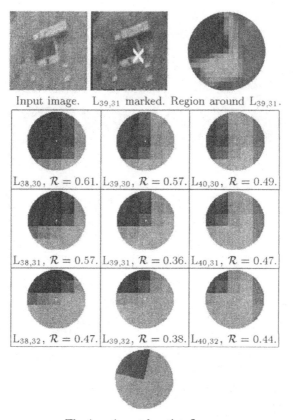

Input image. $L_{39,31}$ marked. Region around $L_{39,31}$.

$L_{38,30}$, $\mathcal{R} = 0.61$.	$L_{39,30}$, $\mathcal{R} = 0.57$.	$L_{40,30}$, $\mathcal{R} = 0.49$.
$L_{38,31}$, $\mathcal{R} = 0.57$.	$L_{39,31}$, $\mathcal{R} = 0.36$.	$L_{40,31}$, $\mathcal{R} = 0.47$.
$L_{38,32}$, $\mathcal{R} = 0.47$.	$L_{39,32}$, $\mathcal{R} = 0.38$.	$L_{40,32}$, $\mathcal{R} = 0.44$.

The junction at location $L_{39,31}$.

Fig. 3. The use of $\mathcal{R}$, to locate the center of the junction. $L_{x,y}$ indicates the x and y coordinates on the image. Note that the location $L_{39,31}$ has the minimum $\mathcal{R}$ in the neighborhood. Incidentally, R_1, the size of the template is the same for all the nine locations.

where,

$$C = \int_0^\infty g(r)r\,dr = R_1 - R_0,$$

$$\tilde{I}(\theta) = \int_0^\infty I(r,\theta)g(r)r\,dr$$

$$(\partial_\theta \tilde{I})_{\theta_p} \equiv \frac{\partial \tilde{I}(\theta)}{\partial \theta}|_{\theta_p} = \frac{\partial \int_0^\infty I(r,\theta)g(r)r\,dr}{\partial \theta}|_{\theta_p}$$

$$\bar{I}_{\theta_p,\theta_{p+1}} = \Delta\theta \sum_{j=j_p}^{j_{p+1}} \tilde{I}(j\,\Delta\theta).$$

Further, $\tilde{I}(\theta)$, $(\partial_\theta \tilde{I})_{\theta_p}$ can be approximated numerically. For the sake of brevity,

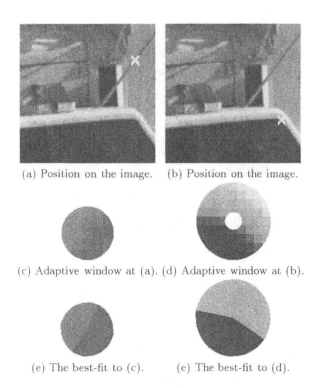

(a) Position on the image.   (b) Position on the image.

(c) Adaptive window at (a). (d) Adaptive window at (b).

(e) The best-fit to (c).   (e) The best-fit to (d).

Fig. 4. An example to show the dynamic computation of the windows at different locations on the image.

we have omitted the details of the derivations here; they appear in [14].

Estimating wedge angles and intensities: Let us assume the number of wedges is fixed. In the next section we discuss how to estimate the number of wedges. We propose a dynamic programming formulation, although in practice we use the simpler version which is reasonably effective (See section 4). Let A_1, A_2, ..., A_K denote the range of admissible intensities, θ_1, θ_2, ..., θ_k, the discretized angles. Then,

$$\mathcal{E}^{ij} = \begin{cases} -2A_j \tilde{I}(\theta_i) + A_j^2 C & i = 1, \\ \min_{1 \leq s \leq K} \left(\mathcal{E}^{(i-1)s} - 2A_j \tilde{I}(\theta_i) + \lambda^2 (C \Delta A_{js}^2 - 2\Delta A_{js} \partial_\theta \tilde{I}(\theta_i)) \right) & i > 1. \end{cases}$$

where $\Delta A_{jk} = A_j - A_k$. The energy is,

$$\overline{E} = \min_{s=1,K} \mathcal{E}^{ks}.$$

The constraint that the number of wedges is fixed can be imposed by increasing the energy to infinity whenever violated. Also, for the dynamic program, we re-arrange θ's so that in the rearrangement, θ_1 is such that $\tilde{I}(\theta_1)$ is closest to $\tilde{I}(\theta_k)$. This ensures that θ_1 and θ_k are part of the same wedge.

Estimating the number of wedges: There are at least two ways of deciding on the optimal number of wedges: one is by penalizing for the increase in the number of junctions by introducing a term such as αn, and, the other is by measuring the amount of decrease in the energy.

The former has a straightforward underlying variational form by adding the term $+\alpha\Delta A_{js}$ to the energy obtained in the previous paragraph. We have observed that, in practice, this criteria has not worked well. Instead, measuring the rate of increase of energy by thresholding the ratio of the energy measurement, $\overline{E}^n$, works better. More precisely, the number of wedges, N, is computed by thresholding the relative error, r^n,

$$r^n = \frac{\overline{E}^{n+1}}{\overline{E}^n}.$$

Note that as the number of parameters increase, $\overline{E}^n$ decreases, i.e., $r^n < 1$. A variational form that may justify this approach is to use, as suggested in the book of Morel and Solimini [19], a split and merge algorithm for the energy $\tilde{E} = log(r^n)$.

4 Implementation

Although the energy equation E of the last section looks fairly complex, it has a remarkably simple and natural interpretation. Once the role of each factor of the energy equation is ascertained, some computations (like evaluating $\mathcal{F}$, for instance), can be omitted without changing the solution. To recapitulate, the factors are used thus:

1. $\lambda^2\mathcal{R}$ is used for scale, i.e., to determine the size of the window, R_1. This is also used to obtain the exact location of the junction in a neighborhood.
2. $\overline{E}$ is used to obtain the junction parameters.

The $\tilde{I}(\theta)$ can be viewed as integrating the intensity along a radial line. Thus the two-dimensional image is projected on to a one-dimensional coordinate $D(\theta)$, where θ is appropriately discretized.

Let $D(\theta_i)$ be defined for $\theta_1, \theta_2, \ldots, \theta_d$, and, $(\theta_{i+1} - \theta_i) = 2\pi/d$, $\forall i$ [2]. For a p-junction, $T_1, T_2, \ldots, T_p$, are the template intensities and the wedge boundaries are at $\theta_{k_1}, \theta_{k_2}, \ldots, \theta_{k_p}$, $k_1 \leq k_2 \ldots \leq k_p$.

Assuming, we know the θ_p's, we can obtain T_p's by setting $\frac{\partial V}{\partial T_p} = 0, \forall p$. When $\lambda^2 = 0$, fixing, θ_{k_i}'s, the T_l's can be shown to be the following:

$$T_l = \frac{\sum_{j=k_l}^{k_{l+1}} D(\theta_j)}{k_{l+1} - k_l}.$$

---

[2] If $i = d$, $1 = i + 1$.

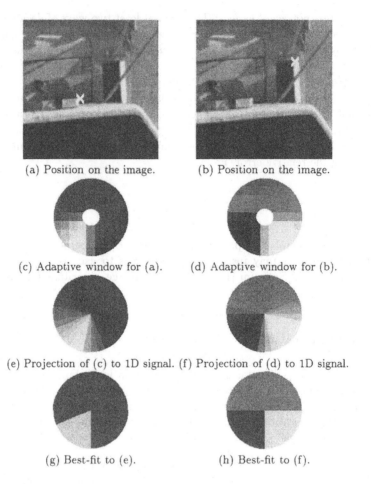

(a) Position on the image.　　(b) Position on the image.

(c) Adaptive window for (a).　　(d) Adaptive window for (b).

(e) Projection of (c) to 1D signal. (f) Projection of (d) to 1D signal.

(g) Best-fit to (e).　　(h) Best-fit to (f).

Fig. 5. Examples of a sharp corner and a T-junction.

In other words, the T_l is a piecewise constant fit which is the average value of the data in that region. The energy for the fit is:

$$\overline{E}^p = \sum_{l=1}^{p} \sum_{j=k_l}^{k_{l+1}} \left(D(\theta_j) - T_l \right)^2 .$$

When $\lambda^2 \neq 0$, $\overline{E}^p$ has some extra terms. Since, the template intensities are close to the image intensities, we make the following approximation:

$$T'_p e_\theta \approx (\partial_\theta \tilde{I})_{\theta_p} .$$

Now, it can be easily verified that the T_l and $\overline{E}^p$ is the same as before. We compute the θ_p's by exploring all possible set of θ_p's. We summarize the dynamic program

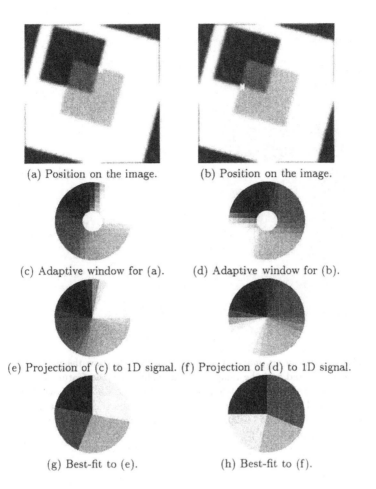

(a) Position on the image. (b) Position on the image.

(c) Adaptive window for (a). (d) Adaptive window for (b).

(e) Projection of (c) to 1D signal. (f) Projection of (d) to 1D signal.

(g) Best-fit to (e). (h) Best-fit to (f).

Fig. 6. A transparent object occludes a dark object in the background. The X-junctions detected by the program.

as follows:

$$C_{jl}^p = \begin{cases} \text{cost of fitting } T_p \text{ to } \theta_j, \theta_{j+1} \ldots \theta_l, & l \geq j, \\ \text{cost of fitting } T_p \text{ to } \theta_l, \theta_{l+1} \ldots \theta_1 \ldots \theta_j, & l < j. \end{cases}$$

$$\mathcal{E}_{sj}^p = \begin{cases} C_{sj}^1 & p = 1, \\ \min_{i<j}\left(\mathcal{E}_{si}^{p-1} + C_{(i+1)j}^p\right) & \text{otherwise.} \end{cases}$$

$$\overline{E} = \min_{s=1,m} \mathcal{E}_{sm}^N$$

$\mathcal{F}$ is a constant (fixed), depending only on the image, and, does not influence the junction parameters. The scenario where $\mathcal{F}$ could play a role is at the time of

 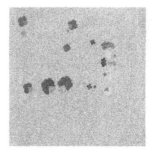

(a) Sharp corners on the image. (b) The sharp corner templates of (a).

 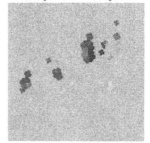

(c) Junctions on the image.   (d) The junction templates of (c).

Fig. 7. Kona is run on an image. The images on the left show the points at which the features were detected and the images on the right show the feature templates at the points, with the size of the template proportional to the size of the window computed by the program. The bi-corners are filtered to show sharp corners (angle < 100) and with not-too-small contrast (> 20). The tri-corners are filtered to show the ones with not-too-small contrast (> 40).

comparing the energy in a neighborhood. But we use $\mathcal{R}$ to filter the neighborhood so $\mathcal{F}$ may be ignored without any damage.

The threshold used to dynamically determine the window size R_1, is the same at all places on the image, irrespective of the local contrast. We achieve this by normalizing the input data (i.e., rescaling the intensities in the input signal to lie in a standard range, say $[0, 1]$). Thus, regions with low contrast get comparable values to regions with high contrast. Hence, a single global threshold works.

To summarize, the following steps are involved in detecting junctions on a large region of an image:

- Compute $\mathcal{R}$, and, R_1, the size of the template on every point.
- Filter the locations using a threshold on $\mathcal{R}$.
- In a neighborhood of a surviving location, pick the one with minimum $\mathcal{R}$, and remove all other locations within a radius of R_1 of this. Repeat this for all the surviving locations.
- Compute the junction parameter for all the surviving locations.

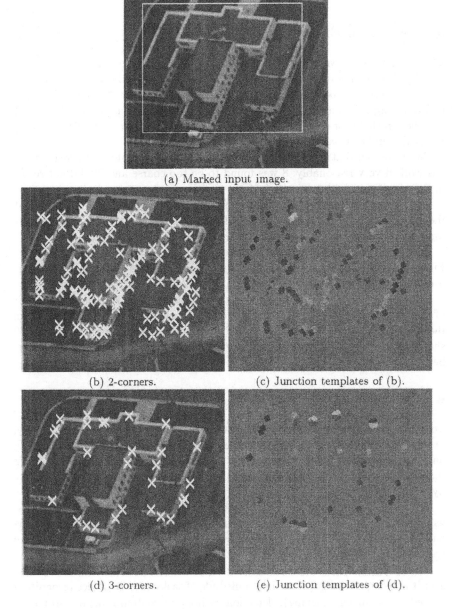

(a) Marked input image.

(b) 2-corners.

(c) Junction templates of (b).

(d) 3-corners.

(e) Junction templates of (d).

Fig. 8. Example of another image showing the results of **Kona**.

Kona[3] is an implementation of this junction model. It is programmed in C. A parallel implementation of this is also available.

5   Results of Experiments

In our experiments we have used $\lambda^2 = 1$.

The threshold for obtaining the scale (and, subsequently R_1), is lower for very sharp images, like binary images, where we use a value of 0.4 and for other real-life images we have used a value of 0.8 with very satisfactory results.

The threshold for deciding N of the junction was set to 0.4, for all the images we used, with very satisfactory results.

We observed that using the number of discretization units of the angle as 16 has worked very reasonably: 8 was found to be too coarse and 32 did not result in any significant higher accuracy [4].

An interesting observation of our experiments is that, using a small hole at the center ($R_0 > 0$) has worked very well. We have also noticed that the sharper images need larger holes. The other alternative is to blur the image first.

Figure 5 shows the function/template that is fit at two points on the image. Figure 6 shows an image where the X-junctions have been detected and Figures 7 and 8 show the results of Kona on regions of images.

We demonstrate the stability of the junction detector by running it on a pair of stereo images as shown in Figure 9. The results of this is used by an algorithm that runs on stereo images and estimates depth of objects in the scene. Figure 10 shows some results of obtaining illusory contours from junctions on an image. See [17] for details of the algorithm.

6   Conclusions

To conclude, we summarize the contributions of this paper as follows. Firstly, an effective modeling of the junction that includes a gradient term in the model, and, the removal of a small disk at the center of the junction. Secondly, using the model to obtain the scale and location of a junction, and, obtaining a simple dynamic programming solution to the optimization problem.

This paper demonstrates the successful use of piecewise constant functions, using a minimum description length principle, to detect features like junctions and corners. Similar piecewise constant functions may be used for features like bar detectors, blobs, end-points etc.

In this paper we have focussed solely on the task of junction detection, however it is being currently tested in a multitude of tasks such as object recognition (based on geometric hashing), detection of illusory contours, depth estimation from stereo pairs of images. It is also being tested in a novel approach to image compression using image diffusion and multi-junctions.

---

[3] The word for "corner" in Hindi is *Kona*.

[4] We choose a multiple of 4 because of the four quadrants - using any arbitrary number could do as well, in principle.

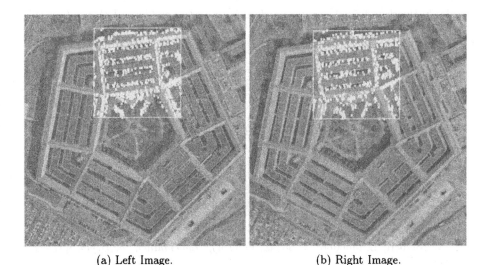

(a) Left Image.   (b) Right Image.

Fig. 9. Kona is run on a pair of stereo images: it detects junctions, with significant contrast, on similar locations on both the images.

Fig. 10. The well known four-packman picture, and, the illusory contours of a square in front, as a result of the algorithm, is shown on the right.

Acknowledgments: We are grateful to J. Morel and T. Binford for their insightful comments and feedback. We also thank E. Hancock for his comments on the paper.

References

1. W. Freeman, E. Adelson, *Junction Detection and Classification*, Proc. ARVO 1991.
2. A. Guzman, *Decomposition of a Visual Scene into Three-Dimensional Bodies*, Proc. AFIPS 1968 Fall Joint Computer Conference, 1968.
3. D.A. Huffman, *A Duality Concept for the Analysis of Polyhedral Scenes*, Machine Intelligence, Vol 6, Edinburgh Univ. Press, Edinburgh, U.K., 1971.
4. M. F. Hueckel, *An operator which locates edges in digitized pictures*, J, Assoc. Compt. Mach. Vol 18, 1971.
5. D. L. Waltz, *Understanding Line Drawings of Scenes with Shadows*, The Psychology of Computer Vision, McGraw-Hill, New York, 1972.

6. M. F. Hueckel, *A local operator which recognizes edges and lines*, J, Assoc. Compt. Mach. Vol 20, 1973.

7. R. Hummel, *Feature Detection Using Basis Functions*, Computer Graphics and Image Processing, Vol 9, 1979.

8. W. Forstner, E. Gulch, *A Fast Operator for Detection and Precise Location of Distinct Points, Corners, and Centres of Circular Features*, Procc of Intercommssion Conference on Fast Processing of Photogrammetric Data, Interlaken, Switzerland, 1987, pp 281-305.

9. R. Deriche, T. Blaszka, *Recovering and Characterizing Image Features Using An Efficient Model Based Approach.* In Proceedings of Computer Vision and Pattern Recognition, New York, 1993.

10. G. Giraudon and R. Deriche. *On corner and vertex detection.* In Proceedings of Computer Vision and Pattern Recognition, Hawaii, 1991.

11. D. Mumford, T. Shah, *Optimal Approximation by Piecewise Smooth Functions and Associated Variational Problems*, Comm. on Pure and Applied Mathematics, Vol XLII, No 5, July 1989.

12. M. Nitzberg, D. Mumford, T. Shiota, *Filtering, Segmentation, and Depth*, Springer Verlag Berlin 1993.

13. D. Beymer, Massachusetts Institute of Technology Master's thesis, *Junctions: Their detection and use for grouping images*, 1989.

14. L. Parida, D. Geiger, B. Hummel, *Junction Detection Using Piecewise Constant Functions*, 1996.

15. J. Rissanen, *A universal prior for integers and estimation by minimum description length*, Annals Statistics, vol. 11, pp, 416-431, 1983.

16. V. Caselles, B. Coll, J. M. Morel, *A Kanizsa Programme*, Technical Report, Universitat de les Illes Balears, Spain, 1996.

17. D. Geiger, K. Kumaran, L. Parida, *Visual Organization for Figure/Ground Separation* , CVPR-96, San Francisco, 1996.

18. Y. Lamdan, H. J. Wolfson, Geometric Hashing: A general and efficient model-based recognition scheme in *Second IEEE International Conference on Computer Vision*, 238-249, 1988.

19. J. Morel, S. Solimini, Variational Methods in Image Segmentation, Birkhauser Boston, 1995.

Restoration of SAR Images Using Recovery of Discontinuities and Non-linear Optimization

Florence Tupin, Marc Sigelle, Ammar Chkeif and Jean-Pierre Véran

Ecole Nationale Supérieure des Télécommunications
Département Images, 46 rue Barrault 75634 Paris Cedex 13 France
E-mail: tupin@ima.enst.fr Phone: 33 1 45 81 76 27 Fax: 33 1 45 81 37 94

Abstract. In this paper, we study the behaviour of contour recovery when filtering radar images. We start from recent methods lying on an equivalence scheme between implicit and explicit boundary processes in image restoration [1, 2]. Here we extend them to the processing of synthetic aperture radar (SAR) images. First we set up a general bayesian frame enabling recovery of discontinuities in such restoration methods. Then we exhibit an extension of the Geman-Reynolds-Charbonnier theorem allowing convenient filtering of SAR images. Due to the high dynamics of radar ERS-1 images, a deterministic algorithm is proposed integrating different statistical hypotheses for observation and regularization parts. Besides, we use a well-adapted SAR edge detector instead of the usual gradient in the boundary estimation step of an iterative boundary/intensity restoration algorithm. Intensities are then estimated with a deterministic non-linear method. Finally, the particular behaviour or radar statistics (χ law) lead us to define a new potential function adapted to speckle regularization while respecting region discontinuities.

1   Introduction

Image reconstruction or restoration can often be formulated as minimizing some energy functional:

$$U(f \mid p) \tag{1}$$

where $f = \{f_s\}_{s \in S}$ is the image to be reconstructed, $p = \{p_s\}_{s \in S}$ a given observation and $S = \{s\}$ the (primary) lattice of sites. It leads generally to non-convex optimization with respect to intensity variables f_s. This is the more so when a regularization term implicitly accounting for discontinuities is used [3, 4]. In the past few years, several methods have been drawn out in order to overcome the intrinsic complexity of these optimization problems:

• Graduated Non-Convexity [3] consists in approaching original energy functional (1) by a sequence of convex functions whose minima are by some means guaranteed to converge to the desired optimum.

• Mean-Field approximation was first designed for the truncated quadratic also called weak-string model [5, 6]. First, average estimation of the boundary value between neighbor sites is obtained by mean-field computations. Then, a gradient-type algorithm allows to estimate intensities.

- Anisotropic diffusion processes have also been deeply investigated (see [7]).
- More recently, there has been renewed interest for restoring an intensity image by simultaneously looking for the explicit line process associated to the primal energy [1, 2, 4]. This approach can be viewed as solving the dual problem of problem (1). It can be viewed as introducing discrete or continuous boundary variables on the dual lattice of the original one [1, 8]. It generally leads to a sequence of convex optimization problems. Moreover, the line process itself can contain some regularization part enabling boundary continuity [9]. Here we shall consider only non-interacting either explicit or implicit line processes.

In this paper we follow this last line of algorithms by extending the method originally designed by P. Charbonnier *et al.* [2]. It was first aimed to reconstruct images blurred with white gaussian noise. We are interested here in the filtering of synthetic aperture radar (SAR) images which suffer from specific speckle effects. Many filters have been proposed in the last twenty years. Most of them are based on the statistical properties of speckle images [10, 11]; maximum homogeneous region detection [12] or structure (strong scatterers, edges and lines) detection [13] improve filtering results. We propose in this paper an adaptation of bayesian regularization methods which preserve discontinuities. More specifically one should possibly process and remove speckle noise while trying to preserve spatial boundaries between regions of interest such as fields or cities, or even to restore thin separating objects such as roads.

2 A Bayesian Model of the Recovery of Boundaries

A bayesian formulation of explicit/implicit boundary processes can be derived as follows. Let us note $\mathcal{C} = \{(r, s)\}$ the set of second order cliques, *i.e.* of neighbor sites pairs. We also note B the boundary process and $b = \{b_{rs}\}_{(r,s) \in \mathcal{C}}$ any realization of it. Up to now we make no hypotheses on the discrete/continuous nature of this process. The joint posterior probability of f and b writes as:

$$\Pr(F = f, B = b \mid P = p) \propto \Pr(P = p \mid F = f, B = b) \, \Pr(F = f, B = b)$$
$$= \Pr(P = p \mid F = f, B = b) \, \Pr(F = f \mid B = b) \, \Pr(B = b) \ (2)$$

From now on we make the following assumptions:

- First, likelihood of data does not depend on boundary realization b, due to a classical site-site independance assumption for data formation. Thus we obtain:

$$\Pr(P = p \mid F = f, B = b) = \Pr(P = p \mid F = f)$$

which can always be put in an exponential form:

$$\Pr(P = p \mid F = f) = \prod_{s \in S} \Pr(P_s = p_s \mid F_s = f_s) = \frac{1}{Z_1} \exp\left\{- U_1(p \mid f)\right\}$$

where Z_1 is a normalization constant which does not depend on f. For example in the classic additive white gaussian noise assumption we have:

$$\Pr(P_s = p_s \mid F_s = f_s) = \frac{1}{\sqrt{2\pi}\sigma} \exp\left\{- \frac{(p_s - f_s)^2}{2\sigma^2}\right\}$$

leading to the quadratic energies:

$$U_s(p_s \mid f_s) = \frac{(p_s - f_s)^2}{2\sigma^2} \text{ and } U_1(p \mid f) = \sum_{s \in S} \frac{(p_s - f_s)^2}{2\sigma^2}$$

- Then, we write the second term of final member of eq.2 as:

$$\Pr(F = f \mid B = b) = \frac{1}{Z_2(b)} \exp\{-U_2(f \mid b)\} = \frac{1}{Z_2(b)} \exp\{-\sum_{(r,s) \in C} b_{rs}\, U_{rs}(f_r, f_s)\}$$

$$(3)$$

meaning that regularization between neighbor sites is accounted for when no boundary exists between them. For example one can assume a gaussian-quadratic expression for U_{rs}: $U_{rs}(f_r, f_s) = \lambda\,(f_r - f_s)^2$ or a more general expression of the type: $\eta\, g(\frac{G_{rs}}{\delta})$, where η is a regularization coefficient, $G_{rs} = f_s - f_r$ the local intensity gradient between sites r and s and δ a suitable gradient normalization coefficient. Notice also that normalization constant Z_2 *does depend* here of the conditional line process realization b.

- Last, third term of eq.2 is the prior distribution for line process. Assuming now boundary variables b_{rs} to be binary and independant, we write it as:

$$\Pr(B = b) = \frac{1}{Z_3} \exp\{-U_3(b)\} = \frac{1}{Z_3} \exp\{-\mu \sum_{(r,s) \in C}(1 - b_{rs})\} = \frac{1}{Z_3} \exp\{-\mu \sum_{(r,s) \in C} \psi(b_{rs})\}$$

i.e. a staticnary binomial model for non-interacting boundaries. Here the value of μ allows to master the rate of contours in posterior image f.

Let us now assume that normalization constant $Z_2(b)$ in equation (3) is nearly independant of b. This consists indeed in *neglecting the contour regularity information* contained in $Z_2(b)$. Joint MAP estimates of f and b result then from:

$$\max_{(f,b)} \Pr(F = f,\ B = b \mid P = p) \ i.e. \ \min_{(f,b)} \{ U(f,\ b \mid p) = U_1(p \mid f) + U_2(f \mid b) + U_3(b) \}$$

The MAP estimate for intensity image itself is thus:

$$\hat{f} = \arg\min_f \{ \min_b U(f, b \mid p) = U_1(p \mid f) + \min_b [U_2(f \mid b) + U_3(b)] \}$$

which enables to define a global effective regularization energy :

$$\tilde{U}_2(f) = \min_b [U_2(f \mid b) + U_3(b)]$$

and also locally, due to the independance assumption between b_{rs} variables:

$$\tilde{U}_{rs}(f_r, f_s) = \min_{b_{rs}} [b_{rs}\, U_{rs}(f_r, f_s) + \mu\, \psi(b_{rs})]$$

$$(4)$$

In the case where all pixel energies are quadratic, this leads to minimize [3] :

$$U(f, b \mid p) = \sum_{s \in S} \frac{(p_s - f_s)^2}{2\sigma^2} + \lambda \sum_{(r,s) \in C} b_{rs}\,(f_r - f_s)^2 + \mu \sum_{(r,s) \in C}(1 - b_{rs})$$

$$(5)$$

This allows estimation of boundary variables once realization f is known:

$$\hat{b}_{rs} = \begin{cases} 0 \text{ if } \lambda\,(f_r - f_s)^2 \geq \mu \text{ (there is boundary between r and s)} \\ 1 \text{ if } \lambda\,(f_r - f_s)^2 < \mu \text{ (no boundary between r and s)} \end{cases}$$

and to write the effective interaction potential also called weak-string model [3]: $\tilde{U}_{rs}(f_r,\ f_s) = \min\,[\lambda\,(f_r - f_s)^2,\ \mu\,]$. Using this implicit model is then equivalent to solve problem (5) with explicit boundary variables. Nevertheless smoother, derivable effective potential functions of the local intensity gradient have been proposed, among them the famous example of Geman-Reynolds-Mc Clure: [1]:

$$\tilde{U}_{rs}(f_r,\ f_s) = \eta\,\phi\big(\,(\frac{G_{rs}}{\delta})^2\,\big)\ \text{ with } \phi(u) = \frac{u}{1+u}$$

Notice that this potential and weak-string model possess the same total variation and curvature at origin characteristics when chosing $\eta = \mu$ and $\lambda = \dfrac{\mu}{\delta^2}$. We shall assume these relations fulfilled in the following. More general requirements for effective potentials have been explicited in [1, 2]. In the next section we present a new, extended theoretical framework for such potentials functions.

3   Extending the Geman-Reynolds-Charbonnier theorem

Here we generalize the Geman-Reynolds-Charbonnier theorem [1, 2] which allows passing from a general implicit to an explicit boundary model for deterministic restoration purposes. Our extension in view of SAR image processing is the following:

Theorem 1 (an extension of Geman-Reynolds-Charbonnier). *Let ϕ and $\mathcal{H}$ two functions defined on $\mathbf{R}^+$ ($\mathcal{H} \geq 0$ and monotonously increasing) such that ϕ is strictly concave increasing, and let L and M be defined as:*

$$L = \lim_{u \to +\infty} \phi'(u) \ \text{ and }\ M = \lim_{u \to 0^+} \phi'(u)$$

Then

- *there exists a strictly decreasing convex function $\psi\colon [L, M] \mapsto [\alpha, \beta]$, such that:*

$$\phi(\mathcal{H}(u)) = \inf_{L \leq b \leq M}\,(b\mathcal{H}(u) + \psi(b)) \quad \text{with}$$

$$\alpha = \lim_{v \to \infty} \gamma(v)\ ,\ \ \beta = \lim_{v \to 0^+} \gamma(v)\ \text{ where } \gamma(v) = \phi(v) - v\phi'(v)$$

- *for any value of u, the value of b reaching the infimum is $b_u = \phi'(\mathcal{H}(u)) \geq 0$.*

It results from Legendre transform applied to $\phi(x)$ and substituting $x = \mathcal{H}(u)$ in it, due to the inversibility of $\mathcal{H} : \mathbf{R}^+ \mapsto \mathbf{R}^+$. In the classic case where $\mathcal{H}(u) = u^2$ we re-obtain the conditions of Geman-Reynolds-Charbonnier Theorem, which states that:

$$\phi(u^2) = \inf_{L \leq b \leq M} \left(bu^2 + \psi(b) \right) \text{ with } \alpha = \lim_{v \to +\infty} \left(\phi(v) - v\phi'(v) \right) \text{ and } \beta = \lim_{v \to 0+} \phi(v)$$

and where the "boundary value" b_u for which infimum is reached is

$$b_u = \phi'(u^2) \tag{6}$$

The theorem is applied to each local interaction energy considered as a function of local intensity gradient: $\tilde{U}_{rs}(f_r, f_s) = \eta \, \phi\left(\left(\frac{f_r - f_s}{\delta} \right)^2 \right)$. It allows then to transform a non-convex, implicit model into a convex, explicit one for optimization purposes. For a gaussian observation model one has:

$$U(f \mid p) = \sum_{s \in S} \frac{(p_s - f_s)^2}{2\sigma^2} + \eta \sum_{(r,s) \in C} \phi\left(\left(\frac{f_r - f_s}{\delta} \right)^2 \right)$$

so that total energy can be put in the convex form:

$$U(f, b \mid p) = \sum_{s \in S} \frac{(p_s - f_s)^2}{2\sigma^2} + \lambda \sum_{(r,s) \in C} b_{rs}(f_r - f_s)^2 + \mu \sum_{(r,s) \in C} \Psi(b_{rs}) \tag{7}$$

with $\mu = \eta$, $\lambda = \frac{\mu}{\delta^2} \geq 0$ and:

$$b_{rs} = \phi'\left(\left(\frac{f_r - f_s}{\delta} \right)^2 \right) \geq 0 \tag{8}$$

In order to optimize an energy function such as (7) we use the ARTUR variant [2] (see fig.1). At some step (N) a new intensity image is computed. Then, boundary variables b_{rs} are estimated from eq.8, allowing in turn to minimize previous energy by a Newton-Raphson-like algorithm. For this purpose, the zeros of every partial derivative $\dfrac{\partial U(f, b \mid p)}{\partial f_s}$ are estimated using the following gradient-descent iterative scheme:

$$f_s^{(n+1)} - f_s^{(n)} = -\frac{\left(\dfrac{\partial U(f, b \mid p)}{\partial f_s} \right)^{(n)}}{\omega} \text{ where } \omega = \left(\dfrac{\partial^2 U(f, b \mid p)}{\partial f_s^2} \right)^{(n)} \forall s \in S \tag{9}$$

pixels being updated in a sequential mode. After some iterations of this kind a new intensity image $f^{(N+1)}$ is obtained, so that boundary values b_{rs} can in turn be re-estimated from eq.8 and so on. Convergence is attained when both boundary and intensity variables are stable [2].

However, the gaussian observation model as well as the truncated gaussian regularization one are not always adapted to the processing of SAR images. Our general aim is to apply extended Theorem 1 when attachment to data functions are no more quadratic and to regularization models which do not necessarily depend on the local intensity gradient.

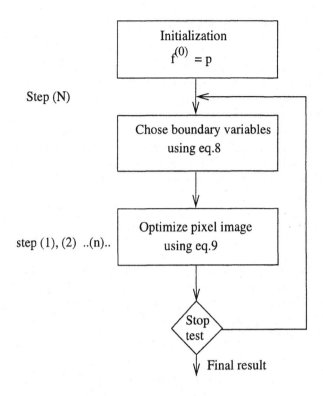

Fig. 1. Modified Artur Algorithm

4 Statistics of SAR images

We shortly describe the well-known statistics of radar images. Denoting $a \exp(i\phi)$ the complex field received by the radar antenna, the intensity is defined by $I = |a|^2$ and the amplitude by $A = \sqrt{I} = |a|$. L-looks images are obtained by averaging L independent images (either by dividing the available bandwith of the SAR system in L parts, or by spatially averaging L pixels [14]). The ERS-1 images, on which results are presented in this paper, are PRI Products (Precision Images) *i.e.* 3-look amplitude images with a resolution of 12.5 meters.

Under some assumptions implying a rough surface compared to the radar wavelength (5.6cm for ERS-1) statistics of an area with constant reflectivity are given by [15]:

$$\Pr(A \mid \alpha) = \frac{2L^L}{\Gamma(L)} \frac{A^{2L-1}}{\alpha^{2L}} \exp\left(-\frac{LA^2}{\alpha^2}\right) \tag{10}$$

denoting by Γ the Gamma function [16] and by α the square root of the mean reflected intensity of the area. This probability density function is called χ in the following and implies the well-known speckle phenomenon which affects radar images. Other probability density functions could be used to take into account textured regions [17] [18].

5 Edge detection on SAR images

The use of the radiometric difference G_{rs} is ill-adapted to SAR image statistics [20]. On radar images, such a detector gives different detection results depending on the radiometric mean of a region since the standard deviation increases proportionally to the mean.

An edge detector widely used in radar imagery is based on the ratio between radiometric means [19] [20]. Denoting $Re(r)$ and $Re(s)$ two adjacent regions associated to each site of a clique (r, s) (horizontal, vertical or diagonal) as shown on figure 2, the edge detector response $\overline{d_{rs}}$ is obtained by:

$$\overline{d_{rs}} = 1 - \min\left(\frac{\overline{A_r}}{\overline{A_s}}, \frac{\overline{A_s}}{\overline{A_r}}\right)$$

with $\overline{A_r}$ the radiometric mean computed on the neighborhood $Re(r)$ around r. To preserve thin structures, the neighborhood size can be chosen of 5×2 pixels, although this implies more false alarms than with larger regions. This detector has proved to have a good behaviour on SAR images [20]. Let us also define a ponctual edge detector:

$$d_{rs} \doteq 1 - \min\left(\frac{A_r}{A_s}, \frac{A_s}{A_r}\right)$$

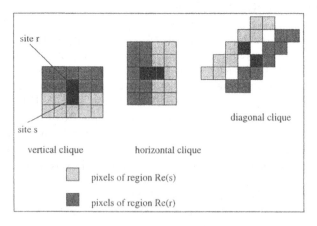

Fig. 2. Used regions to compute $\overline{d_{rs}}$

In the following, we propose to use these results to restore the original scene image while preserving the discontinuities.

6 Methodology of the study

We propose in this paper to do some experiments to analyse the behaviour of restoration techniques with recovery of discontinuities on SAR images.

We test several configurations and analyse the obtained results, particularly the restoration effects on bright and dark regions. The following choices can be made:

- *Choice of the probability density function:*
  We have tested two possibilities, gaussian and χ distribution. The second choice should be more adapted to SAR images as claimed in section 4.
- *Choice of the regularization function $\mathcal{H}$:*
  The usual choice is a quadratic function. We will show in this paper that other functions can be used in the case of SAR images.
- *Choice of the boundary process definition:*
  The right expression is $b_{rs} = \phi'(\mathcal{H}(\frac{G_{rs}}{\delta}))$. Using the remarks made on edge detection in SAR images, we propose to test the boundary process defined by $b_{rs}^* = \phi'(\mathcal{H}(\frac{d_{rs}}{\delta^*}))$ where δ^* is an appropriate control parameter of d_{rs}. Of course, in the case of this modification, we are not any more in the theoretical framework defined by the generalized Geman-Reynolds-Charbonnier theorem, and all the convergence prooves are not valid any more. Therefore, in this case, the results proposed are surely not the MAP estimates. Let us also note that the a new choice of the regularization function $\mathcal{H}$ provides a new boundary process.
  Besides, we propose to introduce a new way to estimate the boundary process, by using average values instead of amplitudes in the gradient or ratio. The boundary process which is estimated using average values is noted $\overline{b_{rs}}$ (or $\overline{b_{rs}}^*$ respectively). Once again, in this case the theoretical framework is not verified any more.

The following table summarizes the different tests we have made (with $G_{rs} = f_r - f_s$ and $R_{rs} = \frac{f_r}{f_s}$).

distribution	gaussian		χ		
reg. function	$x = G_{rs}, \mathcal{H}(x) = x^2$	$x = G_{rs}, \mathcal{H}(x) = x^2$	$x = R_{rs}, \mathcal{H}(x) = x + \frac{1}{x} - 2$		
boundary	b_{rs}	b_{rs}^*	b_{rs}	b_{rs}^*	b_{rs}
section	7.1	7.2	8.1.1	8.1.2	8.2

Table 1. *Summary of the tests and the corresponding sections.*

For all the tested configurations, estimations of the boundary process with ponctual and average values are tried. As for the ϕ function, the following function is used in all tests: $\phi(x) = \frac{x}{1+x}$. For each configuration, the regularized result of a synthetic 3-look amplitude image (fig.3a) is given. Besides, the remarks made on the regularization process are also verified on the boundary process image which shows where edges are detected. Then a comparison of all the obtained results is given in section 9. The best method is applied on a real (ERS-1) SAR image (fig.5a) showing well defined fields and roads.

7 Gaussian probability and quadratic regularization function

Recall that in the case of a gaussian probability and a quadratic $\mathcal{H}$ function, the energy $U(f, b \mid p)$ is expressed by:

$$U(f, b \mid p) = \sum_{s \in S}(p_s - f_s)^2 + \lambda \sum_{c \in C} b_{rs}(f_s - f_r)^2 + \mu \sum_{c \in C} \Psi(b_{rs})$$

With $\phi(x) = \frac{x}{1+x}$ [1], the boundary process is given by:

$$b_{rs} = \phi'(\mathcal{H}(\frac{G_{rs}}{\delta})) = \frac{1}{\left(1 + (\frac{G_{rs}}{\delta})^2\right)^2}$$

Since the first and second derivatives are:

$$\frac{\partial U}{\partial f_s} = 2(f_s - p_s) + 2\lambda \sum_{r \in \mathcal{N}_s} b_{rs}(f_s - f_r) \quad \text{and} \quad \frac{\partial^2 U}{\partial f_s^2} = 2(1 + \lambda \sum_{r \in \mathcal{N}_s} b_{rs})$$

the iterative scheme is given by:

$$f_s^{(n+1)} - f_s^{(n)} = -\frac{1}{1 + \lambda \sum_{r \in \mathcal{N}_s} b_{rs}} \left(f_s^{(n)} - p_s + \lambda \sum_{r \in \mathcal{N}_s} b_{rs}(f_s^{(n)} - f_r^{(n)})\right) \quad (11)$$

The regularization method has been applied on a synthetic 3-look amplitude image (fig.3a), in both cases: right b_{rs} and modified b_{rs}^* (which is equivalent to replace the gradient edge detector by a ratio edge detector). For each case, estimation with the amplitude values and local average values have been tested.

7.1 Using b_{rs}

The results obtained are not very statisfying. A different behaviour in dark and bright regions is observed: the dark areas are strongly regularized, while the bright areas show many variations. Note that these effects, although present in both cases (for b_{rs} or $\overline{b_{rs}}$), are reduced when the average values are used to estimate b_{rs} (fig.3b). Besides, the result contains many isolated bright points in the case of the ponctual b_{rs} estimator.

7.2 Using b_{rs}^*

Since the boundary process is now well adapted to the detection of discontinuities in SAR images, the previous effects have disapeared. Resulting images are satisfying with a good edge preservation and a strong filtering of homogeneous regions (fig.3c, see also section 9). Let us also note that the homogeneous areas are much more regularized in the case of the average estimation $\overline{b_{rs}}^*$, than in ponctual estimation.

These satisfying results seem at first in contradiction with speckle behaviour since a SAR image does not follow a gaussian pdf. An explanation of this result is the behaviour of the filtering process. Indeed, equation (11) can be written as:

$$f_s^{(n+1)} = \frac{1}{1 + \lambda \sum\limits_{r \in \mathcal{N}_s} b_{rs}} \left(p_s + \sum_{r \in \mathcal{N}_s} b_{rs} f_r^{(n)} \right)$$

showing that the filtered value is a weighted mean of the observation and the neighboring values, with weights depending of the edge presence. Therefore, after a few iterations, the probability density function turns out to be almost gaussian.

8 χ probability

8.1 Quadratic regularization function

To improve the restoration method a χ distribution, more adapted to SAR images (§4), has been used [21]:

$$\Pr(p_s|f_s) = k \frac{p_s^{2L-1}}{f_s^{2L}} \exp(-\frac{L p_s^2}{f_s^2})$$

k being a normalization constant depending on the number of looks used to create the SAR image (eq.10). Therefore, the following data attachment energy is deduced:

$$U_1(p|f) = L \left(\sum_{s \in S} 2 \log f_s + \frac{p_s^2}{f_s^2} \right)$$

providing the expression of sequence $f_s^{(n+1)} - f_s^{(n)}$:

$$\frac{-1}{\frac{2L}{f_s^{(n)4}}(3p_s^2 - f_s^{(n)2}) + 2\lambda \sum\limits_{r \in \mathcal{N}_s} b_{rs}} \left(\frac{2L}{f_s^{(n)3}}(f_s^{(n)2} - p_s^2) + 2\lambda \sum_{r \in \mathcal{N}_s} b_{rs}(f_s^{(n)} - f_r^{(n)}) \right)$$

Many problems arise using this expression. First, in order to assure the convergence of the Newton-Raphson method, coefficient ω in eq.9 has to be positive, which implies:

$$\frac{2L}{f_s^{(n)4}}(3p_s^2 - f_s^{(n)2}) + 2\lambda \sum_{r \in \mathcal{N}_s} b_{rs} > 0$$

In practice, starting with the original image p for f initialization, the condition $3p_s^2 > f_s^2$ is always verified and no convergence problem accurs.

Using b_{rs} The previous phenomenon (stronger filtering of the dark areas) is now reversed, which is of course still not satisfying. In the case of a ponctual boundary process estimation, there are many isolated dark points in the result, which is not the case with the average estimation $\bar{b}_{rs}$.

Using b_{rs}^* The same phenomenon of completely different filtering behaviours according to the local radiometric average is observed and the same remark about isolated dark points holds. Of course, the aim of the regularization process is to smooth every homogeneous region of the image in the same way, whatever its radiometric mean. But it is not the case using a χ distribution and a quadratic regularization function. Let us consider two extreme cases:

- when $f_s \to \infty$ (precisely for $f_s^2 \gg \dfrac{KL}{\lambda} \max(1, \dfrac{|f_s - p_s|}{|f_s - f_r|})$, $1 \leq K \leq 10$) :

$$f_s^{(n+1)} \approx \frac{\displaystyle\sum_{r \in \mathcal{N}_s} b_{rs} f_r^{(n)}}{\displaystyle\sum_{r \in \mathcal{N}_s} b_{rs}}$$

therefore, only the regularization term counts on bright regions, leading to very smoothed areas;

- when $f_s \to 0$ (precisely for $f_s^2 \ll \dfrac{KL}{\lambda} \min(1, \dfrac{|f_s - p_s|}{|f_s - f_r|})$, $1 \leq K \leq 10$) :

$$f_s^{(n+1)} \approx f_s^{(n)} + f_s^{(n)} \frac{f_s^{(n)2} - p_s^2}{f_s^{(n)2} - 3p_s^2}$$

thus, the regularization term does not appear any more on dark regions. These two extreme behaviours can be observed in practice. In both cases (right or modified b_{rs}), bright areas are too smoothed, whereas dark ones are not smoothed at all (fig.3 d and e).

8.2 Ratio-based regularization function

To have the same regularization strength in bright and dark areas, the data attachment term and the contextual one should have the same weight whatever the radiometric mean is. To do so, we impose the following constraint: if p and $f^{(n)}$ are replaced by αp and $\alpha f^{(n)}$ then the estimation $f^{(n+1)}$ must be replaced by $\alpha f^{(n+1)}$. But in the case of the χ distribution, each term $\dfrac{\partial U_1}{\partial f_s}(p|f)$ is a homogeneous function of degree -1 with respect to p and f (by this we mean that $\dfrac{\partial U_1}{\partial f_s}(\alpha p|\alpha f) = \dfrac{1}{\alpha}\dfrac{\partial U_1}{\partial f_s}(p|f)$ $\forall \alpha$). Therefore, we have to choose a 0 degree homogeneous function with respect to f_r and f_s for $\mathcal{H}$.

To do so, we propose to indroduce a new variable which is defined for two sites r and s, by $R_{rs} = \dfrac{f_r}{f_s}$. Then, we define the equivalent of G_{rs}^2 in the case of speckle images as $R_{rs} + \dfrac{1}{R_{rs}} - 2$. This (positive) quantity is symmetric in (f_r, f_s), minimal when $f_r = f_s$ and is moreover convex with respect to each of these variables. Besides, since it takes the same values for R_{rs} and $\dfrac{1}{R_{rs}}$, we only consider the interval $[1, \infty[$. Therefore, a natural form for $\mathcal{H}$ on $[1, \infty[$ is:

$$\mathcal{H}(x) = x + \frac{1}{x} - 2$$

Total energy writes then from Theorem 1:

$$U(f,\, b \mid p) = L\left(\sum_{s \in S} 2 \log f_s + \frac{p_s^2}{f_s^2} \right) + \lambda \sum_{(r,s) \in C} b_{rs} \left(\frac{f_r}{f_s} + \frac{f_s}{f_r} - 2 \right) + \mu \sum_{(r,s) \in C} \Psi(b_{rs})$$

with boundary values for the Geman et al. ϕ-function:

$$b_{rs} = \frac{1}{\left(1 + \dfrac{1}{\delta'} \left(R_{rs} + \dfrac{1}{R_{rs}} - 2 \right) \right)^2} \geq 0$$

Once again, we have tested ponctual and average boundary process estimators. The results obtained are satisfying. The regularization effects are constant on the whole image and no isolated bright or dark points are obtained. Nevertheless, the average estimation $\overline{b_{rs}}$ give the better results (but we have in this case no proof of convergence). In the case of ponctual filtering, slightly textured results are obtained, and no ideal parameter set can be found.

9 Comparison with other SAR filtering methods

Let us begin with some general remarks. In any cases, better results have been obtained using average boundary process estimators, either because isolated bright or dark points are suppressed, or because the filtering effects are stronger. In every cases, except §7.2 and for §8.2, different behaviours in dark and bright regions are observed, due to the multiplicative nature of the noise. The best result is given by a new regularization function taking account of amplitude ratios (§8.2). This method has also been tested on real ERS-1 SAR images. An exemple is given in figure 1.

To compare the performance with other filters, some classical filters (proposed by Kuan [11] and by Wu and Maître [12]) have been tested with the synthetic image (figures 3 g and h). We also show the profile of a line in the middle of the image (fig. 4). The following table 2 gives the equivalent number of looks [13] which is often taken to measure the filtering performances (the higher it is, the stronger are the filtering effects).

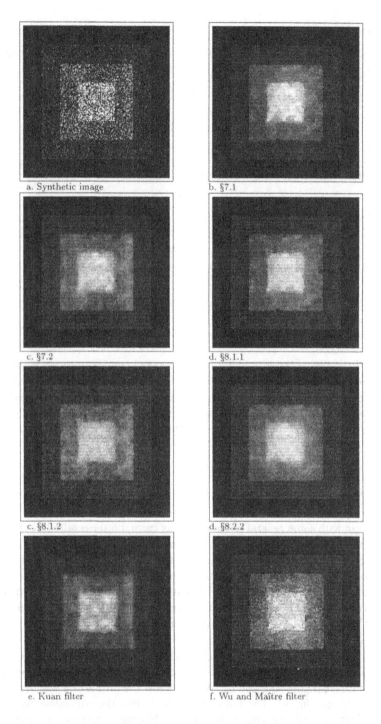

a. Synthetic image

b. §7.1

c. §7.2

d. §8.1.1

c. §8.1.2

d. §8.2.2

e. Kuan filter

f. Wu and Maître filter

Fig. 3. Results obtained on a synthetic image

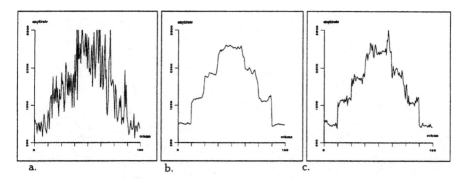

a. b. c.

Fig. 4. Profile of the middle line for a) the original synthetic image, b) for the regularization of section §8.2.2, c) for the Wu and Maître filtered image.

method	equivalent number of looks				
	region 1	region 2	region 3	region 4	average
mire	3.3	3.4	3.3	3.3	3.3
§7.1	23.7	18.3	17.8	16.4	19
§7.2	14.5	17.8	18.7	19.7	17.7
§8.1.1	6.7	12.4	16.8	20.4	14
§8.1.2	4.7	9.3	15.3	19.4	12.2
§8.2	29.4	25.	19.	18.	22.
Kuan filter	1.7	9.8	13.7	15.5	10.1
Wu and Maître filter	11.3	10.6	11.4	12.9	11.5

Table 2. *Equivalent number of looks for the different tests and for each region (1 to 4 from the outside to the center of the image).*

10   Conclusions

In this paper, we have extended the approach of [1, 2] to the restoration of synthetic aperture radar images, dealing in particular with non-gaussian statistics. We have exhibited an adapted edge detector whose response can be injected in a deterministic algorithm with explicit boundaries. Satisfying results have been obtained assuming a gaussian observation pdf, a truncated gaussian regularization model and using this edge detector. The scaling law of the exact speckle pdf has also been considered by devising a new class of regularization potentials based on the ratio of neighbor pixels rather than on their gradient. The best results using this model and χ law were obtained with average boundary estimation, which is not very satisfying, since we move away from theoretical framework. We believe that a real appropriate function $\mathcal{H}$ and a χ distribution should permit good restoration even with ponctual estimation. These results could be improved by testing other functions ϕ and by comparing with simulated annealing results.

a. Original ERS-1 ©ESA

b. Regularization result (gaussian probability)

Fig. 5. Results obtained on a real SAR ERS-1 image

References

1. D. Geman and G. Reynolds. Constrained restoration and the recovery of discontinuities. *IEEE Transactions on Pattern Analysis and Machine Intelligence*, 14(3),
   March 1992.
2. P. Charbonnier, L. Blanc-Féraud, G. Aubert and M. Barlaud. Deterministic Edge-
   Preserving Regularization in Computed Imaging. *IEEE Transactions on Image
   Processing*, 5(12):1-13, 1996.
3. A. Blake and A. Zissermann. *Visual Reconstruction*. MIT Press, 1987.
4. M. Nikolova, A. Mohammad-Djaffari, and J. Idier. Inversion of large-support ill-
   conditioned linear operators using a markov model with a line process. *IEEE
   Transactions on Acoustic Speech and Signal Processing*, 5:357–360, 1994.
5. J. Zerubia and R. Chellapa. Mean Field Annealing for Edge Detection and Image Restoration. *Signal Processing V: Theories and Applications*. L. Torres, E.
   Masgrau and M.A. Lagunas (eds.) Elsevier Science Publishers B.V. 837-840, 1990.
6. D. Geiger and F. Girosi. Parallel and deterministic algorithms from MRF's : surface reconstruction. *IEEE Transactions on Pattern Analysis and Machine Intelligence*, 13(5), 1991.
7. *Geometry-Driven Diffusion in Computer Vision*. Editor: Bart M. ter Haar
   Romeny, Kluwer Academic Publishers, 1994.

8. S. Geman and D. Geman. Stochastic relaxation, Gibbs distribution, and the bayesian restoration of images. *IEEE Transactions on Pattern Analysis and Machine Intelligence*, 6(6):721–741, 1984.

9. L. Bedini, I. Gerace, and A. Tonazzini. A deterministic algorithm for reconstructing images with interactive discontinuities. *Computer Vision and Graphics Image Processing: Graphical Models and Image Processing*, 56(2):109–123, 1993.

10. J.-S. Lee. Speckle analysis and smoothing of synthetic aperture radar images. *Computer Graphics and Image Processing*, 17:24–32, 1981.

11. Kuan, Sawchuk, Strand, and Chavel. Adaptive restoration of images with speckle. *IEEE Transactions on Acoustics, Speech, and Signal Processing*, ASSP-35(3):373–383, 1987.

12. Y. Wu and H. Maître. Smoothing speckled synthetic aperture radar images by using maximum homogeneous region filters. *Optical Engineering*, 31(8):1785–1792, 1992.

13. A. Lopes, E. Nezry, R. Touzi, and H. Laur. Structure detection, and statistical adaptive filtering in SAR images. *Int. J. Remote Sensing*, 14(9):1735–1758, 1993.

14. F.-K. Li, C. Croft, and D. N. Held. Comparison of several techniques to obtain multiple-look SAR imagery. *IEEE Transactions on Geoscience and Remote sensing*, GE-21(3):370–375, July 1983.

15. J.W Goodman. Statistical properties of laser speckle patterns. In *Laser Speckle and Related Phenomena*, volume 9, pages 9–75. J.C Dainty (Springer Verlag, Heidelberg, 1975), 1975.

16. M. Abramowitz and I. Stegun. *Handbook of Mathematical Functions*. Dover Publications, 1972.

17. E. Jakeman and Tough J. A. Generalized K distribution: a statistical model for weak scattering. *J. Opt. Soc. Am.*, 4(9):1764–1772, 1987.

18. C. J. Oliver. A model for non-Rayleigh scattering statistics. *Optica Acta*, 31(6):701–722, 1984.

19. A. C. Bovik. On detecting edges in speckle imagery. *IEEE Transactions on Acoustics, Speech and Signal Processing*, ASSP-36(10):1618–1627, October 1988.

20. R. Touzi, A. Lopes, and P. Bousquet. A statistical and geometrical edge detector for SAR images. *IEEE Transactions on Geoscience And Remote Sensing*, TGARS-26(6):764 – 773, November 1988.

21. J.W. Goodman. Some fundamental properties of speckle. *Journal Optical Society of America*, 66(11):1145–1150, 1976.

Geometrically Deformable Templates for Shape-Based Segmentation and Tracking in Cardiac MR Images

Daniel Rueckert and Peter Burger

Imperial College of Science, Technology and Medicine

Abstract. We present a new approach to shape-based segmentation and tracking of multiple, deformable anatomical structures in cardiac MR images. We propose to use an energy-minimizing geometrically deformable template (GDT) which can deform into similar shapes under the influence of image forces. The degree of deformation of the template from its *equilibrium shape* is measured by a penalty function associated with mapping between the two shapes. In 2D, this term corresponds to the bending energy of an idealized thin-plate of metal. By minimizing this term along with the image energy terms of the classic deformable model, the deformable template is attracted towards objects in the image whose shape is similar to its equilibrium shape. This framework allows for the simultaneous segmentation of multiple deformable objects using intra- as well as inter-shape information. The energy minimization problem of the deformable template is formulated in a Bayesian framework and solved using relaxation techniques: Simulated Annealing (SA), a stochastic relaxation technique is used for segmentation while Iterated Conditional Modes (ICM), a deterministic relaxation technique is used for tracking. We present results of the algorithm applied to the reconstruction of the left and right ventricle of the human heart in 4D MR images.

1 Introduction

The segmentation of images plays a vital role in medical imaging. In many medical applications the segmentation of the acquired images is a necessary step to obtain qualitative measurements, e.g. the visualization of objects of interest, as well as for quantitative measurements such as area or volume. When large group studies are made, the reliable and reproducible manual outlining of the relevant objects requires expert knowledge and is a tedious and time-consuming task, especially with the introduction of 3D and 4D imaging techniques for clinical routine use. However, the automatic segmentation of anatomical structures in cardiac MR images can be problematic due to noise and artefacts which are inherent in these images. The major reason for the sometimes very poor image quality is the fact that objects like the heart are constantly undergoing motion and deformation not only in the three spatial dimensions but also in the temporal dimension. Another common problem in these images are artefacts caused by turbulent blood flow which leads to a loss of signal and temporary occlusion of object boundaries. An example of a typical density-encoded MR image of

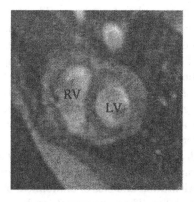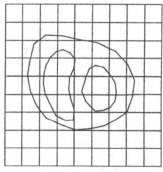

Fig. 1. (a) A gradient echo MR image of the left and right ventricle and (b) its geometric model. In this example the model is composed out of three different objects (in this case contours) whose deformations are highly connected. Note, that a rectangular grid can be used to visualize the deformations of the model. The grid is not part of the model itself.

a human heart is shown in figure 1(a). This image shows a short axis view of the left (LV) and right (RV) ventricle. A geometric model which represents the different anatomical structures in this image is shown in figure 1(b). The model is composed out of three different objects which are represented by the endocardial contours of the LV and RV as well as the epicardium. The segmentation problem in these images cannot be addressed adequately without the anatomical a-priori knowledge which usually aids the radiologist in making decisions about the image segmentation. In this context two major sources of a-priori knowledge can be identified:

– A-priori information about the mean shape and the variability of anatomical objects. We refer to this information as the *intra-shape* knowledge.
– A-priori information about the mean location, orientation and size of anatomical objects with respect to each other and their variability. We refer to this as the *inter-shape* knowledge.

Another important source of a-priori knowledge is information about the intensity and texture of the tissue of different objects. However, these factors are highly dependent on the imaging modality itself, e.g. the same anatomical structures in a spin-echo and gradient-echo MR study can have completely different intensity distributions.

In contrast to many other approaches to deformable templates which model a-priori shape information via their parameterization, we propose to model a-priori shape information in an energy-minimizing framework. We develop a model called Geometrically Deformable Templates (GDT) whose deformation is controlled by an energy or penalty function. This penalty function measures the degree of non-affine deformation of the template from its equilibrium shape which represents the a-priori shape information. At the same time, the penalty function does not penalize affine transformations. To achieve this, we use the bending energy of a thin-plate spline (TPS) mapping function which maps the template from its undeformed equilibrium shape into its deformed shape. Going back to figure 1(b), one can visualize this thin-plate spline mapping function as an rectangular grid associated with the model in its equilibrium. Any deformation of the model would be reflected by a deformation of this grid. The amount of non-affine deformation of this grid corresponds to the bending energy of the thin-plate spline mapping function. Such a model can incorporate not only information about the mean shape and the variability of anatomical objects, but also information about the mean location, orientation and size of anatomical objects with respect to each other and their variability. Thus, the model can be used to segment multiple objects simultaneously.

The remaining part of this paper is organized as follows: The next section reviews some approaches to image segmentation using deformable models and templates. The concept of Geometrically Deformable Templates (GDTs) for shape-based matching in 2D and 3D images is introduced in section 3. Section 4 describes how such an approach can be formulated in a Bayesian framework. The optimization of the model using a stochastic optimization technique, Simulated Annealing (SA) as well as a deterministic relaxation technique, Iterated Conditional Modes (ICM) is described in section 5. Section 6 shows some segmentation and tracking results of left and right ventricle as well as the epi- and endocardium in 4D cardiac MR images. We discuss the results and their implications for future research in section 7.

2 Background

Recently, the application of deformable models and templates for the segmentation and tracking of anatomic structures in medical images has attracted much interest (e.g. an extensive survey is given in [18]). Their increased popularity can be explained by their ability to combine low-level knowledge derived from the image data with a-priori high-level knowledge about the location, size and shape of these anatomic structures. At the same time deformable models can accomodate the shape variability which naturally occurs over time and across individuals. The major difference between deformable models and templates lies in the degree of a-priori knowledge which is used for constraining the segmentation process: While the deformable model approach imposes only generic smoothness constraints on the extracted shape, the deformable template imposes more specific constraints on the extracted shape.

2.1 Deformable Models

Deformable models or *snakes* were first proposed by Kass et al. [14] to segment the contour objects in 2D images. Deformable models are a class of energy minimizing splines which are controlled by an energy function. The energy function has two major terms: on the one hand, the *internal energy* characterizes the energy of the spline due to elastic and bending deformations. The *external energy* on the other hand is characterized by the image forces which attract the model towards image features like edges. Based on an initial estimate, the model is deformed by minimizing its associated energy function. Kass et al. used a gradient descent technique to solve the minimization problem via the Euler-Lagrange method. Other optimization techniques include dynamic programming [1], greedy optimization [28], finite element methods (FEM) [8] and Simulated Annealing [25, 19].

2.2 Deformable Templates

In contrast to deformable models which possess only generic a-priori knowledge, deformable templates possess more specific a-priori knowledge problem and address the problem of matching objects with known shapes. Based on the kind of matching process, two different types of deformable templates can be characterized: Rigid deformable templates are restricted to rigid-body transformations like scaling, rotation and translation. The earliest example of such a model is the Hough-Transform for detecting lines and circles [12] which has been extended to detect arbitrary parameterized shapes [2]. Similar approaches have been used by Yuille et al. [29] to extract features of faces and by Lipson et al. [16] to extract features from medical images. The advantage of this approach is the simplicity of the model due to the limited degrees of freedom. However, a major disadvantage is the fact that these templates have been hand-crafted for specific applications and are not easily applicable to complex objects. Most importantly, the anatomical structures of biological systems can undergo significant non-rigid body deformations (due to their own deformations as well as the deformation of adjacent structures).

Non-rigid deformable templates can undergo rigid- as well as non-rigid body transformations. Such an approach, which is based on a Fourier decomposition of the object contour, has been proposed by Staib et al. [20]. A preference of the template model for specific shapes can be imposed by specifying the probability distribution of the Fourier coefficients or by modal shape analysis [21]. A similar approach has been proposed by Jain et at. [13] in which a parameterized deformation is used to warp the prototype shape into the deformed shape. Again, the preference for specific shapes is expressed by specifying a probability distribution of the parameters of the deformation function. Other researchers have suggested to use deformable superquadrics [24] in order to efficiently capture the global and local a-priori shape knowledge.

Cootes et al. [9] have proposed an alternative approach which is based on learning shapes from training data. Their model uses a point distribution model (PDM) which is based on the statistics of a set of training shapes. Using the largest eigenvectors of the covariance matrix results in a description of the main modes of statistical variation of the shape. These approaches require a number of training sets which are usually obtained by manual outlining to capture the statistics of their shape variability. Such a training process for 3D and 4D deformable objects is very time consuming. Moreover, the training population has to be large enough to capture the shape variability appropriately.

3 Geometrically Deformable Templates

We have developed the general framework of Geometrically Deformable Templates (GDTs) for modelling 2D and 3D deformable templates of multiple objects. We will first give a brief overview of the framework of GDTs before we are going to describe the details of GDTs as 2D and 3D templates: A GDT is a collection of m objects $\mathcal{O} = \{\mathcal{O}^1, \ldots, \mathcal{O}^m\}$. Each object $\mathcal{O}^i$ is described by an ordered set of n_i vertices $\mathcal{V}^i = \{\mathbf{v}_1^i, \ldots, \mathbf{v}_{n_i}^i\}$ which define a contour or surface $\mathcal{C}^i$. Let $\mathcal{V}$ denote the set of vertices given by the union of the vertices of all objects $\mathcal{V} = \{\mathbf{v}_j^i \mid \mathbf{v}_j^i \in \mathcal{V}^1 \cup \ldots \cup \mathcal{V}^i \cup \ldots \cup \mathcal{V}^m\}$. To simplify the notation in the remaining part of this paper we will denote the vertices of a GDT by a single subindex $\mathcal{V} = \{\mathbf{v}_1, \ldots, \mathbf{v}_l, \ldots \mathbf{v}_N\}$ so that

$$l = j + \sum_{k=1}^{i-1} n_k \qquad \text{and} \qquad N = \sum_{k=1}^{m} n_k \qquad (1)$$

Alternatively one can think of the vertices as landmarks[1] which describe the outline of a shape. Informally, a GDT consists of three different parts:

- A set of vertices $\mathcal{V} = \{\mathbf{v}_1, \ldots, \mathbf{v}_N\}$ as defined above which describes the undeformed prototype shape. This undeformed shape constitutes the *equilibrium shape* of our model because the internal shape forces for all vertices are 0.
- A set of vertices $\mathcal{V}' = \{\mathbf{v}_1', \ldots, \mathbf{v}_N'\}$ which describes the deformed prototype shape. This deformed shape is the result of a deformation process which is the result of external image forces acting on the model.
- A penalty function which measures the amount of deformation of the template with respect to its equilibrium shape. The penalty function is associated with the mapping function which maps the undeformed vertices into the deformed ones. The penalty function is invariant to scaling, rotation and translation of the template.

In general we can describe the mapping of a set of undeformed points into a set of deformed points by defining a d-dimensional spline mapping function $\mathbf{v} \to \mathbf{v}' : \mathbf{F}(\mathbf{v}) = (f_1(\mathbf{v}), \ldots, f_d(\mathbf{v}))^T$. The general form of a spline penalty functional [27] is given by

$$J_m^d(f) = \sum_{\alpha_1 + \cdots + \alpha_d = m} \frac{m!}{\alpha_1! \cdots \alpha_d!} \int_{-\infty}^{\infty} \cdots \int_{-\infty}^{\infty} \left(\frac{\partial^m f}{\partial x_1^{\alpha_1} \cdots \partial x_d^{\alpha_d}}\right)^2 \prod_i dx_i \qquad (2)$$

---

[1] It is important to notice that these landmarks are not anatomical landmarks but pseudo-landmarks (or quasi-landmarks [6]).

where m specifies the order of derivatives used. Of special interest are splines which minimize the following quantity:

$$\frac{1}{n}\sum_{i=1}^{n}(y - f(x_1,\ldots,x_d))^2 + \lambda J_m^d(f).\tag{3}$$

The parameter λ controls the smoothness of the spline: For $\lambda = 0$ the spline is an interpolating spline which minimizes the quantity in eq. (2). For $\lambda > 0$ the spline is an approximating spline. In the remaining part of this paper we will focus on splines as interpolants.

3.1 Affine and Non-Affine Deformations in 2D

Let us first discuss the case of deformable templates in two dimensions. The two-dimensional ($d = 2$) penalty-function for $m = 2$ corresponds to the bending energy of a thin-plate of metal which is subject to small deformations and is expressed by the following quantity:

$$\int_{-\infty}^{\infty}\int_{-\infty}^{\infty} (\frac{\partial^2 f}{\partial x^2})^2 + 2(\frac{\partial^2 f}{\partial x\partial y})^2 + (\frac{\partial^2 f}{\partial y^2})^2 dxdy\tag{4}$$

The solution of the variational problem of eq. (3) is the well known thin-plate spline in 2D and has been studied extensively by Bookstein [4, 5]. Each vertex $v_i = (x_i, y_i)^T$ defines a point which is mapped into its homologous deformed vertex $v'_i = (x'_i, y'_i)^T$ in the 2D image plane. Let $\mathbf{F}$ be a vector-valued interpolation function so that $\mathbf{F}(v) = (f_x(v), f_y(v))^T$. For each coordinate x and y, we define an interpolation function f of the following form

$$f(v) = a_1 + a_2 x + a_3 y + \sum_{j=1}^{n} b_j \sigma(|v - v_j|)\tag{5}$$

where the basis function $\sigma(|v - v_j|) = |v - v_j|^2 \log(|v - v_j|)$ is the solution to the biharmonic equation ($\Delta^2\sigma = 0$). The interpolation problem can now be formulated in matrix form

$$\begin{pmatrix} \Sigma & D \\ D^T & 0 \end{pmatrix}\begin{pmatrix} b_x & b_y \\ a_x & a_y \end{pmatrix} = \begin{pmatrix} x' & y' \\ 0 & 0 \end{pmatrix}\tag{6}$$

where $\Sigma_{ij} = \sigma(|v_i - v_j|)$, $x' = (x'_1,\ldots,x'_N)^T$, $y' = (y'_1,\ldots,y'_N)^T$ and the i-th row of D being $(1, x_i, y_i)$. The vectors $a^T = (a_1, a_2, a_3)$ and $b^T = (b_1,\cdots,b_N)$ contain the coefficients of the affine and non-affine part of the transformation. The resulting transformation will interpolate all deformed vertices and is smooth between these vertices. Moreover, it minimizes the quantity given in eq. (4). On the one hand, the coefficients of the affine part of this mapping do not influence the amount of bending energy so that all scaling, rotation and translation transformations do not require any "bending" of the interpolation function and are free of bending energy. On the other hand the amount of bending energy is only zero if all coefficients of the non-affine part of mapping functions are zero, so that the amount of non-affine deformation of a 2D deformable template can be expressed by the bending energy of the thin-plate spline mapping function $\mathbf{F}$.

3.2 Affine and Non-Affine Deformations in 3D

The case of deformable templates in three dimensions is very similar. However, the three-dimensional form of a thin-plate spline is slightly different from its to two-dimensional counterpart: Its penalty-function is expressed by the following quantity:

$$\int_{-\infty}^{\infty} \int_{-\infty}^{\infty} \int_{-\infty}^{\infty} (\frac{\partial^2 f}{\partial x^2})^2 + (\frac{\partial^2 f}{\partial y^2})^2 + (\frac{\partial^2 f}{\partial z^2})^2 + 2[(\frac{\partial^2 f}{\partial xy})^2 + (\frac{\partial^2 f}{\partial xz})^2 + (\frac{\partial^2 f}{\partial yz})^2] dx dy dz \quad (7)$$

Each vertex $\mathbf{v}_i = (x_i, y_i, z_i)^T$ defines a point which is mapped into its homologous deformed vertex $\mathbf{v}_i' = (x_i', y_i', z_i')^T$ in the 3D image volume. Let $\mathbf{F}$ be a vector-valued interpolation function so that $\mathbf{F}(\mathbf{v}) = (f_x(\mathbf{v}), f_y(\mathbf{v}), f_z(\mathbf{v}))^T$. For each coordinate x, y and z, we define an interpolation function f of the following form

$$f(\mathbf{v}) = a_1 + a_2 x + a_3 y + a_4 z + \sum_{j=1}^{n} b_j \sigma(|\mathbf{v} - \mathbf{v}_j|) \quad (8)$$

where $\sigma(|\mathbf{v} - \mathbf{v}_j|) = |\mathbf{v} - \mathbf{v}_j|$ is the solution to the biharmonic equation ($\Delta^2 \sigma = 0$). The interpolation problem can now be formulated in matrix form

$$\begin{pmatrix} \Sigma & \mathbf{D} \\ \mathbf{D}^T & 0 \end{pmatrix} \begin{pmatrix} \mathbf{b}_x & \mathbf{b}_y & \mathbf{b}_z \\ \mathbf{a}_x & \mathbf{a}_y & \mathbf{a}_z \end{pmatrix} = \begin{pmatrix} \mathbf{x}' & \mathbf{y}' & \mathbf{z}' \\ 0 & 0 & 0 \end{pmatrix} \quad (9)$$

where $\Sigma_{ij} = \sigma(|\mathbf{v}_i - \mathbf{v}_j|)$, $\mathbf{x}' = (x_1', \ldots, x_N')^T$, $\mathbf{y}' = (y_1', \ldots, y_N')^T$, $\mathbf{z}' = (z_1', \ldots, z_N')^T$ and the i-th row of $\mathbf{D}$ being $(1, x_i, y_i, z_i)$. Again, the vectors $\mathbf{a}^T = (a_1, a_2, a_3, a_4)$ and $\mathbf{b}^T = (b_1, \cdots, b_N)$ contain the coefficients of the affine and non-affine part of the transformation. The bending energy of the three-dimensional thin-plate spline has the same invariance properties as the corresponding two-dimensional thin-plate spline so that the amount of non-affine deformation of a 3D deformable template can be expressed by the bending energy of the thin-plate spline mapping function $\mathbf{F}$.

4 Bayesian Framework for Geometrically Deformable Templates

The deformation of the template model is driven by the minimization of its associated energy function. Like a deformable model, the energy function of a deformable template is two-fold: The internal energy E_{intern} measures the amount of non-affine deformation of the template with respect to its equilibrium shape.

The external energy E_{extern} is a form of potential created by the image which attracts the template towards image features such as edges. A convenient approach is to view the energy minimization problem in a probabilistic framework. Such a probabilistic framework allows us to incorporate specific prior knowledge about the expected object shape into the segmentation and tracking process. This is formulated by Bayes theorem,

$$P(\mathcal{V}|\mathcal{I}) = \frac{P(\mathcal{I}|\mathcal{V})P(\mathcal{V})}{P(\mathcal{I})} \tag{10}$$

where $P(\mathcal{V}|\mathcal{I})$ expresses the posterior probability of the model $\mathcal{V}$ given an observed image $\mathcal{I}$. Here $P(\mathcal{V})$ corresponds to the prior distribution of shapes and $P(\mathcal{I}|\mathcal{V})$ corresponds to the likelihood of an image $\mathcal{I}$ given a model $\mathcal{V}$.

4.1 Prior Distribution

Let us first consider non-affine deformations of the template. We have already described how we can use the penalty function of the thin-plate spline mapping function to specify the degree of non-affine deformation of the template. We can transform this into a prior probability distribution which indicates which shapes we are expecting by using a Gibbs (or Boltzmann) distribution

$$P(\mathcal{V}) = \frac{1}{Z(T)} \exp(-\frac{E_{intern}(\mathcal{V})}{T}) \tag{11}$$

where $Z(T)$ is the partition function which normalizes the distribution. The parameter T controls the degree of shape variability and has significant influence on the shape of the probability distribution: For large values of T, high- and low-energy configurations have approximately the same probability and the probability distribution is close to a uniform distribution. For small values of T, high-energy configurations become less likely and the probability distribution concentrates on low-energy configurations. The parameter T describes the degree of shape variations which we expect to encounter and can be used to express the confidence in the template model. Figure 2 shows some examples of sampling shapes from the prior distribution of a heart template at different values of T. It can be clearly seen that non-affine body deformations of the template are more likely at high values of T. The amount of non-affine deformation of the template can be expressed by the bending energy of thin-plate splines of the mapping function $\mathbf{F}$. Let $\mathbf{L}$ be a matrix defined as follows:

$$\mathbf{L} = \begin{pmatrix} \Sigma & \mathbf{D} \\ \mathbf{D}^T & 0 \end{pmatrix} \tag{12}$$

Then the bending energy of a thin-plate spline mapping function $\mathbf{F}$ is given by the following quantity [17]

$$E_{bending} = \frac{1}{8\pi} \text{tr}(\mathbf{v}' \mathbf{L}_N^{-1} \mathbf{v}'^T) \tag{13}$$

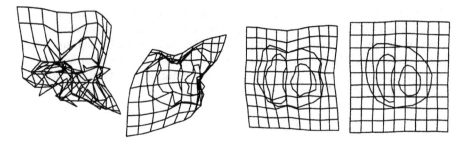

Fig. 2. Sampling of different shapes from a heart template using the the Gibbs distribution: (a) at $T = 1$, (b) at $T = 0.1$, (c) at $T = 0.05$ and (d) at $T = 0.01$.

where $\mathbf{L}_N$ is the left upper $N \times N$ matrix of $\mathbf{L}$. A more efficient way of calculating the bending energy of the deformation exploits the spectrum of $\mathbf{L}_N^{-1}$ by calculating its eigenvectors $\mathbf{e}_i$ and eigenvalues e_i, which represent the principal warps of deformation [4, 5].

Let us now consider affine deformations of the template. Because the thin-plate spline penalty function is invariant to scaling, rotation and translation, the prior distribution expresses no preferences for specific affine deformations of our template which amounts to assuming an uniform probability distribution for affine deformations for the template. In fact the scaling, rotation and translation parameters are largely dependent on user defined imaging parameters, e.g. the size of an object is highly dependent on the selected field-of-view (FOV) during the image acquisition. It is therefore appropriate and convenient to treat the scaling, rotation and translation priors as uniformly distributed.

4.2 Likelihood

The likelihood $P(\mathcal{I}|\mathcal{V})$ expresses the probability of observing an image $\mathcal{I}$ given a model $\mathcal{V}$. One possibility of specifying this likelihood is to use an energy potential E_{extern} so that

$$P(\mathcal{I}|\mathcal{V}) \propto - \exp(E_{extern}(\mathcal{V})) \qquad (14)$$

In our approach we choose an edge-based potential which is based on two differential invariants [22, 23], the gradient and the Laplace operator. The magnitude of the gradient operator $|\nabla \mathcal{I}|$ of the image intensity function measures the strength of an edge. The zero-crossings of the Laplace operator $\Delta \mathcal{I}$, or the second derivative of the image intensity function, indicate a local minimum or maximum of the first derivative which is equivalent to the center of an edge. By computing the distance transform [7] of the zero-crossings of the Laplace operator $|D(\Delta \mathcal{I})|$, the template is attracted towards the center of edges. The external energy is computed as a linear combination of both terms which are biased by constant weighting factors α_i:

$$E_{extern}(\mathcal{V}) = \sum_{i=1}^{n} -\alpha_1 |\nabla \mathcal{I}(\mathbf{v}_i)|^2 + \alpha_2 |D(\Delta \mathcal{I}(\mathbf{v}_i))|^2 \qquad (15)$$

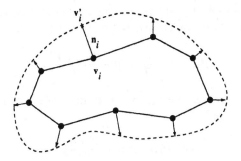

Fig. 3. Non-affine deformations of the template can occur only along the normal direction of the equilibrium shape.

5   Optimization of Geometrically Deformable Templates

Estimating the maximum a posteriori (MAP) solution directly is usually impossible due to the size of the configuration space, even for template models with very few vertices. Instead we have implemented two different optimization techniques: SA as a global minimization technique, which is able to escape local energy minima and ICM as an efficient local minimization technique.

Assuming that the center of mass of the undeformed model is at the origin of the coordinate system, we can express the deformed model by the following equation:

$$\mathbf{v}'_i = \mathcal{T}_{\mathbf{t},\mathbf{s},\theta}(\mathbf{v}_i + \lambda_i \mathbf{n}_i) \quad \text{for} \quad i = 1, \cdots, N \tag{16}$$

Here $\mathcal{T}_{\mathbf{t},\mathbf{s},\theta}$ is an affine deformation which involves a translation $\mathbf{t}$, a scaling $\mathbf{s}$ and a rotation θ. The non-affine deformations are expressed by movements along the normal direction $\mathbf{n}_i$ at each vertex $\mathbf{v}_i$ (see figure 3), thus the search space for each vertex is only one-dimensional. This reduces the search space for the optimization considerably. To solve the segmentation problem we now need to estimate the optimal set of parameters $\{\mathbf{t}, \mathbf{s}, \theta, \lambda_1, \ldots, \lambda_N\}$ which corresponds to the affine and non-affine deformation of the template which matches the image best. The affine parameters of the transformation are determined using an exhaustive search method. Next, we estimate the non-affine parameters of the transformation using Simulated Annealing optimization.

5.1   Stochastic Relaxation

Simulated Annealing (SA) [15], [26] is a stochastic relaxation technique which is based on the analogy to the physical process of annealing a metal: At high temperatures the atoms are randomly distributed. With decreasing temperatures they tend to arrange themselves in a crystalline state which minimizes their energy. Using this analogy, the algorithm generates randomly new configurations by sampling from the probability distribution of the system:

$$P(\mathcal{V}) = \frac{1}{Z(T)} \exp(-\frac{E_{total}(\mathcal{V})}{T}) \qquad (17)$$

New configurations are accepted with a certain acceptance probability $H(T)$ depending on the temperature:

$$H(T) = \exp[-\frac{\Delta E_{total}}{T}] \qquad (18)$$

Since increases of energy can be accepted, the algorithm is able to escape local energy minima. It has been shown [10] that the algorithm converges to a global energy minimum if the temperature at iteration k is

$$T(k) \geq \frac{c}{\log(1 + k)}, \qquad (19)$$

where c is a constant depending on the amount of energy which is necessary to escape local minima.

5.2 Deterministic Relaxation

For tracking an object in an image sequence where the changes between successive time frames is small, we take the deformed model of the previous time frame as the undeformed model of the current time frame and use a deterministic relaxation method. In contrast to stochastic relaxation, which makes random changes, deterministic relaxation makes only changes which improve the configuration and converges much faster. Besag [3] proposed an iterative algorithm, called Iterated Conditional Modes (ICM), which maximizes the conditional probability based on a provisional estimate: suppose $\mathcal{V}$ denotes a provisional estimate of the template and that our goal is to update the position of vertex $\mathbf{v}_i$ in the context of all available information by estimating a new value λ_i. This means that we want to maximize the conditional probability of λ_i given our current estimate $\mathcal{V}$. It should be noted that ICM is equivalent to SA with instantaneous freezing; it converges therefore much faster. ICM is not a global minimization technique but rather a local one, as the results are dependent on the initial estimate. However, it is well suited for tracking objects if the temporal resolution is high enough.

6 Results

We have applied the algorithm for the simultaneous segmentation and tracking of the endocardial surfaces of the left (LV) and right ventricle (RV). These images are 4D MR short axis studies provided by the National Heart and Lung Institute of the Royal Brompton Hospital, London. All images were acquired

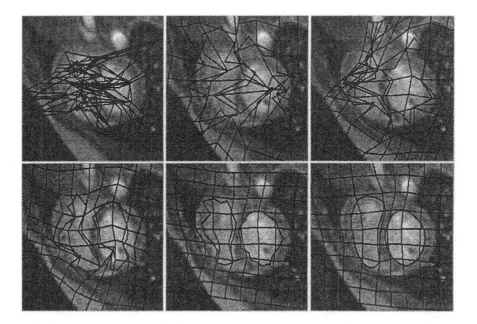

Fig. 4. Evolution of a deformable template of the LV and RV during the SA optimization after (a) 100, (b) 200, (c) 500, (d) 2000 and (e) 5000 iterations.

with a modified Picker scanner (1.5 T with cardiac gating) and have a resolution of $256 \times 256 \times 8$ pixels. Each pixel corresponds to 2.1 mm^2 and the slice thickness is 5 mm. The image sequence usually contains 16 time frames which yields a temporal resolution between 40 and 60 ms.

The test of the algorithm involved the segmentation and tracking of the LV and RV in 2D cine sequences. In this case the initial template in equilibrium state consists of two ellipsoids with 16-32 vertices each. For each image sequence the initial template is randomly placed in the first time frame: We estimate the affine transformation parameters of the model. After that the non-affine transformation parameters are estimated using SA. Subsequent time frames are initialized with the final model of the previous frame and then optimized using ICM. Figure 4 shows the segmentation of the LV and RV as well as the evolution of the deformable template during the SA optimization. Figure 5 shows the tracking of the LV and RV at different time frames during the cardiac cycle. We have compared the automatic segmentation results with a manual outlining of a radiologist and found that the variations for the area of the LV lie within 5%. The outlining of the RV is more difficult and the variations lie within 10%. We have also tested the algorithm on a 3D cine sequence. The results are shown in figure 6. The optimization for such a 3D GDT takes ca. 10 mins. using SA and ca. 1 min. using ICM on a Sun Ultra Sparc.

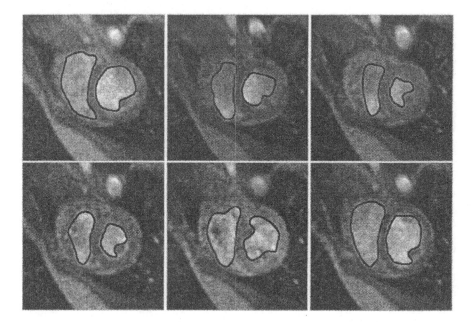

Fig. 5. Simultaneous tracking of the RV and LV at different time frames during the cardiac cycle. The tracking process uses the final result of the previous time frame as initialization for the current time frame which is then optimized using ICM.

Our experimental results have shown that the use of a-priori shape information significantly increases the robustness of the algorithm in situations where parts of the boundary are temporarily occluded by blood flow artefacts. However, the identification of the papillary muscle can be problematic, because it is not visible during all time frames. Consequently, the deformable template might lose the papillary muscle during the tracking. Another problem is the identification of the top and bottom of the LV and RV which are often not identifiable in short-axis studies. A possible solution to avoid this problem is the fusion of short-axis and long-axis studies [11].

7 Discussion

We have been able to successfully reconstruct the epi- and endocardium of the left ventricle as well as the right ventricle completely automatically from clinical 4D MR images. We believe that the combination of high-level a-priori knowledge and low-level image knowledge makes the reliable and accurate segmentation of 4D cardiac MR images not only possible but is essential in order to provide robustness. We think that such an automated segmentation tool is an important step towards accepting 4D MR imaging as a valuable method for assessing cardiac malfunction. Current work focuses on atlas-based initialization of the segmentation process to eliminate the need for the computationally expensive SA optimization. Future work will be directed towards the possibility of incorporating temporal knowledge into the deformable template model.

References

1. A. A. Amini, T. E. Weymouth, and R. C. Jain. Using dynamic programming for solving variational problems in vision. *IEEE Transactions on Pattern Analysis and Machine Intelligence*, 12(9):855–867, September 1990.

2. D. H. Ballard. Generalizing the Hough transform to detect arbitrary shapes. *Pattern Recognition*, 13(2):111–122, 1981.

3. J. Besag. On the statistical analysis of dirty pictures. *Journal of the Royal Stat. Soc. B*, 48(3):259–302, 1986.

4. F. L. Bookstein. Principal Warps: Thin-plate splines and the decomposition of deformations. *IEEE Transactions on Pattern Analysis and Machine Intelligence*, 11(6):567–585, June 1989.

5. F. L. Bookstein. *Morphometric tools for landmark data: Geometry and Biology.* Cambridge University Press, 1991.

6. F. L. Bookstein. Applying landmark methods to biological outline data. In K. V. Mardia, C. A. Gill, and I. L. Dryden, editors, *Image Fusion and Shape Variability Techniques*, pages 59–70, July 1996.

7. G. Borgefors. Distance transformations in digital images. *Computer Vision, Graphics, and Image Processing*, 34:344–371, 1986.

8. L. D. Cohen and I. Cohen. Finite-element methods for active contour models and balloons for 2-D and 3-D images. *IEEE Transactions on Pattern Analysis and Machine Intelligence*, 15(11):1131–1147, November 1993.

9. T. F. Cootes, C. J. Taylor, D. H. Cooper, and J. Graham. Active Shape Models - their training and application. *Computer Vision and Image Understanding*, 61(1):38–59, 1995.

10. S. Geman and D. Geman. Stochastic relaxation, Gibbs distribution, and the Bayesian restoration of images. *IEEE Transactions on Pattern Analysis and Machine Intelligence*, 6:721–741, 1984.

11. A. A. Goshtasby and D. A. Turner. Fusion of short-axis and long-axis cardiac MR images. In *Workshop on Mathematical Methods for Biomedical Image Analysis*, pages 202–211, San Francisco, CA, 1996. IEEE.

12. P. V. C. Hough. Method and means for recognizing complex patterns. U.S. Patent No. 3069654, 1962.

13. A. K. Jain, Y. Zhong, and S. Lakshmanan. Object matching using deformable templates. *IEEE Transactions of Pattern Recognition and Machine Intelligence*, 18(3):267–278, March 1996.

14. M. Kass, A. Witkin, and D. Terzopoulos. Snakes - Active contour models. *International Journal of Computer Vision*, 1(2):259–268, 1987.

15. S. Kirkpatrick, C. D. Gelatt Jr., and M. P. Vecchi. Optimization by Simulated Annealing. *Science*, 220:671–680, May 1983.

16. P. Lipson, A. Yuille, D. O'Keefe, J. Cavanaugh, J. Taaffe, and D. Rosenthal. Deformable templates for feature extraction from medical images. In *Proc. First European Conf. on Computer Vision*, pages 477–484, 1990.

17. K. V. Mardia and T. J. Hainsworth. Image warping and Bayesian reconstruction with grey-level templates. In *Advances in Applied Statistics*, pages 257–280. 1993.

18. T. McInerney and D. Terzopoulos. Deformable models in medical image analysis: A survey. *Medical Image Analysis*, 1(2), 1996.

19. D. Rueckert and P. Burger. Contour fitting using stochastic and probabilistic relaxation for cine MR images. In *Computer Assisted Radiology*, pages 137–142, Berlin, Germany, June 21-24 1995. Springer-Verlag.

20. L. H. Staib and J. S. Ducan. Boundary finding with parametrically deformable models. *IEEE Transactions on Pattern Analysis and Machine Intelligence*, 17(11):1061–1075, 1992.

21. G. Székely, A. Kelemen, Ch. Brechbühler, and G. Gerig. Segmentation of 2-D and 3-D objects from MRI volume data using constrained elastic deformations of flexible fourier contour and surface models. *Medical Image Analysis*, 1(1), 1996.

22. B. M. ter Haar Romeny, L. M. J. Florack, J. J. Koenderink, and M. A. Viergever. Scale-space: Its natural operators and differential invariants. In A. C. F. Colchester and D. J. Hawkes, editors, *Information Processing in Medical Imaging*, pages 239–255. Springer-Verlag, 1991.

23. B. M. ter Haar Romeny, L. M. J. Florack, A. H. Salden, and M. A. Viergever. Higher order differential structure of images. In H. H. Barret and A. F. Gmitro, editors, *Information Processing in Medical Imaging*, pages 77–93. Springer-Verlag, 1993.

24. D. Terzopoulos and D. Metaxas. Dynamic 3D models with local and global deformations - deformable superquadrics. *IEEE Transactions on Pattern Analysis and Machine Intelligence*, 13(7):703–714, 1991.

25. K.D. Toennies and D. Rueckert. Image segmentation by stochastically relaxing contour fitting. In *SPIE Conference on Medical Imaging*, volume 2167, pages 18–27, Newport Beach, USA, February 1994.

26. P. J. M. van Laarhoven and E. H. L. Aarts. *Simulated Annealing: Theory and Applications*. Reidel, 1987.

27. G. Wahba. *Spline Models for Observational Data*. Society for Industrial and Applied Mathematics, 1990.

28. D. J. Williams and M. Shah. A fast algorithm for active contours and curvature estimation. *CVGIP: Image Understanding*, 55(1):14–26, 1992.

29. A. L. Yuille, D. S. Cohen, and P. W. Hallinan. Feature-Extraction from Faces using Deformable Templates. In *Conference on Computer Vision and Pattern Recognition*, pages 104–109. IEEE, 1989.

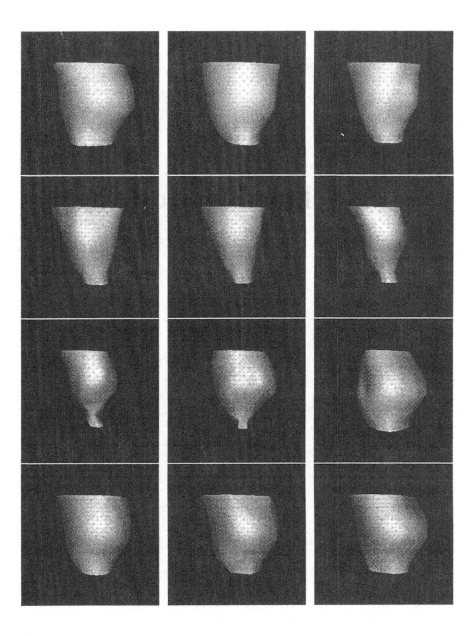

Fig. 6. Reconstructed surface of the LV at different time frames during the cardiac cycle.

Markov Random Fields

Image Segmentation via Energy Minimization on Partitions with Connected Components

Jia-Ping Wang

DIAM/CMLA, ENS Cachan, 61, av. du Président Wilson,
F-94235 Cachan Cedex, France
and
University of Cergy-Pontoise, UFR Sciences et Techniques,
F-95302 Cergy-Pontoise Cedex, France
email: wang@cmla.ens-cachan.fr
Tel: (+33) - 1 47 40 24 89
Fax: (+33) - 1 47 40 21 69

Abstract. We present a new method of segmentation in which images are segmented by partitions with connected components. For this, first we define two different types of neighborhoods on the space of partitions with connected components of a general graph, neighborhoods of the first type are simple but small, while those of the second type are large but complex; second, we give algorithms which are not computationally costly, for probability simulation and simulated annealing on such spaces using the neighborhoods. In particular Hastings algorithms and generalized Metropolis algorithms are defined to avoid heavy computations in the case of the second type of neighborhoods. To realize segmentation, we propose a hierarchical approach which at each step, minimizes a cost function on the space of partitions with connected components of a graph.

1 Introduction

Image segmentation is a basic step in digital image processing. Various methods have been proposed in the literature. This paper is concerned with methods of Markov random fields (MRF) ([7] [1] [6] [15]...) which lead to segmentation by maximizing the a posteriori probability of the partition of the image grid which is classically considered as a labeling of image pixels. In this paper we propose to segment images using *partitions with connected components* (PCC) of the image grid. A PCC is a segmentation where each homogeneous region is *connected* (see Section 3.1 for the precise definition).

A. Why partitions with connected components ?

In most of the model-based segmentation algorithms using MRF, the segmentation space which is the space of all possible partitions of image pixels, is the space of pixel labelings: $\Omega = L^S = \{(l_s)_s : s \in S, l_s \in L\}$, where S is the image grid, $L = \{1, 2, ..., m\}$ with m the number of labels representing different types of homogeneous regions. MRF modeling and stochastic relaxation on Ω can be performed in a classic way like for intensity images [7] [1] [3]. However the fundamental drawback of this modeling is that it requires the number of labels which must be estimated in unsupervised segmentation [4] [12] [18]. However in general this estimation requires prior information or hypothesis, and is usually unreliable and in particular for real images containing complex scene.

In this paper, we define the segmentation space by the set of all PCCs of the image grid. This segmentation model does not require the knowledge of the number of labels, and is particularly suitable for unsupervised cases.

Second, the space of the PCCs is "small" in comparison with a general segmentation space Ω. In fact, let $C(S)$ be the space of PCCs of the image grid S, since we can color connected regions by four different colors (this is the famous four-color problem : the connected regions of an arbitrary partition of a 2D lattice can be colored only by four colors such that two neighbors have different colors), $C(S)$ can then be regarded as a subset of $\{1, 2, 3, 4\}^S$. This means that the PCC space contains less elements than the classic segmentation space with only four labels. (The conjecture of four-color problem has not been mathematically proven, anyway, it is proven that connected components can be colored by five colors). In this way $C(S)$ can be regarded as a subset of Ω (if $m \geq 4$).

Third, there is a natural relation between the product space $\Omega = L^S$ and $C(S)$: the boundaries of a partition in Ω divide S into connected regions which constitute a partition in $C(S)$. Often the optimal segmentation(s) with a model is a PCC. For instance the piecewise constant (or smooth) model of Mumford and Shah [17]: an arbitrary partition in Ω has cost function value greater than the corresponding partition in $C(S)$. Then in these cases, it would be better to segment images directly in the space of the PCCs. Moreover, if we employ boundary detection techniques under the constraint that the boundaries are closed curves, any possible partition is equivalent to a PCC.

B. *Stochastic relaxation on space of partitions with connected components.*

A PCC space with respect to an image (or a general graph of sites) is complex, unlike a general product space such as classic segmentation space $\Omega = L^S$ where there is simple product structure. However stochastic relaxations such as probability distribution simulation and simulated annealing require neighborhood structures to ensure irreducibility and feasibility of the algorithms. In fact, at each step of stochastic relaxation, a sampling of a new state is restricted to a small subset called neighborhood which is determined by current state. On the one hand, neighborhoods must be large enough such that the algorithm is irreducible. On the other hand, neighborhoods should be simple and small enough in order to reduce computation time so that the algorithm is feasible. We have to solve this dilemma to construct neighborhoods over PCC spaces.

The organization of the paper is as follows. In Section 2, we recall the general approach of segmentation and present our energy model on which our segmentation method with PCCs has been tested, a hierarchical segmentation algorithm is developed. In Section 3, we define the neighborhood structures on PCC space of an arbitrary graph. In Section 4, feasible algorithms of stochastic relaxation with the neighborhoods are defined. Application of PCCs to image segmentation is presented in Section 5.

2 General Approach of Segmentation

2.1 General Segmentation Model

We follow the general modeling using random fields. Let Y be the observed intensity image on a rectangular lattice S, let X be the random field representing the partition of the grid S into different homogeneous regions. Let Ω denote the classic labeling space $\Omega = \{1, 2, ..., m\}^S = L^S$. There are two essential ways to model segmentation, both lead to MAP estimate realized by minimizing a cost function which is also called energy. In the first, the model is doubly stochastic : X is a Markov Random field defined by *a priori* regularities of the distribution of the regions, the texture features or natures of homogeneous regions are described by the conditional distribution $P(Y = y \mid X = x)$ of the intensity image given homogeneous regions. The image is segmented by maximizing the conditional probability of X given the intensity image Y (the MAP estimate) [6], [4], [12], [14], [18]: using Bayes' rule, we have $\hat{x} = \arg \max_{x} P(Y = y \mid X = x)P(X = x)$. Let $U_y(x) = -\log P(Y = y \mid X = x) - \log P(X = x)$, then $\hat{x} = \arg \min_{x} U_y(x)$.

In the second kind of modeling, one models directly the interaction energy $U_y(x)$ between the segmentation and the observed image, so that the minimization of U_y tends to group pixels of similar natures into homogeneous region, [8], [13]. In all cases the segmentation becomes a problem of minimization of the cost function U_y on Ω. In the following we denote $U(x) = U_y(x)$ to simplify the notation.

In our application of segmentation, we have used the following energy model, which is suitable for gray level images, color images as well as textured images. For each pixel $s \in S$, let $\xi(s)$ denote the image features around/at s : for textured images, $\xi(s)$ is the texture features of a small window centered at s; for color images, $\xi(s)$ is the color components at s; $\xi(s)$ is simply the gray level for gray level images. Let $D(\xi, \xi')$ be the distance between features. In general D is quadratic for gray level or color images. A non-quadratic distance between textures which doesn't require any normalization is presented in [2]: texture features $\xi = \{\xi_\omega\}$ are an estimate of the spectral density from windowed Fourier filters (in particular Gabor filters), the distance is defined as a symmetrized Kullback distance $D(\xi, \xi') = \sum_\omega (\xi_\omega/\xi'_\omega + \xi'_\omega/\xi_\omega - 2)$.

Let $x = \{R_1, R_2, ...\}$ be an arbitrary segmentation with R_i the homogeneous regions, then

$$U(x) = \sum_i \sum_{s \in R_i} D(\xi(R_i), \xi(s)) - \gamma_1|\partial_\delta x| + \gamma_2|\partial x|, \tag{1}$$

where $\xi(R_i)$ is the centroid of features of the region R_i such that $\xi(R_i) = \arg \min_\xi \sum_{s \in R_i} D(\xi, \xi(s))$; $\partial_\delta x = \{< s, t > \in \partial x : D(\xi(s), \xi(t)) > \delta\}$, $< s, t > \in \partial x$ indicates that the two pixels s and t are neighbors and separated by an edge, $|\partial_\delta x|$ is the number of such pairs of pixels such that the distance between features is greater than δ; $|\partial x|$ is the length of the boundaries of x; γ_1, γ_2 and δ are positive constants which are the parameters of the model. The first term of $U(x)$ is a homogeneousness measure of the regions R_i, it encourages to group together pixels having similar features. The second term of $U(x)$ favors the separation of neighboring pairs of pixels by edges if the distance between features is large enough. The third term of $U(x)$ is a penalty term which limits the length of the boundaries.

Model (1) can be regarded as a variant of Mumford and Shah's piecewise constant model [17] in the discrete case : Mumford and Shah's model is the model (1) for gray level images with the quadratic distance and without the second term (i.e., $\gamma_1 = 0$). For the quadratic distance between gray levels $D(\xi, \xi') = (\xi - \xi')^2$, the centroid $\xi(R)$ of a region R is the average of the gray levels in R. For quadratic distance for vectors of attributes, the centroid $\xi(R)$ is the vector average calculated over R. For the Kullback distance above, let $\xi(s) = \{\xi_\omega(s)\}$ be the (texture) features of a pixel s, then the centroid $\xi(R) = \{\xi_\omega\}$ is calculated by $\xi_\omega = \left(\sum_{s \in R} \xi_\omega(s) / \sum_{s \in R} \xi_\omega^{-1}(s) \right)^{1/2}$

The complete development of a multi-scale segmentation of (textured) images with this energy including the estimation of the parameters is presented in [21] and will be published elsewhere. We focus our attention on simulated annealing for minimizing U.

2.2 Minimizing by Simulated Annealing

Let G_T be the Gibbs distribution with the energy U at temperature T: $\forall x \in \Omega$, $G_T(x) = Z^{-1} \exp[-U(x)/T]$ with $Z = \sum_x \exp[-U(x)/T]$.

Simulated annealing is realized by a non-stationary Markov chain (X_n) associated with a stochastic dynamic and a temperature schedule (T_n). At each time n, the conditional distribution $P(X_n = x' \mid X_{n-1} = x)$ given an element x obtained at the previous step, is the *stochastic dynamic* of the annealing and is written as $Q_n(x, x')$. (Q_n) is the family of the transition probabilities of (X_n). In the domain of image analysis there are two essential stochastic dynamics: Metropolis dynamics [10] and dynamics of Gibbs sampler [7].

Gibbs sampler dynamics: $Q_n(x, \cdot)$ are conditional probabilities of the Gibbs distribution G_{T_n} over suitable subsets $N(n, x)$ of Ω called neighborhoods: $Q_n(x, x') = G_{T_n}(x' \mid N(n, x))$.

Metropolis dynamics: a irreducible symmetric transition probability (or Markov kernel) $q(x, \cdot)$ is used to choose an element x', this element is either accepted or rejected with a probability which depends on the difference of the energies and the temperature T_n:

$$Q_n(x, x') = \begin{cases} q(x, x') \exp\left(-(U(x') - U(x))^+/T_n\right) & \text{if } x' \neq x \\ 1 - \sum_{y \neq x} Q_n(x, y) & \text{if } x' = x \end{cases}, \tag{2}$$

A generalization of Metropolis dynamics is *Hastings dynamics* [11] where the irreducible transition probability h is not necessarily symmetric but the invariant measures of transition probabilities are still Gibbs distributions :

$$Q_n(x, x') = \begin{cases} h(x, x') \alpha_n(x, x') & \text{if } x' \neq x \\ 1 - \sum_{y \neq x} Q_n(x, y) & \text{if } x' = x \end{cases}, \tag{3}$$

where $\alpha_n(x, x') = \rho(x, x') \left(1 + \dfrac{G_{T_n}(x)h(x, x')}{G_{T_n}(x')h(x', x)}\right)^{-1}$, ρ symmetric and insuring

that $0 \leq \alpha_n(x, x') \leq 1$ for all x, x'.

Remarks for the classic segmentation $\Omega = L^S$: (i) At step n, let $s = s(n)$ be the pixel taken from a fixed pixel-visitation schedule, a classic choice of neighborhood is $N(n, x) = x_{S \setminus s}$, where $x_{S \setminus s} = \{y \in \Omega : y_t = x_t \ \forall t \neq s\}$. (ii) For Metropolis dynamics, at each step n, a pixel $s = s(n) \in S$ is selected at random, then take x' with the uniform distribution in the subset $x_{S \setminus s} \setminus \{x\}$.

Note that Hastings dynamics are quite useful in the case when a symmetric Markov kernel is impossible or computation demanding to realize in practice. This will be the case in PCC space (cf. Section 3). It has been proven in [7] that if T_n decreases to zero sufficiently slowly, X_n will converge to the uniform distribution over the minimums of U. Our goal is to construct algorithms to minimize U on $C(S)$ (and simulate Gibbs distribution over $C(S)$, cf. Section 4) as we can do on Ω.

For minimizing over $C(S)$, *we need to define neighborhoods* $N(s, z)$ *for all* $s \in S$ *and* $z \in C(S)$, $N(s, z)$ must verify the *reversibility property* which is required in simulated annealing and also in simulation of probability distribution: $z' \in N(s, z) \iff z \in N(s, z')$.

2.3 Segmentation with Progressive Graphs

Theoretically the annealing schedule must be too slow to reach to a global minimum. In practice because of limited computation time, a faster schedule is used, for instance an exponential schedule as $T_n = T_0 \gamma^n$ with $\gamma \approx 0.95$. The schedule is a compromise between the computation and the performance.

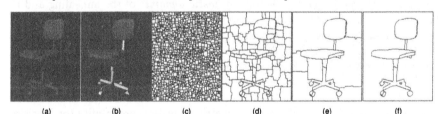

|(a)|(b)|(c)|(d)|(e)|(f)|

Fig. 1. Instance of hierarchical segmentation with progressive graphs. (a) and (b) are the red band and the gray level image of a color image, (c),(d) and (e) are the progressive graphs, (f) is the final segmentation result.

In our application of segmentation, we have used an exponential cooling schedule associated with progressive graphs which is a hierarchical procedure : the algorithm begins with the simulated annealing (X_n) minimizing $U(z)$ over $C(S)$ associated with a suitable stochastic dynamic (see Sections 3 and 4 for stochastic dynamics on $C(S)$), it converges to a local minimum z_0; then we make the regions of z_0 grow in grouping them with simulated annealing to minimize the same energy U. For that, we consider z_0 as a *graph* S_1 whose sites are the regions of z_0, two sites of S_1 are neighbors if the corresponding regions are neighbors. Let $C(S_1)$ be the set of the partitions with connected components of the graph S_1 (see also Section 3 for rigorous definition), $C(S_1)$ is simply the subset of partitions in $C(S)$ which do not divide any region of z_0. In this stage, we minimize U restricted to $C(S_1)$ by a suitable simulated annealing algorithm on $C(S_1)$. The algorithm will reach to a (local) minimum z_1; in the same way, to group the regions in z_1, we consider z_1 as a graph written as S_2, and we minimize the same energy U restricted to $C(S_2)$ using simulated annealing over $C(S_2)$, we continue so on. The procedure is ended when the algorithm can no longer yield any change even if it works on the new graph generated by the segmentation. Fig. 1 is an example of such a hierarchical segmentation for a color image.

On each graph S_k, the algorithm is an annealing, the next graph S_{k+1} makes it escape from the local minimum where it stayed, and favors grouping of similar regions. Although the algorithm is not guaranteed to converge to global minima, it can avoid many undesirable local minima, and yields satisfying segmentation; moreover the rate of convergence is rapid, since we can use fast schedule of annealing such as exponential schedules, and the number of sites in the graph falls quickly while the algorithm advances.

The problem now is that S_k, unlike the image grid S, is a general graph: the number of neighbors of a site is not fixed, it contains complex relations among the sites. As we have seen in the previous paragraph, for simulated annealing on $C(S_k)$, we need to define neighborhoods $N(s, z)$ for all $s \in S, z \in C(S_k)$ (the neighborhoods are written as $\mathcal{A}(\cdot, \cdot)$ and $\mathcal{B}(\cdot, \cdot)$ in the next sections).

The concept of graphs introduced in this paper is different of the one used in some approaches of perceptual organization [16] [20]. In [16], edge curves are represented by a graph structure with the curves considered as arcs, the curve terminations and junctions being nodes of the graph. To form enclosed regions, for any pair of nodes corresponding to the two terminations of two symmetric curves, a curve is proposed to join them. The segmentation is then achieved by rejecting wrong closures on the graph structure under some conditions. In [20], the authors proposed a hierarchical approach to detect structures in images by constructing graphs using voting methods, the nodes of graphs are edge tokens and the arcs represent association under some compatibility relation based on proximity, parallelism, collinearity etc. At any level, each connected component *of the graph* is replaced by a single edge curve. But in our approach of segmentation, the sites (or nodes) of a graph represent pixels and/or regions, neighborhoods are the relationships between sites; *all partitions* (with connected components) of a graph are considered with the aim of minimizing a unique energy and simulating the corresponding probability distribution on the whole space of these partitions.

3 Neighborhood Structures on Partitions with Connected Components of a Graph

3.1 PCC of a General Graph

Throughout this section, S is a general symmetric finite graph of sites : for each site $s \in S$ there is set V_s with $V_s \subset S$, which is the set of neighbors of s, V_s does not contain s. We suppose that V_s are non-empty and symmetric, i.e., $s' \in V_s$ implies $s \in V_{s'}$. Two sites s, t are said neighbors if $s \in V_t$ (or $t \in V_s$).

For instance, if S is an image grid, two sites of S are neighbors if the distance between them is equal to the unity.

Definition 1 (i) A subset R of S is called a connected component (or connected region) if R contains only one site, or for two arbitrary different sites $s, t \in R$, there is a sequence $s_1, s_2, ..., s_n \in R$, such that $s_1 = s, s_n = t$ and $s_i \in V_{s_{i+1}}$ $\forall 1 \leq i < n$. (ii) A region R and a site s are neighbors (or R is a neighboring region of s) if R contains a site t such that s and t are neighbors. (iii) Two disjoint connected regions R_1 and R_2 of S are neighbors if there exists $s \in R_1$ and $t \in R_2$ such that s and t are neighbors.

A partition $x = \{R_1, R_2, ...\}$ is a PCC if every part R_i is a connected region. The space of the PCCs is written as $C(S)$.

3.2 Definitions of Neighborhoods on $C(S)$

For the definition of neighborhood on $C(S)$, we need to define a particular partition written as $[x]_s$ associated with $x \in C(S)$, $s \in S$:

Definition 2 Let $s \in S, x = \{R, R_1, R_2, ..., R_n\} \in C(S)$, where R is the region containing s. Suppose that isolating s from R, R is partitioned into connected components $\{s\}, C_1, C_2, ..., C_l$, (i.e., $C_1, C_2, ..., C_l$ are connected components of $R \backslash s$), then we define the PCC $[x]_s$: $[x]_s = \{\{s\}, C_1, C_2, ..., C_l, R_1, R_2, ..., R_n\}$.

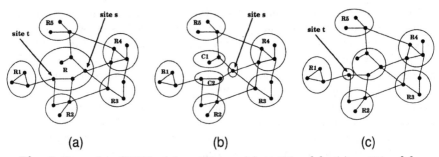

Fig. 2. Examples of PCCs. (a) partition x; (b) partition $[x]_s$; (c) partition $[x]_t$.

Note that $[x]_s$ is simply the PCC obtained from x by isolating s, the other regions remaining unchanged. If s is already isolated in x, then $[x]_s = x$; if $R \backslash s$ is connected, $[x]_s = \{\{s\}, R \backslash s, R_1, R_2, ..., R_n\}$.

Fig. 2(a) shows an example of partition x where the points represent the sites, two sites which are neighbors are linked by a line, the regions are represented by ellipses and circles. Fig. 2(b) and Fig. 2(c) present $[x]_s$ and $[x]_t$ respectively with respect to the sites s, t. In Fig. 2(b), $R \backslash s$ is divided by s into two connected components C_1 and C_2; in Fig. 2(c), $R \backslash t$ is a connected region itself.

Definition 3 For $s \in S, x \in C(S)$, we define the set $\mathcal{A}(s, x)$ of partitions as follows : let R be the region in x containing s, then

- if $R\backslash s$ is connected or R contains only s, then $\mathcal{A}(s,x)$ is the set containing the partition $[x]_s$ and the PCCs which are obtained from $[x]_s$ by merging s with one of the neighboring regions of s in $[x]_s$ and leaving other regions unchanged.
- otherwise, (i.e., if $R\backslash s$ is not connected), $\mathcal{A}(s,x) = \{x\}$.

$\mathcal{A}(s,x)$ is called the *neighborhood of the first type* for s and x on $C(S)$.

Notation Let x be a PCC and R_1, ..., R_k be k regions in x such that their union $\cup_{i=1}^k R_i$ is connected. To simplify the notations, let $(x, \{R_1, ..., R_k\})$ denote the PCC obtained from x merging R_1, ..., R_k and leaving other regions of x unchanged.

In the instance of Fig. 2, since the isolation of s cuts the region R into several connected parts, $\mathcal{A}(s,x)$ contains only x; however the elements of $\mathcal{A}(t,x)$ are :

- $[x]_t$,
- $([x]_t, \{t, R\backslash t\}) = x$, $([x]_t, \{t, R_1\})$, $([x]_t, \{t, R_2\})$.

Note that the reversibility property $y \in \mathcal{A}(s,x) \iff x \in \mathcal{A}(s,y)$, is respected. In fact, if $y \in \mathcal{A}(s,x)$, then $[y]_s = [x]_s$, therefore $x \in \mathcal{A}(s,y)$ following the definition. The reversibility property simply means that if x can become y at a step of the algorithm, then inversely y can also become x at the same step.

The definition of $\mathcal{A}(\cdot,\cdot)$ is natural, the algorithm modifies only locally the partition in distributing the site to the neighboring regions. If a neighborhood associated with x and s contains $[x]_s$ even if the isolation of s divides its region into several connected parts, then according to the reversibility property, conversely the neighborhood has to contain partitions which group different regions through s. This leads to the following definition of neighborhoods of the *second type* which are much larger and more complex.

Definition 4 For $x \in C(S)$ and $s \in S$, the neighborhood of the second type for s and x written as $\mathcal{B}(s,x)$, is composed of $[x]_s$ and the PCCs which are obtained from $[x]_s$ by merging s with some regions in $[x]_s$ which are neighbors of s, such that *there is not any pair of regions among them which are neighbors*, and leaving other regions unchanged.

$\mathcal{B}(s,x)$ is the set of the PCCs of the form $([x]_s, \{s, R_1, ..., R_p\})$ where $R_1, ..., R_p$ are neighbors of s and there are not two regions which are neighbors among $R_1, ..., R_p$ (we suppose that the partition with $p = 0$ is $[x]_s$).
Example Take again the instance of Fig. 2(b), the neighboring regions of s are C_1, C_2, R_3 and R_4, the neighborhood $\mathcal{B}(s,x)$ is comprised of the following PCCs:

- $[x]_s$,
- $([x]_s, \{s, C_1\})$, $([x]_s, \{s, C_2\})$, $([x]_s, \{s, R_3\})$, $([x]_s, \{s, R_4\})$,
- $([x]_s, \{s, C_1, C_2\}) = x$, $([x]_s, \{s, C_1, R_3\})$, $([x]_s, \{s, C_1, R_4\})$, $([x]_s, \{s, C_2, R_3\})$, $([x]_s, \{s, C_2, R_4\})$,
- $([x]_s, \{s, C_1, C_2, R_3\})$, $([x]_s, \{s, C_1, C_2, R_4\})$.

In this example R_3 and R_4 are neighbors, so they can not be grouped in a region through s.

The reversibility property holds for $\mathcal{B}(\cdot, \cdot)$ $y \in \mathcal{B}(s, x) \iff x \in \mathcal{B}(s, y)$, since $y \in \mathcal{B}(s, x)$ implies $[y]_s = [x]_s$, then $x \in \mathcal{B}(s, y)$.

Remarks

- $x \in \mathcal{A}(s, x) \subset \mathcal{B}(s, x)$,
- if $x \in \mathcal{A}(s, y)$ ($x \in \mathcal{B}(s, y)$ resp.), then $\mathcal{A}(s, x) = \mathcal{A}(s, y)$ ($\mathcal{B}(s, x) = \mathcal{B}(s, y)$ resp.),
- if $x \in \mathcal{A}(s, y)$ ($x \in \mathcal{B}(s, y)$ resp.), there may be sites t other than s such that $x \in \mathcal{A}(t, y)$ ($x \in \mathcal{B}(t, y)$ resp.).

In the construction of $\mathcal{B}(s, x)$, s can not merge with two regions which are neighbors. The reason of this consideration is that, in the other case, to satisfy the reversibility property, $\mathcal{B}(s, x)$ would have to contain all partitions which subdivide neighboring regions of s in $[x]_s$ into connected parts which are neighbors of s. Such $\mathcal{B}(s, x)$ would be huge and of infeasible use.

3.3 Stochastic Dynamics with the Neighborhoods $\mathcal{A}(s, x)$ and $\mathcal{B}(s, x)$, Irreducibility

The Markov chain (X_n) is required be irreducible in the sense that any element x is reachable from any other element y, that is, suppose that Q_n is the transition probability at the time n, for any m there exist a finite number of elements $x_m = x, x_{m+1}, ..., x_{m+k} = y$ such that $Q_{m+i}(x_{m+i}, x_{m+i+1}) > 0$ for each $0 \le i < k$. We can show the irreducibility of a Markov chain defined with neighborhood $\mathcal{A}(s, x)$ ($\mathcal{B}(s, x)$ resp.) by the following proposition.

Proposition 1 For any $x, y \in C(S)$ with S a general graph, there exists a sequence of partitions $x_0 = x, x_1, x_2, ..., x_k = y$ and a sequence of sites $s_1, s_2, ..., s_k$, such that $x_i \in \mathcal{A}(s_{i+1}, x_{i+1})$ ($x_i \in \mathcal{B}(s_{i+1}, x_{i+1})$ resp.) for each $0 \le i < k$.

For the proof, we refer to [22].

Using the Markov chain defined with the neighborhood $\mathcal{A}(s, x)$, the change of the state of the chain is much small, and thus requires many steps to reach an element from another. However, in general the neighborhood $\mathcal{A}(s, x)$ is small and simple, in fact, at a step, once a site s has been chosen, it suffices to choose one of the neighboring regions of s which is to be merged with s. Thus the choice of the partition at a step of the algorithm does not need much real computation. On the contrary, the neighborhood $\mathcal{B}(s, x)$ is large and complex.

At a step of a Markov chain defined with $\mathcal{B}(s, x)$, a region can be cut into several connected parts and regions such that there are not two neighbors among them can be merged, then the one-step change of the chain may be great. Therefore we can visit more efficiently partitions at each iteration, it then requires fewer steps to reach a partition from another. But in practice, *determining the elements of a neighborhood $\mathcal{B}(s, x)$ requires much more computation*, since to find elements in the neighborhood, we have to establish a table of neighborhood relations among all the neighboring regions of s and consider all combinations of regions such that there are not two regions which are neighbors among them. Note that it is computation demanding even to determine the number of elements in $\mathcal{B}(s, x)$. In the next section, we present algorithms and practical implementations to avoid the expensive calculation whenever we use neighborhoods of the second type.

4 Algorithms of Probability Distribution Simulation and Simulated Annealing on $C(S)$

4.1 Probability Simulation by Gibbs Sampler and Metropolis Dynamics

We use Gibbs sampler and Metropolis dynamics associated with the neighborhoods $\mathcal{A}(s, x)$ $(\mathcal{B}(s, x)$ resp.) to simulate the distribution G_T. We briefly present the algorithms only for neighborhoods of the first type $\mathcal{A}(s, x)$; the algorithms with $\mathcal{B}(s, x)$ are the same except the neighborhoods $\mathcal{B}(s, x)$ that are to be replaced with $\mathcal{A}(s, x)$.

For Gibbs sampler, it suffices to replace the neighborhoods $N(n, x)$ (cf. Section 2.2) with $\mathcal{A}(s(n), x)$ where $s(n)$ is the site taken at step n.

Similarly, for Metropolis dynamics, at each step n, we choose a partition y in $\mathcal{A}(s(n), x)\backslash\{x\}$ by the uniform distribution if $\mathcal{A}(s(n), x)\backslash\{x\}$ is not empty, where $s(n)$ is a site taken at random. In this case the Markov kernel q (cf. (2)) is as follows : let $I(x, y) = \{s \in S : y \in \mathcal{A}(s, x)\}$, then if $I(x, y)$ is empty or $x = y$, $q(x, y) = 0$; if $I(x, y)$ is not empty and $x \neq y$, $q(x, y) = \frac{1}{|S|} \sum_{s \in I(x,y)} (|\mathcal{A}(s, x)| - 1)^{-1}$. Moreover q is symmetric : first, since $y \in \mathcal{A}(s, x)$ implies $x \in \mathcal{A}(s, y)$, then $I(x, y) = I(y, x)$; second, $y \in \mathcal{A}(s, x)$ implies $\mathcal{A}(s, x) = \mathcal{A}(s, y)$, so that we have $q(x, y) = q(y, x)$.

4.2 Probability Simulation Using Hastings Dynamics and Neighborhoods $\mathcal{B}(s, x)$

The idea consists in selecting a partition in the neighborhood in a simple way, with a transition probability $h(x, y)$ which is not symmetric in general. Then we accept the partition with the probability α which is calculated according to Hastings dynamics such that G_T remains the invariant distribution of the transition probabilities of the Markov chain.

More precisely, at any step n, given $X_{n-1} = x$, X_n will be determined as follows : (i) take a site s with the uniform distribution in S, (ii) choose a partition y in $\mathcal{B}(s, x)\backslash\{x\}$ by a distribution $h_s(x, \cdot)$ (which is not symmetric in general), (iii) set $X_n = y$ with probability $\alpha_s(x, y)$ and set $X_n = x$ with probability $1 - \alpha_s(x, y)$.

We now present how to choose a partition in $\mathcal{B}(s, x)$ by a sampling, which is a random variable written as $w_{s,x}$. Let p be the number of the neighboring regions of s in $[x]_s$, $w_{s,x}$ is realized by successive sampling of regions in $[x]_s$ which are neighbors of s :

Choose a region with the uniform distribution in the set of the neighboring regions of s in $[x]_s$, this region is denoted by R_1. Then we choose a second region at random in the set comprising s itself and the remaining $p-1$ neighboring regions of s; if this region is neighbor of R_1, the sampling is ended and the region is not retained; if the region is not neighbor of R_1, it is denoted by R_2, and we continue ... Suppose that l regions ($l \geq 1$) $R_1, ..., R_l$ have been chosen, then we choose a region at random in the set comprising s and the remaining $p-l$ neighboring regions of s; if the region is neighbor of at least one of the regions $R_1, ..., R_l$, we stop the sampling of regions and this region is not retained; otherwise, we write it as R_{l+1}, and we continue so on.

At the end, let $R_1, ..., R_r$ be the chosen regions ($r \leq p$) which determine a partition $([x]_s, \{s, R_1, ..., R_r\})$ written as $z_{s,x}$.

We set

$$w_{s,x} = \begin{cases} z_{s,x} \text{ if } z_{s,x} \neq x \\ [x]_s \text{ if } z_{s,x} = x \end{cases}.$$

Therefore $w_{s,x} \in \mathcal{B}(s,x)\backslash\{x\}$, since there are not two regions which are neighbors among $R_1, ..., R_r$. Let $h_s(x, \cdot)$ denote the distribution of $w_{s,x}$, $h_s(x,y) > 0$ for any $y \in \mathcal{B}(s,x)\backslash\{x\}$. From this region sampling, we can calculate $h_s(x, \cdot)$: for any $y = ([x]_s, \{s, R_1, ..., R_r\}) \in \mathcal{B}(s,x)\backslash\{x\}$, $(r \geq 1)$, let p be the number of the neighboring regions of s in $[x]_s$, d the number of the neighboring regions of s which are neighbors of at least one of the regions $R_1, ..., R_r$. Then we have

$$h_s(x,y) = \frac{1}{p}\frac{1}{p}\frac{1}{p-1}\frac{1}{p-2}\cdots\frac{1}{p-r+2}\frac{1}{p-r+1}\frac{d+1}{r!} = \frac{d+1}{pC_p^r}. \tag{4}$$

If $[x]_s \neq x$, $h_s(x, [x]_s)$ is also given by (4) where r, d are the numbers with respect to x expressed under the form $x = ([x]_s, \{s, R_1, ..., R_r\})$.

Note that $h_s(x,y)$ is simple to compute by (4), it suffices to know the number r of the regions which are merged with s in y (in x if $y = [x]_s$) and count the neighboring regions of these r united regions.

We now define $\alpha_s(x,y)$ as follows:

$$\alpha_s(x,y) = \rho_s(x,y)\left(1 + \frac{h_s(x,y)}{h_s(y,x)}\exp-\frac{1}{T}(U(x) - U(y))\right)^{-1}, \tag{5}$$

it then suffices to give ρ_s which is symmetric and insuring that $0 \leq \alpha_s(x,y) \leq 1$ for all x, y. For this we could simply set $\rho_s(x,y) = 1$. However we prefer to encourage relaxation of the state of the algorithm, then take ρ_s as large as possible. We may choose

$$\rho_s(x,y) = 1 + \min\{\frac{h_s(x,y)}{h_s(y,x)}\exp-\frac{1}{T}(U(x) - U(y)),$$

$$\frac{h_s(y,x)}{h_s(x,y)}\exp-\frac{1}{T}(U(y) - U(x))\}. \tag{6}$$

The Markov chain (X_n) is stationary with transition probability $Q(x,y) = \frac{1}{|S|} \sum_{s \in S} Q_s(x,y)$, where $Q_s(x,y)$ are Hastings dynamics (cf. (3)) associated with transition probabilities $h_s(x,y)$ and $\alpha_s(x,y)$. X_n converges to G_T since the chain (X_n) is irreducible by Proposition 1, aperiodic, and G_T is the invariant measure. The dynamic of (X_n) is an average of Hastings dynamics. The implementation of this algorithm is simple. In fact at each iteration, the calculation concerns only one partition y in $\mathcal{B}(s,x)$ instead of all partitions in $\mathcal{B}(s,x)$ for Gibbs samplers and Metropolis dynamics.

4.3   Simulated Annealing on $C(S)$

Algorithms of simulated annealing derived from simulation The Markov chains of Sections 4.1 and 4.2 simulate the distribution G_T at the fixed temperature T. From [7], for any Markov chain (X_n) defined previously, i.e., the Metropolis or Gibbs sampling algorithm, or the algorithm using Hastings dynamics and $\mathcal{B}(s,x)$, if at each step n we replace the temperature with a temperature T_n decreasing to 0 slowly enough, then X_n converges to the uniform distribution on the set of the global minima of U.

Generalized Metropolis algorithm using $\mathcal{B}(s,x)$ We will construct an algorithm, using the neighborhoods $\mathcal{B}(s,x)$, which is even simpler than the previous Hastings algorithm, however it does not simulate the distribution G_T at fixed temperature. A generalized Metropolis algorithm is a Metropolis algorithm (cf. (2)) with the transition probability $q(x,y)$ not symmetric.

Let (T_n) be a temperature schedule, at each step n, given $X_{n-1} = x$, the state of the algorithm X_n is determined by carrying out the following steps:

(1) Select a site s at random in S.
(2) Choose a partition y in $\mathcal{B}(s,x)\backslash\{x\}$ by the sampling $w_{s,x}$.
(3) If $U(y) \le U(x)$, choose $X_n = y$; if $U(y) > U(x)$, set $X_n = y$ with probability $\exp{-\frac{1}{T_n}(U(y) - U(x))}$, and set $X_n = x$ with probability $1 - \exp{-\frac{1}{T_n}(U(y) - U(x))}$.

Then the transition probability $Q(x,y) = P(X_n = y \mid X_{n-1} = x)$ can be written as $Q(x,y) = \frac{1}{|S|} \sum_s Q'_s(x,y)$, where

$$Q'_s(x,y) = \begin{cases} h_s(x,y) \exp\left(-(U(y) - U(x))^+ / T_n\right) & \text{if } y \ne x \\ 1 - \sum_{z \ne x} Q'_s(x,z) & \text{if } y = x \end{cases},$$

with $h_s(x,y)$ given by (4). Therefore (X_n) is a generalized Metropolis algorithm of kernel $q(x,y)$:

$$q(x,y) = \begin{cases} 0 & \text{if } I(x,y) \text{ is empty or } x = y \\ \frac{1}{|S|} \sum_{s \in I(x,y)} h_s(x,y) & \text{otherwise} \end{cases}, \qquad (7)$$

where $I(x,y) = \{s \in S : y \in \mathcal{B}(s,x)\}$.

Proposition 2 For any temperature schedule (T_n) decreasing to 0 and satisfying $T_n \geq \frac{c}{\ln n}$ for large n, if c large enough, the probability that X_n is a global minimum tends to 1 as $n \to \infty$.

The proof is given in [22].

5 Application of Simulated Annealing Algorithms on the PCC Space to Image Segmentation

We present briefly our approach of image segmentation using the algorithms of simulated annealing developed in Section 4 and the energy model (1).

The segmentation is completely *unsupervised* and performed following the *hierarchical procedure with progressive graphs* and exponential temperature schedules as presented in Section 2.3. The algorithm starts with the image lattice S (i.e., each pixel is considered as a region). Both types of neighborhoods $\mathcal{A}(s,x)$ and $\mathcal{B}(s,x)$ are used in the segmentation. $\mathcal{A}(s,x)$ yields small change at each iteration of the algorithm, but it requires less computation; however $\mathcal{B}(s,x)$ (used with Hastings algorithm or generalized Metropolis algorithm) can bring about large change and allow to avoid some undesirable partitions rapidly. For example, during the segmentation process, it can happen that two different pieces of the image lattice are misclassified together only through one or few small sites, in this case, $\mathcal{B}(s,x)$ can separate them rapidly, whereas this separation would require a much longer time or be impossible if $\mathcal{A}(s,x)$ is used. In general at the beginning of the segmentation, there are many sites in the graph, and the regions are small, we use $\mathcal{A}(s,x)$ to rapidly create bigger regions and then reduce the number of sites in the next graph. At a time when the number of sites in the new graph is largely reduced, we use the neighborhoods $\mathcal{B}(s,x)$ which allow to visit more efficiently the partitions at each time.

In addition, we can alternate simulated annealing with $\mathcal{A}(s,x)$ and simulated annealing with $\mathcal{B}(s,x)$. Simulated annealing with $\mathcal{A}(s,x)$ smoothing the boundaries : we can free the pixels which are close to the boundaries, these pixels become sites of the new graph, the other sites are the existing regions with these pixels removed, and we minimize the same energy with this new graph and under the constraint that only these pixels are visited. This technique smoothes the boundaries. Then simulated annealing with $\mathcal{B}(s,x)$ regroup the smoothed regions, and so on. Our experiments illustrate that this alternative method improve the quality of the segmentation.

This method can also be extended without difficulty, to multi-scale segmentation : at a fixed resolution, each possible segmentation is a PCC of the coarse grid at the resolution, the result of segmentation at this resolution will be regularized at the finer resolution.

The further details of our approach of segmentation, including multi-scale segmentation and parameter estimation are presented in [21], and will be published elsewhere.

Figures 3 to 5 show the experimental results of segmentation, obtained with the method previously described. Fig. 3 shows the segmentation result for a real color image of size 256×256. We use quadratic distance D (cf. (1)) on LUV ([19]) transformation components. Almost all the regions are correctly segmented although the image is much degraded by the noise. Fig. 4 presents the segmentation result of a real gray level image.

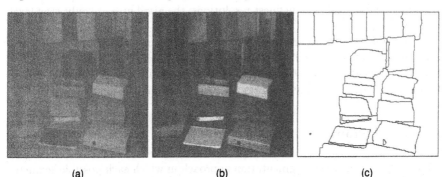

(a)   (b)   (c)

Fig. 3. (a) and (b) are the red band and the gray level image of a real color image of size 256×256 (from INRIA-Syntim); (c) segmentation output.

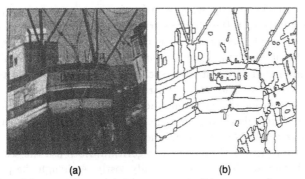

(a)   (b)

Fig. 4. (a) A real image of size 256×256; (b) segmentation output.

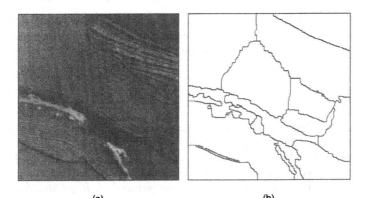

(a)   (b)

Fig. 5. (a) Aerial textured 300×300 image of Calvi; (b) segmentation obtained using multi-scale segmentation method and Gabor filters.

Fig. 5 illustrates the segmentation result for real textured image of sizes 300 × 300, using multi-scale approach. At the two most coarsest resolutions, the texture attributes of a lattice point are extracted within a window centered at the point using Gabor filters, the distance between textures is a symmetrized Kullback distance [2]. At the finest resolutions, the attributes are only gray level information.

Experiments of comparison of our segmentation method using PCCs with the classic labeling method are presented in [22], which show that the algorithm with PCCs yields much better result in terms of quality of segmentation and of minimization of energy, and requires less computation.

6 Conclusion

We have proposed a new segmentation approach in which each possible segmentation is a PCC of the image grid. The advantage of this purpose is clear. This approach is particularly suitable for unsupervised segmentation. In addition, to accelerate the minimization of the cost function, we have used a hierarchical method of progressive graphs which consists in generating a new graph by the result of segmentation on the previous graph and continuing to segment the image on the new graph. Segmentation is then based on stochastic relaxation on spaces of PCCs of general graphs. To construct algorithms of distribution simulation and simulated annealing over such spaces, we have defined two types of neighborhoods on PCC space of an arbitrary graph of sites, the first yields small change at each iteration of algorithms and it requires less computation, whereas the second can bring about large change, but it is complex. In order to be able to handle the second type of neighborhoods, we have constructed a Hastings algorithm and a generalized Metropolis algorithm. Both use the second type of neighborhoods and are not computationally costly. Although the presented algorithms with the neighborhoods on PCC spaces are illustrated for the problem of image segmentation, they can be applied to a variety of other problems.

ACKNOWLEDGMENT The author wishes to thank R. Azencott and L. Younes for valuable guidance, discussions and encouragement throughout this work. This work was supported in part by the SUDIMAGE research group.

References

1. R. Azencott, "Image analysis and Markov fields", *Proc. of the Int. Conf. on Ind. and Appl. Math, SIAM, Paris*, 1987. *SIAM* Philadelphia, 1988.
2. R. Azencott, J.-P. Wang, L. Younes, "Texture classification using windowed Fourier filters", to appear in *IEEE Trans. Pattern Anal. Machine Intell.*.
3. J. Besag, "On the statistical analysis of dirty pictures", *J. Royal Stat. Soc.*, B. 48, pp. 259-302, 1986.
4. C. Bouman, B. Liu, "Multiple resolution segmentation of textured images", *IEEE Trans. Pattern Anal. Machine Intell.*, vol. 13, pp. 99-113, Feb. 1991.

5. O. Catoni, "Rough large deviation estimates for simulated annealing. Application to exponential schedules", *The Annals of Probability*, vol. 20, pp. 1109-1146, 1992.
6. H. Derin, H. Elliott, "Modeling and segmentation of noisy and textured images using Gibbs random fields", *IEEE Trans. Pattern Anal. Machine Intell.*, vol. PAMI-9, pp. 39-55, Jan. 1987.
7. D. Geman, S. Geman, "Stochastic relaxation, Gibbs distribution, and the Bayesian restoration of images", *IEEE Trans. Pattern Anal. Machine Intell.*, vol. PAMI-6, pp. 721-741, Nov. 1984.
8. D. Geman, S. Geman, C. Graffigne, P. Dong, "Boundary detection by constrained optimization", *IEEE Trans. Pattern Anal. Machine Intell.*, vol. 12, pp. 609-628, July 1990.
9. B. Hajek, "Cooling schedules for optical annealing", *Mathematics of Operations Research*, vol. 13, no.2, May 1988.
10. J.M. Hammersley, D.C. Handscomb, *Monte Carlo Methods*, London: Methuen and Company, 1964.
11. W.K. Hastings, "Monte Carlo sampling methods using Markov chains and their applications", *Biometrika*, 57, 97-109, 1970.
12. R. Hu, M.M. Fahmy, "Texture segmentation based on a hierarchical Markov random field model", *Signal Processing*, vol. 26, pp. 285-305, 1992.
13. C. Kervrann, F. Heitz, "A Markov random field model-based approach to unsupervised texture segmentation using local and global statistics", to appear in *IEEE Trans. Image Processing*.
14. S. Lakshmanan, H. Derin, "Simultaneous parameter estimation and segmentation of Gibbs random fields using simulated annealing", *IEEE Trans. Pattern Anal. Machine Intell.* vol. 11, pp. 799-813, Aug. 1989.
15. B.S. Manjunath, R. Chellappa, "unsupervised texture segmentation using Markov random field models", *IEEE Trans. Pattern Anal. Machine Intell.* vol. 13, pp. 478-482, May 1991.
16. R. Mohan, R. Nevatia, "Perceptual organization for scene segmentation and description", *IEEE Trans. Pattern Anal. Machine Intell.* vol. 14, pp. 616-635, June 1992.
17. D. Mumford, J. Shah, "Optimal approximations by piecewise smooth functions and associated variational problems", *Comm. on Pure and Applied Math.*, vol. XLII, pp. 577-685, 1989.
18. H.H. Nguyen, P. Cohen, "Gibbs random fields, fuzzy clustering, and the unsupervised segmentation of textured images", *CVGIP: Graphical Models and Image Processing*, vol. 55, no.1, pp. 1-19, Jan. 1993.
19. W.K. Pratt, *Digital image processing*, Wiley-Interscience, 1991.
20. S. Sarkar, K.L. Boyer, "A computational structure for preattentive perceptual organization: graphical enumeration and voting methods", *IEEE Trans. Sys., Man, Cybern.*, vol. 24, no. 2, pp. 246-267, 1994.
21. J.-P. Wang, "Multiscale Markov fields: applications to the segmentation of textured images and film fusion", (in French) Ph.D. Dissertation, Paris-Sud University, 1994.
22. J.-P. Wang, "Stochastic relaxation on partitions with connected components and its application to image segmentation", Preprint, CMLA, Ecole Normale Supérieure de Cachan, France, 1996.

Restoration of Severely Blurred High Range Images Using Stochastic and Deterministic Relaxation Algorithms in Compound Gauss Markov Random Fields *

Rafael Molina[1]. Aggelos K. Katsaggelos[2]. Javier Mateos[1] and Aurora Hermoso[3]

[1] Departamento de Ciencias de la Computación e I.A. Universidad de Granada. · 18071 Granada. España.
[2] Department of Electrical and Computer Engineering, Northwestern University, Evanston, Illinois 60208-3118.
[3] Departamento de Estadística e I.O. Universidad de Granada. 18071 Granada. España.

Abstract. Over the last few years. a growing number of researchers from varied disciplines have been utilizing Markov random fields (MRF) models for developing optimal, robust algorithms for various problems. such as texture analysis, image synthesis, classification and segmentation, surface reconstruction. integration of several low level vision modules, sensor fusion and image restoration. However, not much work has been reported on the use of this model in image restoration.
In this paper we examine the use of compound Gauss Markov random fields (CGMRF) to restore severely blurred high range images. For this deblurring problem. the convergence of the Simulated Annealing (SA) and Iterative Conditional Mode (ICM) algorithms has not been established. We propose two new iterative restoration algorithms which extend the classical SA and ICM approaches. Their convergence is established and they are tested on real and synthetic images.

1 Introduction

Image restoration refers to the problem of recovering an image. f. from its blurred and noisy observation, g. for the purpose of improving its quality or obtaining some type of information that is not readily available from the degraded image.

It is well known that translation linear shift invariant (LSI) image models do not. in many circumstances. lead to appropriate restoration methods. Their main problem is their inability to preserve discontinuities. To move away from simple LSI models several methods have been proposed.

The CGMRF theory provides us with a mean to control changes in the image model using a hidden random field. A compound random field has two levels: an

* This work has been supported by the "Comisión Nacional de Ciencia y Tecnología" under contract PB93-1110.

upper level which is the real image that has certain translation invariant linear sub-models to represent image characteristics like border regions. smoothness. texture. etc. The lower or hidden level is a finite range random field to govern the transitions between the sub-models. The use of the underlying random field. called the line process. was introduced by Geman and Geman in [4] in the discrete case and extended to the continuous case by Jeng [5]. Jeng and Woods [6. 7] and Chellapa. Simchony and Lichtenstein [3].

Given the image and noise models. the process of finding the maximum *a posteriori* (MAP) estimate for the CGMRF is much more complex. since we no longer have a convex function to be minimized and methods like simulated annealing (SA) (see [4]) have to be used. Although this method leads to the MAP estimate. it is a very computationally demanding method. A faster alternative is deterministic relaxation which results in local MAP estimation. also called *iterative conditional mode* (ICM) [1].

In this paper we extend the use of SA to restore high dynamic range images in the presence of blurring. a case where convergence of this method has not been shown (see [5. 6. 7] for the continuous case without blurring).

In Sect. 2 we introduce the notation we use and the proposed model for the image and line processes as well as the noise model. Both. stochastic and deterministic relaxation approaches to obtain the MAP estimate without blurring are presented in Sect. 3. Reasons why these algorithms may be unstable in the presence of blurring are studied in Sect. 4. In Sect. 5 we modify the SA algorithm and its corresponding relaxation approach in order to propose our modified algorithms. Convergence proofs are given in Sect. 7. In Sect. 6 we test both algorithms on real images and Sect. 7 concludes the paper.

2 Notation and Model

We will distinguish between f. the 'true' image which would be observed under ideal conditions and g. the observed image. The aim is to reconstruct f from g. Bayesian methods start with a prior distribution. a probability distribution over images f by which they incorporate information on the expected structure within an image. It is also necessary to specify $p(g \mid f)$. the probability distribution of observed images g if f were the 'true' image. The Bayesian paradigm dictates that the inference about the true f should be based on $p(f \mid g)$ given by

$$p(f \mid g) = p(g \mid f)p(f)/p(g) \propto p(g \mid f)p(f). \tag{1}$$

Maximization of (1) with respect to f yields

$$\dot{f} = \arg \max_f p(f \mid g). \tag{2}$$

the maximum *a posteriori* estimator. For the sake of simplicity. we will denote by $f(i)$ the intensity of the true image at the location of the pixel i on the lattice. We regard f as a $p \times 1$ column vector of values $f(i)$. The convention applies equally to the observed image g. Let us now examine the image and noise models.

The use of CGMRF was first presented in [4] using an Ising model to represent the upper level and a line process to model the abrupt transitions. Extensions to continuous range models using GMRF were presented in [5]. The CGMRF model used in this paper was proposed by Chellapa. Simchony and Lichtenstein in [3] and it is an extension of the Blake and Zisserman's weak membrane model [2] used for surface interpolation and edge detection. The convergence proof that will be given here can also be extended to the CGMRF defined in [5. 6. 7].

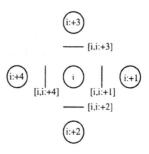

Fig. 1. Image and line sites.

The probability density function (pdf) of the CGMRF is given by

$$-\log p(f,l) = \text{const}$$
$$+\frac{1}{2\sigma_w^2}\sum_i \left[\phi(f(i)-f(i:+1))^2(1-l([i,i:+1])+\beta l([i,i:+1])\right.$$
$$+\ \phi(f(i)-f(i:+2))^2(1-l([i,i:+2]))+\beta l([i,i:+2])+(1-4\phi)f^2(i)\Big]\ .(3)$$

where $l([i,j])$ takes the value zero if pixels i and j are not separated by an active line and one otherwise and $i:+1,\ i:+2,\ i:+3,\ i:+4$ denote the four pixels around pixel i as described in figure 1. That is. we penalize the introduction of the line element between pixels i and j (see figure 1) by the term $\beta l([i,j])$. The intuitive interpretation of this line process is simple; it acts as an activator or inhibitor of the relation between two neighboring pixels depending on whether or not the pixels are separated by an edge. In this paper we shall use this simple image model. The convergence proofs that follow can be easily extended to more complex image model including more neighboring pixels or interactions in the line process.

Let us now describe the noise model. A simplified but very realistic noise model for many applications is the Gaussian model with mean zero and variance σ_n^2. This means that the observed image corresponds to the model $g(i) = (Df)(i)+n(i) = \sum_j d(i-j)f(j)+n(i)$. where D is the $p\times p$ matrix defining the systematic blur. assumed to be known and approximated by a block circulant matrix. $n(i)$ is the additive Gaussian noise with zero mean and variance σ_n^2 and $d(j)$ are the coefficients defining the blurring function.

Then, the probability of the observed image g if f were the 'true' image is

$$p(g \mid f) \propto \exp\left[-\frac{1}{2\sigma_n^2}\|g - Df\|^2\right].$$ (4)

3   MAP Estimation Using Stochastic and Deterministic Relaxation

The MAP estimates of f and l, $\hat{f}, \hat{l}$ are given by,

$$\hat{f}, \hat{l} = \arg\max_{f,l} p(f, l \mid g).$$ (5)

This is an obvious extension of (2) where now we have to estimate both the image and line processes. The modified simulated annealing (MSA), algorithm we are going proposing in this work, ensures convergence to a local MAP estimate regardless of the initial solution. We start by examining the SA procedure as defined in [5].

Since $p(f, l \mid g)$ is nonlinear it is extremely difficult to find $\hat{f}$ and $\hat{l}$ by any conventional method. Simulated annealing is a relaxation technique to search for MAP estimates from degraded observations. It uses the distribution

$$p_T(f, l \mid g) = \frac{1}{Z_T} \exp\left\{ -\frac{1}{T}\frac{1}{2\sigma_n^2}\|g - Df\|^2 \right.$$

$$-\frac{1}{T}\frac{1}{2\sigma_w^2}\sum_i [\phi(f(i) - f(i:+1))^2(1 - l([i, i:+1])) + \beta l([i, i:+1])$$

$$\left. + \phi(f(i) - f(i:+2))^2(1 - l([i, i:+2])) + \beta l([i, i:+2]) + (1 - 4\phi)f^2(i) \right\}$$ (6)

where T is the temperature and Z_T a normalization constant.

We shall need to simulate the conditional *a posteriori* density function for $l([i, j])$, given the rest of l, f and g and the conditional *a posteriori* density function for $f(i)$ given the rest of f, l and g. To simulate the line process conditional *a posteriori* density function, $p_T(l([i, j]) \mid l([k, l]) : \forall [k, l] \neq [i, j], f, g)$, we have

$$p_T(l([i, j]) = 0 \mid l([k, l]) : \forall [k, l] \neq [i, j], f, g) \propto \exp\left[-\frac{1}{T}\frac{\phi}{2\sigma_w^2}(f(i) - f(j))^2\right].$$ (7)

$$p_T(l([i, j]) = 1 \mid l([k, l]) : \forall [k, l] \neq [i, j], f, g) \propto \exp\left[-\frac{1}{T}\frac{\beta}{2\sigma_w^2}\right].$$ (8)

Furthermore, for our Gaussian noise model,

$$p_T(f(i) \mid f(j) : \forall j \neq i, l, g) \sim \mathcal{N}\left(\mu^{l[i]}(i), T\sigma^{2l[i]}(i)\right),$$ (9)

where $\mu^{\underline{l}[i]}(i)$ and $\sigma^{2\underline{l}[i]}(i)$ are given by

$$\mu^{\underline{l}[i]}(i) = \lambda^{\underline{l}[i]}(i)\phi \sum_{j \text{ nhbr } i} \frac{f(j)(1 - l([i,j]))}{nn^{\underline{l}[i]}(i)}$$

$$+(1 - \lambda^{\underline{l}[i]}(i)) \left(\frac{(D^T g)(i) - (D^T Df)(i)}{c} + f(i) \right). \tag{10}$$

$$\sigma^{2\underline{l}[i]}(i) = \frac{\sigma_w^2 \sigma_n^2}{nn^{\underline{l}[i]}(i)\sigma_n^2 + c\sigma_w^2}. \tag{11}$$

where c is the sum of the square of the coefficients defining the blur function. that is. $c = \sum_j d(j)^2$. $nn^{\underline{l}[i]}(i) = \phi \sum_{j \text{ nhbr } i}(1 - l([i,j])) + (1 - 4\phi)$ and

$$\lambda^{\underline{l}[i]}(i) = \frac{nn^{\underline{l}[i]}(i)\sigma_n^2}{nn^{\underline{l}[i]}(i)\sigma_n^2 + c\sigma_w^2}.$$

and $\underline{l}[i]$ is the four dimensional vector representing the line process configuration around image pixel (i).

Then the sequential SA to find the MAP. with no blurring $(D = I)$. proceeds as follows (see [5]):

Algorithm 1 Sequential SA procedure. *Let i_t, $t = 1,2\ldots$, be the sequence in which the sites are visited for updating.*

1. *Set $t = 0$ and assign an initial configuration denoted as f_{-1}, l_{-1} and initial temperature $T(0) = 1$.*
2. *The evolution $l_{t-1} \rightarrow l_t$ of the line process can be obtained by sampling the next point of the line process from the raster-scanning scheme based on the conditional probability mass function defined in (7) and (8) and keeping the rest of l_{t-1} unchanged.*
3. *Set $t = t+1$. Go back to step 2 until a complete sweep of the field l is finished.*
4. *The evolution $f_{t-1} \rightarrow f_t$ of the observed system can be obtained by sampling the next value of the observation of the line process from the raster-scanning scheme based on the conditional probability mass function given in (9) and keeping the rest of l_{t-1} unchanged.*
5. *Set $t = t + 1$. Go back to step 4 until a complete sweep of the field f is finished.*
6. *Go to step 2 until $t > t_f$, where t_f is a specified integer.*

The following theorem from [5] guarantees that the SA algorithm converges to the MAP estimate in the case of no blurring.

Theorem 1. *If the following conditions are satisfied:*

1. *$|\phi| < 0.25$*
2. *$T(t) \rightarrow 0$ as $t \rightarrow \infty$, such that*
3. *$T(t) \geq C/\log(1 + k(t))$,*

then for any starting configuration f_{-1}, l_{-1}, *we have*

$$p(f_t . l_t \mid f_{-1} . l_{-1} . g) \rightarrow p_0(f . l) \ as \ t \rightarrow \infty.$$

where $p_0(\ldots)$ *is the uniform probability distribution over the MAP solutions and* $k(t)$ *is the sweep iteration number at time* t.

Instead of using a stochastic approach, we can use a deterministic method to search for a local maximum. An advantage of the deterministic method is that its convergence is much faster than the stochastic approach, since instead of simulating the distributions, the mode from the corresponding conditional distribution is chosen. The disadvantage is the local nature of the solution obtained. This method can be seen as a particular case of SA where the temperature is always set to zero.

4 Instability of the SA and ICM Solutions

Unfortunately, due to the presence of blurring the convergence of SA has not been established for this problem. The main problem of the methods is that, if c is small, as is the case for severely blurred images, the term $[(D^T g)(i) - (D^T Df)(i)]/c$ in (10) is highly unstable. For the ICM method the problem gets worse because sudden changes in the first stages, due to the line process, become permanent (see [9]).

Let us examine intuitively and formally why we may have convergence problems with algorithm 1 and its deterministic relaxation approximation when severe blurring is present. Let us assume for simplicity no line process and examine the iterative procedure where we update the whole image at the same time: it is important to note that this is not the parallel version of SA but an iterative procedure. We have,

$$f_t = \lambda \phi N f_{t-1} - (1 - \lambda) \left[\frac{D^T D}{c} f_{t-1} - f_{t-1} \right] + (1 - \lambda) \frac{D^T g}{c}$$

$$= A f_{t-1} + \text{const}. \tag{12}$$

where t is the iteration number, understood as sweep of the whole image, and

$$A = \left[I - \lambda(I - \phi N) - (1 - \lambda) \frac{D^T D}{c} \right]. \tag{13}$$

For the method to converge A must be a contraction mapping. However this may not be the case. For instance, if the image suffers from severe blurring then c is close to zero and the matrix $[D^T D/c]$ has eigenvalues greater than one. Furthermore, if the image has a high dynamic range, like astronomical images where ranges $[0, 7000]$ are common, it is natural to assume that σ_w^2 is big and thus, $(1 - \lambda)[D^T D/c]$ has eigenvalues greater than one. Therefore, this iterative method may not converge. It is important to note that, when there is no blurring, $c = 1$ and A is a contraction mapping.

Let us modify A in order to have a contraction. Adding $[(1-\lambda)(1-c)/c]f$ to both sides of (12) we have. in the iterative procedure.

$$(1 + [(1-\lambda)(1-c)/c])\, f_t = [(1-\lambda)(1-c)/c]f_{t-1}$$
$$+Af_{t-1} + \text{const}$$

or

$$f_t = \omega f_{t-1} + (1-\omega)[Af_{t-1} + \text{const}].$$

with $\omega = (1-c)\sigma_w^2/(\sigma_n^2 + \sigma_w^2)$. We then have for this new iterative procedure

$$f_t = \tilde{A}f_{t-1} + (1-\omega)\text{const}.$$

where

$$\tilde{A} = \left[I - \rho(I - \phi N) - (1-\rho)D^T D\right].$$

with $\rho = \sigma_n^2/(\sigma_n^2 + \sigma_w^2)$. is now a contraction mapping.

5   The Modified Simulated Annealing Algorithm

Let us now examine how to obtain a contraction for our iterative procedure. Let us rewrite (10) as an iterative procedure and add $(\alpha(1-nn^{l[i]}(i))+\beta(1-c))f(i)$ to each side of the equation. we have

$$(\alpha + \beta)f_t(i) = (\alpha(1 - nn^{l[i]}(i)) + \beta(1-c))f_{t-1}(i)$$
$$+\alpha\phi \sum_{j\,\text{nhbr}\,i} f_{t-1}(j)(1 - l([i,j]))$$
$$+\beta((D^T g)(i) - (D^T Df)_{t-1}(i) + cf_{t-1}(i)). \tag{14}$$

where $\alpha = 1/\sigma_w^2$ and $\beta = 1/\sigma_n^2$. or.

$$f_t(i) =$$

$$\omega^{l_{t-1}[i]}(i)f_{t-1}(i) + (1 - \omega^{l_{t-1}[i]}(i)) \times \left(\lambda^{l[i]}(i)\phi \sum_{j\,\text{nhbr}\,i} \frac{f_{t-1}(j)(1 - l([i,j]))}{nn^{l[i]}(i)}\right.$$

$$\left. +(1 - \lambda^{l[i]}(i)) \left(\frac{(D^T g)(i) - (D^T Df)_{t-1}(i)}{c} + f_{t-1}(i)\right)\right).$$

where $\omega^{l_{t-1}[i]}(i) = (\sigma_n^2(1 - nn^{l_{t-1}[i]}(i)) + (1-c)\sigma_w^2/(\sigma_n^2 + \sigma_w^2)$.

So. in order to have a contraction. we update the whole image at the same time using the value of $f(i)$ obtained in the previous iteration. $f_{t_{k-1}}(i)$. and. instead of simulating from the normal distribution defined in (9) to obtain the new value of $f(i)$. we simulate from the distribution

$$\mathcal{N}\left(\mu_m^{l[i]}(i), T\sigma_m^2{}^{l_{t-1}[i]}(i)\right) \tag{15}$$

with mean

$$\mu_m^{l[i]}(i) = \omega^{l_{t-1}[i]}(i) f_{t_{k-1}}(i) + (1 - \omega^{l_{t-1}[i]}(i)) \mu^{l_{t-1}[i]}(i) \tag{16}$$

and

$$\sigma_m^{2\,l_{t-1}[i]}(i) = (1 - (\omega^{l_{t-1}[i]})^2) \sigma^{2l_{t-1}[i]}(i). \tag{17}$$

The reason to use this modified variance is clear if we take into account that, if

$$X \sim \mathcal{N}(m, \sigma^2)$$

and

$$Y|X \sim \mathcal{N}\left(\lambda X + (1 - \lambda)m, (1 - \lambda^2)\sigma^2\right),$$

where $0 < \lambda < 1$, then

$$Y \sim \mathcal{N}(m, \sigma^2).$$

We then have for this iterative method that the transition probabilities are

$$\pi_{T(t_k)}(f_{t_k} \mid f_{t_{k-1}}, l_{t_k}, g) \propto$$
$$\exp[-\frac{1}{2T(t_k)}[f_{t_k} - \underline{M}^{l_{t_k}} f_{t_{k-1}} - \underline{Q}^{l_{t_k}} g]^t [\underline{Q}_1^{l_{t_k}}]^{-1} [f_{t_k} - \underline{M}^{l_{t_k}} f_{t_{k-1}} - \underline{Q}^{l_{t_k}} g]], \tag{18}$$

where

$$\underline{M}^{l_{t_k}} = \Omega^{l_{t_k}} + (I - \Omega^{l_{t_k}})(C^{l_{t_k}} - (D^T D)_*^{l_{t_k}}). \tag{19}$$
$$\underline{Q}^{l_{t_k}} = (I - \Omega^{l_{t_k}}) B^{l_{t_k}}. \tag{20}$$

where

$$C^{l_{t_k}[i]} * f_{t_k}(i) = \phi \lambda^{l_{t_k}[i]}(i) \sum_{j \,\mathrm{nhbr}\, i} \frac{(1 - l([i,j]))}{nn^{l_{t_k}[i]}(i)} f_{t_k}(j).$$

and

$$(D^T D)_*^{l_{t_k}[i]} * f_{t_k}(i) = (1 - \lambda^{l_{t_k}[i]}(i)) \left(\frac{(D^T D f)(i)}{c} - f(i) \right).$$

$\Omega^{l_{t_k}}$ is a diagonal matrix with entries $\omega^{l_{t_k}[i]}(i)$ and $\underline{Q}_1^{l_{t_k}}$ is a diagonal matrix with entries $\sigma_m^{2\,l[i]}(i)$.

In the coming section we apply the modified SA and ICM algorithms, whose convergence is established in the appendix to restore astronomical images.

The algorithms are the following:

Algorithm 2 Sequential MSA procedure. *Let i_t, $t = 1, 2, \ldots$, be the sequence in which the sites are visited for updating.*

1. *Set $t = 0$ and assign an initial configuration denoted as f_{-1}, l_{-1} and initial temperature $T(0) = 1$.*

2. *The evolution $l_{t-1} \rightarrow l_t$ of the line process can be obtained by sampling the next point of the line process from the raster-scanning scheme based on the conditional probability mass function defined in (7) and (8) and keeping the rest of l_{t-1} unchanged.*

3. *Set $t = t+1$. Go back to step 2 until a complete sweep of the field l is finished.*

4. *The evolution $f_{t-1} \rightarrow f_t$ of the observed system can be obtained by sampling the next value of the whole image based on the conditional probability mass function given in (15)*

5. *Go to step 2 until $t > t_f$, where t_f is a specified integer.*

The following theorem guarantees that the MSA algorithm converges to a local MAP estimate, even in the presence of blurring.

Theorem 2. *If the following conditions are satisfied:*

1. *$|\phi| < 0.25$*
2. *$T(t) \rightarrow 0$ as $t \rightarrow \infty$, such that*
3. *$T(t) \geq C / \log(1 + k(t))$,*

then for any starting configuration $f_{-1}.l_{-1}$, we have

$$\mathrm{p}(f_t.l_t \mid f_{-1}.l_{-1}.g) \rightarrow \mathrm{p}_0(f.l) \ as \ t \rightarrow \infty.$$

where $\mathrm{p}_0(...)$ is a probability distribution over local MAP solutions and $k(t)$ is the sweep iteration number at time t.

The modified ICM procedure is obtained by selecting in steps 2 and 4 of Algorithm 2 the mode of the corresponding transition probabilities.

6 Test Examples

Let us examine how the modified ICM algorithm works on a synthetic star image. blurred with an atmospherical point spread function (PSF). D. given by

$$d(i) \propto \left(1 + (u^2 + v^2)/R^2\right)^{-\delta}. \tag{21}$$

with $\delta = 3$. $R = 3.5$, $i = (u.v)$. and Gaussian noise with $\sigma_n^2 = 64$. If we use $\sigma_w^2 = 24415$. which is realistic for this image. and take into account that. for the PSF defined in (21). $c = 0.02$. A defined in (13) is not a contraction. Figures 2a and 2b depict the original and corrupted image, respectively. Restorations from the original and modified ICM methods with $\beta = 2$ for 2500 iterations are depicted on Fig. 2c and Fig. 2d. respectively. Similar results are obtained with 500 iterations.

The methods were also tested on images of Saturn which were obtained at the Cassegrain f/8 focus of the 1.52-m telescope at Calar Alto Observatory (Spain) on July. 1991. Results are presented on a image taken through a narrow-band interference filter centered at the wavelength 9500 Å.

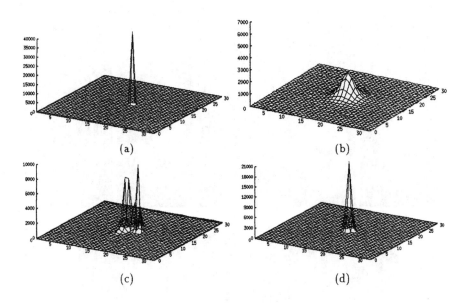

Fig. 2. (a) Original image. (b) Observed image. (c) ICM restoration. (d) Restoration with the proposed ICM method.

The blurring function defined in (21) was used. The parameters δ and R were estimated from the intensity profiles of satellites of Saturn that were recorded simultaneously with the planet and of stars that were recorded very close in time and airmass to the planetary images. We found $\delta \sim 3$ and $R \sim 3.4$ pixels.

Figure 3 depicts the original image and the restorations after running the original ICM and our proposed ICM methods for 500 iterations and the original SA and our proposed SA methods for 5000 iterations. In all the images the improvement in spatial resolution is evident. To examine the quality of the MAP estimate of the line process we compared it with the position of the ring and disk of Saturn, obtained from the Astronomical Almanac, corresponding to our observed image. Although all the methods detect a great part of the ring and the disk, the ICM method, Fig. 4a, shows thick lines. The SA method, on the other hand, gives us thinner lines and the details are more resolved, Fig. 4b. Obviously there are some gaps in the line process but better results would be obtained by using 8 neigbors instead of 4 or, in general, adding more l-terms to the energy function.

Table 1 shows the computing time per iteration of the studied methods. They are referred to the computing time of the ICM method. The little difference between the ICM and SA methods is due to the fact that most of the time is spent in convolving images.

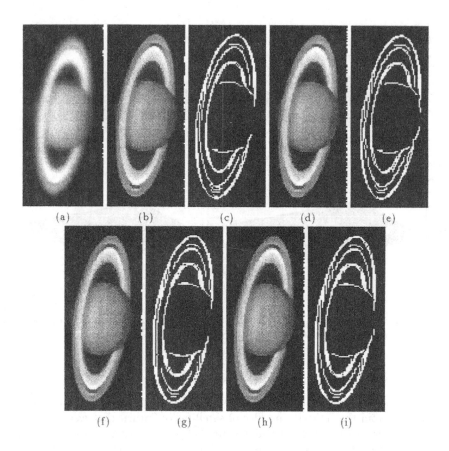

Fig. 3. (a) Original image. (b) restoration with the original ICM method and (c) its line process, (d) restoration with the original SA method and (e) its line process. (f) restoration with the proposed ICM method and (g) its line process, (h) restoration with the proposed SA method and (i) its line process.

7   Conclusions

In this paper we have presented two new methods that can be used to restore high dynamic range images in the presence of severe blurring. These methods extend the classical ICM and SA procedures, so that convergence of the algorithms is now guaranteed. The experimental results verify the derived theoretical results. Further extensions of the algorithms are under consideration.

Appendix: Convergence of the MSA Procedure

In this section we shall examine the convergence of the MSA algorithm. It is important to make clear that in this new iterative procedure we simulate $f(i)$

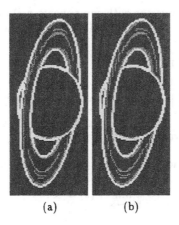

(a)   (b)

Fig. 4. Comparison between the real edges (light) and the obtained line process (dark). (a) Proposed ICM method, (b) Proposed SA method

Table 1. Computing times per iteration of the methods referred to the ICM computing time.

Method	Original ICM	Original SA	Proposed ICM	Proposed SA
Relative Time	1.00	1.13	0.12	0.20

using (15) and to simulate $l([i, j])$ we keep using (7) and (8). We shall denote by π_T the corresponding transition probabilities. That is, $\pi_{T(t_k)}(f_{t_k}|f_{t_{k-1}}, l_{t_k}, g)$ is obtained from (18) and $\pi_{T(t_k)}(l_{t_k}|f_{t_{k-1}}, l_{t_{k-1}})$ is obtained from (7) and (8).

Since updating the whole image at the same time prevents us from having $P_t P_{T(t)} = P_{T(t)}$ we will not be able to show the convergence to the global MAP estimates using the same proofs as in [4, 6].

To prove the convergence of the chain we need some lemmas and definitions as in [5, 6].

We assume a measure space (Ω, Σ, μ) and a conditional density function $\pi_n(s_n|s_{n-1})$ which defines a Markov chain $s_1, s_2, \ldots, s_n, \ldots$. In our application, the s_i are vectors valued with a number of elements equal to the number of pixels in the image. For simplicity, we assume Ω is R^d and μ is a Lebesgue measure on R^d. Define a Markov operator $P_n : L^1 \to L^1$ as follows

$$P_n f(s_n) = \int_{\Omega} \pi_n(s_n|s_{n-1}) f(s_{n-1}) ds_{n-1}. \qquad (22)$$

By P_n^m we mean the composite operation $P_{n+m} P_{n+m-1} \cdots P_{n+2} P_{n+1}$. The convergence problem we are dealing with is the same as the convergence of P_0^m as $m \to \infty$.

Definition 3. Let x be a vector with components $x(i)$ and Q be a matrix with components $q(i,j)$. We define $\| x \|_2$ and $\| Q \|_2$ as follows

$$\| x \|_2 = (\sum_i |x(i)|^2)^{1/2}.$$

$$\| Q \|_2 = \sup_x \frac{\| Qx \|_2}{\| x \|_2} = \max_i (\rho(i))^{1/2}.$$

where $\rho(i)$ are the eigenvalues of matrix $Q^t Q$.

Definition 4. A continuous nonnegative function $V : \Omega \rightarrow R$ is a Liapunov function if

$$\lim_{\|s\| \rightarrow \infty} V(s) = \infty. \tag{23}$$

where $\| s \|$ is a norm of s.

Denote by D the set of all pdfs with respect to Lebesgue measure and the L_1 norm defined as follows:

$$\| f \|_1 = \int_\Omega |f(s)| ds \quad \forall f \in L^1.$$

Definition 5. Let $P_n : L^1 \rightarrow L^1$ be a Markov operator. Then $\{P_n\}$ is said to be asymptotically stable if, for any $f_1, f_2 \in D$.

$$\lim_{m \rightarrow \infty} \| P_0^m (f_1 - f_2) \|_1 = 0. \tag{24}$$

Let us prove the following lemma.

Lemma 6. *If $|\phi| < 0.25$ then, $\forall l$,*

$$\| \underline{M}^l \|_2 < 1.$$

where $\underline{M}^l$ has been defined in (19).

Proof. First we note that from (14)

$$f_t(i) = f_{t-1}(i) - \rho(\phi \sum_{j \, \text{nhbr} \, i} (f_{t-1}(i) - f_{t-1}(j))(1 - l([i,j])) + (1 - 4\phi) f_{t-1}(i))$$

$$+ (1 - \rho)((D^T g)(i) - (D^T D f)_{t-1}(i)).$$

where $\rho = \alpha/(\alpha + \beta)$.

So, $\underline{M}^l$ is symmetric and for any vector x

$$x^T \underline{M}^l x = \sum_i x(i)^2 - \rho(\sum_i \phi(x(i) - x(i:+1))^2 (1 - l([i,i:+1]))$$

$$- \rho(\sum_i \phi(x(i) - x(i:+2))^2 (1 - l([i,i:+2])) + (1 - 4\phi) \sum_i x^2(i))$$

$$- (1 - \rho) x^T D^T D x$$

Obviously if $|\phi| < 0.25$, $\forall x \neq 0$, $x^T \underline{M}^l x < \sum x(i)^2$. Furthermore,

$$x^T \underline{M}^l x \geq \sum_i x(i)^2 - \rho(\sum_i \phi(x(i) - x(i:+1))^2 + \sum_i \phi(x(i) - x(i:+2))^2$$

$$+(1 - 4\phi)\sum_i x^2(i)) - (1 - \rho)x^T D^T D x$$

$$= x^T(I - \rho(I - \phi N) - (1 - \rho)D^T D)x$$

and if $|\phi| < 0.25$, $-I < (I - \rho(I - \phi N) - (1 - \rho)D^T D)$. So, if $|\phi| < 0.25$,

$$-I < \underline{M}^l < I$$

and

$$x^T \underline{M}^{l^T} \underline{M}^l x < x^T x,$$

which proves that $\underline{M}^l$ is a contraction matrix for $|\phi| < 0.25$. $\qquad \square$

We shall also use the following lemma from [5, 6].

Lemma 7. *Assume B is a d-dimensional positive definite matrix with eigenvalues $\rho(1) \geq \rho(2) \geq \ldots \geq \rho(d) > 0$ and $B = J^t D J$, where D is a diagonal matrix which consists of the eigenvalues. Let $b > 0$, then*

$$\frac{1}{\sqrt{(2\pi)^d |B|}} \int_{\|x\|_2 > b} \exp[-x^t B^{-1} x] dx \geq q\left(\frac{b}{\sqrt{\rho(d)}}\right)^{d-2} \exp\left[-\frac{b^2}{2\rho(d)}\right].$$

The following theorem from [6] gives the sufficient conditions on the convergence of P_0^m in terms of transition density functions.

Theorem 8. *Let (Ω, Σ, μ) be a measure space and μ be Lebesgue measure on R^d. If there exists a Liapunov function, $V : \Omega \to R$, such that*

$$\int_\Omega V(s_n)\pi_n(s_n | s_{n-1}) ds_n \leq \alpha V(s_{n-1}) + \beta \quad \text{for } 0 \leq \alpha < 1 \text{ and } \beta \geq 0 \quad (25)$$

and

$$\sum_{i=1}^\infty \| h_{m_i} \|_1 = \infty, \quad m_i = i\tilde{m} \text{ for any integer } \tilde{m} > 0, \tag{26}$$

where

$$h_{m_i}(s_{m_i}) = \inf_{\|s_{m_i-1}\| \leq r} \pi_{m_i}(s_{m_i} | s_{m_i-1}) \tag{27}$$

and r is a positive number satisfying the following inequality:

$$V(s) > 1 + \frac{\beta}{1 - \alpha} \quad \forall \| s \| > r$$

then, for the Markov operator, $P_n : L^1 \to L^1$, defined by (22) we have that P_0^m is asymptotically stable.

We are going to show that the sufficient conditions of Theorem 8 are satisfied by the Markov chain defined by our MSA procedure. The proof follows the same steps as the one given in [5. 6].

Let $V(f.l)$ be the Liapunov function

$$V(f.l) = \| f \|_2 + \| l \|_2 . \tag{28}$$

Step 1: Show that

$$\sum_{l_{t_k}} \int_\Omega V(f_{t_k}.l_{t_k}) \pi_{T(t_k)}(f_{t_k}.l_{t_k}|f_{t_{k-1}}.l_{t_{k-1}}.g) df_{t_k} \leq \beta + \alpha V(f_{t_{k-1}}.l_{t_{k-1}}).$$

First we show that

$$\int_\Omega \| f_{t_k} \|_2 \, \pi_{T(t_k)}(f_{t_k}|f_{t_{k-1}}.l_{t_k}.g) df_{t_k} \leq \beta_1 + \alpha \| f_{t_{k-1}} \|_2 \quad \forall l_{t_k}. \tag{29}$$

We have

$$\int_\Omega \| f_{t_k} \|_2 \, \pi_{T(t_k)}(f_{t_k}|f_{t_{k-1}}.l_{t_k}.g) df_{t_k} = \qquad \text{(by change of variable)}$$

$$= \int_\Omega \| \bar{f}_{t_k} + \underline{M}^{l_{t_k}} f_{t_{k-1}} + \underline{Q}^{l_{t_k}} g \|_2 \text{ const exp} \left[-\frac{1}{2T(t_k)} \bar{f}_{t_k}^t [\underline{Q}_1^{l_{t_k}}]^{-1} \bar{f}_{t_k} \right] d\bar{f}_{t_k}$$

$$\leq \int_\Omega (\| \bar{f}_{t_k} \|_2 + \| \underline{M}^{l_{t_k}} f_{t_{k-1}} \|_2 + \| \underline{Q}^{l_{t_k}} g \|_2) \text{const}$$

$$\text{exp} \left[-\frac{1}{2T(t_k)} \bar{f}_{t_k}^t [\underline{Q}_1^{l_{t_k}}]^{-1} \bar{f}_{t_k} \right] d\bar{f}_{t_k}$$

$$\leq \beta_1 + \alpha \| f_{t_{k-1}} \|_2. \tag{30}$$

where

$$\alpha = \max_l \| \underline{M}^l \|_2.$$

$$\beta_1 = \max_l \left[T(t_k) \right]^{1/2} [trace(\underline{Q}_1^l)]^{1/2} + \| \underline{Q}^{l_{t_k}} g \|_2 \right] .$$

with $\alpha < 1$. since for Lemma 6. $\underline{M}^l$ is a contraction. $\forall l$.

Furthermore. it can be easily shown that

$$\sum_{l_{t_k}} \pi_{T(t_k)}(l_{t_k}|f_{t_{k-1}}.l_{t_{k-1}}) \| l_{t_k} \|_2 \leq \beta_1 + \alpha \| l_{t_{k-1}} \|_2. \tag{31}$$

since l_{t_k} has only a finite number of levels. choosing β_1 big enough. the above inequality obviously holds.

Let us now show that (29) holds. We have, using (30) and (31),

$$\sum_{l_{t_k}} \int_\Omega V(f_{t_k}, l_{t_k})\pi_{T(t_k)}(f_{t_k}, l_{t_k}|f_{t_{k-1}}, l_{t_{k-1}}; g)df_{t_k} =$$

$$= \sum_{l_{t_k}} \int_\Omega \| f_{t_k} \|_2 \, \pi_{T(t_k)}(f_{t_k}, l_{t_k}|f_{t_{k-1}}, l_{t_{k-1}}; g)df_{t_k}$$

$$+ \sum_{l_{t_k}} \int_\Omega \| l_{t_k} \|_2 \, \pi_{T(t_k)}(f_{t_k}, l_{t_k}|f_{t_{k-1}}, l_{t_{k-1}}; g)df_{t_k}$$

$$\leq \beta_1 + \alpha \| f_{t_{k-1}} \|_2 + \beta_2 \| l_{t_{k-1}} \|_2 = \beta + \alpha V(f_{t_{k-1}}, l_{t_{k-1}}).$$

Step 2: Step 2 is the same that in [5, 6] using

$$\delta_{\max} = \max\left\{ \sup_{\|f\|_2 \leq a} [\frac{\phi}{2\sigma_w^2}(f(i) - f(j))^2, \frac{\beta}{2\sigma_w^2}] \right\}$$

and

$$\delta_{\min} = \min\left\{ \inf_{\|f\|_2 \leq a} ([\frac{\phi}{2\sigma_w^2}(f(i) - f(j))^2, \frac{\beta}{2\sigma_w^2}] \right\}.$$

References

1. Besag, J. (1986), "On the Statistical Analysis of Dirty Pictures", *J. Royal Statistics Soc.* B 1 48, 259–302.
2. Blake, A. and Zisserman, A. (1987), "Visual Reconstruction", Cambridge, MIT Press.
3. Chellapa, R., Simchony, T. and Lichtenstein, Z. (1991), "Image Estimation Using 2D Noncausal Gauss-Markov Random Field Models", in *Digital Image Restoration*, Katsaggelos, A.K. (ed.), Springer Series in Information Science, vol. 23, Springer–Verlag.
4. Geman, S., Geman D. (1984), "Stochastic Relaxation, Gibbs Distributions, and the Bayesian Restoration of Images", *IEEE Trans. on PAMI*, vol. PAMI-9, (1 6), 721–742.
5. Jeng, F.C., (1988), "Compound Gauss-Markov Random Fields for Image Estimation and Restoration", *Ph.D Thesis*, Rensselaer Polythenic Institute.
6. Jeng, F.C., and Woods, J.W. (1988), "Simulated Annealing in Compound Gaussian Random Fields", *IEEE Trans. Inform. Theory*, 1 36, 94–107.
7. Jeng, F.C. and Woods, J.W. (1991), "Compound Gauss-Markov Models for Image Processing", in *Digital Image Restoration*, Katsaggelos, A.K. (ed.), Springer Series in Information Science, vol. 23, Springer–Verlag.
8. Molina, R., Ripley, B.D., Molina, A., Moreno, F. and Ortiz, J.L. (1992), "Bayesian Deconvolution with Prior Knowledge of Object Location: Applications to Ground-Based Planetary Images", *AJ*, 1 104, 1662–1668.
9. Molina, R., Katsaggelos, A.K., Mateos, J. and Abad, J. (1996), "Restoration of Severely Blurred High Range Images Using Compound Models", *Proceeding of ICIP-96*.
10. Ripley, B.D. (1981) "Spatial Statistics", Wiley, New York.

Maximum Likelihood Estimation of Markov Random Field Parameters Using Markov Chain Monte Carlo Algorithms

Xavier Descombes, Robin Morris, Josiane Zerubia, Marc Berthod

INRIA, 2004, route des Lucioles BP 93
06902 Sophia Antipolis Cedex, France
tel. (33) 93 65 78 66
Fax (33) 93 65 76 43
email: *name*@sophia.inria.fr

Abstract. Recent developments in statistics now allow maximum likelihood estimators for the parameters of Markov Random Fields to be constructed. We detail the theory required, and present an algorithm which is easily implemented and practical in terms of computation time. We demonstrate this algorithm on three MRF models, the standard Potts model, an inhomogeneous variation of the Potts model and a long-range interaction model, better adapted to modelling real-world images. We estimate the parameters from a synthetic and a real image, and then resynthesise the models to demonstrate which features of the image have been captured by the model.

1 Introduction

Early vision algorithms extract some information from observed data without any specific knowledge about the scene. However, these data (remote sensing data, medical images,...) are usually disturbed by noise. To improve the algorithms, regularization techniques are used, incorporating constraints on the solution. These constraints represent a general knowledge about what a natural scene should be. A popular way to define these constraints is to consider a probabilistic model (the prior) of the expected result. Using the Bayesian approach, we search for a realization which optimizes the probability of the solution, given the data. A key point to obtain unsupervised algorithms in this paradigm is to be able to estimate the different parameters involved in the prior. Accurate estimators of these parameters are necessary to control the impact of the prior on the properties desired for the solution.

Because of their ability to model global properties using local constraints, Markov Random Fields (MRFs) are very popular priors. Several optimization algorithm converging either toward a global minimum of the energy [1] or a local one [2], [3] are now well defined. But accurate estimation of the parameters is still an open issue. Indeed, the partition function (normalization constant) leads to intractable computation. Parameter estimation methods are then either devoted to very specific models [4], [5] or based on approximations such as

Maximum Pseudo Likelihood [6], [7], [8]. Unfortunately, these approximations lead to inaccurate estimators for the prior parameters. A good behavior of the estimation can be reached by Maximum Likelihood estimators, whose statistical properties, such as consistency, are proved by B. Gidas in [9].

Markov Chain Monte Carlo algorithms (MCMC) [10] are very popular in image processing to derive optimization methods when using a Markovian prior [1]. In fact, MCMC algorithms can be developped for other purposes such as estimation. The partition function of Gibbs Fields can be estimated using an MCMC procedure. A Maximum Likelihood estimation using an MCMC algorithm is proposed in [11]. The convergence of this algorithm is adressed in [12]. This method can be applied to a wide range of models such a Point Processes [13] or Markov Random Fields. In this paper, we propose an estimation algorithm for Markovian prior parameters based on an MCMCML procedure. We validate this algorithm on three different priors.

In section 2, we compute the Maximum Likelihood estimators of a given Gibbs Field whose energy is linear with respect to parameters. Besides, the importance sampling [11] is also introduced. It allows us to compute statistics of the model associated with given parameters using samples obtained with other parameter values. These results lead to an MCMCML estimation method described in section 3. Results are detailed in section 4. We consider three different Markovian priors: the Potts model, an inhomogeneous variation of the Potts model and the Chien-model [14]. For the Potts model, we also consider the case of inhomogeneous parameters. This Maximum Likelihood estimation allows us to derive some comments about the priors. Section 5 is devoted to a comparison between the three priors considered. We conclude in section 6.

2 Maximum Likelihood estimators

2.1 The log-likelihood

Let P_Θ be a random field define on S, parameterized by vector $\Theta = (\theta_i)$. We consider P_Θ to be a Gibbs Field, whose energy is linear with respect to the parameters θ_i. We then have :

$$P_\Theta(Y) = \frac{1}{Z(\Theta)} \exp - \langle \Theta, Y \rangle = \frac{1}{Z(\Theta)} \exp \left[-\sum_i \theta_i N_i(Y) \right], \qquad (1)$$

where $N_i(Y)$ are function of the configuration Y. In this paper, we consider a continuous framework for the state space Λ. Results are still valid in the discrete case by changing integrals into sums. The partition function $Z(\Theta)$ is then written:

$$Z(\Theta) = \int_{\Lambda^S} \exp \left[-\sum_i \theta_i N_i(X) \right] dX, \qquad (2)$$

where S is the site set and Λ is the state space.

We consider that we have data Y. We want to fit the model on the data. The log-likelihood is then defined by :

$$\log P(Y|\Theta) = \log \left[\frac{1}{Z(\Theta)} \exp - \sum_i \theta_i N_i(Y) \right], \tag{3}$$

$$\log P(Y|\Theta) = -\sum_i \theta_i N_i(Y) - \log Z(\Theta). \tag{4}$$

The Maximum Likelihood estimators are obtained by maximizing the log-likelihood. We then have:

$$\forall i, \frac{\partial \log P(Y|\Theta)}{\partial \theta_i} \left(\hat{\Theta} \right) = 0, \tag{5}$$

and then:

$$\forall i, -N_i(Y) + \frac{\int_{\Lambda^S} N_i(X) \exp \left[-\sum_i \hat{\theta}_i N_i(X) \right] dX}{\int_{\Lambda^S} \exp \left[-\sum_i \hat{\theta}_i N_i(X) \right] dX} = 0, \tag{6}$$

where $\hat{\theta}_i$ is the Maximum Likelihood estimator of θ_i.

Denoting by $< a(x) >_\Theta$, the expectation of $a(x)$ with respect to P_Θ, we finally get:

$$\forall i, \langle N_i(X) \rangle_{\hat{\Theta}} = N_i(Y). \tag{7}$$

To evaluate the log-likelihood function, we have to compute the partition function. The partial derivatives of the log-likelihood requires the computation of the different $\langle N_i(X) \rangle_\Theta$. Unfortunately, the computation of these quantities is untractable. We can estimate the $\langle N_i(X) \rangle_\Theta$ by sampling the distribution. Nevertheless, to sample the distribution for each value of Θ is inconceivable from CPU time considerations.

2.2 Importance sampling

We introduce importance sampling [11] to avoid having to sample the model for each value of Θ. Indeed, importance sampling allows us to estimate statistical moments corresponding to P_Θ using samples obtained from P_Ψ.

Consider first the partition function. We have:

$$Z(\Theta) = \int_\Omega \exp \left[-\sum_i \theta_i N_i(X) \right] dX, \tag{8}$$

where $\Omega = \Lambda^S$ is the configuration space, then:

$$Z(\Theta) = \int_\Omega \exp \left[-\sum_i (\theta_i - \psi_i) N_i(X) \right] \exp \left[-\sum_i \psi_i N_i(X) \right] dX$$

$$Z(\Theta) = \int_\Omega \exp \left[-\sum_i (\theta_i - \psi_i) N_i(X) \right] Z(\Psi) dP_\Psi(X). \tag{9}$$

For each couple (Θ, Ψ), the partition functions ratio is given by:

$$\frac{Z(\Theta)}{Z(\Psi)} = E_\Psi \left(\exp \left[-\sum_i (\theta_i - \psi_i) N_i(X) \right] \right), \tag{10}$$

where E_Ψ refers to the expectation with respect to the law P_Ψ.

The partition function corresponding to P_Θ can thus be estimated from the sampling of P_Ψ. We just have to sample the law with parameter Ψ to get an estimator of the ratio $\frac{Z(\Theta)}{Z(\Psi)}$ for all Θ by computing from the samples the expectation given by formula (10).

Consider now the log-likelihood. The maximum likelihood estimator is given by the vector Θ which maximize formula (3). This is equivalent to minimizing the following expression:

$$-\log P_\Theta(Y) = \sum_i \theta_i N_i(Y) + \log \frac{Z(\Theta)}{Z(\Psi)}. \tag{11}$$

The partial derivative of the partition function can be written:

$$\frac{\partial Z(\Theta)}{\partial \theta_i} = \int_\Omega -N_i(X) \exp \left[-\sum_j (\theta_j - \psi_j) N_j(X) \right] Z(\Psi) dP_\Psi(X)$$

$$\frac{\partial Z(\Theta)}{\partial \theta_i} = -Z(\Psi) E_\Psi \left(N_i(X) \exp \left[-\sum_j (\theta_j - \psi_j) N_j(X) \right] \right). \tag{12}$$

Then, we have:

$$\frac{\partial -\log P_\Theta(Y)}{\partial \theta_i} = N_i(Y) - \frac{E_\Psi \left(N_i(X) \exp \left[-\sum_j (\theta_j - \psi_j) N_j(X) \right] \right)}{E_\Psi \left(\exp \left[-\sum_j (\theta_j - \psi_j) N_j(X) \right] \right)}. \tag{13}$$

From a sampling of P_Ψ we thus can theoretically estimate the log-likelihood of P_Θ and its partial derivatives for all Θ. The same kind of computation allows us to compute the Hessian, and we have:

$$\frac{\partial^2 -\log P_\Theta(Y)}{\partial \theta_i \partial \theta_j} = N_i(Y) N_j(Y) - \frac{E_\Psi \left(N_i(X) N_j(X) \exp -[\sum_k (\theta_k - \psi_k) N_k(X)] \right)}{E_\Psi \left(\exp -[\sum_k (\theta_k - \psi_k) N_k(X)] \right)}. \tag{14}$$

3 An MCMCML algorithm

3.1 Estimate a robustness criterion

Consider an image Y from which we want to compute the maximum likelihood estimator of Θ using P_Θ as a model. From the image we can extract the value of the $N_i(Y)$. Then, we can sample the law P_Ψ for a given Ψ. From the samples, the different expectations involved in formulas (10) and (13) can be estimated. Then, for all Θ, we can estimate the log-likelihood and its derivatives. An optimization algorithm (gradient descent, conjugate gradient,...) leads then to the Maximum Likelihood estimator of Θ, when the log-likelihood is a convex function. Otherwise, a more complex optimization technique has to be used.

Nevertheless, if the two parameters Θ and Ψ are too far from each other, the estimation of the expectations will be inaccurate. Indeed, the robustness of the estimation of the expectations requires the overlap between the two distributions P_Θ and P_Ψ to be large enough. The proposed method is practically valid only in a neighborhood of parameter Ψ. During the optimization, when the current value of Θ is too far from Ψ, we have to re-sample the model using a new value for Ψ (we take the current value of Θ for Ψ). Such a sampling requires CPU time. So, we need a criteria to define the neighborhood of Ψ on which the estimation is robust to avoid un-necessary sampling. A first idea is to use a metric which quantifies the overlap between the distributions P_Ψ and P_Θ and given by:

$$d\left(P_\Theta, P_\Psi\right) = \frac{1}{2} \int |P_\Theta(X) - P_\Psi(X)| \, dX. \tag{15}$$

By definition, we have:

$$P_\Theta(X) - P_\Psi(X) = \frac{\exp - \langle X, \Theta \rangle}{Z(\Theta)} - \frac{\exp - \langle X, \Psi \rangle}{Z(\Psi)}, \tag{16}$$

$$P_\Theta(X) - P_\Psi(X) = \left(\frac{Z(\Psi)}{Z(\Theta)} \exp\left[-\langle X, \Theta \rangle + \langle X, \Psi \rangle\right] - 1 \right) \frac{\exp - \langle X, \Psi \rangle}{Z(\Psi)}. \tag{17}$$

Thus, we define a distance between the distribution by:

$$\int |P_\Theta(X) - P_\Psi(X)| \, dX = \int \left| \left(\frac{Z(\Psi)}{Z(\Theta)} \exp\left[-\langle X, \Theta \rangle + \langle X, \Psi \rangle\right] - 1 \right) \right| dP_\Psi(X),$$

$$= E_\Psi \left(\left| \frac{Z(\Psi)}{Z(\Theta)} \exp\left[-\langle X, \Theta \rangle + \langle X, \Psi \rangle\right] - 1 \right| \right). \tag{18}$$

By using formula (10), we then have:

$$d\left(P_\Theta, P_\Psi\right) = \frac{1}{2} \times$$

$$E_\Psi \left(\left| E_\Psi \left(\exp\left[-\sum_i (\theta_i - \psi_i) N_i(X) \right] \right) \exp\left[-\langle X, \Theta \rangle + \langle X, \Psi \rangle\right] - 1 \right| \right) \tag{19}$$

We can compute this distance to test the robustness of estimates and decide whether we should sample the model once more or not. However, this distance is also estimated and can be biased. Therefore, we define a heuristical criterion, considering the current samples used for expectation estimation. For each sample X_i, we define a weight by:

$$\omega_i = U_\Theta(X_i) - U_\Psi(X_i), \tag{20}$$

$$\omega_i = \sum_j (\Theta_j - \Psi_j) N_j(X_i). \tag{21}$$

Computing the expectations, we use the following trick to avoid overflow and numerical instabilities:

$$\sum_{samples\ i} \exp[-\omega_i] = exp[-\omega_{max}] \sum_{samples\ i} \exp[-(\omega_i - \omega_{max})], \tag{22}$$

where $\omega_{max} = \max_{samples,}\ \omega_i$.

Consider the different samples. If ω_{max} is too far from most of the ω_i the quantity $\exp[-(\omega_i - \omega_{max})]$ will be close to 0 and results in a poor estimation. So, we can consider the estimation robust only if $\omega_{max} - \omega_{min}$ is lower than a given threshold.

3.2 Estimation algorithm

We now can derive an algorithm based on the conjugate gradient principle. Consider the current parameter estimate Θ and a sampling of $P_{\hat{\Theta}}$. We can estimate the gradient and the Hessian of the log-likelihood function at Θ. We then compute the conjugate directions [15]. Along each conjugate direction we define an interval using the distance defined by equation (19), where the log-likelihood estimation is robust. We then maximize the log-likelihood along these intervals.

The algorithm is then written in the following way:

1. Compute the $N_i(Y)$
2. Initialize $\hat{\Theta}_0$, $n = 0$
3. Sample the distribution $P_{\hat{\Theta}_n}$
4. Estimate the gradient and the Hessian of the log-likelihood at $\hat{\Theta}_n$, using equations (13) and (14)
5. Compute the conjugate directions Δ_i
6. For each conjugate direction define a search interval using either the distance defined in equation (19): $I_i = \left[\hat{\Theta}_n - \alpha_i \Delta_i, \hat{\Theta}_n + \beta_i \Delta_i\right]$ where $\alpha_i = sup_{\alpha \in \mathbb{R}^+}\left\{\alpha : d\left(P_{\hat{\Theta}_n}, P_{\hat{\Theta}_n - \alpha \Delta_i}\right) < T\right\}$,
   $\beta_i = sup_{\beta \in \mathbb{R}^+}\left\{\beta : d\left(P_{\hat{\Theta}_n}, P_{\hat{\Theta}_n + \beta \Delta_i}\right) < T\right\}$ where T is a threshold, or the proposed heuristic criterion.
7. Compute $\hat{\Theta}_{n+1}$ by maximizing the log-likelihood along each search interval using the golden section principle [15]
8. if $\|\hat{\Theta}_{n+1} - \hat{\Theta}_n\| > T_2$ put $n = n + 1$ and go back to 3, where T_2 is another threshold, otherwise exit.

4 Validation on Markovian priors

In this section, we consider different Markov models used as priors in image processing. We validate the estimation method on these models and demonstrate the generality of its applicability.

4.1 The Potts model

The Potts model is commonly used as a prior in image segmentation. It depends on a single parameter β and is defined by:

$$P_\beta(X) = \frac{1}{Z(\beta)} \exp\left[-\beta \sum_{c=\{s,s'\}\in\mathcal{C}} \delta_{r_s \neq r_{s'}}\right],\tag{23}$$

where $\mathcal{C}$ is the set of cliques. In this case, a clique consists in two neighboring pixels. We consider the case where the lattice S is a subset of $\mathbb{Z}^2$. For simulations and estimations we have considered the 4 nearest-neighbors. The Potts model can be embedded in the general form of equation (1):

$$P_\beta(X) = \frac{1}{Z(\beta)} \exp\left[-\beta N_0(X)\right] = \frac{1}{Z(\beta)} \exp\left[-\beta\#x\right],\tag{24}$$

where $N_0(X) = \#x$ is the number of inhomogenous cliques in the configuration X. The model depends on one single parameter, so the proposed algorithm is simplified as we do not have to compute the conjugate directions. Table 1 shows estimates obtained using the MCMCML method for several values of β.

Parameters	$\beta = 0.53$ ($N_0 = 48070$)	$\beta = 0.5493$ ($N_0 = 35699$)
Estimates	$\hat{\beta} = 0.529$ ($\langle N_0 \rangle = 48072$)	$\hat{\beta} = 0.5488$ ($\langle N_0 \rangle = 35699$)
Sample		

Table 1. Estimation of the Potts model parameter

4.2 An inhomogeneous variation of the Potts model

We can extend the procedure to the case of a non-stationary Potts model. Consider a Potts model for which parameter β depends on the localization of the clique. We suppose for simplicity that this dependency is linear and that β is written:

$$\beta_{c=\{x_{i,j},x_{p,q}\}} = a\left(\frac{i+p}{2}\right) + b\left(\frac{j+q}{2}\right) + c. \tag{25}$$

To estimate β we have to estimate a, b, and c. The associated distribution is written:

$$P_{a,b,c}(X) = \frac{1}{Z(a,b,c)} \exp\left[-\sum_{c=\{s,s'\}\in C}\left(a\left(\frac{i+p}{2}\right) + b\left(\frac{j+q}{2}\right) + c\right)\delta_{x_s \neq x_{s'}}\right]. \tag{26}$$

This model can be written in the form of equation (1):

$$P_{a,b,c}(X) = \frac{1}{Z(a,b,c)} \exp\left[-cN_0(X) - bN_1(X) - aN_2(X)\right], \tag{27}$$

where:

$$N_0(X) = \#_X, \text{ the number of inhomogeneous cliques}$$

$$N_1(X) = \sum_{\text{inhomogeneous cliques}} \frac{j+q}{2} = N_0(X)\left\langle\frac{j+q}{2}\right\rangle_{inh.cl.}$$

$$N_2(X) = \sum_{\text{inhomogeneous cliques}} \frac{i+p}{2} = N_0(X)\left\langle\frac{i+p}{2}\right\rangle_{inh.cl.}$$

4.3 The chien-model

To improve segmentations some more complex model have been proposed in the last few years. These models consider cliques of more than two pixels to define more accurately local configurations and their contribution to the model. Such a model based on 3×3 cliques was proposed in [16]. Another model on an hexagonal lattice can be found in [17]. These models consider only the cliques configurations. In [14], a binary model (the chien-model) taking into account links between neighboring cliques is proposed. This model has been generalized to the m-ary case in [18]. This model, although regularizing, preserves fine structures and linear shapes in images. In this model, the set of cliques is composed by 3×3 squares. The chien-model is defined from the discrimination between noise, lines and edges. Three parameters (n, l and e) are associated with these patterns.

Before constructing the model the different configurations induced by a 3×3 square are classified using the symetries (symetry black-white, rotations, etc.) This classification and the number of elements in each class are described in Figure 1. A parameter is associated to each class and refers to the value of the potential function for the considered configuration. So, under the hypothesis of isotropy of the model which induces the symmetries, we have for such a topology

Table 2. Estimation of an inhomogeneous variation of the Potts model.

Parameters	c	0.3	N_0	26603		c	0.5	N_0	29171
	b	0.005	N_1	1703201		b	0.005	N_1	1816390
	a	0.002	N_2	2777495		a	0.0	N_2	3704620
Estimates	$\hat{c}$	0.3002	$\langle N_0 \rangle$	27960		$\hat{c}$	0.535	$\langle N_0 \rangle$	30495
	$\hat{b}$	0.0052	$\langle N_1 \rangle$	1771015		$\hat{b}$	0.0052	$\langle N_1 \rangle$	1859293
	$\hat{a}$	0.0025	$\langle N_2 \rangle$	2757615		$\hat{a}$	0.0003	$\langle N_2 \rangle$	3760871

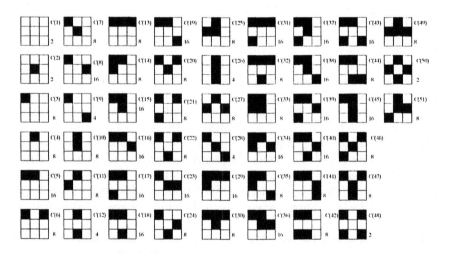

Fig. 1. The different classes induced by a binary 3×3 model and their number of elements

(cliques of 3×3) fifty one degrees of freedom. The construction of the model consists in imposing constraints by relations between its parameters. Two energy functions which differ only by a constant are equivalent, so we suppose that the minimum of the energy is equal to 0. The global realization of 0 energy are called the ground states of the model and represent the realization of maximal probability. We suppose that uniform realizations are ground states, so we have the first equation for the parameters given by $C(1) = 0$. We then define the different constraints with respect to those two uniform realizations. The first class of constraints concerns the energy of edges which is noted e per unit of length. Thanks to symetries and rotations we just have to define three orientations of edges corresponding to the eight ones induced by the size of cliques. These constraints and the derived equations are represented on figure 2. These

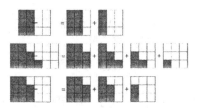

Fig. 2. Equations associated with edges constraints

constaints are defined for features which width is at least equal to 3. For other features, we have to define other constraints. When the width of the considered object is one pixel, it is referred as a line and has energy per unit l. For larger features (double and triple lines), we consider that the energy per unit is given by $2 \times e$, which correspond to left and right edge, and get more equations. All these constraints induce eleven equations which depend on fourteen parameters leading to the following solution (see [14] for full details):

$$C(3) = C(5) = \tfrac{e}{4} \quad C(26) = l - e \quad C(14) = \tfrac{\sqrt{2}e}{4}$$

$$C(16) = C(23) = \tfrac{\sqrt{5}}{6}l - \tfrac{e}{4} \quad C(11) = C(28) = \tfrac{\sqrt{2}l}{3} - \tfrac{e}{6}$$

$$C(35) = \tfrac{\sqrt{2}e}{2} \quad C(29) = \tfrac{\sqrt{5}e}{6} \quad C(13) = C(9) = C(19) = \tfrac{e}{2}$$

Noise is defined by assigning to every other configuration a positive value n.

To extend the binary chien-model in an m-ary model, we define the energy of a given configuration as the sum of several energies given by the binary model. Consider a configuration and a given label σ_0. We put every pixels of the configuration which are in state σ_0 to 0 and others to 1. We then have a binary configuration. The energy of the m-ary model is the sum of the energies obtained by these deduced binary configurations for the m labels (see figure 3). The potential associated with each configuration is then a linear combination of the three parameters e, l and n:

$$\forall i = 0, ..., 51 \; C(i) = \epsilon(i)e + \lambda(i)l + \eta(i)n. \tag{28}$$

Fig. 3. M-ary extension of the chien-model

The resulting distribution is written:

$$P_{e,l,n}(X) = \frac{1}{Z(e,l,n)} \exp\left[-eN_0(X) - lN_1(X) - nN_2(X)\right], \qquad (29)$$

where:

$$N_0(X) = \sum_{i=1,\dots,51} \epsilon(i)\#_i(X),$$

$$N_1(X) = \sum_{i=1,\dots,51} \lambda(i)\#_i(X),$$

$$N_2(X) = \sum_{i=1,\dots,51} \eta(i)\#_i(X).$$

$\#_i(X)$ being the number of configurations of type i in the realization X.

Results are summarized in table 3. The chosen parameter values show the properties of the model. Indeed, we can control the total length of edges as well as the total length of lines. Moreover, parameter n allows to control the amount of noise.

5 Pros and cons of the priors

5.1 Image constraints modelled by priors

In this section, we provide test to evaluate the properties the different models can incorporate in a segmentation result for example. First, we consider a binary synthetic image (see figure 4.a). A segmented SPOT image is the second proposed test (see figure 4.b). We estimate the corresponding parameters for each model and then synthetize the result. In that way, we can observe the properties of the initial image which are captured by the different models. We first consider the synthetic image shown in figure 4.a. Results obtained for the three models using a MCMCML estimation are summarized in table 4.

Parameters	ϵ 0.2 N_0 32950 l 0.4 N_1 11724 n 0.6 N_2 49708	ϵ 0.4 N_0 21089 l 0.8 N_1 1710 n 1.0 N_2 2880
Estimates	$\hat{\epsilon}$ 0.2008 $\langle N_0\rangle$ 32857 $\hat{l}$ 0.4038 $\langle N_1\rangle$ 11669 $\hat{n}$ 0.5997 $\langle N_2\rangle$ 49606	$\hat{\epsilon}$ 0.3905 $\langle N_0\rangle$ 21358 $\hat{l}$ 0.7843 $\langle N_1\rangle$ 1585 $\hat{n}$ 0.9993 $\langle N_2\rangle$ 2947
Sample		

Table 3. Estimation of chien-model parameters

a: Binary synthetic image

b: Segmented SPOT image, 5 classes

Fig. 4. Test images: 256×256

Model	N_0	Es. par.	As. $< N_0 >$	N_1	Es. par.	As. $< N_1 >$
Potts	8706	0.4981	8734			
Chien	3259	0.82	3261	1462	1.5	1464

Model	N_2	Es. par.	As. $< N_2 >$			As. $< N_3 >$
Potts						
Chien	1101	1.6	1094			

Model	Sample with estimated parameters	Comments
Potts		Inhomogeneous cliques are represented. The simulation is far from the original image. It represents noise in a homogeneous background.
Chien		Edge and line lengths are captured. Surface mean of black areas is greater than in the original image due to the double and triple lines in the original image (bone, birds, horizontal line...)

Table 4. Comparison of Potts model and chien-model as prior for the binary synthetic image

Model	N_0	Es. par.	As. $< N_0 >$	N_1	Es. par.	As. $< N_1 >$
Potts	18915	0.6043	18129			
Chien	17856	0.4261	18585	1605	1.0203	1651

Model	N_2	Es. par.	As. $< N_2 >$	N_3	Es. par.	As. $< N_3 >$
Potts						
Chien	11175	0.7353	11750			

Model	Sample with estimated parameters	Comments
Potts		The Potts model results in a noisy uniform image. The amount of noise is defined by the number of inhomogeneous cliques in the SPOT image.
Chien		The resulting image is composed by homogeneous areas. The edge length is given by the SPOT image. The lines in the SPOT image are represented by little segments in the synthetic realization.

Table 5. Comparison of Potts model and chien-model as prior for a segmented SPOT image

5.2 Sampling considerations

In the proposed algorithm, more than 99% of the required CPU time consists in sampling the model. Computing the log-likelihood and its derivatives is very fast when we have the samples. This sampling is obtained using a Metropolis-Hasting algorithm [10]. We first have to iterate the algorithm until we reach convergence and then achieve enough iterations to get accurate estimates of the different statistical moments involved in the MCMCML estimation. Among Metropolis-Hasting algorithms, the Gibbs Sampler is the most used in image processing. However, when considering the Potts model (homogeneous or not), the Swendsen-Wang algorithm [19] is more efficient. The Swendsen-Wang algorithm considers clusters instead of pixels. The convergence rate is then faster than a Gibbs Sampler. Moreover, as it moves freely within the distribution, we need less samples to obtain accurate estimates of the statistical moments than when using a Gibbs Sampler. Unfortunately, this algorithm can not be applied to the Chien-model. Finding an auxiliary variable to define clusters in this case is still an open issue. In a CPU time point of view, users may then prefer the Potts model.

Notice that, for given parameters, we only ever have to sample the model once. To compute the estimation, we need for each sample the values of the N_i. We can store these values in a data base. The parameter space can be discretized. The discretization step depends on the robustness of the importance sampling. Once we have sample the model for each value of the discrete parameter space the proposed algorithm requires a few seconds on a SUN 20. We can initialize the parameters with the values corresponding to the closest $< N_i >$ in the data base and derive the estimators without sampling the model.

6 Conclusion

In this paper, we have used recent developments in statistics to propose an algorithm performing a Maximum Likelihood estimation of Markovian prior parameters. Using importance sampling, the proposed algorithm avoids too much sampling which requires huge CPU time. Moreover, a data base can be computed which suppresses sampling. We are currently working on such a data base.

Using the Maximum Likelihood criterion leads to accurate estimators of the prior parameters. Therefore, we can compare the different priors and the regularizing properties they handle. In this paper, we have considered three Markovian priors: the Potts model, the inhomogeneous Potts model and the Chien-model. The later seems more appropriate to image processing as it controls image features (edge length, line length, noise) independently. On the other hand, this model requires more CPU time as it considers higher order interactions.

References

1. S. Geman, D. Geman. Stochastic relaxation, Gibbs distribution, and the Bayesian restoration of images. *IEEE trans. on Pattern Analysis and Machine Intelligence*, 6(6):721–741, 1984.
2. J. Besag. Spatial interaction and statistical analysis of lattice systems. *Academic Royal Statistical Society Series B*, 36:721–741, 1974.
3. J. Zerubia, R. Chellappa. Mean field approximation using Compound Gauss Markov Random fields for edge detection and image estimation. *IEEE trans. on Neural Networks*, 8(4):703–709, July 1993.
4. J.K. Goutsias. Mutually compatible Gibbs random fields. *IEEE trans. on Information Theory*, 35:1233–1249, 1989.
5. J.K. Goutsias. Unilateral approximation of Gibbs random fiel images. *Computer Vision, Graphics and Image Processing: Graphical Models and Image Processing*, 53:240–257, 1991.
6. J. Besag. On the statistical analysis of dirty pictures. *J. Roy. Statis. Soc., Series B*, 48:259–302, 1986.
7. B. Chalmond. Image restoration using an estimated Markov model. *Signal Processing*, 15:115–129, 1988.
8. A.J. Gray, J.W. Kay, D.M. Titterington. On the estimation of noisy binary Markov Random Fields. *Pattern Recognition*, 25:749–768, 1992.
9. B. Gidas. *Markov Random Fields (Theory and Application)*, chapter 17, Parameter Estimation for Gibbs Distributions from Fully Observed Data, pages 471–498. Ed. R. Chellappa, A.K. Jain Academic Press Inc., 1993.
10. W.K. Hastings. Monte Carlo sampling methods using Markov Chains and their applications. *Biometrika*, 57:97–109, 1970.
11. C. J. Geyer, E.E. Thompson. Constrained Monte Carlo Maximum Likelihood for dependent data. *J. R. Statist. Soc. B*, 54(3):657–699, 1992.
12. C.J. Geyer. On the convergence of Monte Carlo Maximum Likelihood calculations. *Journal of Royal Statistical Society B*, 56:261–274, 1994.
13. Y. Ogata, M. Tanemura. Estimation for interaction potentials of spatial point patterns through the maximum likelihood procedure. *Annals of the Institute of Statistical Mathematics, B*, 33:315–338, 1981.
14. X. Descombes, J.F. Mangin, E. Pechersky, M. Sigelle. Fine structures preserving model for image processing. In *Proc. 9th SCIA 95 Uppsala, Sweden*, pages 349–356, 1995.
15. W. Press, S. Teukolski, W. Vetterling, B. Flannery. *Numerical Recipes in C: The Art of Scientific Computing*. Cambridge University Press, 2nd ed., 1992.
16. G. Wolberg, T. Pavlidis. Restoration of binary images using stochastic relaxation with annealing. *Pattern Recognition Letters*, 3:375–388, 1985.
17. H. Tjelmeland, J. Besag. Markov Random Fields with higher order interactions. submitted to JASA. Preprint.
18. X. Descombes. Application of stochastic techniques in image processing for automatic tissue classification in MRI and blood vessel restoration in MRA. Technical Report KUL/ESAT/MI2/9603, Laboratory for Medical Imaging Research (ESAT-Radiology), K.U.Leuven, Belgium, 1996.
19. R.H. Swendsen, J.S. Wang. Nonuniversal critical dynamics in Monte Carlo simulations. *Physical Review Letters*, 58(2):86–88, January 1987.

Noniterative Manipulation of Discrete Energy-Based Models for Image Analysis

Patrick Pérez and Jean-Marc Laferté

IRISA/INRIA
Campus de Beaulieu, F-35042 Rennes cedex, France.

tel: (+33) 2.99.84.72.73
fax: (+33) 2.99.84.71.71

e-mail : perez@irisa.fr, laferte@irisa.fr

Abstract. With emphasis on the graph structure of energy-based models devoted to image analysis, we investigate efficient procedures for sampling and inferring. We show that triangulated graphs, whom trees are simple instances of, always support causal models for which noniterative procedures can be devised to minimize the energy, to extract probabilistic descriptions, to sample from corresponding prior and posterior distributions, or to infer from local marginals. The relevance and efficiency of these procedures are illustrated for image restoration problems.

1 Introduction and background

Many issues of image analysis can be modeled and coped with by designing an *energy* function $U(x, y)$ which captures the interaction between the unknown variables $x = (x_i)_i$ to be estimated, and the observed variables –the measurements or data–, $y = (y_j)_j$. Such an energetic modeling is encountered both in Markov random fields (MRFs)-based approaches and partial differential equations (PDEs)-based approaches. In the former class of approaches x and y are random vectors and the energy function is naturally related to the *posterior distribution* through $P(x|y) \propto \exp\{-U(x, y)\}$.

An important ingredient of functions usually used is their decomposition as a sum of simple *interaction potentials* depending just on a few "neighboring" variables. This key notion of local functional dependencies is naturally captured by defining an *independence graph* associated to U. This graph structure turns out to be a powerful tool to account for important local and global structural properties of the model. As we shall see, in some specific cases it suffices to deduce *causality* properties, thus allowing the design of *efficient* estimation algorithms. This paper is particularly dedicated to the exploration of this type of situations in case of discrete models (i.e., x_i's take values in a finite set).

After the specification of an energetic model, one deals with the problem of actually inferring the "best" estimate of x given y, relative to a criterion to be devised. In case of discrete models, there exist two standard estimators stemming from Bayesian estimation theory. The *maximum a posteriori* (MAP) estimator which is the most widely used, makes the best estimate of the most probable x given y: $\hat{x} = \arg\max_x \mathsf{P}(x|y) = \arg\min_x U(x, y)$; In contrast, the so-called MPM (for *marginal posterior modes*) defines site-wise estimate at vertex i as the most probable given y : $\forall\, i$, $\hat{x}_i = \arg\max_{x_i} \mathsf{P}(x_i|y)$.

For most energy-based models suitable for image analysis problems, the use of these common estimators requires to devise deterministic or stochastic iterative algorithms that exploit the locality of the model to get tractable single-step computations, but which, in turn, result in a very slow propagation of information. As a consequence, these iterative procedures may converge very slowly. This motivates the search for specific models allowing noniterative or efficient inference.

In this spirit, *causal* models have been already thoroughly studied [3, 4, 6, 7, 14, 15]. As we shall recall later, they usually rely on a purely probabilistic causality concept that is captured by the factorization of $\mathsf{P}(x)$ in terms of *causal transition kernels*.

We examine here the causality from a more graphical point of view, in order to identify causal models *at first sight*, based on simple characteristics of the independence graph of the model. We then explain how noniterative two-sweep algorithms can be devised on particular graph structures whose simplest instances are *trees*. On trees, the general setting we intend to develop here is very much related to discrete classification models by Bouman *et al.* [2] and by Laferté *et al.* [11]. It is also formally similar to Gaussian models on trees designed by Chou *et al* in seminal papers [9] and which have been applied to various image processing problems (optical flow estimation [12], texture analysis [13], remote sensing [5]).

2   Independence graph

Let choose for the moment a general notational setting in which all the variables (observed or not) of the problem are gathered into a single vector $z = (z_i)_{i=1}^n$ associated to an energy function $U(z)$. An important characteristic of the energy function is its usual decomposition as a sum of local terms

$$U(z) = \sum_{c \in C} v_c(z_c),$$

where elements of C are "small" subsets of indices (usually one or two), and the *interaction potential* v_c only depends on $z_c \triangleq (z_i)_{i \in c}$. Equivalently, the joint distribution *factorizes* into a product of positive *factor potentials* :

$$\mathsf{P}(z) \propto \prod_c g_c(z_c),$$

where $g_c \triangleq \exp\{-v_c\}$. The interaction structure such introduced is conveniently captured by a graph:

> Definition: the independence graph associated to energy function $U(z) = \sum_c v_c(z_c)$ is the simple undirected graph $\mathbb{G} = [S, \mathcal{N}]$ with vertex set $S = \{1, \dots, n\}$, and neighborhood system $\mathcal{N} = (n(i))_i$ defined as: $j \in n(i) \Leftrightarrow i \in n(j) \Leftrightarrow \exists c \in \mathcal{C} : \{i, j\} \subset c$.

As a consequence of this definition, elements of $\mathcal{C}$ are *cliques* of $\mathbb{G}$ (i.e., complete subgraphs of $\mathbb{G}$). The vertex set $n(i)$ contains the neighbors of i in $\mathbb{G}$.

The *key* probabilistic information conveyed by $\mathbb{G}$ is an independence relation lying within the *absence* of edge between two sites. Indeed, one can easily show that if i and j are not neighbors, then random variables z_i and z_j are *independent given all the remaining variables*:

$$P(z_i, z_j | z_{S-\{i,j\}}) = P(z_i | z_{S-\{i,j\}}) P(z_j | z_{S-\{i,j\}}).$$

This probabilistic statement constitutes the **pairwise Markov property**. To prove it, it suffices to note that posterior distribution factorizes into a product of two functions, one of which *not* depending on z_i, and the other one not depending on z_j. More generally, one can prove the following **Global Markov property**: If a vertex subset a separates two other disjoint subsets b and d in $\mathbb{G}$ (i.e., all chains from $i \in b$ to $j \in d$ intersect a), then random vectors z_b and z_d are independent given z_a: $P(z_b, z_d | z_a) = P(z_b | z_a) \times P(z_d | z_a)$.

When handling an energy-based model, one might extensively use two "mechanisms": *(i)* **Summing out:** to compute probabilistic quantities or distributions, one has to sum $\exp\{-U(z)\}$ over all possible values of one or several variables, which then "disappear" from the model; *(ii)* **Maximizing out:** when dealing with MAP estimation, the global maximization of $\exp\{-U(z)\}$ is often performed through coordinate-wise maximizations (i.e., w.r.t. a few variables at a time). As it turns out, these two operations i and ii result in the same structural transformations of independence graphs.

Namely, for some subset $a \subset S$, the summation or the maximization of $\exp\{-U(z)\}$ w.r.t. to $z_{\bar{a}}$ (where $\bar{a} = S - a$) generally results in turning complete the neighborhood of each connected component of $\bar{a}$. In case $\bar{a}$ reduces to a singleton $\{i\}$, the neighbors of i become mutually neighboring through summation or maximization of the joint distribution w.r.t. z_i (see Fig. 1). Let us briefly sketch the proof in this particular case. Since $n(i)$ separates i from the rest, $P(z)$ factorizes as

$$P(z) \propto g_a(z_a) g_i(z_i, z_{n(i)}),$$

where $S = a \cup \{i\}$. As a consequence:

$$\sum_{z_i} P(z) \propto g_a(z_a) \times \underbrace{\sum_{z_i} g_i(z_i, z_{n(i)})}_{\triangleq G_i(z_{n(i)})}, \tag{1}$$

$$\max_{z_i} P(z) = g_a(z_a) \times \underbrace{\max_{z_i} g_i(z_i, z_{n(i)})}_{\triangleq \mathcal{G}_i(z_{n(i)})} + \mathrm{cst}. \tag{2}$$

This means that, in both cases, the components of $z_{n(i)}$ become *in general* mutually dependent through functions G_i or $\mathcal{G}_i$.

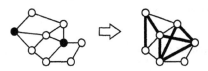

Fig. 1. Appearance of new edges in summing or maximizing out variables on • vertices.

This, of course, remains a *graphical* viewpoint. Depending on the analytical form of original distribution, simplifications (factorization, or actual dependence on less variables) may occur either in G_i or in $\mathcal{G}_i$, thus reducing the actual number of appearing edges (if any). Such simplifications occur with causal models, as we shall see. However, it is very unlikely that simplifications simultaneously occur in both G_i and $\mathcal{G}_i$.

3 Causality and graphs

The concept of causality relies on an ordering of sites (from 1 to n), and expresses that the conditional distribution of a component z_i given its "past" $\mathrm{pa}(i) \triangleq \{1, \ldots, i-1\}$ reduces to the conditional distribution given a "small" neighborhood in the past:

$$\forall i > 1, \ P(z_i | z_{i-1}, \ldots, z_1) = P(z_i | z_{\tilde{n}(i)}), \tag{3}$$

where $\tilde{n}(i) \subset \mathrm{pa}(i)$ is a small subset of i's past. If (3) holds, the distribution of $(z_1, \ldots, z_k)$, for any k takes the following remarkable factorized form:

$$P(z_1, \ldots, z_k) = \prod_{i=1}^{k} P(z_i | z_{\tilde{n}(i)}), \tag{4}$$

where, for notational convenience, we let $\tilde{n}(1) = \emptyset$, which means that $z_{\tilde{n}(1)}$ has to be ignored. There are no unknown normalizing constants within the joint distribution (4), and a noniterative forward recursive sampling of this Markov chain-type distribution can be easily performed.

As for practical use of the nice properties offered by causality, the following design problem has to be addressed: the set of sites S being ordered, how to design an energy function $U(z) = \sum_c v_c(z_c)$, with independence graph $\mathbb{G} = [S, \mathcal{N}]$, such that random vector z with distribution $P(z) \propto \exp\{-U(z)\} = \prod_c g_c(z)$ is causal with *small* past neighborhoods. By successively considering marginals of vectors $z_{\mathsf{pa}(n)}, z_{\mathsf{pa}(n-1)}, \cdots, z_1$, one can establish two ways of getting such a *local causality*. Before we detail them, note that $\prod_c g_c$ can be rearranged as $\prod_i g_i$, where g_i is the product of g_c's for all cliques containing i and no further site: $g_i \overset{\triangle}{=} \prod_{c:\max c=i} g_c$. Then g_i depends on $(z_i, z_{\mathsf{n}(i) \cap \mathsf{pa}(i)})$ only. By convention $g_i \equiv 1$ if no clique c verifies $\max c = i$.

3.1 Functional characterization

As explained in §2, the summation of $\prod_i g_i$ w.r.t. z_n makes all sites of $\mathsf{n}(n) \cap \mathsf{pa}(n) = \mathsf{n}(n)$ mutually neighbors through function $G_n(z_{\mathsf{n}(n)}) \overset{\triangle}{=} \sum_{z_n} g_n(z_n, z_{\mathsf{n}(n)})$, *except if this function drastically simplifies*. If it collapses into a constant, then no new edge appears through summing out z_n, and random vector $z_{\mathsf{pa}(n)}$ has joint distribution proportional to $\prod_{i=1\ldots n-1} g_i$ whose independence graph is simply the *subgraph* generated by $\mathbb{G}$ on $\mathsf{pa}(n)$. By repeating the argument according to a backward induction, one obtains the following characterization of causality [8]:

$$\forall i, \quad \sum_{z_i} g_i(z_i, z_{\mathsf{n}(i) \cap \mathsf{pa}(i)}) \equiv k_i \text{ (constant).} \tag{5}$$

The model then verifies (3) with past neighborhoods $\tilde{\mathsf{n}}(i) = \mathsf{n}(i) \cap \mathsf{pa}(i)$ which are small for $\mathsf{n}(i)$'s are. This way to introducing causality is at the heart of the so-called *unilateral, mutually compatible* or *recursive* MRFs [3, 6, 8]. The marginal $P(z_1)$ and the *causal transition kernels* (and consequently *exact* factorized distributions) are easily obtained:

$$P(z_1) = \frac{g_1(z_1)}{k_1}, \ P(z_i|z_{\tilde{\mathsf{n}}(i)}) = \frac{g_i(z_i, z_{\tilde{\mathsf{n}}(i)})}{k_i},$$
$$\text{and } P(z_1, \ldots, z_k) = \prod_{i=1}^k \frac{g_i(z_i, z_{\tilde{\mathsf{n}}(i)})}{k_i}.$$

As we already said, this causal probabilistic decomposition allows to recursively draw samples from $P(z)$, starting from node 1. However, in the prospect of MAP estimation, there is no reason for the maximization counterpart of (5) to hold on corresponding functions $\mathcal{G}_i \overset{\triangle}{=} \max_{z_i} g_i$.

3.2 Graphical characterization

Graphical considerations will allow to circumvent the aforementioned limitations of general causality. First return to function $G_n(z_{\mathsf{n}(n)})$ that possibly makes new edges appear. A simple graphical way to prevent from this structural change is to consider $n(n)$ is *already complete*. As a consequence random vector $z_{pa(n)}$ exhibits the *subgraph* generated by $\mathbb{G}$ on $pa(n)$ as independence graph. Its joint distribution is proportional to $\prod_{i=1\ldots n-1} g_i \times G_n$. Let $\overline{n} \triangleq \max n(n)$ be the "greater" vertex of $n(n)$. Function G_n depends on $z_{n(n)}$ where $n(n) \subset n(\overline{n}) \cap pa(\overline{n}) \cup \{\overline{n}\}$, since $n(n)$ is complete. Therefore G_n can be seen as "aggregated" to $g_{\overline{n}}$ in the joint distribution of $z_{pa(n)}$: $g_{\overline{n}} \leftarrow g_{\overline{n}} \times G_n$. We can start again with reduced vector $z_{pa(n)}$. By repeating the *graphical* argument according to a backward induction, one obtains the following sufficient characterization of causality [1]:

$$\forall i,\ n(i) \cap pa(i) \text{ is complete in } \mathbb{G}. \tag{6}$$

Fig. 2 shows a graph which satisfies this condition w.r.t. the indicated site ordering (other orderings were possible). *Any* energy function of six variables admitting this graph as its independence graph defines a causal model (i.e., verifying (3)) with past neighborhoods generated by $\mathcal{N}$ as: $\forall i, \tilde{n}(i) = n(i) \cap pa(i)$.

Let us make more precise the recursion behind the above induction. Functions G_i's are recursively defined for all i as:

$$G_i(z_{\tilde{n}(i)}) = \begin{cases} \sum_{z_i} g_i(z_i, z_{\tilde{n}(i)}), & \text{if } \underline{i} = \emptyset \\ \sum_{z_i} [g_i(z_i, z_{\tilde{n}(i)}) \prod_{j \in \underline{i}} G_j(z_{\tilde{n}(j)})], \\ \quad \text{otherwise}, \end{cases} \tag{7}$$

where $\underline{i} \triangleq \{j \in S : \max \tilde{n}(j) = i\}$. One can show that (6) along with the connectedness of $\mathbb{G}$ ensures that $\tilde{n}(i) \neq \emptyset$, $\forall i > 1$ (therefore $\bar{\imath} \triangleq \max \tilde{n}(i)$ exists). In this case, it clearly turns out that one deals with an *upward recursion on a tree structure* $T_{\mathbb{G}}$ defined as: $\forall i > 1$, its father is $\bar{\imath}$ and its child set is $\underline{i}$. The root is vertex 1. The nodes for which $\underline{i} = \emptyset$ (the first to be considered) are the *leaves*. The relevant recursive structure for defining algorithms is not anymore the ordering of sites, but the underlying tree structure which can be defined if (6) holds.

The root prior distribution and transition kernels are then obtained:

$$P(z_1) = \frac{g_1(z_1)}{G_1} \prod_{j \in \underline{1}} G_j(z_1), \quad P(z_i | z_{\tilde{n}(i)}) = \frac{g_i}{G_i} \prod_{j \in \underline{i}} G_j,$$

from which the normalized joint distribution is deduced. From §2, we know that the completeness of $\tilde{n}(i)$'s ensures that the *maximization counterpart* of these derivations exists as well. It yields a noniterative way to find energy minimizers, as we shall see later in particular cases. Also, the upward recursive definition (7) holds both for prior model ($z \equiv x$) and for posterior model ($z \equiv x|y$) [2]. In the later case, it allows either to compute (and sample) posterior distribution, or

---

[1] In the course of the recursion, others G_i's (if any) such that $\max n(i) \cap pa(i) = \overline{n}$ will similarly "aggregate" to $g_{\overline{n}}$.

[2] In these cases, we shall change notation G_i into F_i and $\mathbb{F}_i$ respectively.

to compute (and maximize) local posterior marginals, within a single downward sweep.

A nice result shows that the graphs for which exists an ordering of sites verifying (6) are *triangulated* (or *chordal*), i.e. they contain no cycles of length ≥ 4 without a chord. This is obviously the case of graph in Fig. 2. A complete proof can be found in [16].

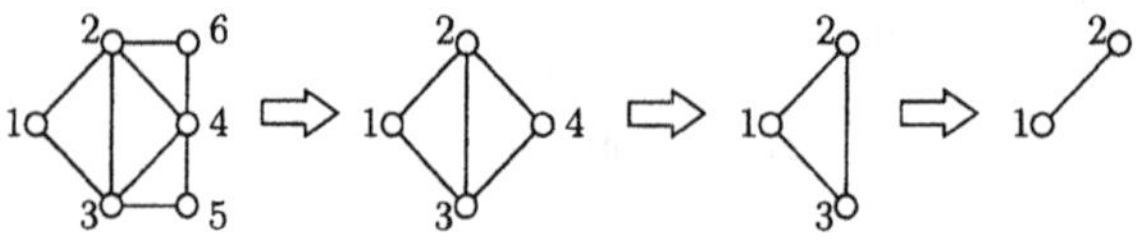

Fig. 2. Example of graph supporting *causal* energy-based models and subgraphs obtained by summing out (or maximizing out) (z_5, z_6), z_4, and z_3 successively.

The functional characterization of causality is the most general, but necessitates the prior definition of a site ordering and of all transition probabilities (up to multiplicative constants). It therefore relies on potential forms more than on structural information. Besides, it is strongly related to the ordering originally defined. A new causal representation w.r.t. another ordering of sites is not possible in general.

The second viewpoint is associated to a class of special graphical models. It thus allows to identify at first glance graphical structures which *always* support causal models, without need of any computational or probabilistic argument. The use of such independence graph structures will give access to noniterative sampling, energy minimization, posterior marginal computation and normalization constant computation. In particular, for *any compatible ordering* (there are several of them in general), one can get back to the classical causal representation (4) based on transition kernels, by means of simple noniterative computations. This probabilistic representation which can be derived afterward is used for noniterative sampling and marginal computation/maximization.

In the following, we will focus on particular case of *trees*. They are triangulated for they don't have cycles by definition. For them, each $ñ(i)$ reduces to a singleton with the *parent* of i, and $\mathbb{G} \equiv T_{\mathbb{G}}$ obviously.

4   Models on trees

Consider a model defined on a tree as:

$$\exp\{-U(x,y)\} = \prod_i f_i(x_i, x_{\bar{i}}) h_i(y_i, x_i),$$

with $\sum_{y_i} h_i(y_i, x_i) \equiv m_i$. This means that $P(y|x) = \prod_i P(y_i|x_i) = \prod_i \frac{h_i(y_i,x_i)}{m_i}$ and $P(x) \propto \prod_i f_i$. Recall $\bar{\imath}$ denotes the unique parent of i (with convention $\bar{1} = \emptyset$, and $x_{\bar{1}}$ having to be ignored) and $\underline{i}$ is the set of i's children. Also introduce *ancestor* site set $\bar{\bar{\imath}}$ composed of sites of the chain between i and 1 (except i itself) and *descendant* site set $\underline{\underline{i}} \triangleq \{j : i \in \bar{\bar{\jmath}}\}$ (see Fig. 3).

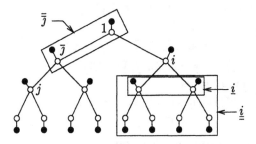

Fig. 3. Independence graph whose prior component is a (dyadic) tree: o vertices are for x_i's while • vertices are for pointwise measurements y_i's.

As in (7) (with $z \equiv x$, $\tilde{n}(i) = \{\bar{\imath}\}$, and appropriate changes of notations) we can recursively define functions F_i's. The causal probabilistic specification of the prior model is then obtained:

$$P(x_i|x_{\bar{\imath}}) = \frac{f_i(x_i, x_{\bar{\imath}})}{F_i(x_{\bar{\imath}})} \prod_{j \in \underline{i}} F_j(x_i), \text{ and } P(x) = \frac{1}{F_1} \prod_i f_i.$$

This allows to easily draw sample from the prior distribution according to a root-to-leaves recursive procedure.

4.1 Leaves-to-root maximizations

Using maximization instead of summation in the upward scheme provides a two-sweep Viterbi-like method to globally maximize energy $U(x, y)$ w.r.t. x. The maximization counterpart of (7) provides function $\mathcal{F}_i$'s which, in this case, "collect" dependencies to more and more data as the recursion proceeds: $\mathcal{F}_i$ not only depends on $x_{\bar{\imath}}$, but also on $(y_i, y_{\underline{i}}) \triangleq y_i^+$.

The maximizer (i.e., MAP estimate) has then to be recovered component by component according to a downward recursion where one has simply to read look-up tables built during the previous sweep:

> **Two-sweep MAP computation on a tree**
> ▲ upward sweep
> Leaves
> $$\begin{cases} \mathcal{F}_i(x_{\bar{\imath}}, y_i) = \max_{x_i} h_i(y_i, x_i) f_i(x_i, x_{\bar{\imath}}) \\ x_i^*(x_{\bar{\imath}}, y_i) = \arg\max_{x_i} h_i f_i \end{cases}$$
> Recursion
> $$\begin{cases} \mathcal{F}_i(x_{\bar{\imath}}, y_{\underline{i}}^+) = \max_{x_i} h_i f_i \prod_{j \in \underline{i}} \mathcal{F}_j(x_i, y_{\underline{j}}^+) \\ x_i^*(x_{\bar{\imath}}, y_{\underline{i}}^+) = \arg\max_{x_i} h_i f_i \prod_{j \in \underline{i}} \mathcal{F}_j \end{cases}$$
> Root
> $$\begin{cases} \mathcal{F}_1(y) = \max_{x_1} h_1 f_1 \prod_{j \in \underline{1}} \mathcal{F}_j(x_1, y_{\underline{j}}^+) \\ x_1^*(y) = \arg\max_{x_1} h_1 f_1 \prod_{j \in \underline{1}} \mathcal{F}_j \end{cases}$$
> ▼ downward sweep
> $$\hat{x}_1 = x_1^*(y) \text{ and } \forall i > 1, \ \hat{x}_i = x_i^*(\hat{x}_{\bar{\imath}}, y_{\underline{i}}^+)$$

4.2 Leaves-to-root summing given data

A similar two-sweep procedure can be devised to exactly compute MPM estimate. Let us start with introducing $x_{\bar{\imath}}$ within local posterior marginal $P(x_i|y)$:

$$\forall i > 1, \ P(x_i|y) = \sum_{x_{\bar{\imath}}} P(x_i|x_{\bar{\imath}}, y) P(x_{\bar{\imath}}|y), \tag{8}$$

where $P(x_i|x_{\bar{\imath}}, y) = P(x_i|x_{\bar{\imath}}, y_{\underline{i}}^+)$ due to separation property. This makes appear a *downward recursion*, provided that the posterior marginal at root, $P(x_1|y)$, and the posterior transition probabilities $P(x_i|x_{\bar{\imath}}, y_{\underline{i}}^+)$ are available. This is achieved by a *previous upward sweep* corresponding to successively summing out x_i's from leaves to vertex 1, as in (7) for $z \equiv x|y$ (i.e., $\forall i, \ g_i \equiv h_i f_i$) and $\tilde{n}(i) = \{\bar{\imath}\}$, yielding functions $\mathbb{F}_i$'s. The Markov chain-type representation is then obtained as with prior model:

$$P(x_i|x_{\bar{\imath}}, y) = P(x_i|x_{\bar{\imath}}, y_{\underline{i}}^+) = \frac{h_i f_i}{\mathbb{F}_i(x_{\bar{\imath}}, y_{\underline{i}}^+)} \prod_{j \in \underline{i}} \mathbb{F}_j(x_i, y_{\underline{j}}^+),$$
$$\text{and } P(x|y) = \frac{1}{\mathbb{F}_1(y)} \prod_i h_i(y_i, x_i) f_i(x_i, x_{\bar{\imath}}). \tag{9}$$

A noniterative sampling from the posterior distribution can be performed thanks to this probabilistic representation. Also the joint likelihood of data $P(y)$ is accessible: from $P(y|x) = \prod_i \frac{h_i(y_i, x_i)}{m_i}$, $P(x) = \frac{1}{F_1} \prod_{i>1} f(x_i, x_{\bar{\imath}})$ and $P(x|y)$ given above, it comes $P(y) = \frac{\mathbb{F}_1(y)}{F_1 \times \prod_i m_i}$.

The upward sweep computing $\mathbb{F}_i$'s provides the necessary ingredients for the downward recursion (8). We end up with the following two-sweep procedure:

> **Two-sweep MPM computation on a tree**
>
> ▲ downward sweep
>
> Initialization
> $$\mathbb{F}_i(x_{\bar{\imath}}, y_i) = \sum_{x_i} h_i(y_i, x_i) f_i(x_i, x_{\bar{\imath}})$$
>
> Recursion
> $$\mathbb{F}_i(x_{\bar{\imath}}, y_{\underline{i}}^+) = \sum_{x_i} h_i(y_i, x_i) f_i(x_i, x_{\bar{\imath}}) \prod_{j \in \underline{i}} \mathbb{F}_j(x_i, y_{\underline{j}}^+)$$
>
> Root
> $$\mathbb{F}_1(y) = \sum_{x_1} h_1(y_1, x_1) f_1(x_1) \prod_{j \in \underline{1}} \mathbb{F}_j(x_1, y_{\underline{j}}^+)$$
>
> ▼ downward sweep
>
> Initialization
> $$P(x_1|y) = \frac{h_1(y_1, x_1)}{\mathbb{F}_1(y)} \prod_{j \in \underline{1}} \mathbb{F}_j(x_1, y_{\underline{j}}^+)$$
>
> Recursion
> $$P(x_i|y) = \sum_{x_{\bar{\imath}}} P(x_{\bar{\imath}}|y) \frac{h_i(y_i, x_i) f_i(x_i, x_{\bar{\imath}})}{\mathbb{F}_i(x_{\bar{\imath}}, y_{\underline{i}}^+)} \prod_{j \in \underline{i}} \mathbb{F}_j(x_i, y_{\underline{j}}^+)$$
>
> Leaves
> $$P(x_i|y) = \sum_{x_{\bar{\imath}}} P(x_{\bar{\imath}}|y) \frac{h_i(y_i, x_i) f_i(x_i, x_{\bar{\imath}})}{\mathbb{F}_i(x_{\bar{\imath}}, y_{\underline{i}}^+)}$$

where the MPM estimates are obtained within the top-down part by maximizing the sitewise posterior marginals obtained.

It is interesting noting that Bouman *et al.* [2] define a very similar noniterative estimator on tree structure. Starting from an original Bayesian estimator they call "sMAP", devised to improve MAP estimates, they obtain a downward recursive *approximation* of it which goes as follows:

$$\hat{x}_1 \approx \arg\max_{x_1} P(x_1|y),$$
$$\hat{x}_i \approx \arg\max_{x_i} P(y_{\underline{i}}^+|x_i) P(x_i|\hat{x}_{\bar{\imath}}) \tag{10}$$
$$= \arg\max_{x_i} P(x_i|\hat{x}_{\bar{\imath}}, y_{\underline{i}}^+), \ \forall i > 1,$$

where the partial data likelihoods $P(y_{\underline{i}}^+|x_i)$ are computed within a previous upward sweep, similar to the one we have just described. At root, their estimator actually provides the MPM estimate. As for the estimates at other sites, the influence of observations which are not on descendants is simply replaced by the dependency with respect to the parent variable, set at its optimal value already computed. This inference scheme can be plugged into our two-sweep procedures to produce an alternate estimator close to MPM, that we could refer as to *"semi-*MPM*"*. Note that the corresponding (exact) top-down recursive estimation is formally very similar to the one of the MAP estimation: in both cases, the estimate at a site is obtained by maximizing a function of the estimated value on the parent vertex (contrary to MPM estimation).

Table 1 gathers in a structured and synthetic way the different two-sweep procedures presented so far, but within the general setting of triangulated graphs (i.e., not necessarily with $\tilde{n}(i)$ reducing to an unique parent node): it concerns a discrete energy-base model with triangulated independence graph and $\exp\{-U(x, y)\} = \prod_{i>1} f_i(x_i, x_{\tilde{n}(i)}) \times \prod_i h_i(y_i, x_i)$, with $\sum_{x_i} h_i(y_i, x_i) = m_i$. Note however that for sake of simplicity, downward recursions (indicated with a black symbol) which would require summations over possible values of past neighborhood, i.e., w.r.t. $x_{\bar{n}(i)}$, are only written down for a tree, when $\tilde{n}(i)$ reduces to $\{\bar{\imath}\}$.

Apart from providing a practical reference summary of the different noniterative computations on these models, this table allows to emphasize the profound similarity of these procedures.

5   Experimental results

To demonstrate the practicability and the relevance of the causal models we have presented, for low level image analysis problems, we report experimental results in case of two level restoration of noisy images. We built two versions of a 256×256 image involving uniform dark geometrical patterns of different shapes and sizes, before a uniform light background. The first one is a binary image (luminance 1 for the background and 0 for the patterns) which has been corrupted by 20% (resp. 30 %) of "channel noise". The second version is a gray level image (luminance 80 for the patterns and 160 in the background) which has been corrupted by a Gaussian white noise of standard deviation 50 (resp. 110). See Fig. 4.

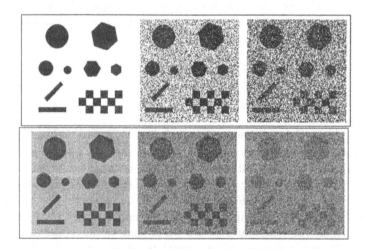

Fig. 4. Original 256×256 binary and gray level images, and their noisy versions.

The restoration model we used is based on a standard quadtree as for its independence graph, with the 256×256 leaves fitting the pixels of the image to restore. The same simple energy function has been chosen for both experiments:

$$U(x,y) = \sum_{i>1} \frac{\alpha}{4^{d(i)}} \|x_i - x_{\bar{\imath}}\|^2 + \sum_i \beta \|y_i - x_i\|^2 \qquad (11)$$

▲ Upward sweep ▲

leaves	$\mathbb{F}_i(x_{\tilde{n}(i)}) = \sum_{x_i} f_i$	$\mathcal{F}_i(x_{\tilde{n}(i)}, y_i) = \max_{x_i} h_i f_i$
recursion	$\mathbb{F}_i(x_{\tilde{n}(i)}) = \sum_{x_i} f_i \prod_{j\in\underline{i}} F_j(x_{\tilde{n}(j)})$	$\mathcal{F}_i(x_{\tilde{n}(i)}, y_{\underline{i}}^+) = \max_{x_i} h_i f_i \prod_{j\in\underline{i}} \mathcal{F}_j(x_{\tilde{n}(j)}, y_{\underline{i}}^+)$
root	$\mathbb{F}_1 = \sum_{x_1} \prod_{j\in\underline{1}} F_j(x_1)$	$\mathcal{F}_1(y) = \max_{x_1} h_1 \prod_{j\in\underline{1}} \mathcal{F}_j(x_1, y_{\underline{i}}^+)$

▼ Downward sweep ▼

	Prior sampling □ / Prior marginals $(\tilde{n}(i) = \{i\})$ ■	Posterior sampling ◇ / Semi MPM inference ○	Posterior marginals $(\tilde{n}(i) = \{\hat{z}\})$ ◆ / MPM inference $(\tilde{n}(i) = \{\hat{z}\})$ •	MAP inference
root	$\square\blacksquare\ \mathrm{P}(x_1) = \dfrac{1}{\mathbb{F}_1} \prod_{j\in\underline{1}} F_j(x_1)$	$\diamond\blacklozenge\ \mathrm{P}(x_1\mid y) = \dfrac{h_1}{\mathbb{F}_1(y)} \prod_{j\in\underline{1}} \mathbb{F}_j(x_1, y_{\underline{i}}^+)$ $\circ\bullet\ \hat{x}_1 = \arg\max_{x_1} h_1 \prod_{j\in\underline{1}} \mathbb{F}_j(x_1, y_{\underline{i}}^+)$		$\hat{x}_1 = \arg\max_{x_1} h_1 \prod_{j\in\underline{1}} \mathcal{F}_j(x_1, y_{\underline{i}}^+)$
recursion	$\square\ \mathrm{P}(x_i\mid x_{\tilde{n}(i)}) = \dfrac{f_i}{\mathbb{F}_i} \prod_{j\in\underline{i}} F_j$ $\blacksquare\ \mathrm{P}(x_i) = \sum_{x_{\underline{i}}} \mathrm{P}(x_{\underline{i}}) \dfrac{f_i}{\mathbb{F}_i} \prod_{j\in\underline{i}} F_j$	$\diamond\ \mathrm{P}(x_i\mid x_{\tilde{n}(i)}, y_{\underline{i}}^+) = \dfrac{h_i f_i}{\mathbb{F}_i} \prod_{j\in\underline{i}} \mathbb{F}_j$ $\circ\ \hat{x}_i = \arg\max_{x_i} h_i f_i \prod_{j\in\underline{i}} \mathbb{F}_j$ with $x_{\tilde{n}(i)} = \hat{x}_{\tilde{n}(i)}$	$\blacklozenge\ \mathrm{P}(x_i\mid y) = \sum_{x_{\underline{i}}} \mathrm{P}(x_{\underline{i}}\mid y) \dfrac{h_i f_i}{\mathbb{F}_i} \prod_{j\in\underline{i}} \mathbb{F}_j$ $\bullet\ \hat{x}_i = \arg\max_{x_i} \sum_{x_{\underline{i}}} \mathrm{P}(x_{\underline{i}}\mid y) h_i f_i \prod_{j\in\underline{i}} \mathbb{F}_j$	$\hat{x}_i = \arg\max_{x_i} h_i f_i \prod_{j\in\underline{i}} \mathcal{F}_j$ with $x_{\tilde{n}(i)} = \hat{x}_{\tilde{n}(i)}$

Table 1.

where α and β are two positive parameters, and $d(i)$ denotes the graph distance of vertex i to the root: $d(1) = 0$, and $d(i) = 8$ for leaves, in these experiments. The *a priori* energy term corresponds to an Ising-type prior encouraging likeness of children with parents. The particular weighting according to the "resolution" level (averaging w.r.t. to the number of vertices of the level) is reminiscent of the Gaussian fractal prior defined on quadtrees in [12] and used in [5]. It has proved to be also well suited for our discrete modeling.

On the four noisy images we compared the three noniterative inference procedures on the quadtree, and the iterative ICM algorithm running on the spatial counterpart of energy (11). The restored images are shown in Fig. 5 and Fig. 6 [3] while Table 2 indicates the corresponding amount of discrepancy relative to original images.

	quadtree			2d grid
	MAP	sMPM	MPM	ICM
binary, $p = 0.2$	2.5	2.7	2.4	1.5
binary, $p = 0.3$	4.3	4.3	3.7	6.6
gray level, $\sigma = 50$	2.4	2.4	3.2	1.0
gray level, $\sigma = 110$	4.6	4.5	5.9	7.1

Table 2. Comparative percentages of misclassification.

In both binary and gray level restoration experiments, the three noniterative estimates provide good results: they do slightly less well than iterative ICM for low degradation, but they keep on doing well when noise level increases, contrary to ICM whose performances notably decrease.

The three estimators thus seem quite robust to noise for this particular application. A closer look at results show that quadtree-based MAP and semi-MPM estimators behave in a very similar way, with a lighter computational load for the former. The quadtree-based MPM estimator, which is more expensive that two others, allows a better binary restoration, while it provides results of inferior quality for gray level image restoration.

Another particular aspect of MPM estimator, is that is naturally provides a measure of relative *confidence* at each site, through the numerical value of the probabilities $P(\hat{x}_i|y)$. Fig. 7 shows these "confidence maps". It clearly appears that the locations of reduced confidence loosely demarcate the contours of the image. These confidence measures, reminiscent of error covariance matrices of Gaussian models on trees [12], can be useful for a better appreciation and use of obtained estimates.

Visually, the restoration provided by the three noniterative estimators exhibit a "blocky" aspect, reminding the underlying prior quadtree structure. In the

---

[3] semi-MPM estimates which are *extremely similar* to MAP restorations are actually not displayed.

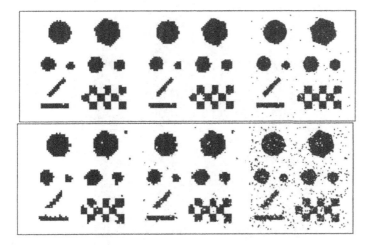

Fig. 5. From left to right: MAP, MPM estimates on the quadtree, and ICM iterative estimate on the pixel grid, for the restoration of the two binary noisy images.

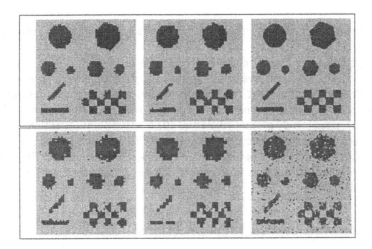

Fig. 6. From left to right: MAP, MPM estimates on the quadtree, and ICM iterative estimate on the pixel grid, for the restoration of the two noisy gray level images.

check region (lower right part of images) one can see that the amount of such artifact depends on the relative location of spatial patterns with respect to the block partition induced on the pixel grid by the quadtree. Also, these artifacts are more apparent in the restoration of more noisy images, where the role of quadtree-based prior has to be enforced to get rid of noise. In the prospect of parameter estimation, this is not a serious problem, provided that the overall estimate is good (i.e., the percentage of misclassification is low). However, if the visual rendering of the estimate is at the heart of the concerned application, a

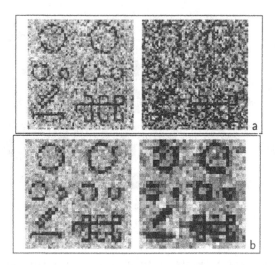

Fig. 7. "Confidence maps" for restoration (a) of binary images, and (b) of gray level images.

single ICM smoothing sweep suffices to remove the "blockyness" at reasonable cost.

As regards computational complexity, the noniterative nature of the two-sweep procedures we have presented results in a *fixed complexity per site*. In other words, they exhibit an $\mathcal{O}(n)$ complexity. We experimentally determined (using MATLAB implementations) that MAP, semi-MPM, and MPM inferences are achieved with respectively around 79, 94 and 107 floating point operations (flops) per site, when x_i's can take two possible values. With a similar implementation, standard ICM estimation on bidimensional grid [1] costs around 52 flops/site, whereas the overall procedure is *iterative* with no guarantee on the required number of iterations.

6 Conclusions and further directions

In this paper, we intended to provide a comprehensive and unified picture of models on "causal graphs". We presented in detail the manipulation of such discrete models, with emphasis on (a) the use of graph theoretic concepts as tools to devise models and get insight into algorithmic procedures; (b) the profound unity which underlies the different procedures whether they compute probabilities, draw samples, or infer estimates.

In particular, we presented three generic *exact noniterative* inference algorithms devoted to models exhibiting a triangulated independence graph. On simple quadtrees, these two-sweep procedures can be suited for discrete image analysis problems such as detection, segmentation or classification. The first algorithm allows to compute the MAP estimate, and then can be set up apart from any probabilistic framework. The second one, whose aim is intrinsically probabilistic, allows to compute local posterior marginals which can be used to get the MPM estimate or to estimate parameters within an EM-like algorithm. The third one mixes, to some extent, the characteristics of the two others.

Further extensions of this study concern (i) the design of light parameter estimation procedures based on noniterative two-sweep computations, and (ii) the effective use of more complex triangulated graphs, such as augmented trees with nodes grafted on branches (thus exhibiting three vertex cycles) allowing to design *robust* energy-based model with auxiliary variables.

References

1. J. BESAG. Spatial interaction and the statistical analysis of lattice systems. *J. Royal Statist. Soc.*, 36 B:192–236, 1974.
2. C. BOUMAN and M. SHAPIRO. A multiscale image model for bayesian image segmentation. *IEEE Trans. Image Proc.*, 3(2):162–177, March 1994.
3. H. DERIN and P.A. KELLY. Discrete-index Markov-type random processes. *Proc. IEEE*, 77(10):1485–1509, 1989.
4. P.A. DEVIJVER. Real-time modeling of image sequences based on hidden Markov Mesh random field models. Technical Report M-307, Philips Research Lab., June 1989.
5. P. FIEGUTH. *Application of multiscale estimation to large scale multidimensional imaging and remote sensing problems.* PhD thesis, MIT Dept. of EECS, June 1995.
6. J. GOUTSIAS. Mutually compatible Gibbs random fields. *IEEE Trans. Information Theory*, 35(6):1233–1249, 1989.
7. J. GOUTSIAS. Unilateral approximation of Gibbs random field images. *Graph. Mod. Image Proc.*, 53:240–257, 1991.
8. J. GOUTSIAS. Markov random fileds: interacting particles systems for statistical image modeling and analysis. Technical Report JHU/ECE 96-01, The Johns Hopkins Univ., 1996.
9. A. WILLSKY K. CHOU and A. BENVENISTE. Multiscale recursive estimation, data fusion, and regularization. *IEEE Trans. Automatic Control*, 39(3):464–477, 1994.
10. J.-M. LAFERTÉ, F. HEITZ, P. PÉREZ, and E. FABRE. Hierarchical statistical models for the fusion of multiresolution image data. In *Proc. Int. Conf. Computer Vision*, Cambridge, USA, June 1995.
11. M. LUETTGEN, W. KARL, and A. WILLSKY. Efficient multiscale regularization with applications to the computation of optical flow. *IEEE Trans. Image Processing*, 3(1):41–64, 1994.
12. M. LUETTGEN and A. WILLSKY. Likelihood calculation for a class of multiscale stochastic models, with application to texture discrimination. *IEEE Trans. Image Processing*, 4(2):194–207, 1995.
13. J. MOURA and N. BALRAM. Recursive structure of noncausal Gauss-Markov random fields. *IEEE Trans. Information Theory*, 38(2):335–354, 1992.
14. D. PICKARD. Unilateral Markov fields. *Advances in Applied Probability*, 12:655–671, 1980.
15. J. WHITTAKER. *Graphical models in applied multivariate statistics.* Wiley, 1990.

Unsupervised Image Segmentation Using Markov Random Field Models

S.A.Barker and P.J.W.Rayner

Signal Processing and Communications Group,
Cambridge University Engineering Dept.,
Cambridge CB2 1PZ, England

Abstract. We present an unsupervised segmentation algorithm based on a Markov Random Field model for noisy images. The algorithm finds the the most likely number of classes, their associated model parameters and generates a corresponding segmentation of the image into these classes. This is achieved according to the MAP criterion. To facilitate this, an MCMC algorithm is formulated to allow the direct sampling of all the above parameters from the posterior distribution of the image. To allow the number of classes to be sampled, a reversible jump is incorporated into the Markov Chain. The jump enables the possible splitting and combining of classes and consequently, their associated regions within the image. Experimental results are presented showing rapid convergence of the algorithm to accurate solutions.

1 Introduction

The segmentation of noisy or textured images into a number of different regions comprises a difficult optimisation problem. This is compounded when the number of regions into which the image is to be segmented is also unknown.

If each region within an image is described by a different model class then the observed image may be viewed as a sample from a realisation of an underlying class map. Image segmentation can therefore be treated as an incomplete data problem, in which the intensity data is observed, the class map is missing and the associated class model parameters need to be estimated. In the unsupervised case, the number of model classes may also be unknown.

The unsupervised segmentation problem has been approached by several authors. [1] [7] and [8] propose algorithms comprising of two steps. The image is assumed to be composed of an unknown number of regions, each modelled as individual Markov Random Fields.

The first of these steps is a coarse segmentation of the image into the most 'likely' number of regions. This is achieved by dividing the image into windows, calculating features or estimating model parameters, then using a measure to combine closely related windows. The resulting segmentation is then used to estimate model parameters for each of the classes, before a supervised high-resolution segmentation is carried out via some form of relaxation algorithm.

A similar methodology is used in [5] but the measure used, the Kolmogorov-Smirnov distance, is a direct measure of similarity of the distributions of grayscale values (in the form of histograms) between adjacent windows. Windows are then combined into a single region if the distance between their distributions is relatively small. A variant of this algorithm [2] is based on the same distance function but the distribution of grayscales in each window is compared with the distribution functions of the samples comprising each class over the complete image. If the distribution of one class is found to be close enough to that of the window then it is designated as being a member of that class. Otherwise, a new outlier class is created. When the field stabilises, usually after several iterations, new classes are created from the outliers if they constitute more than one percent of the image. If not, the algorithm is re-run.

A split and merge algorithm is proposed in [6]. The image is initially split into large square windows but these are then re-split to form four smaller windows if a uniformity test for each window is not met. The process ends when windows as small as 4 × 4 pixels are reached. The windows are then merged to form regions using a distance measure based on the pseudo-likelihood.

In [3] segmentations and parameter estimates were obtained by alternately sampling the label field and calculating maximum pseudo likelihood estimates of the parameter values. The process was repeated over differing numbers of label classes and the resulting estimates were applied to a model fitting criteria to select the optimum number of classes and hence, the image segmentation. The criterion used compensates the likelihood of the optimised model with a penalty term that offsets image size against the number of independent model parameters used. The penalty term and its associated parameter values were selected arbitrarily.

This method of exhaustive search over a varying number of classes was developed further in [4]. An EM algorithm was first used to estimate parameters while alternately segmenting the image. To select between the resulting optimsations of the differing models the function of increasing likelihood against increasing model order was fitted to a rising exponential model. The exponential model parameters were selected in a least squares sense. The optimum model order was then found at a pre-specified knee point in the exponential curve.

The approach to unsupervised segmentation presented here comprises a Markov Chain Monte Carlo (MCMC) algorithm to sample from the posterior distribution so that simulated annealing may be used to estimate the MAP solution. This methodology is similar to that used in [13] to segment an image using a known MRF model. Here the method is extended so that the MAP estimate is over not just the segmentation of the image into classes but the number of classes and their respective model parameters.

The algorithm differs from those reviewed in that no windowing is required to estimate region model parameters. The algorithm's MCMC methodology removes the necessity for an exhaustive search over a subsection of the parameter space. This ensures an improvement in efficiency over algorithms that require a separate optimisation to be carried out for each model before a model order selection is made.

The remainder of this paper is divided as follows: section 2 specifies the image model used throughout the paper. The posterior distribution for this model is derived. Section 3 describes the algorithms employed to sample from this posterior distribution. In section 3.1 the segmentation process or allocation of class labels to pixel sites is described. Section 3.2 shows how the noise and MRF model parameters may be sampled from their conditional densities. Section 3.3 describes how reversible jumps are incorporated into the Markov Chain to enable the number of classes into which the image is to be segmented to be sampled. Experimental results of such an algorithm are presented in section 4 and the paper is concluded in section 5.

2 Image Model

Let Ω denote an $M \times N$ lattice indexed by (i, j) so that $\Omega = \{(i, j); 1 \leq i \leq M, 1 \leq j \leq N\}$. Let $Y = \{Y_s = y_s; s \in \Omega\}$ be the observed grayscale image where pixels take values from the interval $(0, 1]$. Then let $X = \{X_s = x_s; s \in \Omega\}$ correspond to the labels of the underlying Markov Random Field which have values taken from $\Lambda = \{0, 1, ..., k - 1\}$.

The neighbours of the pixel at site s are denoted η_s and the model parameter vector is denoted Ψ. If a Gibbs MRF is used to model the image, the joint conditional density for an observed pixel grayscale value and class label at site s may be expressed,

$$p(Y_s = y_s, X_s = x_s \mid \eta_s, \ \Psi) = \frac{1}{Z_s} e^{-U(Y_s=y_s, X_s=x_s|\eta_s, \ \Psi)} \tag{1}$$

where $U(\cdot)$ is the energy function and Z_s is the normalising constant or partition function of the Gibbs distribution. If we write $\Psi = [\{\Theta_c, \beta_c^{(0)}; c \in \Lambda\}, \beta^{(1)}]$, where Θ_c corresponds to the noise model parameter vector, $\beta_c^{(0)}$ to the external field parameter, and $\beta^{(1)}$ is the inter-pixel interaction strength, the Gibbs distribution may be factorised so that,

$$p(Y_s = y_s, X_s = x_s \mid \eta_s, \ \Psi) =$$
$$\frac{1}{Z_s} e^{\{-U_1(Y_s=y_s|X_s=x_s, \ \Theta_{x_s}) - U_2(X_s=x_s|\eta_s, \ \beta_{x_s}^{(0)}, \ \beta^{(1)})\}} \tag{2}$$

The partition function Z over the complete image is far too complex to evaluate, so it is unfeasible to compare the likelihoods of two differing Markov Random Field realisations. The closest one can come is to compare their Pseudo-Likelihoods [9]. The Pseudo-Likelihood, given the above described model is given,

$$PL(Y = y, X = x \mid \Psi) =$$

$$\prod_{s \in \Omega} \frac{1}{z_{x_s}(\Theta_{x_s})} \, e^{\{-U_1(Y_s=y_s \mid X_s=x_s, \, \Theta_{x_s})\}}$$

$$\times \; \frac{e^{\left\{-\sum_{s \in L} U_2(X_s=x_s \mid \eta_s, \, \beta_{x_s}^{(0)}, \, \beta^{(1)})\right\}}}{\prod_{s \in \Omega} \sum_{c \in \Lambda} e^{\left\{-U_2(X_s=c \mid \eta_s, \, \beta_c^{(0)}, \, \beta^{(1)})\right\}}} \tag{3}$$

where $z_c(\Theta_c)$ is the normalising function for the grayscale value conditional distribution. Using Bayes law, the above factorisation of the Pseudo-Likelihood and incorporating the model order k, the posterior probability for the image model may now be approximated,

$$p(X = x, \Psi, k \mid Y = y) \; \propto \; p(Y = y \mid X = x, \Theta) \, PL(X = x \mid \beta)$$

$$\times \left(\prod_{c=0}^{k-1} p_r(\Theta_c) \, p_r(\beta_c^{(0)}) \right) \tag{4}$$

$$\times \; p_r(\beta^{(1)}) \, p_r(k)$$

where $p_r(\cdot)$ are priors, β represents the parameter vector $[\beta_c^{(0)}, \beta^{(1)}; c \in \Lambda]$.

Assuming a Gaussian noise model for each of the classes, the parameter vector $\Theta_c = [\mu_c, \sigma_c]$. If a nearest neighbour Gibbs MRF is chosen to model the image, then the posterior density may be written,

$$p(X = x, \Psi, k \mid Y = y) \propto$$

$$\frac{1}{\sqrt{2\pi\sigma_{x_s}^2}} \exp\left\{ -\frac{1}{2} \sum_{s \in \Omega} \left(\frac{y_s - \mu_{x_s}}{\sigma_{x_s}} \right)^2 \right\}$$

$$\times \; \frac{\exp\left\{ -\sum_{s \in \Omega} \left(\beta_{x_s}^{(0)} + \beta^{(1)} \, V(x_s, \eta_s) \right) \right\}}{\prod_{s \in \Omega} \sum_{c \in \Lambda} \exp\left\{ -\left(\beta_c^{(0)} + \beta^{(1)} \, V(c, \eta_s) \right) \right\}} \tag{5}$$

$$\times \; p_r(\beta^{(1)}) \, p_r(k) \prod_{c \in \Lambda} p_r(\mu_c) \, p_r(\sigma_c) \, p_r(\beta_c^{(0)})$$

where $V(c, \eta_s)$ is the potential function at site s when it is allocated to class c. Throughout this paper the potential function is defined, $V(c, \eta) = \frac{1}{4} \sum_{t \in \eta} (c \oplus x_t)$, where $\oplus$ is an operator defined to take the value -1 if its arguments are equal, otherwise, $+1$.

Non-informative reference priors are chosen for the noise model parameters to ensure that the observed intensity data dominates any prior information incorporated into the model. Uniform priors are selected for $\{\mu_c, \beta_c^{(0)}; c \in \Lambda\}$ and k. For $\{\sigma_c, \forall c \in \Lambda\}$ the reference priors may be found using Jeffrey's formula for non-informative priors [10]. Normally these priors are improper, but here their range is restricted to facilitate normalisation and ensure that the model selection described later is valid.

3 MCMC Sampling from the Posterior Distribution

To obtain the MAP image segmentation via a stochastic relaxation algorithm an MCMC algorithm is used to sample from the posterior distribution.

The sampling scheme in this paper is based on the Gibbs Sampler [13] but Metropolis-Hastings sub-chains [11] are incorporated to enable the model parameters and number of classes to be sampled.

The sampling process comprises a sequential scan, updating the pixel sites and various model parameters in a specific order. The algorithm used here consists of the following moves:

(i)   re-segment the image,
(ii)   sample noise model parameters,
(iii) sample MRF model parameters,
(iv)   sample the number of classes.

These moves are described in detail in the following sections of this paper.

3.1 Image Segmentation

The conditional density functions for the allocation of pixel s to class c may be derived from equation 5,

$$p(x_s = c \mid y_s, \eta_c, \Psi_c) \propto$$

$$\frac{1}{\sqrt{2\pi\sigma_c^2 T_t}} \exp\left\{-\frac{1}{T_t}\left[\frac{1}{2}\left(\frac{y_s - \mu_c}{\sigma_c}\right)^2 + \left(\beta_c^{(0)} + \beta^{(1)} V(c, \eta_s)\right)\right]\right\}$$

$$(6)$$

where T_t is the annealing temperature at iteration t of the algorithm. Gibbs sampling is used to update the allocation of class labels to pixel sites using the above conditional density function.

3.2 Sampling Noise and MRF Model Parameters

Metropolis-Hastings samplers are used to update noise and MRF model parameters. The proposal densities used are zero mean Gaussian with variances dependent on the parameter being sampled. The conditional density function for the noise model parameters for class c is,

$$p(\mu_c, \sigma_c \mid Y,\ X) \propto \prod_{s:x_s=c} p(y_s \mid \mu_c, \sigma_c)\ p_r(\mu_c) p_r(\sigma_c)$$

$$= \frac{1}{\sigma_c\ (2\pi\sigma_c^2 T_t)^{n_c}} \exp\left\{-\frac{1}{2T_t} \sum_{s:x_s=c} \left(\frac{y_s - \mu_c}{\sigma_c}\right)^2\right\} \tag{7}$$

where $n_c = \#(s : x_s = c)$. The conditional probability density functions for the external field model parameters, $\{\beta_c^{(0)}, c \in \Lambda\}$ are given by,

$$p(\beta_c^{(0)}, c \in \Lambda \mid X)$$
$$= p(X \mid \beta_c^{(0)}, c \in \Lambda)\ p_r(\beta_c^{(0)}, c \in \Lambda)$$
$$= \prod_{(c\in\Lambda, \forall\eta)} \left(\frac{\exp\left(-\frac{1}{T_t}[\beta_c^{(0)} + \beta^{(1)}\ V(c,\eta)]\right)}{\sum_{i\in\Lambda} \exp\left(-\frac{1}{T_t}[\beta_i^{(0)} + \beta^{(1)}\ V(i,\eta)]\right)}\right)^{n_{(c,\eta)}}$$
$$= \prod_{(c\in\Lambda)} \left(\frac{\exp\left(-\frac{1}{T_t}[\beta_c^{(0)}]\right)}{\sum_{i\in\Lambda} \exp\left(-\frac{1}{T_t}[\beta_i^{(0)}]\right)}\right)^{n_c} \tag{8}$$
$$\times \prod_{(c\in\Lambda, \forall\eta)} \left(\frac{\exp\left(-\frac{1}{T_t}[\beta_c^{(0)} + \beta^{(1)}\ V(c,\eta)]\right) \sum_{i\in\Lambda} \exp\left(-\frac{1}{T_t}[\beta_i^{(0)}]\right)}{\sum_{i\in\Lambda} \exp\left(-\frac{1}{T_t}[\beta_i^{(0)} + \beta^{(1)}\ V(i,\eta)]\right)}\right)^{n_{(c,\eta)}}$$

where $n_{(c,\eta)} = \#(s : x_s = c, \eta_s = \eta)$. If the parameters $\beta_i^{(0)}$ are normalised so that, $\sum_{i\in\Lambda} exp(-\beta_i^{(0)}) = 1$, then the term $exp(-\beta_i^{(0)})$ becomes analogous to a weight term in a mixture density. By introducing this dependency between $\beta_i^{(0)}$ parameters it becomes possible to maintain a balance between the external field strength and the strength of interaction between neighbouring pixels. This makes it possible to set the pixel interaction strength *a priori*. The introduction of this weight term also proves highly convenient for proposing reversible jumps, as will be seen in the following section.

It is theoretically possible to sample the $\beta^{(1)}$ parameter from the conditional density,

$$p(\beta_c^{(1)}, c \in \Lambda \mid X) = p(X \mid \beta_c^{(1)}, c \in \Lambda)\ p_r(\beta_c^{(1)}, c \in \Lambda)$$
$$= \prod_{(c\in\Lambda, \forall\eta)} \left(\frac{\exp\left(-\frac{1}{T_t}\beta_c^{(1)}\ V(c,\eta)\right)}{\sum_{i\in\Lambda} \exp\left(-\frac{1}{T_t}[\beta_i^{(0)} + \beta^{(1)}\ V(i,\eta)]\right)}\right)^{n_{(c,\eta)}} \tag{9}$$

Unfortunately, under particular underlying label map configurations the posterior density for $\beta^{(1)}$ will not be proper.

$$\lim_{\beta^{(1)} \to -\infty} p(X = x', \Psi \mid Y = y) = \alpha \tag{10}$$

where α is a positive constant. This is a direct consequence of approximating the likelihood by the pseudo-likelihood. It may be possible to overcome this problem by choosing a suitable prior but for simplicity, the results presented in section 4 of this paper are obtained with $\beta^{(1)}$ given *a priori*.

3.3 Reversible Jumps to sample the Number of Classes

Reversible jumps were developed in [12] to allow a Metropolis-Hastings sampler to sample from a variable sized class space, $\Lambda = \{0, 1, ..., k\}$, i.e. where k changes. When k increases the model parameters associated with the new class are derived from the old parameter values and random variables. This allows the dimension of the parameter vector to be preserved.

If two models are considered, labelled $m1$ and $m2$, and $\Theta^{(1)}$ and $\Theta^{(2)}$ are their associated parameter vectors of dimension n_1 and n_2 respectively, then to jump between their parameter spaces requires the generation of random vectors $u^{(1)}$ and $u^{(2)}$ such that, $\#(\Theta^{(1)}) + \#(u^{(1)}) = \#(\Theta^{(2)}) + \#(u^{(2)})$, where $\#(\cdot)$ indicates the dimension of the inclosed vector.

If y represents observed data, the acceptance ratio based on sampling the posterior distribution, for the transition of $x = (m1, \Theta^{(1)})$ to $x' = (m2, \Theta^{(2)})$ is derived in [12],

$$min \left\{ 1, \frac{p(2, \Theta^{(2)}) \, p(1, \Theta^{(1)} \mid 2, \Theta^{(2)}) \, p(u^{(1)})}{p(1, \Theta^{(1)}) \, p(2, \Theta^{(2)} \mid 1, \Theta^{(1)}) \, p(u^{(2)})} \left| \frac{\partial(\Theta^{(2)}, u^{(2)})}{\partial(\Theta^{(1)}, u^{(1)})} \right| \right\} \tag{11}$$

where $\left| \frac{\partial(\Theta^{(2)}, u^{(2)})}{\partial(\Theta^{(1)}, u^{(1)})} \right|$ is the Jacobian determinant for the mapping functions of the transformation of $[\Theta^{(1)}, u^{(1)}]$ to $[\Theta^{(2)}, u^{(2)}]$.

This methodology was applied in [14] to the problem of fitting a Gaussian mixture model with an unknown number of components to observed data. The posterior distribution was Gibbs sampled with sequential sweeps, each of which allocated classes, updated model parameters and a reversible jump was incorporated to update the number of mixture components, k. At each sweep the algorithm would randomly choose between proposing to increment or decrement the number of classes.

If the number of classes was to be incremented then a class was randomly chosen to be split and new parameters generated for each of the two new classes. The observed data samples allocated to the splitting class were reallocated using a Metropolis Sampler based on an acceptance ratio incorporating their conditional density functions.

If the number of classes was to decrease, two classes that were in some relevant way adjacent, were chosen to be merged. New parameters for the merged class were then generated from the two old sets of parameters. All data samples allocated to either of the two classes being split were then automatically assigned to the new merged class with probability one.

The problem of splitting a region of a Markov Random Field labelled by a single class, c, into a region composed of two classes, c_1, c_2, is similar to the splitting of a component of the mixture distributions described in [14]. Hence a similar approach may be followed. Each class is defined by a set of parameters, $\Psi_c = \{\mu_c, \sigma_c, \beta_c^{(0)}\}$. When splitting one class into two, three new parameters need to be created and the values of all six can then be set with three degrees of freedom. To preserve the dimensionality of the parameter space three random variables are generated, u_1, u_2, u_3. So when splitting state c into c_1 and c_2 a transform between $[\mu_c, \sigma_c, \beta_c^{(0)}, u_1, u_2, u_3]$ and $[\mu_{c1}, \sigma_{c1}, \beta_{c1}^{(0)}, \mu_{c2}, \sigma_{c2}, \beta_{c2}^{(0)}]$ has to be defined.

The three parameters for each of the two new classes may be derived from the old values, $\mu_c, \sigma_c, \beta_c^{(0)}$, and the random variables u_1, u_2, u_3. The new parameters are calculated to preserve the 0th, 1st and 2nd order moments across the transformation. The resulting values given by the following set of equations:

$$\beta_{c1}^{(0)} = \beta_c^{(0)} - T_t \ln(u_1) \qquad \beta_{c2}^{(0)} = \beta_c^{(0)} - T_t \ln(1 - u_1)$$

$$\mu_{c1} = \mu_c - u_2 \, \sigma_c \sqrt{\tfrac{1-u1}{u1}} \qquad \mu_{c2} = \mu_c + u_2 \, \sigma_c \sqrt{\tfrac{u1}{1-u1}} \tag{12}$$

$$\sigma_{c1}^2 = u_3 \, (1 - u_2^2) \, \sigma_c^2 \, \tfrac{1}{u_1} \qquad \sigma_{c2}^2 = (1 - u_3) \, (1 - u_2^2) \, \sigma_c^2 \, \tfrac{1}{1 - u_1}$$

The choice of random variables for, u_1, u_2, u_3, must be such that, $\{u_1, u_2, u_3 \in (0, 1]\}$. For this reason and to allow a bias towards splitting the data into roughly equal partitions, beta distributions are used to sample u_1, u_2, u_3.

The Jacobian determinant of these mapping functions, needed in the calculation of the acceptance ratio is,

$$\left| \frac{\partial(\Psi_{c1}, \Psi_{c2})}{\partial(\Psi_c, u_1, u_2, u_3)} \right| = \frac{T_t \sigma^2}{u_1^2(1 - u_1^2) \sqrt{u3(1 - u3)}} \tag{13}$$

The pixel sites allocated to the class or classes selected in the split or merge reversible jump need to be reallocated on the basis of the new parameters generated. If a merge is being proposed, then all sites allocated to the two old classes are relabelled with the new merged class, with probability one.

The difficulty occurs when splitting one class into two. If a reasonable probability of acceptance is to be maintained, the proposed reallocation of the sites needs to be completed in such a way as to ensure the posterior probability of that particular segmentation is relatively high. To achieve this it would be desirable to propose a reallocation of pixels using the conditional density given in equation 6. Unfortunately, this is not possible since the allocation of classes in the neighbourhood η_s has not yet been calculated.

By using a distance measure based on the new class parameters and the observed grayscale values of the surrounding region of pixels it is possible to make a 'guess' to which class the neighbouring pixels might be allocated. The measure used here has a precedent in this type of algorithm: the Kolmogorov-Smirnov distance was used in [5] to allocate pixel sites between classes based on grayscale values or transformations of grayscale, indicative of texture type.

The Kolmogorov-Smirnov distance is a measure of the closeness of two distribution functions. It may be applied to two samples of data to ascertain whether they have been drawn independently from the same distribution. If $\hat{F}_1(k)$ and $\hat{F}_2(k)$ are two independent sample distribution functions (i.e. histograms) defined,

$$\hat{F}(k) = \frac{1}{n} \#(i : y_i \leq k) \tag{14}$$

where n is the number of data samples, y_i so that $1 \leq i \leq n$. Then the Kolmogorov-Smirnov distance is the maximum difference between distributions over all k,

$$d(y^{(1)}, y^{(2)}) = \max_k \left| \hat{F}_1(k) - \hat{F}_2(k) \right| \tag{15}$$

The Kolmogorov-Smirnov distance is a useful for two reasons; its value is independent of the underlying distribution function and it is unaffected by outlying data values.

To propose a likely neighbourhood configuration so that the conditional probability in equation 6 may be calculated, the Kolmogorov-Smirnov distance between the distributions of pixel grayscales in windows centered on each of the pixels comprising the neighbourhood and the distribution functions of the classes to which they might be allocated is calculated. The class giving the smallest distance at each of the neighboring pixel sites is then used as the best 'guess' for substitution in equation 6.

The two properties described above ensure the suitability of this measure because its value will be independent of the class distribution functions and its insensitivity to outlying pixel values means it will closely model the interactions of a Gibbs MRF.

The acceptance ratio for splitting region c into $c1$ and $c2$, thus increasing the number of classes from k to k^+, is given by,

$$\frac{p(X = x^+, \psi^+, k^+ \mid Y = y)}{p(X = x, \psi, k \mid Y = y)} \frac{1}{p_\beta(u_1) p_\beta(u_2) p_\beta(u_3)}$$
$$\times \frac{1}{p(segmentation)} \left| \frac{\partial(\Psi_{c1}, \Psi_{c2})}{\partial(\Psi_c, u_1, u_2, u_3)} \right| \tag{16}$$

where, $p(X = x, \psi, k \mid Y = y)$ is the approximation to the posterior density defined by equation 5, $p_\beta(u)$ is the probability of proposing the random variable u, $p(segmentation)$ is the probability of the segmenting region c into $c1$ and $c2$ $| \cdot |$ is the Jacobian determinant given by equation 13. The acceptance ratio for the jump combining two states into one is simply the inverse of that given in equation 16. In this case $p(segmentation)$ is found in retrospect and u_1, u_2, u_3 are calculated by back-substitution into equation 12.

It is therefore possible to incorporate into the algorithm any of the information criteria used is [4] [3] by adding their compensatory terms as priors on model order k to the posterior probabilities of the reversible jump acceptance ratio.

4   Experimental Results

The segmentation algorithm, described in the previous sections has been applied to various computer synthesised mosaics. A geometric annealing temperature schedule was chosen so that the algorithm would converge in a reasonable time. The schedule is given by,

$$T_t = (1 + \alpha_1)^{\alpha_2 (1 - \frac{t}{N_t})} \tag{17}$$

where t is the iteration number, N_t is the total number of iterations, and α_1 and α_2 are constants (which were arbitrarily set to 1.1 and 10.0, respectively).

For the purposes of these experiments, $\beta^{(1)}$, which prescribes the overall strength of interactions between pixels within the image, was set a priori to a value of 1. 5. In proposing a reversible jump, the Kolmogorov-Smirnov distances for were calculated using 9×9 windows to generate 40 bin histograms of the pixel grayscale distribution functions.

Figure 1 shows the convergence of a 100 iteration run on a 6 class image. The segmentation, although not perfect is a good representation of the image after so few iterations and the number of classes has been correctly diagnosed. The results of a 500 iteration run are shown in figure 2. The original grayscale densities of the five classes are far closer than in the previous example (as shown by the grayscale histogram) but the algorithm has still converged to a good estimate of the underlying image.

A greyscale image of a house is segmented in Figure 3. The algorithm was repeated from various starting conditions and the results reached remained consistent. It could be argued that a better segmentation was arrived at in the intermediate steps but the algorithm then fits to a statistically if not visually better model in the final iterations.

5   Conclusion

In this paper we have presented an unsupervised segmentation algorithm for noisy images. The class model parameters, number of classes and pixel labels are all directly sampled from the posterior distribution using an MCMC algorithm. A single parameter is defined prior to the data (or at least an informative prior distribution needs to be defined) which defines the overall strength of neighbouring pixel interactions within the image. Excepting this, the algorithm is completely unsupervised. Experiments results have been presented in which synthesised images have been rapidly segmented to give accurate estimate of the original underlying image.

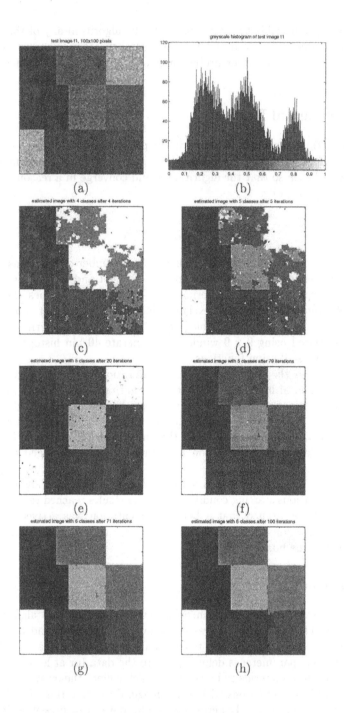

Figure 1: 100 iteration experiment on an image with six classes and beginning the algorithm with an arbitrary initial guess of four classes

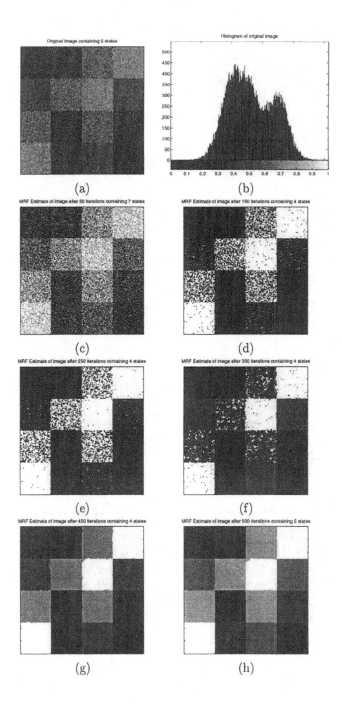

Figure 2: 500 iteration experiment on an image with five classes and beginning the algorithm with an arbitrary initial guess of six classes

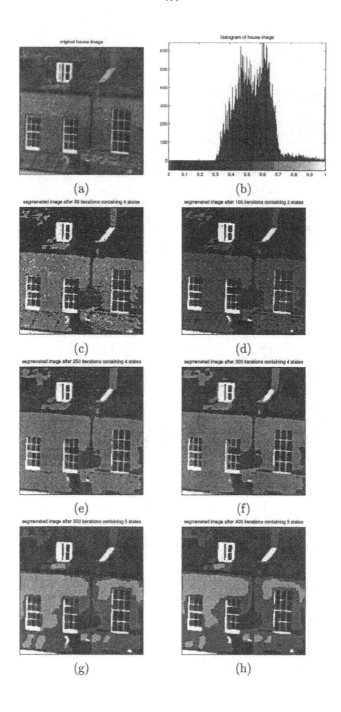

Figure 3: 400 iteration experiment on a greyscale image of a house. The algorithm begins with an arbitrary initial guess of six classes and consistently converges to five.

References

[1] B.S.Manjunath and R.Chellappa. Unsupervised texture segmentation using Markov Random Fields. *IEEE Trans. Patt. Anal & Machine Intell.*, 13(5):478–482, May 1991.

[2] C.Kervrann and F.Heitz. A Markov Random Field model-based approach to unsupervised texture segmentation using local and global statistics. *IEEE Trans. Image Processing*, 4(6):856–862, June 1995.

[3] C.S.Won and H.Derin. Unsupervised Segmentation of Noisy and Textured Images using Markov Random Fields. *CVGIP:Graphical Models and Image Processing*, 54(4):308–328, Jult 1992.

[4] J.W.Modestino D.A.Langan and J.Zhang. Cluster Validation for Unsupervised Stochastic model-based Image Segmentation. *Proc. ICIP94*, pages 197–201, 1994.

[5] C.Graffigne D.Geman, S.Geman and P.Dong. Boundary Detection by Constrained Optimization. *IEEE Trans. Patt. Anal & Machine Intell.*, 12(7):609–628, July 1990.

[6] D.K.Panjwani and G.Healey. Markov Random Field models for unsupervised segmentation of textured color images. *IEEE Trans. Patt. Anal & Machine Intell.*, 17(10):939–954, Oct 1995.

[7] F.S.Cohen and Z.Fan. Maximum Likelihood unsupervised texture segmentation. *CVGIP:Graphical Models and Image Processing*, 54(3):239–251, May 1992.

[8] H.H.Nguyen and P.Cohen. Gibbs Random Fields, Fuzzy Clustering, and the unsupervised segmentation of images. *CVGIP:Graphical Models and Image Processing*, 55(1):1–19, Jan 1993.

[9] J.Besag. On the statistical analysis of dirty pictures. *J. Royal Statist. Soc., Series B*, 48:259–302, 1986.

[10] J.M.Bernardo and A.F.M.Smith. *Bayesian Theory*. Wiley, 1994.

[11] L.Tierny. Markov Chains for exploring posterior distributions. *Annals of Statistics*, 22(5):1701–1762, 1994.

[12] P.J.Green. Reversible jump Markov Chain Monte Carlo computation and Bayesian model determination. *Biometrika*, 82(4):711–732, 1996.

[13] S.Geman and D.Geman. Stochastic Relaxation, Gibbs Distributions and the Bayesian Restoration of Images. *IEEE Trans. Patt. Anal & Machine Intell.*, 6(6):721–741, Nov 1984.

[14] S.Richardson and P.J.Green. On Bayesian analysis of mixtures with an unknown number of components. -, Feb 1996.

Adaptive Anisotropic Parameter Estimation in the Weak Membrane Model

Toshiro Kubota *, Terry Huntsberger *

Intelligent Systems Laboratory, Department of Computer Science
University of South Carolina, Columbia, SC 29208, USA
kubota@cs.sc.edu, terry@cs.sc.edu
Ph: (803) 777-8306, FAX:(803) 777-3767

Abstract. The weak membrane model uses Markov Random Fields within the Bayesian inference framework for image reconstruction and segmentation problems. Recently, the model has been extended for the 4D Gabor feature vector space and was applied to texture segmentation. A limitation of this technique is that the parameters in the model have to be adjusted for each different input image and they are fixed throughout the image. This paper proposes a technique to alleviate this limitation by estimating the parameters using local feature statistics. The technique has the following desirable properties: 1) the whole segmentation process is done in an unsupervised fashion, 2) robustness to noise and contrast variation, and 3) increased connectivity of boundaries.

Keywords: *texture segmentation, weak membrane model, Bayesian inference, Gaussian filters,*

1 Introduction

The main task of the low-level computer vision process is to extract meaningful features from an input image (or a set of images) and to divide the image into separate regions based on discontinuities in the feature space. This task is called *segmentation*. Good segmentation algorithms should separate the input image into physically meaningful areas.

Modeling the image formation process through a discretized system of partial differential equations (PDEs) is one way to address this problem [16, 18]. This approach serves as the underlying basis for a number of surface reconstruction techniques [26, 29], and texture synthesis methods for computer graphics [11, 30, 31].

Inclusion of a explicit representation of discontinuities between regions in any model is a key element for robust segmentation [2, 3, 14, 15, 22, 24, 28]. In general these techniques involve the minimization of a functional of the form [28]:

$$\mathcal{E}(v, \mathbf{w}) = \mathcal{S}(v, \mathbf{w}) + \mathcal{P}(v) + \mathcal{D}(\mathbf{w}), \tag{1}$$

---
* Research supported in part under ONR Grant No. N00014-94-1-1163 and ARO Grant No. DAAH04-96-10326.

where v is an estimate of the image structure, $\mathbf{w}$ is a continuity control function, $\mathcal{S}(v, \mathbf{w})$ is a functional that measures the smoothness of v, $\mathcal{P}(v)$ measures the discrepancy between v and the given data, and $\mathcal{D}(\mathbf{w})$ constrains the solution to have good continuity structure. As pointed out in [2, 28], the choice of $\mathcal{D}(\mathbf{w})$ will have a large effect on the coherence of the solution. The non-convex nature of the energy functional limits the available methods that can be used to solve the resulting system of Euler-Lagrange equations. What is ideally needed is a formulation that has good convergence and computational characteristics.

One way to achieve this goal is to use Bayesian inference and neighborhood constraints to derive the maximum *a posteriori* estimate of the regions and the boundaries [3, 12, 14, 22]. Markov random field (MRF) or Gibbs random field (GRF) models have recently received attention for texture synthesis [7] and image representation/segmentation [1, 6, 10, 13, 19, 20, 21, 25, 27, 32, 33]. The Bayesian approach is called the *weak membrane model*, since it is related to the physical model of an elastic sheet draped over a wire frame. The objective is to find the global minimum of the energy function described as

$$E = \int \left[\alpha(f-g)^2 + \mu\|\nabla f\|^2(1-l) + \nu l \right] dx \, dy \,, \tag{2}$$

where $g(x,y)$ is the measured local statistics of data or the extracted local features for segmentation, $f(x,y)$ is the surface process which represents the global statistics of the particular region, $l(x,y)$ is the line process which represents the boundaries between different regions, ∇ is the gradient operator, and $\|\cdot\|$ is the norm in the feature vector space. Throughout the paper g will be called *observation* or *observed data*. The parameters α, μ, and ν need to be determined before any minimization algorithm is used.

Gabor wavelet filters can be used to give a multiscale description of line processes in images [8, 9, 17, 22]. In [22], the concept of the weak membrane model was extended to the 4D Gabor feature vector space. The surface interpolation process is performed not only in the (x,y) space, but also in the scale space (σ) and the orientation space (θ). The energy function to be minimized is

$$E = \int \left[\alpha(f-g)^2 + \gamma_\sigma \left(\frac{\delta f}{\delta \sigma} \right)^2 + \gamma_\theta \left(\frac{\delta f}{\delta \theta} \right)^2 + \mu\|\nabla f\|^2(1-l) + \nu l \, d\theta \, d\sigma \right] dx \, dy \,, \tag{3}$$

where γ_σ and γ_θ are two additional parameters that need to be determined before minimization. Lee called this model the "coupled membrane model". Like other segmentation algorithms, one of the difficulties associated with the weak membrane model is the determination of a good set of parameters for the energy model. In most cases, the parameters are input image dependent and the final segmentation results are sensitive to the parameter values chosen.

Designing a segmentation algorithm using the weak membrane model can be divided into three stages:

1. decide which features are to be extracted,

2. choose the model and its parameter values, Equation (2), and

3. select a method for minimizing the function.

The main focus of this paper is on the second stage, the parameter estimation. We present a new estimation method based on the local feature statistics computed by a combined set of concentric and directional Gaussian filters. This method gives the segmentation algorithm relative image independence. The new segmentation process is:

- less sensitive to noise,

- immune to contrast variation due to the localized adaptation, and

- increases connectivity of boundaries.

The next section gives a more detailed description of the weak membrane model, and discusses its limitations. This is followed by a description of the adaptive, anisotropic segmentation algorithm, which includes a discussion of the parameter estimation and adaptation technique. Finally, we present the results of some experimental studies and conclusions.

2 Weak Membrane Model

Each term in Equation (2) represents a constraint on the weak membrane model. The first term constrains the observation to be close to the global statistics of the region. The second term determines that the global statistic should be smooth except at the region boundaries. Finally, the third term controls the smoothness in the x-y space except at region boundaries. The last constraint is often called a "penalty". The additional two terms in Equation (3) constrain the smoothness of the global statistics in the scale space and the smoothness in the orientation space.

The solutions to both (2) and (3) are not convex functions, and it is not straightforward to reach the global minimum without being trapped in a local minimum. Stochastic optimization methods such as simulating annealing (SA) are often too time consuming, and various different optimization methods have been proposed [3, 12, 15].

In order to perform segmentation in an unsupervised fashion, the set of parameter describing (2) have to be estimated somehow. One way to do in the Bayesian framework is to incorporate the parameter estimation into the optimization process using maximum likelihood estimate [23][4]. Assuming both surface and line processes in (2) obey GRF, the optimization process can be divided into two sub-optimization processes.

$$\{f^*, l^*\} = \arg\max_{f,l} \frac{1}{Z(\Theta^*)} e^{-E(f,l,|\Theta^*)}, \text{ and} \tag{4}$$

$$\{\Theta^*\} = \arg\max_{\Theta} \frac{1}{Z(\Theta)} e^{-E(\Theta|f^*,l^*)} \tag{5}$$

Fig. 1. *Synthetic Test Image.* This is a test image generated synthetically with two quadratic functions.

where Z is the partition function, E is the energy function of (2) or (3) and Θ is the set of the parameters. This is an approximation of

$$\{f^*, l^*, \Theta^*\} = \arg\max_{f,l,\Theta} \frac{1}{Z} e^{-E(f,l,\Theta)} \tag{6}$$

which is computationally too expensive in most cases. Equation (5) is still costly to compute since it involves evaluating the partition function. An approximation to (5) can be made using pseudo-likelihood to reduce the computation.

Another issue associated with the parameter estimation is how to control the parameters adaptively within an image. A natural image consists of surfaces/regions with different characteristics, different lighting conditions, and different noise characteristics. The parameters have to be adapted to the changes in order for a segmentation algorithm to succeed. For example, Fig. 1 has the top half and the bottom half generated by different quadratic functions. The top half is generated with $1 - 0.2(x - a)^2$, and the bottom half is generated with $1 - 0.1(x - a)^2$. When the image is segmented using the weak membrane model with $\alpha = \mu = 1.0$ and $\nu = .002$ throughout the image, the left image in Fig. 2 is obtained as a result. The boundary between the top and the bottom half of the image is only extended for less than 2/3 of the width of the image. On the other hand, when the image is segmented with $\alpha = \mu = 1.0$ and $\nu = .001$, the right image in Fig. 2 is obtained. Quadratic slopes are also picked up as boundaries, while the boundary between the top and the bottom half is slightly extended. In the above example, there is a trade-off between extending the true boundary and picking up spurious boundaries. This example image is generated artificially, but similar effects can be seen on specularly reflecting surfaces.

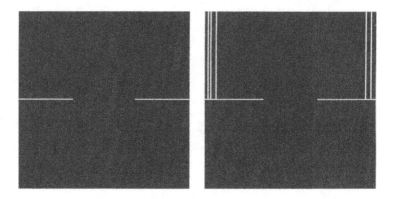

Fig. 2. *Test Result I* This shows the results of applying the segmentation algorithm to the test image (??) without parameter adaptation.

3 Estimation Technique

Problems with the probabilistic parameter estimation techniques such as Maximum-likelihood estimate and pseudo-likelihood estimate are 1) the amount of computation required for the estimation is large, 2) if the techniques are used on the membrane model without introducing additional constraints on the parameters, the optimization of (5) converges to the trivial solution where all the parameters are zeros, and 3) the result is not necessarily the best solution in terms of our subjective sense since the optimality is based on the Gibbs distribution assumption.

Because of the above problems, our approach for the parameter estimation is not based on the probabilistic model but based on the local feature statistics and is derived in a heuristic way. The technique involves much less computation, it does not need other artificial constraints to be introduced, and it tries to produce results which agree with the human visual perception.

From the previous experiments on the test image (Figure 1), it is clear that no single set of parameters for the membrane model can extract the boundaries reliably, and an adaptive scheme for adjusting the parameters locally is necessary. The estimation technique has to be adjusted to the local contrast of the image so that weak boundaries in a low contrast regions can be detected as well as strong boundaries in a high contrast regions. It can be also observed that the human visual system tends to extrapolate a strong boundary beyond the end-point of the boundary. This effect can be seen in various visual illusion experiments such as Kanizsa triangles. Based on the above arguments, three objectives are chosen for designing the estimation technique. They are 1) the segmentation is insensitive to the local contrast of the boundaries, 2) it extrapolates a strong boundary, and 3) it is robust to noise.

In order to develop the adaptive parameter estimation technique, it is necessary to examine the dynamics of the line and surface processes during the energy minimization process. By employing the mean field technique on the weak membrane model (2), the line process is controlled by the following equation [12],

$$l(x, y; T) = \frac{1}{1 + e^{(\nu(x,y) - \mu|\nabla f|^2)/T}}, \tag{7}$$

where T is analogous to the temperature in SA and $T \to 0$ gradually as the minimization process proceeds. It is easy to see in Equation (7) that $\sqrt{(\nu/\mu)}$ acts as a threshold for the line process. When $\sqrt{(\nu/\mu)}$ is fixed globally, it influences the number of boundaries in the final segmentation result. Smaller $\sqrt{(\nu/\mu)}$ leads to more boundaries.

The surface process is controlled by

$$\frac{df}{dt} \propto \alpha(g - f) + \mu\nabla \cdot ((1 - l)\nabla f). \tag{8}$$

This is obtained from the Euler-Lagrange equation on (2). Note that for a large α, the first term dominates and the surface will converge to the observed data. Little smoothing will be introduced. When $\alpha = 0$, the surface process is not constrained by the observation and it will be smoothed out everywhere except where the line process is on. Thus, it can be suggested that α should be large if the observation contains little noise and should be small if the observation is noisier.

3.1 Global parameters

Since scaling the parameters by the same amount does not affect the segmentation result, there are only 2 free parameters in (2) and 4 in (3). For both (2) and (3), μ is fixed globally and other parameters are derived in reference to μ.

We introduce another global parameter, ν_0, which controls the amount of detail extracted in the final segmentation result. With a small ν_0, the result may contain boundary between each brick on a wall, while with a large ν_0, it may extract only the boundary of the wall. Our intention is to make the segmentation process more flexible by providing user controllable parameter, and not to introduce a tweakable parameter to improve the segmentation. This is similar to the scale parameter in the scale-space analysis.

We also set both γ_σ and γ_θ in (3) to 1.0. Our experiments showed that these two parameters are less influential to the final results than ν and α, and estimation/adaptation techniques for these parameters remain in our future research.

3.2 Estimating α

As stated above, with fixed μ, the amount of the surface process smoothing can be controlled by α. When the observation is noisy, the influence of the first constraint should be small and more smoothing should be introduced, which implies that a small α should be used. Thus, the effect of the noise can be reduced by appropriately controlling α, and the third objective can be achieved. Assume we can estimate the amount of noise on the image through the observation and denote the estimate by $\mathcal{N}(g)$. Take a monotonically decreasing function $\mathcal{H}_1$, then α can be adaptively estimated as

$$\alpha = \mathcal{H}(\mathcal{N}(g)) \ . \tag{9}$$

Assume the observation g is the sum of a piece-wise constant surface and the zero-mean Gaussian noise. Then,

$$g(x,y) = \tilde{f}(x,y) + n(x,y) \tag{10}$$

where $\tilde{f}$ is the surface and n is the Gaussian noise with

$$Pr\{n(x,y)\} = e^{-n^2/\sigma_n(x,y)} \tag{11}$$

Note that the Gaussian variance σ_n is space-variant. Ideally, the surface process should converge to $\tilde{f}$. Within a region boundary, the variance of the observation is equal to the variance of the noise. Hence, the local variance of the observed data can serve as the noise estimate. However, the variance is high at the region boundary even though the noise in the observation is low. Therefore, ideally the local variance computation should be constrained within the same region and should not go beyond region boundaries. Of course, the purpose of segmentation is to find where the region boundaries are and this information is not available at the estimation stage.

One way to possibly increase the accuracy of the noise estimate is to use an iterative segmentation/estimation approach. First, segment the image with some initial set of α. Then the noise estimate is performed using the initial segmentation and α is computed based on the noise estimate. The same image is again segmented using the new α. The iteration continues for a sufficient number of times or until the convergence. This iteration technique is similar to the probabilistic approach in a sense that it performs the segmentation multiple times. The amount of computation increases drastically.

A more computationally affordable way is to update the noise estimate as the region boundaries are being formed. A problem with this method associated with the weak membrane model is that there is no labeling information available on the surface process and the line process does not guarantee to produce closed boundaries. Therefore, it is not straightforward to distinguish one region from another.

In our experiment, the noise measure n is simply set to the ratio of the local feature variance and the global feature variance. Thus,

$$n = \frac{v}{\bar{v}} \tag{12}$$

where v is the local variance and $\bar{v}$ is the global variance. The function $\mathcal{H}_1$ is set to

$$\mathcal{H}(n) = \mu e^{-n^2} \ . \tag{13}$$

3.3 Estimating ν

The first two objectives for the adaptive parameter estimation technique are more relevant to ν than α since ν controls the line process directly as shown in (7), while α only influences the line process through the surface process.

To achieve the first objective, a contrast independent *boundary-ness* measure is required. Some priors for a boundary are 1) there tend to be a discontinuity at a boundary in the feature space, 2) there are only limited number of boundaries in a finite area, 3) all the boundaries are closed, and 4) the boundaries tend to be smooth. In our experiment, the first and second priors are considered. Other two will be added in our future work. Note that the first prior is already incorporated into (7) by the use of the magnitude of the surface process gradient ($|\nabla f|$). To incorporate the second prior into the estimation of ν, the density of the boundaries needs to be estimated. In our experiment, it is estimated by a weighted local average of $|\nabla g|$ using a concentric Gaussian filter. The estimate for the boundary density is

$$\mathcal{G} = |\nabla f| \star G(x, y) \tag{14}$$

where G is a concentric Gaussian filter. A weighted local average of l is another candidate for the measure.

To achieve the second objective, a strong boundary should lower ν in the direction along the boundary so that the corresponding line process extrapolates the boundary. One way to achieve this effect is to follow the line process and lower ν along the direction at a high curvature point. However, the line process takes a continuous value between 0 and 1 until it converges to either 0 or 1, and it is not straight forward to follow the contour of the intermediate process. Instead, we use a set of directional Gaussian filters equally distributed in orientation $[0, \pi]$ and apply them to the intermediate line process. The scheme incorporates the fuzziness of the process and can estimate the directional strength of the line process by the ratio of the maximum filter response and the average of the responses. Thus, the directional strength estimate $\mathcal{B}$ is

$$\mathcal{B}(x, y) = \frac{M \max_k G_k(x, y) \star l(x, y)}{\sum_k G_k(x, y) \star l(x, y)} \tag{15}$$

where G_k is the directional Gaussian filter at the orientation θ_k and M is the number of the filters.

Using the boundary density estimate and the directional strength of the line process, ν is adaptively estimated as

$$\nu = \nu_0 \mathcal{G}(x, y)^2 \left(\frac{1 - \mathcal{B}}{M - 1} \right) \tag{16}$$

where ν_0 is the global scale-space parameter. The second product term maps the range of $\mathcal{B}$, $[1, M]$, linearly to $[1, 0]$. Note that $\mathcal{G}$ is squared so that ν matches with $|\nabla f|^2$ in (7).

Fig. 3. *Line Process Outputs for the Test Image.* This is the result of the segmentation algorithm with parameter estimation/adaptation applied on the test image (Fig. 1).

By incorporating this adaptive method into the weak membrane model and applying the segmentation algorithm on the test image shown in Fig. 1, the result shown in Fig. 3 is obtained. The boundary between the top and the bottom half is extended further than Fig. 2, but the quadratic slopes are not picked up as boundaries.

4 Experimental Results

This section shows some preliminary results using our adaptive parameter estimation technique. The weak membrane model is used for the region segmentation experiments and the coupled membrane model is used for the texture segmentation experiments. The result with the adaptive algorithm is compared to the result without adaptation. The minimization strategy, the rate of temperature decrease and the convergence criteria, are identical for both schemes.

The size of the concentric Gaussian filter, G, is 21×21pixels, the standard deviation of the filter is 12pixels. The number of the orientaional Gaussian filters, M, is set to 16, the size of the filters is 11×11pixels, the standard deviations of the proto-type filter ($\theta = 0$) are 6 and 3 pixels for the horizontal and vertical directions, respectively.

For the non-adaptation results, the parameters are set to $\alpha = \gamma_\sigma = \gamma_\theta = 1.0$. For the region segmentation experiments, ν_0 is set to 1.0, while for the texture segmentation experiments, it is set to 0.6. The reason for this adjustment is that the features extracted for texture segmentation are more subtle than pixel intensities in the gray scale image due to the pixel-wise non-linear transform and the local averaging described below. Thus, it was necessary to lower the scale-space level for texture segmentation. It was also possible to scale the outputs of the texture feature extractor by some constant so that this adjustment of ν_0 was unnecessary.

The mean field technique described in [12] is used to optimize the line process, and the deterministic relaxation method is used to optimize the region process. For (2), the direction of descent is given in (8) and for (3), it is computed as

$$\frac{df}{dt} \propto \alpha(g - f) + \gamma_\sigma \frac{\delta^2 f}{\delta \log \sigma^2} + \gamma_\theta \frac{\delta^2 f}{\delta \theta^2} + \mu \nabla \cdot ((1 - l) \nabla f). \tag{17}$$

The temperature T in (7) is decreased gradually to reach the zero temperature state.

4.1 Texture Segmentation

Features extracted for this experiments are those suggested in [22] and [17]. First, the input image is normalized so that its mean is zero and its variance is 1.0. A set of Gabor filters described in [22] is applied to the image to produce a multi-resolution representation of the image. The Gabor filters are described as

$$g_b(x, y : \omega, \theta) = A_c e^{-\frac{\tilde{x}^2}{\sigma_x} - \frac{\tilde{y}^2}{\sigma_y}} e^{j\omega\tilde{x}}, \tag{18}$$

where ω is the radial frequency, θ is the orientation, $\tilde{x} = x\cos\theta + y\sin\theta$, $\tilde{y} = -x\sin\theta + y\cos\theta$, and A_c is the normalization coefficient. For our experiment, the total of 24 Gabor filters (8 orientations and 3 frequencies) are used, and the aspect ratio of the Gaussian (σ_y/σ_x) is set to 2,

A pixel-wise non-linear transform described in [17] is applied next to each filtered image. The transform is

$$\psi(x) = \tanh(\rho x), \tag{19}$$

where ρ is set to 1.0. The transform has an effect similar to thresholding, and increases the contrast of significant features. Finally, the local average of each non-linear transformed image is computed. The average absolute deviation described in [17] is used.

Fig. 4 shows test images composed of 2 different Brodatz textures [5]. The left image has fieldstone texture and ricepaper texture, while the right image has pellets texture and pig skin texture. Fig. 5 shows the results of the segmentation algorithm applied to the fieldstone-ricepaper image and Fig. 6 shows the results for the pellets-pig image. The right images in both figures are the results without adaptation and the left ones are those with adaptation. For the non-adaptation cases, ν is set globally to $\frac{\nu_0 \sum_{x,y} |\nabla f|^2}{N^2}$, where N^2 is the number of pixels in the image. This value corresponds to the special case of the adaptation of ν with the standard deviation of both concentric and directional Gaussian filters being ∞. In this case, the Gaussian window extends over the whole image and the statistical measurement of (16) is no longer localized. The results with the adaptation are less noisier and has thinner and smoother boundaries than those without.

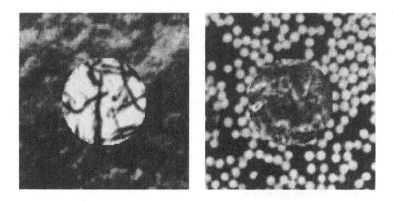

Fig. 4. *Textured Test Images.* These are the test images used for the texture segmentation experiments. The left image is a mosaic of fieldstone and ricepaper textured obtained from Brodatz's photo album ([5]).

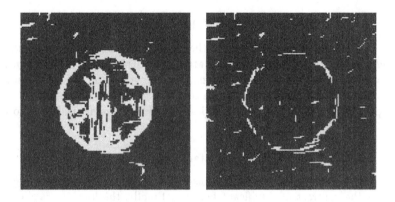

Fig. 5. *Texture Segmentation Result I.* These are the results of the segmentation algorithm applied to the fieldstone-ricepaper test image. The left is the result without adaptation and the right is the result with adaptation.

4.2 Region Segmentation

Natural gray scale images of $256 \times 256 \times 8$ bits are used for this series of experiments. The pixel intensity is used as a feature.

Fig. 7 shows the test images. Fig. 8 shows the results of segmentation for the house image (the left image in Fig. 7), and Fig. 9 shows the results for the car image. The left images are the results without adaptation and the right ones are those with adaptation. Without the parameter adaptation, the value of ν is computed as described above. For the house image, the result with adapta-

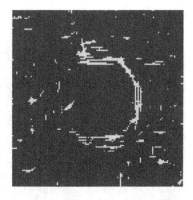 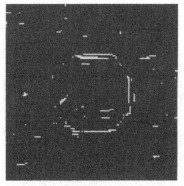

Fig. 6. *Texture Segmentation Result II.* These are the results of the segmentation algorithm applied to the pellets-pig test image. The left is the result without adaptation and the right is the result with adaptation.

Fig. 7. *Original House and Car Images.* These are the test images used for the region segmentation experiments.

tion shows subtle boundaries such as the roof under shadow and tree branches whereas the result without adaptation did not. However, the latter picked up spurious boundaries in the gutter of the roof.

For the car image, the result without adaptation could not pick up boundaries of the cars, but the result with adaptation delineated much more complete boundaries of the cars.

Fig. 8. *Region Segmentation Result I.* These images show the boundaries detected by the segmentation algorithm applied to the house image
shown in Fig. 7 The left is the result without parameter adaptation and
the right is the result with adaptation.

5 Conclusions

We have presented an adaptive parameter selection method based on local feature variance, boundary density and boundary strength. This method was combined with energy minimization techniques for segmentation of textured and
natural images.

The preliminary results are quite encouraging in that the adaptive method
outperformed the non adaptive techniques for boundary completion and region
identification. However, the results still show some unclosed boundaries especially for the texture segmentation. The third prior given in the Section 3 needs
to be incorporated into the algorithm somehow to ensure the closed boundaries.

The second issue is to remove small spurious boundaries in a textured region.
One possible way to solve the issue is to place a lower limit on the parameter,
ν, based on the local feature statistics. Within a textured region, the average of
the directional Gaussian responses is very small, and the noise in the region is
amplified in the directional strength measure, which affects the selection of ν.
Another approach is to introduce spatial smoothness to the parameter selection.
A small low-pass filter can be applied to the parameter space after the selection
to reduce noise in the space.

The third issue is to increase smoothness of the line process along curved
boundaries. Our experiments show that discrete gaussian type filters sampled
on the rectangular lattice produce strongest responses on horizontally or vertically oriented edges. This non-isotropical filter property gives the line process
more preference to horizontal and vertical boundaries, which appears in the final

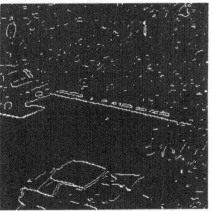

Fig. 9. *Region Segmentation Result II.* These images show the boundaries detected by the segmentation algorithm applied to the car image shown in Fig. 7. The left is the result without parameter adaptation and the right is the result with adaptation.

results (See Figs. 5 and 6). A better sampling scheme (eg. super sampling of the filters) or weighted outputs of the filters may fix the problem.

References

1. J. Besag. Spatial interaction and the statistical analysis of lattice systems. *J. Royal Statistical Soc., Ser. B*, 36:192–236, 1974.
2. A. Blake. The least–disturbance principle and weak constraints. *Pattern Recog. Lett.*, 1:393–399, 1983.
3. A. Blake and A. Zisserman. *Visual Reconstruction.* MIT Press, Cambridge, MA, 1987.
4. C. Bouman and B. Liu. Multiple resolution segmentation of textured images. *IEEE Trans. Pattern Recog. and Machine Intel.*, 13(2):259–302, 1991.
5. P. Brodatz. *Texture: A photographic album for artists and designers.* Dover, NY, NY, 1966.
6. P. Chou and C. Brown. The theory and practice of Bayesian image labeling. *Intern. J. Computer Vision*, 4:185–210, 1990.
7. G. R. Cross and A. K. Jain. Markov random field texture models. *IEEE Trans. Pattern Analysis and Machine Intel.*, 5(1):25–39, 1983.
8. J. G. Daugman. Two–dimensional spectral analysis of cortical receptive field profiles. *Vision Research*, 20:847–856, 1980.
9. J. G. Daugman. Uncertainty relation for resolution in space, spatial-frequency, and orientation optimized by two–dimensional cortical filters. *J. Optical Soc. Amer.*, 2(7):1160–1169, 1985.

10. H. Derin and H. Elliott. Modeling and segmentation of noisy and textured images using Gibbs random fields. *IEEE Trans. Pattern Analysis and Machine Intel.*, 9(1):39–55, 1987.

11. K. W. Fleischer, D. H. Laidlaw, B. L. Currin, and A. H. Barr. Cellular texture generation. In *ACM Computer Graphics, Proc. SIGGRAPH '95*, volume 29, pages 239–248, Los Angeles, CA, August 1995.

12. D. Geiger and F. Girosi. Parallel and deterministic algorithms from MRF's: Surface reconstruction. *IEEE Trans. Pattern Analysis and Machine Intel.*, 13(5):401–412, 1991.

13. D. Geiger and A. Yuille. A common framework for image segmentation. *Int. Journal of Computer Vision*, 6(3):227–243, 1991.

14. S. Geman and D. Geman. Stochastic relaxation, Gibbs distribution, and the Bayesian restoration of images. *IEEE Trans. Pattern Analysis and Machine Intel.*, 6(6):721–741, 1984.

15. S. Geman, D. Geman, C. Graffigne, and P. Dong. Boundary detection by constrained optimization. *IEEE Trans. Pattern Analysis and Machine Intel.*, 12(7):609–628, 1990.

16. A. K. Jain. Partial differential equations and finite difference methods in image processing–Part I: Image representation. *J. Optimiz. Theory and Applications*, 23:65–91, September 1977.

17. A. K. Jain and F. Farrokhnia. Unsupervised texture segmentation using Gabor filters. *Pattern Recognition*, 24(12):1167–1186, 1991.

18. A. K. Jain and J. R. Jain. Partial differential equations and finite difference methods in image processing–Part II: Image restoration. *IEEE Trans. on Automatic Control*, 23(5):596–613, October 1978.

19. A. K. Jain and S. G. Nadabar. MRF model–based segmentation of range images. In *Proc. IEEE ICCV3*, pages 667–671, Osaka, Japan, 1990.

20. I. Y. Kim and H. S. Yang. An integration scheme for image segmentation and labeling based on Markov random field model. *IEEE Trans. Pattern Analysis and Machine Intel.*, 18(1):69–73, 1996.

21. S. Lakshmanan and H. Derin. Simultaneous parameter estimation and segmentation of Gibbs random fields using simulated annealing. *IEEE Trans. Pattern Analysis and Machine Intel.*, 11:799–813, 1989.

22. T. S. Lee. A Bayesian framework for understanding texture segmentation in the primary visual cortex. *Vision Res.*, 35(18):2643–2657, 1995.

23. S. Z. Li. *Markov random field modeling in computer vision*. Springer-Verlag, New York, NY, 1995.

24. S. G. Nadabar and A. K. Jain. Parameter estimation in Markov random field contextual models using geometric models of objects. *IEEE Trans. Pattern Analysis and Machine Intel.*, 18(3):326–329, 1996.

25. N. E. Nahi and T. Assefi. Bayesian recursive image estimation. *IEEE Trans. Comput.*, 21:734–737, July 1972.

26. P. Perona and J. Malik. Scale-space and edge detection using anisotropic diffusion. *IEEE Trans. Pattern Analysis and Machine Intel.*, 12(7):629–639, 1990.

27. J. A. Stuller and B. Kurz. Two dimensional Markov representations of sampled images. *IEEE Trans. Commun.*, 24:1148–1152, October 1976.

28. D. Terzopoulos. Regularization of inverse visual problems involving discontinuities. *IEEE Trans. Pattern Analysis and Machine Intel.*, 8(4):413–424, July 1986.

29. D. Terzopoulos. The computation of visible–surface representations. *IEEE Trans. Pattern Analysis and Machine Intel.*, 10(4):417–438, July 1988.

30. G. Turk. Generating textures for arbitrary surfaces using reaction–diffusion. In *ACM Computer Graphics, Proc. SIGGRAPH '91*, volume 25, pages 289–298, July 1991.

31. A. Witkin and M. Kass. Reaction–diffusion textures. In *ACM Computer Graphics, Proc. SIGGRAPH '91*, volume 25, pages 299–308, July 1991.

32. E. Wong. Two dimensional random fields and representation of images. *SIAM J. Appl. Math*, 16:756–770, July 1968.

33. J. W. Woods. Two dimensional discrete Markov fields. *IEEE Trans. Inform. Th.*, 18:232–240, March 1972.

Deterministic Methods

Twenty Questions, Focus of Attention, and A*: A Theoretical Comparison of Optimization Strategies

A. L. Yuille[1] and J. Coughlan[2]

[1] Smith-Kettlewell Eye Research Institute, San Francisco, California, CA 94115, USA.
[2] Department of Physics, Harvard University, Cambridge, MA 02139. USA

Abstract. Many vision problems involve the detection of the boundary of an object, like a hand, or the tracking of a one-dimensional structure, such as a road in an aerial photograph. These problems can be formulated in terms of Bayesian probability theory and hence expressed as optimization problems on trees or graphs. The twenty questions, or minimum entropy, algorithm has recently been developed by Geman and Jedynak (1994) as a highly effective, and intuitive, tree search algorithm for road tracking. In this paper we analyse this algorithm to understand how it compares to existing algorithms used for vision, and related, optimization problems. First we show that it is a special case of the focus of attention planning strategy used on causal graphs, or Bayes nets, [18]. We then show its relations to standard methods, already successfully applied to vision optimization problems, such as dynamic programming, decision trees, the A* algorithm used in artificial intelligence [22] and the, closely related, Dijkstra algorithm of computer science [4]. These comparisons show that twenty questions is often equivalent to an algorithm, which we call A+, which tries to explore the most probable paths first. We show that A+ is a greedy, and suboptimal, variant of A*. This suggests that A+ and twenty questions will be faster than A* and Dijkstra for certain problems but they may occasionally converge to the wrong answer. However, the fact that A+ and twenty questions maintain a probabilistic estimate of how well they are doing may give warning of faulty convergence and also allow intelligent pruning to speed up the search.

1 Introduction

A promising approach to object detection and recognition assumes that we represent the objects by deformable templates [8, 12, 13, 5, 20, 21, 23, 24]. These deformable templates have been successfully applied in such special purpose domains as, for example, medical images [21], face recognition [8, 24, 5, 23], and galaxy detection [20]. Deformable templates specify the shape and intensity properties of the objects and are defined probabilistically so as to take into account the variability of the shapes and the intensity properties. Objects are typically represented in terms of tree or graph structures with many nodes.

There is a formidable computational problem, however, in using such models for the detection and recognition of complex objects from real images with background clutter. The very flexibility of the models means that we have to do tree/graph search over a large space of possible object configurations in order to determine if the object is present in the image. This is possible if the objects are relatively simple, there is little background clutter, and/or if prior knowledge is available to determine likely configurations of the objects. But it becomes a very serious problem for the important general case where the objects are complex and occur in natural scenes.

Statistical sampling algorithms [12, 20], and in particular the jump diffusion algorithm [13], have been very successful but do not, as yet, work in real time except on a restricted, though important, class of problems. Moreover, the only time convergence bounds currently known for such algorithms are extremely large. Dynamic programming [3] can also be used to find the optimal solutions for a limited, though important, class of problems [17], [1],[9],[6], [14] and the time complexity is typically a low order polynomial in the parameters of the problem. Unfortunately, these algorithms are still too slow for the harder problem of real time detection of complex objects in cluttered backgrounds.

This motivates the need to investigate algorithms which perform fast intelligent search over trees and graphs. Several algorithms of this type have been recently proposed and demonstrated to run extremely quickly. These include the novel *twenty questions* algorithm for tree search [11], and adaptions of existing algorithms such as Dijkstra's algorithm [4] for special cases of graph search [10]. The twenty questions algorithm is intuitively very attractive because it uses information theory [7] to guide the search through the representation tree/graph. More recently, it has been rediscovered by Kontsevich and applied to analysing psychophysical data [15]. The basic intuition of twenty questions has also been proposed as a general approach to vision in order to explain how the human visual system might be able to solve the enormous computatational problems needed to interpret visual images and interpret visual scenes [19].

In section (2) we define the types of deformable template models we consider in the paper and give examples of their representations in terms of trees and graphs. Section (3) describes the twenty questions algorithm and shows its relation to the focus of attention method used in Bayes nets [18]. In Section (4) we define the A+ algorithm and show how it relates to twenty questions. The A* and Dijkstra algorithms are introduced in section (5) and related to A+ and hence to twenty questions. Finally we discuss the results in Section (6) and discuss the relative strengths of the algorithms.

2 Deformable Templates

The deformable templates we consider in this paper will only specify intensity properties at the boundaries of objects (i.e. they will ignore all regional intensity information). They will represent the template configuration X by a tree or a graph, see figures (1,2). There will be a probabilistic model $P(I|X)$ for generating an image I given the configuration $X \in \chi$ of the deformable template. As stated above, this model will only specify the intensity at positions at the bounding contour and will assume that the intensity is generated by a uniform probability distribution elsewhere. There will also be a prior probability $P(X)$ on the set of possible configurations of the template. The goal is to find the most probable configuration of the template. In mathematical terms, we wish to the *a posteriori* estimate X^* such that:

$$X^* = \arg\max_{X \in \chi} P(I|X)P(X). \tag{1}$$

The possible configurations in χ can be represented as trees or graphs. χ is typically enormous and it is impractical to evaluate all its possibilities. Figure (1) shows three different representations for deformable templates. In (A) we have the standard representation for Dynamic Programming (DP), see for example [6], [14]. The complexity of DP will be of order NQM where N is the number of lattice points in the relative region of the image, Q is the fan out factor, and M is the (quantized) length of the deformable template. For the road tracking problem this will be roughly of order NL which is too big for large images. By contrast, the twenty question algorithm, using the representation (B), has an empirical complexity of order L [11]. The representation (C) is based directly on the image lattice and is suitable for graph search algorithms, see for example [10]. Observe that if the fan out factor Q of DP only allows nearest neighbour interactions then representation (A) can be tranformed directly into representation (C). Moreover, we see that the twenty questions' representation, (B), ignores the fact that paths can cross over each other.

One advantage, however, of Dynamic Programming is that for these type of problems its complexity does not increase significantly even if the start and finish points of the deformable template are unknown, see figure (2) from [6].

3 Twenty Questions and focus of attention

Geman and Jedynak [11] design a deformable template model for describing roads in satellite images and a novel algorithm *twenty questions* for tracking them given an initial position and starting direction.

They represent roads in terms of a tree of straight-line segments, called 'arcs', each approximately twelve pixels long with the root arc being specified by the user. Each arc has three 'children' which can be in the same direction as its 'parent' or may turn slightly to the left or the right by a small, fixed angle. In this way the arcs form a discretization of a smooth, planar curve with bounded curvature, see figure (1). A road is defined to be a sequence of L arcs (not counting the root arc). The set χ of all possible roads has 3^L members. The set A of all arcs has $(1/2)(3^{L+1} - 1)$ members. Many of the following results will depend only on the representation being a tree (i.e. not including closed loops) and so other branching patterns are possible.

Geman and Jedynak assume a priori that all roads are equally likely and hence $P(X) = 3^{-L}$ for each X. This is equivalent to assuming that at each

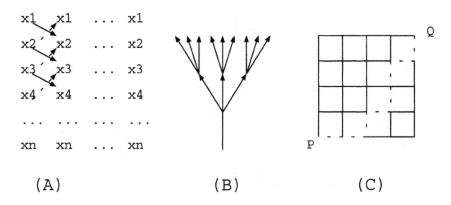

Fig. 1. Examples of representation trees or graphs. On the left, fig (A), we have the standard representation for Dynamic Programming. The columns represent the N lattice points $x1, ..., xn$ in the image and the M rows label the number of points on the deformable template. The arrows show the fan out from each lattice point and put restrictions on the set of paths the algorithm considers. Fig (B) shows the ternary representation tree used in Geman and Jedynak. The arcs represent segments in the image some of which correspond to the road being tracked. The start and end point of each arc will be points in the image lattice. The root arc, at bottom, is specified by the user. To track the road the algorithm must search through subsequent arcs. In fig (C) we represent the lattice points in the image directly. A boundary segment of a person's silhouette can be represented by points on a lattice linking salient points P and Q (see Geiger and Tyng 1996). To determine the boundary involves searching for the best path through the graph. If the fan out factor in Dynamic Programming is restricted so that each point is only connected to its neighbouring points on the image lattice then representation (A) can be re-expressed in form (C).

branch the road has an equal probability of going straight, left or right. Much of the analysis below is independent of the specific prior probabilities $P(X)$.

They assume that there are a set of test observations which can be made on the image using non-linear filters. For each arc $a \in A$, a test Y_a consists of applying a filter whose response $y_a \in \{1, ..., 10\}$ is large when the image near arc a is road-like. (An arc a is considered road-like if the intensity variation of pixels along the arc is smaller than the intensity differences between pixels perpendicular to the arc.) The distribution of the tests $\{Y_a\}$ (regarded as random variables) depends only on whether or not the arc a lies on the road candidate X and the tests are assumed to be conditionally independent given X. Thus the probabilities can be specified by

$$P(Y_a|X) = p_1(Y_a) \ if \ a \ lies \ on \ X,$$
$$P(Y_a|X) = p_0(Y_a) \ otherwise. \tag{2}$$

The probability distributions $p_1(.)$ and $p_2(.)$ are determined by experiment (i.e. by running the tests on and off the road to gain statistics). These distributions

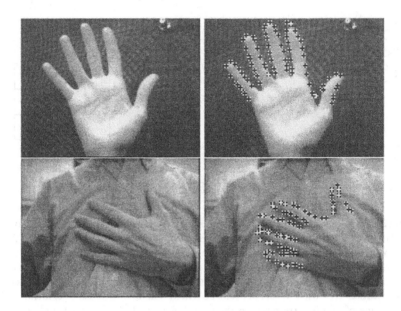

Fig. 2. Examples of a deformable template using Dynamic Programming, from Coughlan (1995). The input images are shown on the left and the outputs on the right. The deformable templates, marked by the positions of the crosses, find the true maximum a posteriori estimate, hence locating the correct positions of the hands, without knowing the positions of the start and finish points.

overlap, otherwise the tests would give unambiguous results (i.e. "road" or "not-road") and the road could be found directly. The theoretical results we obtain are independent of the precise nature of the tests and indeed the algorithm can be generalized to consider a larger class of tests, but this will not be done in this paper.

The true road may be determined by finding the MAP estimate of $P(X|\ all\ tests)$. However there is an important practical difficulty in finding the MAP: the number of possible candidates to search over is 3^L, an enormous number, and the number of possible tests is even larger (of course, these numbers ignore the fact that some of the paths will extend outside the domain of the image and hence can be ignored. But, even so, the number of possible paths is exorbitant). To circumvent this problem, Geman and Jedynak propose the *twenty questions* algorithm that uses an intelligent testing rule to select the most informative test at each iteration.

They introduce the concept of partial paths and show that it is only necessary to calculate the probabilities of these partial paths rather those of all possible road hypotheses. They define the set C_a to consist of all paths which pass through arc a. Observe, see figure (5), that this condition specifies a unique path from the root arc to a. Thus $\{X \in C_a\}$ can be thought of as the set of all possible extensions of this partial path. Their algorithm only needs to store the probabilities of certain partial paths, $z_a = P(X \in C_a|\ test\ results)$, rather than the probabilities of all the 3^L possible road paths. Geman and Jedynak describe rules for updating these probabilities z_a but, in fact, the relevant probabilities can be calculated directly (see Section (4)). It should be emphasized, that calculating these probabilities would be significantly more difficult for general graph structures where the presence of closed loops introduces difficulties which require algorithms like dynamic programming to overcome [16].

The testing rule is the following: after having performed tests Y_{π_1} through Y_{π_k}, choose the next test $Y_{\pi_{k+1}} = Y_c$ so as to minimize the conditional entropy $H(X|b_k, Y_c)$ given by:

$$H(X|b_k, Y_c) = -\sum_{y_c} P(Y_c = y_c|b_k)\{\sum_X P(X|b_k, Y_c = y_c) \log P(X|b_k, Y_c = y_c)\},$$

(3)

where $b_k = \{y_{\pi_1}, ..., y_{\pi_k}\}$ is the set of test results from steps 1 through k (we use capitals to denote random variables and lower case to denote numbers such as the results of tests). The conditional entropy criterion causes tests to be chosen which will be excepted to maximally decrease the uncertainty of the distribution $P(X|b_{k+1})$.

We also point out that their strategy for choosing tests has already been used in Bayes Nets [18]. Geman and Jedynak state that there is a relationship to Bayes Nets [11] but they do not make it explicit. This relationship can be seen from the following theorem.

Theorem 1. *The test which minimizes the conditional entropy is the same test that maximizes the mutual information between the test and the road conditioned on the results of the proceeding tests. More precisely,* $\arg\min_c H(X|b_k, Y_c) = \arg\max_c I(Y_c; X|b_k)$.

Proof. This result follows directly from standard identities in information theory [7]:

$$I(Y_a; X|b_k) = H(X|b_k) - H(X|b_k, Y_a) = H(Y_a|b_k) - H(Y_a|X, b_k), \quad (4)$$

This maximizing mutual information approach is precisely the *focus of attention* strategy used in Bayes Nets [18]. It has proven an effective strategy in medical probabilistic expert systems, for example, where it can be used to determine which diagnostic test a doctor should perform in order to gain most information about a possible disease [16]. Therefore the twenty questions algorithm can be considered as a special case of this strategy. Focus of attention, however, is typically applied to problems involving graphs with closed loops and hence it is difficult to update probabilities after a question has been asked (a test has been performed). Moreover, on graphs it is both difficult to evaluate the mutual information and to determine which, of many possible, tests will maximize the mutual information with the desired hypothesis state X.

By contrast, Geman and Jedynak are able to specify simple rules for deciding which tests to perform. This is because: (i) their tests, equation (2), are simpler that those typically used in Bayes Nets and (ii) their tree structure (i.e. no closed loops) makes it easy to perform certain computations.

The following theorem, which is stated and proven in their paper, simplifies the problem of selecting which test to perform. As we will show later, this result is also important for showing the relationship of twenty questions to A+. The theorem is valid for any graph (even with closed loops) and for arbitrary prior probabilities. It relies only on the form of the tests specified in equation (2). The key point is the assumption that roads either contain the arc which is being tested or they do not.

Theorem 2. *The test Y_c which minimizes the conditional entropy is the test which minimizes a convex function $\phi(z_c)$ where $\phi(z) = H(p_1)z + H(p_0)(1-z) - H(zp_1 + (1-z)p_0)$.*

Proof. From the information theory identities given in equation (4) it follows that minimizing $H(X|b_k, Y_c)$ with respect to a is equivalent to minimizing $H(Y_c|X, b_k) - H(Y_c|b_k)$. Using the facts that $P(Y_c|X, b_k) = P(Y_c|X)$, $z_c = P(X \in C_c|b_k)$, $P(Y_c|b_k) = \sum_X P(Y_c|X)P(X|b_k) = p_1(Y_c)z_c + p_0(Y_c)(1-z_c)$, where $P(Y_c|X) = p_1(Y_c)$ if arc c lies on X and $P(Y_c|X) = p_0(Y_c)$ otherwise, we find that:

$$H(Y_c|X, b_k) = \sum_X P(X|b_k)\{-\sum_{Y_c} P(Y_c|X) \log P(Y_c|X)\}$$
$$= z_c H(p_1) + (1 - z_c)H(p_0),$$
$$H(Y_c|b_k) = H(z_c p_1 + (1 - z_c)p_0). \tag{5}$$

The main result follows directly. The convexity can be verified directly by showing that the second order derivative is positive definite.

For the tests chosen by Geman and Jedynak it can be determined that $\phi(z)$ has a unique minimum at $\bar{z} \approx 0.51$. For the game of twenty questions, where the tests give unambiguous results, it can be shown that the minimum occurs at $\bar{z} = 0.5$ (In this case the tests will obey $p_1(Y_c = y_c)p_0(Y_c = y_c) = 0$, $\forall y_c$ and this enforces that $H(z_c p_1 + (1 - z_c)p_0) = z_c H(p_1) + (1 - z_c)H(p_0) - z_c \log z_c - (1 - z_c)\log(1 - z_c)$ and so $\phi(z) = z \log z + (1 - z)\log(1 - z)$ which is convex with minimum at $z = 0.5$).

Thus the minimal entropy criterion says that we should test the next untested arc which minimizes $\phi(z_c)$. By the nature of the tree structure and the prior there can be very few (and typically no) untested arcs with $z_c > \bar{z}$ and most untested arcs will satisfy $z_c \leq \bar{z}$. Restricting ourselves to this subset, we see that the convexity of $\phi(.)$, see figure (3), means that we need only find an arc c for which z_c is as close to $\bar{z}$ as possible. It is straightforward to show that most untested arcs, particularly distant descendants of the tested arcs, will have probabilities far less than $\bar{z}$ and so do not even need to be tested (each three way split in the tree will introduce a prior factor $1/3$ which multiplies the probabilities of the descendant arcs, so the probabilities of descendants will decay exponentially with the distance from a tested arc). It is therefore simple to minimize $\phi(z_c)$ for all arcs such that $z_c \leq \overline{z}$ and then we need simply compare this minimum to the values for the few, if any, special arcs for which $z_c > \overline{z}$. This, see [11], allows one to quickly to determine the best test to perform. Observe, that because the prior is uniform there may often be three or two arcs which have the same probability. To see this, consider deciding which arc to test when starting from the root node – all three arcs will be equally likely. It is not stated in [11] what their algorithm does in this case but we assume, in the event of a tie, that the algorithm picks one winner at random.

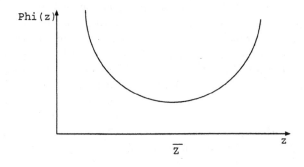

Fig. 3. Test selection for twenty questions is determined by the $\phi(z)$ function. This is convex with at minimum at $\overline{z}$. Most untested arcs a with have probabilities z_a less than $\overline{z}$ and twenty questions will prefer to explore the most probable of these paths. It is conceivable that a few untested arcs have probability greater than $\overline{z}$. In this case they may or may not be tested. The exact form of the $\phi(.)$ function depends on specific details of the problem.

4   A+ and twenty questions

In this section we define an algorithm, which we call $A+$, which simply consists of testing the most probable untested arc. We then show that this is usually equivalent to twenty questions. In the following section we show that $A+$ is also very similar to the standard Artificial Intelligence algorithm $A*$ and to Dijkstra's algorithm.

The algorithm $A+$ is based on the same model and the same array of tests used in Geman and Jedynak's work. What is different is the rule for selecting the most promising arc c on which to perform the next test Y_c. The arc c that is chosen is the arc with the highest probability z_c that satisfies two requirements: Test Y_c must not have been performed previously and c must be the child of a previously tested arc. For twenty questions the best test will typically be the child of a tested arc though occasionally, as we will describe later, it might be a grandchild or some other descendant.

Theorem 3. *A+ and Twenty questions will test the same arc provided $z_c \leq \overline{z}$ for all untested arcs c. Moreover, the only cases when the algorithms will differ is when A+ chooses to test an arc both siblings of which have already been tested.*

Proof. The first part of this result follows directly from Theorem 2: $\phi(z)$ is convex with minimum at $\overline{z}$ so, provided $z_c \leq \overline{z}$ for all untested c, the most probable untested arc is the one that minimizes the conditional entropy, see figure (3). The second part is illustrated by figure (4). Let c be the arc that A+ prefers to test. Since A+ only considers an arc c that is the child of previously tested arcs, there are only three cases to consider: when none, one, or two of c's siblings have been previously tested. In the first two cases, when none or one of c's siblings has been tested, the probability z_c is bounded: by $z_c < 1/3 < \overline{z}$ or by $z_c < 1/2 < \overline{z}$. Clearly, since c is the arc with the maximum probability, no other arc can have a probability closer to $\overline{z}$; thus arc c minimizes $\phi(z_c)$ and both algorithms are consistent. In the third case, however, when both of c's siblings have been tested, it is possible for z_c to be larger than $\overline{z}$. In this case it is possible that other arcs with smaller probabilities would lower ϕ more than $\phi(z_c)$. For example, if $\phi(z_c/3) < \phi(z_c)$, then the twenty questions algorithm would prefer any of c's (untested) children, having probability $z_c/3$, to c itself. But conceivably there may be another untested arc elsewhere with probablity higher than $z_c/3$, and lower than $\overline{z}$, which twenty questions might prefer.

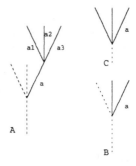

Fig. 4. The three possible possibilities for A+'s preferred arc a where dashed lines represent tested arcs. In A, both a's siblings have been tested. In this case the twenty question algorithm might prefer testing one of a's three children or some other arc elsewhere on the tree. In cases B and C, at most one of a's siblings have been tested and so both twenty questions and A+ agree.

Thus the only difference between the algorithms may occur when the previous tests will have established c's membership on the road with such high certainty that the conditional entropy principle considers it unnecessary to test c itself. In this case twenty questions may perform a "leap of faith" and test c's children or it may test another arc elsewhere. If twenty questions chooses to test c's children then this would make it potentially more efficient than A+ which would waste one test by testing c. But from the backtracking histogram in [11] it seems that testing children in this way never happened in their experiments. There may, however, have been cases when untested arcs are more probable than $\bar{z}$ and the twenty questions algorithm tested other unrelated arcs. If this did indeed happen, and the structure of the problem might make this impossible, then it is seems that twenty questions might be performing an irrelevant test. We expect therefore that A+ and twenty questions will usually pick the same test and so should have almost identical performance on the road tracking problem.

This analysis can be generalized to alternative branching structures and prior probabilities. For example, for a binary tree we would expect that the twenty questions algorithm might often make leaps of faith and test grandchildren. Conversely, the wider the larger the branching factor then the more similar A+ and twenty questions will become. In addition, a non-uniform prior, might also make it advisable to test other descendants. Of course we can generalize A+ to allow it to skip children too if the children have high probability of being on the path. But we will not do this here because, as we will see, such a generalization will reduce the similarity of A+ with A*.

Our next theorem shows that we can give an analytic expression for the probabilities of the partial paths. Recall that these are the probabilities z_a that the road goes through a particular tested arc a, see figure (5). (Geman and Jedynak give an iterative algorithm for calculating these probabilities). This leads to a formulation of the A+ algorithm which makes it easy to relate to A*. The result holds for arbitrary branching and priors.

Theorem 4. *The probabilities* $z_a = P(X \in C_a | y_1, ..., y_M)$ *of partial paths to an untested arc* a, *whose parent arc has been tested, can be expressed as:*

$$P(X \in C_a | y_1, ..., y_M) = \frac{1}{Z_M} \prod_{j=1}^{M_a} \frac{p_1(y_{a_j})}{p_0(y_{a_j})} \psi(a_j, a_{j-1}), \qquad (6)$$

where $A_a = \{a_j : j = 1...M_a\}$ *is the set of (tested) arcs lying on the path to* a, *see figure (5), and* $\psi(a_i, a_{i-1})$ *is the prior probability of arc* a_i *following arc* a_{i-1}.

Proof. Suppose a is an arc which has not yet been tested but which is a child of one that has. Assume we have test results $(y_1, ..., y_M)$, then there must be a unique subset $A_a = \{a_1, ..., a_{M_a}\}$ of tests which explore all the arcs from the starting point to arc a, see figure (5).

The probability that the path goes through arc a is given by:

$$P(X \in C_a | y_1, ..., y_M) = \sum_{X \in C_a} P(X | y_1, ..., y_M) = \sum_{X \in C_a} \frac{P(y_1, ..., y_M | X) P(X)}{P(y_1, ..., y_M)}.$$
$$(7)$$

The factor $P(y_1, ..., y_M)$ is independent of a and so we can remove it (we will only be concerned with the relative values of different probabilities and not their

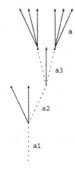

Fig. 5. For any untested arc a, there is a unique path $a_1, a_2, \ldots$ linking it to the root arc. As before, dashed lines indicate arcs that have been tested.

absolute values). Recall that the tests are independent and if arc i lies on, or off, the road then a test result y_i is produced with probability $p_1(y_i)$ or $p_0(y_i)$ respectively. We obtain:

$$P(X \in C_a | y_1, \ldots, y_M) \propto \sum_{X \in C_a} P(X) \Big(\prod_{i : X \in C_i \cap C_a} p_1(y_i) \prod_{i : X \notin C_i \cap C_a} p_0(y_i) \Big)$$

$$= \sum_{X \in C_a} P(X) \Big(\prod_{i : X \in C_i \cap C_a} \frac{p_1(y_i)}{p_0(y_i)} \prod_{i : X \notin C_i \cap C_a} p_0(y_i) \Big) \quad (8)$$

where the notation $X \in C_i \cap C_a$ means the set of all roads which contain the (tested) arc i and arc a, with $i = 1, \ldots, M$. The final factor $\prod_i p_0(y_i)$ can be ignored since it is also independent of a.

Now suppose none of arc a's children have been tested. Then since the sum in equation (8) is over all paths which go through arc a this means that set of arcs $i : X \in C_i$ on the road X for which tests are performed *must be precisely those in the unique subset A_a going from the starting point to arc a*. More precisely, $\{i = 1, \ldots, M : X \in C_i \cap C_a\} = A_a$. Therefore:

$$\prod_{i=1,\ldots,M : x \in C_i \cap C_a} \frac{p_1(y_i)}{p_0(y_i)} = \prod_{i \in A_a} \frac{p_1(y_i)}{p_0(y_i)} = \prod_{j=1}^{M_a} \frac{p_1(y_{a_j})}{p_0(y_{a_j})}. \quad (9)$$

Now $\sum_{X \in C_a} P(X)$ is simply the prior probability that the path goes through arc a. We can denote it by P_a. Because of the tree structure, it can be written as $P_a = \prod_{1=1}^{M_a} \psi(a_i, a_{i-1})$, where $\psi(a_i, a_{i-1})$ is the prior probability that the road takes the child arc a_i given that it has reached its parent a_{i-1}. If all paths passing through a are equally likely (using Geman and Jedynak's prior on the ternary graph) then $\psi(a_i, a_{i-1}) = 1/3$ for all a and we have:

$$P_a \equiv \sum_{X \in C_a} P(X) = \frac{3^{L - |A_a| - 1}}{3^L}, \quad (10)$$

where L is the total length of the road and $|A_a|$ is the length of the partial path. Therefore in the general case:

$$P(X \in C_a|y_1, ..., y_M) = \frac{1}{Z_M} \prod_{j=1}^{M_a} \frac{p_1(y_{a_j})}{p_0(y_{a_j})} \psi(a_j, a_{j-1}), \qquad (11)$$

where Z_M is a normalization factor.

5 A* and Dijkstra's algorithm

An alternative search strategy of tree search strategy, taken from the artificial intelligence literature (e.g. see [22]), is the A* graph-search algorithm. This algorithm is used to find the path of maximum cost between a start node A and a goal node B in a graph. The cost of a particular path is the sum of the costs of each edge traversed. The A* procedure maintains a tree of partial paths already explored, and computes a measure f^* of the "promise" of each partial path (i.e. leaf in the search tree). The measure f^* for any node C is defined as $f^*(C) = g^*(C) + h^*(C)$, where $g^*(C)$ is the best cumulative cost found so far from A to C and $h^*(C)$ is an overestimate of the remaining cost from C to B. The closer this overestimate is to the true cost then the faster the algorithm will run. (A* can also be expressed in terms of cost minimization in which case the overestimate must become an underestimate. For example, the arcs might represent lengths of roads connecting various "cities" (nodes), and $h^*(C)$ could be estimated as the straight-line distance from city C to B.)

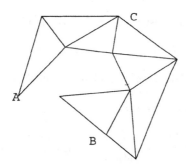

Fig. 6. The A* algorithm tries to find the most expensive path from A to B. For a partial path AC the algorithm stores $g^*(C)$, the best cost to go from A to C, and an overestimate $h^*(C)$ of the cost to go from C to B.

New paths are considered by extending the most promising node one step. If at any time two or more paths reach a common node, then all the paths but the best (in terms of f^*) are deleted. (This provision is unnecessary in searching a tree, in which case there is only one path to each leaf.)

Dijkstra's algorithm [4] can be considered as a special case of A* for which the the overestimate h^* is always zero. Since it often seems possible to redefine g^* to ensure this, see an example later this section, there seems little real difference between the two algorithms. Like A*, Dijkstra is typically expressed in terms of cost minimization. Dijkstra's algorithm is particularly relevant for us because it has been successfully applied to detecting deformable shapes in computer vision [10].

To adapt A* to apply to the road tracking problem we must convert the ternary road representation tree into a graph by introducing a terminal node to which all the leaves of the tree are connected. We set the cost of getting to this terminal node from any of the leaves of the tree to be constant. Then deciding to go from one node to an adjacent node, and evaluating the cost, is equivalent to deciding to test the arc between these nodes and evaluating the test result.

It follows directly from Theorem 4, or see [11], that the bext road is the one which maximizes:

$$E(X) = \sum_i \{log \frac{p_1(y_{ax,i})}{p_0(y_{aX,i})} + \log \psi(a_{X,i}, a_{X,i-1})\} \tag{12}$$

where $X = \{a_{X,1}, ..., a_{X_L}\}$ and $\psi(a_{X,i}, a_{X,i-1})$ is the prior probability that arc $a_{X,i}$ follows $a_{X,i-1}$.

By Theorem 4 again, the cost for a partial path of length M_a which terminates at arc a is given by:

$$g^*(a) = \sum_{j=1}^{M_a} \{log \frac{p_1(y_{ax,i})}{p_0(y_{aX,i})} + \log \psi(a_j, a_{j-1})\}. \tag{13}$$

An overestimate of the cost to the end of the road is:

$$h^*(a) = (L - M_a)\{\Lambda_0 + \Lambda_p\}, \tag{14}$$

where $\lambda_0 == \max_y \log p_1(y)/p_0(y)$ and $\lambda_p = \max \log \psi(.,,)$ over all possible prior branching factors in the tree.

The A* algorithm therefore uses a cost f* given by:

$$f^*(a) = g^*(a) + h^*(a) = \sum_{j=1}^{M_a} \{log \frac{p_1(y_{ax,i})}{p_0(y_{aX,i})} + \log \psi(a_j, a_{j-1})\} + (L - M_a)\{\Lambda_0 + \Lambda_p\}. \tag{15}$$

To obtain Dijkstra observe that we can rewrite equation (15) as

$$f^* = \sum_{a \in path} (\log \frac{p_1(y_a)}{p_0(y_a)} + \log \psi(a_j, a_{j-1}) - \Lambda_0 - \Lambda_p) + L\{\Lambda_0 + \Lambda_p\}, \tag{16}$$

and, because the length of all roads are assumed to be the same, the final term $L\{\Lambda_0 + \Lambda_p\}$ is a constant and can be ignored. This can be directly reformulated as Dijkstra with $g^* = \sum_a (\log \frac{p_1(y_a)}{p_0(y_a)} + \log \psi(a_j, a_{j-1}) - \Lambda_0 - \Lambda_p)$ and $h^* = 0$.

Observe that the size of $\Lambda_0 + \Lambda_p$ has a big influence in determining the order in which paths get searched. The bigger $\Lambda_0 + \Lambda_p$ then the bigger the overestimate cost, see equation (14). The larger the overestimate then the more A* will prefer to explore paths with a small number of tested arcs (because these paths will have overgenerous estimates of their future costs). This induces a *breadth first* search strategy [22] and may slow down the search.

We now compare A* to A+. The result is summarized in Theorem 5.

Theorem 5. *A+ is a variant of A* which does not necessarily obey the overestimate condition.*

Proof. From Theorem 4 we see that A+ picks the path which minimizes equation (13). In other words, it minimizes the $g^*(a)$ part of A* but has no overestimate term. In other words, it sets $h^*(a) = 0$ by default. There is no reason to believe that this is an overestimate for the remaining part of the path. Of course, if $\Lambda_0 + \Lambda_p \leq 0$ then $h^*(a) = 0$ would be an acceptable overestimate. For the special case considered by Geman and Jedynak this would require that $\max_y \log\{p_1(y)/p_0(y)\} - \log 3 \leq 0$. For their probability distributions it seems that this condition is not satisfied, see figure 5 in [11].

This means that A+, and hence twenty questions, are typically suboptimal and are not guaranteed to converge to the optimal solution. On the other hand, the fact that A* uses upper bounds means that it prefers paths with few arcs to those with many, so it may waste time by exploring in breadth. We will return to these issues in the discussion.

6 Discussion

This report has explored connections between twenty questions, focussed attention search, A* and Dijkstra. We described how twenty questions and focussed attention search use the same heuristic but because focussed attention search is typically applied only to the harder problem of estimation on graphs (with closed loops) it has not been as well analyzed and fewer results can be proven about it.

We showed that twenty questions and A+ (following the most probable path) are very similar. Our analysis showed that twenty questions might sometimes takes leaps of faith which might make it faster than A+, particularly when there are not too many false road paths. But there seemed to be no evidence for such jumps in the results reported in [11] and on balance we concluded that both algorithms should give similar results on most problems.

Finally we proved that A+ is a variant of A* and Dijkstra which does not necessarily satisfy the overestimation condition for the remaining part of each path. This means that A+, and by extension twenty questions, is not guaranteed to find the best path and is hence suboptimal. In practice, however, the number of long false road paths is small [11] and so once we have reached a leaf node there is unlikely to be a better path elsewhere. Moreover, the fact that twenty questions maintains an estimate of the probabilities of partial paths gives it an absolute measure of how well partial paths are doing. In fact, Geman and Jedynak make use of this property to prune paths whose probabilities are below a threshold. In particular, if the probability of a partial path is above a threshold then they assume it is correct and re-initialize it as a new root node. Observe also that A+ and twenty questions may often be faster than A* and Dijkstra *precisely* because they may violate the overestimation requirement. This violation means that they will be biased towards longer paths and so may avoid searching many short paths (breadth first search) which can slow down Dijkstra/A* for certain problems. We conjecture that this advantage will be greater the less the amount of background clutter in the image. We are currently investigating this issue.

In summary, both twenty questions and A* offer speed ups over A*/Dijkstra at the cost of sometimes converging to the wrong answer. However, the fact that they maintain probabilities of paths does allow them to check how well they are performing and give possible indications of faulty convergence (of course, these estimate are based on the assumption that the probabilities used by the models are correct for the images being processed). On the other hand, both A* and Dijkstra are designed to work on graphs with closed loops and it seems difficult to extend twenty questions and A+ to to such representations.

Acknowledgements

This report was partially inspired by an interesting talk by Donald Geman and by David Mumford wondering what relation there was between the twenty question algorithm and A*. One of (ALY) is grateful to Davi Geiger for discussions of the Dijkstra algorithm and to M.I. Miller and N. Khaneja for useful discussions about the results in this paper and their work on Dynamic Programming. This work was partially supported by NSF Grant IRI 92-23676 and the Center for Imaging Science funded by ARO DAAH049510494. ALY was employed by Harvard while some of this work was being done and would like to thank Harvard University for many character building experiences. He would also like to thank Prof's. Lei Xu and Irwin King for their hospitality at the Engineering Department of the Chinese University of Hong Kong where this work was completed.

References

1. M. Barzohar and D. B. Cooper, "Automatic Finding of Main Roads in Aerial Images by Using Geometric-Stochastic Models and Estimation," *Proc. IEEE Conf. Computer Vision and Pattern Recognition,* pp. 459-464, 1993.
2. R. Basri, L. Costa, D. Geiger, and D. Jacobs. "Determining shape similarity." In *IEEE workshop on Physics Based Vision,* Boston, June 1995.
3. R. E. Bellman, *Applied Dynamic Programming,* Princeton University Press, 1962.
4. D. Bertsekas. *Dynamic Programming and Optimal Control.* Vol. 1. (2nd Ed.) Athena Scientific Press. 1995.
5. T. F. Cootes and C. J. Taylor, "Active Shape Models - 'Smart Snakes'," *British Machine Vision Conference,* pp. 266-275, Leeds, UK, September 1992.

6. J. Coughlan. "Global Optimization of a Deformable Hand Template Using Dynamic Programming." Harvard Robotics Laboratory. Technical report. 95-1. 1995.

7. T.M. Cover and J.A. Thomas. **Elements of Information Theory**. Wiley Interscience Press. New York. 1991.

8. M.A. Fischler and R.A. Erschlager. "The Representation and Matching of Pictorial Structures". *IEEE. Trans. Computers.* C-22. 1973.

9. D. Geiger, A. Gupta, L.A. Costa, and J. Vlontzos. "Dynamic programming for detecting, tracking and matching elastic contours." *IEEE Transactions on Pattern Analysis and Machine Intelligence*, PAMI-17, March 1995.

10. D. Geiger and T-L Liu. "Top-Down Recognition and Bottom-Up Integration for Recognizing Articulated Objects". Preprint. Courant Institute. New York University. 1996.

11. D. Geman. and B. Jedynak. "An active testing model for tracking roads in satellite images". Preprint. Dept. Mathematics and Statistics. University of Massachusetts. Amherst. 1994.

12. U. Grenander, Y. Chow and D. M. Keenan, *Hands: a Pattern Theoretic Study of Biological Shapes,* Springer-Verlag, 1991.

13. U. Grenander and M.I. Miller. "Representation of Knowledge in Complex Systems". *Journal of the Royal Statistical Society,* Vol. 56, No. 4, pp 569-603. 1994.

14. N. Khaneja, M.I. Miller, and U. Grenander. "Dynamic Programming Generation of Geodesics and Sulci on Brain Surfaces". Submitted to *PAMI.* 1997.

15. L. Kontsevich. Private Communication. 1996.

16. S.L. Lauritzen and D.J. Spiegelhalter. "Local Computations with Probabilities on Graphical Structures and their Application to Expert Systems". *Journal of the Royal Statistical Society.* B. Vol. 50. No. 2., pp 157-224. 1988.

17. U. Montanari. "On the optimal detection of curves in noisy pictures." *Communications of the ACM*, pages 335–345, 1971.

18. J. Pearl. **Probabilistic Reasoning in Intelligent Systems**. San Mateo, CA:Morgan Kauffman. 1988.

19. W. Richards, and A. Bobick. "Playing twenty questions with nature." In: **Computational Processes in Human Vision: An Inter- disciplinary Perspective.** Z. Pylyshyn, Ed; Ablex, Norwood, NJ. 1988.

20. B. D. Ripley. "Classification and Clustering in Spatial and Image Data". In **Analyzing and Modeling Data and Knowledge**. Eds. M. Schader. Springer-Verlag. Berlin. 1992.

21. L.H. Straib and J.S. Duncan. "Parametrically deformable contour models". *Proceedings of Computer Vision and Pattern Recognition*, pp 98-103. San Diego, CA. 1989.

22. P.H. Winston. **Artificial Intelligence**. Addison-Wesley Publishing Company. Reading, Massachusetts. 1984.

23. L. Wiscott and C. von der Marlsburg. "A Neural System for the Recognition of Partially Occluded Objects in Cluttered Scenes". Neural Computation. 7(4):935-948. 1993.

24. A.L. Yuille "Deformable Templates for Face Recognition". *Journal of Cognitive Neuroscience.* Vol 3, Number 1. 1991.

Deterministic Annealing for
Unsupervised Texture Segmentation

Thomas Hofmann, Jan Puzicha and Joachim M. Buhmann *

Institut für Informatik III, Römerstraße 164
D-53117 Bonn, Germany
email: {th,jan,jb}@cs.uni-bonn.de, http://www-dbv.cs.uni-bonn.de

Abstract. In this paper a rigorous mathematical framework of *deterministic annealing* and *mean-field approximation* is presented for a general class of partitioning, clustering and segmentation problems. We describe the canonical way to derive efficient optimization heuristics, which have a broad range of possible applications in computer vision, pattern recognition and data analysis. In addition, we prove novel convergence results. As a major practical application we present a new approach to the problem of unsupervised texture segmentation which relies on statistical tests as a measure of homogeneity. More specifically, this results in a formulation of texture segmentation as a *pairwise data clustering* problem with a sparse neighborhood structure. We discuss and compare different clustering objective functions, which are systematically derived from invariance principles. The quality of the novel algorithms is empirically evaluated on a large database of Brodatz–like micro-texture mixtures and on a representative set of real–word images.

1 Introduction

The *unsupervised segmentation* of textured images is widely recognized as a difficult and challenging computer vision problem. It possesses a multitude of important applications, ranging from vision–guided autonomous robotics and remote sensing to medical diagnosis and retrieval in large image databases. In addition, object recognition, optical flow and stereopsis algorithms often depend on high quality image segmentations. The segmentation problem can be informally described as partitioning an image into homogeneous regions. For textured images one of the main conceptual difficulties is the definition of a homogeneity measure in mathematical terms. Many explicit texture models have been considered in the last three decades. For example, textures are often represented by feature vectors, by the means of a filter bank output [1], wavelet coefficients [2] or as parameters of an explicit Markov random field model [3]. Feature–based approaches suffer from the inadequacy of the metric utilized in parameter space to appropriately represent visual dissimilarities between different textures, a problem which is severe for unsupervised segmentation. It is an important observation [4], that the segmentation problem can be defined in terms of pairwise dissimilarities between textures without extracting explicit texture features.

Once an appropriate homogeneity measure has been identified, unsupervised texture segmentation can be formulated as a constrained combinatorial optimization problem known as *pairwise data clustering* [5], which is NP–hard in the general case. It is the aim of this paper to develop practicable efficient optimization heuristics.

* Supported by the German Research Foundation (DFG # BU 914/3–1) and by the Federal Ministry for Education, Science and Technology (BMBF # 01 M 3021 A/4).

Our approach to unsupervised texture segmentation is based on four cascaded design decisions, concerning the questions of image representation, texture homogeneity measures, objective functions and optimization procedures.

1. We use a *Gabor wavelet* scale–space representation with frequency–tuned filters as a natural image representation.
2. Homogeneity between pairs of texture patches is measured by a *non–para-metric* statistical test applied to the empirical feature distribution functions of locally sampled Gabor coefficients.
3. Due to the nature of the pairwise proximity data, we systematically derive a family of *pairwise clustering objective functions* based on invariance properties to formalize the segmentation problem. The objective functions are extended to sparse data in order to achieve additional computational efficiency.
4. As an optimization technique we apply *deterministic annealing* to derive heuristic algorithms for efficient minimization of the clustering objective functions.

This novel optimization approach combines advantages of simulated annealing with the efficiency of a deterministic procedure and has been applied successfully to a variety of combinatorial optimization problems [6–10] and computer vision tasks [11,12]. The method is presented in a unifying way for a larger class of partitioning problems and extend the pairwise clustering algorithm derived in [5] to sparse dissimilarity data. To demonstrate the capability of this optimization approach, we present a rigorous mathematical framework for the development of continuation, 'GNC–like' [13] algorithms. This also clarifies the intrinsic connection between mean–field approximation and Gibbs sampling [14]. Novel convergence proofs significantly extending [15] are given.

2 Image Representation and Non–parametric Homogeneity Measures

In the following we summarize some of the details specific to our texture segmentation approach [16,17]. The choice of a *scale space* image representation overcomes one of the key difficulties in unsupervised texture segmentation, which is the detection of the characteristic scale of a texture. Since natural textures arise at a wide range of scales, scale space methods are a promising approach for texture segmentation and texture classification. We choose a Gabor filter representation, as their good discrimination properties for textures are well-known [1,18].

The idea of applying statistical tests to compare local feature distributions is due to Geman et al. [4], where the Kolmogorov–Smirnov distance was proposed as a similarity measure. We have intensively investigated additional non–parametric tests with respect to their texture discrimination ability [16]. As a result throughout this work a χ^2–statistic is used. To apply the test, the image is partitioned into overlapping blocks, which are centered on a regular grid. For each such block $\mathbf{B}_i$ of size n and each Gabor channel $1 \leq r \leq L$ the empirical distribution of Gabor coefficients $(b_s^r)_{1 \leq s \leq n}$, $f_i^r(t) = |\{t_{k-1} \leq b_s^r \leq t_k\}|/n, t \in [t_{k-1}, t_k]$, is calculated, where $(t_k)_{0 \leq k < M}$ represents an appropriate binning. The dissimilarity between two blocks $(\mathbf{B}_i, \mathbf{B}_j)$ with respect to channel r is then given by

$$D_{ij}^{(r)} = \sum_{k=1}^{M} \frac{\left(f_i^r(t_k) - \hat{f}^r(t_k)\right)^2}{\hat{f}^r(t_k)}, \quad \text{where} \quad \hat{f}^r(t_k) = \frac{f_i^r(t_k) + f_j^r(t_k)}{2} \ . \quad (1)$$

These values are finally combined to obtain $D_{ij} = \sum_{r=1}^{L} D_{ij}^{(r)}$. There are several advantages in using a statistical test in this context. First, the result of a statistical test is directly interpretable in terms of statistical confidence and is largely independent of the specific representation and the image domain. Second, the empirical distribution functions of features preserve significantly more information than commonly used moment statistics. Third, the problem of finding the appropriate metric in the feature space is avoided.

To guarantee computational efficiency the evaluation of dissimilarity values for a block $\mathbf{B}_i$ is restricted to a substantially reduced *neighborhood* $\mathcal{N}_i$, $|\mathcal{N}_i| \ll N$, where a *neighborhood system* $\mathcal{N} = (\mathcal{N}_i)_{i=1,\dots,N}$, $\mathcal{N}_i \subset \{1,\dots,N\}$ is defined as an irreflexive and symmetric binary relation. Notice, that long range interactions are essential to correctly segment unconnected areas of identical textures [4].

3 Deterministic Annealing for Partitioning, Clustering and Segmentation Problems

3.1 Partitioning and Clustering Problems

In this section we consider combinatorial optimization problems, where a set of N objects is assigned to a certain number of K groups or labels. In the texture segmentation problem these 'objects' are image blocks $\mathbf{B}_i$ and the labels represent different texture types. If the number of distinctive classes K is known a priori, an assignment is simply given by a total mapping $\Pi : \{1,\dots,N\} \to \{1,\dots,K\}$, which we represent by indicator functions $M_{i\nu} \in \{0,1\}$ for each predicate $\Pi(i) = \nu$. All assignments are summarized in terms of a Boolean assignment matrix $\mathbf{M} \in \mathcal{M}$, where

$$\mathcal{M} = \left\{ \mathbf{M} \in \{0,1\}^{N \times K} : \sum_{\nu=1}^{K} M_{i\nu} = 1, \ 1 \le i \le N \right\}.$$

Throughout this paper any function $\mathcal{H} : \mathcal{M} \to \mathbb{R}$ will be called an *partitioning objective function* or *partitioning problem*. In this work we focus on objective functions that measure the intra–cluster compactness and depend only on the homogeneity of a cluster. The simplest choice of a cost function, which corresponds to the one proposed in [4], is the (*unnormalized*) standard graph partitioning cost function:

$$\mathcal{H}^{\mathrm{un}}(\mathbf{M}) = \sum_{\nu=1}^{K} \sum_{i=1}^{N} \sum_{j \in \mathcal{N}_i} M_{i\nu} M_{j\nu} D_{ij} \ . \quad (2)$$

We adopt the principles of *invariance with respect to additive shifts* and *invariance with respect to rescaling* of the dissimilarities as major guidelines to derive alternative *normalized* clustering objective functions. The most obvious advantage of shift invariance is the independence on the origin of the dissimilarity function. Note that $\mathcal{H}^{un}$ is not shift–invariant. For example $\mathcal{H}^{un}$ applied to non–negative data as is typical for statistical tests favors equipartitionings, because the costs for a cluster C_ν scale quadratically with the number of assigned blocks. In the opposite case, the formation of large clusters is favored. Indeed, it has been noticed [4], that the data have to be shifted adequately in order to obtain plausible segmentations. However, if a large number of different textures exists in an image, it is often impossible to globally shift the data, such that all textures are well-discriminated by the objective function $\mathcal{H}^{un}$. We have empirically verified these arguments in our simulations.

Under weak additional regularity assumptions it has been shown [16], that only four shift– and scale–invariant cost functions for sparse dissimilarities exist, which measure intra–cluster compactness.

1. Two normalized objective functions which are equivalent for complete neighborhoods combine average homogeneities proportional to the cluster size.

$$\mathcal{H}^{no}(\mathbf{M}) = \sum_{\nu=1}^{K} \sum_{i=1}^{N} M_{i\nu} \frac{\sum_{j\in\mathcal{N}_i} M_{j\nu} D_{ij}}{\sum_{j\in\mathcal{N}_i} M_{j\nu}}, \tag{3}$$

$$\mathcal{H}^{nc}(\mathbf{M}) = \sum_{\nu=1}^{K} \left[\sum_{i=1}^{N} M_{i\nu} \right] \frac{\sum_{i=1}^{N} \sum_{j\in\mathcal{N}_i} M_{i\nu} M_{j\nu} D_{ij}}{\sum_{i=1}^{N} \sum_{j\in\mathcal{N}_i} M_{i\nu} M_{j\nu}}. \tag{4}$$

2. In addition, there are two normalized objective functions, which combine homogeneities independent of the cluster size. Again, both versions are equivalent for complete neighborhoods.

$$\mathcal{H}^{sno}(\mathbf{M}) = \sum_{\nu=1}^{K} \sum_{i=1}^{N} \frac{M_{i\nu}}{\sum_{i=1}^{N} M_{i\nu}} \cdot \frac{\sum_{j\in\mathcal{N}_i} M_{j\nu} D_{ij}}{\sum_{j\in\mathcal{N}_i} M_{j\nu}}, \tag{5}$$

$$\mathcal{H}^{snc}(\mathbf{M}) = \sum_{\nu=1}^{K} \frac{\sum_{i=1}^{N} \sum_{j\in\mathcal{N}_i} M_{i\nu} M_{j\nu} D_{ij}}{\sum_{i=1}^{N} \sum_{j\in\mathcal{N}_i} M_{i\nu} M_{j\nu}}. \tag{6}$$

There are two properties, which distinguish the four cost functions. The first property is only induced by the sparseness of the neighborhood system and vanishes in the complete data limit. It concerns the question, whether every object in a cluster should have the same influence on the total costs ($\mathcal{H}^{no}$ and $\mathcal{H}^{sno}$) or whether the contribution should be proportional to the number of known dissimilarities in the assigned cluster ($\mathcal{H}^{nc}$ and $\mathcal{H}^{snc}$). For the typical neighborhood size used in the segmentation application this difference turns out to be of minor importance. The second property is fundamental, since it concerns the way cluster compactness measured for single clusters is summed up to give the total clustering costs. Cluster homogeneities can either be weighted with the cluster sizes ($\mathcal{H}^{no}, \mathcal{H}^{nc}$) or combined irrespective of their size ($\mathcal{H}^{sno}, \mathcal{H}^{snc}$). The later has the tendency to create small clusters, because it is always simpler to find clusters of higher homogeneity with few objects. For this reason, we propose to utilize prior costs to penalize unbalanced data partitionings. In addition, taking advantage of the fact that image segments for natural scenes are expected to form connected components, we also include a topological prior,

$$\mathcal{H}^{\mathrm{pr}}(\mathbf{M}) = \lambda_s \sum_{\nu=1}^{K} \left(\sum_{i=1}^{N} M_{i\nu} \right)^2 + \lambda_t \sum_{\nu=1}^{K} \sum_{i=1}^{N} M_{i\nu} \sum_{j \in \mathcal{T}_i} (1 - M_{j\nu}) , \lambda_s, \lambda_t \in \mathbb{R}^+. \quad (7)$$

Here $\mathcal{T}_i$ denotes a topological neighborhood of $\mathbf{B}_i$, e.g., the four–connected neighborhood of image blocks left, right, above and below of $\mathbf{B}_i$. More complex topological priors to forbid small and thin regions can be introduced by hard constraints as proposed in [4], but additional constraints restrict the development of efficient optimization algorithms. For this reason, we decided to extend the optimization by a post-processing stage, where the clustering solution is used as an initial configuration for an MRF–model to find a valid image partitioning respecting all constraints.

3.2 Principles of Deterministic Annealing

In recent years the stochastic optimization strategy *Simulated Annealing* has become popular to solve image processing tasks [14]. The random search is modeled by an inhomogeneous discrete–time Markov chain $(\mathbf{M}^{(t)})_{t \in \mathbb{N}}$, which stochastically samples the solution space. Since the configuration space for partitioning problems naturally decomposes into single site configurations $\mathcal{M} = \bigotimes_i \mathcal{M}_i$, we focus on a restricted class of *local* algorithms, that perform only state transitions between configurations, which differ in the assignment of at most one site. Denote by $\tilde{\mathbf{M}}_\alpha = \mathrm{s}_i(\mathbf{M}, \mathrm{e}_\alpha)$ the matrix obtained by substituting the i–th row of $\mathbf{M}$ by the unity vector e_α. For convenience we introduce a *site visitation schedule* as a map $v : \mathbb{N} \to \{1, \ldots, N\}$ fulfilling $\lim_{U \to \infty} \# \{t \leq U : v(t) = i\} \to \infty$ for all i. A sampling scheme known as the *Gibbs sampler* [14] is advantageous, if it is possible to efficiently sample from the conditional distribution at site $v(t)$, given the assignments at all other sites $\{j \neq v(t)\}$. For a given site visitation schedule v the Gibbs sampler is defined by the non–zero transition probabilities

$$S_t \left(\mathrm{s}_i(\mathbf{M}, \mathrm{e}_\alpha), \mathbf{M} \right) = \frac{\exp\left[-\mathcal{H}\left(\mathrm{s}_i(\mathbf{M}, \mathrm{e}_\alpha) \right) / T(t) \right]}{\sum_{\nu=1}^{K} \exp\left[-\mathcal{H}\left(\mathrm{s}(\mathbf{M}, \mathrm{e}_\nu) \right) / T(t) \right]}, i = v(t) . \quad (8)$$

The site visitation schedule guarantees the irreducibility of the Markov chain. For a constant temperature $T = T(t)$, the Markov chain defined by (8) will converge towards its equilibrium distribution, which is the *Gibbs distribution*

$$P_{\mathcal{H}}(\mathbf{M}) = \frac{1}{\mathcal{Z}_T} \exp(-\mathcal{H}(\mathbf{M})/T), \qquad \mathcal{Z}_T = \sum_{\mathbf{M} \in \mathcal{M}} \exp(-\mathcal{H}(\mathbf{M})/T) . \quad (9)$$

Formally, denote by $\mathcal{P}_{\mathcal{M}} = \left\{ P : \mathcal{M} \to [0,1] : \sum_{\mathbf{M} \in \mathcal{M}} P(\mathbf{M}) = 1 \right\}$ the space of probability distributions on $\mathcal{M}$ and by

$$\mathcal{F}_T(P) = \langle \mathcal{H} \rangle_P - TS(\mathbf{P}) = \sum_{\mathbf{M} \in \mathcal{M}} P(\mathbf{M})\mathcal{H}(\mathbf{M}) + T \sum_{\mathbf{M} \in \mathcal{M}} P(\mathbf{M}) \log P(\mathbf{M}) \quad (10)$$

the *generalized free energy*, which plays the role of an objective function over $\mathcal{P}_{\mathcal{M}}$. For arbitrary partitioning problems $\mathcal{H}$ the Gibbs distribution $P_{\mathcal{H}}$ minimizes the generalized free energy, i.e., $P_{\mathcal{H}} = \arg\min_{P \in \mathcal{P}_{\mathcal{M}}} \mathcal{F}_T(P)$. The basic idea of annealing is to use Gibbs sampling, but to gradually lower the temperature $T(t)$, on which the transition probabilities depend. For the zero temperature limit a deterministic local optimization algorithm known as *Iterative Conditional Mode* (ICM) [19] is obtained. Both algorithms are used for benchmarking in the segmentation experiments.

After a transient phase, a stochastic search according to a Markov process samples from the canonical Gibbs distribution. Gibbs expectation values for random variables $X(\mathbf{M})$ can thus be approximated by ergodic time–averages. The main disadvantage is the fact that stochastic techniques can be extremely slow. On the other hand, a slow annealing will often produce solutions of a very high quality, while gradient based methods are very sensible to (bad) local minima. An approach, known as *Deterministic Annealing* (DA), combines the advantages of a temperature controlled continuation method with a fast, purely deterministic computational scheme.

The key idea of DA is to calculate the relevant expectation values of system parameters, e.g., the variables of the optimization problem, analytically. In DA a combinatorial optimization problem with objective function $\mathcal{H}$ over $\mathcal{M}$ is relaxed to a family of stochastic optimization problems with objective functions $\mathcal{F}_T$ over a subspace $\mathcal{Q}_\mathcal{M} \subseteq \mathcal{P}_\mathcal{M}$. Obviously, the discrete search space $\mathcal{M}$ can be canonically embedded in $\mathcal{P}_\mathcal{M}$ by the injective mapping $e : \mathcal{M} \to \mathcal{P}_\mathcal{M}$, where $e(\mathbf{M}) = P_\mathbf{M}$ is defined as the Dirac distribution at $\mathbf{M}$. In order for $\mathcal{Q}_\mathcal{M}$ to be a true relaxation we demand $e(\mathcal{M}) \subseteq \mathcal{Q}_\mathcal{M}$. The subspace $\mathcal{Q}_\mathcal{M}$, which we will discuss in the context of partitioning problems, is the space of all factorial distributions given by

$$\mathcal{Q}_\mathcal{M} = \left\{ Q \in \mathcal{P}_\mathcal{M} \ : \ Q(\mathbf{M}) = \prod_{i=1}^{N} \sum_{\nu=1}^{K} M_{i\nu} q_{i\nu}, \ \forall \mathbf{M} \in \mathcal{M} \right\} \ . \qquad (11)$$

$\mathcal{Q}_\mathcal{M}$ is distinguished from other subspaces of $\mathcal{P}_\mathcal{M}$ in many respects. First, the dimensionality of $\mathcal{Q}_\mathcal{M}$ increases only linearly with N. Second, an efficient alternation algorithm exists for a very general class of objective functions, which converges towards a local minimum of $\mathcal{F}_T$ in $\mathcal{Q}_\mathcal{M}$. Third, in the limit of $T \to 0$ solutions to the combinatorial optimization problem can be recovered, which are locally optimal with respect to single site changes [16].

While we recover the original combinatorial problem for $T \to 0$, the generalized free energy $\mathcal{F}_T$ becomes convex at high temperatures, since the entropy S is convex. Furthermore $\mathcal{F}_T$ also becomes convex over $\mathcal{Q}_\mathcal{M}$ for sufficiently large T (cf. Theorem 4). Thus $\mathcal{F}_T$ is an entropy–smoothed version of the original optimization problem, where more and more details of the original objective function appear as T is lowered. In DA a solution is tracked from high temperatures, where $\mathcal{F}_T$ is convex, to low temperatures, where the minimization of $\mathcal{F}_T$ becomes as hard as minimizing $\mathcal{H}$ over $\mathcal{M}$. This approach relies on the possibility of minimizing the generalized free energy over $\mathcal{Q}_\mathcal{M}$. For the unrestricted case of $\mathcal{Q}_\mathcal{M} = \mathcal{P}_\mathcal{M}$ we know, that the solution is the temperature dependent Gibbs distribution $P_\mathcal{H}$. As a consequence, DA will only result in a tractable procedure for $\mathcal{P}_\mathcal{M}$, if an explicit summation over $\mathcal{M}$ can be avoided, since the calculation of assignment probabilities would require an exhaustive overall evaluation of $\mathcal{H}$. In this perspective, the relaxation to factorial distributions is an approximation of a continuation method, which is intractable in $\mathcal{P}_\mathcal{M}$. The approximation accuracy can be expressed by the cross entropy $\mathcal{I}(Q\|P_\mathcal{H})$, which is automatically minimized by minimizing $\mathcal{F}_T$ over $\mathcal{Q}_\mathcal{M}$, as $\mathcal{F}_T(Q) = \frac{1}{T}[\mathcal{I}(Q\|P_\mathcal{H}) - \log \mathcal{Z}_T]$ for all $Q \in \mathcal{P}_\mathcal{M}$.

There is a strong motivation for the maximum entropy framework. First, maximizing the entropy yields the least biased inference method being *maximally noncommittal with respect to missing data* [20]. Second, the maximum entropy probability distribution changes the least in terms of the L_2 norm if the expected costs $\langle \mathcal{H} \rangle$ are lowered or raised by changes of the temperature [21], which stresses the robustness of this inference technique. We conclude that a stochastic search heuristic, which starts with a large noise level and which gradually reduces stochasticity to zero, should ideally follow the trajectory defined by the family of Gibbs distributions with decreasing temperature.

3.3 Mean–Field Approximation

Now we concentrate on the space of factorial distribution. The resulting scheme is known as *mean–field approximation*. We will use the more specific term *Mean–Field Annealing* (MFA) instead of DA, if $P_{\mathcal{H}} \notin Q_{\mathcal{M}}$. A factorial distributions Q can be transformed into the Gibbs normal form.

$$Q(\mathbf{M}) = \exp \left[-\frac{1}{T} \sum_{i=1}^{N} \sum_{\nu=1}^{K} M_{i\nu} \left(-T \log q_{i\nu} \right) \right]. \tag{12}$$

Thus, factorial distributions could alternatively be defined by Gibbs distributions with linear Hamiltonians of the type $\mathcal{H}^0(\mathbf{M}) = \sum_{i=1}^{N} \sum_{\nu=1}^{K} M_{i\nu} h_{i\nu}$, where $h_{i\nu} \in \mathbb{R}$ are $N \cdot K$ variational parameters, which are often called *mean–fields* by physical analogy. The most important relations for factorial distributions are summarized in the following proposition, the proof of which can be found in [16].

Proposition 1. *Let $\mathcal{H}^0(\mathbf{M})$ be a linear partitioning objective function. Denote by $Q = P_{\mathcal{H}^0}$ the associated Gibbs distribution.*

1. *The partition function and the free energy are given by*

$$\mathcal{Z}_T^0 = \prod_{i=1}^{N} \sum_{\nu=1}^{K} \exp\left[-h_{i\nu}/T \right], \qquad \mathcal{F}_T^0 = -T \sum_{i=1}^{N} \log \sum_{\nu=1}^{K} \exp\left[-h_{i\nu}/T \right] \ .$$

2. *An equivalent reparametrization of Q according to (11) is obtained by*

$$q_{i\nu} = \langle M_{i\nu} \rangle_Q = \frac{\partial \mathcal{F}_T^0}{\partial h_{i\nu}} = \frac{\exp\left[-\frac{1}{T} h_{i\nu} \right]}{\sum_{\mu=1}^{K} \exp\left[-\frac{1}{T} h_{i\mu} \right]} \ .$$

The inverse transformation is only unique up to an additive constant and is given by $h_{i\nu} = -T \log q_{i\nu} + c_i$, where c_i is arbitrary. Thus the parameters $q_{i\nu}$ can be identified with the Q–averages $\langle M_{i\nu} \rangle$.

3. *All correlations w.r.t. Q vanish for assignment variables at different sites, e.g.,*

$$\langle M_{i\nu} M_{j\mu} \rangle_Q = \langle M_{i\nu} \rangle_Q \langle M_{j\mu} \rangle_Q, \nu \neq \mu \ . \tag{13}$$

Calculating stationary conditions from (10), a system of coupled transcendental, so–called *mean–field equations*, is obtained, which can be efficiently solved by a convergent iteration scheme. For factorial distributions the equation system takes the following general form.

Proposition 2. *Let $\mathcal{H}$ be an arbitrary partitioning cost function. The factorial distribution $Q^* \in \mathcal{Q}_\mathcal{M}$, which minimizes the generalized free energy $\mathcal{F}_T$ over $\mathcal{Q}_\mathcal{M}$, is characterized by the stationary conditions*

$$h_{i\nu}^* = \frac{\partial \langle \mathcal{H} \rangle_{Q^*}}{\partial q_{i\nu}} = \frac{1}{q_{i\nu}^*} \langle M_{i\nu} \mathcal{H} \rangle_{Q^*} . \tag{14}$$

3.4 Mean–Field Equations and Gibbs Sampling

There is a tight relationship between the quantities $g_{i\nu} = \mathcal{H}(s_i(M, e_\nu))$ involved in implementing the Gibbs sampler in (8) and the mean–field equations. Rewriting (14) we arrive at

$$h_{i\nu}^* = \sum_{M \in \mathcal{M}} \frac{M_{i\nu}}{q_{i\nu}^*} \mathcal{H}(M)\, Q^*(M) = \sum_{M \in \mathcal{M}} \mathcal{H}(s_i(M, e_\nu))\, Q^*(M) . \tag{15}$$

This proofs the following theorem.

Theorem 3. *The mean–fields $h_{i\nu}^*$ are a Q–averaged version of the local costs $g_{i\nu}$. Thus Q^* is characterized by*

$$q_{i\nu}^* = \frac{\exp\left[-\frac{1}{T} h_{i\nu}^*\right]}{\sum_{\mu=1}^K \exp\left[-\frac{1}{T} h_{i\mu}^*\right]}, \qquad h_{i\nu}^* = \langle g_{i\nu} \rangle_{Q^*} . \tag{16}$$

This relationship can be further clarified by the Markov blanket identity, also known as the Callen equation [5].

$$\langle M_{i\nu} \rangle_{P_\mathcal{H}} = \frac{1}{\mathcal{Z}_T} \sum_{M \in \mathcal{M}} M_{i\nu} \exp\left[-\mathcal{H}(M)/T\right] = \left\langle \frac{\exp\left[-g_{i\nu}/T\right]}{\sum_{\mu=1}^K \exp\left[-g_{i\nu}/T\right]} \right\rangle_{P_\mathcal{H}} . \tag{17}$$

The Markov blanket identity is a relation between Gibbs expectations, corresponding to the probabilistic equation of the Gibbs sampler in (8) at equilibrium. From this perspective, the mean–field approximation is seen to be equivalent to a two step approximation, which interchanges the averages with the non–linearity in (17) and neglects fluctuations in averaging the exponents.

3.5 Convergence of Mean–Field Annealing

Theorem 3 implies an optimization procedure, which converges to a local minimum of the generalized free energy.

Theorem 4. *For any site visitation schedule v and arbitrary initial conditions, the following asynchronous update scheme converges to a local minimum of the generalized free energy (10):*

$$q_{i\nu}^{\text{new}} = \frac{\exp\left[-\frac{1}{T} h_{i\nu}\right]}{\sum_{\mu=1}^K \exp\left[-\frac{1}{T} h_{i\mu}\right]}, \qquad \text{where } h_{i\nu} = \langle g_{i\nu} \rangle_{Q^{\text{old}}} \text{ and } i = v(t) . \tag{18}$$

Furthermore $\mathcal{F}_T$ is strictly convex over $\mathcal{Q}_\mathcal{M}$ for T sufficiently large.

A proof can be found in [16]. Notice, that the variables $h_{i\nu}$ are only auxiliary parameters to compactify the notation. The update scheme is essentially a non-linear Gauß–Seidel relaxation to iteratively solve the coupled transcendental equations. For polynomial $\mathcal{H}$ it is straightforward to compute the expectations of the Gibbs–fields because of Proposition 1.2 and 1.3. The convergent update scheme together with the convexity for large T leads to a GNC–like [13] algorithm, a result which does not extend to non–binary MFA-algorithms in general [22].

MFA Algorithm

```
INITIALIZE q_iν randomly, temperature T ← T₀;
WHILE T > T_FINAL
      add a small random perturbation to all q_iν;
      REPEAT
            generate a permutation π ∈ S_N;
            FOR i=1,...,N
                  update all q_π(i)ν according to (18);
      UNTIL converged ;
      T ← η·T, 0 < η < 1;
END
```

3.6 Gibbs Sampling and Deterministic Annealing for Pairwise Clustering

To efficiently implement the Gibbs sampler one has to optimize the evaluation of $\mathcal{H}$ for a sequence of locally modified assignment matrices. It is an important observation that the quantities $g_{i\nu}$ only have to be computed up to an additive shift, which may depend on the site index i, but not on ν. The choice of $g_{i\nu}(\mathbf{M}) = \mathcal{H}\left(s_i\left(\mathbf{M}, e_\nu\right)\right) - \mathcal{H}\left(s_i\left(\mathbf{M}, 0\right)\right)$ leads to compact analytical expressions, because the contributions of the reduced system without site i are subtracted.

Following Theorem 3 the problem of calculating the mean–fields $h_{i\nu}$ is reduced to the problem of Q–averaging the quantities $g_{i\nu}$. The main technical difficulty in calculating the mean–field equations are the averages of the normalization constants. Although every Boolean function has a polynomial normal form, which would in principle eliminate the denominator, to avoid exponential order in the number of conjunctions some approximations have to be made. We do this by independently averaging the numerator and the normalization in the denominator. Using Proposition 1.3 this leads to $h_{i\nu}(\mathbf{M}) = g_{i\nu}(\langle\mathbf{M}\rangle)$, which is exact in the limit of $T \to 0$, since the susceptibilities $\langle M_{i\nu}\rangle(1 - \langle M_{i\nu}\rangle)$ vanish exponentially fast at low temperatures. The approximation quality as well as an efficient implementation by proper book–keeping is further discussed in [16]. As an example we explicitly display the result for the cost function $\mathcal{H}^{nc}$. With $Q_{i\nu}^- = \sum_{j \neq i} \sum_{k \in \mathcal{N}_j, k \neq i} \langle M_{j\nu}\rangle\langle M_{k\nu}\rangle$ and $Q_{i\nu}^+ = Q_{i\nu}^- + 2\sum_{j \in \mathcal{N}_i} \langle M_{j\nu}\rangle$ we obtain

$$h_{i\nu} = \frac{2}{Q_{i\nu}^+} \sum_{j \in \mathcal{N}_i} \langle M_{j\nu}\rangle D_{ij} - \frac{2\sum_{j \in \mathcal{N}_i}\langle M_{j\nu}\rangle}{Q_{i\nu}^+ Q_{i\nu}^-} \sum_{j \neq i} \sum_{k \in \mathcal{N}_j, k \neq i} \langle M_{j\nu}\rangle\langle M_{k\nu}\rangle D_{jk} \ . \quad (19)$$

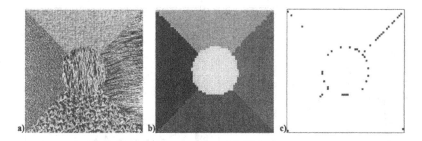

Fig. 1. Typical segmentation result with $K = 5$: (a) Randomly generated image. (b) Segmentation on the basis of the normalized costs $\mathcal{H}^{no}$. (c) Misclassified blocks (depicted in black).

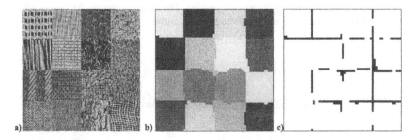

Fig. 2. Typical segmentation result with $K = 16$: (a) Randomly generated image. (b) Segmentation on the basis of the normalized costs $\mathcal{H}^{nc}$. (c) Misclassified blocks (depicted in black). For the segmentation an average neighborhood size of $|\mathcal{N}_i| = 300$ was used.

4 Results

To empirically test the segmentation algorithms on a wide range of textures we selected a representative set of 40 Brodatz–like micro–patterns. From this collection a database of random mixtures of size 512x512 pixels, containing 100 entities of five textures (as depicted in Fig. 1(a)) was constructed. All segmentations are based on a filter bank of twelve Gabor filters at four orientations and three octave scales. Each image was divided into 64x64 overlapping blocks of size 16x16 pixels each. Dissimilarities have been evaluated for an average neighborhood size of $|\mathcal{N}_i| = 80$, including the four–connected neighborhood in the image. Typical segmentation examples using the normalized cost functions are shown in Fig. 1 and 2. It has been empirically verified that the algorithms are insensitive to variation of parameters such as neighborhood size or cooling schedule, which were chosen conservatively. Typical run–times on a Sun Ultra-Sparc are about 3 minutes for the clustering stage. The used database and additional examples are available via World Wide Web (WWW).

The first question, which is empirically investigated, addresses the problem of how adequate texture segmentation is modeled by the extracted proximity data and the presented cost functions. Figure 3 shows the distribution of misclassified blocks. The distributions for the other normalized cost functions under examination are similar. For $\mathcal{H}^{no}$ a median segmentation error rate as low as 2.83% (6.84% before post-processing)

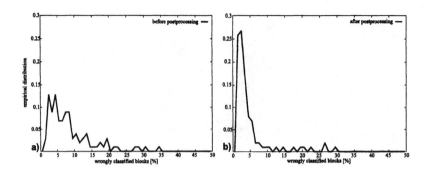

Fig. 3. Empirical density of the percentage of misclassified blocks for the database with five textures each: before (a) and after (b) post-processing. The diagram depicts the results achieved for the normalized cost function $\mathcal{H}^{no}$ with the MFA algorithm.

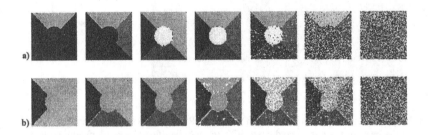

Fig. 4. Segmentations for two example images obtained by $\mathcal{H}^{un}$ for several data shifts. From the left segmentations with a mean dissimilarity of $-0.05, 0, 0.05, 0.1, 0.15, 0.2$ and 0.25 are depicted. Segments start collapsing for negative shifts. For large positive shifts the obtained segmentations become random, because the sampling noise induced by the random neighborhood system dominates the data contributions.

was obtained, which was only beaten by the $\mathcal{H}^{nc}$ cost function with a median error of 2.65% (7.12% before post-processing). For $\mathcal{H}^{snc}$ the error was 3.56% (7.50%). $\mathcal{H}^{sno}$ was excluded from the empirical investigations, because the MFA and Gibbs sampling implementation is inefficient compared to $\mathcal{H}^{snc}$ and the quality differences are expected to be marginal. We conclude, that in most cases the normalized cost functions based on a pairwise data clustering formalization capture the true structure. As can be seen in Fig. 1 (c) the misclassified blocks mainly correspond to errors at texture borders. The post-processing step improves the segmentations by a significant noise reduction. The unnormalized cost function $\mathcal{H}^{un}$ severely suffers from the missing shift–invariance property as shown in Fig. 4. Depending on the shift the unnormalized cost function often misses several full texture classes. As seen in Fig. 4 (b) there may not even exist any parameter value to find all five textures. Even worse the optimal value depends on the data at hand and varies for different images. With the unnormalized cost function $\mathcal{H}^{un}$ we achieved a median error rate of 3.86% (9.50% before post-processing) after ex-

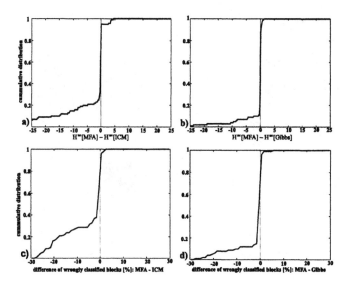

Fig. 5. The empirical density of the cost difference/misclassification rate of deterministic annealing versus the ICM algorithm (a)/(c) and versus the Gibbs sampler (b)/(d).

tensive tuning to find the appropriate data shift. A further deterioration on images with largely varying texture sizes was observed.

Another important question concerns the quality of the MFA algorithm as opposed to stochastic procedures. The quality of the proposed clustering algorithm was evaluated by comparing the costs of the achieved segmentation with the deterministic ICM algorithm and with Gibbs sampling. Exemplary for the normalized cost functions the cost differences for $\mathcal{H}^{nc}$ using MFA versus ICM (Fig. 5(a)) and MFA versus Gibbs sampler (Fig. 5(b)) are depicted. Compared with the ICM algorithm a substantial improvement has to be noted, since the ICM algorithm gets frequently stuck in bad local minima. For the comparison with the Gibbs sampler we decided to use the same number of updates for both MFA and Gibbs sampling, although the running time for the Gibbs sampler is slightly superior. As depicted in Fig. 5 MFA yields much better results. In the few cases where the other algorithms yield better solutions the achievements are insignificantly small. We have also compared the algorithms w.r.t. the percentage of misclassifications instead of energy, see 5 (c),(d). The better optimization procedure leads to substantial improvements in the segmentation quality, which is not trivial, as the global optimum of the cost function does not necessarily correspond to the ground truth segmentation.

To visualize the annealing process, we have taken the example displayed in Fig. 1 and show solutions with different number of effective clusters [7] at different temperatures. Obviously we obtain more information than just a single image segmentation. For $K = 5$ effective clusters the decrease of the mean energy starts to flatten and no phase transition occurred for the maximal range of ≈ 0.02 units. This information can be used to decide upon the question of the optimal number of clusters.

To demonstrate the applicability of the presented MFA algorithm for $\mathcal{H}^{nc}$ to real–world images we performed tests on three types of images. An important application is the

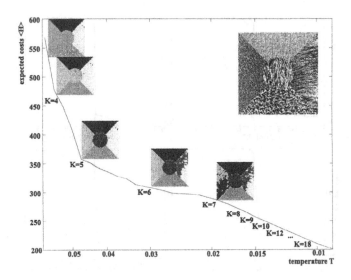

Fig. 6. Mean energy $\langle \mathcal{H}^{nc} \rangle$ and effective number of clusters as a function of T.

segmentation of Synthetic Aperture Radar (SAR) images. In Fig. 7 the segmentation into three texture classes of a SAR image is depicted. The achieved segmentation is both visually and semantically correct. Mountains, valleys and plain areas are well–separated. Even small valley structures are detected. A second interesting class of images are aerial images, as many aerial images contain texture–like structures as for example seen in Fig. 8, where an aerial image of San Francisco is segmented. The solution for $K = 8$ is visually satisfying. Tilled area and parks as well as water are well–discriminated. A third class of applications for texture segmentation are indoor and outdoor images, which contain textured objects. Unsupervised segmentation has important applications in autonomous robotics and the presented algorithms are currently implemented on the autonomous robot RHINO [23]. An example image of a typical office environment is presented in Fig. 9. Untextured parts of the image are grouped together irrespective of their absolute luminance and the discrimination of the remaining three textures is very plausible.

5 Discussion

The main contribution of the paper with respect to the development of efficient and scalable optimization algorithms is the rigorous mathematical framework for applying the optimization principle of deterministic annealing to arbitrary partitioning problems. Also guided by physical insight the framework has been developed from a purely algorithmic perspective to construct efficient GNC–like continuation methods with guaranteed convergence. The canonical way to obtain mean–field equations as well as an efficient implementation of Gibbs sampling for the proposed objective functions have been presented. The intrinsic connection with the Gibbs–sampler has been exploited

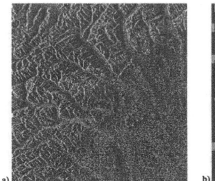 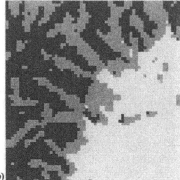

Fig. 7. SAR image of a mountain landscape: (a) original image, (b) segmentation into three clusters ($\lambda_t = 0.01$) without post-processing.

to derive efficient MFA–algorithms. The framework is general enough to adopt to a broad range of other possible clustering and partitioning applications. For the problem of unsupervised texture segmentation we have demonstrated that statistical tests are a powerful technique for texture discrimination without the need of parametric assumptions or explicit texture models. Moreover, objective functions were derived which have proven to be in very good agreement with ground truth data for an image database generated from a large collection of textures. In all these simulations covering a wide range of image domains, we have been using the same algorithms without the need of parameter tuning or learning. This is the reason, why we consider our approach to be *unsupervised* in a strict sense. As is generally true for optimization approaches to computer vision problems, this would nevertheless not be of practical use without the existence of efficient optimization algorithms. Our derivation of a deterministic annealing algorithm provides a solution to this problem. We strongly believe that deterministic annealing algorithms for related computer vision problems can be derived along the same lines.

References

1. A. Jain and F. Farrokhnia, "Unsupervised texture segmentation using Gabor filters," *Pattern Recognition*, vol. 24, no. 12, pp. 1167–1186, 1991.
2. O. Pichler, A. Teuner, and B. Hosticka, "A comparison of texture feature extraction using adaptive Gabor filtering, pyramidal and tree–structured wavelet transforms," *Pattern Recognition*, vol. 29, no. 5, pp. 733–742, 1996.
3. J. Mao and A. Jain, "Texture classification and segmentation using multiresolution simultaneous autoregressive models," *Pattern Recognition*, vol. 25, pp. 173–188, 1992.
4. D. Geman, S. Geman, C. Graffigne, and P. Dong, "Boundary detection by constrained optimization," *IEEE Transactions on Pattern Analysis and Machine Intelligence*, vol. 12, pp. 609–628, July 1990.
5. T. Hofmann and J. Buhmann, "Pairwise data clustering by deterministic annealing," *IEEE Transactions on Pattern Analysis and Machine Intelligence*, vol. 19, 1997.
6. C. Peterson and B. Söderberg, "A new method for mapping optimization problems onto neural networks," *International Journal of Neural Systems*, vol. 1, no. 1, pp. 3–22, 1989.

227

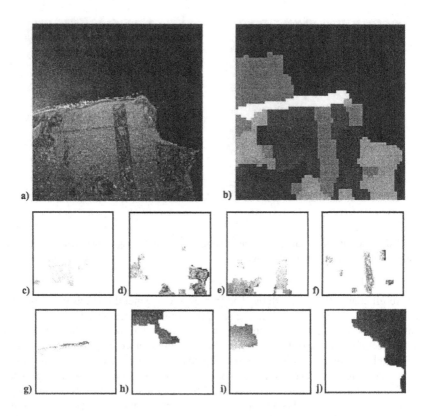

Fig. 8. Aerial image of San Francisco: (a) original grey-scale image, (b) segmentation for $K = 8$ ($\lambda_t = 0.01$) after post-processing, (c) - (j) visualization of the solution.

7. K. Rose, E. Gurewitz, and G. Fox, "Statistical mechanics and phase transition in clustering," *Physical Review Letters*, vol. 65, no. 8, pp. 945–948, 1990.

8. J. Buhmann and H. Kühnel, "Vector quantization with complexity costs," *IEEE Transactions on Information Theory*, vol. 39, pp. 1133–1145, 1993.

9. J. Kosowsky and A. Yuille, "The invisible hand algorithm: Solving the assignment problem with statistical physics," *Neural Networks*, vol. 7, no. 3, pp. 477–490, 1994.

10. S. Gold and A. Rangarajan, "A graduated assignment algorithm for graph matching," *IEEE Transactions on Pattern Analysis and Machine Intelligence*, 1996.

11. D. Geiger and F. Girosi, "Parallel and deterministic algorithms from MRF's: Surface reconstruction," *IEEE Transactions on Pattern Analysis and Machine Intelligence*, pp. 401–412, 1991.

12. J. Zerubia and R. Chellappa, "Mean field annealing using compound Gauss-Markov random fields for edge detection and image estimation," *IEEE Transactions on Neural Networks*, vol. 4, no. 4, pp. 703–709, 1993.

13. A. Blake and A. Zisserman, *Visual Reconstruction*. MIT Press, 1987.

14. S. Geman and D. Geman, "Stochastic relaxation, Gibbs distributions, and the Bayesian restoration of images," *IEEE Transactions on Pattern Analysis and Machine Intelligence*, vol. 6, no. 6, pp. 721–741, 1984.

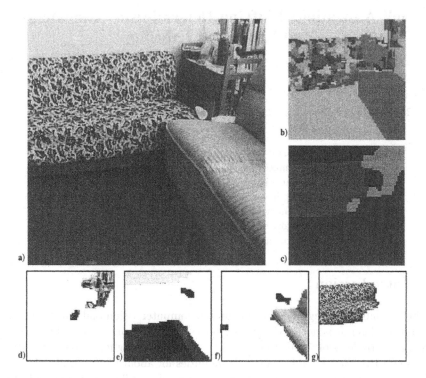

Fig. 9. (a) Indoor image of a typical office environment containing an old–fashioned sofa, (b) contrast based image segmentation with a region merging algorithms, (c) a texture segmentation with $K = 4$ ($\lambda_t = 0.01$). The image partitioning is visualized in (d) - (g).

15. J. Zhang, "The convergence of mean field procedures for MRF's," *IEEE Transactions on Image Processing*, vol. 5, no. 12, pp. 1662–1665, 1996.

16. T. Hofmann, J. Puzicha, and J. Buhmann, "A deterministic annealing framework for textured image segmentation," Tech. Rep. IAI-TR-96-2, Institut für Informatik III, 1996.

17. T. Hofmann, J. Puzicha, and J. Buhmann, "Unsupervised segmentation of textured images by pairwise data clustering," in *Proceedings of the IEEE International Conference on Image Processing, Lausanne*, 1996.

18. J. Puzicha, T. Hofmann, and J. Buhmann, "Unsupervised texture segmentation on the basis of scale space features.," in *Proceedings of the Workshop on Classical Scale–Space Theory, TR DIKU 96/19, University of Copenhagen*, 1996.

19. J. Besag, "On the statistical analysis of dirty pictures," *Journal of the Royal Statistical Society, Series B*, vol. 48, pp. 25–37, 1986.

20. E. Jaynes, "Information theory and statistical mechanics," *Physical Review*, vol. 106, no. 4, pp. 620–630, 1957.

21. Y. Tikochinsky, N. Tishby, and R. Levine, "Alternative approach to maximum–entropy inference," *Physical Review A*, vol. 30, no. 5, pp. 2638–2644, 1984.

22. M. Nielsen, "Surface reconstruction: GNCs and MFA," in *Proceedings of the International Congress on Computer Vision*, 1995.

23. J. Buhmann, W. Burgard, A. Cremers, D. Fox, T. Hofmann, F. Schneider, I. Strikos, and S. Thrun, "The mobile robot RHINO," *AI Magazin*, vol. 16, no. 1, 1995.

Self Annealing: Unifying Deterministic Annealing and Relaxation Labeling

Anand Rangarajan

Department of Diagnostic Radiology, Yale University, New Haven, CT, USA

Abstract. Deterministic annealing and relaxation labeling algorithms for classification and matching are presented and discussed. A new approach —self annealing—is introduced to bring deterministic annealing and relaxation labeling into accord. Self annealing results in an emergent linear schedule for winner-take-all and assignment problems. Also, the relaxation labeling algorithm can be seen as an approximation to the self annealing algorithm for matching and labeling problems.

1 Introduction

Labeling and matching problems abound in computer vision and pattern recognition (CVPR). It is not an exaggeration to state that some form or the other of the basic problems of template matching or data clustering has remained central to the CVPR and neural networks communities for about three decades. Due to the somewhat disparate natures of these communities, different frameworks for formulating and solving these two problems have emerged and it is not immediately obvious how to go about reconciling some of the differences between these frameworks so that they can benefit from each other.

In this paper, we pick two such frameworks, deterministic annealing [18, 24, 8, 19] and relaxation labeling [21] which arose mainly in the neural networks and pattern recognition communities respectively. Deterministic annealing has its origins in statistical physics and more recently in Hopfield networks [10]. It has been applied with varying degrees of success to a variety of image matching and labeling problems. In the field of neural networks, deterministic annealing developed from its somewhat crude origins in the Hopfield-Tank networks [10] to include fairly sophisticated treatment of constraint satisfaction and mean-field dynamics by drawing from statistical physics. Recently, for both matching and classification problems, a fairly coherent framework and suite of algorithms has emerged. These algorithms range from using the softmax or softassign for constraint satisfaction and discrete-time dynamics that mimic the Expectation–Maximization (EM) algorithm. The term relaxation labeling originally referred to a heuristic technique developed in [21] in the mid 70's. Relaxation labeling specified a discrete-time update rule by which class labels (typically in image segmentation problems) were refined while taking relationships in the pixel and label array into account. As interest in the technique grew, many bifurcations and off shoots of the basic idea developed, spanning the spectrum from *ad hoc* fixes to principled modifications and justifications [5, 11, 9, 17, 16, 3] based on probability, optimization and dynamical systems theories. Relaxation labeling in its basic form is a discrete-time update equation that is suitably (and fairly obviously) modified depending on the problem of interest—image matching, segmentation, or classification. Deviations from the basic form of relaxation labeling replaced the discrete-time update rule by gradient descent and projected gradient descent [11, 5] on the objective functions. Much of this development prefigured the evolution of optimizing neural networks; from the original Hopfield–Tank dynamics via the softmax dynamics [18, 7] to projected gradient descent [6] or softassign dynamics for the quadratic assignment problem [19, 8].

Here, we return to the heuristic origins of relaxation labeling since ironically, it is in the original discrete-time RL dynamical system that we find the closest parallel to recent deterministic annealing algorithms (which have a completely different line of development from energy functions via mean field theory to algorithms). A new approach—self annealing (SA)—is presented which promises to unify relaxation labeling (RL) and deterministic annealing (DA).

2 Deterministic Annealing

Deterministic annealing arose as a computational shortcut to simulated annealing. Closely related to *mean field* theory, the method consists of minimizing the *free energy* at each temperature setting. The free energy is separately constructed for each problem. The temperature is reduced according to a pre-specified annealing schedule. DA has been applied to a variety of combinatorial optimization problems—winner-take-all (WTA), linear assignment (AP), quadratic assignment (QAP) including the traveling salesman problem, graph matching and graph partitioning, quadratic winner-take-all (QWTA) problems including pairwise clustering, line process models in visual reconstruction etc. with varying degrees of success.

In this paper, we focus on the relationship between DA and RL with emphasis on matching and labeling problems. The archetypal problem at the heart of labeling problems is the winner-take-all and similarly for matching problems, it is linear assignment that is central. Consequently, our development dwells considerably on these two problems.

2.1 The winner take all

The WTA problem is stated as follows: Given a set T_i, $i \in \{1, \ldots, N\}$, find $i^* = \arg\max_i(T_i, i \in \{1, \ldots, N\})$ or in other words, find the index of the maximum number. Using N binary variables s_i, $i \in \{1, \ldots, N\}$, the problem is restated as:

$$\max_s \sum_i T_i s_i$$

$$\text{s. to } \sum_i s_i = 1, \text{ and } s_i \in \{0,1\}, \forall i \ . \tag{1}$$

The DA free energy is written as follows:

$$F_{\text{wta}}(v) = -\sum_i T_i v_i + \lambda(\sum_i v_i - 1) + \frac{1}{\beta}\sum_i v_i \log v_i \ . \tag{2}$$

In (2), v is a new set of *analog* mean field variables summing to one. The transition from binary variables s to analog variables v is deliberately highlighted here. Also, β is the *inverse temperature* to be varied according to an annealing schedule. λ is a Lagrange parameter satisfying the WTA constraint. The $x \log x$ form of the barrier function keeps the v variables positive and is also referred to as an *entropy* term.

We now proceed to solve for the v variables and the Lagrange parameter λ. We get (after eliminating λ)

$$v_i^{(\beta)} = \frac{\exp(\beta T_i)}{\sum_j \exp(\beta T_j)}, \ \forall i \in \{1, \ldots, N\} \ . \tag{3}$$

This is referred to as the *softmax* nonlinearity [1]. DA WTA uses the nonlinearity within an annealing schedule. (Here, we gloss over the technical issue of propagating the solution at a given temperature $v^{(\beta_n)}$ to be the initial condition at the next temperature β_{n+1}.) When there are no ties, this algorithm finds the single winner for any reasonable annealing schedule—quenching at high β being one example of an "unreasonable" schedule.

2.2 The linear assignment problem

The AP is written as follows: Given a matrix of numbers A_{ai}, $a, i \in \{1, \ldots, N\}$, find the *permutation* that maximizes the assignment. Using N^2 binary variables s_{ai}, $a, i \in \{1, \ldots, N\}$, the problem is restated as:

$$\max_s \sum_{ai} A_{ai} s_{ai}$$

$$\text{s. to } \sum_i s_{ai} = 1, \sum_a s_{ai} = 1, \text{ and } s_{ai} \in \{0, 1\}, \ \forall a, i \ . \tag{4}$$

The DA AP free energy is written as follows:

$$F_{\text{ap}}(v) = -\sum_{ai} A_{ai} v_{ai} + \sum_a \mu_a(\sum_i v_{ai}-1) + \sum_i \nu_i(\sum_a v_{ai}-1) + \frac{1}{\beta}\sum_{ai} v_{ai} \log v_{ai} \ . \tag{5}$$

In (5), v is a doubly stochastic mean field matrix with rows and columns summing to one. (μ, ν) are Lagrange parameters satisfying the row and column WTA constraints. As in the WTA case, the $x \log x$ form of the barrier function keeps the v variables positive.

We now proceed to solve for the v variables and the Lagrange parameters (μ, ν) [15, 24]. We get

$$v_{ai}^{(\beta)} = \exp(\beta A_{ai} - \beta[\mu_a + \nu_i]) \ \forall a, i \in \{1, \ldots, N\} \ . \tag{6}$$

AP is distinguished from the WTA by requiring the satisfaction of two-way WTA constraints as opposed to one. Consequently, the Lagrange parameters cannot be solved for in closed form. Rather than solving for the Lagrange parameters using steepest ascent, an iterated row and column normalization method is used to obtain a doubly stochastic matrix at each temperature [15, 19]. Sinkhorn's theorem [22] guarantees the convergence of this method. (This method can be independently derived as coordinate ascent w.r.t. the Lagrange parameters.) With Sinkhorn's method in place, the overall dynamics at each temperature is referred to as the *softassign* [19]. DA uses the softassign within an annealing schedule. (Here, we gloss over the technical issue of propagating the solution at a given temperature $v^{(\beta_n)}$ to be the initial condition at the next temperature β_{n+1}.) When there are no ties, this algorithm finds the optimal permutation for any reasonable annealing schedule.

2.3 Related problems

Having specified the two archetypal problems, the WTA and AP, we turn to other optimization problems which frequently arise in computer vision, pattern recognition and neural networks.

2.4 Clustering and Labeling

Clustering is a very old problem in pattern recognition [4, 12]. In its simplest form, the problem is to separate a set of N vectors in dimension d into K categories. The precise statement of the problem depends on whether central or pairwise clustering is the goal. In central clustering, prototypes are required, in pairwise clustering, a distance measure between any two patterns is needed [2]. Closely related to pairwise clustering is the labeling problem where a set of compatibility coefficients are given and we are asked to assign one unique label to each pattern vector. In both cases, we can write down the following general energy function:

$$\max_s \frac{1}{2} \sum_{aibj} C_{ai;bj} s_{ai} s_{aj}$$

$$\text{s. to } \sum_a s_{ai} = 1, \text{ and } s_{ai} \in \{0,1\}, \ \forall \, a, i \ . \tag{7}$$

(This energy function is a simplification of the pairwise clustering objective function used in [2], but it serves our purpose here.) If the set of compatibility coefficients C is positive definite in the subspace of the one-way WTA constraint, the local minima are WTAs with binary entries. We call this the quadratic WTA (QWTA) problem, emphasizing the quadratic objective with a one-way WTA constraint.

For the first time, we have gone beyond objective functions that are linear in the binary variables s to objective functions quadratic in s. This transition is very important and entirely orthogonal to the earlier transition from the WTA constraint to the permutation constraint. Quadratic objectives with binary variables obeying simplex like constraints are usually much more difficult to minimize than their linear objective counterparts. The DA QWTA free energy is written as follows

$$F_{\text{qwta}}(v) = -\frac{1}{2} \sum_{aibj} C_{ai;bj} v_{ai} v_{bj} + \sum_i \lambda_i (\sum_a v_{ai} - 1) + \frac{1}{\beta} \sum_{ai} v_{ai} \log v_{ai}. \quad (8)$$

Notwithstanding the increased difficulty of this problem, a DA algorithm which is fairly adept at avoiding poor local minima is:

$$q_{ai} \stackrel{\text{def}}{=} \sum_{bj} C_{ai;bj} v_{bj}, \quad (9)$$

$$v_{ai}^{(\beta)} = \frac{\exp(\beta q_{ai})}{\sum_b \exp(\beta q_{bi})} . \quad (10)$$

The intermediate q variables have an increased significance in our later discussion on RL. The algorithm consists of iterating the above equations at each temperature. It has been shown to converge to a fixed point provided C is positive definite in the subspace of the WTA constraint [23]. Central and pairwise clustering energy functions have been used in image classification and segmentation or labeling problems in general.

2.5 Matching

Template matching is also one of the oldest problems in vision and pattern recognition. Consequently, the subfield of image matching has become increasingly variegated over the years. In our discussion, we restrict ourselves to feature matching. Akin to labeling or clustering, there are two different styles of matching depending on whether a *spatial mapping* exists between the features in one image and the other. When a spatial mapping exists (or is explicitly modeled), it acts as a strong constraint on the matching. The situation when no spatial mapping is known between the features is similar to the pairwise clustering case. Here, a distance measure between pairs of features in the model and pairs of features in the image is assumed. This results in the QAP objective function—for more details see [8]:

$$\max \frac{1}{2} \sum_{aibj} C_{aibj} s_{ai} s_{bj}$$

$$\text{s. to } \sum_i s_{ai} = 1, \sum_a s_{ai} = 1, \text{ and } s_{ai} \in \{0, 1\}, \ \forall \, a, i \quad (11)$$

If the quadratic benefit matrix C is positive definite in the subspace spanned by the row and column constraints, the minima are permutation matrices. This result was shown in [24]. Once again, a DA free energy and algorithm can be written down after spotting the basic form (linear or quadratic objective, one-way or two-way constraint): The DA QAP free energy is written as follows:

$$F_{\text{qap}}(v) = -\frac{1}{2}\sum_{aibj}C_{ai;bj}v_{ai}v_{bj} + \sum_a \mu_a\left(\sum_i v_{ai} - 1\right) + \sum_i \nu_i\left(\sum_a v_{ai} - 1\right)$$
$$+\frac{1}{\beta}\sum_{ai}v_{ai}\log v_{ai}\,(12)$$

And the DA QAP algorithm is

$$q_{ai} \stackrel{\text{def}}{=} \sum_{bj}C_{ai;bj}v_{bj}, \tag{13}$$

$$v_{ai}^{(\beta)} = \exp(\beta q_{ai} - \beta[\mu_a + \nu_i]) \ . \tag{14}$$

The two Lagrange parameters μ and ν are specified by Sinkhorn's theorem and the softassign. These two equations (one for the q and one for the v) are iterated until convergence at each temperature. The softassign QAP algorithm is guaranteed to converge to a local minimum provided the Sinkhorn procedure always returns a doubly stochastic matrix [20].

We have written down DA algorithms for two problems (QWTA and QAP) while drawing on the basic forms given by the WTA and the AP. The common features in the two DA algorithms and their differences (one-way versus two-way constraints) [13] have been highlighted as well. We now turn to relaxation labeling.

3   Relaxation Labeling

Relaxation labeling as the name suggests began as a method for solving labeling problems [21]. While the framework has been extended to many applications [17, 3] the basic feature of the framework remains: Start with a set of nodes i (in feature or image space) and a set of labels λ. Derive a set of compatibility coefficients (as in Section 2.4) r for each problem of interest and then apply the basic recipe of RL for updating the node-label (i to λ) assignments:

$$q_i(\lambda) = \sum_{j\mu}r_{ij}(\lambda, \mu)p_j(\mu), \tag{15}$$

$$p_i^{(n+1)}(\lambda) = \frac{p_i^{(n)}(\lambda)(1 + \alpha q_i^{(n)}(\lambda))}{\sum_\mu p_i^{(n)}(\mu)(1 + \alpha q_i^{(n)}(\mu))} \ . \tag{16}$$

Here the p's are the node-label (i to λ) labeling probabilities, the q are intermediate variables similar to the q's defined earlier in DA. α is a parameter greater than zero used to make the numerator positive (and keep the probabilities positive.) We have deliberately written the RL update equation in a quasi-canonical form while suggesting (at this point) similarities most notably to the pairwise clustering update equation. To make the semantic connection to DA more obvious, we now switch to the old usage of the v variables rather than the p's in RL.

$$q_{ia}^{(n)} = \sum_{jb} C_{ai;bj} v_{bj}, \tag{17}$$

$$v_{ia}^{(n+1)} = \frac{v_{ia}^{(n)}(1 + \alpha q_{ia}^{(n)})}{\sum_b v_{ib}^{(n)}(1 + \alpha q_{ib}^{(n)})} . \tag{18}$$

As in the QAP and QWTA DA algorithms, a Lyapunov function exists [16] for RL.

We can now proceed in the reverse order from the previous section on DA. Having written down the basic recipe for RL, specialize to WTA, AP, QWTA and QAP. While the contraction to WTA and QWTA may be obvious, the case of AP and QAP are not so clear. The reason: two-way constraints in AP are not handled by RL. We have to invoke something analogous to the Sinkhorn procedure. Also, there is no clear analog to the iterative algorithms obtained at each temperature setting. Instead the label probabilities directly depend on their previous state which is never encountered in DA. How do we reconcile this situation so that we can clearly state just where these two algorithms are in accord? The introduction of self annealing promises to answer some of these questions and we now turn to its development.

4 Self annealing

Self annealing has one goal, namely, the elimination of a temperature schedule. As a by-product we show that the resulting algorithm bears a close similarity to both DA and RL. The SA update equation for any of the (matching or labeling) problems we have discussed so far is derived [14] by minimizing

$$F(v, \sigma) = E(v) + \frac{1}{\alpha} d(v, \sigma) \tag{19}$$

where $d(v, \sigma)$ is a distance measure between v and an "old" value σ. (The explanation of the "old" value will follow shortly.) When F is minimized w.r.t v, both terms in (19) come into play. Indeed, the distance measure $d(v, \sigma)$ serves as an "inertia" term with the degree of fidelity between v and σ determined by the parameter α. For example, when $d(v, \sigma)$ is $\frac{1}{2}\|v - \sigma\|^2$, the update equation obtained after taking derivatives w.r.t. v and σ and setting the results to zero is

$$\sigma_i = v_i^{(n)}$$
$$v_i^{(n+1)} = \sigma_i - \alpha \left. \frac{\partial E(v)}{\partial v_i} \right|_{v=v^{(n+1)}} . \tag{20}$$

This update equation reduces to "vanilla" gradient descent provided we approximate $\left. \frac{\partial E(v)}{\partial v_i} \right|_{v=v^{(n+1)}}$ by $\left. \frac{\partial E(v)}{\partial v_i} \right|_{v=v^{(n)}}$. α becomes a step-size parameter. However, the distance measure is not restricted to just quadratic error measures. Especially, when positivity of the v variables is desired, a Kullback-Leibler (KL) distance measure can be used for $d(v, \sigma)$. In [14], the authors derive many linear on-line prediction algorithms using the KL divergence. Here, we apply the same approach to the QWTA and QAP.

Examine the following QAP objective function using the KL divergence as the distance measure:

$$F_{\text{saqap}}(v, \sigma, \mu, \nu, \alpha) = -\frac{1}{2} \sum_{aibj} C_{ai;bj} v_{ai} v_{bj} + \frac{1}{\alpha} \sum_{ai} \left(v_{ai} \log \frac{v_{ai}}{\sigma_{ai}} - \sigma_{ai} + v_{ai} \right)$$
$$+ \sum_{a} \mu_a (\sum_i v_{ai} - 1) + \sum_i \nu_i (\sum_a v_{ai} - 1) \quad (21)$$

We have used the generalized KL divergence $d(x,y) = \sum_i (x_i \log \frac{x_i}{y_i} - x_i + y_i)$ which is guaranteed to be greater than or equal to zero without requiring the usual constraints $\sum_i x_i = \sum_i y_i = 1$. This energy function looks very similar to the earlier DA energy function (12) for QAP. However, it has no temperature parameter. The parameter α is fixed and positive. Instead of the entropy barrier function, this energy function has a new KL measure between v and a new variable σ. Without trying to explain the SA algorithm in its most complex form (QAP), we specialize immediately to the WTA.

$$F_{\text{sawta}}(v, \sigma, \lambda, \alpha) = -\sum_i T_i v_i + \lambda (\sum_i v_i - 1) + \frac{1}{\alpha} \sum_i \left(v_i \log \frac{v_i}{\sigma_i} - \sigma_i + v_i \right) .$$
$$(22)$$

Equation (22) can be alternately minimized w.r.t. v and σ (using a closed form solution for the Lagrange parameter λ) resulting in

$$v_i^{(n+1)} = \frac{v_i^{(n)} \exp(\alpha T_i)}{\sum_j v_j^{(n)} \exp(\alpha T_j)}, \quad v_i^{(0)} > 0, \ \forall i, \ i \in \{1, \ldots, N\} . \quad (23)$$

The new variable σ is identified with $v_i^{(n)}$ in (23). When an alternating minimization (between v and σ) is prescribed for F_{sawta}, the update equation (23) results. Initial conditions are an important factor. A reasonable choice is $v_i^{(0)} = 1/N$, $\sigma_i^{(0)} = v_i^{(0)}$, $\forall i, i \in \{1, \ldots, N\}$ but other positive, initial conditions may work as well. To summarize, in the WTA, the new variable σ is identified with the "past" value of v. We have not yet shown any relationship to DA or RL.

Moving to the QAP, the main update equation used by the algorithm is

$$q_{ai} \overset{\text{def}}{=} \sum_{bj} C_{ai;bj} v_{bj}^{(n)}, \quad (24)$$

$$v_{ai}^{(n+1)} = \sigma_{ai} \exp(\alpha q_{ai} - \alpha[\mu_a + \nu_i]) . \quad (25)$$

Convergence of the SA QAP algorithm to a local minimum can be easily shown when we assume that the Sinkhorn procedure always returns a doubly stochastic matrix. Our treatment follows [20]. A discrete-time Lyapunov function for the SA QAP algorithm is (21). (The Lagrange parameter terms can be eliminated since we are restricting v to be doubly stochastic.) The change in energy is written as

$$F_{\text{saqap}}(v^{(n)}, \sigma) - F_{\text{saqap}}(v^{(n+1)}, \sigma) \stackrel{\text{def}}{=} \Delta F_{\text{SAQAP}} =$$

$$= -\frac{1}{2} \sum_{aibj} C_{ai;bj} v_{ai}^{(n)} v_{bj}^{(n)} + \frac{1}{\alpha} \sum_{ai} v_{ai}^{(n)} \log \frac{v_{ai}^{(n)}}{\sigma_{ai}}$$

$$+ \frac{1}{2} \sum_{aibj} C_{ai;bj} v_{ai}^{(n+1)} v_{bj}^{(n+1)} - \frac{1}{\alpha} \sum_{ai} v_{ai}^{(n+1)} \log \frac{v_{ai}^{(n+1)}}{\sigma_{ai}} . \tag{26}$$

The Lyapunov energy difference has been simplified using the relation $\sum_{ai} v_{ai} = N$. Using the update equation for SA in (25), the energy difference is rewritten as

$$\Delta F_{\text{saqap}} = \frac{1}{2} \sum_{aibj} C_{ai;bj} \Delta v_{ai} \Delta v_{bj} + \sum_{ai} v_{ai}^{(n)} \log \frac{v_{ai}^{(n)}}{v_{ai}^{(n+1)}} \geq 0 \tag{27}$$

where $\Delta v_{ai} \stackrel{\text{def}}{=} v_{ai}^{(n+1)} - v_{ai}^{(n)}$. The first term in (27) is non-negative due to the positive definiteness of C in the subspace spanned by the row and column constraints. The second term is non-negative by virtue of being a KL distance measure. We have shown the convergence to a fixed point of the SA QAP algorithm.

We now write down the QAP SA algorithm:

Self annealing QAP
Initialize v_{ai} to $\frac{1}{N}$, σ_{ai} to v_{ai}
Begin A: Do A until row dominance and $(1 - p_{\text{norm}}) < p_{\text{thr}}$.
   Begin B: Do B until $e_{\text{diff}} < e_{\text{thr}}$.
   $q_{ai} \leftarrow \sum_{bj} C_{ai;bj} v_{bj}$
   $v_{ai} \leftarrow \sigma_{ai} \exp(\alpha q_{ai})$
      Begin C: Do C until $s_{\text{norm}} < s_{\text{thr}}$.
      Update v_{ai} by normalizing the rows:
      $v_{ai} \leftarrow \frac{v_{ai}}{\sum_i v_{ai}}$
      Update v_{ai} by normalizing the columns:
      $v_{ai} \leftarrow \frac{v_{ai}}{\sum_a v_{ai}}$
      End C
   End B
   $\sigma_{ai} \leftarrow v_{ai}$
End A

The various parameters are defined as: $p_{\text{norm}} \stackrel{\text{def}}{=} \frac{\sum_{ai} v_{ai}^2}{N}$, $e_{\text{diff}} \stackrel{\text{def}}{=} \Delta F_{\text{saqap}}$, and $s_{\text{norm}} \stackrel{\text{def}}{=} \sqrt{\frac{\sum_a (\sum_i v_{ai} - 1)^2}{N}}$. p_{thr}, e_{thr}, and s_{thr} are the permutation, energy difference and Sinkhorn convergence thresholds respectively. Row dominance implies that thresholding v returns a permutation matrix [15]. This is the full blown SA QAP algorithm with Sinkhorn's method and the softassign used for the constraints but more importantly a built in delay between the "old" value of v namely σ and the current value of v.

5 Self annealing and deterministic annealing

SA and DA are closely related. To see this, we return to our favorite example—the WTA. The SA and DA WTAs are now brought into accord: Assume uniform rather than random initial conditions for SA. $v_i^{(0)} = 1/N$, $\forall i$, $i \in \{1, \ldots, N\}$. With uniform initial conditions, it is trivial to solve for $v_i^{(n)}$:

$$v_i^{(n)} = \frac{\exp(n\alpha T_i)}{\sum_j \exp(n\alpha T_j)}, \; \forall i, \; i \in \{1, \ldots, N\} \; . \tag{28}$$

The correspondence between SA and DA is clearly established by setting $\beta_n = n\alpha$, $n = 1, 2, \ldots$ We have shown that the SA WTA corresponds to a particular *linear* schedule for the DA WTA.

Since the case of AP is more involved than WTA, we present anecdotal experimental evidence that SA and DA are closely related. In Figure 1, we have shown the evolution of the permutation norm and the AP free energies. A linear schedule with $\beta = n\alpha$ was used. The correspondence between DA and SA is nearly exact for the permutation norm despite the fact that the free energies evolve in a different manner. The correspondence is exact only when we match the linear schedule DA parameter α to the SA parameter α. It is important that SA and DA be in lockstep, otherwise we cannot make the claim that SA corresponds to DA with an emergent linear schedule.

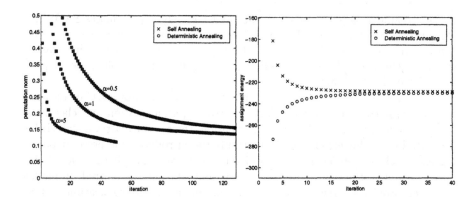

Fig. 1. Left: 100 node AP with three different schedules. The agreement between SA and DA is obvious. Right: The evolution of the SA and DA AP free energies for one schedule.

The SA and DA QAP objective functions are also quite general. The QAP or QWTA benefit matrix $C_{ai;bj}$ is preset based on the chosen problem—weighted, graph matching, or pairwise clustering. Note the basic similarity between the SA and DA QAP algorithms. In SA, a separation between past (σ) and present (v) replaces relaxation at a fixed temperature. Moreover, in the WTA and AP, SA results in an emergent linear schedule. A similar argument can be made for QAP as well but requires experimental validation due to the presence of bifurcations. We return to this topic in Section 7.

6 Self annealing and relaxation labeling

Rather than present the RL update equation in its "canonical" labeling problem form, we once again return to the WTA problem where the similarities between SA and RL are fairly obvious. The RL WTA update equation is

$$v_i^{(n+1)} = \frac{v_i^{(n)}(1 + \alpha T_i)}{\sum_j v_j^{(n)}(1 + \alpha T_j)}, \quad v_i^{(0)} > 0, \ \forall i, \ i \in \{1, \ldots, N\} \ . \tag{29}$$

Equations (23) and (29) are very similar. The main difference is the $1 + \alpha T_j$ factor in RL instead of the $\exp(\alpha T_j)$ factor in SA Expanding $\exp(\alpha T_j)$ using the Taylor-MacLaurin series gives

$$f(\alpha) = \exp(\alpha T_j) = 1 + \alpha T_j + R_2(\alpha) \tag{30}$$

where

$$R_2(\alpha) \leq \frac{\exp(\alpha|T_j|)\alpha^2 T_j^2}{2} \ . \tag{31}$$

If the remainder $R_2(\alpha)$ is small, the RL WTA closely approximates SA WTA. This will be true for small values of α. Increased divergence between RL and SA can be expected as α is increased—faster the rate of the *linear* schedule, faster the divergence. If $|T_j| > \frac{1}{\alpha}$, the non-negativity constraint is violated leading to breakdown of the RL algorithm.

Comparison at the WTA level is not the end of the story. RL in its heyday was applied to image matching, registration, segmentation and classification problems. Similar to the QAP formulation, the benefit matrix C called the compatibility coefficients in the RL literature was introduced and preset depending on the chosen problem. Because of the bias towards labeling problems, the all important distinction between matching and labeling was blurred. In model matching problems (arising in object recognition and image registration), a two way constraint is required. Setting up one-to-one correspondence between features on the model and features in the image requires such a two-way assignment constraint. On the other hand, only a one way constraint is needed in segmentation, classification, clustering and coloring problems since i) the label and the data fields occupy different spaces and ii) many data features share membership under the same label. (Despite sharing the multiple membership feature of these labeling problems, graph partitioning has a two-way constraint because of the requirement that all multiple memberships be equal in number—an arbitrary requirement from the standpoint of labeling problems arising in pattern recognition.)

Due to the bias towards labeling, RL almost never tried to enforce two-way constraints either using something like the Sinkhorn procedure in discrete-time algorithms or using projected gradient descent in continuous time algorithms. This is an important difference between SA and DA on one hand and RL on the other.

Another important difference is the separation of past and present. Due to the close ties of both SA and DA to simulated annealing, the importance of relaxation at a fixed temperature is fairly obvious. Otherwise, a very slow annealing schedule has to be prescribed to avoid poor local minima. Due to the entirely heuristic origin of RL and due to the lack of an analog of a temperature parameter, the importance of relaxation at fixed temperature was not recognized. Examining the SA and RL QAP algorithms, it is clear that RL roughly corresponds to one iteration at each temperature. This issue is orthogonal to constraint satisfaction. Even if Sinkhorn's procedure is implemented in RL—and all that is needed is non-negativity of each entry of the matrix $1 + \alpha Q_{ai}$—the separation of past (σ) and present (v) is still one iteration. Put succinctly, step B in SA is allowed only one iteration.

A remaining difference is the positivity constraint, We have already discussed the relationship between the exponential in SA and the $(1 + \alpha T_i)$ RL term in the WTA context. There is no need to repeat the analysis for QAP—note that positivity is guaranteed by the exponential whereas it must be checked in RL.

In summary, there are three principal differences between SA and RL: (i) The positivity constraint is strictly enforced by the exponential in SA and loosely enforced in RL, (ii) the use of the softassign rather than the softmax in matching problems has no parallel in RL and finally (iii) the discrete-time SA QAP update equation introduces an all important delay between past and present (roughly corresponding to multiple iterations at each temperature) whereas RL having no such delay forces one iteration per temperature with consequent loss of accuracy (as demonstrated in the next section).

7 Results

We conducted several hundreds of experiments comparing the performance of DA, RL, and SA discrete-time algorithms. The chosen problems were QAP and QWTA.

In QAP, we randomly generated benefit matrices C (of size $N \times N \times N \times N$) that are positive definite in the subspace spanned by the row and column constraints. The procedure is as follows: Define a matrix $r \stackrel{\text{def}}{=} I_N - e_N e_N^T / N$ where e_N is the vector of all ones. Generate a matrix R by taking the Kronecker product of r with itself ($R \stackrel{\text{def}}{=} r \otimes r$). Rewrite $\hat{C}$ as a two-dimensional $N^2 \times N^2$ matrix $\hat{c}$. Project $\hat{c}$ into the subspace of the row and column constraints by forming the matrix $R\hat{c}R$. Determine the smallest eigenvalue $\lambda_{\min}(R\hat{c}R)$. Then the matrix $c \stackrel{\text{def}}{=} \hat{c} - \lambda_{\min}(R\hat{c}R)I_{N^2} + \epsilon I_{N^2}$ (where ϵ is a small, positive quantity) is positive definite in the subspace spanned by the row and column constraints.

Four algorithms were executed on the QAP. Other than the three algorithms mentioned previously, we added a new algorithm called exponentiated relaxation (ER). ER is closely related to SA. The only difference is that the inner B loop in SA is performed just once ($I_B = 1$). ER is also closely related to RL. The main difference is that the positivity constraint is enforced via the exponential. Since the QAP has both row and column constraints, the Sinkhorn procedure is used in ER just as in SA. However, RL enforces just one set of constraints. To avoid this asymmetry in algorithms, we replaced the normalization procedure in RL by the Sinkhorn procedure, thereby avoiding unfair comparisons. As long as the positivity constraint is met in RL, we are guaranteed to obtain doubly stochastic matrices. There is overall no proof of convergence, however, for this "souped up" version of RL.

The common set of parameters shared by the four algorithms were kept exactly the same: $N = 25$, $\epsilon = 0.001$, Sinkhorn norm threshold $s_{\text{thr}} = 0.0001$, energy difference threshold $e_{\text{thr}} = 0.001$, permutation norm threshold $p_{\text{thr}} = 0.001$, and initial condition $v^{(0)} = e_N e_N^T / N$. The stopping criterion chosen was $p_{\text{thr}} = 0.001$ and row dominance [15]. In this way, we ensured that all four algorithms returned permutation matrices. A linear schedule $\beta = n\alpha$ was used in DA. The parameter α was varied logarithmically from $\log(\alpha) = -2$ to $\log(\alpha) = 1$ in steps of 0.1. 100 experiments were run for each of the four algorithms. The common benefit matrix $\hat{c}$ shared by the four algorithms was generated using independent, Gaussian random numbers. $\hat{c}$ was then made symmetric by forming $\frac{\hat{c}+\hat{c}^T}{2}$. The results are shown in Figure 2(a).

The most interesting feature emerging from the experiments is that there is an intermediate range of α in which self annealing performs at its best. (The negative of the QAP minimum energy is plotted on the ordinate.) Contrast this with ER and RL which do not share this feature. We conjecture that this is due to the "one iteration per temperature" policy of both these algorithms. RL could not be executed once the positivity constraint was violated but ER had no such problems. Also, notice that the performances of both SA and DA are nearly identical after $\alpha = 0.2$. The emergent linear schedule in SA derived analytically for the WTA and demonstrated in AP seems to be valid only after a certain value of α in both QAP and QWTA.

Figure 2(b) shows the results of QWTA. The behavior is very similar to the QAP. In QWTA the benefit matrices were projected onto the subspace of only one of the constraints (row or column). In other respects, the experiments were carried out in exactly the same manner as QAP. Since there is only one set of constraints, the canonical version of RL [21] was used. Note that the negative of the minimum energy is consistently higher in QWTA than QAP; this is due to the absence of the second set of constraints.

Next we studied the behavior of self annealing with changes in problem size. In Figure 3(a), the problem size is varied from $N = 2$ to $N = 25$ in steps of one. We normalized the QAP minimum energy at $\log(\alpha) = -2$ for all values of N.

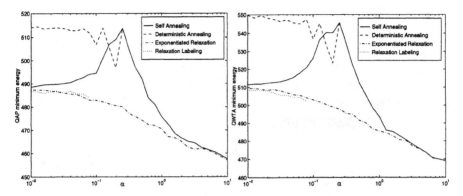

Fig. 2. Median of 100 experiments at each value of α. Left: (a) QAP. Right (b) QWTA. The negative of the QAP and QWTA minimum energies is plotted on the ordinate.

Not only is the overall pattern of behavior more or less the same, in addition there is an impressive invariance to the choice of the broad range of α. This evidence is very anecdotal however.

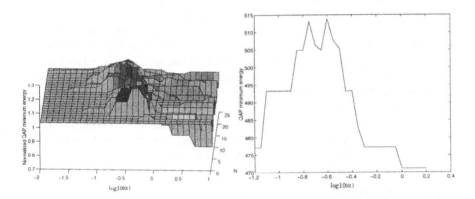

Fig. 3. Self annealing: Left: (a) Normalized negative QAP minimum energy plot for problem size N varying from 2 to 25 in steps of one. The performance is somewhat invariant to the broad range of α. Right. (b) Negative QAP minimum energy plot in a more finely sampled range of α.

Finally, we present some evidence to show that there is a qualitative change in the behavior of the self annealing algorithm roughly around $\alpha = 0.15$. The energy plot in Figure 3(b), the contour and "waterfall" plots in Figure 4 indicate the presence of different regimes in SA. The change in the permutation norm with iteration and α is a good qualitative indicator of this change in regime. Our results are very preliminary and anecdotal here. We do not as yet have any understanding of this qualitative change in behavior of SA with change in α.

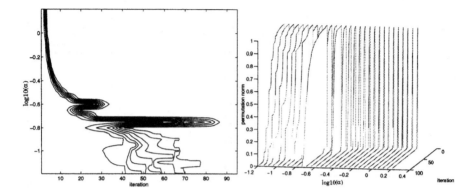

Fig. 4. Self Annealing: Left: A contour plot of the permutation norm versus α and the number of iterations. Right: A "waterfall" plot of the permutation norm versus α and the number of iterations. Both plots illustrate the abrupt change in behavior around $\alpha = 0.1$.

8 Conclusions

We have demonstrated that self annealing has the potential to reconcile relaxation labeling with deterministic annealing when applied to matching and labeling problems. While the relaxation labeling dynamical system has a Lyapunov energy function [16], we have shown that there exists a class of hitherto unsuspected self annealing energy functions that are also closely related to relaxation labeling. Our experiments and analyses suggest that relaxation labeling can be extended in a self annealing direction until the two become almost indistinguishable. The same cannot be said for deterministic annealing since it has more formal origins in mean field theory. Also, it remains to be seen if some of the more recent modifications to relaxation labeling like probabilistic relaxation [3] can be brought under the same rubric as deterministic annealing.

Acknowledgements

We acknowledge Manfred Warmuth for a helpful conversation. We thank Haili Chui, Steven Gold, Eric Mjolsness and Paul Stolorz for stimulating discussions.

References

1. J. S. Bridle. Training stochastic model recognition algorithms as networks can lead to maximum mutual information estimation of parameters. In D. S. Touretzky, editor, *Advances in Neural Information Processing Systems 2*, pages 211–217, San Mateo, CA, 1990. Morgan Kaufmann.
2. J. Buhmann and T. Hofmann. Central and pairwise data clustering by competitive neural networks. In J. Cowan, G. Tesauro, and J. Alspector, editors, *Advances in Neural Information Processing Systems 6*, pages 104–111. Morgan Kaufmann, San Francisco, CA, 1994.

3. W. J. Christmas, J. Kittler, and M. Petrou. Structural matching in computer vision using probabilistic relaxation. *IEEE Trans. Patt. Anal. Mach. Intell.*, 17(5):749–764, Aug. 1995.

4. R. Duda and P. Hart. *Pattern Classification and Scene Analysis.* Wiley, New York, NY, 1973.

5. O. Faugeras and M. Berthod. Improving consistency and reducing ambiguity in stochastic labeling: an optimization approach. *IEEE Trans. Patt. Anal. Mach. Intell.*, 3(4):412–424, Jul. 1981.

6. A. H. Gee and R. W. Prager. Polyhedral combinatorics and neural networks. *Neural Computation*, 6(1):161–180, Jan. 1994.

7. D. Geiger and A. L. Yuille. A common framework for image segmentation. *Intl. Journal of Computer Vision*, 6(3):227–243, Aug. 1991.

8. S. Gold and A. Rangarajan. A graduated assignment algorithm for graph matching. *IEEE Transactions on Pattern Analysis and Machine Intelligence*, 18(4):377–388, 1996.

9. E. R. Hancock and J. Kittler. Discrete relaxation. *Pattern Recognition*, 23(7):711–733, 1990.

10. J. J. Hopfield and D. Tank. 'Neural' computation of decisions in optimization problems. *Biological Cybernetics*, 52:141–152, 1985.

11. R. Hummel and S. Zucker. On the foundations of relaxation labeling processes. *IEEE Trans. Patt. Anal. Mach. Intell.*, 5(3):267–287, May 1983.

12. A. K. Jain and R. C. Dubes. *Algorithms for Clustering Data.* Prentice Hall, Englewood Cliffs, NJ, 1988.

13. B. Kamgar-Parsi and B. Kamgar-Parsi. On problem solving with Hopfield networks. *Biological Cybernetics*, 62:415–423, 1990.

14. J. Kivinen and M. K. Warmuth. Exponentiated gradient versus gradient descent for linear predictors. Technical Report UCSC-CRL-94-16, Univ. Calif. Santa Cruz, June 1994.

15. J. J. Kosowsky and A. L. Yuille. The invisible hand algorithm: Solving the assignment problem with statistical physics. *Neural Networks*, 7(3):477–490, 1994.

16. M. Pelillo. On the dynamics of relaxation labeling processes. In *IEEE Intl. Conf. on Neural Networks (ICNN)*, volume 2, pages 606–1294. IEEE Press, 1994.

17. M. Pelillo. Learning compatibility coefficients for relaxation labeling processes. *IEEE Trans. Patt. Anal. Mach. Intell.*, 16(9):933–945, Sept. 1994.

18. C. Peterson and B. Söderberg. A new method for mapping optimization problems onto neural networks. *Intl. Journal of Neural Systems*, 1(1):3–22, 1989.

19. A. Rangarajan, S. Gold, and E. Mjolsness. A novel optimizing network architecture with applications. *Neural Computation*, 8(5):1041–1060, 1996.

20. A. Rangarajan, A. L. Yuille, S. Gold, and E. Mjolsness. A convergence proof for the softassign quadratic assignment algorithm. In *Advances in Neural Information Processing Systems (NIPS) 9*. MIT Press, 1997. (in press).

21. A. Rosenfeld, R. Hummel, and S. Zucker. Scene labeling by relaxation operations. *IEEE Trans. Syst. Man, Cybern.*, 6(6):420–433, Jun. 1976.

22. R. Sinkhorn. A relationship between arbitrary positive matrices and doubly stochastic matrices. *Ann. Math. Statist.*, 35:876–879, 1964.

23. F. R. Waugh and R. M. Westervelt. Analog neural networks with local competition. I. Dynamics and stability. *Physical Review E*, 47(6):4524–4536, June 1993.

24. A. L. Yuille and J. J. Kosowsky. Statistical physics algorithms that converge. *Neural Computation*, 6(3):341–356, May 1994.

Multidimensional Scaling by Deterministic Annealing

Hansjörg Klock & Joachim M. Buhmann

Rheinische Friedrich–Wilhelms–Universität
Institut für Informatik III, Römerstraße 164
D-53117 Bonn, Germany
{joerg,jb}@cs.uni-bonn.de

Abstract. Multidimensional scaling addresses the problem how proximity data can be faithfully visualized as points in a low-dimensional Euclidian space. The quality of a data embedding is measured by a cost function called stress which compares proximity values with Euclidian distances of the respective points. We present a novel *deterministic annealing* algorithm to efficiently determine embedding coordinates for this continuous optimization problem. Experimental results demonstrate the superiority of the optimization technique compared to conventional gradient descent methods. Furthermore, we propose a transformation of dissimilarities to reduce the mismatch between a high-dimensional data space and a low-dimensional embedding space.

1 Introduction

Visualizing experimental data arises as a fundamental pattern recognition problem for exploratory data analysis in empirical sciences. Data are quite frequently represented as vectors in an often high-dimensional Euclidian vector space. Visualization in this context requires to project high-dimensional data to informative low-dimensional planes or manifolds. In contrast, *proximity* data represent object information by pairwise dissimilarity values instead of feature vectors. Such data occur in psychology, linguistics, genetics and other experimental sciences. Due to the relational nature of these data, their visualization poses a difficult optimization problem. Multidimensional scaling (MDS) is known as a collection of visualization techniques for proximity data which yield a set of representative data points in a suitable embedding space such that the distances between data points match the respective proximity values as faithful as possible. Section 2 provides a brief introduction to this topic.

Kruskal has formulated the search for such a set of representative data points as a continuous optimization problem [13]. Deterministic algorithms, the most frequently used candidates to solve such a problem, often converge quickly but display a tendency to get trapped in local minima. Stochastic techniques like simulated annealing treat the embedding coordinates as random variables and circumvent local minima at the expense of computation time. The merits of both techniques, speed and the capability to avoid local minima, are combined by the *deterministic annealing* approach. This design principle for optimization algorithms is reviewed in section 3. Sections 4 and 5 present the new algorithm and its derivation. The applicability of the novel algorithm to realistic problems is demonstrated in section 6.

2 Multidimensional Scaling

Multidimensional scaling refers to a class of algorithms for exploratory data analysis which visualize *proximity* relations of objects by distances between points in a low-dimensional Euclidian space. Proximity values are represented in the following as *dissimililarity* values. The reader is refered to [9] for a detailed discussion on proximity structures. Mathematically, the dissimilarity of object i to object j is defined as a real number δ_{ij}. Throughout this paper we assume symmetric dissimilarity values, i.e. $\delta_{ij} = \delta_{ji}$. The MDS algorithm determines a spatial representation of the objects, i.e. each object i is represented by coordinates $\mathbf{x}_i \in \mathbb{R}^M$ in a M-dimensional space. We will use $\mathcal{X} = \{\mathbf{x}_1, \ldots, \mathbf{x}_N\}$ to denote the entire *embedding* configuration. The distance between two points $\mathbf{x}_i$ and $\mathbf{x}_j$ of $\mathcal{X}$ is usually measured by the Euclidian distance $d_{ij} \equiv d(\mathbf{x}_i, \mathbf{x}_j) = \|\mathbf{x}_i - \mathbf{x}_j\|$. Quite often, the raw dissimilarity data are not suitable for Euclidian embedding and an additional processing step is required. To model such data transformations we assume a monotonic non-linear transformation $\mathcal{D}(\delta_{ij})$ of dissimilarities into *disparities*. Ideally, after an iterative refinement of $\mathcal{D}(.)$ and $\mathcal{X}$, the transformation $\mathcal{D}(.)$ should project the dissimilarities δ_{ij} to disparities that closely match the distances d_{ij} of the embedded points, i.e. $d_{ij} \cong \mathcal{D}(\delta_{ij})$. In section 5 we will discuss a new function $\mathcal{D}(.)$ which compensates for a potential dimensionality mismatch between dissimilarities and Euclidian distances.

Least Squares Scaling: Let us assume that the transformed dissimilarities $\mathcal{D}_{ij} = \mathcal{D}(\delta_{ij})$ match sufficiently well metric distances in an embedding space. Under this condition, MDS can be formulated as an optimization problem with the cost function

$$\mathcal{H}^{\mathrm{MDS}}(\{\mathbf{x}_i\}) = \sum_{i=1}^{N} \sum_{k=1}^{N} w_{ik} \left(\|\mathbf{x}_i - \mathbf{x}_k\|^2 - \mathcal{D}_{ik} \right)^2 \tag{1}$$

with *squared* Euclidian distances for computational simplicity. Despite the fact that many different choices are possible, e.g. based on other metrics, we will restrict the discussion in this paper to the minimization of (1). An application of the approach to other variants, e.g. Sammon mapping [20], can be found in [12]. Note that the squaring of dissimilarities is subsumed into the choice of the function $\mathcal{D}$. Eq. (1) is known as SSTRESS [3,23] in the literature. The weighting factors w_{ik} are introduced to weight the disparities individually and, thereby, to gauge the scale of the stress function, i.e., to normalize out the absolute values of the disparities $\mathcal{D}_{ij}$. Dependent on the data analysis task at hand, it might be appropriate to use a local, a global or an intermediate normalization

$$w_{ik}^{(l)} = \frac{1}{N(N-1)\mathcal{D}_{ik}^2}; \quad w_{ik}^{(g)} = \frac{1}{\sum_{i,k=1}^{N} \mathcal{D}_{ik}^2}; \quad w_{ik}^{(m)} = \frac{1}{\mathcal{D}_{ik} \sum_{l,m=1}^{N} \mathcal{D}_{lm}^2} \tag{2}$$

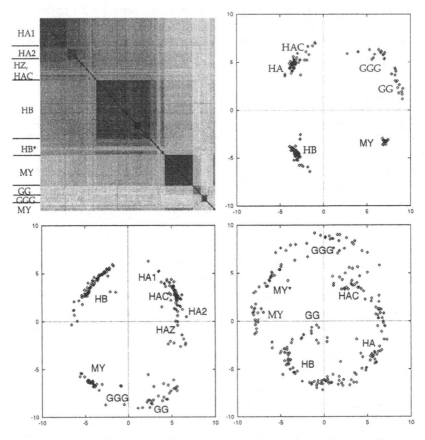

Fig. 1. Similarity matrix (a) of 226 protein sequences of the globin family. Dark grey levels correspond to high similarity values. (b)-(d) show the embeddings derived by deterministic annealing algorithm: (b) global (c) intermediate and (d) local normalization of the cost function (see text).

which corresponds to the minimization of relative, absolute or intermediate error [6]. The w_{ik} weighting might also be used to discount disparities with a high degree of experimental uncertainty. For the sake of simplicity $w_{ii} = 0$, $\forall\, i$ in the sequel. MDS methods which minimize an objective function of the type (1) are commonly referred to as *least squares scaling* (LSS) and belong to the class of *metric multidimensional scaling* algorithms. The term *metric* characterizes the type of transformation $\mathcal{D}(.)$ used to preprocess the dissimilarities and does not refer to a property of the embedding space [3]. Fig. 1 gives an idea of how MDS might be used in practice. Starting with the dissimilarity matrix (a) of 226 protein sequences from the globin family (dark grey levels correspond to small dissimilarities), embeddings are derived by minimizing (1) with global (b), intermediate (c) or local (d) weighting. The embeddings clearly reveal the cluster structure of the data with different accuracy in the representation of inter- and intra-cluster dissimilarities.

Nonmetric Scaling and ALSCAL: Often it is not possible to construct an explicit functional form $\mathcal{D}(.)$ such that the mapped dissimilarities $\mathcal{D}_{ij}$ of an empirical data set match sufficiently well metric distances. In such a situation the space of possible transformations $\mathcal{D}(.)$ has to be enlarged and should only be restricted by the monotonicity constraint $\delta_{ij} < \delta_{lk} \Rightarrow \mathcal{D}(\delta_{ij}) \leq \mathcal{D}(\delta_{lk})$. Order preserving but otherwise unconstraint transformations of the dissimilarities describe the class of *nonmetric MDS* algorithms invented by Shepard [21] and Kruskal [14]. In Kruskal's approach not the transformation $\mathcal{D}(.)$ but the disparity matrix is modified. His objective function slightly differs form (1).

A popular algorithm to perform MDS is *Alternating Least Squares Scaling* (ALSCAL) [23]. Its core routine is the minimization of the SSTRESS cost function (1) with a weighted Euclidian distance by alternating two phases until convergence. The *model estimation phase* is a diagonal method deriving an embedding $\mathcal{X}$ from the disparities $\mathcal{D}_{ik}$ and adapting a weighting. This phase is mainly equivalent to the minimization problem discussed in this paper and is based on equations that correspond to the *Dirac model* discussed below. The *optimal scaling phase* transforms the disparities $\mathcal{D}_{ik}$ to minimize the SSTRESS for the current configuration $\mathcal{X}$. The reader is refered to [3] for further details on ALSCAL and other MDS algorithms.

3 The Maximum Entropy Approach to Optimization

Stochastic Optimization and Deterministic Annealing: Stochastic optimization [11], an alternative to gradient descent techniques, has found widespread acceptance in the pattern recognition and computer vision community. Applying this approach to MDS, stochastic optimization simulates a random walk through the space Ω of possible embeddings $\mathcal{X} \in \Omega$. Such a Markov process converges to an equilibrium probability distribution known as *Gibbs distribution* with density

$$P^G(\mathcal{X}) = \exp(-\frac{1}{T}(\mathcal{H}(\mathcal{X}) - \mathcal{F})); \quad \mathcal{F} = -T \log \int_\Omega d\mathcal{X} \exp\left(-\frac{1}{T}\mathcal{H}(\mathcal{X})\right). \tag{3}$$

If we denote by $\mathcal{P}_\Omega$ the space of probability densities over Ω, then the Gibbs density P^G minimizes an objective function over $\mathcal{P}_\Omega$ called the *generalized free energy*

$$\mathcal{F}_P = \langle \mathcal{H} \rangle_P - T\mathcal{S}(P) \equiv \int_\Omega d\mathcal{X} P(\mathcal{X})\mathcal{H}(\mathcal{X}) + T \int_\Omega d\mathcal{X} P^G(\mathcal{X}) \log P^G(\mathcal{X}). \tag{4}$$

$\langle \mathcal{H} \rangle_P$ and $\mathcal{S}$ denote the *expected energy* and the *entropy* of the system with state space Ω and probability density P. The computational *temperature* T serves as a Lagrange multiplier to control the expected energy $\langle \mathcal{H} \rangle$. Obviously, entropy maximization with fixed expected costs minimizes $\mathcal{F}_P$, cf. [10].

Simulated and Deterministic Annealing: Equation (4) motivates the idea to slowly reduce the temperature during an optimization process. Analogous to experimental annealing, solutions for an optimization problem are heated and cooled in simulations. To prevent the system from falling into a poor local minimum, one starts at a high temperature T where the free energy landscape (4) is dominated by the entropy term and appears to be smoothed out. A decrease of the temperature then gradually reveals the structure of the original cost function defined by $\mathcal{H}$.

In *simulated annealing* [11], the interesting expectation values of the system parameters, e.g., the expected embedding coordinates in MDS, are estimated by sampling the Gibbs distribution P^G using a Monte Carlo method. For a logarithmically slow decrease of the temperature convergence to a global optimum [7] has been proven, but the technique is well-known for being slow compared to deterministic approaches. This drawback is cured by a technique, called *deterministic annealing*, which exactly or approximately calculates the relevant expectation values w.r.t. the Gibbs distribution. *Deterministic annealing* has first been applied to data clustering [19,2]. The convincing success advocated its application to other combinatorial optimization problems such as pairwise data clustering [24], graph matching [8] and multidimensional scaling [1]. The interested reader is refered to [24] for a more detailed discussion.

Mean Field Approximation: The computation of the free energy $\mathcal{F}$ (3) and, consequently, of all other interesting expectation values is computationally intractable due to the high-dimensional integrals $\int_\Omega f(\mathcal{X})d\mathcal{X}$. We, therefore, reside to an approximation techniques, called *mean field* approximation, which neglects specific correlations between optimization variables and only takes their average effect into account. The Gibbs $P^G(\mathcal{X})$ is approximated by a factorized distribution $P^0(\mathcal{X}|\Theta)$:

$$P^0(\mathcal{X}|\Theta) = \prod_{i=1}^{N} q_i(\mathbf{x}_i|\Theta_i) \tag{5}$$

with *mean field parameters* $\{\Theta_i | 1 \le i \le N\}$. To determine the optimal parameters Θ_i, we have to minimize the Kullback–Leibler (KL) divergence of the factorial density $P^0(\mathcal{X})$ w.r.t. to the Gibbs density $P^G(\mathcal{X})$,

$$\mathcal{I}(P^0(\mathcal{X}|\Theta)\|P^G(\mathcal{X})) \equiv \int_\Omega P^0(\mathcal{X}|\Theta) \log\left(\frac{P^0(\mathcal{X}|\Theta)}{P^G(\mathcal{X})}\right) d\mathcal{X} \tag{6}$$

EM-Algorithm: The introduction of the mean field parameters Θ_i suggests an alternating algorithm to estimate the expectation values of the embedding coordinates. Iteratively, the parameters Θ_i are optimized given a vector of statistics Φ_i that contains all relevant information about the other sites (M-step). This step is followed by a recomputation of the statistics Φ_k, $k \ne i$ on the basis of the new parameters Θ_i (E-step). The resulting alternation algorithm can be viewed as a generalized *expectation-maximization* algorithm [5].

4   Derivation of the Mean Field Approximations

Utilizing the symmetry $\mathcal{D}_{ik} = \mathcal{D}_{ki}$ and neglecting constant terms an expansion of $\mathcal{H}^{\mathrm{MDS}}$ yields the expected costs

$$\langle \mathcal{H}^{\mathrm{MDS}} \rangle = \sum_{i,k=1}^{N} w_{ik} \Bigg[2\langle \|\mathbf{x}_i\|^4 \rangle - 8\langle \|\mathbf{x}_i\|^2 \mathbf{x}_i \rangle^T \langle \mathbf{x}_k \rangle + 2\langle \|\mathbf{x}_i\|^2 \rangle \langle \|\mathbf{x}_k\|^2 \rangle$$

$$+ 4\,Tr\left[\langle \mathbf{x}_i \mathbf{x}_i^T \rangle \langle \mathbf{x}_k \mathbf{x}_k^T \rangle \right] - 4\,\mathcal{D}_{ik}(\langle \|\mathbf{x}_i\|^2 \rangle - \langle \mathbf{x}_i \rangle^T \langle \mathbf{x}_k \rangle) \Bigg], \quad (7)$$

$Tr\,[A]$ denoting the trace of matrix $\mathbf{A}$. Expectation values in (7) are taken w.r.t. the factorized distribution P^0 (5), i.e.,

$$\langle g \rangle = \int_{-\infty}^{\infty} \prod_i d\mathbf{x}_i\, g(\mathbf{x}_i)\, q_i(\mathbf{x}_i|\Theta_i) \qquad (8)$$

A Statistics for any Mean Field Approximation: Before we discuss computationally tractable model densities $q_i(\mathbf{x}_i|\Theta_i)$, we calculate the statistics $\Phi = (\Phi_1, \ldots, \Phi_N)$ for an *arbitrary* mean field approximation. Using (7) we determine the Kullback–Leibler divergence of P^0 with respect to the Gibbs density P^G

$$\mathcal{I}(P^0\|P^G) = \sum_{i=1}^{N} \langle \log q_i(\mathbf{x}_i|\Theta_i) \rangle - \frac{1}{T}\left[\langle \mathcal{H}^{\mathrm{MDS}} \rangle - \mathcal{F} \right] \qquad (9)$$

$\mathcal{F}$, the correct free energy of the system, does not depend on the mean field parameters and can be neglected in the minimization problem. A variation with respect to the parameters θ_{ip} of P^0 leads to a system of transcendental equations

$$0 = T\frac{\partial \mathcal{I}(P^0\|P^G)}{\partial \theta_{ip}} = \sum_{i=1}^{N}\left(\alpha_i^0 \frac{\partial \langle \mathbf{x}_i^4 \rangle}{\partial \theta_{ip}} + \hat{\mathbf{h}}_i^T \frac{\partial \langle \|\mathbf{x}_i\|^2 \mathbf{x}_i \rangle}{\partial \theta_{ip}} + Tr\left[\mathbf{H}_i \frac{\partial \langle \mathbf{x}_i \mathbf{x}_i^T \rangle}{\partial \theta_{ip}} \right] \right.$$

$$\left. + \mathbf{h}_i^T \frac{\partial \langle \mathbf{x}_i \rangle^T}{\partial \theta_{ip}} \right) + T\frac{\partial}{\partial \theta_{ip}}\langle \log q_i \rangle \qquad (10)$$

Terms independent of the parameters θ_{ip} are collected in the statistics $\Phi_i = (\alpha_i^0, \mathbf{h}_i, \mathbf{H}_i, \hat{\mathbf{h}}_i)$ with

$$\hat{\mathbf{h}}_i = -8\sum_{k=1}^{N} w_{ik}\langle \mathbf{x}_k \rangle \qquad \alpha_i^0 = 2\sum_{k=1}^{N} w_{ik} \qquad (11)$$

$$\mathbf{h}_i = 8\sum_{k=1}^{N} w_{ik}(\mathcal{D}_{ik}\langle \mathbf{x}_k \rangle - \langle |\mathbf{x}_k|^2 \mathbf{x}_k \rangle) \qquad (12)$$

$$\mathbf{H}_i = \sum_{k=1}^{N} w_{ik}(8\langle \mathbf{x}_k \mathbf{x}_k^T \rangle + 4\mathbf{I}(\langle |\mathbf{x}_k|^2 \rangle - \mathcal{D}_{ik})) \qquad (13)$$

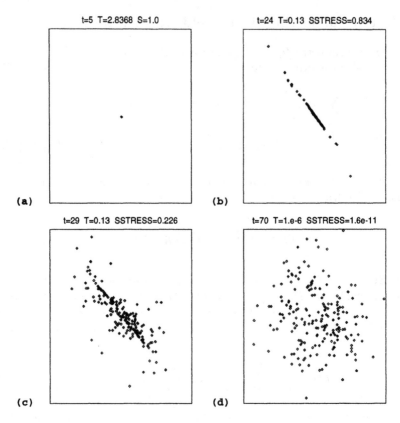

Fig. 2. Evolution of the coordinates at different temperature levels

The reader should note that the derivation up to this point does not depend on the choice of the model density (5). Φ_i is a statistics to compute *any* mean field approximation to the Gibbs density P^G with cost function (1).

We propose the following algorithm to compute the statistics $\Phi = (\Phi_1, \ldots, \Phi_N)$ and the parameter estimates $\Theta = (\Theta_1, \ldots \Theta_N)$ in an iterative fashion: The algorithm decreases the temperature exponentially ($0 < \eta < 1$) while an estimate of the statistics Φ (E-like step) is alternated with an optimization of the parameters Θ (M-like step). This can be carried out in parallel (with potential convergence problems caused by oscillations) or sequentially with an immediate update of the statistics Φ. The sequential variant of the generalized EM-algorithm with a random site visitation schedule and immediate update is known to exhibit satisfactory convergence properties [15]. It will converge to a local minimum of the KL divergence since Θ_i is uniquely determined by the $\{\Phi_k\}_{1 \leq k \leq N, k \neq i}$ which do not explicitly depend on Θ_i. The expected coordinates for Euclidian dissimilarities are displayed for four different temperatures in Fig. 2a-d. The algorithm finds a nearly perfect reconstruction ($\mathcal{H}^{\text{MDS}} < 10^{-11}$) at $T = 0$.

Algorithm: MDS by Deterministic Annealing

INITIALIZATION:
  Initialize the parameters Θ^0 of $P^0(\mathcal{X}|\Theta^0)$ randomly.
WHILE $T > T_{min}$ DO
  DO
    FOR $1 \leq i \leq N$ in random order DO
      E-like step:
        Calculate $\langle \mathbf{x}_i \rangle^1$, $\langle \mathbf{x}_i \mathbf{x}_i^T \rangle^1$ and $\langle \|\mathbf{x}_i\|^2 \mathbf{x}_i \rangle^1$
        w.r.t. $P^0(\mathcal{X}|\Theta^0)$ and compute $\Phi_k^1, 1 < k < N, k \neq i$.
      M-like step:
        Minimize $\mathcal{I}(P^0(\mathcal{X}|\Theta^1)\|P^G(\mathcal{X})) = G(\Theta^1|\Phi^1)$ by a variation of Θ_i^1.
      $\Phi^0 \leftarrow \Phi^1; \quad \Theta^0 \leftarrow \Theta^1$
    UNTIL $\mathcal{I}(P_0^0\|P^G) - \mathcal{I}(P_0^1\|P^G) < \varepsilon$
  $T \leftarrow \eta T$
END

To complete the derivation, we have to insert the derivatives of the expectation values $\langle \mathbf{x}_i \rangle$, $\langle \mathbf{x}_i \mathbf{x}_i^T \rangle$, $\langle \mathbf{x}_i \|\mathbf{x}_i\|^2 \rangle$, $\langle \|\mathbf{x}_i\|^4 \rangle$ and the entropy $S = -\langle \log q_i(\mathbf{x}_i|\Theta_i) \rangle$ into the stationary equation (10). Depending on the chosen model $q_i(\mathbf{x}_i|\Theta_i)$ these values can be computed analytically or they have to be estimated by Monte Carlo integration. The rest of this section will be devoted to a detailed discussion of some variants in the choice of $q_i(\mathbf{x}_i|\Theta_i)$.

Exact Model: In principle, we can use the Ansatz $\Theta_i = \Phi_i$ for the factorizing density

$$q_i^0(\mathbf{x}_i|\Theta_i) = \frac{1}{\mathcal{Z}_i^0} \exp(-\frac{1}{T} f_i(\mathbf{x}_i)) \quad \text{with} \quad \mathcal{Z}_i^0 = \int_{-\infty}^{\infty} d\mathbf{x}_i \exp(-\frac{1}{T} f_i(\mathbf{x}_i)) \quad (14)$$

$$f_i(\mathbf{x}_i) = \alpha_i^0 \|\mathbf{x}_i\|^4 + \|\mathbf{x}_i\|^2 \mathbf{x}_i^T \hat{\mathbf{h}}_i + Tr\left[\mathbf{x}_i \mathbf{x}_i^T \mathbf{H}\right] + \mathbf{x}_i^T \mathbf{h}_i . \quad (15)$$

The factorial density is directly parameterized by the statistics Φ_i. From (14) we yield the mean field approximation $\mathcal{F}_0$ of the free energy $\mathcal{F}$.

$$\mathcal{F}_0 = -T \sum_{i=1}^{N} \log \mathcal{Z}_i^0 = -T \sum_{i=1}^{N} \log \int_{-\infty}^{\infty} d\mathbf{x}_i \, \exp(-\frac{1}{T} f_i(\mathbf{x}_i)) \quad (16)$$

The Ansatz (14) exactly models the marginals of the Gibbs density (3) with the Hamiltonian $\mathcal{H}^{\text{MDS}}$ and, therefore, is called the *exact model* in this paper. The moments of $\mathbf{x}_i$ are dependent on the mean field parameters $\Theta_i = \Phi_i$. The former are related to the free energy $\mathcal{F}_0$ by the so-called self-consistency equations, i.e. the derivatives of $\mathcal{F}_0$ with respect to the elements $\mathbf{h}_i$, $\mathbf{H}_i$, $\hat{\mathbf{h}}_i$ and α_i^0 of the field vector.

$$\frac{\partial \mathcal{F}_0}{\partial \mathbf{h}_i} = \langle \mathbf{x}_i \rangle \quad \frac{\partial \mathcal{F}_0}{\partial \mathbf{H}_i} = \langle \mathbf{x}_i \mathbf{x}_i^T \rangle \quad \frac{\partial \mathcal{F}_0}{\partial \hat{\mathbf{h}}_i} = \langle \|\mathbf{x}_i\|^2 \mathbf{x}_i \rangle \quad \frac{\partial \mathcal{F}_0}{\partial \alpha_i^0} = \langle \|\mathbf{x}_i\|^4 \rangle$$

$$(17)$$

Unfortunately the integral (16) cannot be evaluated analytically. A Taylor-series expansion of the argument $f_i(\mathbf{x}_i)$ of the exponential at the minima $\mathbf{x}_{ip}$ with $\nabla f_i|_{\mathbf{x}_{ip}} = 0$ yields satisfactory results for low temperatures but it turns out to numerically unstable at intermediate temperatures.

Dirac Model: To derive tractable approximations for the statistics Φ we consider the Dirac delta distribution

$$q_i(\mathbf{x}_i|\boldsymbol{\mu}_i) = \delta(\mathbf{x}_i - \boldsymbol{\mu}_i). \tag{18}$$

centered at the location $\boldsymbol{\mu}_i$. This model can be considered as the zero temperature limit $T \longrightarrow 0$ of the density (14) with the moments being

$$\langle \mathbf{x}_i \rangle = \boldsymbol{\mu}_i; \quad \langle \mathbf{x}_i \mathbf{x}_i^T \rangle = \boldsymbol{\mu}_i \boldsymbol{\mu}_i^T; \quad \langle \|\mathbf{x}_i\|^2 \mathbf{x}_i \rangle = \|\boldsymbol{\mu}_i\|^2 \boldsymbol{\mu}_i; \quad \langle \|\mathbf{x}_i\|^4 \rangle = \|\boldsymbol{\mu}_i\|^4 \tag{19}$$

Inserting the derivatives with respect to $\boldsymbol{\mu}_i$ into the stationary equations (27) yields the gradient of an M-dimensional potential

$$T\mathcal{I}_i(q_i) = \alpha^0 \|\boldsymbol{\mu}_i\|^4 + \hat{\mathbf{h}}_i^T \boldsymbol{\mu}_i \|\boldsymbol{\mu}_i\|^2 + Tr\left[\boldsymbol{\mu}_i \boldsymbol{\mu}_i^T H_i\right] + \mathbf{h}_i^T \boldsymbol{\mu}_i. \tag{20}$$

$\mathcal{I}_i$ quantifies the *partial costs* of assigning site i the model q_i given the statistics Φ_i. It is a fourth degree vector polynomial that can be minimized by gradient decent methods, e.g. conjugate gradient [17] or a technique described in [12] to explicitly compute all minima.

Gaussian Models: The Dirac model for $q_i(\mathbf{x}_i|\boldsymbol{\mu}_i)$ neglects all temperature effects and, consequently, does not exploit the smoothing effects of deterministic annealing at finite T. A refined model based on a multivariate Gaussian with expectation value $\boldsymbol{\mu}_i$ and covariance $\boldsymbol{\Sigma}_i$ captures finite T effects and preserves the benefits of deterministic annealing,

$$q_i(\mathbf{x}_i) = \frac{1}{\mathcal{Z}_i} \exp(-\frac{1}{2T} Tr\left[\Sigma_i^{-1}(\mathbf{x}_i - \boldsymbol{\mu}_i)(\mathbf{x}_i - \boldsymbol{\mu}_i)^T\right])$$
$$\text{with} \quad \mathcal{Z}_i = |\Sigma|^{\frac{1}{2}}(2\pi T)^{\frac{M}{2}}. \tag{21}$$

$|\Sigma_i|$ denotes the determinant. In practice, however, the full multivariate Gaussian model can be restricted to a radial basis function model with a diagonal covariance matrix $\Sigma_i = \sigma_i^2 \mathbf{I}$ ($\mathbf{I}$ denotes the unit matrix). The moments of this isotropic model q_i are given by

$$\langle \mathbf{x}_i \rangle = \boldsymbol{\mu}_i \tag{22}$$

$$\langle \mathbf{x}_i \mathbf{x}_i^T \rangle = T\sigma_i^2 \mathbf{I} + \boldsymbol{\mu}_i \boldsymbol{\mu}_i^T \tag{23}$$

$$\langle \|\mathbf{x}_i\|^2 \mathbf{x}_i \rangle = KT\sigma_i^2 \boldsymbol{\mu}_i + \|\boldsymbol{\mu}_i\|^2 \boldsymbol{\mu}_i \tag{24}$$

$$\langle \mathbf{x}_i^4 \rangle = 2MT^2\sigma_i^4 + 4T\|\boldsymbol{\mu}_i\|^2\sigma_i^2 + (MT\sigma_i^2 + \|\boldsymbol{\mu}_i\|^2)^2 \tag{25}$$

$$-\langle \log q_i \rangle = \frac{1}{2} + \frac{M}{2}\log\sigma_i^2 + \frac{M}{2}\log(2\pi T) \tag{26}$$

with $K = M + 2$. Inserting these moments into the stationary equations (10) yields

$$T\frac{\partial \mathcal{I}}{\partial \boldsymbol{\mu}_i} = \|\boldsymbol{\mu}_i\|^2 (4\alpha_i^0 \boldsymbol{\mu}_i + \hat{\mathbf{h}}_i) + 2\boldsymbol{\mu}_i \boldsymbol{\mu}_i^T \hat{\mathbf{h}}_i$$

$$+ \left[2\mathbf{H}_i + 4KT\sigma_i^2 \alpha_i^0 \mathbf{I}\right] \boldsymbol{\mu}_i + \mathbf{h}_i + KT\sigma_i^2 \hat{\mathbf{h}}_i \tag{27}$$

$$T\frac{\partial \mathcal{I}}{\partial \sigma_i} = 4\alpha_i^0 KMT^2 \sigma_i^3 + (4K\alpha_i^0 \|\boldsymbol{\mu}_i\|^2 + 2K\boldsymbol{\mu}_i^T \hat{\mathbf{h}}_i + 2Tr\,[\mathbf{H}_i])T\sigma_i - \frac{MT}{\sigma_i} \tag{28}$$

Again the stationary equations (27, 28) define the gradient of the partial costs

$$T\mathcal{I}_i(q_i) = \alpha^0 \langle \|\mathbf{x}_i\|^4 \rangle + \hat{\mathbf{h}}_i^T \langle \mathbf{x}_i \|\mathbf{x}_i\|^2 \rangle + Tr\,[\langle \mathbf{x}_i \mathbf{x}_i^T \rangle H_i] + \mathbf{h}_i^T \langle \mathbf{x}_i \rangle - \frac{MT}{2}\log \sigma_i^2 \tag{29}$$

w.r.t. the mean field parameters $\boldsymbol{\mu}_i$ and σ_i. Note that given a fixed value σ_i^2, Eq. (27) defines the gradient of a quartic vector potential in $\boldsymbol{\mu}_i$ as in the Dirac case. On the other hand, given a fixed value of $\boldsymbol{\mu}_i$, (28) defines a quadratic equation in σ_i^2 with a unique solution

$$\sigma_i^2 = -\frac{p}{2} + \sqrt{\frac{p^2}{4} - q} \qquad \text{with} \tag{30}$$

$$p = \frac{(4K\alpha_i^0 \|\boldsymbol{\mu}_i\|^2 + 2K\boldsymbol{\mu}_i^T \hat{\mathbf{h}}_i + 2Tr\,[\mathbf{H}_i])}{4\alpha_i^0 KMT} \quad \text{and} \quad q = -\frac{1}{4\alpha_i^0 KMT} \tag{31}$$

since $\sigma^2 > 0$, $q < 0$ and therefore $-\frac{p}{2} < \sqrt{\frac{p^2}{4} - q}$ $\forall p$. In the performed MDS experiments, the system (27,28) of equations has been solved in an iterative fashion, alternating the computation $\boldsymbol{\mu}_i$ given σ_i^2 and of σ_i^2 given $\boldsymbol{\mu}_i$.

5 Reducing Stress Induced by Embedding Data from High Dimensional Spaces

It has been noticed by several authors [4,22] that embeddings of real-world data in low-dimensional Euclidian spaces exhibit a tendency to arrange points in a circular fashion, especially when minimizing the SSTRESS criterion (1). This effect is aggravated for similarity matrices with only a limited number of levels or, in the extreme case, with binary values [22]. For real-valued dissimilarities δ_{ij} this behavior can be altered by choosing an appropriate transformation $\mathcal{D}(\delta_{ij})$ into disparities which are more suitable for Euclidian embedding than the original dissimilarities. For this purpose we model the distribution of the squared interpoint dissimilarities $\delta_{\mathbf{xy}}$ between two points $\mathbf{x}, \mathbf{y}$

$$\delta_{\mathbf{xy}} = \sum_{d=1}^{n} (x_d - y_d)^2. \tag{32}$$

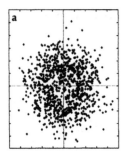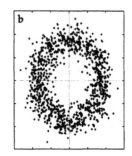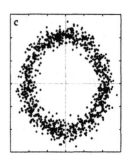

Fig. 3. Evolution of the ring structure with increasing dimensionality n of the object space. The figures show the resulting embeddings of three simulations with 1000 points. The coordinates where drawn independently for each dimension from a normal distribution with dimension (a) $n = 5$, (b) $n = 30$ and (c) $n = 100$.

In case of n i.i.d. Gaussian random coordinates x_d, y_d $1 \leq d \leq n$ with vanishing mean and variance $\sigma^2/2$ the density of δ_{xy} is given by the χ_n^2-density [16] with n degrees of freedom

$$f_{(n)}(\delta) = \frac{1}{2^{n/2}\sigma^n \Gamma(n/2)} \delta^{(n-2)/2} \exp(-\delta/2\sigma^2)\Theta(\delta), \tag{33}$$

with the gamma function $\Gamma(x)$ and the Heaviside step function $\Theta(x)$. The first two moments of (33) are given by

$$\langle \delta \rangle = 2\sigma^2 \frac{\Gamma(\frac{n}{2} + 1)}{\Gamma(\frac{n}{2})} = n\sigma^2 \qquad \langle \delta^2 \rangle = 4\sigma^4 \frac{\Gamma(\frac{n}{2} + 1)}{\Gamma(\frac{n}{2})} = (n^2 + 2n)\sigma^4. \tag{34}$$

Apparently the expected distance $\langle \delta \rangle$ increases linearly with n causing *poor scaling with high dimensionality.* Embeddings are strongly dominated by an annular ring for large n. Figure 3 demonstrates this behavior for three different values of n.

The data analyst is confronted with the problem that dimensionality mismatch stress dominates the possible embeddings for large n and distorts or destroys data structure of interest. Under the assumption that data are drawn from a model distribution with density (33), we are able to compensate this dimensionality mismatch by a monotonic transformation $\mathcal{D}(\delta)$. The goal of this data preprocessing is to divide the total stress into a part which accounts for the difference in dimensionality and a part which carries information about the underlying structure in the data. The model assumption of a χ^2 density (33) for disparities seems to be a natural candidate for this transformation since an "uninteresting" Gaussian structure in high dimensions is approximately represented by a Gaussian in two dimensions.

We therefore search for a transformation $\mathcal{D}(\delta)$ such that $F_{(n)}$ distributed dissimilarities are transformed into $F_{(2)}$ distributed disparities which corresponds to a Gaussian distribution of the embedding coordinates. δ is the random distance variable in the (hypothetical) data space, $\mathcal{D} = \mathcal{D}(\delta)$ the transformed random variable in the (two-dimensional) embedding space:

$$F_{(2)}(\mathcal{D}(\delta)) = \int_0^{\mathcal{D}(\delta)} f_{(2)}(z)dz = \int_0^\delta f_{(n)}(x)dx = F_{(n)}(\delta). \tag{35}$$

Assuming the densities (33) of the distances for the object and the embedding space, we derive the transformation

$$\mathcal{D}(\delta) = F_{(2)}^{-1} \circ F_{(n)}(\delta) = -2\sigma^2 \log \left[1 - P(\frac{n}{2}, \frac{\delta}{2\sigma^2}) \right] \tag{36}$$

with the incomplete gamma function

$$P(a, x) = \frac{1}{\Gamma(a)} \int_0^x e^{-t} t^{a-1} dt \quad (a > 0) \tag{37}$$

If we turn to the application of our transform to real-world data, we have to estimate the effective "dimension" n and the variance σ of the distance distribution. Based on (33) the parameters can be found directly from the mean $\langle \delta \rangle$ and the variance $\langle \delta^2 \rangle$ of the observed dissimilarities, i.e.,

$$n = \frac{2\langle \delta \rangle^2}{\langle \delta^2 \rangle - \langle \delta \rangle^2} \qquad \sigma = \sqrt{\frac{\langle \delta \rangle}{n}}. \tag{38}$$

Thus the transformation involves a computation of mean and variance of the dissimilarities δ, estimation of the parameters n and σ by (38) and the projection by (36).

6 Simulation Results

Visualization of Protein Data: In the first experiment an embedding for a real-world data set of 226 protein sequences has been calculated. The similarity values between pairs of sequences were determined by a sequence alignment program that took biochemical an structural information into account. The sequences belong to different globin families abbreviated by the displayed capital letters. Fig.1 displays both a grey level visualization of the dissimilarity matrix (dark values denote high similarity) and the discovered embedding which is in good agreement with the similarity values of the data. Note the significant differences between the three embeddings. Results are consistent with the biochemical classification.

Dimensionality Reduction for a Virus Data Set: A second experiment was performed on a data-set described in B. Ripley's book [18]. The data consists of 60 vectors with 18 entries describing the biochemical features of a virus under investigation. According to Ripley [18], it exhibits a large number of bad local minima when examined with the Sammon mapping. This problem was less severe

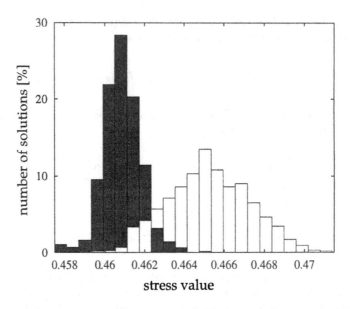

Fig. 4. Bimodal random data: Histograms of the final stress of 1000 runs of the deterministic annealing algorithm (gray) versus 1000 runs of the zero temperature version (white) with local weighting.

with the SSTRESS cost function when using the intermediate weighting condition (2), but still the zero temperature algorithm got stuck in one of a number of local minima at least every second trial. The deterministic annealing algorithm, used with an exponential annealing schedule, found the best minimum available in 93.7% of the trials.

Algorithm	$\mathcal{H} = 0.0938$	$\mathcal{H} = 0.100$	$\mathcal{H} = 0.102$	$\mathcal{H} \geq 0.124$
Gradient descent $(T = 0)$	563	143	231	63
Det. Annealing	937	14	49	0

The table lists the local minima and the corresponding number of trials out of 1000 randomly initialized experiments with the intermediate weighting. Apparently, deterministic annealing significantly reduces the dependency on good starting solutions.

Embedding of Random Dissimilarities: Random dissimilarities pose a particularly difficult problem for embedding since a lot of Euclidian constraints are violated. We have performed this experiment to demonstrate the power of the deterministic annealing technique in situations where the energy landscape becomes very rugged. Dissimilarities in the data set have been randomly drawn from a bimodal Gaussian mixture with $\mu_1 = 1.0$ and $\mu_2 = 2.0$, both mixture components with standard deviation $\sigma = 0.1$. It turns out that the probability to reach the global optimum by a random starting solution shrinks significantly compared to the virus data-set. Histograms of deterministic annealing solutions and gradient descend solutions are shown in Fig. 4. 95 percent of the deterministic annealing solutions can be found in the top 10 percent range of the gradient descent solutions.

Dissimilarity Transformation: Finally we will demonstrate the effect of the dissimilarity transformation introduced in section 5. We have simulated the effects of the transformation on several real-world data-sets. The improvement in visual quality is particularly pronounced for local normalization. Fig.5 demonstrates how the method can be applied to a synthetical data set: Four projections of a set of $n = 200$-dimensional vectors are shown. The set contains eight clusters of Gaussian distributed points, each cluster with a different center. As expected, these clusters are separated by *principal component analysis* (PCA), see e.g.[18] (d). The proposed transform serves even better when combined with local normalized LSS as in (b). This is not the case with LSS alone (a). The clusters appear to be smeared out in the annular ring. Non-metric methods as *isotonic regression* [3] (shown in 5c) can partially improve the projection quality. The dissimilarity transformation for dimensionality adaptation, however, unravels the hidden mixture component structure best.

7 Conclusion

A novel algorithm for least–squares multidimensional scaling has been presented and applied to real–world data sets. It shares the robustness properties of maximum entropy inference. To our knowledge this is the first application of the concept of deterministic annealing to a continuous optimization problem. This work has been percieved as a case-study yet to be generalized to more complex continuous cost functions [12].

A well-known deficit of MDS algorithms, the annular structure of embedded data sets, is cured by a transformation of proximity values into disparities. The intrinsic volume mismatch in projections from high-dimensional space to low-dimensional ones is reduced by a parametric transformation which factors out the null hypothesis and, thereby, substantially improves the visualization quality.

Current research focuses on techniques to alleviate the computational burden posed by a large number N of objects, e.g. $N \approx 10000 - 50000$ for realistic biochemical data bases. Active sampling techniques allow us to estimate the statistics Θ on the basis of a sparsely sampled dissimilarity matrix.

Acknowledgement: This work was supported by the Federal Ministry of Education and Research (BMBF).

References

1. J. Buhmann and T. Hofmann. Central and pairwise data clustering by competitive neural networks. In *Advances in Neural Information Processing Systems 6*, pages 104–111. Morgan Kaufmann Publishers, 1994.
2. J. M. Buhmann and H. Kühnel. Vector quantization with complexity costs. *IEEE Transactions on Information Theory*, 39(4):1133–1145, July 1993.

3. T. F. Cox and M.A.A. Cox. *Multidimensional Scaling*. Number 59 in Monographs on Statistics and Applied Probability. Chapman & Hall, London, 1994.

4. J. deLeeuw and I. Stoop. An upper bound for SSTRESS. *Psychometrika*, 51:149–153, 1986.

5. A. P. Dempster, N. M Laird, and D. B. Rubin. Maximum likelihood from incomplete data via the em algorithm. *J. Royal Statist. Soc. Ser. B (methodological)*, 39:1–38, 1977.

6. R. O. Duda and P. E. Hart. *Pattern Classification and Scene Analysis*. Wiley, New York, 1973.

7. S. Geman and D. Geman. Stochastic relaxation, Gibbs distribution, and the Bayesian restoration of images. *PAMI*, 6:721–741, 1984.

8. S. Gold and A. Rangarajan. A graduated assignment algorithm for graph matching. *IEEE Transactions on Pattern Analysis and Machine Intelligence*, 18(4):377–388, 1996.

9. J.A. Hartigan. Representations of similarity matrices by trees. *J.Am.Statist.Ass.*, 62:1140–1158, 1967.

10. E. T. Jaynes. Information theory and statistical mechanics. *Physical Review*, 106:620–630, 1957.

11. S. Kirkpatrick, C.D. Gelatt, and M.P. Vecchi. Optimization by simulated annealing. *Science*, 220:671–680, 1983.

12. H. Klock and J.M. Buhmann. Data visualization by multidimensional scaling: A deterministic annealing approach. Technical Report IAI-TR-96-8, Universität Bonn, Institut für Informatik III, Römerstraße 194, October 1996.

13. Joseph B. Kruskal. Multidimensional scaling by optimizing goodness of fit to a nonmetric hypothesis. *Psychometrika*, 29(1):1–27, März 1964.

14. Joseph B. Kruskal. Nonmetric multidimensional scaling: a numerical method. *Psychometrika*, 29(2):115–129, Juni 1964.

15. R.M Neal and G.E. Hinton. A new view of the em algorithm that justifies incremental and other varienats. *Submitted to Biometrica*, 1993.

16. A. Papoulis. *Probability, Random Variables and Stochastic Processes*. McGraw-Hill, 1965.

17. William Press, Saul Teukolsky, William Vetterling, and Brian Flannery. *Numerical Recipes in C*. Cambridge University Press, 2. edition, 1992.

18. B.D Ripley. *Pattern Recognition and Neural Networks*. Cambridge University Press, 1996.

19. K. Rose, E. Gurewitz, and G. Fox. Statistical mechanics and phase transitions in clustering. *Physical Review Letters*, 65(8):945–948, 1990.

20. J.W. Sammon. A nonlinear mapping for data structure analysis. *IEEE Trans. Comp.*, C-18(5):401–409, May 1969.

21. R.N. Shepard. The analysis of proximities: Multidimensional scaling with an unknown distance function i. *Psychometrica*, 27:125–140, 1962.

22. M. W. Simmen, G.J. Goodhill, and D.J. Willshaw. Scaling and brain connectivity. *Nature*, 369:448–450, 1994.

23. Yoshio Takane and Forest W. Young. Nonmetric individul differences multidimensional scaling: An alternating least squares method with optimal scaling features. *Psychometrika*, 42(1):7–67, March 1977. ALSCAL.

24. T.Hofmann and J.M.Buhmann. Pairwise data clustering by deterministic annealing. *IEEE Transactions on Pattern Analysis and Machine Intellegence*, 1997. to appear.

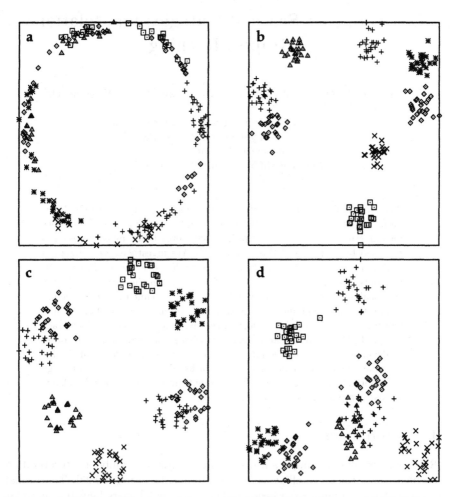

Fig. 5. Embeddings of eight clusters from a $m = 200$ dimensional space. a) LSS without transform, b) LSS with parametric transform, c) LSS alternated with *isotonic regression* (see text), d) PCA using the first two principal components. The stress in the LSS experiments is locally normalized. Note that PCA is not directly applicable if only a dissimilarity matrix is available.

Deterministic Search Strategies for Relational Graph Matching

Mark L. Williams[1], Richard C. Wilson[2], and Edwin R. Hancock[2]

[1] Defence Research Agency, St Andrews Road,
Malvern, Worcestershire, WR14 3PS, UK.
[2] Department of Computer Science,
University of York, York, Y01 5DD, UK.

Abstract. This paper describes a comparative study of various deterministic discrete search-strategies for graph-matching. The framework for our study is provided by the Bayesian consistency measure recently reported by Wilson and Hancock [47–49]. We investigate two classes of update process. The first of these aim to exploit discrete gradient ascent methods. We investigate the effect of searching in the direction of both the local and global gradient maximum. An experimental study demonstrates that although more computationally intensive, the global gradient method offers significant performance advantages in terms of accuracy of match. Our second search strategy is based on tabu search. In order to develop this method we introduce memory into the search procedure by defining context dependant search paths. We illustrate that although it is more efficient than the global gradient method, tabu search delivers almost comparable performance.

1 Introduction

Relational graph matching is a process that is central to symbolic interpretation problems in artificial intelligence and pattern recognition [20,23]. The formal aspects of the problem have been studied for over 30 years [45]. In particular topics such as subgraph isomorphism [46], maximal clique finding [2] and graph partitioning [14] have attracted considerable interest in the fields of discrete mathematics and the theory of algorithms. Each of these problems is known to be NP-complete, and the quest for efficient algorithms of polynomial complexity still raises many important theoretical issues.

However, from the perspective of practical problem-solving the issue of theoretical complexity is of less importance than the ability to find useful, though suboptimal solutions using finite computing resources. In any case, since the graph-structures under study are likely to be inexact due to the presence of noise and segmentation errors, approximate solutions may be the best that is achievable [38,40,41]. Indeed, the idea of posing graph-theoretic problems as optimisation tasks has recently attracted considerable interest in the literature [18,17,35,43]. Mean-field networks have been applied to a variety of graph-theoretic topics including graph-partitioning [31], the travelling salesman problem [51] and graph-matching [18,35]. Although these examples can all be regarded as instances of continuation methods, discrete configurational optimisation methods have also been used to great effect. For instance, Cross, Wilson and Hancock have used genetic search for graph-matching [6]. Heuristic search techniques have also proved to be highly effective. In the classical pattern analysis literature Haralick and Elliot [23] have used forward-checking backtracking to search for consistent labellings. More recently, Messmer and Bunke [34] have addressed the issue of exponential complexity by demonstrating how subgraph isomorphisms can be located in polynomial-time if a form of structural-hashing is used to prune the search-space.,

In fact, the idea of using domain-specific heuristics to improve the efficiency of search was central to much of the pioneering work on artificial intelligence of the 1970's [37]. Perhaps the most popular of these is the A* algorithm which has been widely exploited in applications such as planning and feature extraction. With the advent of more generally applicable global configurational optimisation strategies such as simulated annealing [11], mean-field theory [31,51,52] and most recently evolutionary optimisation (genetic search), heuristic search has been largely neglected in the literature. However, as recently observed by Glover [13-16], the abandonment of the method may be somewhat premature, since the use of domain-specific knowledge can prove highly effective in rapidly locating useful though suboptimal solutions. It is this observation that has lead to the development of a new class of heuristic optimisation techniques known as tabu search.

Tabu-search [13-16] exploits constraints known to apply in a specific domain to take maximum advantage of the available computational resources. Rather than adopting a computationally demanding exploration of the state-space using stochastic (e.g. simulated annealing and genetic search) or continuation methods(e.g. mean-field annealing), tabu search deploys the resources to preferentially search potentially profitable areas. In essence, the search procedure possesses memory. This memory can be both short-term and long-term. In the long term, regions of unprofitable search are deemed tabu and are not revisited. Short term memory can be invoked to intensify search in certain regions. If intensification fails to yield a useful solution, then diversification strategies can be invoked over a longer time-scale. In the broadest sense, this process can be viewed as planning the deployment of computational resources to gain maximum yield in terms of solution quality.

This paper aims to investigate the use of different deterministic search strategies for graph matching. In a recent series of papers we have developed a Bayesian framework which allows the consistency of graph-matching to be gauged using probability distributions [47,48]. These distributions are defined over the Hamming distances between partially consistent subgraphs and a set of model subgraphs residing in a dictionary. We have explored the optimisation of this global consistency measure using a number of stochastic [5,6] and continuation methods [8,9]. In this paper we aim to compare the use of steepest gradient methods with a heuristic search method inspired by tabu-search.

2 Relational Graphs

We abstract the matching process in terms of purely symbolic relational graphs [4,10,30,41]. We use the notation $G = (V, E)$ to denote the graphs under match, where V is the set of nodes and E is the set of arcs. Our aim in matching is to associate nodes in a graph $G_1 = (V_1, E_1)$ representing data to be matched against those in a graph $G_2 = (V_2, E_2)$ representing an available relational model. This matching process is facilitated using constraints provided by suitable relational subunits of the model graph G_2. In order to accommodate the possibility of unmatchable data-graph nodes, we augment the model-graph nodes with a null-label ϕ. This node acts as an attractor for extraneous nodes in the data graph that may, for instance, be due to the presence of noise or occlusion. Formally, the matching is represented by a function $f : V_1 \rightarrow V_2$ from the nodes in the data graph G_1 to those in the augmented model graph G_2. The function f consists of a set of Cartesian pairs drawn from the space of possible matches between the two graphs, i.e. $f \subseteq V_1 \times V_2 \cup \phi$; it provides a convenient device for indexing the nodes in the data graph G_1 against their matched counterparts in the model graph G_2. We use the notation $(u, v) \in f$ to denote the match of node $u \in V_1$ against node $v \in V_2$.

In performing the matches of the nodes in the data graph G_1 we will be interested in exploiting structural constraints provided by the model graph G_2. These constraints are purely symbolic in nature and are represented by configurations of matched labels drawn from the model graph. We use representational units or subgraphs that consist of neighbourhoods of nodes interconnected by arcs. For convenience we refer to these structural subunits or N-ary relations as super-cliques. The super-clique of the node indexed j in the graph G_1 with arc-set E_1 is denoted by the set of nodes $C_j = j \cup \{i | (i, j) \in E_1\}$. The matched realisation of this super-clique is denoted by the relation $\Gamma_j = (f(u_1), f(u_2), ..., f(u_{|C_j|}))$. In order to facilitate comparison between super-cliques of different size, we pad-out the smaller unit with dummy nodes so as to raise it to the same cardinality as the larger unit. Our aim is to modify the match to optimise a measure of global consistency with the constraints provided by the model graph G_2. The constraints available to us are provided by the N-ary symbol relations on the super-cliques of the model graph G_2. The critical ingredient in developing our matching scheme is the set of feasible mappings between each super-clique of graph G_1 and those of graph G_2. The set of feasible mappings, or dictionary, for the super-clique C_j is denoted by $\Theta_j = \{S_i\}$ where $S_i = i \cup \{j | (i, j) \in E_2\}$. q

Each element S_i of Θ_j, is therefore a relation formed on the nodes of the model graph; we denote such consistent relations by $S_i = (v_1, v_2, ...)$. The dictionary of feasible mappings for the super-clique C_j consists of all the consistent relations that may be elicited from the graph G_2. In practice these relations are formed by performing permutation of the non-centre nodes for each super-clique with the requisite number of dummy nodes. An example of this mapping process is shown in Figure 1. This process effectively models the disruption of the adjacency structure of the model graph caused by the addition of clutter elements.

Since it is intrinsically symbolic in nature, the resulting dictionary is invariant to scene translations, scalings or rotations.

It is the size of the dictionary which poses the main computational bottleneck in the application of our matching scheme. For instance, if we are considering the matching of super-cliques of the same size, i.e. no padding is required, then there are $|C_j|$ cyclic dictionary items of the super-clique C_j. If, on the other hand, the cyclicity constraint is lifted then there are $|C_j|!$ items. When padding is introduced, then the complexity is increased. If the model-graph relation S_i is being compared with the match residing on the data-graph clique C_j, then there are $\frac{(|S_i|-1)!}{(|C_j|-1)!(|S_i|-|C_j|)!}$ cyclic dictionary items and $\frac{(|S_i|-1!|C_j|}{(|S_i|-|C_j|)!}$ non-cyclic dictionary items. In Section 4 we consider how the underlying complexity of our method can be restricted by pruning the set of dictionary items in a tabu search strategy.

Fig. 1. Example super-clique mapping

3 Bayesian Consistency Measure

In this section we review the development of a refinement of the relational consistency measure originally reported by Wilson and Hancock [47,48]. As we noted in Section 2, the consistent labellings available for gauging the quality of match are represented by the set of relational mappings from C_j onto G_2, i.e. Θ_j. As demanded by the Bayes rule, we compute the probability of the required super-clique matching by expanding over the basis configurations belonging to the dictionary Θ_j

$$P(\Gamma_j) = \sum_{S_i \in \Theta_j} P(\Gamma_j|S_i).P(S_i) \tag{1}$$

The development of a useful graph-mapping measure from this expression requires models of the processes at play in matching and of their roles in producing errors. These models are represented in terms of the joint conditional matching probabilities $P(\Gamma_j|S_i)$ and of the joint priors $P(S_i)$ for the consistent relations in the dictionary. In developing the required models we will limit our assumptions to the case of matching errors which are memoryless and occur with uniform probability distribution.

To commence our modelling of the conditional probabilities, we assume that the various types of matching error for nodes belonging to the same super-clique are memoryless. In direct consequence of this assumption, we may factorize the required probability distribution over the symbolic constituents of the relational mapping under consideration. As a result the conditional probabilities $P(\Gamma_j|S_i)$ may be expressed in terms of a product over label confusion probabilities

$$P(\Gamma_j|S_i) = \prod_{k=1}^{|S_i|} P(f(u_k)|v_k) \tag{2}$$

Our next step is to propose a two component model of the processes which give rise to erroneous matches. The first of these processes is initialisation error, which we aim to rectify be iterative label updates. We assume that initialisation errors occur with a uniform and memoryless probability P_e. This probability is distributed over the $|V_2| - 1$ possible matching errors that can occur. The second source of error is structural disturbance of the relational graphs caused by noise, clutter or segmentation error. We assume that structural errors can also be modelled by a uniform distribution which occurs with probability P_ϕ. This probability is distributed over both the possibility of null-labelling of the data-graph nodes and the possibility of dummy insertions in the dictionary item S_i. Under these dual assumptions concerning the nature of matching errors the confusion probabilities appearing under the product of equation (2) may be assigned according to the following distribution rule

$$P(f(u_k)|v_k) = \begin{cases} (1 - P_\phi)(1 - P_e) & \text{if } f(u_k) = v_k \\ (1 - P_\phi)\frac{P_e}{|V_2|-1} & \text{if } f(u_k) \neq v_k \text{ and } v_k \neq \text{dummy} \\ P_\phi & \text{if } f(u_k) = \phi \text{ or } v_k \neq \text{dummy} \\ P_\phi \frac{1}{|V_2|} & \text{if } f(u_k) \neq \phi \text{ or } v_k \neq \text{dummy} \end{cases} \tag{3}$$

The four cases under this distribution rule require further explanation. The first case corresponds to the situation in which there is agreement between the current match and that demanded by the dictionary item S_i. The second case corresponds to matching disagreements. In this case, there are $|V_2|-1$ erroneous labels over which the error-probability P_e may be distributed. The third case arrises when the super-clique under consideration contains more nodes than the dictionary item S_i. In this case the matching configuration Γ_j is padded-out with dummy nodes. Since the dummy nodes are not mapped onto specific nodes in the model-graph, the null-match probability is assigned. In the fourth, and final case, the dictionary item contains fewer nodes than the data-graph super-clique. In this case the dictionary item is padded with dummy nodes. Since there are V_2 model graph nodes that can be dummied in this way, the null-match probability is distributed uniformly.

As a natural consequence of this distribution rule the joint conditional probability is a function of three physically meaningful variables. The first of these is the Hamming distance $H(\Gamma_j, S_i)$ between the assigned matching and the feasible relational mapping S_i. This quantity counts the number of conflicts between the current matching assignment Γ_j residing on the super-clique C_j and those assignments demanded by the relational mapping S_i. The second variable is the sum of the number dummy nodes padding the data graph clique C_j which we denote by $\psi_{i,j}$. This second quantity is equal to the size difference between the structure preserving mapping S_i and the data graph clique C_j, i.e. $\psi_{i,j} = |S_i| - |C_j|$. The third quantity is the number of null-labels assigned to the non-dummy nodes of the data clique C_j, which we denote by $\Psi(\Gamma_j)$. With these ingredients, the resulting expression for the joint conditional probability acquires an exponential character

$$
\begin{aligned}
P(\Gamma_j|S_i) = & \left[(1 - P_\phi)(1 - P_e) \right]^{|C_j| - H(\Gamma_j, S_i) - \Psi(\Gamma_j, S_i) - \psi_{i,j}} \\
& \times \left[(1 - P_\phi)\frac{P_e}{|V_2| - 1} \right]^{H(\Gamma_j, S_i)} \\
& \times \left[P_\phi \right]^{\Psi(\Gamma_j)} \\
& \times \left[P_\phi \frac{1}{|V_2|} \right]^{\psi_{i,j}}
\end{aligned}
\tag{4}
$$

Finally, in order to compute the super-clique matching probability $P(\Gamma_j)$, we require a model of the joint-priors for the dictionary items. Here we assume that the unit probability mass is uniformly distributed over the relevant items, i.e.

$$
P(S_i) = \frac{1}{|\Theta_j|}
\tag{5}
$$

Collecting together terms in the expression for $P(\Gamma_j|S_i)$ and substituting for the joint priors for the dictionary items we obtain the following expression for the super-clique matching probability

$$
P(\Gamma_j) = \frac{K_{C_j}}{|\Theta_j|} \sum_{S_i \in \Theta_j} \exp \left[-\left(k_e H(\Gamma_j, S_i) + k_\phi \left\{ \psi_{i,j} + \Psi(\Gamma_j) \right\} - \ln |V_2| \psi_{i,j} \right) \right]
\tag{6}
$$

where and $K_{C_j} = [(1 - P_e)(1 - P_\phi)]^{|C_j|}$. The two exponential constants appearing in the above expression are related to the matching-error probability and the null match probability, i.e. $k_e = \ln \frac{(1 - P_e)(|V_2| - 1)}{P_e}$ and $k_\phi = \ln \frac{(1 - P_e)(1 - P_\phi)}{P_\phi}$. The probability distribution may be regarded as providing a natural way of softening the hard relational constraints operating in the model graph. The most striking and critical feature of the expression for $P(\Gamma_j)$ is that the consistency of match is gauged by a series of exponentials that are compounded over the dictionary of consistently mapped relations.

We use the super-clique matching probabilities to construct a global consistency measure for the current state of match. For the sake of simplicity we average the consistency measure over the data-graph nodes using the following quantity

$$
Q(f) = \frac{1}{|V_1|} \sum_{j \in V_1} P(\Gamma_j)
\tag{7}
$$

In the next section of this paper we discus various alternative strategies for searching for matching configurations which maximise this global consistency measure.

4 Search Strategies

In the previous section we reviewed the development of a Bayesian consistency measure that can be utilised in the search for graph-matches. This measure is based on a purely symbolic representation of the matching process and does not for instance draw on attribute information to establish consistency of match. In this section we describe some alternative ways in which the consistency measure can be used in the search for graph matches.

4.1 Gradient ascent

In the continuous domain gradient ascent involves selecting parameter updates which are aligned in the direction of maximum slope on the optimisation surface. When the optimisation surface is defined over a set of discrete entities, then the definition of the steepest gradient requires more care. Suppose that $\Delta_{a,\alpha}Q(f)$ is the change in the global consistency measure when the match on the node a in the data graph is switched from its current value $f(a)$ to the new value α. With the definition of the global consistency measure given in equation (7) the change is evaluated over those super-cliques modified by the label update, i.e.

$$\Delta_{a,\alpha}Q(f) = \sum_{b \in C_a} \left[P(\alpha, f(c), \forall c \in C(b) - a) - P(f(a), f(c), \forall c \in C(b) - a) \right] \quad (8)$$

With this definition of gradient, there are two ways in which the match can be updated.

Local steepest gradient The simplest way of searching for consistent matches is to apply steepest gradient methods in sequential order. Here the graph nodes are considered one after the other in pre-specified order and the matching updates made in according to the following rule

$$f(a) = \arg\max_{\alpha \in V_2} \Delta_{a,\alpha}Q(f) \quad (9)$$

The update selected is the one that results in the greatest increase in consistency. Unfortunately, this simple updating scheme does not necessarily follow the direction of steepest positive gradient. The search is limited by the fact that it is only the node currently under consideration that can have its matching assignment changed. The reason for this is that although the state-space of the optimisation surface is $|V_1 \times V_2|$ dimensional, each move to a new solution is constrained to lie within a $|V_2|$ dimensional subspace. The number of computations required at the node a is of order $|C_a|.|V_2|.|\Theta_a|$. The consequence of this is that in general the path to the global maximum of the surface will be longer than the one dictated by true gradient ascent. Moreover, the chance of encountering a local maxima is increased.

Global steepest gradient True gradient requires the computation of the consistency metric under the complete set of possible mappings for all the nodes in the graph. In other words rather than choosing the data-graph node in some pre-specified order, we visit the node $a \in V_1$ which possesses the largest value of $\Delta_{a,\alpha}Q(f)$ over the set of model graph nodes. The update process involves identifying the Cartesian pair (a, α) which maximises the gradient and updating the state of match accordingly, i.e.

$$(a, \alpha) = \arg \max_{(a,\alpha) \in V_1 \times V_2} \Delta_{a,\alpha}Q(f) \Rightarrow f(a) = \alpha \qquad (10)$$

At first sight this would appear prohibitively expensive since it implies an increase in the number of computations required by a factor $|V_1|$. In fact the number of computations required for the update decision at node a is $|V_1|.|V_2|.|\Theta_a|$. However, in practice it is only necessary to re-evaluate the consistency measure for those super-cliques modified by a matching re-assignment. In other words, the full set of consistency values need only be calculated in the first iteration. In fact the number of required calculations increases by a factor equal to the average number of nodes in each super-clique. By monitoring the super-cliques modified by label updates, the complexity at subsequent iterations is no greater than that for local-gradient search.

4.2 Heuristic Planning - the Jigsaw Puzzle Algorithm

The idea of grading the entire state-space of possible matches included in the set of Cartesian pairs $V_1 \times V_2$ according to a confidence measure provides an interesting departure from the conventional sequential search by discrete relaxation. Although this is closer in spirit to true gradient ascent on the optimisation surface, this is only achieved at the expense of greater computational overheads. The main computational bottleneck is the requirement to evaluate the super-clique matching probabilities over the complete set of dictionary items. It is interesting to note, however, that in our derivation of the matching-probabilities we assumed that the different dictionary items were equiprobable. In practice, however, we can refine our viewpoint and make the probabilities context-dependant. In this way we can impose a distribution on the different dictionary items which effectively favours certain search paths over others. In a nutshell, we aim to enhance the probability of consistently abutting dictionary items. This can be viewed as a form of tabu search which uses memory concerning the structure of the model-graph to limit the search space so as to preferentially explore the most potentially profitable regions [13–16].

The adopted approach is to make the dictionary Θ_j both context and iteration dependant. Suppose that we are considering the consistency of the match

α on the node a of the data graph. According to our definition of consistency, we gauge confidence in this match by the quantity

$$q_{a,\alpha} = \sum_{j \in C_a} \sum_{S_i \in \Theta_j} P(\Gamma_j | S_i) P(S_i) \tag{11}$$

We modify this confidence measure by introducing the concept of a conditional dictionary for the super-cliques modified by the label update. We let $\tilde{\Theta}_{j|f(a)=\alpha}$ be the set of structure-preserving mappings permitted on the super-clique C_j given that the match α resides on the data-graph node a. In this case the confidence of match is gauged by quantity

$$q_{a,\alpha} = \sum_{S_i \in \Theta_a} P(\Gamma_a | S_i) P(S_i) + \sum_{\substack{j \in C_a \\ j \neq a \\ f(a)=\alpha}} \sum_{S_i \in \tilde{\Theta}_j} P(\Gamma_j | S_i) P(S_i) \tag{12}$$

The conditional dictionaries for the neighbouring super-cliques are pruned so as to remove those configurations that can not abut with the match $f(a) = \alpha$.

This strategy for computing the confidence of match has many similarities to the problem of solving a jigsaw puzzle. Here pieces of the puzzle are sorted according to their saliency. In the initial stages of search it is only the salient pieces that are used to construct islands of consistency. At later stages these islands are joined together to construct the completed global solution. Moreover, this concept of making compound moves in the search procedure has much in common with Glover's ejection chains [13]. By contrast, the sequential search procedure described in the previous section would be akin to overlooking the role of saliency and exhaustively checking for consistency of match.

The basic idea underpinning the tabu-search strategy described in this Section is to invoke memory to rank the pieces according confidence of match. This rank is used to determine an order of search so that computational resources can be concentrated in an intensified search of islands of consistency. These islands eventually merge to form a global solution. In this way areas of low consistency are only visited when the islands of high consistency encroach. In this way computational resources are not wasted fruitlessly updating matches which are unstable or fluctuate between ambiguous states. Moreover, because it is context-dependant, the confidence measure embodies the concept of using an ejection-chain structure in the search procedure [13]. Based on these observations, we adopt the following search strategy

- The algorithm commences by assigning random matches to the data graph nodes. Based on these random matches, the confidence measure $q_{a,\alpha}$ is evaluated over the complete space of potential updates, $\forall (a, \alpha) \in V_1 \times V_2$. The confidence measures are then used to rank the nodes of the data graph according to the value of $\rho_a = \max_{\alpha \in V_2} q_{a,\alpha}$. According to our jigsaw-puzzle analogy, this corresponds to drawing pieces at random from the box and retaining the salient ones as seeds from which to build the solution.
- The best-N ranked matches are then selected as seeds for the search procedure. The number of nodes is selected to reflect the fraction of correct

matches anticipated to be present in the initial random configuration. Using the pruned dictionaries, each neighbour of the initial seeds is then updated so as to select the match of maximum confidence. Again, according to our jigsaw analogy, this corresponds to building out from the seeds by drawing from pools of likely matches.

- Once all neighbours of the initial seeds have been visited and updated, the confidence measures are re-evaluated and the nodes re-ranked. An enlarged set of seeds is then selected. The updating step described above is then repeated, incrementally increasing the population of seeds. In this way islands of consistency naturally develop. Computational resources are concentrated on extending the boundaries of the islands. This process is iterated until the islands of consistency merge and the match stabilises. This corresponds to linking seed patches in the jigsaw by extending the scope of the search.

The philosophy underpinning the tabu search strategy contrasts with the global gradient method. Rather than concentrating resources on regions of the search space where the gradient is largest, it attempts to consolidate regions of consistency by preferentially making moves that are more likely to result in improvements. The basic difference resides in the ranking of matches. This endows the search procedure with memory. Is is this feature that is distinctive of tabu search.

5 Experiments

In this section we provide some experimental evaluation of our deterministic search methods. We pose our evaluation as a Monte-Carlo study using randomly generated synthetic graphs. The graphs are generated in the following way. We commence by randomly distributing points on the image plane. These points are used to seed a Voronoi tessellation of the image plane. The relational structure that we use in our experiments is the Delaunay triangulation, i.e. the region adjacency graph for the Voronoi regions.

To simulate the effects of relational corruption, we both randomly add and delete a controlled fraction of the nodes from the dot patterns used to seed the Delaunay graphs. We compare matching performance as a function of this corruption fraction. Our measure of performance is the fraction of the nodes correctly matched. Each experimental data-point is based on the averaging of matching performance over a sample of ten random graphs each containing 30 nodes.

We commence by comparing the results of local and global gradient ascent methods. The solid curve in Figure 2 shows the best possible fraction of correct matches achievable as a function of the fraction of added clutter. The dashed curve is the result of applying global gradient ascent while the dotted curve is the result of applying local gradient ascent. The main conclusion to be drawn from this plot is that the global method consistently outperforms the local method at all levels of structural corruption. In both cases, the update process has been applied to the exponential consistency measure.

Our next set of experiments aim to compare global gradient ascent with the tabu search strategy. In Figure 3 the solid curve and the dashed curve are again respectively the best-achievable result and the result of global gradient ascent. The dotted curve now shows the result of applying the tabu search strategy to the exponential consistency measure. The performance of the tabu search method is consistently marginally lower than the global gradient ascent method. However, it is significantly higher in performance than the local gradient ascent method. Figure 4 illustrates how the accuracy match scales with graph-size for tabu search. The log-linear plot exhibits an linear increase in matching accuracy with the number of graph-nodes. In other words, the underlying increase in performance is polynomial with graph-size.

To give some idea of the computational tradeoff between accuracy of match and convergence rate, timings suggest that the local gradient method and the tabu search strategy require comparable resources. Both are twenty times faster than the global gradient method. This accords with our discussion of complexity in Section 4, since the average neighbourhood connectivity of the Delaunay graph is approximately twenty. In other words, the tabu search method compares favourably with the global-gradient method in terms of accuracy of match both offers significant advantages in terms of computational overheads.

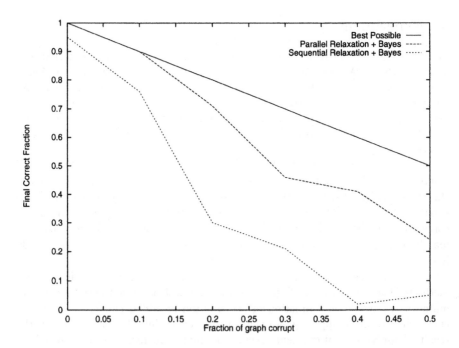

Fig. 2. *Comparing the two gradient-based methods; the solid curve is the maximum achievable fraction of correct matches; the dashed curve is the result obtained with global gradient; the dotted curve is the result obtained with local gradient.*

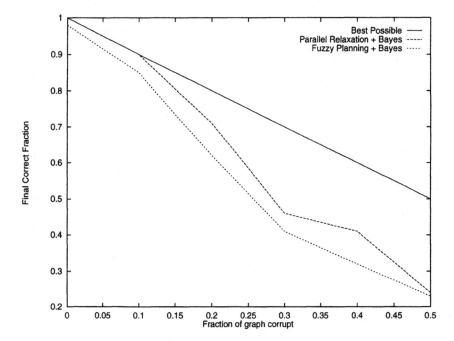

Fig. 3. *Comparing global gradient and tabu search; the solid curve is the maximum achievable fraction of correct matches; the dashed curve is the result of applying the global gradient method; the dotted curve is the result of applying tabu search.*

6 Conclusion

Our main contribution in this paper has been to compare three deterministic search methods for graph-matching. Two of these revolve around computing a discrete approximation to the maximum gradient direction. Here we demonstrate the advantages to be gained from searching for updates in the direction of the global maximum gradient. In other words we show that nodes should be visited in an order determined by the value of the gradient, rather than by some predetermined sequence.

Our second contribution has been to develop a tabu search strategy. This algorithm has been inspired by the strategies adopted in solving jigsaw-puzzles. The basic idea is to rank potential matches according to saliency and to grow islands of consistency from a population of high ranking seeds. The resulting algorithm offers matching accuracy that is comparable to global gradient search. However, it requires computational resources of only the same order as local sequential search.

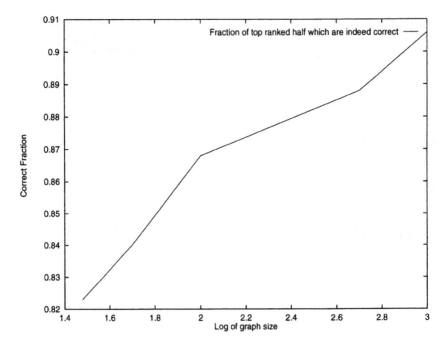

Fig. 4. *Performance of tabu search as a function of graph-size.*

References

1. Amit Y. and A. Kong, "Graphical Templates for Model Registration", *IEEE PAMI*, **18**, pp. 225–236, 1996.
2. Barrow H.G. and R.M Burstall, "Subgraph Isomorphism, Matching Relational Structures and Maximal Cliques", *Information Processing Letters*, **4**, pp.83–84, 1976.
3. Barrow H.G. and R.J. Popplestone, "Relational Descriptions in Picture Processing", *Machine Intelligence*, **6**, 1971.
4. Boyer K. and A. Kak, "Structural Stereopsis for 3D Vision", *IEEE PAMI*, 10, pp 144-166, 1988.
5. Cross A.D.J. and E.R. Hancock, "Relational Matching with Stochastic Optimisation" *IEEE International Symposium on Computer Vision*, pp. 365–370, 1995.
6. Cross A.D.J., R.C.Wilson and E.R. Hancock, "Genetic Search for structural matching", *Proceedings ECCV96*, **LNCS 1064**, pp. 514–525, 1996.
7. Finch A.M., Wilson R.C. and Hancock E.R., "Matching Delaunay Graphs", to appear in Pattern Recognition, 1996.
8. Finch A.M., Wilson R.C. and Hancock E.R., "Relational Matching with Mean-Field Annealing", *Proceedings of the 13th International Conferrence on Pattern Recognition*, Volume II, pp. 359–363, 1996.
9. Finch A.M., Wilson R.C. and Hancock E.R., "Softening Discrete Relaxation", *to appear in Neural Information Processing Systems 9*, MIT Press 1997.
10. Flynn P.J. and A.K.Jain, "CAD-Based Vision - from CAD Models to Relational Graphs", *IEEE PAMI*, **13**, pp 114-132, 1991.

11. Geman D. and S. Geman, "Stochastic Relaxation, Gibbs Distributions and Bayesian Restoration of Images", *IEEE PAMI*, **6**, pp 721-741, 1984.
12. Geiger D. and F. Girosi, "Parallel and Deterministic Algorithms from MRF's: Surface Reconstruction", *IEEE PAMI*, **13**, pp 401-412, 1991.
13. Glover F., "Ejection chains, reference structures and alternating path methods for traveling salesman problems", *Discrete Applied Mathematics*, **65** , pp.223-253, 1996.
14. Rolland E., H. Pirkul and F. Glover, "Tabu search for graph partitioning", *Annals of Operations Research*, **63**, pp. 290-232, 1996.
15. Glover F., "Genetic algorithms and tabu search - hybrids for optimisation", *Discrete Applied Mathematics*, **49**, pp. 111-134, 1995.
16. Glover F., "Tabu search for nonlinear and parametric optimisation (with links to genetic algorithms)", *Discrete Applied Mathematics*, **49**, pp. 231-255, 1995.
17. Gold S., A. Rangarajan and E. Mjolsness, "Learning with pre-knowledge: Clustering with point and graph-matching distance measures", *Neural Computation*, **8**, pp. 787-804, 1996.
18. Gold S. and A. Rangarajan, "A Graduated Assignment Algorithm for Graph Matching", *IEEE PAMI*, **18**, pp. 377-388, 1996.
19. Hancock E.R. and J. Kittler, "Discrete Relaxation," *Pattern Recognition*, **23**, pp.711-733, 1990.
20. Haralick R.M. and J. Kartus, "Arrangements, Homomorphisms and Discrete Relaxation", *IEEE SMC*, **8**, pp. 600-612, 1978.
21. Haralick R.M. and L.G. Shapiro, "The consistent labelling problem- part I", *IEEE PAMI*, *1*, pp. 173-184, 1979.
22. Haralick R.M. and L.G. Shapiro, "The consistent labelling problem- part II", *IEEE PAMI*, *2*, pp. 193-203, 1980.
23. Haralick R.M. and G. Elliott, "Increasing Tree Search Efficiency for Constraint Satisfaction Problems" *Artificial Intelligence*, **14**, pp. 263-313, 1980.
24. Harary F. , "Graph Theory", *Addison Wesley, Reading, MA*, 1969.
25. Henderson T.C., "Discrete Relaxation Techniques", *Oxford University Press*, 1990.
26. Horaud R., F.Veilon and T.Skordas, "Finding Geometric and Relational Structures in an Image", *Proceedings of the First European Conference on Computer Vision*, pp 374-384, 1990.
27. Horaud R. and T. Skordas, "Stereo Correspondence through Feature Grouping and Maximal Cliques", *IEEE PAMI*, **11**, pp. 1168-1180, 1989.
28. Herault L., R. Horaud, F. Veillon and J-J. Niez, "Symbolic Image Matching by Simulated Annealing", *Proceedings of First British Machine Vision Conference*, pp. 319-324, 1990.
29. Hummel R.A. and S. W. Zucker, "On the foundations of relaxation processes", *IEEE PAMI*, **5**, pp. 267-287, 1983.
30. Kittler J., W.J. Christmas and M.Petrou, "Probabilistic Relaxation for Matching Problems in Machine Vision", *Proceedings of the Fourth International Conference on Computer Vision*, pp. 666-674, 1993.
31. Kosowsky J.J. and Yuille A.L., "The Invisible Hand Algorithm: Solving the Assignment Problem with Statistical Physics", *Neural Networks*, **7**, pp 477-490, 1994.
32. Lades M., J.C. Vorbruggen, J. Buhmann, J. Lange, C. von der Malsburg, R.P. Wurtz and W. Konen, "Distortion Invariant Object Recognition in the Dynamic Link Architecture", *IEEE Transactions on Computers*, **42**, pp. 300-311, 1992.
33. Li S.Z., "Matching Invariant to Translations, Rotations and Scale Changes", *Pattern Recognition*, **25**, pp. 583-594, 1992.

34. Messmer B.T. and Bunke H., "Efficient Error-tolerant Subgraph Isomorphism Detection", *Shape, Structure and Pattern Recognition, Edited by D. Dori and A. Bruckstein*, pp. 231–240, 1995.

35. Mjolsness E., G. Gindi and P. Anandan, "Optimisation in model matching and perceptual organisation", *Neural Computation*, **1**, pp. 218–219, 1989.

36. Motzkin T.S. and E.G. Straus, "Maxima for graphs and a new proof of a theorem of Turan", *Canadian Journal of Mathematics*, **17**, pp. 533–540, 1965.

37. Nilsson N.J., "Problem solving Methods in Artificial Intelligence", *McGraw-Hill, New York*, 1971.

38. Sanfeliu A. and Fu K.S., "A Distance Measure Between Attributed Relational Graphs for Pattern Recognition", *IEEE SMC*, **13**, pp 353–362, 1983.

39. Sarker S. and K.L. Boyer, "Perceptual Organisation in Computer Vision: A Review and Proposal for a Classificatory Structure", *IEEE SMC*, **23**, pp 382–399, 1993.

40. Shapiro L.G. and R.M. Haralick, "Structural Description and Inexact Matching", *IEEE PAMI*, **3**, pp 504–519, 1981.

41. Shapiro L.G. and R.M.Haralick, "A Metric for Comparing Relational Descriptions", *IEEE PAMI*, **7**, pp 90-94, 1985.

42. Simic P., "Constrained nets for graph matching and other quadratic assignment problems", *Neural Computation*, **3** , pp. 268–281, 1991.

43. Suganathan P.N., E.K. Teoh and D.P. Mital, "Pattern Recognition by Graph Matching using Potts MFT Networks", *Pattern Recognition*, **28**, pp. 997–1009, 1995.

44. Tang Y.C. and C.S.G. Lee, "A Geometric Feature Relation Graph Formalism for Consistent Sensor Fusion", *IEEE SMC*, **22**, pp 115–129, 1992.

45. Ullman J.R., "Associating parts of patterns", *Information and Control*, **9**, pp. 583–601, 1966.

46. Ullman J.R., "An algorithm for subgraph isomorphism", *Journal of the ACM*, **23**, 31-42, 1976.

47. Wilson R.C. and E.R Hancock, "Graph Matching by Discrete Relaxation", *Pattern Recognition in Practice IV: Multiple Paradigms, Comparative Studies and Hybrid Systems*, **North Holland** pp. 165–177, 1994.

48. Wilson R.C., A.N. Evans and E.R Hancock, "Relational Matching by Discrete Relaxation", *Image and Vision Computing*, **13**, pp. 411–422, 1995.

49. Wilson R.C. and E.R.Hancock, "A Bayesian Compatibility Model for Graph Matching", *Pattern Recognition Letters*, **17**, pp. 263-276, 1996.

50. Yang D. and J. Kittler, "MFT-Based Discrete Relaxation for Matching High-Order Relational Structures", *Proceedings 12th International Conference on Pattern Recognition*, pp. 219–223, 1994.

51. Yuille A., "Generalised Deformable Models, Statistical Physics and Matching Problems", *Neural Computation*, **2**, pp. 1-24, 1990.

52. Yuille A.L. and Kosowsky J.J., "Statistical Physics Algorithms that Converge", *Nueral Computation*, **6**, pp 341–356, 1994.

Object Recognition

Object Localization Using Color, Texture and Shape

Yu Zhong and Anil K. Jain

Dept. of Computer Science
Michigan State University
E. Lansing, MI 48823, USA
{zhongyu, jain}@cps.msu.edu

Abstract. We address the problem of localizing objects using color, texture and shape. Given a handrawn sketch for querying an object shape, and its color and texture, the algorithm automatically searches the database images for objects which meet the query attributes. The database images do not need to be presegmented or annotated. The proposed algorithm operates in two stages. In the first stage, we use local texture and color features to find a small number of candidate images, and identify regions in the candidate images which share similar texture and color as the query example. To speed up the processing, the texture and color features are directly extracted from the Discrete Cosine Transform (DCT) compressed domain. In the second stage, we use a deformable template matching method to match the query shape to the image edges at the locations which possess the desired texture and color attributes. This algorithm is different from the other content-based image retrieval algorithms in that: (i) no presegmentation of the database images is needed, and (ii) the color and texture features are directly extracted from the compressed images. Experimental results show that substantial computational savings can be achieved utilizing multiple image cues.

1 Introduction

Content-based retrieval methods use pictorial cues instead of textual cues to retrieve desired images from the database. Shape, texture, and color are commonly used image content cues due to their significant roles in human vision perception. For example, the QBIC system [11] formulates the queries in terms of texture, shape, and color features to retrieve images. Photobook [12] provides a set of interactive tools for browsing and retrieving images based on texture. Vinod and Murase have proposed to locate an object image by matching the corresponding DCT coefficients in the transformed domain [17]. Color, texture and shape features have also been applied to index and browse digital video databases [20].

In most of the approaches, the challenge is to extract appropriate features such that they are representative of a specific image attribute and at the same time, are able to discriminate images with different attributes. Color histogram

[14] is a commonly used color feature; responses to specially tuned spatial-temporal filters are widely used to characterize a texture. Invariant moments and histograms of edge turning angles are used as shape features [15]. Once features are extracted to characterize the image property of interest, the matching and retrieval problem is reduced to computing the similarity in the feature space and finding database images which are most similar to the query image.

Feature-based matching methods have the drawback that it is not always clear whether a given set of features is appropriate for a specific application. Furthermore, they can not be applied when the image attributes of interest have not been segmented from the background. Deformable template-based methods [5, 7, 10, 16, 19] do not compute any specific shape features. Various deformable template models have been proposed to perform tasks including image registration, object detection and localization, feature tracking, and object matching. These deformable models are popular because (i) they combine both the structural knowledge and local image features, and (ii) they are versatile in incorporating the within-object-class variations. One such method for shape matching is proposed by Jain et al. [7]. The advantage of this method is that it does not require specific shape features, and no segmentation of the input image is necessary. However, the ability to deform the template is achieved at the cost of a high-dimensional parameter space. Object matching requires either a global optimization of a non-concave (usually complex with many local extrema) [5] objective function or a good initialization of the template near the true location of the object in the image domain [10, 19]. Although much work has been done on deformable template models, very little attention is paid on how to automatically find a good initialization of the template.

In this paper we address the problem of object retrieval using several image cues, including shape, texture, and color. In particular, texture and color features are used as supplemental clues to help locate promising regions in the image which are likely to contain the desired objects. This eliminates a large portion of the database images from further screening. Once a small set of candidate regions is obtained, we then use the deformable template matching method to localize the objects in the proximity of these regions. The motivation of this work is threefold: (i) the region cues (texture and color) may come naturally as a constraint in the retrieval task, (ii) the region cues may be used to expedite the localization process: the deformable template matching process need not be executed where the region cues are quite different from the desired ones, and (iii) region-based matching methods are more robust to misalignment and position shift than edge-based methods. We use the region information to obtain some good yet coarse initializations. The contributions of this work are as follows: (i) we extract the color texture features directly from the compressed image data, (ii) we use the region attributes to direct the shape-based search to save computational costs, and (iii) we sensibly fuse multiple content cues to efficiently retrieve images from a nonannotated image database where the only information available is the bit stream of the images.

The remainder of the paper is organized as follows. In section 2 we describe the screening process using color and texture, where features extracted from the DCT domain are used to browse the database for a small number of images as well as identify specific locations in these images. In section 3 we solve the shape matching problem using a deformable template approach, where the query shape is used as a prototype template which can be deformed. We integrate the color, texture, and shape matching in section 4 and present a two-stage matching algorithm. Experimental results are presented in section 5. Section 6 summarizes the paper and proposes future work.

2 Matching Using Color and Texture

Texture and color features have been used in several content-based image database systems to retrieve objects or images of a specific texture and color composition [4, 12]. We use texture and color cues in addition to shape information to local-ize objects. For example, one may be interested in finding a golden fish, with a particular shape, color and texture. The texture and color information can be specified in terms of a sample pattern, as in the case "I want to retrieve all fish images with the same color and texture as the fish in this picture". When such image region information is available, we use these features to quickly screen the input image for a small set of candidate positions where we can initialize the deformable template-based shape matching process.

As the color and texture cues are used as supplemental tools for examining an image for the presence of a candidate object, we need to use features which are easy to compute and at the same time, characterize the desired color and texture properties. For this purpose, we extract the features from the block DCT coefficients of an image. These coefficients can be obtained directly from DCT compressed images and videos (JPEG [18], MPEG [3]) without first decom-pressing them. This is very appealing since more and more images and videos are stored in compressed format for efficient storage and transfer [13, 20].

2.1 DCT Compressed Images

DCT-based image compression techniques encode a two-dimensional image by the block DCT coefficients. To compress an image, the DCT coefficients of each $N \times N$ image block (macroblock) are computed and quantized. These com-pression techniques take advantage of the fact that most of the high frequency components of the transformed image are close to zero. The low-order coeffi-cients are quantized to save the bits, and then further compressed using either the Huffman coding or the arithmetic coding method. The JPEG images and Intra frames of MPEG videos are compressed this way, where the value of N is set to 8.

The DCT coefficients $\{c_{uv}\}$ of an $N \times N$ (N is usually a power of 2) image region $\{I_{xy},\ 0 \leq x < N, 0 \leq y < N\}$ are computed as follows:

$$c_{uv} = \frac{1}{N}\mathcal{K}_u\mathcal{K}_v \sum_{x=0}^{N-1}\sum_{y=0}^{N-1} I_{xy} \cos\frac{\pi u(2x+1)}{2N} \cos\frac{\pi v(2y+1)}{2N} \tag{1}$$

where u and v denote the horizontal and vertical frequencies ($u, v = 0, 1, \ldots, N-1$), and $\mathcal{K}_w = \frac{1}{\sqrt{2}}$ for $w = 0$ and $\mathcal{K}_w = 1$, otherwise. The DC component (c_{00}) of the transformed coefficients represents the average of the spatial domain signals I_{xy} in the macroblock, and the AC components (c_{uv}, $u \neq 0$ or $v \neq 0$) capture the frequency (characterized by u and v) and directionality (by tuning the u and v values) properties of the $N \times N$ image block.

One property of the Discrete Cosine Transform is that for a typical image, its energy is dominant at the low frequency components. This means that the coefficients of the high frequency components are close to zero, and therefore negligible in most cases. Most of the image information is contained in the low frequency components, which represent a "coarse" or "blurred" version of the spatial image. We will now show how we extract texture and color features from DCT coefficients.

2.2 Texture Features

An image region is textured if it contains some repetitive gray level patterns. Texture is usually characterized by the spatial variation, directionality, and coarseness in the image. Textured images provide rich information about the image content. It is desirable to determine whether texture-based methods are suitable for processing the given image [9]. Multichannel filtering approach has been used extensively in texture analysis. This includes the Gabor filter based approach by Jain and Farrokhnia [6], the wavelet transform model by Chang and Kuo [2], and the subband approach by Jernigan and D'Astous [8], to name a few.

As the Discrete Cosine Transform converts the spatial image information into the spatial frequency domain, we define texture features as the spectrum energies in different channels of a local macroblock. The absolute values of the AC components of the quantized DCT coefficients of each macroblock indexes the channel spectrum. We use them as the texture features which are expected to capture the spatial variation and directionality of the image texture. The DC component, which is the average greyscale value of the macroblock, is not considered a texture measure. This is reasonable because we usually subtract the mean or normalize the image before extracting texture features.

2.3 Color Features

The **YCrCb** color model is widely used to encode color images in TV and video and in compression standards, including JPEG and MPEG. This color space is obtained by applying a linear transformation to the **RGB** color space where the **Y** plane represents the luminance information, and the **Cr** and **Cb** planes encode the chrominance differences. The advantage of this color model is that human eyes are usually more sensitive to the luminance changes than to the chrominance changes. As a result, the chrominance frames can be encoded at a lower bit rate than the luminance frame for compression purposes, without significantly affecting the quality of the perceived image.

283

In line with the JPEG and MPEG standards, we use the **YCrCb** model for representing color images. We use the DC components of the DCT coefficients of the three frames **Y**, **Cr** and **Cb** to represent the color for a macroblock. We note that although the intensity (the **Y** plane) is subject to lighting conditions, the **Cr** and **Cb** components are more robust indicators of the color attribute. However, for image retrieval tasks, people do distinguish between bright red and dark red. So, the intensity also plays a role in color perception.

We should note that although we use the DC component of DCT for representing the color attribute and AC components for texture, we believe that texture and color properties are mingled together. The variation in color results in color texture. It is difficult to draw a clear boundary between color and texture.

2.4 Feature Selection

There are N^2 DCT coefficients for an $N \times N$ image block; for an 8×8 macroblock, there are 64 coefficients. Not all the coefficients contain useful information. As mentioned earlier, for a typical image a large portion of the high frequency components have negligible coefficients. We use the following two different criteria to choose only M features out of the N^2 total number of features:

1. We take the M lowest frequency components. That is, we pick $|c_{10}|$, $|c_{01}|$, $|c_{20}|$, $|c_{11}|$, $|c_{02}|$, ... and so on, until we have selected M features;
2. This criteria adapts to the query image. It finds the M features which maximize the energy for the query image. It proceeds as follows:
   (a) obtain the quantized DCT coefficients for all the DCT blocks for the query object region;
   (b) compute the absolute values of the AC components as features;
   (c) sum up the energies for each frequency component over all the DCT blocks in the region;
   (d) select those M features that have the most energy over all the blocks.

The texture features are extracted separately for each of the three color frames (Y, Cr, Cb). It turns out that for most cases, the two criteria select the same set of features. When the query image presents very fine texture, the second criteria selects a set of features which outperforms the first one.

2.5 Representing the Query Image Region

The query image is represented by a set of feature vectors. Each vector corresponds to an $N \times N$ block in the query image region. We allow the overlapping of the macroblocks so that the blocks densely cover the query region, and all the $N \times N$ configurations in the query region are covered. The DCT coefficients of a non-aligned block can be computed from the DCT coefficients of its four overlapping, aligned macroblocks using the algorithm proposed by Chang and Messerschmitt [1]. Each feature vector consists of the color and texture features which are extracted as specified in sections 2.2 and 2.3. If there is a large number of feature vectors, we perform a cluster analysis on all the feature vectors, and only keep the features corresponding to the cluster centers to maintain a small set of representative features.

2.6 Similarity Computation

We have represented the query region attributes using a set of feature vectors (sec. 2.5) which characterize color and texture. In the same manner, we can also extract a set of feature vectors to represent a region in the test image, one vector for each macroblock in this region. Then we can match the query region to an arbitrary region in the database image by comparing the two characteristic feature vector sets. We have derived a symmetric distance measure between query feature set Q and a test region feature set R. First, we define the color and texture distances of the ith feature vector in set R to vector set Q as the minimum distance to each of the vector in Q:

$$\text{dist}_{text}(R_i, Q) = \text{Min}_{j \in Q} \frac{1}{N} \sum_{k=0}^{N-1} \frac{(ftext_{ik} - ftext_{jk})^2}{vartext_k} \qquad (2)$$

$$\text{dist}_{color}(R_i, Q) = \text{Min}_{j \in Q} \frac{1}{3} \sum_{k=1}^{3} \frac{(fcolor_{ik} - fcolor_{jk})^2}{varcolor_k}, \qquad (3)$$

where R_i denotes the ith feature vector in R, $ftext_{ik}$ ($fcolor_{ik}$) denotes the texture (color) feature k for vector i, and $vartext_k$ ($varcolor_k$) denotes the variance of texture (color) feature k in the database. The weighted distance measure is used because the DC component usually has a very large variation, the low frequency AC features have a smaller variation, and the high frequency AC components have the least variation. We weigh the contribution of each feature by the variance of each feature component computed from all the macroblocks in the database images. (This is equivalent to the Mahalanobios distance with a diagonal covariance matrix.) The distance of the ith vector in R to the query set Q is the summation of the distances in color and texture:

$$\text{Dist}(R_i, Q) = \text{dist}_{text}(R_i, Q) + \text{dist}_{color}(R_i, Q). \qquad (4)$$

The distance of set R to set Q is defined as the average distance of vectors in R to Q:

$$\overline{\text{Dist}(R_i, Q)} = \sum_{i=1}^{N_R} Dist(R_i, Q)/N_R. \qquad (5)$$

where N_R is the number of feature vectors in R. Note that this distance is asymmetric. We define a symmetric distance measure between R and Q as follows:

$$\text{DIST}(R, Q) = \frac{1}{2}(\overline{\text{Dist}(R_i, Q)} + \overline{\text{Dist}(Q_i, R)}). \qquad (6)$$

3 Deformable Template Matching

Shape-based matching is a difficult problem in content-based retrieval due to the following factors:

- For a query shape, one generally has no prior information about its presence in database images, including the number of occurrences and its location, scale, and orientation.
- Often, the desired object has not been segmented from the background in the image.
- There is a need to accommodate both rigid and nonrigid deformations in the query shape.
- Most quantitative shape features cannot efficiently represent different query shapes.

Jain et al. have proposed a deformable template matching model to retrieve objects using handrawn sketches [7], where prior knowledge of an object shape is described by a handrawn prototype template which consists of its representative contours. The shape variations in an object class are accommodated using a set of probabilistic deformation transformations on the template. The deformed shape template then interacts with the input image via a directional edge potential field calculated from the salient edge features (edge positions and directions). A Bayesian scheme, which is based on the prior knowledge and the likelihood (edge information) in the input image, is employed to find a match between the deformed template and objects in the image. The fitness of the template to a subimage of the input edge map is measured by an objective function $\mathcal{E}$.

To determine the presence of a desired object in the neighborhood of a given location, the prototype template is initialized at the proximity of this location. The gradient descent method is used to find the largest value of the objective function $\mathcal{E}$ with respect to the deformation parameters and the other transformation parameters (translation, rotation, and scale). If $\mathcal{E}$ is less than a threshold value, then the desired object is assumed to be present, and the final configuration of the deformed template gives the detected object shape and location; otherwise, it is decided that the desired object is not present. A multiresolution algorithm searches for the desired object in a coarse-to-fine manner.

We use the above-mentioned deformable template approach [7] to perform shape matching. Some deformed versions of a handrawn sketch are shown in figure 1 to illustrate the deformations that are allowed for this approach, where figure 1(a) is the prototype template on a grid, and figures 1(b)-(d) are the deformed templates using the deformation transform in [7].

In spite of the multiresolution scheme, the deformable template matching is computationally expensive. To improve the performance, we use the texture and color features to prune the search space for the localization process. We apply the deformable template matching process only at the image locations which match the query region in texture and color.

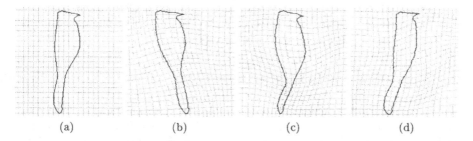

Fig. 1. Deformations of a handrawn template.

4 Integrating Texture, Color and Shape

We have integrated texture, color, and shape cues to improve the performance of the retrieval process. The integrated system operates in two stages. Since region-based matching methods are relatively robust to minor displacements as long as the two matching regions substantially overlap, we browse the database using color and texture in the first stage, so that only a small set of images, and a small number of locations in the candidate images are obtained. In the second stage, the identified regions with the desired texture and color are used to direct the shape-based search, so that the iterative matching process is only performed in the proximity of those candidate locations.

The integrated matching algorithm is described as follows:

Region-based screening:
- Compute feature vectors for the query region:
  - extract the quantized DCT coefficients for the macroblocks in the sample region;
  - compute DCT coefficients for the other displaced 8 × 8 blocks from the DCT coefficients of the 4 overlapping macroblocks;
  - form the color and texture feature vectors for each block, as described in section 2;
  - if the number of sample blocks exceeds a threshold, cluster the sample feature vectors; keep the cluster centers as the representative sample feature vectors;
- Compute similar images in the database:
  - for each database image,
    - for each macroblock in the database image:
      - compute the color and texture feature vectors;
    - place the masked query shape at evenly spaced positions, and over a discretized set of orientations, compute the distance between the query texture and color attributes and the masked input image region as described in section 2.6. If the distance is less then a threshold, initialize the shape-based matching.

Shape-based matching:

- initialize the query template at the computed configurations from the previous stage for M iterations; if the final objective function value is less than a threshold, report the detection;

5   Experimental Results

We have applied the integrated retrieval algorithm to an image database of 592 color images containing people, animals, birds, fishes, flowers, outdoor and indoor scenes, etc. These images are of varying size from 256×384 to 420×562. They have been collected from different sources including HP Labs, the Kodak Photo CD, and web sites (Electronic Zoo/Net Vet - Animal Image Collection URL: http://netvet.wustl.edu/pix.htm). Some sample images from the database are illustrated in Fig. 2.

Fig. 2. Some sample images from the database. They have been "scaled" for display purposes.

To gain some insight about the DCT spectrums we have used as texture and color features, Fig. 3 shows the absolute value of block DCT coefficients of a color image of houses (Fig. 3(a)). Figures 3(b)-(d) show the absolute values of the DCT coefficients for the three color components separately. Each small image (block) corresponds to the spectrum of a specific channel, that is, one feature for all the macroblocks in the image. The x axis (across the features) indicates horizontal variations, and the y axis (across the features) indicates vertical variations, with increasing frequencies from left to right, top to bottom. So, the block at the top left corner corresponds to the DC component, which is the averaged and subsampled version of the input image, and the small images on the top row, from left to right, correspond to channels of zero vertical frequency, and increasing horizontal frequencies. This figure shows that the top left channels, which represent the low frequency components, contain most of the energy, while the high frequency channels, which are located at the bottom right corner of each figure, are mostly blank. It also indicates that the channel spectrums capture the directionality and coarseness of the spatial image; for all the vertical edges in the input image, there is a corresponding high frequency component in the horizontal frequencies, and vice versa. Furthermore, diagonal variations are captured by the channel energies around the diagonal line. This example illustrates that the DCT domain features do characterize the texture and color attributes.

We now show the retrieval results using only texture and color, as described by the first stage of the integrated algorithm. Figure 4 shows one example of color matching, where the image in the subwindow in Fig. 4(a) is the query sample, and Fig. 4(b) gives the top-4 retrieved images from the database. The three DC components of the color frames are used as the color features.

Figure 5 shows one matching result using the texture features. Five features are selected from each of the **Y**, **Cr**, and **Cb** frames, so that a total of 15 features are used. Figure 5(a) specifies the query textured region, and Fig. 5(b) shows the matching macroblocks in the same image, and Fig. 5(c) shows the top-10 retrieved regions with similar texture.

One example of object localization using color and shape is illustrated in Fig. 6, where the rectangular region in Fig. 6(a) specifies the sample color. Matching macroblocks in the same images are identified by 'x', as shown in Fig. 6(c). Note that almost all the blocks on the fish where the query is extracted are marked. So is part of another fish with a similar blueish color. No blocks in the background pass the color matching test. Shape matching using the handrawn sketch in Fig. 6(b) is then processed around the two detected regions. The final matched result is shown in Fig. 6(d). The final configuration of the deformed templates agrees in most part with the fish boundaries. The deviations from the fish boundary are due to the edges extracted in the textured background. Note that although there is another striped fish in the image, it is not localized due to its different color.

We show another example of the integrated retrieval in Fig. 7. One region is extracted from a cardinal to specify the query color and texture, as shown in Fig. 7(a). A sketch of a side view of a bird is used as the shape template (Fig. 7(b)). One cardinal image is retrieved from the database using the combined shape and region information (Fig. 7(c)).

The performance of the system is summarized in Table 1. Using texture and color, we can eliminate a large portion of the database images. A total of 18 color and texture features are used. Given a query image, it typically takes about 180 sec to perform a retrieval on our database containing 592 images on a SGI Indigo 2 workstation. Query images are successfully retrieved.

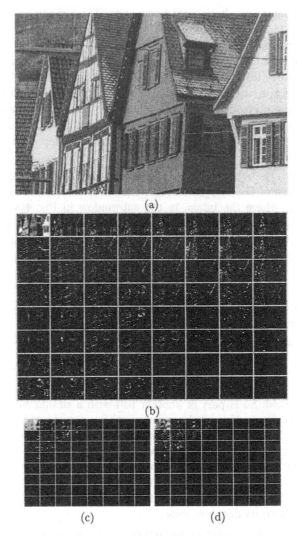

Fig. 3. Features extracted from the block DCT coefficients. **(a)** 250 × 384 input color image; **(b)** DCT features for the **Y** frame (intensity); **(c)** DCT features for the **Cr** frame (chrominance); **(d)** DCT features for the **Cb** frame (chrominance);

	images retrieved	computation time [0]
Stage 1	11%	0.1 sec
stage 2	1.2%	1.76 sec

Table 1. Performance of the two-stage algorithm; the database contains 592 color images.

[0] CPU time per 256 × 384 image on a SGI Indigo 2

(a)

(b)

Fig. 4. Retrieval based on color. **(a)** query example is given by the rectangular region; **(b)** top-4 retrieved images from the database which contain blocks of similar color.

6 Conclusion

In this paper we have proposed an algorithm for object localization using shape, color, and texture. Shape-based deformable template matching methods have the potential in object retrieval because of their versatility and generalizability in handling different classes of objects and different instances of objects belonging to the same shape class. But, one disadvantage in adopting them in content-based image retrieval systems is their computational cost. We have proposed efficient methods to compute texture and color features to direct the initialization of the shape-based deformable template matching method. These texture and color features can be directly extracted from compressed images. This filtering stage allows the deformable template matching to be applied to a very small subset of database images, and only to a few specific positions in the candidate images. Preliminary experimental results show computational gains using these supplemental features.

The proposed method assumes no preprocessing of the database. The input is the raw image data. We believe that our system can be used as an auxiliary tool to annotate, organize, and index the database using color, texture, and shape attributes off-line, where features (shape, color and texture) of retrieved items are computed and stored to index the database.

Fig. 5. Retrieval based on texture. (a) query example is specified by the rectangular region; (b) matching macroblocks are marked with crosses in the query image; (c) other nine retrieved images from the database which contain regions of similar texture.

We are currently investigating whether shape matching can also be performed in the compressed domain, which may be feasible now that the edge detectors are available for compressed data. An integrated and efficient content-based retrieval system for compressed digital library will offer a great potential with the rapid accumulation of image and video data, which are typically compressed for storage and transmission efficiency. We will also look into extracting more reliable texture features, which capture texture structure that go beyond the size of a DCT macroblock.

Acknowledgments

The authors would like to thank Dr. Hongjiang Zhang of the HP labs for providing some of the test images.

References

1. S.F. Chang and D.G. Messerschmitt. A new approach to decoding and compositing motion compensated DCT-based images. In *Proc IEEE Int. Conf. Acoust. Speech Signal Proc.*, pages 421–424, 1993, Minneapolis, MN.

Fig. 6. Retrieval based on color and shape. **(a)** query color example is specified by the rectangular region; **(b)** sketch for the shape; **(c)** matching macroblocks are marked with crosses in the query image; **(d)** retrieved shapes.

2. T. Chang and C.J. Kuo. Texture analysis and classification with tree-structured wavelet transform. *IEEE Trans. Image Processing*, 2(4):429–441, October 1994.

3. D. L. Gall. MPEG: a video compression standard for multimedia applications. *Communications of the ACM*, 34(4):47–58, 1991.

4. M. M. Gorkani and R. W. Picard. Texture orientation for sorting photos "at a glance". *Proc. of the 12th Int. Conf. on Pattern Recognition, Jerusalem, Israel,* 67(5):A459–A464, October 1994.

5. U. Grenander and M. I. Miller. Representation of knowledge in complex systems. *J. of Royal Statistical Society (B)*, 56(3):1–33, 1994.

6. A. K. Jain and F. Farrokhnia. Unsupervised Texture Segmentation Using Gabor Filters. *Pattern Recognition*, 24(12):1167–1186, 1991.

7. A.K. Jain, Y. Zhong, and S. Lakshmanan. Object matching using deformable templates. *IEEE Trans. Pattern Anal. and Machine Intell.*, 18(3):267–278, March 1996.

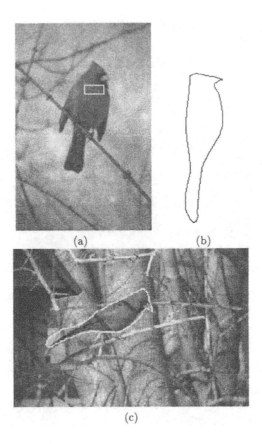

Fig. 7. Retrieval based on color, texture, and shape. **(a)** query region example is given by the rectangular region; **(b)** sketch for the shape; **(c)** retrieved shape.

8. M.E. Jernigan and F. D'Astous. Entropy-based texture analysis in the spatial frequency domain. *IEEE Trans. Pattern Anal. and Machine Intell.*, 6(2), March 1984.

9. K. Karu, A. K. Jain, and R. M. Bolle. Is there any texture in the image? *Pattern Recognition*, 29(9):1437–1446, 1996.

10. M. Kass, A. Witkin, and D. Terzopoulos. Snakes: Active contour models. *Int. J. Comput. Vision*, 1(4):321–331, 1988.

11. W. Niblack, R. Barber, and W. Equitz. The QBIC project: Querying images by content using color, texture, and shape. *Proc. SPIE Conf. on Storage and Retrieval for Image and Video Databases*, 1908:173–187, 1993.

12. A. Pentland, R. W. Picard, and S. Sclaroff. Photobook: tools for content-based manipulation of image databases. *Proc. SPIE Conf. on Storage and Retrieval for Image and Video Databases II*, 2185-05, February 1994.

13. B. Shen and I.K. Sethi. Direct feature extraction from compressed images. In *Proc. SPIE Conf. on Storage and Retrieval for Image and Video Databases IV*, volume 2670, 1995.

14. M.J. Swain and D.H. Ballard. Color indexing. *Int. J. Comput. Vision*, 7(1):11–32, 1991.
15. A. Vailaya, Y. Zhong, and A. K. Jain. A hierarchical system for efficient image retrieval. In *Proc. 13th Int. Conf. on Patter Recognition (ICPR)*, pages 356–360, Vienna, Austria, 1996.
16. B.C. Vemuri and A. Radisavljevic. From global to local, a continuum of shape models with fractal priors. *Proc. IEEE Conf. on Computer Vision and Pattern Recognition (CVPR)*, pages 307–313–627, New York City, NY, June 1993.
17. V.V. Vinod and H. Murase. Object location using complementary color features: histogram and DCT. In *Proc. 13th Int. Conf. on Patter Recognition (ICPR)*, pages 554–559, Vienna, Austria, 1996.
18. G.K. Wallace. The JPEG still picture compression standard. *Communications of the ACM*, 34(4):31–44, 1991.
19. A. L. Yuille, P. W. Hallinan, and D. S. Cohen. Feature extraction from faces using deformable templates. *Int. J. Comput. Vision*, 8(2):133–144, 1992.
20. H. J. Zhang, C. Y. Low, and S. W. Smoliar. Video parsing and browsing using compressed data. *Multimedia Tools and Applications*, pages 89–111, 1995.

Visual Deconstruction: Recognizing Articulated Objects

Tyng-Luh Liu and Davi Geiger

Courant Institute of Mathematical Sciences
251 Mercer Street
New York, NY 10012, USA

Abstract. We propose a deconstruction framework to recognize and find articulated objects. In particular we are interested in human arm and leg articulations.

The deconstruction view of recognition naturally decomposes the problem of finding an object in an image, into the one of (i) extracting key features in an image, (ii) detecting key points in the models, (iii) segmenting an image, and (iv) comparing shapes. All of these subproblems can not be resolved independently. Together, they reconstruct the object in the image. We briefly address (i) and (ii) to focus on solving together *shape similarity* and *segmentation*, combining top-down & bottom-up algorithms.

We show that the *visual deconstruction* approach is derived as an optimization for a Bayesian-Information theory, and that the whole process is naturally generated by the guaranteed Dijkstra optimization algorithm.

1 Introduction

We investigate the problems of recognizing and finding articulated and deformable objects. In particular we study human arm and leg articulations, restricting the class of objects to the one that can be represented as contours. Our approach is extendible to three dimensional objects, which we discuss, but our main focus is on two dimensional contours. Still, it allows for a large variety of objects and applications. Our aims are applications to aid video editing, database content retrieval, animation and medical imaging. In real world, articulated shapes are encountered almost everywhere. However, most of the (invariant-based) object recognition systems [12] do not have the capability to recognize articulated or deformable targets. Methods based on multiple views [16, 21, 22] are interesting but, can not account for large deformations or articulations. They lack a method that can realize the similarity between an object and its articulated/deformed counterparts.

Our approach is a *Deconstruction* one. We break the problem of finding an object in the image that is most similar to the model into the one of (i) extracting key features in an image, (ii) detecting key points in the models, (iii) segmenting an image, (iv) comparing shapes. These problems can be used to reconstruct the object in the image, and so the deconstruction is this process of breaking a model and an image to reconstruct a solution (another "similar" object in the image).

To illustrate our approach we briefly discuss (i) and (ii) then focus on the integration of two methods, snakes (active contours) and shape comparison. The ability of judging the degree of similarity between two shapes (contours) provides a global shape property not encountered on previous snake model. The snake model was introduced in [9] and we follow a formulation based on dynamic programming [7]. In shape analysis we draw from the shape similarity work in [2], where a pseudo metric was established to measure articulations and some deformations.

From (i) and (ii) we extract model points and features in images that are believed to have a correspondence. The top-down method guides the search for reconstructing the object in the image. It hypothesizes candidate matches between a pair of model points and a pair of image features. Then, feeds the bottom-up module with the object part that connects the pair of model points. The bottom-up method extracts edges, then groups edges to link the hypothesized pair of image features (growing a snake), and finally compares the snakes with the object parts given by the top-down module. It feeds the result of this process to the top-down module to guide the search for a new match hypothesis. We show that these methods are derived as an optimization for a Bayesian-Information theory, and that the whole process is naturally generated by the guaranteed Dijkstra optimization algorithm.

Methods combining snakes with shapes have previously been discussed, e.g. [6]. Differently from their work, we model the deformations explicitly accounting for articulations. Moreover, we claim, our formulation can provide a foundation for object recognition. Interesting new ideas on recognition appeared in [1, 5, 18, 19, 21, 24] with related aspects to our approach.

To reduce the computation complexity of our method, we adopt an "integration by parts" technique to approximately solve the global optimization problem. Our rational is that the shape similarity measure [2] prefers deformations that preserve the part structures of objects over deformations that modify the parts. Previous work that describes objects by their parts can be found in [3, 10, 13]. We present experimental results for recognizing articulated human shapes.

2 Deconstructing Recognition

Given an image I and model Γ, we first establish the difference and similarity between the processes of recognizing and of finding Γ in I.

Definition 1: Recognizing an object Γ in the image is equivalent to responding "yes" to the question " Is an object model present in the image ?" , i.e.,

$$P(\Gamma|I) > 0.5 \quad ?$$

Definition 2: Finding an object Γ in the image is equivalent to computing among all possible objects in the image the one closest to Γ, i.e., to find

$$\Gamma^{T*} = arg \max_{\Gamma^T} P(\Gamma^T|\Gamma, I).$$

Note that, if $P(\Gamma^T, \Gamma|I)$ is given, we can compute both Γ^{T*} and $P(\Gamma|I)$, since

$$\Gamma^{T*} = arg\max_{\Gamma^T} P(\Gamma^T, \Gamma|I) = arg\max_{\Gamma^T} P(\Gamma^T|\Gamma, I)$$

$$P(\Gamma|I) = \sum_{\Gamma^T} P(\Gamma^T, \Gamma|I) \approx P(\Gamma^{T*}, \Gamma|I),$$

where the last approximation is only valid if the distribution $P(\Gamma^T, \Gamma|I)$ is sharply peaked on Γ^{T*}.

2.1 Deconstructing with key points and features

The focus now is to compute the optimal Γ^{T*}. We introduce the possibility of detecting localized features in the image represented by a set $\{y_k : k = 1, ..., K\}$. They can represent corners, junctions, high curvature points, etc. Since our models are contour models, we use an ordered set of model features $[x_s : s = 1, ..., S]$ representing possibly high curvature points, or bending points.

The key points of a model contour are points that convey a lot/most of information about the contour (see Figure-1(a)). These points connected by straight lines can give a good caricature of the contour, even when this contour undergoes deformations/articulations. All the points of a contour figure that are allowed to bend (articulation points) are included. It is beyond the scope of this paper to derive/detect these points from an information-theoretic modeling. We will simply manually select them for each contour model.

Note that the key points of the model can, in a limit case, be all of the contour points. The distance between two points in the model, s and r are given by $d_S(s, r)$ and can be precomputed by following the contour. We then decompose $P(\Gamma^T|\Gamma, I)$ as

$$
\begin{aligned}
P(\Gamma^T|\Gamma, I) &= \sum_{[x_s], \{y_k\}} P(\Gamma^T, [x_s], \{y_k\}|\Gamma, I) \\
&= \sum_{[x_s], \{y_k\}} P(\Gamma^T|[x_s], \{y_k\}, \Gamma, I)\, P([x_s], \{y_k\}|\Gamma, I) \\
&= \sum_{[x_s], \{y_k\}} P(\Gamma^T|[x_s], \{y_k\}, \Gamma, I)\, P(\{y_k\}|[x_s], \Gamma, I)\, P([x_s]|\Gamma, I) \\
&\approx \sum_{[x_s], \{y_k\}} P^{shape}(\Gamma^T|[x_s], \{y_k\}, \Gamma)\, P^{snake}(\Gamma^T|\{y_k\}, I) \\
&\qquad\qquad P^{features}(\{y_k\}|[x_s], \Gamma, I)\, P^{model-points}([x_s]|\Gamma), \qquad (1)
\end{aligned}
$$

where in the approximation we did consider the model points, $[x_s]$, to be independent of the image I, i.e., $P^{model-points}([x_s]|\Gamma) = P^{model-points}([x_s]|\Gamma, I)$. $P(\Gamma^T|[x_s], \{y_k\}, \Gamma, I)$ is decomposed into a shape model, $P^{shape}(\Gamma^T|[x_s], \{y_k\}, \Gamma)$

and a snake model $P^{snake}(\Gamma^T|\{y_k\}, I)$. We say the whole process is a deconstruction because we not only decompose the recognition into various terms, but later we reconstruct the final object in the image through this decomposition.

Ideally, the image features $\{y_k\}$ are originated from the model points $[x_s]$. A model of the geometric projection as well as illumination and reflectance is necessary. However, in our experiments we have neglected this issues and simply used the "SUSAN" feature detector [17] to generate a set of key features in the image. They are candidates for matching the model key features. These features usually capture corner points, junction points, and salient edges and we have found them useful for our experiments (see Figure-1(b)). Clearly, the total number of detected features affect the algorithm complexity and we do require a reasonable amount of them to be capable of detecting the target. Roughly speaking, the feature resolution should be fine enough to sample a similar distribution like the one found by those model key features.

Formally, we are making the assumption that the distribution over all possible features are sharply peaked at a set of features detected by SUSAN operator, say $\{y_k^{SUSAN}\}$. Moreover, we will manually produce $[x_s]$, say $[x_s^{manual}]$ and assume the distribution over all possible $[x_s]$ is also sharply peaked. These two assumptions can be formally written as

$$P^{features}(\{y_k\}|[x_s], \Gamma, I) = \prod_{k=1}^{K} \delta(y_k - y_k^{SUSAN}),$$

$$P^{model-points}([x_s]|\Gamma) = \prod_{s=1}^{S} \delta(x_s - x_s^{manual}) \tag{2}$$

where $\delta(x) = 1$ if $x = 0$ and $\delta(x) = 0$ otherwise.

Matching key points and features: In the above model we have not made explicit that the model points , $[x_s]$, have a correspondence in the feature set $\{y_k\}$. We can make so by introducing binary matching variables $\{M_{s,k} : s = 1, ..., S : k = 1, ..., K\}$, so that

- $M_{s,k} = \begin{cases} 1, & \text{when } y_k \text{ is matched to } x_s, \\ 0, & \text{otherwise.} \end{cases}$
- $\sum_{s=1}^{S} M_{s,k} = 0$ or 1. 0 occurs when y_k is not part of the model contour.
- $\sum_{k=1}^{K} M_{s,k} = 1$.

In this paper, we have not experimented with occlusions; otherwise we would need to consider the case $\sum_{k=1}^{k} M_{s,k} = 0$. We can now rewrite (1) as

$$P(\Gamma^T | \Gamma, I)$$

$$\approx \sum_{[x_s],\{y_k\}} \{ \prod_{s,i,j=1}^{S,K,K} [(1 - M_{s,i}M_{s-1,j}) + M_{s,i}M_{s-1,j}P_{s,i,j}^{shape}((\Gamma^T)_{y_j}^{y_i}|(\Gamma)_{x_{s-1}}^{x_s})$$

$$P_{i,j}^{snake}((\Gamma^T)_{y_j}^{y_i}|y_i,y_j,I)\, P_{s,i}^{features}(y_i|x_s,\Gamma,I)\, P_s^{modelpoints}(x_s|\Gamma)\,]\} \qquad (3)$$

$$\approx \prod_{s,i,j=1}^{S,K,K} [(1 - M_{s,i}M_{s-1,j})$$

$$+ M_{s,i}M_{s-1,j}P_{s,i,j}^{shape}((\Gamma^T)_{y_j}^{y_i}|(\Gamma)_{x_{s-1}}^{x_s})P_{i,j}^{snake}((\Gamma^T)_{y_j}^{y_i}|y_i,y_j,I)]\,,$$

where in the last step we have used (2), that is, the assumption (approximation) that image features obtained by SUSAN and the manually detected model points are optimal and sharply peaked. We also simply use $\{y_k\}, [x_s]$ to refer to $\{y_k^{SUSAN}\}, [x_s^{manual}]$.

Thus, the focus of our work is reduced to the snake and shape integration (decomposition and reconstruction). One could criticize having spent this effort on writing about probabilities of features and not using them. We argue that by following the approach fully, and the making of this assumption, helps to (1) clearly understand where the assumptions are being made; (2) In the future, extend the work to account for these probabilities, including a system that could evaluate feature detectors based on the recognition system; (3) The main technical difficulty of decomposing and reconstructing are left present to analyze the two remaining probabilities, for shape analysis and snakes.

3 Snake and Shape Models

In this section, we establish both the snake model, $P(\Gamma^T|I,\{y_k\})$ which is a simple model for detecting contours, and the shape model, $P(\Gamma|\Gamma^T,[x_s],\{y_k\})$.

3.1 Snake

A snake model [9] is a deformable contour usually applied to detect contour boundaries (see Figure-1(c),(d) for results). Within a Bayesian rational, we need to construct the probability distribution of contours in images, $P(\Gamma^T)$, and the probability of generating images and features given contours, $P(I,\{y_k\}|\Gamma^T)$ to obtain $P(\Gamma^T|I,\{y_k\}) = P(I,\{y_k\}|\Gamma^T)P(\Gamma^T)$. We have considered the prior model of contours to be similar to the Elastica [11], i.e.

$$P(\Gamma^T) = C_1 e^{-\int_{\Gamma^T}[\lambda_1|k|_{\Gamma^T}(x(t),y(t))+\lambda_2]\,dt}$$

or

$$P_{i,j}((\Gamma^T)_{y_j}^{y_i}) = C'_1 e^{-\int_{\Gamma^T=y_j}^{y_i}[\lambda_1|k(t)|+\lambda_2]\,dt}, \qquad (4)$$

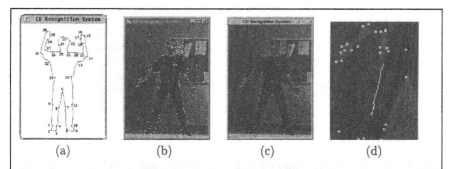

Fig. 1. (a) Original model with its key points. (b) Original image with key features detected by "SUSAN" detector. (c) Snake result connecting two key features. (d) Same as (c), with a large scale of the snake region.

where the contour is parameterized by t, the parameters λ_1 and λ_2 have to be estimated, $k_{\Gamma^T}(x(t), y(t))$, or simply $k(t)$, are the contour curvature at $(x(t), y(t)) \in \Gamma^T$, and C_1 is a normalization constant. This model differs from the elastica model [11] in that we require the curvature term to be scale invariant.

For the image generation, given the contour Γ^T, we have assumed that

$$P(I|\Gamma^T) = C_2 e^{-[A + \int_{\Gamma^T} \frac{1}{|\nabla I|^2_{(x(t), y(t))} + \epsilon} dt]}$$

or

$$P_{ij}(I, y_i, y_j | \Gamma^T) = C'_2 e^{-[A + \int_{\Gamma^T = y_j}^{y_i} \frac{1}{|\nabla I|^2_{(x(t), y(t))} + \epsilon} dt]}, \tag{5}$$

where $|\nabla I|_{(x(t), y(t))}$, or simply $|\nabla I|_t$, is the image gradient at $(x(t), y(t)) \in \Gamma^T$. A is a constant reflecting a uniform distribution of intensity outside the contour boundary, and C_2 is a normalization constant. We then obtain the posterior distribution,

$$P(\Gamma^T, \{y_k\} | I) = C \prod_{i,j=1}^{K,K} e^{-\int_{\Gamma^T = y_j}^{y_i} \left[\frac{1}{|\nabla I|^2(t) + \epsilon} + \lambda_1 |k(t)| + \lambda_2 \right] dt}, \tag{6}$$

where $C = C'_1 C'_2 e^{-A}$. In order to maximize this probability alone, one can use the Dijkstra algorithm (single source optimal path).

3.2 Shape analysis and Kullback Leibler distance

In [2], it is argued that two contours are similar according to the amount of deformation, stretching and bending, to bring one into the other. It assumes that two shape contours are similar when their local components are similar. This assumption is particularly useful when modeling articulations, since an object

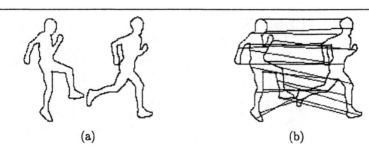

(a)   (b)

Fig. 2. (a) Two similar contours with articulations and stretchings. Note that locally both contours are similar almost everywhere. (b) Correspondences $\{t(s)\}$ derived from minimizing the spring model ($p = 2$) cost function.

undergoing articulations is untouched (similar) almost everywhere (see Figure-2(a)).

Finally we consider the Dijkstra algorithm at the top-down level, to minimize for the set of matchings, i.e., to determine M^*.

Our interest is to model $P^{shape}(\Gamma^T|\Gamma)$ or $P^{shape}_{s,i,j}((\Gamma^T)^{y_i}_{y_j}|(\Gamma)^{x_s}_{x_{s-1}})$. So, this is to say that given a contour Γ the probability of generating a "similar" contour Γ^T should be high. We notice that different correspondences can be established between two contours, say Γ and Γ^T, and a measure of similarity between them may depend on which correspondence is used. We can formalize this as follows: we parameterize the contours $\Gamma(s)$; $s = 1, ..., S$ and $\Gamma^T(t)$: $t = 1, ..., T$. Then,

$$P^{shape}(\Gamma^T|\Gamma) = \sum_{\{t(s)\}} P(\{t(s)\}, \Gamma^T|\Gamma).$$

The sum over all possible correspondences can sometimes be reduced to the optimal correspondence, i.e., we may consider

$$P^{shape}(\Gamma^T|\Gamma) \approx P(\{t(s)^*\}, \Gamma^T|\Gamma),$$

where $\{t(s)^*\} = arg \max_{\{t(s)\}} P(\{t(s)\}, \Gamma^T|\Gamma)$. Given the correspondence $t(s)$, we can then express the Kullback Leibler distance between the "true" contour, $\Gamma(s)$, and the detected one, $\Gamma^T(t(s))$, as

$$\mathcal{D}_{\{t(s)\}}(\Gamma^T\|\Gamma) = \sum_{s=1}^{S} P(\Gamma(s)) log \frac{P(\Gamma(s))}{P(\Gamma^T(t(s)))},$$

where we are indeed considering $\{\Gamma(s)$: $s = 1, 2, ..., S\}$ to be a sequence of samples from the distribution of the "true" contour. Analogously, $\{\Gamma^T(t(s))$: $s = 1, ..., S\}$ are the sequence samples from the "targeted" contour. Assuming again the prior (4) distribution on Γ, we obtain

$$\mathcal{D}_{\{t(s)\}}(\Gamma^T\|\Gamma) = \int \{e^{-[|k(s)|+\lambda]}[|k^T(t(s))|dt - |k(s)|ds + \lambda(dt - ds)]\}$$

$$= \int ds\{e^{-[|k(s)|+\lambda]}[|k^T(t(s))||t'(s) - |k(s)| + \lambda(t'(s) - 1)]\}\,.(7)$$

where $t' = dt/ds$, $\lambda = \frac{\lambda_2}{\lambda_1}$. The problem is again to find $t^*(s)$ that minimizes $\mathcal{D}_{\{t(s)\}}(\Gamma^T\|\Gamma)$.

This is a non-symmetric shape comparison measure, which may be desired since there is a "true" contour, the model contour Γ and it is possible that human perception does not utilize symmetric measures. Another (symmetric) distance we have considered [2] is

$$E^{shape}_{\{t^*(s)\}}(\Gamma, \Gamma^T)$$

$$= \min_{\{t(s)\}} E(\Gamma, \Gamma^T, \{t(s)\}) = \int ds \frac{|k^T t'^*(s) - k|^p}{(|k^T t'^*(s)| + |k|)^{(p-1)}} + \lambda \frac{|t'^*(s) - 1|^p}{(t'^*(s) + 1)^{p-1}}, \qquad (8)$$

where p is constant (we use $p = 2$). The first term in the integral (8) is the bending cost and the second one is the stretching cost. Notice that the cost is rotation and translation invariant, since it is solely based on the curvature measure of the contour. The bending cost is scale invariant. The parameter λ weights the relative contributions of stretching and bending. One important property of the model is accounting of articulations. Since articulations occur at high curvature points, it will cost relatively less to bend them (because of the denominator of the bending cost).

In order to compute this distance we need to optimize for $t(s)$. This is possible using Dijkstra algorithm (single source optimal path).

Coarse computation Since the Dijkstra algorithm efficiency may still leads to long computations (when this module is called many times), we investigate a coarse approach to shape similarity. The shape energy can be computed in a coarse way as

$$E^{sh}_{s,i,j} = \frac{[\Theta_S(s) - \Theta_T(i)]^p}{[|\Theta_S(s)| + |\Theta_T(i)|]^{p-1}} + \lambda \frac{|t'(s,i,j) - 1|^p}{(t'(s,i,j) + 1)^{p-1}}, \qquad (9)$$

where $\Theta_S(s)$ and $\Theta_T(i)$ are the angles of the contours at the points x_s and y_i, respectively. The stretching is computed by

$$t'^*(s) = t'^*((\Gamma^S)^s_{s-1}, (\Gamma^T)^{f_i}_{f_j}) = \frac{d^S(s, s-1)}{d^T(y_j, y_i)},$$

where $d^T(y_j, y_i)$ is computed from the contour connecting y_j and y_i, i.e., depends on the choice of $(\Gamma^T)^{y_i}_{y_j}$, while $d^S(s, s-1)$ is a precomputed distance between x_s and x_{s-1} in the contour model (following the contour). These computations are done much faster than with Dijkstra algorithm. We have considered

$$P(\Gamma^T|\Gamma) = C \prod_{s,i,j=1}^{S,K,K} e^{-E_{s,i,j}^{sh}} \ .$$

4   Optimization: Top-down & Bottom-up

From (3) we have obtained

$$P(\Gamma^T|\Gamma, I) \approx \prod_{s,i,j=1}^{S,K,K} e^{-M_{s,i}M_{s-1,j}[E_{i,j}^{sn}((\Gamma^T)_{y_j}^{y_i},I) + \beta \ E_{s,i,j}^{sh}((\Gamma^T)_{y_j}^{y_i},(\Gamma)_{x_{s-1}}^{x_s})]} \ , \quad (10)$$

where

$$E_{i,j}^{sn}((\Gamma^T)_{y_j}^{y_i}, I) = \int_{(\Gamma^T)_{y_j}^{y_i}} \left[\frac{1}{|\nabla I|^2(t) + \epsilon} + \lambda_1 k^T(t) + \lambda_2 \right] dt \ ,$$

and

$$E_{s,i,j}^{sh} = \frac{[\Theta_S(s) - \Theta_T(i)]^p}{[|\Theta_S(s)| + |\Theta_T(i)|]^{p-1}} + \lambda \frac{|t'(s,i,j) - 1|^p}{(t'(s,i,j) + 1)^{p-1}} \ .$$

Notice that $\{M_{s,i}\}$ have been rearranged, moved to the top of the exponential, without any change in the theory. When $M_{s,i} = 0$ the correspondence is not established and the costs do not contribute for the probability estimation.

We now give an intuitive account, the rational, of the top-down & bottom-up processes. Following that we derive this rational from the optimization method, Dijkstra algorithm, to compute the solution.

4.1   The rational

From the top-down view of the problem, we need to select the optimal choice of M, i.e., the optimal matching correspondence between model key points and image key features. The algorithm must not search for all possible configurations of M to be efficient. The guidance of the top-down model is to decide which pairs, say $M_{s-1,j} = 1$ and $M_{s,i} = 1$, to consider, without searching for all possible ones.

The top-down module hypothesizes a pair of correspondences, say $M_{s-1,j} = 1$ and $M_{s,i} = 1$, and feeds the model contour Γ_{s-1}^s to the bottom-up module.

The bottom-up process test the hypothesis that (x_{s-1}, x_s) corresponds to (y_j, y_i), i.e., $M_{s-1,j}^* = 1$ and $M_{s,i}^* = 1$, taking the contour part Γ_{s-1}^s as input. There is freedom to select different contours $(\Gamma^T)_{y_j}^{y_i}$ connecting y_j to y_i. The bottom-up process returns the cost induced by the best contour choice, $(\Gamma^{T*})_{y_j}^{y_i}$. This cost takes into account the snake cost and the shape comparison cost with Γ_{s-1}^s.

The top-down will then decide which other pair of correspondences to hypothesize for its search.

To simplify and approximate the solution, the bottom-up approach groups the edges between y_i and y_j, growing a snake and optimizing for E^{sn}, regardless the shape analysis measure E^{sh}. The bottom-up algorithm then computes E^{sh}, to deliver the total cost, $E^{sn} + \beta E^{sh}$, for this pair of hypothesis. An illustration of the control loop is given in Figure-3.

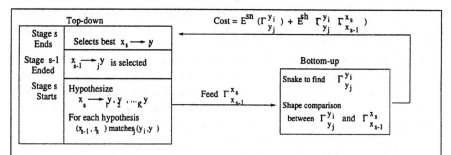

Fig. 3. Control loop of the top-down and bottom-up algorithm. The stage $s-1$ has been resolved with x_{s-1} matching y_j, i.e., $M^*_{s-1,j} = 1$. Then the algorithm finds the best y_i such that $M^*_{s,j} = 1$. It also finds the contour connecting y_j and y_i, i.e., $(\Gamma^{T*})^{y_i}_{y_j}$.

More precisely, the solution of the problem is to obtain a maximum a posteriori probability estimate (MAP) of

$$(\Gamma^{T*}, M^*) = arg \min_{\Gamma^T, M} log P(\Gamma^T | \Gamma, I)$$

$$= arg \min_{\Gamma^T, M} \sum_{s,i,j=1}^{s=S, i=K, j=k} M_{s,i} M_{s,j-1} [E^{sn}_{i,j}((\Gamma^T)^{y_i}_{y_j}, I) + \beta \, E^{sh}_{s,i,j}((\Gamma^T)^{y_i}_{y_j}, (\Gamma)^{x_s}_{x_{s-1}})].$$

We then approximate this solution by

$$M^* = arg \min_{M} \sum_{s,i,j=1}^{s=S, i,j=N} M_{s,i}, M_{s-1,j} [E^{sn}((\Gamma^{T*})^{y_i}_{y_j}) + \beta E^{sh}((\Gamma^{T*})^{y_i}_{y_j})]$$

$$(\Gamma^{T*})^{y_i}_{y_j} = arg \min_{(\Gamma^T)^{y_i}_{y_j}} E^{sn}_{i,j}((\Gamma^T)^{y_i}_{y_j}, I) \qquad \text{if } M^*_{s,i} = M^*_{s-1,j} = 1. \tag{11}$$

4.2 Different levels of Dijkstra algorithm

At the bottom-up level, we can solve for $(\Gamma^{T*})^{y_i}_{y_j}$ using dynamic programming [7], and since the energy costs are all positive we can replace it with Dijkstra algorithm with a gain in efficiency of a factor 4 to 10 (see Figure-1(c)(d) for results).

At the next level, still bottom-up, a Dijkstra algorithm has also been used to test the shape similarity model, i.e. to find $\{t^*(s)\}$ (see Figure-2 (a),(b)).

Finally we consider the Dijkstra algorithm at the top-down level, to minimize for the set of matchings, i.e., to determine M^*. The advantage of using Dijkstra at the top-down level is that, due to its greedy characteristic, not all possible matches are considered. Indeed most matches will not be considered. The Dijkstra search at the top-down level will command which matching hypothesis to consider given its current state and evaluation. The bottom-up Dijkstra algorithm will simply compute the cost of each hypothesis. This is in a unique way the interaction between top-down and bottom-up algorithms.

In order to justify the algorithm we use the dynamic programming principle (and the fact that the costs are all positive) since it is easier to convey the idea.

The dynamic programming algorithm works as follows (as shown in Figure-4 where each vertex is a possible matching combination, e.g., $M_{s,i} = 1$ indicates that a feature point y_i is matched to the model contour point $x_S(s)$.)

(a) Top-down: For each match candidate, $M_{s,i} = 1$, we compute all the transition cost $E^{sn} + \beta E^{sh}((\Gamma^{T*})^{y_i}_{y_j})$ for $j = 1, 2, ..., N$ of going from any of the pairs $(x_S(s-1), y_j)$ $(M_{s-1,j} = 1)$ to the current candidate $(x_S(s), y_i)$ (We don't need to consider all key features, but only the ones within reasonable distances from the current one.)

(b) Bottom-up: This transition cost is obtained by running a snake algorithm between the two key features, using Dijkstra algorithm, to obtain $(\Gamma^{T*})^{y_i}_{y_j}$. Then the shape comparison is used to estimate $t'(s)$, or one could use Dijkstra again to estimate $\{t(s)\}$ at more computational time.

(c) we repeat the computations for all key points, i.e., loop for $s = 1, ..., S$

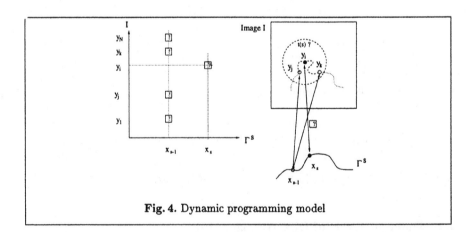

Fig. 4. Dynamic programming model

4.3   Further simplifications:

We discuss two further simplifications of the algorithm.

Optimization with Integration by Parts: We now consider to represent the objects by parts to simplify further the computations. A part is a partial model contour between two consecutive partition points that we have marked as *partition*-points (see Figure-5(b)). The set of partition-points is a subset of all key points from the model.

The globally optimal solution becomes a sum of optimizations done on each part of the model contour and we refer this process as "integration by parts". Whenever a snake recovered a new part in the optimization (and the solution has been verified by the shape comparison), we content that a new part is found and it is added into the previously recovered optimal solution. We then start a new optimization process from the last vertex recovered. We have used this simplification in our experiments.

Verifying the correctness of a target contour: Observe that if the articulations and deformations of a human shape do not introduce self-occlusions, the region enclosed by the polygon when orderly connecting the partition-points can be considered as a rigid part. Also, most of human articulations are caused by movements of parts such as hands, legs or head. This provides us a good measurement of how correctly a derived target contour is. For example, one can simply compute then compare the enclose rigid areas for the model and target contour to explicitly test a possible solution. We have not used this simplification in our experiments.

5   Experimental Results

In Figure-5, we show the results of testing our proposed shape contour recognition method. Given an input image as shown in Figure-5, we carried out the algorithm with respect to three different model contours as in Figure-5 (a), (b) and (c). Note that contour (a) is part of the whole human shape model contour (b). Satisfactory results are derived as seen in Figure-5 (e), (f), (h), (k) and (l). It is worth to point out that the image being tested does contain a complex background and our method has successfully recovered the corresponding contour of human shape in each experiment though there is still room for improvement such as in result (h), the right hand was not picked up very well.

Currently, our methods have been implemented in two different versions: one for the SGI machines and the other for PC with Linux. On a Pentium 150, the algorithm takes about 5 minutes to complete (including displaying the evolution of detected contours on the window interface of our softwares).

6   Extensions and Conclusions

We have introduced a new method to recognize and detect shape contours for articulated and deformed objects. The basis of the approach is a carefully Bayesian-Information formulation and manipulation of the problem variables. We have

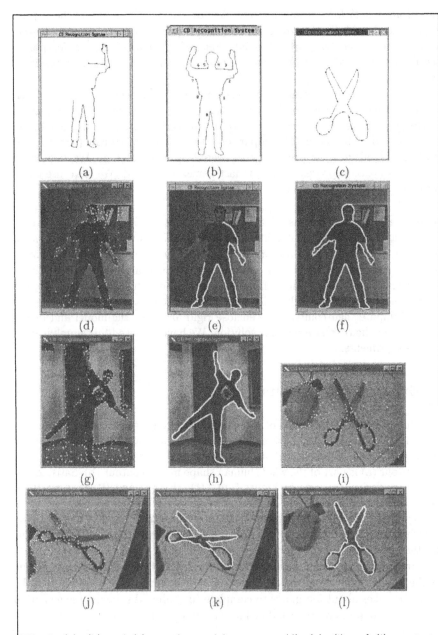

Fig. 5. (a), (b) and (c) are the model contours. (d), (g), (i) and (j) are test images with detected features. (e) (with model (a)), (f)(h) (with model (b)) and (k)(l) (with model (i)) are the corresponding detected shape boundaries.

relied on the use of Dijkstra algorithm as the main engine of computations. Combining shape and snakes have been part of the system and we have shed light on combining top-down & bottom-up approaches to recognition in unique way. The global optimization is approximately completed by optimization with "integration by parts".

A limitation of our experiments and formulation is the use of contour models, 1 dimensional graphs, allowing the use of Dijkstra algorithms. As one moves to 3 dimensions, the use of surfaces would destroy the efficiency of Dijkstra algorithm. Another limitation of the approach is the non-use of symmetries along the contours. A natural way to overcome both limitations is to consider the axis of symmetry of an object. If we represent objects by their axes of symmetry, we naturally include the symmetries and represent 3D objects by 1D graphs (the axis of symmetry). The approach can then be easily extendible to 3D objects and account for symmetry properties.

Acknowledgments

The authors would like to thank Stuart Geman and Alan Yuille for interesting discussions. We thank the AFOSR grant #:F49620-96-1-0519 for sponsoring this research.

References

1. Y. Amit, D. Geman, and K. Wilder, "Recognizing Shapes from Simple Queries about Geometry," Technical Report, University of Chicago, 1995.
2. B. Basri, L. Costa, D. Geiger, and D. Jacobs, "Determine Shape Similarity," *IEEE workshop in Physics Based Vision*, Boston, June 1995.
3. I. Biederman, "Human Image Understanding: Recent Research and a Theory," *Computer Graphics, Vision, and Image Processing*, (32):29-73, 1985.
4. M. C. Burl, P. Perona, "Recognition of Planar Object Classes," *IEEE Conf. on Computer Vision and Pattern Recognition*, pp. 223-230, San Francisco, June 1996.
5. D. Forsyth, J. Malik, M. Fleck, Leung, Bregler, Carson, Greenspan, "Finding objects by grouping," *Proc. of Workshop on Object Representation, ECCV, England, 1996*.
6. T. Cootes, C. Taylor, D. Cooper and J. Graham, "Active Shape Models - Their Training and Application," *Computer Vision and Image Understanding.*, Vol. 61, No 1, pp. 38-59, January. 1995.
7. D. Geiger, A. Gupta, L. A. Costa, and J. Vlontzos, "Detecting, Tracking and Matching Elastic Contours with Dynamic Programming," *IEEE Transactions on Pattern Analysis and Machine Intelligence*, PAMI-17, March 1995.
8. U. Grenander, Y. Chow and D. M. Keenan, " Hands: a Pattern Theoretic Study of Biological Shapes," Springer-Verlag, 1991.
9. M. Kass, A. Witkin, and D. Terzopoulos, "Snakes: Active Contour Models," *Proceedings of the First International Conf. on Computer Vision*, pp. 259-268, 1987.
10. K. Kupeev and H. Wolfson, "On Shape Similarity," *Proceedings Int. Conf. on Pattern Recognition*, pp. 227-237, 1994.

11. D. Mumford. Elastica and computer vision. In C. L. Bajaj, editor, *Algebraic Geometry and Its Applications*. Springer-Verlag, New York, 1993.
12. J. L. Mundy and A. Zisserman (editors), "Geometric Invariance in Computer Vision," MIT Press, 1992.
13. A. Pentland, "Recognition by Parts," *Proceedings of the First International Conf. on Computer Vision*, pp. 612-620, 1987.
14. A. Pentland and B. Horowitz, "Recovery of Non-rigid Motion and Structure," *IEEE Trans. Pattern Analysis and Machine Intelligence*, **13**(7), 730-742, 1991.
15. A. Pentland and S. Sclaroff, " Closed-form Solutions for Physically Based Shape Modeling and Recognition," *IEEE Trans. Pattern Analysis and Machine Intelligence*, **13**(7), 715-729, 1991.
16. T. Poggio and D. Beymer, "Learning Networks for Face Analysis and Synthesis," *Proceedings of the International Workshop on Automatic Face- and Gesture-Recognition*, Zurich, Switzerland, June 26-28, 1995.
17. S. Smith and J. Brady, "SUSAN - a New Approach to Low Level Image Processing," *Int. Journal of Computer Vision*, 1996, In publication.
18. K. Siddiqi and B. Kimia, "Parts of Visual Form: Computational Aspects," *IEEE Transactions on Pattern Analysis and Machine Intelligence*, PAMI-17, March 1995.
19. K. Siddiqi and B. Kimia, "Toward a Shock Grammar for Recognition," *IEEE Conf. on Computer Vision and Pattern Recognition*, 1996.
20. M. Turk and A. Pentland, "Face Recognition Using Eigenfaces," *IEEE Conf. on Computer Vision and Pattern Recognition*, pp. 586-591, 1991.
21. S. Ullman, "High-level vision", MIT Press, Cambridge, 1996.
22. S. Ullman and R. Basri, "Recognition by Linear Combinations of Models," *IEEE Transactions on Pattern Analysis and Machine Intelligence*, PAMI-13 (10), pp. 992-1006, 1991.
23. A. L. Yuille and P. W. Hallinan, "Deformable Templates for Recognition and Tracking," *Active Vision*, editors A. Blake and A. L. Yuille, MIT Press, Cambridge, 1992.
24. S. C. Zhu and A.L. Yuille, "A Flexible Object Recognition and Modeling System, " *Proceedings International Conference on Computer Vision*, 1995. To appear in IJCV, 1996.

Optimization Problems in Statistical Object Recognition

Joachim Hornegger and Heinrich Niemann

Lehrstuhl für Mustererkennung (Informatik 5),
Martensstraße 3, D–91058 Erlangen, Germany,
email: {hornegger,niemann}@informatik.uni-erlangen.de
Tel.: 0049/9131/85–7826   Fax: 0049/9131/303811

Abstract This paper treats the application of statistical principles for 3D computer vision purposes. Both the automatic generation of probabilistic object models, and the localization as well as the classification of objects in compound scenes result in complex optimization problems within the introduced statistical framework. Different methods are discussed for solving the associated optimization problems: the Expectation–Maximization algorithm forms the basis for the learning stage of stochastic object models; global optimization techniques — like adaptive random search, deterministic grid search or simulated annealing — are used for localization. The experimental part utilizes the abstract formalism for normally distributed object features, proves the correctness of 3D object recognition algorithms, and demonstrates their computational complexity in combination with real gray–level images.

1 Introduction

Optimization problems are very much a part of pattern recognition and computer vision [28]. Within the field of object recognition and scene analysis one of the most challenging tasks is the computation of symbolic descriptions which optimally fit together sensor data and models as well as available domain knowledge [4]. The acquisition of object models and domain knowledge should be done automatically out of a set of representative training views [24, 27]. The methods for solving these hard computer vision problems are quite different and vary for particular approaches.

Recent trends show that the use and the extension of classical statistical pattern recognition algorithms [18] apply to image processing with an increasing interest. Examples for successfully tested probabilistic methods in the field of computer vision are:

- Bayesian parameter estimation techniques for surface segmentation and the computation of lower bounds for achievable errors [5],
- theory of probabilistic relaxation for matching symbolic structures [17, 20],
- Markov random field based image segmentation [14] and model–based image interpretation [23], and
- Bayesian networks for image labeling and interpretation [6, 21, 26].

Here we combine probabilistic and optimization methods for solving high–level vision tasks. We introduce statistical concepts for transforming sensor data into a symbolic description and show that knowledge acquisition, object localization, and classification are associated with complicated maximizations. In contrast to [33], both the matching and the projection from the model into the image space are part of statistical models.

This paper is divided up into seven sections: The introduction is followed by the suggestion of a probabilistic formalism which combines continuous and discrete probability density functions for object and scene modeling. The stochastic object models are parameterized with respect to feature– and pose–specific parameters. The third section provides a mathematical representation of the involved optimization problems; model generation as well as object localization are defined as parameter estimation problems. The computation of feature–specific parameters corresponds to a parameter estimation problem with *incomplete data*. This is due to the loss of range information during the projection into the image space and the missing matching between image and model primitives. Just as the model generation, the localization reduces to the estimation of an optimal set of pose parameters. Methods and strategies for solving the introduced optimization problems are discussed in section four and five. The experimental evaluation illustrates how the investigated theory solves 3D computer vision problems. The paper ends with a brief summary of the main results, draws some conclusions, and gives some hints for future research.

2 Statistical Modeling of Objects

A wide range of different object recognition strategies has been proposed. Recognition systems, for instance, distinguish into sensor data, into features, into localization and classification algorithms, or into representation formalisms for object models and domain knowledge [29]. Because of the objects' geometric nature, most approaches to object modeling prefer geometric representations, like CAD models, wire frame models, or simply 3D line and point features [22]. In general, those pure geometric models do not or not sufficiently consider the probabilistic behavior of features available from sensor data, although these primitives constitute the input data for classification and localization. For a suitable and complete statistical description of an object and its appearance in images, the following components require an adequate probabilistic modeling [15]:

- statistical behavior of single features, for example, point or line features,
- object rotation and translation,
- projection from the model into the image space,
- occlusion,
- correspondence between image and model features, and
- relations between features, for instance, neighborhood relationships.

Classical pattern recognition theory and statistical classifiers expect non–transformed feature vectors of fixed dimension for each pattern [18]. Therefore an extension of common principles becomes necessary. An explicit or implicit statistical formalization of above items is introduced in the following subsections.

2.1 Statistical Modeling of Features

Object features occur in different domains, the model and the image space. Let D_m and D_o denote the dimensions of model and image spaces, respectively. For 3D object recognition in gray–level images, for example, we set $D_m = 3$ and $D_o = 2$. The set $\{\Omega_\kappa | 1 \le \kappa \le K\}$ contains the considered object classes, where K denotes the number of models. Let $\boldsymbol{C}_\kappa = \{\boldsymbol{c}_{\kappa,1}, \boldsymbol{c}_{\kappa,2}, \ldots, \boldsymbol{c}_{\kappa,n_\kappa}\}$ be the set of model features of an object from class Ω_κ including n_κ different D_m–dimensional feature vectors $\boldsymbol{c}_{\kappa,l}$, where $l = 1, 2, \ldots, n_\kappa$. Usually, objects differ in the number of model features, i.e. $n_\kappa \ne n_\lambda$ for almost all $\kappa \ne \lambda$. With each single model feature $\boldsymbol{c}_{\kappa,l}$ we associate a random vector; thus a feature can be considered as a probabilistic event, which underlies a parametric distribution $p(\boldsymbol{c}_{\kappa,l} | \boldsymbol{a}_{\kappa,l})$. Here $\boldsymbol{a}_{\kappa,l}$ is the parameter set belonging to $\boldsymbol{c}_{\kappa,l}$. A rotation and translation of a rigid object within the model space is mathematically described by a bijective, affine transform given by the (parametric) matrix $\boldsymbol{R}_{rot} \in \mathbb{R}^{D_m \times D_m}$ and the vector $\boldsymbol{t}_{rot} \in \mathbb{R}^{D_m}$. If model primitives are attached features, i.e. for the transformed feature $\boldsymbol{c}'_{\kappa,l}$ we have $\boldsymbol{c}'_{\kappa,l} = \boldsymbol{R}_{rot}\boldsymbol{c}_{\kappa,l} + \boldsymbol{t}_{rot}$, then we get the density function $p(\boldsymbol{c}'_{\kappa,l} | \boldsymbol{a}_{\kappa,l}, \boldsymbol{R}_{rot}, \boldsymbol{t}_{rot})$ including two different types of parameters: *feature–* and *pose*–specific parameters. The integration of pose specific parameters can be done by a standard density transform [1]. The same holds for extension of the model density with respect to the projection from the model into the image space [15].

Object rotation, translation, and orthographic projection, for instance, causes for each D_m–dimensional model feature $\boldsymbol{c}_{\kappa,l_k}$ a corresponding D_o–dimensional image feature $\boldsymbol{o}_k$. The relational dependency of image and model features

$$\boldsymbol{o}_k = \boldsymbol{R}\boldsymbol{c}_{\kappa,l_k} + \boldsymbol{t} \quad , \tag{1}$$

is given by an affine transform, where $\boldsymbol{R} \in \mathbb{R}^{D_o \times D_m}$ and $\boldsymbol{t} \in \mathbb{R}^{D_o}$. If the random variable in the model space is normally distributed with mean vector $\boldsymbol{\mu}_{\kappa,l_k}$ and covariance matrix $\boldsymbol{\Sigma}_{\kappa,l_k}$, the observed feature vector $\boldsymbol{o}_k$ is also Gaussian with the modified mean vector $\boldsymbol{R}\boldsymbol{\mu}_{\kappa,l_k} + \boldsymbol{t}$ and covariance matrix $\boldsymbol{R}^T \boldsymbol{\Sigma}_{\kappa,l} \boldsymbol{R}$ (see [1], p. 25).

If the corresponding pairs $[\boldsymbol{o}_k, \boldsymbol{c}_{\kappa,l_k}]$ of model and image features are known, the density function for observing a set $\boldsymbol{O} = \{\boldsymbol{o}_1, \boldsymbol{o}_2, \ldots, \boldsymbol{o}_m\}$ of image features for a given transformation is

$$p(\boldsymbol{O} | \{\boldsymbol{a}_{\kappa,1}, \boldsymbol{a}_{\kappa,2}, \ldots, \boldsymbol{a}_{\kappa,n_\kappa}\}, \boldsymbol{R}, \boldsymbol{t}) = \prod_{k=1}^{m} p(\boldsymbol{o}_k | \boldsymbol{a}_{\kappa,l_k}, \boldsymbol{R}, \boldsymbol{t}) \quad , \tag{2}$$

provided that all features are pairwise statistical independent.

2.2 Statistical Modeling of Matching

In practice, the major problem results from the missing assignment of image and model features. But the obvious computation or estimation of an assignment function applying heuristic or threshold methods would be a contradiction to the intended goal of a closed statistical framework for object modeling. For that reason, we define a hidden correspondence function

$$\zeta_\kappa : \begin{cases} \boldsymbol{O} \to \{1, 2, \ldots, n_\kappa\} \\ \boldsymbol{o}_k \mapsto \qquad l_k \end{cases} , \quad k = 1, 2, \ldots, m \tag{3}$$

Each set of correspondence pairs $\{[o_k, c_{\kappa,l_k}] | 1 \le k \le m\}$ including elements of $O \times C_\kappa$ can be associated with an integer vector

$$\zeta_\kappa = \begin{pmatrix} \zeta_\kappa(o_1) \\ \zeta_\kappa(o_2) \\ \vdots \\ \zeta_\kappa(o_m) \end{pmatrix} = \begin{pmatrix} l_1 \\ l_2 \\ \vdots \\ l_m \end{pmatrix} \in \{1, 2, \dots, n_\kappa\}^m \quad , \tag{4}$$

and each correspondence ζ_κ can be understood as a random vector. Thus, the discrete probability $p(\zeta_\kappa)$ can be computed, giving stochastic measures for correspondence functions ζ_κ [33].

An example shows Figure 1. The assignment ζ_κ, illustrated by arrows, induces the random vector $\zeta_\kappa = (3, 3, 2, 1, 5, 4, 4, 5)^T$.

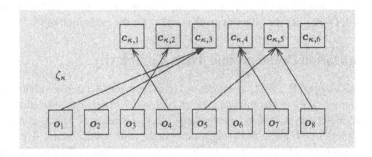

Figure 1. Assignment of image and model features

2.3 Construction of Model Densities

With the suggested statistical modeling of assignment functions and the probabilistic characterization of image features, the density function for observing a set of features O with an assignment function ζ_κ and a transform, given by R and t, is

$$p(O, \zeta_\kappa | B_\kappa, R, t) = p(\zeta_\kappa) \prod_{k=1}^{m} p(o_k | a_{\kappa, \zeta_\kappa(o_k)}, R, t) \quad . \tag{5}$$

Herein, B_κ subsumes all involved parameters of the density, i.e. $B_\kappa = \{p(\zeta_\kappa), a_{\kappa,1}, a_{\kappa,2}, \dots, a_{\kappa,n_\kappa}\}$. Usually, the matching ζ_κ is not part of the observation. Within the statistical context the missing matching is considered by computing the marginal density of (5) with respect to ζ_κ, i.e. ζ_κ is integrated out, and we get

$$p(O | B_\kappa, R, t) = \sum_{\zeta_\kappa} p(O, \zeta_\kappa | B_\kappa, R, t) = \sum_{\zeta_\kappa} p(\zeta_\kappa) \prod_{k=1}^{m} p(o_k | a_{\kappa, \zeta_\kappa(o_k)}, R, t) \tag{6}$$

Since $p(O|B_\kappa, R, t)$ represents a statistical description of the object of class Ω_κ appearance in the image plane with an eliminated correspondence function, it is called a *model density*. The complexity of evaluating the model density (6) for a given observation $O = \{o_1, o_2, \ldots, o_m\}$ is bounded by $\mathcal{O}(n_\kappa^m)$.

This exponential run–time behavior can be reduced by special independency assumptions for the components of ζ_κ. Let, for instance, all components of ζ_κ be pairwise statistically independent, then we have

$$p(\zeta_\kappa) = \prod_{k=1}^{m} p(\zeta_\kappa(o_k) = l_k) = \prod_{k=1}^{m} p_{\kappa, l_k} \quad , \tag{7}$$

and (6) combined with (7) results in

$$p(O|B_\kappa, R, t) = \prod_{k=1}^{m} \sum_{l=1}^{n_\kappa} p_{\kappa, l} \, p(o_k|a_{\kappa, l}, R, t) \quad , \tag{8}$$

with the linear complexity $\mathcal{O}(mn_\kappa)$. In general, it can be shown that a statistical dependency of order g implies the complexity $\mathcal{O}(mn_\kappa^{g+1})$ for the evaluation of (6).

3 Optimization Problems and Their Complexity

Model densities $p(O|B_\kappa, R, t)$ as introduced in the previous section are characterized by two different types of parameters. Within the model generation stage the *model–specific* parameter set B_κ has to be estimated. The localization of objects corresponds to the computation of R and t. Both stages are — in the mathematical sense — parameter estimation problems, which can be solved by different techniques [30]. One established and widely used method is, for instance, the maximum–likelihood approach.

3.1 Estimation of Model Parameters

For model generation purposes it is assumed that N different views are available and that for each view ϱ, $1 \leq \varrho \leq N$, the set of features ${}^\varrho O = \{{}^\varrho o_1, {}^\varrho o_2, \ldots, {}^\varrho o_m\}$ and the transformation parameters ${}^\varrho R$ and ${}^\varrho t$ are known. The maximum–likelihood estimation (ML estimation) of B_κ expects a set of statistically independent observations and solves the optimization problem

$$\widehat{B}_\kappa = \operatorname*{argmax}_{B_\kappa} \prod_{\varrho=1}^{N} p({}^\varrho O|B_\kappa, {}^\varrho R, {}^\varrho t) \quad . \tag{9}$$

The number of unknown parameters depends on the existing model features, on the chosen parametric density functions for single feature distributions, and on the dependencies of the correspondence function ζ_κ. If, for instance, normally distributed 3D vectors are used as model features and statistically independent assignments are present, the number of unknown parameters is $n_\kappa + 3n_\kappa + n_\kappa \cdot 3(3+1)/2$. For a 3D cube with eight ($n_\kappa = 8$) corners this results in 80 parameters. Consequently, the ML estimation has to be done in a fairly high dimensional parameter space from possibly projected data, since $D_m \geq D_o$, and unsupervised with respect to feature correspondences. The parameter estimation has to deal with incomplete sample data.

3.2 Estimation of Pose Parameters

The localization of one object in a single image results in the global optimization problem

$$\{\widehat{R}, \widehat{t}\} = \underset{R, t}{\operatorname{argmax}} \, p(O|B_\kappa, R, t) \quad , \tag{10}$$

where the parameters R and t of the transform from the model into the image space are estimated. In contrast to the estimation of model–specific parameters B_κ the set of data for parameter estimation is here restricted to a single view. The number of pose parameters does not depend on the number of model features, but on the parametric function which maps model features to image features. Assuming that objects are rotated, translated, and projected into the image plane by a perspective projection. Independent of the model features' present distribution the search space is six–dimensional, fixed by rotation angles ϕ_x, ϕ_y and ϕ_z and components t_1, t_2 and t_3 of the translation vector.

3.3 Classification of Objects

If the optimal pose parameters for all model densities are known, the class decision is based on the Bayesian decision rule, i.e. the discrete optimization problem

$$\kappa = \underset{\lambda}{\operatorname{argmax}} \, p(\Omega_\lambda|O, B_\lambda, R, t) \tag{11}$$

has to be solved for the observed feature set. This maximization process is bounded by $\mathcal{O}(K)$, where K denotes the number of object classes.

The previous discussion introduced three different types of optimization problems involved in the object recognition process. While the solution of the class decision problem (11) is obvious, model generation (9) and pose estimation (10) are incomparably hard problems. The presentation of possible solutions of both maximization tasks is the challenge of subsequent sections.

4 Model Generation: Incomplete Data Estimation

Object models including statistical properties of primitives should be learned out of a set of training views including non–corresponding features. The manual and painstaking construction of object models should be avoided and computers should learn the appearance of object features in images automatically.

4.1 The Expectation Maximization Algorithm

First, we consider the model generation problem using model densities as introduced in section 2, before we turn to the discussion of practical examples. We have already mentioned the incompleteness of the available training data and the infeasibility of a direct ML estimation due to the high dimension of the search space. The basic idea of the *Expectation Maximization algorithm* (EM algorithm) [8] is the augmentation of the observable data with latent data to simplify the parameter estimation algorithm. This technique leads — in most applications — to a reduction of one complicated optimization problem into a series of independent simpler maximizations. In an informal and colloquial manner we describe the available information for parameter estimation by the difference

> observed information = complete information − missing information .

For simplicity, let us assume that the observable random variables are X and the missing random variables are Y. If the associated densities are parameterized with respect to B, we have $p(X, Y|B) = p(X|B)p(Y|X, B)$. Taking the logarithm on both sides, we get an information theoretic formalization of above difference:

$$(-\log p(X|B)) = (-\log p(X, Y|B)) - (-\log p(Y|X, B)) \quad . \tag{12}$$

By multiplying with $p(Y|X, B)$ and integrating out the latent random variable Y it results the *key–equation* of the EM algorithm [8]

$$E[\log p(X|\widehat{B}^{(i+1)})|X, \widehat{B}^{(i)}] = Q(\widehat{B}^{(i+1)}|\widehat{B}^{(i)}) - H(\widehat{B}^{(i+1)}|\widehat{B}^{(i)}) \quad , \tag{13}$$

where $\widehat{B}^{(i+1)}$ is the re–estimation of the parameter set $\widehat{B}^{(i)}$ in the $(i + 1)$–st iteration,

$$\log p(X|\widehat{B}^{(i+1)}) = \int_Y p(Y|X, \widehat{B}^{(i)}) \log p(X|\widehat{B}^{(i+1)}) \, dY \quad , \tag{14}$$

$$Q(\widehat{B}^{(i+1)}|\widehat{B}^{(i)}) = \int_Y p(Y|X, \widehat{B}^{(i)}) \log p(X, Y|\widehat{B}^{(i+1)}) \, dY \quad , \tag{15}$$

and

$$H(\widehat{B}^{(i+1)}|\widehat{B}^{(i)}) = \int_Y p(Y|X, \widehat{B}^{(i)}) \log p(Y|X, \widehat{B}^{(i+1)}) \, dY \quad . \tag{16}$$

The main properties of equations (13)–(16) can be summarized as follows: The integral of the left hand side of (13) is equal to the original log–likelihood function $\log p(X|\widehat{B}^{(i+1)})$. Changes in the parameter set $\widehat{B}^{(i+1)}$ induce a decrease of $H(\widehat{B}^{(i+1)}|\widehat{B}^{(i)})$ (Jensen's inequality [8]), thus an increase of the *Kullback–Leibler statistics* $Q(\widehat{B}^{(i+1)}|\widehat{B}^{(i)})$ causes a reduction of $H(\widehat{B}^{(i+1)}|\widehat{B}^{(i)})$. Consequently, a maximum–likelihood estimation can be *simulated* by an iterative maximization of $Q(\widehat{B}^{(i+1)}|\widehat{B}^{(i)})$. The final success of the EM iterations depends on the initial estimate $\widehat{B}^{(0)}$, because the EM algorithm is a local optimization technique and provides a linear convergence behavior [34]. The already mentioned advantage of EM iterations instead of a straightforward ML estimation is that in most applications dealing with missing data the search space splits into independent lower dimensional sub–spaces. Furthermore, due to its iterative procedure the storage requirements remain constant. An impressive example out of the field of computer vision will be discussed in the following subsection.

4.2 Modeling of Line and Point Features

A D_m–dimensional line feature c_{κ,l_k} is identified by a sequence $[c_{\kappa,l_k,1},\ldots,c_{\kappa,l_k,q}]$ of D_m–dimensional points. Each component vector $c_{\kappa,l_k,s} \in \mathbb{R}^{D_m}$ ($s = 1,2,\ldots,q$; $l_k = 1,2,\ldots,n_\kappa$) represents a supporting point of the D_m–dimensional polygon c_{κ,l_k} (see Figure 2), and is assumed to be normally distributed with mean vector $\mu_{\kappa,l_k,s}$ and covariance matrix $\Sigma_{\kappa,l_k,s}$. In accordance with subsection 2.1 the density for a feature sequence is

$$p(c_{\kappa,l_k}|a_{\kappa,l_k}) = \prod_{s=1}^{q} p(c_{\kappa,l_k,s}|a_{\kappa,k,s}) = \prod_{s=1}^{q} \mathcal{N}(c_{\kappa,l_k,s}|\{\mu_{\kappa,l_k,s},\Sigma_{\kappa,l_k,s}\}) \quad . \ (17)$$

Obviously, if we set $q = 1$, feature c_{κ,l_k} degenerates to a point feature.

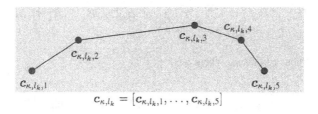

$$c_{\kappa,l_k} = [c_{\kappa,l_k,1},\ldots,c_{\kappa,l_k,5}]$$

Figure2. A polygon represented as a sequence of supporting points

Let the mapping from the D_m–dimensional model into the D_o–dimensional image space be an affine transform, represented by $R \in \mathbb{R}^{D_o \times D_m}$ and $t \in \mathbb{R}^{D_o}$. The sequence of observable image points is $o_k = [o_{k,1}, o_{k,2}, \ldots, o_{k,q}]$, where $o_{k,s} \in \mathbb{R}^{D_o}$ is also normally distributed. In addition to the lost dimensions during the projection process, the orientation of an observable sequence o_k is also latent. Mathematically, we formalize this change of ordering by the introduction of a permutation $\tau \in \Upsilon$, which acts on the sequence elements and assigns each s of $c_{\kappa,k,s}$ to the index $\tau(s) = 1,\ldots,q$ of the corresponding image element $o_{l_k,\tau(s)}$. In general, an identification of initial and final sequence points is impossible without a given matching ζ_κ of model and image features.

The permutation τ and the matching function ζ_κ are part of the missing data, where each permutation and matching is weighted by discrete probabilities $p(\tau)$ and $p(\zeta_\kappa)$. The available training data consist of a N sample views $\{^\varrho O|1 \leq \varrho \leq N\}$ and the corresponding transformation parameters $\{^\varrho R, ^\varrho t|1 \leq \varrho \leq N\}$.

The computation of the Kullback–Leibler statistics (15) and the calculation of the zero crossings of its gradient vector results in the following iteration formulas for estimating the discrete probabilities of the assignment function (cmp. [15])

$$\hat{p}_{\kappa,l}^{(i+1)} = \frac{1}{\sum_{\varrho=1}^{N} {}^\varrho m} \sum_{\varrho=1}^{N} \sum_{k=1}^{{}^\varrho m} \frac{\hat{p}_{\kappa,l}^{(i)} p(^\varrho o_k|\hat{a}_{\kappa,l}^{(i)}, {}^\varrho R, {}^\varrho t)}{p(^\varrho o_k|\hat{B}_\kappa^{(i)}, {}^\varrho R, {}^\varrho t)} \quad , \tag{18}$$

and the mean vectors

$$
\widehat{\boldsymbol{\mu}}_{\kappa,l,s}^{(i+1)} = \left(\sum_{\varrho=1}^{N} \sum_{k=1}^{\varrho_m} \sum_{\tau \in \Upsilon} p(^{\varrho}o_k | l, \tau, \widehat{\boldsymbol{B}}_{\kappa}^{(i)}, {}^{\varrho}\boldsymbol{R}, {}^{\varrho}\boldsymbol{t}) \, {}^{\varrho}\boldsymbol{R}^T ({}^{\varrho}\boldsymbol{R} \widehat{\boldsymbol{\Sigma}}_{\kappa,l,s}^{(i+1)} {}^{\varrho}\boldsymbol{R}^T)^{-1} {}^{\varrho}\boldsymbol{R} \right)^{-1}
$$
$$
\sum_{\varrho=1}^{N} \sum_{k=1}^{\varrho_m} \sum_{\tau \in \Upsilon} p(^{\varrho}o_k | l, \tau, \widehat{\boldsymbol{B}}_{\kappa}^{(i)}, {}^{\varrho}\boldsymbol{R}, {}^{\varrho}\boldsymbol{t}) {}^{\varrho}\boldsymbol{R}^T ({}^{\varrho}\boldsymbol{R} \widehat{\boldsymbol{\Sigma}}_{\kappa,l,s}^{(i+1)} {}^{\varrho}\boldsymbol{R}^T)^{-1} (^{\varrho}o_k - {}^{\varrho}\boldsymbol{t}) \quad , \tag{19}
$$

where $1 \leq l \leq n_\kappa$ and $1 \leq s \leq q$. Unfortunately, no closed–form solution exists for the estimation of the covariance matrices. The zero crossings of the Kullback–Leibler statistics gradient

$$
\nabla_{\widehat{\boldsymbol{\Sigma}}_{\kappa,l,s}^{(i+1)}} Q(\widehat{\boldsymbol{B}}_{\kappa}^{(i+1)} | \widehat{\boldsymbol{B}}_{\kappa}^{(i)}) = - \sum_{\varrho=1}^{N} \sum_{k=1}^{\varrho_m} \sum_{\tau \in \Upsilon} p(^{\varrho}o_k | l, \tau, \widehat{\boldsymbol{B}}_{\kappa}^{(i)}, {}^{\varrho}\boldsymbol{R}, {}^{\varrho}\boldsymbol{t}) \, \widehat{\boldsymbol{M}}_{\kappa,k,l,\tau,s}^{(i+1)} \, , \tag{20}
$$

results in nonlinear equations, where we set

$$
{}^{\varrho}\widehat{\boldsymbol{S}}_{\kappa,k,l,\tau,s}^{(i+1)} = \left({}^{\varrho}o_{k,\tau(s)} - {}^{\varrho}\boldsymbol{R} \widehat{\boldsymbol{\mu}}_{\kappa,l,s}^{(i+1)} - {}^{\varrho}\boldsymbol{t} \right) \left({}^{\varrho}o_{k,\tau(s)} - {}^{\varrho}\boldsymbol{R} \widehat{\boldsymbol{\mu}}_{\kappa,l,s}^{(i+1)} - {}^{\varrho}\boldsymbol{t} \right)^T \, , \tag{21}
$$

$$
{}^{\varrho}\widehat{\boldsymbol{D}}_{\kappa,l,s}^{(i+1)} = {}^{\varrho}\boldsymbol{R} \widehat{\boldsymbol{\Sigma}}_{\kappa,l,s}^{(i+1)} {}^{\varrho}\boldsymbol{R}^T \, , \tag{22}
$$

and

$$
\widehat{\boldsymbol{M}}_{\kappa,k,l,\tau,s}^{(i+1)} = {}^{\varrho}\boldsymbol{R}^T \left({}^{\varrho}\widehat{\boldsymbol{D}}_{\kappa,l,s}^{(i+1)} \right)^{-1} \left({}^{\varrho}\widehat{\boldsymbol{D}}_{\kappa,l,s}^{(i+1)} - {}^{\varrho}\widehat{\boldsymbol{S}}_{\kappa,k,l,\tau,s}^{(i+1)} \right) \left({}^{\varrho}\widehat{\boldsymbol{D}}_{\kappa,l,s}^{(i+1)} \right)^{-1} {}^{\varrho}\boldsymbol{R} \tag{23}
$$

For an iterative computation of the zero crossings of (20) numerical methods like the algorithm of Fletcher and Powell must be applied. In this case the EM algorithm yields a two stage iteration procedure: an iterative maximization of Kullback–Leibler statistics within each single EM iteration is necessary.

Above iteration algorithms allow the estimation of density parameters of the higher dimensional model space using projected observations. The search space is splitted up into separate optimization tasks for the estimation of matching parameters, mean vectors, and covariance matrices. It is remarkable that the parameter estimation step using the EM algorithm requires *no* explicit computations of the assignment functions. The model generation works unsupervised with respect to feature matching.

Specializations of the introduced estimation formulas were already published in [16], where $q = 1$, or can be found in [11], where $q = 1$ and no feature transform is considered, i.e. ${}^{\varrho}\boldsymbol{R} = \mathbf{1}$ and ${}^{\varrho}\boldsymbol{t} = \mathbf{0}$.

parameter	3D features [sec]	2D features [sec]	1D features [sec]
assignement (18)	10	7	4
mean vector (19)	28	27	23
covariance Matrix (20)	37	150	125
total	75	184	152
# iterations	5	20	25

Table1. Computation time for EM iterations using 400 training views of synthetic point features ($q = 1$) of different dimension. Each image includes 10 point features.

4.3 Experimental Results

The EM based model generation routines were implemented in C++ and tested on a HP 735 (100 MHz, 64 MB, 124 MIPS). The iteration formulas allow the estimation of 3D distribution parameters out of 3D, 2D, and 1D data. Table 1 summarizes the computation times and the required number of iterations. For the training of 3D model densities out of 2D views, we use a calibrated robot [9], such that for each random view the position of the camera is known (extrinsic camera parameters). The initialization of mean vectors is based on 2D features of a reference view. All range values are set to zero. The disadvantage of the introduced model generation is that n_κ, the number of model features, has to be known in advance. Up to now, there exists no reliable, robust, and feasible method for the automatic computation of n_κ.

5 Object Localization: Global Optimization

In contrast to geometric based methods, we do not hypothesize a matching of corresponding image and model features for the analytical computation of object's pose, but solve a parameter estimation problem for a smooth density function (see eq. (10)).

The dimension of the search space depends on the used projection model and only the mapping of the model into the image space influences the number of pose parameters. For instance, in the case of perspective projection the object's pose has six degrees of freedom, whereas the orthographic projection results in a five dimensional search problem. The translation parallel to the optical axis is omitted. The density function parameterized in pose parameters is a highly multimodal function. In general, local optimization techniques will not succeed in computing the global maximum. An initialization close to the global maximum is not possible without any additional knowledge. The reasonably low dimensional search space and the necessity of global optimization techniques do not suggest the use of the local optimizing EM algorithm for pose estimation. Nevertheless, in [33] an EM based localization procedure for pose refinement is discussed. The initialization of pose parameters is done by indexing techniques and geometric relations.

 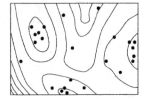

Figure3. Deterministic and probabilistic search in a 2D contour map. The points show the chosen initial values for a local search.

5.1 Deterministic Localization

Widely applied deterministic procedures for the computation of global maxima are grid search techniques, where equidistant initial points are distributed over the finite search space. Figure 3 (left) illustrates this for the 2D case. At the inserted initial points, local optimization algorithms can be started for a pose refinement. Of course, the success of a grid search method for object localization extremely depends on the chosen mesh, i.e. the distance of sample points.

A simple counter example proves the limited use of deterministic search algorithms, even if local optimization steps are left out: Let us assume, we have orthographic projection without scaling. The parameter space has five dimensions, three rotation angles $0° \leq \phi_x, \phi_y, \phi_z \leq 360°$ and two components $0 \leq t_1, t_2 \leq 100$ of the translation vector. Let the step–size for angles be $10°$ and the step–size for the translation 10. If the density function is evaluated at these grid points only and if one function evaluation takes 7 ms (cmp. Section 5.3), the computation of the global maximum will take $4.6 \cdot 10^6$ function evaluations, i.e. approx. 9 hours. This is intolerable for practical applications, and it furthermore proves the necessity of coarse–to–fine grid search or randomized optimization algorithms, which select prospective areas of the search space.

5.2 Probabilistic Localization

A recommended overview of probabilistic optimization techniques can be found in [10]. For solving the object localization problem, we choose the following basic idea: we randomly select a certain number of uniformly distributed initial points and evaluate the density function at these points. In a second step, additional random points are picked out, but their distribution should depend on hitherto computed density values. The random process, which controls the generation of new points, should take the observed density values into account and adapt to the density function's contour. A higher density value of a selected point implies a higher probability for the generation of a sample close to this area (see Figure 3, right). This process is repeated until a termination criterion is satisfied. Figure 4 shows a sketch of this adaptive random search technique. A frequently used termination criterion results from the usage of thresholds. For example, the difference of the lowest and highest entry of the included ordered list should reduce to a predefined threshold. The adaptive behavior of the random generator

/* **Adaptive Random Search** */
INPUT: model density, observed features
evaluate the model density at *a* randomly chosen initial points in the search space; store the best *b* of these points in a sorted list
as long as no stop criterion is satisfied repeat
generate new points in the view of the fact that the elements of *b* were already observed
add the new points to the ordered list
eliminate the worst points out of the list
adapt the parameters which guide the random process for the generation of points
select the global maximum and its position
OUTPUT: coordinates of the global maximum

Figure4. The principle of probabilistic search

can be controlled, for example, by a mixture density of Gaussians, which is iteratively updated by the observed function values.

5.3 Experimental Results

Within the experimental evaluation of different optimization techniques, we compare the following global search techniques:

V1: adaptive random search [12],
V2: adaptive random search combined with a locally operating downhill simplex algorithm [13],
V3: simulated annealing for continuous functions [3, 7],
V4: multi–start algorithm [31, 32],
V5: grid simplex algorithm [25], and
V6: pure probabilistic search [2, 31].

The average number of function evaluations required for the detection of the global maximum, and the average runtime on a monoprocessor system is shown in Table 2, (a). In our experiments with synthetic data ($D_m = 3, D_o = 2, n_\kappa = m = 10, q = 1$), the adaptive random search technique (V1) and modifications of this algorithm (V2) yield the best results. The probabilistic algorithm could find the global maximum with 87% success.

For a sample set of 400 real images the pose parameters were correctly found in average for 47% using adaptive random search (cmp. Table 2, (b)). The used objects can be found in Figure 5. Since the model densities do not take into account self occlusion of objects, both pose estimates shown in Figure 6 result in similar density values. The difference between the rotation angles around one coordinate axis is equal to π for both sets of pose parameters, because models are treated as transparent objects. But above experimental evaluation considers only one parameter set to be physically correct. Indeed, if we formally interpret both pose parameters to be equivalent, the correct localization rate increases to 78% for real data using the adaptive random search technique.

alg.	# eval.	time [sec]
V1	10010	75
V2	8560	64
V3	41300	310
V4	585000	4380
V5	1820000	13600
V6	10000000	74500

(a) Global optimization

3D object	correct pose [%]		comp. time [sec]	
	$q = 1$	$q = 2$	$q = 1$	$q = 2$
Q1	55	52	88	384
Q2	42	47	112	484
Q3	51	47	76	257
Q4	43	37	67	296
mean	48	46	86	355

(b) Localization results

Table2. Comparison of global optimization algorithms and pose estimation results

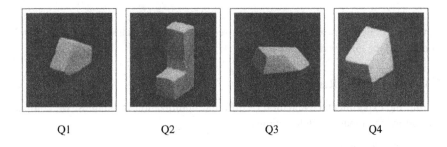

| Q1 | Q2 | Q3 | Q4 |

Figure5. Polyhedral 3D objects (Q1–Q4) used for recognition and pose estimation experiments.

6 Object Recognition

If the pose parameters for each model density are known, the classification is simply done by computing and by comparing the a posteriori probabilities. Since we have seen in previous experiments that the probabilistic search for pose parameters is responsible for about 22% localization errors, the expected recognition rate will be bounded by 78%.

Table 3 shows the classification results for point and straight line features ($q = 1, 2$) using 1600 randomly chosen images with varying illumination. The recognition rate of approximately 70% is due to the fact that the segmentation results are sometimes insufficient for classification, and the statistical behavior of point features is approximated by Gaussians. The chosen test objects show few corners, and segmentation errors often lead image features of low discriminating power.

7 Conclusions and Future Research Problems

This paper has introduced a general uniform statistical framework for object modeling, localization, and recognition. The statistical models include the assignment of features, the transformation of objects, and the projection from the model into the image space.

 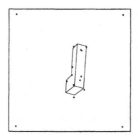 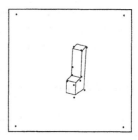

Figure6. The two best pose hypotheses for a polyhedral object. If objects are considered to be transparent, both pose parameter sets are considered to be equal.

3D–object	recognition [%]		time [sec]	
	$q = 1$	$q = 2$	$q = 1$	$q = 2$
Q1	47	44	466	1882
Q2	78	82	485	2101
Q3	58	36	465	1933
Q4	89	76	471	1520
mean	68	59	472	1859

Table3. Recognition rates and runtime on a HP 735 for 3D experiments (1600 real gray–level images using point ($q = 1$) and line ($q = 2$) features).

In contrast to many object recognition systems, all three stages of model generation, pose estimation, and class decision are defined as optimization problems. These were solved using different maximization algorithms.

The estimation of model parameters has shown to be a search problem in a high dimensional parameter space. Even for simple polyhedral objects the model generation has to deal with incomplete training data. The learning problem was solved here by the application of the EM algorithm with reasonable costs. This is the first approach in computer vision which deals with the estimation of model parameters from projected data without taking the matching into consideration.

The pose estimation is related to a global optimization problem. The EM algorithm could be applied, but requires an initialization within the area of attraction of the global maximum [33]. For that reason and due its low convergence rate, we did the localization without the EM technique. A comparison of different optimization algorithms showed that an adaptive random search combined with the downhill simplex algorithm gives best results regarding the runtime behavior. Especially in this application, probabilistic optimization techniques beat deterministic algorithms.

For future research the use of different views for classification and localization might improve and speed up the algorithms. The more data are available, the more reliable are the estimated parameters. Additionally, a parallelization of search algorithms can easily be done by partitioning the search space. It will lead to faster recognition modules. For an improvement of the recognition rates, however, it will be necessary to choose features different from point features, which will also require some extensions and modifications within the introduced theoretical framework.

Acknowledgement

The authors wish to thank the German Research Foundation (DFG), who partially funded the work reported here under grant SFB 182.

References

1. T. W. Anderson. *An Introduction to Multivariate Statistical Analysis.* Wiley Publications in Statistics. John Wiley & Sons, Inc., New York, 1958.
2. C. G. E. Boender, A. H. G. Rinnoy Kan, G. T. Timmer, and L. Stougie. A stochastic method for global optimization. *Mathematical Programming*, 22:125–140, 1982.
3. M. E. Bohachevsky, M. E. Johnson, and M. L. Stein. Generalized simulated annealing for function optimization. *Technometrics*, 28(3):209–217, 1986.
4. T. Caellei, M. Johnston, and T. Robinson. 3D object recognition: Inspirations and lessons from biological vision. In Jain and Flynn [19], pages 1–16.
5. B. Cernuschi–Frias, D. P. Cooper, Y. P. Hung, and P. N. Belhumeur. Toward a model–based Bayesian theory for estimating and recognizing parameterized 3–D objects using two or more images taken from different positions. *IEEE Trans. on Pattern Analysis and Machine Intelligence*, 11(10):1028–1052, October 1989.
6. P. B. Chou and C. M. Brown. The theory and practice of Bayesian image labeling. *International Journal of Computer Vision*, 4(3):185–210, June 1990.
7. A. Corana, M. Marchesi, and S. Ridella. Minimizing multimodal functions of continuous variables with the "simulated annealing" algorithm. *ACM Transactions on Mathematical Software*, 13(3):209–217, 1987.
8. A.P. Dempster, N.M. Laird, and D.B. Rubin. Maximum Likelihood from Incomplete Data via the EM Algorithm. *Journal of the Royal Statistical Society, Series B (Methodological)*, 39(1):1–38, 1977.
9. J. Denzler, R. Beß J. Hornegger, H. Niemann, and D. Paulus. Learning, tracking and recognition of 3D objects. In V. Graefe, editor, *International Conference on Intelligent Robots and Systems – Advanced Robotic Systems and Real World*, volume 1, pages 89–96, 1994.
10. L. C. W. Dixon and G. P. Szegö, editors. *Towards Global Optimisation*, volume 2, Amsterdam, 1978. North–Holland.
11. R.O. Duda and P.E. Hart. *Pattern Classification and Scene Analysis.* John Wiley & Sons, Inc., New York, 1973.
12. S. M. Ermakov and A. A. Zhiglyavskij. On random search of global extremum. *Probability Theory and Applications*, 28(1):129–136, 1983.
13. F. Gallwitz. Lokalisierung von 3D–Objekten in Grauwertbildern. Technical report, Diploma thesis, Lehrstuhl für Mustererkennung (Informatik 5), Universität Erlangen–Nürnberg, Erlangen, 1994.
14. S. Geman and C. Graffigne. Markov random field image models and their applications to computer vision. *Proceedings of the International Congress of Mathematicians*, pages 1496–1517, August 1986.
15. J. Hornegger. *Statistische Modellierung, Klassifikation und Lokalisation von Objekten.* Shaker, Aachen, 1996.

16. J. Hornegger and H. Niemann. Statistical learning, localization, and identification of objects. In *Proceedings of the 5th International Conference on Computer Vision (ICCV)*, pages 914–919, Boston, June 1995. IEEE Computer Society Press.

17. R. Hummel and S. Zucker. On the foundations of relaxation labeling processes. *IEEE Trans. on Pattern Analysis and Machine Intelligence*, 5:267–287, 1983.

18. A. K. Jain. Advances in statistical pattern recognition. In P. A. Devijver and J. Kittler, editors, *Pattern Recognition Theory and Applications*, volume 30 of *NATO ASI Series F: Computer and System Sciences*, pages 1–19. Springer, Heidelberg, 1987.

19. A. K. Jain and P. J. Flynn, editors. *Three–Dimensional Object Recognition Systems*, Amsterdam, 1993. Elsevier.

20. J. Kittler, W. J. Christmas, and M. Petrou. Probabilistic relaxation for matching problems in computer vision. In *Proceedings of the 4th International Conference on Computer Vision (ICCV)*, pages 666–673, Berlin, May 1993. IEEE Computer Society Press.

21. W. B. Mann and T. O. Binford. An example of 3–D interpretation of images using Bayesian networks. In *Proceedings of Image Understandig Workshop*, pages 793–801, San Diego, California, January 1992. Morgan Kaufmann Publishers, Inc.

22. D. Marr. *Vision: A Computational Investigation into the Human Representation and Processing of Visual Information*. W.H. Freeman and Company, San Francisco, 1982.

23. J.W. Modestino and J. Zhang. A Markov random field model–based approach to image interpretation. *IEEE Trans. on Pattern Analysis and Machine Intelligence*, 14(6):606–615, June 1992.

24. H. Niemann, H. Brünig, R. Salzbrunn, and S. Schröder. A knowledge–based vision system for industrial applications. In *Machine Vision and Applications*, pages 201–229, New York, 1990. Springer Verlag.

25. W.H. Press, B.P. Flannery, S. Teukolsky, and W.T. Vetterling. Numerical recipes - the art of numerical computing, c version. Technical report, 35465-X, 1988.

26. S. Sarkar and K. L. Boyer. Integration, inference, and management of spatial information using Bayesian networks: Perceptual organization. *IEEE Trans. on Pattern Analysis and Machine Intelligence*, 15(3):256–274, March 1993.

27. J. Segen. Model learning and recognition of nonrigid objects. In *Proceedings of Computer Vision and Pattern Recognition*, pages 597–602, San Diego, June 1989. IEEE Computer Society Press.

28. Y. Shang and B. W. Wah. Global optimization for neural network training. *Computer*, 29(3):45–54, 1996.

29. P. Suetens, P. Fua, and A. J. Hanson. Computational strategies for object recognition. *ACM Computing Surveys*, 24(1):5–61, March 1992.

30. M. A. Tanner. *Tools for Statistical Inference: Methods for the Exploration of Posterior Distributions and Likelihood Functions*. Springer Series in Statistics. Springer, Heidelberg, 1993.

31. G. T. Timmer. Global optimization: A stochastic approach. PhD thesis, Rotterdam, 1984.

32. A. A. Törn. A programm for global optimization, multistart with clustering (msc). In P. A. Samet, editor, *European Conference on Applied Information Technology, International Federation for Information Processing (EURO IFIP)*, pages 427–434, London, September 1979. Amsterdam North-Holland Publ. Co.

33. W. M. Wells III. Statistical Object Recognition. PhD thesis, MIT, Department of Electrical Engineering and Computer Science, Massachusetts, February 1993.

34. C. F. J. Wu. On the convergence properties of the EM algorithm. *The Annals of Statistics*, 11(1):95–103, 1983.

Evolutionary Search

Object Recognition Using Stochastic Optimization

Shimon Ullman and Assaf Zeira

Department of Applied Mathematics
The Weizmann Institute of Science
Rehovot 76100, Israel

Abstract

We describe an approach to object recognition in which the image-to-model match is based on stochastic optimization. During the recognition process, an internal model is matched with a novel object view. To compensate for changes in viewing conditions (such as illumination, viewing direction), the model is controlled by a number of parameters. The matching is obtained by seeking a setting of the parameters that minimizes the discrepancy between the image and the model. The search is performed in our examples in a six-dimensional space with multiple local minima. We developed an efficient minimization method based on the stochastic optimization approach (Mockus 1989). The search is bidirectional (applied to both the model and the image) and avoids the difficult problem of establishing image-to-model correspondence. It proceeds by evolving a population of candidate solutions using simple generation rules, based on the autocorrelation of the search space. We describe the method, its application to objects in several domains (cars, faces, printed symbols), and experimental comparisons with alternative methods, such as simulated annealing.

1   Introduction

In performing visual object recognition, we are trying to determine whether an image we currently see corresponds to an object we have seen in the past. A general problem in recognition is that the two often fail to match exactly, due to changes in size, position, viewing direction, and the like, and considerable processing is needed in order to overcome these differences. One general approach has been to compensate for the differences by storing a parametric model that depends on viewing direction, illumination, articulation, etc., and then search for the set of parameters that minimizes the discrepancy between the model and the novel view.

Many recent approaches to recognition fall under this general category. For example, the linear combination method (Ullman & Basri 1991), and related extensions such as the trilinear tensor scheme (Shashua 1995), can be viewed as parametric models of the object's appearance. A novel view is matched by a combination of stored views. Each combination is controlled by a set of coefficients, and recognition is obtained by determining the coefficients that yield an optimal match to the novel view. The deformable templates method (Yuille, Cohen & Hallinan 1989, Yuille & Hallinan 1992) is another example of this general approach. Again, the model is controlled by a set of parameters, and an optimal setting of these parameters, leading to the best possible match with the novel view, is determined by the recognition algorithm.

Searching for the matching parameters can be formally described in the following way: Find a such that

$$\min_{a} D(V, M(a))$$

where D is a distance function, a is the set of transformation parameters applied to the model, M is the model and V is the viewed object. We assume for simplicity that the viewed object is compared against a single candidate model M that can vary with the transformation parameters a. The problem of selecting a candidate model will not be considered here. We also assume for now that only the model M depends on a. As we shall see, it is also possible to apply the transformations to the viewed object V. The problem of matching the viewed object and the internal model now becomes a search for the optimal set of parameters, a.

One general approach to this problem is based on the establishment of correspondence between image and model features (Grimson 1990, Poggio 1990, Ullman & Basri 1991). If such correspondence can be established, it often becomes straightforward to determine the transformation that brings the model and the viewed image into optimal match. However, correspondence proved to be a major difficulty. Correspondence methods are often based on optical flow-type computation (Beymer & Poggio 1996), that apply to situations where the model and the viewed image do not differ by much in viewing direction or illumination. In general, correspondence is difficult to establish reliably and with sufficient accuracy, and therefore an alternative approach has been to perform a search in the space of possible parameter values (Baird 1985, Cass 1992, Hill, Taylor & Cootes 1992). The search problem is challenging because the search is for a global minimum of a multivariate, multi-modal matching function (figure 1 depicts the complex landscape in two dimensions). In addition, to achieve human-like performance the entire recognition process is expected to be fast. (Humans often obtain recognition within a few hundred milliseconds; Rosch 1975, Rosch et al. 1976, Biederman 1988).

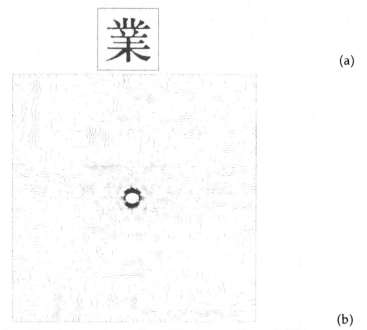

(a)

(b)

Figure 1 The objective function to be minimized contains multiple minima. The level contours in (b) describes the degree of match between the image in (a) and a noisy variant of (a) displaced in x and y.

To achieve fast and reliable recognition, we have developed and tested a search method for the best matching parameters. The search process uses the following general structure. At each stage in the search, there is a population of K possible solutions, for the unknown matching parameters. These solutions are evaluated, and new solutions are generated in the vicinity of the most promising current solutions. The quality of a candidate solution is based on its degree of match as well as the density of solutions already explored in its vicinity. This general structure is common to the class of algorithms known as Evolutionary algorithms (Fogel 1994, Goldberg 1994). These algorithms are similar to Genetic algorithms (Holland 1975) which were used before in the context of object recognition (Hill *et al.* 1992). Unlike Genetic algorithms which simulate evolutionary processes at the level of genes and chromosomes, Evolutionary algorithms simulate evolutionary processes in the level of the individual, without using, for example, genetic coding and cross-over process. Within this general class, our method is particularly close in spirit to the family of stochastic optimization methods (Mockus 1989). In this approach, it is assumed that the function to be minimized is drawn from a stochastic process. Statistical properties of the generating process, such as its autocorrelation function, are used to guide the search process. Our tests show that this method is more efficient than alternative schemes for global optimization such as simulated annealing (Kirkpatrick *et al.* 1983). The method can be naturally applied to a parallel computation in which multiple solutions are generated and evaluated simultaneously.

Before we proceed to describe the optimization procedure in more detail, we describe in the next section the representation of the model and image used by the computation, and the matching function used to compare the image with an internal model.

2   The representation and matching function

Patterns are represented in the system by intensity edges and valleys (figure 2). Edges are defined as sharp boundaries between lighter and darker regions in the image. Valleys are defined as curves that correspond to thin and elongated dark regions in the image (Canny 1986, Marr & Hildreth 1980).

Figure 2   The source image (left) and the corresponding edges (middle) and valleys (right). Edges are less invariant to illumination than valleys. They are stable along the silhouette, but not in the inner facial features (such as the eyes and mouth). The image is of size 512x352 pixels.

The edges and valleys (referred to as "features") are obtained in a similar manner. First, the image is filtered with directional operators to yield a vector field (we use first and second order directional derivatives for edges and valleys respectively), and then a non-maximal suppression process to omit features that carry little information. These are common pre-processing stages, for more detail see, e.g., (Canny 1986).

The matching function $D(\cdot)$ measures the degree of similarity between the viewed image and the model. In comparing two patterns, P_A and P_B, each pattern is represented by a collection of features, $\{\phi^A\}$ and

$\{\phi^B\}$. A feature ϕ (an edge or valley segment) is encoded by its position, direction and intensity $\phi = (x, y, o, i)$. The matching function $D(P_A, P_B)$ is not symmetric; it measures the degree to which the features of pattern P_A fit in the pattern P_B. It is defined as follows: for each feature ϕ^A we choose the nearest neighbor in $\{\phi^B\}$ and sum up all the distances. "Nearest neighbor" here is not merely separation in image space, since the distance between two features depends on the differences in position, orientation and intensity, combined in the following manner:

$$D(P_A, P_B) = \sum_{\phi^A} \min_{\phi^B}\{dist(\phi^A, \phi^B)\} \tag{1}$$

where

$$dist(\phi^A, \phi^B) = 1 - \delta_1(d_1)\, \delta_2(d_2)\, \delta_3(d_3)$$
$$d_1 = \sqrt{(x_A - x_B)^2 + (y_A - y_B)^2}$$
$$d_2 = |o_A - o_B|$$
$$d_3 = |i_A - i_B| / \max(i_A, i_B)$$

The summation is done separately for edges and valleys. The δ functions are non-linear functions of Gaussian shape. These functions determine the relative weight of each attribute; σ_1 was set to 0.1 (in units of image width), σ_2 was set to 40 degrees and σ_3 was set to 1.

Different representation schemes and metric functions were tested and those described here were found to be the most useful. For example, we found that the inclusion of intensity valleys provides an improved representation, and that the matching function described above performed better than many alternatives. The details of these tests are outside the scope of this paper and will appear elsewhere. The choice of feature attributes is not limited to the set described here and other attributes such as color, degree of curvature, depth, and so on, can be used as well.

3   The search algorithm

The search algorithm is characterized by the following general properties: it is bi-directional, stochastic, and it is governed by evolutionary-like rules. These properties are independent of each other in the sense that it is possible, for example, to make the algorithm uni-directional, and at the same time keep it stochastic and evolutionary. Similarly, it is possible to employ bi-directionality in search schemes other than the stochastic-evolutionary scheme used here. In the following sections we describe each of these properties in detail.

3.1 Bi-directional search

From a computational standpoint, it is often advantageous in object recognition to use bi-directional processing, and to apply transformations both to the incoming pattern and the stored models. Some transformations can only be applied reasonably to the stored models; for example, the input pattern may not contain enough depth cues to enable accurate rotations in depth, and therefore it would be more accurate to apply such transformations to the stored model. The model, which is constructed from multiple examples of the object, is more likely to contain an accurate and complete description of the object. Other transformations such as translation, scaling, rotation in the image plane (or, more generally, projective transformations) are best applied to the input pattern, since they can save time and resources by avoiding transforming all models to match the size, position, etc. of the input pattern. It is therefore natural to use in recognition a bi-directional processing, in which some of the transformations are applied to the incoming image ("bottom-up" process), and others to the stored models ("top-down" processes).

There is an additional advantage for bi-directional processing that stems from a combinatorial consideration. Assuming that the computational cost of a pattern generation is higher than the cost of a comparison between patterns, it would be advantageous to minimize the number of patterns explored. This situation may also be applicable to biological systems, where the vast connectivity might be exploited for making "inexpensive" pattern comparisons. The overall number of patterns generated during the computation can be reduced by generating a relatively small number of patterns in each of the two directions, and comparing all possible counter pairs.

To illustrate the possible saving, consider an input image and a stored model that differ in translation in the x and y directions. To compensate for the unknown translation in a bi-directional manner, the bottom-up direction can generate n different instances of the image translated along the x coordinate, and the top-down direction can generate n instances of the model translated in y. The two sets of generated patterns can then be compared in all n^2 possible combinations, to find the best matching pair. Such a scheme requires a total of $2n$ patterns to determine the unknown displacement. This provides a considerable saving compared with a strictly bottom-up or top-down search, that would require n^2 patterns for all possible combinations of x and y translations.

Bi-directional search algorithms were explored in the past mainly in the context of shortest path problems (Pohl 1971, De Champeaux 1977). Although the motivation for the bi-directional search is similar, the problems and the algorithms are different. The complicated machinery used in Pohl's and De Champeaux's algorithms is not required here, and the generation of new offspring is guided by the stochastic-evolutionary constituent of the algorithm.

3.2 Stochastic-evolutionary search

The general idea in evolutionary search is to evolve a population of candidate solutions (also referred to as a population of search probes) until some members of the population become sufficiently close to the global minimum. The population changes by simple rules, according to which the "fittest" among the population create the next generation in their vicinity.

As described in the bi-directional search, the population is divided into two parts, one for the top-down direction and the other for the bottom-up direction. Different transformations are allowed in each part of the population. For example, the bottom-up part generates K different versions of the input patterns, at different displacements, scales, and orientations in the image plane. At the same time, the top-down part generates K different versions of the model, for different possible rotations in depth. The fitness is determined by comparing members of one part of the population with all members of the other part. Each of the K copies produced by the bottom-up part is compared with the K top-down versions, for a total of K^2 comparisons. Each copy gets a score that depends on the best match it achieves with its counterparts.

$$s_i = \min_{P_j} D(P_i, \bar{P}_j) \qquad (2)$$

where $\bar{P}_j$ is a pattern that belongs to the counter population. This score is used to determine the reproduction rate for that copy; the lower the score, the higher is the reproduction rate.

In order to avoid the concentration of many probes within a relatively small region, the reproduction rate depends also on density; the higher the density, the lower the reproduction rate. The density for each probe is determined by the distance to nearby probes:

$$density_i = \sum_{i \neq j} \frac{1}{(\mathbf{x}_j - \mathbf{x}_i)^2} \qquad (3)$$

where the vector x is the location of the probe in the multi-dimensional search space. The reproduction rate combine the score and the density in the following way:

$$r_i = \psi(s_i) \cdot \max(1, \frac{density_0}{density_i}) \tag{4}$$

where ψ is a non-negative, monotonically decreasing function of the score s_i, and $density_0$ is a parameter that determines the threshold from which the penalty for density is applied. This parameter depends on the size of the population - K, and the autocorrelation function that will be discussed below. In order to keep the population diverse and to enable a continuous search for new minima, a part of the new population is always generated at random. The total number of offspring k_i that are generated for a given member is:

$$k_i = (1 - \rho) \cdot K \cdot \frac{r_i}{\sum r_i} \quad , \qquad 0 \le \rho \le 1 \tag{5}$$

where ρ defines the portion of K that is determined at random (a typical value for ρ is 0.25).

Once the number of offspring is known for each member, the locations of the new members are determined by the stochastic constituent of the algorithm. This process is related to the method of Bayesian optimization (Mockus 1989). It is termed "stochastic optimization" since the family of functions to be minimized is assumed to constitute a stochastic Gaussian process, usually taken to be stationary. We will not describe this method in detail, only give a brief general description.

In a stochastic optimization process, the likelihood of a new probe increases in the vicinity of successful probes in the current generation, and decreases with the population density in this neighborhood. To make the computation efficient, some knowledge regarding the autocorrelation function of the underlying process is required. The reason is that the autocorrelation determines the natural distance measure used by the computation. For example, if a particular pattern receives a very low score, we would like subsequent probes to be "far away" from the low-score probe. "Far away" can be naturally defined as a new pattern whose correlation with the low-score one is sufficiently low. The autocorrelation for this process is assumed here to be known although it can be acquired using a simple learning procedure. We assume therefore that the autocorrelation is known for each variable of the multi-variate objective function, and we denote the range at which each autocorrelation functions drop to half by the vector α.

The location of offspring members is drawn at random from a Gaussian probability distribution with a mean located at the parent member, and a standard deviation that depends on the autocorrelation functions and the score of the parent. In this manner, probes of the next generation will be generated closed to high-score parents and further away from low score parent, and all the distances are scaled relative to the width of the autocorrelation α.

In our implementation the reproduction range is given by:

$$\sigma_i = \alpha \cdot \varphi(s_i) \qquad (6)$$

where φ is a monotonically increasing function of the score s_i.

In summary, the search for the global optimum proceeds by updating a population of candidate solutions using the following steps:
1. produce the top and bottom populations at random.
2. compute the score s_i (equation 2) for each probe in the two populations.
3. compute the number of offspring k_i based on the reproduction rate and the density (equation 3,4,5).
4. compute the reproduction range σ_i (equation 6) and generate the new populations.
5. go back to step 2, unless the stopping condition is met.

4   Experimental Results

The stochastic algorithm was tested with three different domains of objects: Kanji logographs, faces and cars. The results presented here were produced mainly with the cars and the Kanji databases. We evaluated the performance of the algorithm by two different criteria. The algorithm was evaluated in terms of the amount of computation required to achieve a sufficient discrimination between two similar objects, and also relative to another search algorithm - simulated annealing, that is frequently used in complex minimization problems. Before we describe the experiments and the results, we will define the search space for the algorithm.

In defining the search space we assumed that the initial alignment between the image and the model can be quite rough. As can be seen from figure 3, the initial agreement between the image and the model can be low, especially if two or more transformations are combined together. Because the initial error can be large, we assume that similar and probably better starting conditions can be attained by a simple process of rough alignment. In the examples below the transformation applied in the search was a 6-parameter affine transformation; in other tests we also used 3-D rotation of the model. The affine parameters $z_0, ..., z_5$ are bounded between -0.5 and 0.5 units to make a 6-dimensional cube of volume one. The parameters are related to the transformations in the following way (the first three applied to the image, the last three to the model):

translation in X : $x' = x + z_0 W, \quad y' = y$ (±0.5 of image width)

translation in Y : $x' = x, \quad y' = y + z_1 H$ (±0.5 of image height)

scaling factor : $x' = (1 + z_2)x, \quad y' = (1 + z_2)y$ (factor between [0.5, 1.5])

rotation : $x' = x + z_3 y, \quad y' = y - z_3 x$ (rotation between ±26.6°)

stretch along X : $x' = (1 + z_4)x, \quad y' = y$

shear along X : $x' = x + z_5 y, \quad y' = y$

Figure 3 A demonstration of the maximal range of the six basic transformations: translation along X coordinate, translation along Y coordinate, scaling, rotation, stretch and shear. Each image contains two faces, one in neutral position and another transformed maximally relative to the first one. When several basic transformations are applied together, the disparity between the neutral and the transformed image becomes much larger.

The purpose of the first two experiments was to estimate the performance of the algorithm in terms of the number of patterns and comparisons that were required in order to achieve a sufficient discrimination between two similar car models. The first experiment was performed with size 32 populations (top and bottom). Figure 5 describes an example of two runs of the algorithm. In the first run the model and the image for recognition were taken from different but similar car models; for the model we used a Chevrolet model 1940, and for the image a Chrysler Windsor model 1946 (see figure 4). In the second run the model and image were taken from a similar car model - that of the Chrysler. In order to make the problem more realistic, the image in the second run was taken from a slightly different viewing direction. In both cases the image was transformed prior to the search process. The parameters for the transformation were selected at random from the search domain $[-0.5, 0.5]^6$, with a uniform distribution.

Figure 4 The Chrysler (right) and the Chevrolet (left) that were used in the first experiment.

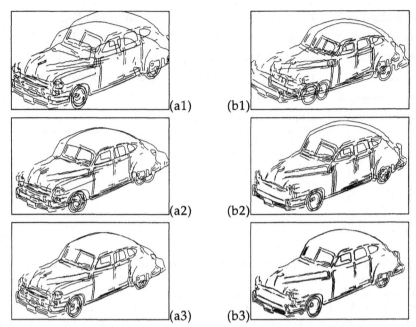

Figure 5 The figure shows an example of two runs of the algorithm. In the first run (figures a1,a2,a3), the model and the image to be recognized were taken from different car models. In the second run (figures b1,b2,b3), the model and image were taken from a similar car model. The top image (a1,b1) describes the configuration of the best matching image and model after 1 iteration, the middle image (a2,b2) describes the configuration after 5 iterations, and the bottom image (a3,b3), after 9 iterations. At this stage an accurate match is obtained despite the large initial discrepancy.

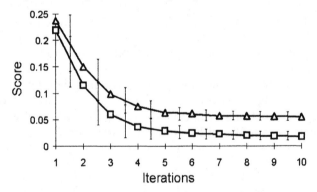

Figure 6 The result of the first experiment shows that after 10 iterations, the discrimination between the two car models becomes clear (can be inferred from the error bars). The triangles curve describe the "different car models" case, and the squares curve describes the "similar car model" case. The graphs describe the mean and standard deviation of 100 runs.

The graph in figure 6 summarizes the result of 100 runs with the two modes described above (different vs. same car model). The graph shows that after 10 iterations, the two car models can be reliably discriminated (discriminability d'=5.2 $\Rightarrow$ 99.4% correct answers). The average distance of the best solution from the true global minimum obtained after 10 iterations was 0.04 in each axis. This means that the result places the global minimum in a sub-cube of volume $1/25^6$. Each run requires a total of 640=10x2x32 patterns to be generated, and 10240=10x32x32 comparisons to be performed.

The second experiment, like the first one, aimed at testing the performance of the algorithm in terms of the number of patterns and comparisons used. In this experiment the model and the image were allowed to differ in rotation in depth, as well as the six affine transformations. We used rotation along the Y axis. The experiment was performed with faces. For the model we used two images of one face (SB), taken from different viewing positions. Using the Linear Combination method (Ullman and Basri 1991), we computed the appearance of the face from any viewing positions (see figure 7). For the image we used images of the same face as the model (SB), and also images of a different face (SK) (see figure 8). The images were taken under slightly different illumination conditions.

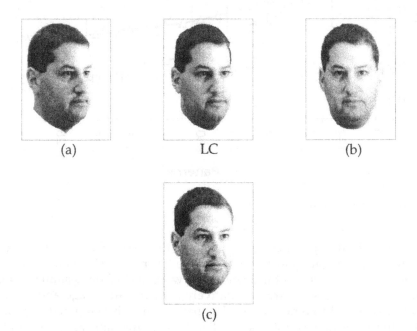

(a)   LC   (b)

(c)

Figure 7 The two model pictures (a) and (b) are linearly combined to generate the picture (LC). The picture in (c) is a real image, taken from the same viewing direction and illumination as (LC).

The experiment procedure was slightly different and less efficient than the first experiment. We used a variant of the bi-directional search that contained 7 levels of depth (instead of two), and we used a population of size 8 (instead of 32) in each level. The results are summarized in figure 9.

Figure 8 The two faces that were used as test images in the second experiment.

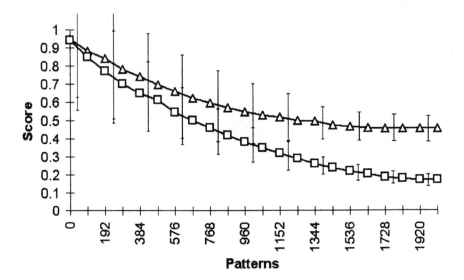

Figure 9 The result of the second experiment.

In the third experiment we compared the performance of the algorithm relative to simulated annealing (see figure 10). The model and the image that were used in this experiment were taken from a similar Kanji logograph (the results are qualitatively similar with image and model that belong to different objects). The performance is compared in terms of patterns generated; this means that in simulated annealing all candidate steps were counted.

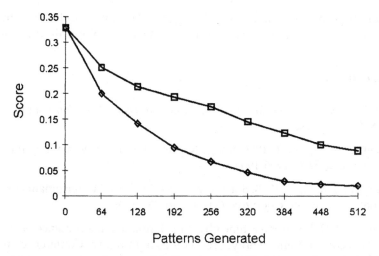

Figure 10 A comparison between bi-directional stochastic search and simulated annealing. The stochastic algorithm (diamonds curve) performed better than simulated annealing (squared curve) in terms of the number of patterns generated in the course of the search for global minimum.

5   Summary

In this paper we presented an algorithm for object recognition that uses bi-directional stochastic minimization in order to find the optimal alignment between an input image and a stored model. The algorithm is stochastic in the sense that it uses statistical properties of the ensemble of objective functions to guide the search process, and it is bi-directional in the sense that it allows both the image and the model to be transformed in the course of the search process.

The algorithm is simple; it evolves a population of solutions that reproduces by simple generation rules. In computational experiments, it proved to be efficient in terms of the number of search probes required. The algorithm shows good results in term of the recognition capability and relative to alternative search algorithms. These properties are useful for machine vision, especially in parallel system, and potentially for biological systems that are inherently slow but highly parallel.

One of the most important problems that should be addressed in future research is the problem of multiple models. The naïve way would be to apply the search method and find the optimal alignment between the input image and each of the models. This would not be feasible if the set of models is very large. One way to cope with this problem would be to apply the search between the input image and a small set of models that are representative of larger classes of models, then to proceed in a hierarchical way and to find the best model within the class.

References

Baird, H.S. 1985. *Model-Based Image Matching Using Location.* Cambridge, MA: MIT Press.

Beymer, D. & Poggio, T. 1996. Image Representations for Visual Learning. *Science,* **272**, 5270, 1905-1909.

Biederman, I. & Ju, G. 1988. Surface versus Edge-Based Determinants of Visual Recognition. *Cognitive Psychology,* **20**, 38-64.

Cass, T.A. 1992. Polynomial time object recognition in the presence of clutter, occlusion, and uncertainty. Proceedings of European Conference on Computer Vision, 834-842.

Canny, J. 1986. A computational approach to edge detection. IEEE PAMI, 8,6:679-698.

De Champeaux, D., Sint, L. 1977. An Improved Bidirectional Heuristic Search Algorithm. *J. of the Association for Computing Machinery,* 24, 2, 177-191.

Fogel, D. B. 1994. An Introduction to Simulated Evolutionary Optimization. IEEE *Transactions on Neural Networks,* 5(1),3-14.

Goldberg, D. E. 1994. Genetic and Evolutionary Algorithms Come of Age. *Communications of the ACM.* 37(3), 113-119.

Grimson, W.E.L. 1990. The combinatorics of heuristic search termination for object recognition in cluttered environments. *Proceedings of the European Conference on Computer Vision,* 552-556.

Hill, A., Taylor, C.J. & Cootes, T. 1992. Object Recognition by Flexible Template Matching using Genetic Algorithms. *Proceedings of the European Conference on Computer Vision,* 852-856.

Holland, J.H. 1975. *Adaptation in Neural and Artificial Systems.* Ann Arbor: University of Michigan Press.

Kirkpatrick, S., Gelatt, C.D. & Vecchi, M.P. 1983. Optimization by simulated annealing. *Science,* **220**, 671.

Mockus, J. 1989. *Bayesian Approach to Global Optimization.* Boston: Kluwer Academic Publishers.

Marr, D. & Hildreth, E.C. 1980. Theory of edge detection. *Proceedings of the Royal Society, London, B,* 207, 187-217.

Poggio, T. 1990. 3D object recognition: on result by Basri and Ullman. Technical Report # 9005-03, IRST, Povo, Italy.

Pohl, I. 1971. Bi-Directional Search. *Machine Intelligence*. 6, 127-140.

Rosch, E. 1975. The nature of mental codes for color categories. *Journal of Experimental Psychology: Human Perception and Performance*, 1, 303-322.

Rosch, E., Mervis, C.B., Gray, W.D., Johnson, D.M. and Boyes-Bream, P., 1976. Basic objects in natural categories. *Cognitive Psychology*, 8, 382-439.

Shashua, A. 1995, Algebraic function for recognition. IEEE *Transaction on Pattern Analysis and Machine Perception*, 17(8), 779-789.

Ullman, S. and Basri, R. 1991. Recognition by linear combinations of models. IEEE PAMI, **13**,10:992-1006.

Yuille, A.L., Cohen, D.S. & Hallinan, P.W. 1989. Feature extraction from faces using deformable templates. *Proceedings of IEEE Conference on Computer Vision and Pattern Recognition*, 104-109.

Yuille, A.L. & Hallinan, P.W. 1992. Deformable templates. In: A. Blake and A. Yuille (eds.), *Active Vision*, Cambridge: MIT Press.

Genetic Algorithms for Ambiguous Labelling Problems

Richard Myers and Edwin R Hancock

Department of Computer Science,
University of York,
York Y01 5DD,
United Kingdom.

Abstract. Consistent labelling problems frequently have more than one solution. Most work in the field has aimed at disambiguating early in the interpretation process, using only local evidence. This paper starts with a review of the literature on labelling problems and ambiguity. Based on this review, we propose a strategy for simultaneously extracting multiple related solutions to the consistent labeling problem. In a preliminary experimental study, we show that an appropriately modified genetic algorithm is a robust tool for finding multiple solutions to the consistent labelling problem. These solutions are related by common labellings of the most strongly constrained junctions. We have proposed three run-time measures of algorithm performance: the maximum fitness of the genetic algorithm's population, its Shannon entropy, and the total Hamming distance between its distinct members. The results to date indicate that when the Shannon entropy falls below a certain threshold, new solutions are unlikely to emerge and that most of the diversity in the population disappears within the first few generations.

1   Introduction

A hallmark of intelligence is the ability to simultaneously entertain several hypotheses until there is sufficient evidence to drop all but one. This paper concerns ambiguous consistent labelling problems, and suggests a framework for maintaining populations of related solutions based on the genetic algorithm.

The consistent labelling problem was formulated by Haralick and Shapiro in the 1970s. A set of units must be assigned labels subject to constraints [1,2]; examples include graph colouring, subgraph isomorphism, inexact matching, the Boolean satisfiability problem and scene labelling. The problem is known to be NP-complete and is often solved using deterministic search [1,3]. Operators such as forward checking and back marking [3], and Waltz filtering (discrete relaxation) [4], which prune incompatible unit-label assignments from the search space, improve the efficiency of search. However, search is of little use when no totally consistent solution exists, such as is the case with inexact matching or analysis of "impossible" scenes; and neither search nor discrete relaxation use global contextual evidence, relying instead on pre-defined local constraint dictionaries.

Most recent work involving consistent labelling has adopted Hummel and Zucker's paradigm: the problem is to find a set of unit-label assignments which maximises some global consistency measure [5]; this is usually done by gradient ascent [5–8]. Gradient ascent techniques are appropriate when there are no local optima between the initial guess and the solution; this is not usually the case. It is therefore preferable to use techniques known to posses global convergence properties such as simulated annealing [9,10], mean field annealing [11,12] or genetic search [13], which is the method used here.

Many consistent labelling problems have more than one possible solution. This was recognised in Waltz's original paper [4], but no strategy for handling ambiguity was developed. In the machine vision literature, ambiguity has been seen as a "bad thing" - to be resolved *locally* as quickly as possible, rather than as a necessary part of scene interpretation. Waltz used search to extract an arbitrary solution [4]; Hummel and Zucker used a simple definition of "unambiguous labelling" as a *sine qua non* for consistency [5]; and Faugeras and Berthod developed a measure of ambiguity which was minimised in their relaxation scheme [6]. Much work concerning ambiguity has been done by linguists and psychologists since language understanding is fraught with ambiguity [14]. MacDonald and coworkers suggest Hummel and Zucker's relaxation framework [5] as a computational model for the disambiguation of sentences based on lexical constraints [14]. Observed frequency and context appear to be the major factors in determining the final interpretation of a word [15,16]; Kawamoto has used a connectionist model to demonstrate this dependency [15].

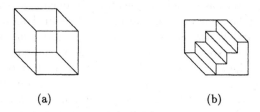

(a)   (b)

Fig. 1. Two Ambiguous Drawings: (a) Necker Cube, (b) Shröder Staircase.

Ambiguities also occur in visual perception. Connectionist systems have been used to model visual perceptual alternation of ambiguous visual stimuli, in which the interpretation of drawings such as the Necker cube and Shröder staircase (see figure 1) periodically switches between several alternatives [17–20]. Bialek and Deweese show that the alternation rate depends on *a priori* hypotheses [15,18–20]. Kawabata has observed that the visual fixation point determines the perception of depth and alternation rates in such figures [21]. He suggests that a local interpretation at the fixation point propagates to generate a stable global interpretation. These observations chime with the selective attention hypothesis [22,23], in which *a priori* expectations combined with focussed attention lead to stable unambiguous interpretations of ambiguous figures. Calliari and Ferrie have recently developed a model-based vision system which can cope with ambiguity [24]. The system makes a set of initial guesses which are refined by subsequent data gathering. This approach has produced promising results, and would seem to complement an active vision strategy.

Early disambiguation may be appropriate if there is compelling local evidence for a particular interpretation, but if not, backtracking is generally inefficient [3]. Although the use of *global* contextual information in scene interpretation is a major unsolved problem in machine vision; premature commitment to a particular interpretation does not help - rather, it makes the problem worse. Following the principle of least commitment, the initial stage of scene interpretation should yield several plausible, and perhaps related, solutions from which the system can choose without having to backtrack.

2   Line Labelling by Optimisation

Line drawing interpretation has been an active area of investigation in machine vision for over 25 years: it was the work of Huffman and Clowes on the consistent labelling of line drawings of polyhedral scenes that led Waltz to his seminal discrete relaxation algorithm [25,26,4]. Waltz's contribution was to show how a dictionary of consistent junction labellings could be used in an efficient search for consistent interpretations of polyhedral objects. Such dictionaries are derived from the geometric constraints on the projection of 3D scenes onto 2D planes [4,27]. The interpretation of line drawings remains an important topic in machine vision, and has obvious applications in document analysis, processing architects' sketches, engineering drawings and so-on. Following the work of Huffman, Clowes and Waltz, Sugihara developed a grammar for skeletal polyhedra [27]. Malik has extended the theory to include curved surfaces [28], and Williams has used labelled line drawings to reconstruct smooth objects [29]. Kirousis has developed several efficient algorithms for determining "labellability" and labelling [30]. Most recently, Parodi and Piccioli have developed a method for reconstructing 3D scenes from labelled line drawings given known vanishing points [31].

Hancock and Kittler have built on the work of Faugeras and Berthod [6] and Hummel and Zucker [5] by developing a Bayesian framework for measuring consistency [7]. This framework can be applied at various levels in image analysis from pixel labelling operations through edge and line labelling to relational matching. Its novelty lies in using an explicit dictionary representation of constraints, as adopted by Waltz, in conjunction with a Bayesian model of the constraint corruption process. The constraint corruption model is based on the premise that the representation of an initially consistent scene is subject to the action of a memoryless label-error process [7]. With this model they formulated a probabilistic measurement of the consistency of a labelling: scene interpretation was done by searching for the label configuration which optimised the probability criterion: this was originally done in [7] by gradient ascent.

In a recent preliminary study, Hancock has applied this framework to labelling polyhedral scenes [32]. Suppose that a polyhedral scene under consideration consists of lines drawn from a set $\mathcal{U} = \{u_1, ..., u_n\}$. Each junction in the scene can be characterised by the set of indices J_k of the lines from which it is constructed. We can form a set $\mathcal{J} = \{J_1, ..., J_K\}$ whose elements are the tuples of line indices making up each junction.

Each of the ELL, TEE, FORK or ARROW junction types has a distinct dictionary which is a compilation of the permitted label configurations. Suppose that Λ_k denotes the dictionary for the kth junction. If the label-set applying to the scene interpretation task is $\Lambda = \{+, -, \rightarrow, \leftarrow\}$, then the cardinality of the junction dictionary $|\Lambda_k|$ is usually much smaller than the number of possible configurations $|\Lambda^{|J_k|}|$. For example, there are only five consistent labellings for a FORK junction (figure 2), whereas $4^3 = 64$ combinatorial possibilities exist.

Fig. 2. Legal Labellings for a FORK Junction.

A candidate solution to this labelling problem is a list of labels, $L = <\lambda_1, ..., \lambda_n>$, where $\lambda_i \in \Lambda$. According to Hancock and Kittler's relaxation framework [7], the global probabilistic criterion is given by summing the probabilities associated with the labellings of each junction. Hancock applies a Bayesian model of label corruption in which consistency of junction labellings is related to the Hamming distance $(H_{k,l})$ of a labelling l of the junction J_k from a dictionary of the consistent labellings of that junction type [32]. Under certain limits, it can be shown that maximising the consistency of a labelling is equivalent to minimising its *cost*.

$$C(L) = \sum_{k=1}^{|\mathcal{J}|} \min_{l \in \Lambda_k} H_{k,l} \tag{1}$$

3 Line Labelling with a Genetic Algorithm

Optimisation algorithms based on Darwinian evolution have been proposed by several authors [33–35,13], but it is Holland's formulation [13] which is regarded as the standard. Genetic algorithms simulate evolution to solve problems: candidate solutions model organisms which exist in an environment modelled by the problem itself. Good solutions to a problem "evolve" over time. The variety of organisms in the world suggests that the problem of survival has many good solutions. It is tempting, therefore, to suppose that a genetic algorithm would produce several alternative optimal solutions. However, this behaviour has not generally been observed: one solution becomes dominant since selection biases the population in favour of fit individuals. This *genetic drift* can be observed even when survival of individuals is equiprobable. A genetic algorithm could also be suitable for "impossible" objects, where the drawings are not consistently labellable but we nevertheless wish to find one or more of the "next best" labellings.

The algorithm takes a set of bit-strings, the *chromosomes* or *individuals*, and iteratively applies crossover (mixing) and mutation (random change) operators to them. At every iteration, the fitness of all individuals is evaluated according to some problem-specific measure. Individuals are then selected for the next generation based on their scores. Most implementations terminate when either a specified number of iterations has been performed or a maximally fit individual has emerged. The algorithm has several *control parameters*. These are the crossover rate, which is the probability of information-exchange between individuals; the mutation rate, which in this study is the probability of a single bit-change in an individual; and the population size. The type of crossover used may also be considered to be a parameter. Where the maximum number of iterations is fixed, this too is a parameter.

Recall from the previous section that a candidate solution to the labelling problem is a list of labels, $L = < \lambda_1, ..., \lambda_n >$, where $\lambda_i \in \Lambda$. If this list is given a binary encoding, $E(L) : L \mapsto I$, where $I \in \{0, 1\}^{(n \cdot \lceil \lg |\Lambda| \rceil)}$, then the problem can be solved using a genetic algorithm, provided some suitable fitness measure $F(I) : I \mapsto [0, 1]$ can be derived.

Fitness Measure We can derive a linear fitness measure directly from the labelling cost in equation 1: to turn $C(L)$ into a fitness measure for use in a genetic algorithm (i.e. one with range $[0, 1]$), we exponentiate.

$$F_L(I) = \exp\left[-\beta \cdot C(E^{-1}(I))\right] \tag{2}$$

This measure falls off rapidly with increasing cost. The steepness of the falloff can be adjusted by changing the scaling parameter, β (in the work reported here, $\beta = 1$). The function never tolerates more than a few label-errors regardless of the number of junctions, for example: F_L has a value of 1 when there are no errors, 0.37 for errors involving one junction, 0.14 for errors involving two junctions, 0.05 for errors involving three junctions, and 0.00 for errors involving six or more junctions.

Crossover Crossover operators generate two offspring from two parent chromosomes. There are two main classes: uniform crossovers exchange information in a bitwise manner; multi-point crossovers exchange whole sequences of bits at a time. The crossover strategy is derived from consideration of the algorithmic variant used, and the relationship between regions in the individual chromosomes and lines in the drawing to be labelled. In a standard genetic algorithm, disruptive crossovers (i.e. uniform) have been shown to explore the search space better [36,37]. However, in a hybrid genetic algorithm with gradient ascent, much exploration will be accomplished by the gradient ascent step, which will tend to create "islands of consistency". In this case, a more conservative crossover (i.e. multi-point), which will preserve and coalesce these islands, should be used.

The use of multi-point crossover raises the more subtle question of how the structure of the chromosome relates to the structure of the drawing. The crossover will recombine chunks of chromosome: neighbouring bits will segregate together, a phenomenon known as *linkage* in genetics. It is therefore important that those loci which are close in the chromosome should correspond to lines which occupy the same region of the drawing - i.e. lines which are relatively closely connected. This is not a problem with synthetic data, since humans have a natural tendency to segment line drawings and number junctions and arcs accordingly: thus data can be primed subconsciously to yield solutions. However, the same is not true of real world data, such as edge-detector output. Our method uses a heuristic to number the arcs. In general, TEE junctions represent occlusions of part of the scene by an overlying plane [25]. A crude segmentation can be achieved by numbering the arcs depth-first, backtracking at TEE junctions. This is sufficient to satisfy the requirement that strongly linked loci in the chromosome map to similar locales in the drawing.

4   Monitoring the Progress of Genetic Search

Although the eventual convergence of genetic algorithms using elitist selection is guaranteed [38], it may take arbitrarily long. Some way of ascertaining the current status of the algorithm is needed. The simplest statistics are the maximum and mean fitnesses of individuals. The maximum fitness clearly shows how close the population is to the solution: the mean fitness rapidly approaches the maximum fitness as a result of selection pressure; when a new optimum is found, the mean fitness tends to lag behind the maximum fitness and is not therefore an especially useful statistic.

Probably because of the lack of a coherent, robust theory for genetic algorithms, there has been relatively little effort put in to devising measures of the algorithm's progress at run-time. Many researchers use average fitness to measure the performance (e.g. Cedeño et al., [39]). This is somewhat naïve since the average fitness will either rapidly approach the maximum fitness as the population converges on an optimum, or provide no specific information if the population is distributed over several local optima. When the positions of the optima are known, the numbers of individuals occupying them or close to them can measure the convergence. However, the positions of optima are usually unknown (or there would not be a problem to solve), and the definition of "close" may entail ungeneralisable assumptions (e.g. Beasley and coworkers [40]).

Louis and Rawlins use the average Hamming distance between members of the population as a measure of diversity [41]. They successfully use this to give an upper bound on the convergence time of the algorithm, but the measure gives no indication of whether the algorithm is actively exploring the search space or stagnating. Furthermore, as they observed, (traditional) crossover - a key operator in the genetic algorithm - does not affect the average Hamming distance.

The essence of the genetic algorithm is that the crossover and mutation operators generate diverse solutions which are tested by the selection operator. The notion of "diversity" in a population really incorporates two distinct attributes: the degree of clustering and the extent to which the individuals span the search space.

Clustering From an information-theoretic point of view, the genetic algorithm's search space is the alphabet from which a population of symbols is drawn. We wish to obtain information about this space by considering the population. The Shannon entropy is a natural measure of how much information about the space is contained in the population [42], and corresponds to the degree of clustering.

Consider replacing some string x with a new string y and the effects of this on the entropy, S, and the average Hamming distance, $\bar{H}$. There are four cases shown in table 1 - we use $N_t(x)$ to denote the number of strings x at time t in the population. According to Shannon's observation that any averaging operation will monotonically increase the entropy [42], if $N_t(x) > (N_t(y) + 1)$, S must increase when an x is replaced by a y.

a	$N_t(x) = 1$, $N_{t+1}(y) = 1$	S unchanged		H unknown
b	$N_t(x) > 1$, $N_{t+1}(y) = 1$	S increased		H unknown
c	$N_t(x) = 1$, $N_{t+1}(y) > 1$	S decreased		H unknown
d	$N_t(x) > 1$, $N_{t+1}(y) > 1$	S $\begin{cases} \text{increased} \\ \text{unchanged} \\ \text{decreased} \end{cases}$	$\begin{array}{l} N_t(x) > (N_t(y) + 1) \\ N_t(x) = (N_t(y) + 1) \\ N_t(x) < (N_t(y) + 1) \end{array}$	$\bar{H}$ unknown

Table 1. Properties of Entropy, S and Average Hamming Distance, $\bar{H}$.

The entropy monotonically increases as new information is introduced (cases a and b), and monotonically decreases as information is removed (cases a and c). The former behaviour corresponds to exploration of the search space by the genetic algorithm; the latter to convergence of the algorithm. Even when no distinct string has been added or removed, changes in S are predictable. By contrast, $\bar{H}$ is unpredictable in all cases and furthermore tells us nothing about the homogeneity of the population. In fact, $\bar{H}$ is equivalent to $2.n.q(1-q)$, where q is the proportion of high bits amongst the distinct strings in the population, and hence says very little about the distribution of the strings themselves.

Span As a first approximation, we can measure the extent to which the population spans the search space by considering the total inter-cluster Hamming distance, H_T, which compares favourably with $\bar{H}$ because it will be increased by any crossover event which adds new clusters without deleting existing ones. H_T will almost certainly be changed by mutation, reflecting the way in which these operators sample the search space.

5 Experiments

The algorithm was tested on three labelling problems with and without gradient ascent and Waltz filtering. Several different parameter sets were tried. The convergence speed and solution-yield were recorded, as were the entropy and total inter-cluster Hamming distance.

5.1 Method

A generational algorithm was used. The initial population was created at random, and at each generation, all individuals were subject to crossover and mutation at rates determined by the control parameters. The population for successive generations was selected from the current population and its offspring. "Roulette-wheel" selection was used. The algorithm terminated after a set number of iterations regardless of whether any solutions had been found.

The algorithm was run on the problems shown in figure 3. These problems can be made arbitrarily more complex by adding disconnected copies; this is reasonable because the constraints in the problem are local. In the work reported here, two copies of each drawing had to be labelled. Several parameter sets were tested with and without gradient ascent, and with and without Waltz filtering [4]. Statistics were gathered over sets of 1000 trials.

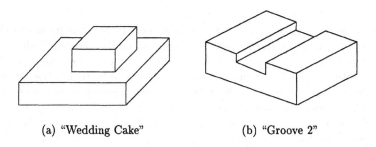

(a) "Wedding Cake"   (b) "Groove 2"

Fig. 3. Test Drawings.

Control Parameters Control parameters for the genetic algorithm are notoriously difficult to set [43]. The literature recommends two alternative parameter suites as set out in table 2. These parameters are based on the standard test suite for the genetic algorithm developed by DeJong [44]. Several other sets were tried (table 3).

	DJS (DeJong and Spears [45])	Gref (Grefenstette [46])
Population size	100	30
Crossover type	2 point	Uniform
Crossover rate	0.6	0.9
Mutation rate	0.001	0.01

Table 2. Parameter Sets from the Literature.

	Set A	Set B	Set C	Set D	Set E
Population size	100	100	100	100	100
Crossover type	Uniform	Weighted	HUX	1 point	2 point
Crossover rate	0.9	0.9	0.9	0.9	0.9
Mutation rate	0.03	0.03	0.03	0.03	0.03

Table 3. Additional Parameter Sets.

5.2 Results

The results are summarised in tables 4 and 5 (no consistent labellings were found for the impossible object). The algorithm performed best with gradient ascent, and especially well when this was combined with multi-point crossover (Sets D and E), having the highest convergence rate and highest yields. Waltz filtering completely confounded the algorithm. The multi-point crossovers generally outperformed the uniform ones.

Progress Measures Figure 5 shows sample plots of the maximum fitness, entropy and total inter-cluster Hamming distance of single successful (left column) and unsuccessful (right column) trials. The correlation between the entropy and the total inter-cluster Hamming distance was found to be high (above 0.9) with the gradient ascent hybrid and lower with the plain algorithm (around 0.7). The correlation between the two measures did not depend on the success of the algorithm. Figure 6 shows the average population entropy over 1000 trials for plain and hybrid algorithms.

5.3 Discussion

Labelling The most convincing results were produced when the algorithm was augmented by gradient ascent. All populations converged within five generations on average. Yields were highest with multi-point crossover: this suggests that the algorithm is combining consistent sub-labellings, something which uniform crossovers would impair. The number of generations to convergence (five) compares favourably with the 20 or so needed by multi-niche crowding [39].

The failure of the algorithm with Waltz filtering may appear surprising: Waltz filtering is known to prune the search space of consistent labellings. However,

	DJS	Gref	Set A	Set B	Set C	Set D	Set E
Standard	c: 2.30%	c: 17.8%	c: 29.3%	c: 30.2%	c: 30.4%	c: 35.5%	c: 38.8%
	$\bar{y}$: 0.06	$\bar{y}$: 0.54	$\bar{y}$: 2.10	$\bar{y}$: 2.27	$\bar{y}$: 1.87	$\bar{y}$: 3.17	$\bar{y}$: 3.45
	$\bar{g}$: 595	$\bar{g}$: 528	$\bar{g}$: 281	$\bar{g}$: 269	$\bar{g}$: 305	$\bar{g}$: 237	$\bar{g}$: 245
With Gradient Ascent	c: 99.2%	c: 76.1%	c: 99.4%	c: 97.8%	c: 99.2%	c: 100%	c: 100%
	$\bar{y}$: 17.0	$\bar{y}$: 3.34	$\bar{y}$: 17.3	$\bar{y}$: 13.5	$\bar{y}$: 17.6	$\bar{y}$: 25.2	$\bar{y}$: 33.0
	$\bar{g}$: 2.47	$\bar{g}$: 3.45	$\bar{g}$: 2.37	$\bar{g}$: 2.54	$\bar{g}$: 2.34	$\bar{g}$: 2.29	$\bar{g}$: 2.22

Table 4. Results for the Wedding Cake problem.
c is the proportion of trials yielding consistent labellings,
$\bar{y}$ is the average solution yield over all trials,
$\bar{g}$ is the average generation at which the first solutions are found.
No solutions were found with Waltz filtering (c : 0% in all cases).

	DJS	Gref	Set A	Set B	Set C	Set D	Set E
Standard	c: 3.80%	c: 23.3%	c: 38.3%	c: 37.4%	c: 33.3%	c: 42.6%	c: 42.9%
	$\bar{y}$: 0.04	$\bar{y}$: 0.34	$\bar{y}$: 1.02	$\bar{y}$: 0.99	$\bar{y}$: 0.80	$\bar{y}$: 1.11	$\bar{y}$: 1.10
	$\bar{g}$: 687	$\bar{g}$: 508	$\bar{g}$: 230	$\bar{g}$: 270	$\bar{g}$: 250	$\bar{g}$: 244	$\bar{g}$: 224
With Gradient Ascent	c: 98.6%	c: 75.9%	c: 99.2%	c: 99.4%	c: 98.4%	c: 99.9%	c: 99.9%
	$\bar{y}$: 9.78	$\bar{y}$: 3.23	$\bar{y}$: 15.1	$\bar{y}$: 13.4	$\bar{y}$: 15.3	$\bar{y}$: 17.8	$\bar{y}$: 19.8
	$\bar{g}$: 2.96	$\bar{g}$: 4.23	$\bar{g}$: 2.76	$\bar{g}$: 2.77	$\bar{g}$: 2.77	$\bar{g}$: 2.47	$\bar{g}$: 2.61

Table 5. Results for the Groove 2 problem.
c is the proportion of trials yielding consistent labellings,
$\bar{y}$ is the average solution yield over all trials,
$\bar{g}$ is the average generation at which the first solutions are found.

genetic algorithms work by exploring the fitness landscape; Waltz filtering sharpens this landscape since partially consistent labellings are regarded as being unacceptable. Thus the algorithm is faced with a landscape consisting of several deep troughs, the local minima, from which it cannot readily escape through mutation. The population rapidly converges and no progress can be made.

Similarity of Solutions The solutions found tended to be invariant with respect to FORK junctions. The results of a typical trial which found 11 distinct labellings for one of the two "wedding cakes" are given in figure 4. The convex interpretation of the two FORKs predominates. This cannot be explained simply by the proximity of the arcs in the drawing (and hence their strong linkage in the chromosomes), since other arc-groups (e.g. 15, 16 and 17) do not show this consistency.

It is likely that a random change in the labelling of a consistently labelled junction will yield a less good labelling. Consider an ELL junction: there are 16 combinatorial labelling possibilities, six have Hamming distances of zero from the Huffman dictionary (i.e. they are consistent), and ten have Hamming distances of one; none have Hamming distances of two. This means that a random replacement of a consistent labelling has a probability of $\frac{5}{15} = 0.\dot{3}$ of yielding another consistent labelling and a probability of $\frac{10}{15} = 0.\dot{6}$ of yielding a labelling

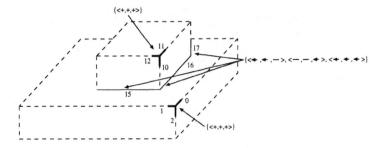

Fig. 4. Related Labellings. Labellings of line-triples with strong chromosomal linkage (proximity) found in 11 distinct solutions. Note that the lines incident at FORK junctions only have one label, but the others may have several. Lines are labelled in numerical order.

with a single error. By contrast, a FORK junction has 64 combinatorial possibilities of which five are consistent; the outcomes of a replacement of a consistent labelling are: another consistent labelling with probability $\frac{4}{63} = 0.06$, a labelling with Hamming distance one with probability $\frac{39}{63} = 0.62$, or a labelling with Hamming distance two with probability $\frac{20}{63} = 0.32$. Thus, the expectation of the Hamming distance from a consistent labelling following a labelling change is 0.6 for an ELL junction and 1.25 for a FORK junction, so FORKs can be said to be more strongly constrained than ELLs. We would therefore expect the labellings of FORK junctions to be relatively immune to the effects of gradient ascent, crossover and selection; and the final population will probably only contain individuals with one labelling for any particular FORK.

Our results reinforce the findings of Trueswell and others. Trueswell and coworkers have suggested that rapid disambiguation occurs in regions of strong constraint [47]; Kawabata has suggested that a local interpretation tends to propagate when humans are faced with ambiguous scenes [21]. With this in mind, FORK junctions can be seen as models for strongly constrained localities which tend to dictate the interpretation of their surroundings. This chimes with the notion that the alternative interpretations of a drawing should all be plausible given *a priori* evidence, and suggests that the search can be controlled by seeding the initial population appropriately.

Progress Measures As can be seen from figure 5, for populations of 100 individuals, the entropy always starts at 4.6. This is reassuring: the first generation is initialised at random, and for a population size of 100, the maximum entropy is $\ln 100 = 4.61$. As the population becomes saturated, the entropy usually falls to some minimum below about 2, but the variations in entropy and total intercluster Hamming distance after saturation indicate that the algorithm is still attempting to explore the search space. The presence of a set of relatively fit individuals reduces the likelihood that new chromosomes will persist.

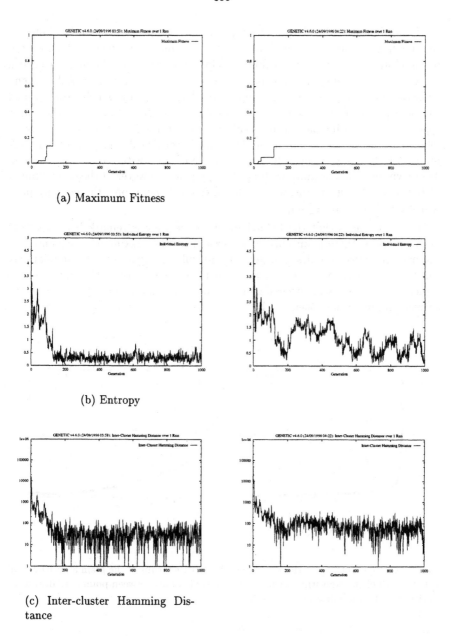

(a) Maximum Fitness

(b) Entropy

(c) Inter-cluster Hamming Distance

Fig. 5. Measurements on a Genetic Algorithm. Left column: successful run, right column: unsuccessful run. A log scale is used for the inter-cluster Hamming distance.

Some, but not all, of the major peaks in entropy coincide with jumps in the maximum fitness - i.e. finding a new optimum. Those peaks which do not presumably represent unsuccessful forays in the search space. Those peaks which do coincide with jumps in maximum fitness may either precede or follow them. This can be explained by proposing several methods by which new optimal solutions can arise. The algorithm may explore some fruitful avenue in the search space, causing an increase in entropy, then an optimal solution may be found following a crossover or mutation. Thus an entropy peak can precede a fitness jump. Alternatively, a new solution may arise *de novo* without extensive search. There will be a fitness jump with no entropy peak. However, if the copy-number of the new solution increases over the next few generations, the entropy peak will succeed the fitness jump.

Figure 6 shows that the behaviour of the entropy is remarkably consistent between trials: there is an abrupt decrease from the maximum to around $\frac{2}{3}$ of the maximum over the first few generations followed by a fall to some relatively constant minimum value (< 2) after 20 to 40 generations. This minimum is typically lower (< 1) in successful trials. New optima are rarely found once the entropy minimum has been reached.

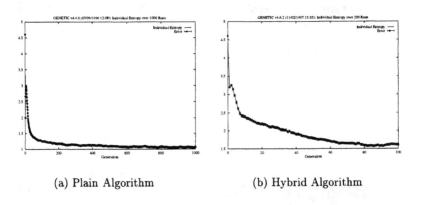

(a) Plain Algorithm   (b) Hybrid Algorithm

Fig. 6. Average Entropy of the Population for (a) 1000 runs of the plain algorithm and (b) 200 runs of the algorithm with gradient ascent. Lines between points are drawn for clarity: the data are discrete.

The initial selection removes most of the diversity from the population: the total inter-cluster Hamming distance falls from around 100 000 to around 1 000 and the entropy loses $\frac{1}{3}$ of its initial value. This is almost certainly the reason for the high correlations observed between entropy and total inter-cluster Hamming distance. The especially high correlations observed with gradient ascent may arise from the fact that the clusters are relatively stable since they all represent locally optimal solutions.

6 Conclusion

Consistent labelling problems frequently have more than one solution. In order that global contextual information be brought to bear in image analysis, several interpretations of locally ambiguous regions should be maintained. We have argued that most work in the field has aimed at disambiguating such regions early in the interpretation process, using only local evidence.

We have shown that the genetic algorithm is a robust tool for solving the line labelling problem and hence other consistent labelling problems. When combined with gradient ascent and using a multi-point crossover, the algorithm robustly finds multiple solutions to the problem. These solutions are related by common labellings of FORK junctions, which are the most strongly constrained of all junction types considered. The number of generations to convergence of the algorithm compares very favourably with that reported for multi-niche crowding, which also finds several solutions [39].

There is no solid theory to predict the behaviour of genetic algorithms or suggest appropriate parameter values. As a result, most of the run-time performance measures found in the literature are naïve. We have proposed three run-time performance measures: the maximum fitness of the population, the Shannon entropy of the population, and the total Hamming distance between distinct clusters of individuals. The maximum fitness and Shannon entropy provide useful information about the status of the algorithm. The total inter-cluster Hamming distance appears to be highly correlated with the Shannon entropy, especially with the gradient ascent hybrid. The results to date indicate that a population with a Shannon entropy of less than 2 has become saturated, and that new solutions are unlikely to emerge from such a population for some considerable time. Furthermore, most of the diversity in the population disappears in the first few iterations.

References

1. R. M. Haralick and L. G. Shapiro. The consistent labelling problem: Part 1. *IEEE PAMI*, 1:173–184, 1979.
2. R. M. Haralick and L. G. Shapiro. The consistent labelling problem: Part 2. *IEEE PAMI*, 2:193–203, 1980.
3. R. M. Haralick and G. L. Elliott. Increasing search tree efficiency for constraint satisfaction problems. *IJCAI 6*, pages 356–364, 1979.
4. D. Waltz. Understanding line drawings of scenes with shadows. In P. H. Winston, editor, *The Psychology of Computer Vision*, pages 19–91. McGraw-Hill, 1975.
5. R. A. Hummel and S. W. Zucker. On the foundations of relaxation labeling processes. *IEEE PAMI*, 5:267–287, 1983.
6. O. D. Faugeras and M. Berthod. Improving consistency and reducing ambiguity in stochastic labeling: An optimisation approach. *IEEE PAMI*, 3:412–424, 1981.
7. E. R. Hancock and J. Kittler. Discrete relaxation. *Pattern Recognition*, 23:711–733, 1990.

8. R. C. Wilson and E. R. Hancock. Graph matching by discrete relaxation. In E. S. Gelsema and L. N. Kanal, editors, *Pattern Recognition in Practice*, volume 4, pages 165–176. Elsevier, 1994.

9. C. D. Gelatt S. Kirkpatrick and M. P. Vecchi. Optimisation by simulated annealing. *Science*, 220:671–680, 1983.

10. S. Geman and D. Geman. Stochastic relaxation, gibbs distributions, and the Bayesian restoration of images. *IEEE PAMI*, 6:721–741, 1984.

11. D. Geiger and F. Girosi. Parallel and deterministic algorithms from MRFs: Surface reconstruction. *IEEE PAMI*, 13:401–412, 1991.

12. A. L. Yuille and J. J. Kosowsky. Statistical physics algorithms that converge. *Neural Computation*, 6:341–356, 1994.

13. J. H. Holland. *Adaptation in Natural and Artificial Systems*. MIT Press, 1975.

14. N. J. Pearlmutter M. C. MacDonald and M. S. Seidenberg. The lexical nature of syntactic ambiguity resolution. *Psychological Review*, 101:676–703, 1994.

15. A. H. Kawamoto. Nonlinear dynamics in the resolution of lexical ambiguity: A parallel distributed processing account. *Journal of Memory and Language*, 32:474–516, 1993.

16. N. J. Pearlmutter and M. C. MacDonald. Individual differences and probabilistic constraints in syntactic ambiguity resolution. *Journal of Memory and Language*, 34:521–542, 1995.

17. J. A. Feldman and D. H. Ballard. Connectionist models and their properties. *Cognitive Science*, 6:205–254, 1982.

18. M. Riani F. Masulli and E. Simonotto. Neural network models of perceptual alternation of ambiguous patterns. In S. Levialdi V. Cantoni, L. P. Cordella and G. Sanniti di Baja, editors, *Progress in Image Analysis*, pages 751–758. World Scientific, 1990.

19. M. Riani and E. Simonotto. Stochastic resonance in the perceptyal interpretation of ambiguous figures - a neural network model. *Physical Review Letters*, 72:3120–3123, 1994.

20. W. Bialek and M. Deweese. Random switching and optimal processing in the perception of ambiguous signals. *Physical Review Letters*, 74:3077–3080, 1995.

21. N. Kawabata. Visual fixation points and depth perception. *Vision Research*, 18:853–854, 1978.

22. N. Kawabata and T. Mori. Disambiguating ambiguous figures by a model of selective attention. *Biological Cybernetics*, 67:417–425, 1992.

23. K. L. Horlitz and A. O'Leary. Satiation or availability - effects of attention, memory and imagery on the perception of ambiguous figures. *Perception and Psychophysics*, 53:668–681, 1993.

24. F. G. Callari and F. P. Ferrie. Active recognition: Using uncertainty to reduce ambiguity. *Proceedings of the 13th International Conference on Pattern Recognition*, pages 925–929, 1996.

25. D. A. Huffman. Impossible objects as nonsense sentences. In B. Meltzer and D. Michie, editors, *Machine Intelligence*, volume 6, pages 295–323. Edinburgh University Press, 1971.

26. M. B. Clowes. On seeing things. *Artificial Intelligence*, 2:79–116, 1971.

27. K. Sugihara. Picture language for skeletal polyhedra. *Computer Graphics and Image Processing*, 8:382–405, 1978.

28. J. Malik. Interpreting line drawings of curved objects. *International Journal of Computer Vision*, 1:73–103, 1987.

29. L. R. Williams. Topological reconstruction of a smooth manifold-solid from its occluding contour. In *ECCV 92*, pages 36–47, 1992.

30. L. M. Kirousis. Effectively labeling planar projections of polyhedra. *IEEE PAMI*, 12:123–130, 1990.
31. P. Parodi and G. Piccioli. 3D shape reconstruction by using vanishing points. *IEEE PAMI*, 18:211–217, 1996.
32. E. R. Hancock. An optimisation approach to line labelling. In S. Impedovo, editor, *Progress in Image Analysis and Processing*, volume 3, pages 159–165. World Scientific, 1994.
33. A. S. Fraser. Simulation of genetic systems by automatic digital computers. *Australian Journal of Biological Science*, 10:484–491, 1957.
34. H. J. Bremermann. The evolution of intelligence. The nervous system as a model of its environment. Technical report, Deparment of Mathematics, University of Washington, Contact No. 477(17), 1958.
35. R. Toombs J. Reed and N. A. Barricelli. Simulation of biological evolution and machine learning. *Journal of Theoretical Biology*, 17:319–342, 1967.
36. G. Syswerda. Uniform crossover in genetic algorithms. In *Proceedings of the Third International Conference on Genetic Algorithms*, pages 2–9, 1989.
37. L. J. Eshelman. The CHC adaptive search algorithm: How to have safe search when engaging in nontraditional genetic recombination. In G. J. E. Rawlins, editor, *Foundations of Genetic Algorithms*, volume 1, pages 265–283. Morgan Kaufmann, 1991.
38. G. Rudolph. Convergence analysis of canonical genetic algorithms. *IEEE Transactions on Neural Networks*, 5:96–101, 1994.
39. V. R. Vemuri W. Cedeño and T. Slezak. Multiniche crowding in genetic algorithms and its application to the assembly of DNA restriction-fragments. *Evolutionary Computation*, 2:321–345, 1995.
40. D. R. Bull D. Beasley and R. R. Martin. A sequential niche technique for multimodal function optimisation. *Evolutionary Computation*, 1:101–125, 1993.
41. S. J. Louis and G. J. E. Rawlins. Syntactic analysis of convergence in genetic algorithms. In D. Whitley, editor, *Foundations of Genetic Algorithms*, volume 2, pages 141–151. Morgan Kaufmann, 1993.
42. C. E. Shannon. A mathematical theory of communication. *Bell System Techincal Journal*, 27:379–423, 1948.
43. L. J. Eshelman J. D. Schaffer, R. A. Caruna and R. Das. A study of control parameters affecting online performance of genetic algorithms for function optimisation. In *Proceedings of the Third International Conference on Genetic Algorithms*, pages 51–60, 1989.
44. K. A. DeJong. *An Analysis of the Behaviour of a Class of Genetic Adaptive Systems*. PhD thesis, University of Michigan, Department of Computer and Communication Sciences, 1975.
45. K. A. DeJong and W. M. Spears. An analysis of the interacting rôles of population size and crossover in genetic algorithms. In *Proceedings of the First Workshop on Parallel Problem Solving from Nature*. Springer-Verlag, 1990.
46. J. J. Grefenstette. Optimisation of control parameters for genetic algorithms. *IEEE SMC*, 16:122–128, 1986.
47. M. K. Tanenhaus J. C. Trueswell and S. M. Garnsey. Semantic influences on parsing: Use of thematic rôle information in syntactic disambiguation. *Journal of Memory and Language*, 33:285–318, 1994.

Toward Global Solution to
MAP Image Estimation:
Using Common Structure of Local Solutions

Stan Z. Li

School of Electrical and Electronic Engineering
Nanyang Technological University, Singapore 639798
szli@szli.eee.ntu.ac.sg

Abstract. The maximum a posteriori (MAP) principle is often used in image restoration and segmentation to define the optimal solution when both the prior and likelihood distributions are available. MAP estimation is equivalent to minimizing an energy function. It is desirable to find the global minimum. However, the minimization in the MAP image estimation is non-trivial due to the use of contextual constraints between pixels. Steepest descent methods such as ICM quickly finds a local minimum but the solution quality depends much on the initialization. Some initializations are better than others. In this paper, we present an iterative optimization algorithm, called the Comb algorithm, for approximating the global minmum. The Comb maintains a number of best local minima found so far. It uses the Common structure of Best local minima (hence "Comb") to derive new initial configurations. Because the derived configurations contain some structure resembling that of the global minimum, they may provide good starting points for local search to approach the global minimum. Experimental comparisons show that the Comb produces solutions of quality much better than ICM and comparable to simulated annealing.

1 Introduction

Image restoration is to recover a degraded image and segmentation is to partition an image into regions of similar image properties. Efficient restoration and segmentation are very important for numerous image analysis applications. Both problems can be posed generally as one of image estimation where the underlying image or segmentation map is to be estimated from the degraded image. Due to various uncertainties, an optimal solution is sought. A popular optimality criterion is the maximum *a posteriori* (MAP) probability principle in which both the prior distribution of the true image class and the conditional (likelihood) distribution of the data are taken into account. Contextual constraints, *i.e.* constraints between pixels, are important in image analysis. Markov random fields (MRFs) or equivalently Gibbs distributions provide a convenient tool for modeling prior distributions of images which encode contextual constraints. Maximizing the posterior is equivalent to minimizing the energy function in the corresponding Gibbs distribution. The MAP principle and MRF together form the MAP-MRF framework [5, 9].

Minimization methods are an important part of the energy minimization approach. When the pixels of the image to be recovered take discrete values, as is the case dealt with in this paper, the minimization is combinatorial. It is desirable to find the global minimum. However, no practical algorithms guarantee a global minimum. The complication increases due to contextual constraints used in the MAP-MRF image estimation.

Combinatorial optimization methods that are often used in statistical image analysis literature include the iterative conditional modes (ICM) [2] and simulated annealing (SA) [8, 5]. The deterministic ICM uses the *steepest descent* strategy to perform local search. Although it quickly finds a local minimum but the solution quality depends much on the initialization. Some initializations are better than others. An extension to steepest descent is the *multi-start* method: initialize a set of random configurations drawn from a uniform distribution, apply steepest descent independently to everyone configuration, and choose, among all resultant local minima, the one with the lowest energy value as the final solution. The SA is a stochastic algorithm, as opposed to deterministic ones. It is shown that the SA with a slow enough schedule finds a global solution with probability approaching one [5]. But such a slow schedule is impractical in applications and therefore in practice, a quick annealing schedule is usually used with the loss of the guaranteed convergence to the global minimum.

There have been developments in population-based methods such as genetic algorithms (GAs) [6] in recent years. Unlike the above mentioned methods which operate on a single configuration, a population-based method maintains and operates on a population of individuals, *i.e.* a collection of configurations. Two operations are used to produce offspring: crossover and mutation. The resulting offspring update the population according to the fittest survive principle. Heuristics can be incorporated into GAs to constitute hybrid GAs [6]. Combining local (minimization) search with a GA yields a hybrid GA also called hill-climbing GA or memetic algorithm [11, 13]. Applications of GAs in the image and vision area have also taken place; see for example [3, 7, 14].

In this paper, we present a new random search method, called the Comb method, for discrete optimization in MRF-based image restoration and segmentation. The Comb method maintains a number of the best local minima found so far, as a population-based method. It uses the Common structure of Best local minima (hence "Comb") to infer the structure of the global minimum. More specifically, it derives, from two chosen best local minima, one (or two) new initial configuration in such a way: For each pixel location, if the pixel labels (values) of the two local minima are the same (in common), the label is copied to the corresponding location of the new configuration; otherwise, a random label is generated and assigned to it. The configuration thus derived contains about the same percentage of common labels as the two local minima (assuming the two have about the same percentage of common labels). However, because it is no longer a local minimum, it may be improved by using a local minimization procedure to achieve a new local minimum. If the new one has a lower energy value, it updates the existing set of the best ones. This process is repeated until some termination conditions are satisfied.

The resulting Comb algorithm is equivalent to a GA hybridized with steepest descent, in which the Comb initialization works like a uniform crossover operator with a uniform selection. There have been various interpretations for the crossover operation. The intuitive motivation of encouraging the common structure provides a new perspective for interpreting the crossover operation in GA.

Experiment results in both image restoration and segmentation are provided to compare the Comb method with the ICM, HCF [4] and SA. The results show that the Comb yields better quality solutions than the ICM and HCF and comparable to SA.

The rest of the paper is organized as follows: Section 2 describes the Comb method for MAP-MRF image restoration and segmentation. Sections 3 discusses relationship between the Comb and GA. Section 4 presents the experimental comparisons.

2   The Comb Method for MAP-MRF Image Estimation

In this section, we formulate the energy function for MAP-MRF Image Restoration and Segmentation, define local energy minima, and describe the Comb method for obtaining good local minima.

2.1   MAP-MRF Image Restoration and Segmentation

Let $S = \{1, \ldots, m\}$ index the set of sites corresponding to image pixels and denote the underlying image as $f = \{f_1, f_2, \ldots, f_m\} = \{f_i \mid i \in S\}$. In our image estimation problem, every pixel can take on a discrete value in the label set $\mathcal{L} = \{1, \ldots, M\}$, i.e. $f_i \in \mathcal{L}$. Therefore, f is a configuration in the solution space $\mathbb{F} = \mathcal{L}^m$.

The spatial relationship of the sites, each of which is indexed by a single number in S, is determined by a neighborhood system $\mathcal{N} = \{\mathcal{N}_i \mid i \in S\}$ where $\mathcal{N}_i$ is the set of sites neighboring i. A single site or a set of neighboring sites form a clique denoted by c. In this paper, only up to pair-site cliques defined on the 8-neighborhood system are considered.

The type of the underlying image f can be blob-like regions or a texture pattern. Different types are due to different ways of interaction between pixels, i.e. due to different contextual interactions. Such contextual interactions can be modeled as MRFs or Gibbs distributions of the form $P(f) = Z^{-1} \times e^{-\sum_{c \in C} V_c(f)}$ where $V_c(f)$ is the potential function for clique c, C is the set of all cliques, and Z is the normalizing constant.

Among various MRFs, the multi-level logistic (MLL) model is a simple yet powerful mechanism for encoding a large class of spatial patterns such as textured or non-textured images. In MLL, the pair-site clique potentials take the form: $V_2(f_i, f_{i'}) = \beta_c$ if sites on clique $\{i, i'\} = c$ have the same label or $V_2(f_i, f_{i'}) = -\beta_c$ otherwise where β_c is the parameter for type-c cliques; while the single site potentials is defined by $V_1(f_i) = \alpha_I$ where α_I is the potential for the label $I = f_i$.

When the true pixel values are contaminated by identical independently distributed (i.i.d.) Gaussian noise, the observed data, or the likelihood model, is $d_i = f_i + e_i$ where $e_i \sim N(0, \sigma^2)$ is the zero mean Gaussian distribution with standard deviation σ. With these prior and likelihood models, the energy in the posterior distribution $P(f \mid d) \propto e^{-E(f)}$ is

$$E(f) = \sum_{i \in S} (f_i - d_i)^2 / [2\sigma^2] + \sum_{\{i\} \in C} V_1(f_i) + \sum_{\{i, i'\} \in C} V_2(f_i, f_{i'}) \qquad (1)$$

The MAP estimate for the restoration or segmentation is defined as

$$f^* = \arg \min_{f \in \mathbb{F}} E(f) \qquad (2)$$

The above minimization is combinatorial because the minimization of $E(f)$ is performed in the discrete space $\mathbb{F}$.

In this paper, we assume that the objective function, $i.e.$ the energy function $E(f)$, has been fully defined, which means that the MRF and noise parameters α, β and σ are known; we concentrate on the problem of minimizing $E(f)$.

2.2 Local Minima

The minimal solution defined in (2) is meant to be the global one, $i.e.$ the one with the lowest possible energy value. Finding the global solution of a combinatorial optimization problem is usually intractable, and therefore a local solution, hopefully a good one, is found instead.

A local minimum f is said with respect to its neighborhood $\mathcal{N}(f)$ composed of all the configurations neighboring f. We may define the following "k-neighborhood of a configuration f^*

$$\mathcal{N}^k(f^*) = \{x \in \mathbb{F} \mid x \text{ differs from } f^* \text{ by at most } k \text{ labels}\} \qquad (3)$$

For example, assuming that $\mathcal{L} = \{a, b, c\}$ is the set of allowable label for every f_i ($i = 1, \ldots, 5$), then $\{a, b, a, a, a\}$ is a 1-neighbor of $\{a, a, a, a, a\}$ and $\{b, a, a, a, c\}$ is a 2-neighbor of it. Note that $\{a, b, a, a, a\}$ is also a 2-neighbor of $\{a, a, a, a, a\}$ (due to the phrase "at most" in the definition) but not vice versa.

A point f^* is a $local\ minimum$ of E with respect to $\mathcal{N}$ if

$$E(f^*) < E(f) \quad \forall f \in \mathcal{N}(f^*) \qquad (4)$$

A local minimum is also the $global\ minimum$ if the neighborhood is defined to include all the other configurations, $\mathcal{N}(f^*) = \mathbb{F} - \{f^*\}$. Local solutions are often defined with respect to the 1-neighborhood, $\mathcal{N}^1$, because finding such a local solution is computationally more economical than using higher k-neighborhood.

```
initialize f = (f₁, ..., fₘ);
repeat
    changed=0;
    for each i ∈ S in turn
        fᵢⁿᵉʷ = arg min_{fᵢ∈ℒ} E(fᵢ | f − {fᵢ});
        if fᵢⁿᵉʷ ≠ fᵢ then
            fᵢ = fᵢⁿᵉʷ, changed=1;
until (changed==0);
return f as f*;
```

Fig. 1. A steepest descent algorithm for finding a local minimum with respect to $\mathcal{N}^1$.

The *steepest descent* is a fast algorithm for finding a local solution. Let $E(f_i \mid f - \{f_i\})$ be the local energy of label f_i given all the other labels. Such an algorithm iteratively minimizes $E(f_i \mid f - \{f_i\})$ for each $i \in S$. Fig.1 gives a sequential version of it. The "coding method" [1] may be incorporated for a parallel implementation.

Although fast, steepest descent has two major drawbacks: First, once reaching a local minimum, it can no more improve it. This is unlike the SA in which occasional jump from a lower energy configuration to a higher one is allowed so that improvements are still possible. Second, the local solution found by the steepest descent depends very much on the initial configuration. A good initialization scheme is always desired. A question is how to derive a good initial configuration. The Comb provides an answer.

2.3 The Comb Method

The Comb method maintains a number of N best local minima found so far, denoted $F = \{f^{[1]}, \ldots, f^{[N]}\}$, as a population-based method. In every iteration, it derives a new initial configuration from F, and perform steepest descent using the derived initial configurations. If the found local minimum is better than an existing one in F, it replaces it.

Ideally, we desire that all local minima in F should converge towards the global minimum $f^{[global]}$, in which case, there must be

$$f_i^{[n]} = f_i^{[global]} \qquad 1 \le n \le N \tag{5}$$

for all $i \in S$. We call $f_i^{[global]}$ the *minimal label* at i. To achieve (5), all the labels at i, $\{f_i^{[n]} \mid \forall n\}$, should finally converge to the minimal label $f_i^{[global]}$. The Comb is aimed to perform towards this objective.

The following heuristic is the basis for deriving new initial configurations: Although $f^{[1]}, \ldots, f^{[N]}$ are local minima, they share some structure with the

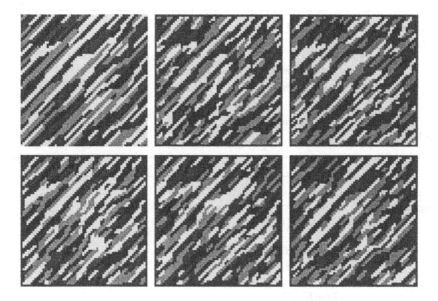

Fig. 2. The global minimum (upper-left) and 5 local minima. The local minima share some structure with the global minimum.

global minimum $f^{[global]}$. More specifically, some local minima $f^{[n]}$ have the minimal label $f_i^{[n]} = f_i^{[global]}$ for some $i \in S$. Fig.2 shows the (approximate) global minimum for an MAP-MRF restoration problem and some local minima found by using the multi-start method with initially random configurations. A statistic over a number of $N = 10$ local minima is made to see how many minimal labels they have. Table 1 shows the statistic in terms of the percentile of the sites (pixels) $i \in S$ at which at least k local minima $f^{[n]}$ have the minimal label $f_i^{[n]} = f_i^{[global]}$.

The Comb initialization is aimed to derive configurations having a substantial number of minimal labels so as to improve F towards the objective of (5). Although a configuration with a larger number of minimal labels does not necessarily have a lower energy value, we hope that it serves as a good initial configuration for a steepest descent algorithm.

k	0	1	2	3	4	5	6	7	8	9	10
%	100	98	95	87	75	60	43	28	16	7	2

Table 1. Percentile (rounded-up to integers) of the sites (pixels) $i \in S$ at which *at least* k local minima $f^{[n]}$ have the same label $f_i^{[n]} = f_i^{[global]}$ as the global minimum $f^{[global]}$.

```
comb_initialization(f^{[a]}, f^{[b]}, F)
begin
        for all i ∈ S:
                if (f_i^{[a]} == f_i^{[b]} && rand[0, 1] < 1 − τ)
                        then f_i^{[0]} = f_i^{[a]};
                else
                        f_i^{[0]} = rand(L);
end
```

```
Comb_Algorithm
begin
        initialize the set F = {f^{[1]}, . . . , f^{[N]}};
        do {
                random_selection(f^{[a]}, f^{[b]}, F);
                comb_initialization(f^{[0]}, f^{[a]}, f^{[b]});
                steepest_descent(f*, f^{[0]});
                update(F, f*);
        } until (termination condition satisfied);
        return(arg min_{f∈F} E(f));
end
```

Fig. 3. The Comb algorithm with a standard Comb-initialization scheme.

The Comb algorithm is described in Fig.3. The initialization at the beginning of the Comb algorithm is done according to a uniform distribution as the multi-start method. This is followed by iterations of four steps. Firstly, two local minima in F, $f^{[a]}$ and $f^{[b]}$, $(a \neq b)$ are randomly selected according to a uniform distribution. Secondly, a new initial configuration $f^{[0]}$ is derived from $f^{[a]}$ and $f^{[b]}$ using the standard Comb initialization, which will be explained shortly. Thirdly, steepest descent is applied to $f^{[0]}$ to produce a local minimum f^*. Then, the worst solution in F is replaced by f^* if the former has a higher energy than the latter, $\max_{f∈F} E(f) > E(f^*)$. The termination condition may be that either all configurations in F are the same or a certain number of local minima have been performed. The algorithm returns the best local minimum in F, *i.e.* the one having the lowest energy.

The central part of the Comb method is the derivation of new initial configurations. The Comb is aimed to derive $f^{[0]}$ in such a way that $f^{[0]}$ contains as many minimal labels as possible. Because the minimal labels are not known *a priori*, the Comb attempts to use the common structure, or *common labels*, of $f^{[a]}$ and $f^{[b]}$ to infer the minimal labels. We say that f_i^{comm} is a common label of $f^{[a]}$ and $f^{[b]}$ if $f_i^{comm} = f_i^{[a]} = f_i^{[b]}$. The Comb makes a hypothesis that f_i^{comm}

is a minimal label if $f_i^{[a]} = f_i^{[b]}$. The Comb initialization schemes are illustrated as follows:

1. The *basic Comb* initialization. For each $i \in S$, if $f_i^{[a]}$ and $f_i^{[b]}$ are identical, then set $f_i^{[0]} = f_i^{[a]}$; otherwise set $f_i^{[0]} = rand(\mathcal{L})$ which is a label randomly drawn from $\mathcal{L}$. The use of the common label in the initial configuration encourages the enlargement of the common structure in the local minimum to be found subsequently.

2. The *standard Comb* initialization (the one in Fig.3). The basic Comb initialization is accepted with a probability $1 - \tau$ where $0 < \tau < 1$ (in Fig.3, $rand[0, 1]$ is a uniformly distributed number in $[0, 1]$). The probabilistic acceptance of common labels diversifies the search and prevents F from converging to a local minimum too soon.

Then, how many minimal labels are retained in $f^{[0]}$ as the result of inferring minimal labels using common labels? In supervised tests where the (near) global minimum is known, we find that the percentages of minimal labels in $f^{[0]}$ is usually only slightly (about 1.0-2.0%) lower than those in $f^{[a]}$ and $f^{[b]}$. That is, the number of minimal labels retained in $f^{[0]}$ is about the same as those in $f^{[a]}$ and $f^{[b]}$. Given this and that $f^{[0]}$ is no longer a local minimum as $f^{[a]}$ and $f^{[b]}$, there is room to improve $f^{[0]}$ using a subsequent local minimization. This makes it possible to yield a better local minimum from $f^{[0]}$.

There are two parameters in the Comb algorithm, N and τ. $N = 10$ seems a good choice as the size of F for producing good quality solutions. Roughly speaking, the solution quality increases, *i.e.* the minimized energy value decreases, as N increases from 2 to 10. After that, the solution quality remains about the same (probabilistically) for greater N values. Empirically, when $\tau = 0$, all $f \in F$ converge sooner or later to a unique configuration and a smaller N makes such convergence quicker. The value of 0.01 is empirically a good choice for τ.

3 Relationship with GA

The Comb algorithm corresponds to a hybrid GA. Fig.4 describes a GA-like version of the Comb. The standard Comb initialization is effectively the same as a crossover operation followed by a mutation operation, the major and minor operations in genetic algorithms (GA) [6]. More exactly,

- the basic Comb corresponds to uniform crossover and
- the probability acceptance in the standard Comb corresponds to mutation.

In GA, two offspring, $f_i^{[01]}$ and $f_i^{[02]}$, are produced as the result of crossover. In the uniform crossover, either of the following two settings are accepted with equal probability:

(i) $f^{[01]} = f_i^{[a]}$ and $f^{[02]} = f_i^{[b]}$,
(ii) $f^{[01]} = f_i^{[b]}$ and $f^{[02]} = f_i^{[a]}$.

GA_comb_initialization($f^{[a]}$, $f^{[b]}$, F)
begin

      for each $i \in S$
          /* uniform crossover */
          if $(f_i^{[a]} == f_i^{[b]})$
              then $f_i^{[01]} = f_i^{[02]} = f_i^{[a]}$;
          else if $(rand[0, 1] < 0.5)$
              $f_i^{[01]} = f_i^{[a]}$ and $f_i^{[02]} = f_i^{[b]}$;
          else

              $f_i^{[01]} = f_i^{[b]}$ and $f_i^{[02]} = f_i^{[a]}$;

          /* mutation */
          if $(rand[0, 1] < \tau)$
              $f_i^{[01]} = rand(\mathcal{L})$;
          if $(rand[0, 1] < \tau)$
              $f_i^{[02]} = rand(\mathcal{L})$;

end

GA_Comb_Algorithm
begin

      initialize $F = \{f^{[1]}, \ldots, f^{[N]}\}$;
      do {
          random_selection($f^{[a]}$, $f^{[b]}$, F);
          GA_comb_initialization($f^{[01]}$, $f^{[02]}$, $f^{[a]}$, $f^{[b]}$);
          steepest_descent(f^{*1}, $f^{[01]}$);
          steepest_descent(f^{*2}, $f^{[02]}$);
          update(F, f^{*1}, f^{*2});
      } until (termination condition satisfied);
      return($\arg\min_{f \in F} E(f)$);

end

Fig. 4. A GA-like Comb algorithm.

So, if $f_i^{[a]} = f_i^{[b]}$, there must be $f_i^{[01]} = f_i^{[02]} = f_i^{[a]}$, just as in the Comb initialization. In effect, the crossover encourages common labels because common labels are copied to the new initial configurations while non-common labels are subject to the swap. Although this about the *uniform* crossover, it should be noted that even the simplest *one-point* crossover also works in a way that encourages common labels.

The discussion suggests that the essence of both the Comb and GA is captured by the use of the common structure of local minima. This is supported by the fact that the original Comb and the GA-like Comb yield comparable results: In the GA-like Comb algorithm (Fig.4), when $f_i^{[a]} \neq f_i^{[b]}$, $f_i^{[01]}$ and $f_i^{[02]}$ inherit the values of $f_i^{[a]}$ and $f_i^{[b]}$, as does a crossover operator. However, setting $f_i^{[01]}$ and $f_i^{[02]}$ to a random label $rand(\mathcal{L})$, i.e. not necessarily inheriting $f_i^{[a]}$ and $f_i^{[b]}$, leads to comparable results, as long as the common labels are copied to $f_i^{[0]}$ when $f_i^{[a]} = f_i^{[b]}$. Moreover, whether to derive one initial configuration $f^{[0]}$ or two initial configurations $f^{[01]}$ and $f^{[02]}$ makes little difference; both schemes yield comparable results. In summary, the Comb and the GA-like Comb produce comparable results; and this suggests that retaining common labels is important and provides an interpretation for the crossover operation in GA.

The Comb produces much better results than the multi-start method. The former uses the best local minima to get an initial estimate whereas the latter uses but random initialization. Therefore, Comb has a much higher efficiency of descending to good local minima.

4 Experimental Results

In the following, we present two experiments, one for MAP-MRF image restoration and the other for segmentation, to compare the performance of the following algorithms: (1) the Comb; (2) the ICM [2]; (3) the HCF (the parallel version) [4]; (4) the SA with the Metropolis sampler [8]. For the Comb, the parameters are $N = 10$ and $\tau = 0.01$. The implementation of SA is based on a procedure given in [12]. The schedules for the SA are set to $T^{(t+1)} \leftarrow 0.999 T^{(t)}$ with $T^{(0)} = 10^4$. The initial configuration for the ICM, HCF and SA is taken as the ML estimate whereas those in F for the Comb is entirely random; the difference will be explained later. The termination condition for the Comb is that all configurations in F are the same or that a number of 10000 new local minima have been generated.

Image	σ	α_I	β_1	β_2	β_3	β_4
No.1	1	0	-1	-1	-1	1
No.2	1	0	-2	-2	1	1
No.3	1	0	1	1	1	1

Table 2. The MRF parameters (α and β) and noise parameter σ for generating the three images.

The first set of experiments is for MAP-MRF restoration performed on three synthetic images of $M = 4$ gray levels, shown in Figs.5-7. The original have the label set $\mathcal{L} = \{1, 2, 3, 4\}$, and the pixel gray values also in $\{1, 2, 3, 4\}$. Table 2 gives the clique potential parameters α_I and $\beta_1, \cdots, \beta_4$ for generating the three types of textures and the standard deviation σ of the Gaussian noise.

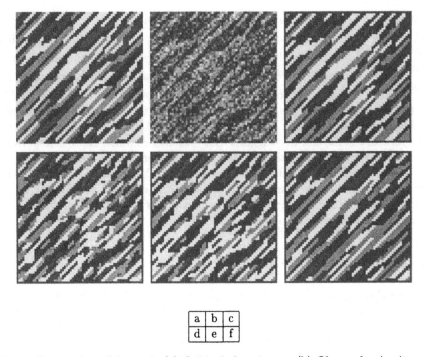

a	b	c
d	e	f

Fig. 5. Restoration of image 1. (a) Original clean image. (b) Observed noisy image (input data). (c) Comb solution. (d) ICM solution. (e) HCF solution. (f) SA solution.

The second experiment compares the algorithms in performing MAP-MRF segmentation on the Lenna image of size 256×240 into a tri-level segmentation map. The results are illustrated in Fig.8. The input image is the original Lenna image corrupted by the i.i.d. Gaussian noise with standard deviation 10. The observation model is assumed to be the Gaussian distribution superimposed on the mean values of 40, 125 and 200 for the three-level segmentation. An isometric MRF prior is used with the four β parameters being $(-1, -1, -1, -1)$.

Table 3 compares the quality of restoration and segmentation solutions in terms of the minimized energy values. We can see that the Comb outperforms the ICM and the HCF and is comparable to SA. A subjective evaluation of the resultant images would also agree to the objective numerical comparison. The quality of the Comb solutions is generally also better than that produced by using the continuous method of augmented Lagrange-Hopfield developed in [10].

The Comb as a random search method needs many iterations to converge, the number being increasing as τ decreasing. All the Comb solutions with $\tau = 0.01$ are obtained when the limit of generating 10000 local minima is reached. This is about 1000 times more than the fast converging ICM and HCF. Nonetheless, the Comb takes about 1/20 of the computational effort needed by the SA.

The Comb algorithm does not rely on initial configurations at the very beginning of the algorithm to achieve better solutions. The ML initialization has

Fig. 6. Restoration of image 2. Legends same as Fig.5.

a significantly effect on improving the ICM, HCF and SA results. But for the Comb, the ML and random initializations make little difference. This insensitivity is probably due to that the Comb operates on multiple, rather than a single, configurations.

	Comb	ICM	HCF	SA
No.1	-12057	-10003	-10269	-11988
No.2	-10944	-8675	-9650	-11396
No.3	-27511	-25881	-26629	-27526
Lenna	-175647	-171806	-167167	-173301

Table 3. The minimized energy values for the restoration of images 1–3 and the segmentation of the Lenna image.

5 Conclusions

The Comb attempts to derive good initial configurations from the best local minima found so far in order to achieve better solutions. To do so, it uses the common structure of the local minima to infer the label values in the global

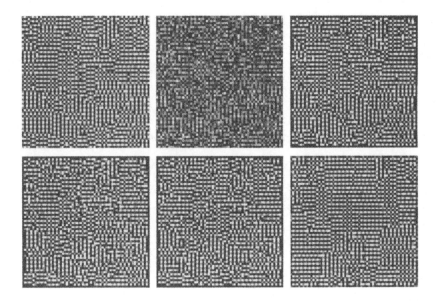

Fig. 7. Restoration of image 3. Legends same as Fig.5.

minimum. An initial configuration thus derived has about the same number of minimal labels as the two local minima from which it is derived. However, it is no longer a local minimum and thus its quality can be improved by a subsequent local minimization. This makes it possible to yield a better local minimum and thus increments the solution quality step by step. The comparisons shows that the Comb produces better results than the ICM and HCF though at higher computational costs and comparable results to the SA at lower costs. This suggests that the Comb can provide a good alternative to the well-known global minimizer SA.

References

1. J. Besag. "Spatial interaction and the statistical analysis of lattice systems" (with discussions). *Journal of the Royal Statistical Society, Series B*, 36:192–236, 1974.
2. J. Besag. "On the statistical analysis of dirty pictures" (with discussions). *Journal of the Royal Statistical Society, Series B*, 48:259–302, 1986.
3. B. Bhanu, S. Lee, and J. Ming. "Adaptive image segmentation using a genetic algorithm". *IEEE Transactions on Systems, Man and Cybernetics*, 25:1543–1567, 1995.
4. P. B. Chou, P. R. Cooper, M. J. Swain, C. M. Brown, and L. E. Wixson. "Probabilistic network inference for cooperative high and low level vision". In R. Chellappa and A. Jain, editors, *Markov Random Fields: Theory and Applications*, pages 211–243, Boston, 1993. Academic Press.

a	b	c
d	e	f

Fig. 8. Segmentation of the Lenna image. (a) The noisy Lenna image. (b) ML configuration. (c) Comb solution. (d) ICM solution. (e) HCF solution. (f) SA solution.

5. S. Geman and D. Geman. "Stochastic relaxation, Gibbs distribution and the Bayesian restoration of images". *IEEE Transactions on Pattern Analysis and Machine Intelligence*, 6(6):721–741, November 1984.

6. D. E. Goldberg. *Genetic Algorithms in Search, Optimization, and Machine Learning*. Addison-Wesley, 1989.

7. Y. Huang, K. P. abd X. Zhuang, and J. Cavanaugh. "Optic flow field segmentation and motion estimation using a robust genetic partitioning algorithm". *IEEE Transactions on Pattern Analysis and Machine Intelligence*, 17:1177–1190, 1995.

8. S. Kirkpatrick, C. D. Gellatt, and M. P. Vecchi. "Optimization by simulated annealing". *Science*, 220:671–680, 1983.

9. S. Z. Li. *Markov Random Field Modeling in Computer Vision*. Springer-Verlag, New York, 1995.

10. S. Z. Li. "MAP image restoration and segmentation by constrained optimization". *IEEE Transactions on Image Processing*, page accepted for publication, 1997.

11. P. Moscato. "On evolution, search, optimization, genetic algorithms and martial arts: Towards memetic algorithms". C3P Report 826, Caltech Concurrent Computation Program, 1989.

12. W. H. Press, S. A. Teukolsky, W. T. Vetterling, and B. P. Flannery. *Numerical recipes in C*. Cambridge University Press, 2 edition, 1988.

13. N. J. Radcliffe and P. D. Surry. Formal memetic algorithms. In T. Fogarty, editor, *Evolutionary Computing: AISB Workshop*, Lecture Notes in Computer Science, pages 1–14. Springer-Verlag, 1994.

14. G. Roth and M. D. Levine. "Geometric primitive extraction using a genetic algorithm". *IEEE Transactions on Pattern Analysis and Machine Intelligence*, 16:901–905, 1994.

Figure–Ground Separation: A Case Study in Energy Minimization via Evolutionary Computing

Suchendra M. Bhandarkar and Xia Zeng

Department of Computer Science, The University of Georgia
Athens, Georgia 30602-7404, U.S.A.

Abstract. It is known that the problem of figure–ground separation can be modeled as one of energy minimization using the Ising system model from quantum physics. The Ising system model for the figure–ground separation problem makes explicit the definition of shape in terms of attributes such as cocircularity, smoothness, proximity and contrast and is based on the formulation of an energy function that incorporates pairwise interactions between local image features in the form of edgels. This paper explores a class of stochastic optimization techniques based on evolutionary algorithms for the problem of figure–ground separation using the Ising system model. Experimental results on synthetic edgel maps and edgel maps derived from gray scale images are presented. The advantages and shortcomings of evolutionary algorithms in the context of figure–ground separation are discussed.

1 Introduction

In spite of several recent advances, state-of-the-art computer vision systems have yet to emulate the preattentive capability of human vision in being able to effortlessly separate figure from ground. In this paper, the problem of figure-ground separation is treated as one of combinatorial optimization. The shape and noise elements and their spatial interactions are modeled as an interacting spin (Ising) system from quantum physics[10]. In conformity with the Ising system model, an energy function is defined over predefined image elements that consist of both shape and noise elements. The energy function serves to reinforce the grouping of local shape elements that represent objects of possible interest into global shapes and also simultaneously eliminate noise elements. The figure-ground separation problem thus becomes one of combinatorial optimization where the global minimum of the energy function corresponds to the optimal separation (i.e., classification) of the image elements into figure and noise elements.

Figure-ground separation was first studied by Gestalt psychologists[13] in their research on perceptual grouping where certain image elements are organized to construct an emergent figure. Researchers in computer vision and image processing have studied figure-ground separation from the viewpoint of edge/contour grouping where short edge segments or *edgels* are grouped into long continuous contours of perceptual significance. Parent and Zucker[14] characterize local edgel shape on the basis of curvature computed on a local grid.

They cast the curve inference problem as one of global optimization and use a relaxation labeling algorithm to compute the optimum. However, relaxation is a local search-based optimization process that is vulnerable to the presence of local optima in the search space and hence needs good initialization. A similar approach can be found in Sha'ashua and Ullman[18] where curve inference is modeled as search for the best sequence of edge elements that would result in the longest and smoothest image curves. The search itself is carried out using dynamic programming which is also a deterministic optimization process that calls for good initialization to prevent it from getting trapped in a local optimum.

In Gutfinger and Sklansky[9] curve/noise separation is viewed as a classification problem where the classification is done using a method that uses supervised and unsupervised training. Their technique though theoretically appealing, is impractical on real image data. Carnevali et al.[4] have used simulated annealing in conjunction with a pixel interaction model to classify pixels in a binary image as object or noise. Simulated annealing is a stochastic optimization technique that is capable of eluding local optima while maintaining asymptotic convergence towards the global optimum with unit probability[7, 12, 15]. Acton and Bovik[1] have applied mean field annealing, which is a deterministic approximation to simulated annealing, to the problem of edge detection and edgel grouping. Sejnowski and Hinton[17] showed the limitations of using deterministic optimization techniques in their formulation of the figure-ground separation problem where the image elements are classified into two possible labels: region and noise. With an initial random labeling the gradient descent procedure, which is a deterministic optimization technique, is seen to get trapped in one of several local optima of the energy function. A stochastic optimization technique such as simulated annealing, on the other hand, is shown to converge to an optimal solution in which the region elements are bounded by the edge elements. Roth and Levine[16] have applied a genetic algorithm based on a minimal subset representation of a geometric primitive to the problem of feature extraction. Their technique however, requires that the geometric primitive have an underlying parametric representation which restricts its applicability.

Herault and Horaud[10] have explored simulated annealing, mean field annealing and microcanonical annealing in the context of figure-ground separation via edgel grouping. The mathematical model used to encode the figure-ground separation problem is shown to fit the constraints of an Ising system model. The results presented in their paper were impressive and brought out the advantages of using the Ising system model in conjunction with stochastic optimization techniques for the figure-ground separation problem.

This paper explores a more recent class of stochastic optimization techniques termed as *evolutionary* algorithms[6]. Evolutionary algorithms emulate the process of biological evolution and are based on the Darwinian *principle of natural selection*; popularly known as *survival of the fittest*. Of specific interest in the wider class of evolutionary algorithms, is the genetic algorithm (GA)[8, 11]. This paper extends our previous work in evolutionary algorithms[2] and the recent work of Herault and Horaud[10] by exploring two variations of the GA in the context of the figure–ground separation problem.

2 Ising System Model for Figure–Ground Separation

The mathematical formulation of the figure-ground separation problem addressed in this paper is based largely on the Ising system model of Herault and Horaud[10]. The problem is cast as one in which figure edgels (i.e., straight and short edge segments) are to be separated from noise edgels. In the interest of making this paper self-contained, we present a brief synopsis of the Ising system model; the interested reader is referred to the paper by Herault and Horaud[10] for a more detailed exposition.

The Ising system model is commonly used in quantum physics to explain electromagnetic phenomena. The state of the Ising system is described by a spin state vector consisting of N elements $\sigma = [\sigma_1, \sigma_2, \ldots, \sigma_N]$ such that $\sigma_i \in \{+1, -1\}$ i.e., each spin is described by a discrete label *up* $(+1)$ or *down* (-1). A symmetric matrix $\mathbf{J}$ describes the interaction between spins. Element $J_{i,j}$ describes the interaction between spins σ_i and σ_j. We require that $J_{i,i} = 0$ for all $1 \le i \le N$. A vector $\mathbf{B} = [B_1, B_2, \ldots, B_N]$ describes the external field that the Ising system is subject to where B_i is value of the field viewed by spin σ_i. The energy function associated with an Ising system subject to an external field $\mathbf{B}$ is given by:

$$E(\sigma_1, \sigma_2, \ldots, \sigma_N) = -\frac{1}{2}\sum_{i=1}^{N}\sum_{j=1}^{N} J_{i,j}\sigma_i\sigma_j - \sum_{i=1}^{N} B_i\sigma_i \tag{1}$$

The *ground state* of the Ising system model is the one that results in the minimization of the energy E.

2.1 Formulation of the Model

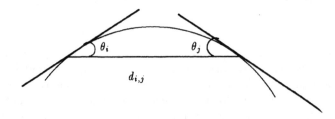

Fig. 1. Edgel interaction parameters

Four types of interaction between edgels are modeled based on very *generic* notions of desired shapes: cocircularity, smoothness, proximity, and contrast.

Incorporation of generic shape properties spares one from having to make very constraining assumptions about the shapes that underlie the figure edgels.

Cocircularity: Two edgels are considered to be cocircular if they are tangent to the same circle at their respective edgel centers (Figure 1). From Figure 1, let $\delta_{i,j} = |\theta_i - \theta_j|$ where smaller values of $\delta_{i,j}$ imply a greater degree of cocircularity. The cocircularity coefficient is defined as:

$$c_{i,j}^{COCIRC} = \left(1 - \frac{\delta_{i,j}^2}{\pi^2}\right) \exp\left(-\frac{\delta_{i,j}^2}{k}\right) \tag{2}$$

where k is chosen such that $c_{i,j}^{COCIRC}$ vanishes gradually under conditions of noncircularity. A value of $k = 10$ was found to give good results in practice.

Parallelism: Two edgels i and j are deemed to be parallel if the sum of θ_i and θ_j equals π (Figure 1). The parallelism coefficient is defined as:

$$c_{i,j}^{PARA} = \begin{cases} \cos\left(\frac{\pi|\pi - \theta_i - \theta_j|}{2\epsilon}\right) & \text{if } |\pi - \theta_i - \theta_j| \le \epsilon \\ 0 & \text{if } |\pi - \theta_i - \theta_j| > \epsilon \end{cases} \tag{3}$$

where ϵ is an angle threshold. A value of $\epsilon = 5^{\circ}$ was found to be a good choice in practice.

Smoothness: Two edgels i and j are deemed to be collinear or smooth if $\theta_i = \theta_j = 0$ (Figure 1). The smoothness coefficient is defined as:

$$c_{i,j}^{SMOOTH} = \left(1 - \frac{\theta_i \theta_j}{\pi^2}\right)\left(1 - \frac{(\pi - \theta_i)(\pi - \theta_j)}{\pi^2}\right) \tag{4}$$

Proximity: Two edgels i and j are deemed to be proximate if the distance $d_{i,j}$ between their centers is small compared to the standard deviation σ_d of all the pairwise edgel distances in the edgel map. The proximity coefficient is defined as:

$$c_{i,j}^{PROX} = \exp\left(-\frac{d_{i,j}^2}{2\sigma_d^2}\right) \tag{5}$$

Contrast: If the average intensities of the two edgels are g_i and g_j then the contrast coefficient is defined as:

$$c_{i,j}^{CONTRAST} = \frac{g_i g_j}{g_{max}^2} \tag{6}$$

where g_{max} is the maximum of the average intensities of all the edgels in the edgel map.

Intensity: Two edgels having the same average intensity g_i and g_j should reinforce each other. An intensity coefficient for this purpose is defined as follows:

$$c_{i,j}^{INTY} = \begin{cases} \cos\left(\frac{\pi|g_i - g_j|}{2\delta}\right) & \text{if } |g_i - g_j| \le \delta \\ 0 & \text{if } |g_i - g_j| > \delta \end{cases} \tag{7}$$

where δ is a threshold for intensity change. We have found $\delta = 5$ to give reliable results when the total number of gray levels is 256 (i.e., 1 byte per pixel).

The overall interaction coefficient is computed as:

$$c_{i,j} = \max\left(c_{i,j}^{COCIRC}, c_{i,j}^{PARA}\right) c_{i,j}^{SMOOTH} c_{i,j}^{PROX} \max\left(c_{i,j}^{CONTRAST}, c_{i,j}^{INTY}\right) \tag{8}$$

The energy function associated with the *orderliness* of the edgel map can be written as:

$$E(\sigma_1, \sigma_2, \ldots, \sigma_N) = -\frac{1}{2} \sum_{i=1}^{N-1} \sum_{j=i+1}^{N} (c_{i,j} - \alpha)(1 + \sigma_i \sigma_j + \sigma_i + \sigma_j) \tag{9}$$

Here, σ_i takes on a value of $+1$ or -1 depending on whether or not the corresponding edgel is labeled as *figure* (i.e., included in the final edgel map) or *noise* (i.e., excluded from the final edgel map). Note that α is a threshold value that is estimated from the signal-to-noise ratio (SNR). If the value of $c_{i,j}$ falls below the threshold α then the corresponding edgels are deemed to be weakly interacting and they result in an increase in the total energy E. Edgel maps with higher E values may be deemed to contain a large number of weakly interacting edgels. The goal therefore is to be able to find an edgel map with the lowest E value i.e., containing edgels that maximally reinforce each other.

Comparing equations (1) and (9) one can show that the Ising system model underlying equation (9) is given by:

$$E(\sigma_1, \sigma_2, \ldots, \sigma_N) = C - \frac{1}{2} \sum_{i=1}^{N} \sum_{j=1}^{N} J_{i,j} \sigma_i \sigma_j - \sum_{i=1}^{N} B_i \sigma_i \tag{10}$$

where

$$C = \frac{1}{4} \sum_{i=1}^{N} \sum_{j=1}^{N} (c_{i,j} - \alpha) \tag{11}$$

$$J_{i,j} = \frac{1}{2}(c_{i,j} - \alpha) \tag{12}$$

$$B_i = \frac{1}{2} \sum_{j=1}^{N} (c_{i,j} - \alpha) \tag{13}$$

In order to ensure that $J_{i,i} = 0$, $1 \leq i \leq N$ in conformity with the Ising system model, one chooses $c_{i,i} = \alpha$, $1 \leq i \leq N$. The energy function of the edgel map is similar to the Ising system model except for a constant bias term given by equation (11). The desired edgel map, (i.e., one in which the noise edgels are separated from the figure edgels), corresponds to the ground state of the Ising system model represented by equation (10) (i.e., the state which minimizes the energy E given by equation (10)).

3   Evolutionary Algorithms

The energy function E (equation (10)) associated with the *orderliness* of the edgel map is a multivariate combinatorial function whose landscape is fraught with several local minima. *Deterministic* combinatorial optimization algorithms based on a strictly local search of the energy landscape are prone to get trapped in one of the several local minima thus entailing the use of a *stochastic* combinatorial optimization procedure that is capable of forgoing the several local minima in favor of the global minimum.

This paper explores a class of stochastic combinatorial optimization techniques based on the paradigm of evolutionary computation in the context of the figure-ground separation problem. Evolutionary computation is a population-based optimization process that mimics the process of biological evolution encountered in nature[6]. This paper explores variations of the genetic algorithm (GA)[8, 11] which is an important member of the wider class of evolutionary algorithms.

3.1   The Genetic Algorithm - A Brief Overview

Central to the GA are the concepts of *population, fitness, chromosomes, selection, crossover* and *mutation*. Potential solutions to a combinatorial optimization problem are represented as bit strings or *chromosomes*. A collection of potential solutions or chromosomes constitutes a *population*. With each chromosome is attached a *fitness* value which is computed using a *fitness function* derived from the objective function to be optimized and the constraints underlying the combinatorial optimization problem. The chomosomes from a given population are chosen using a *selection* operator to form a mating pool for reproduction. The *roulette wheel* selection operator which selects each chromosome with a probability proportional to the ratio of the fitness of the chromosome to the overall fitness of the population, is a popular choice. An alternate choice is the *tournament* selection operator which selects two members at random from the current generation, compares their fitness values and inserts the fitter chromosome in the mating pool.

Two mates, selected at random from the mating pool, reproduce via the *crossover* operator. The crossover operator randomly selects a point along the length of the chromosome and swaps the ends of the mating chromosomes with a predefined crossover probability to generate a pair of offspring for the following generation (Figure 2). Each of the offspring is subject to random localized change via a *mutation* operator, which typically amounts to flipping each bit of the offspring with a predefined mutation probability.

There are two principal variants of the genetic algorithm based on the evolution strategy employed: the canonical genetic algorithm (CGA) and the steady state genetic algorithm (SSGA). In the CGA, the offspring created from the mating pool replace the entire current generation. In the SSGA only a few of the weakest members of the current population are replaced by the offspring created from the mating pool. The pseudocode descriptions of the CGA and the

SSGA are given in Figures 3 and 4 respectively. A more detailed comparison between the CGA and SSGA can be found in [5].

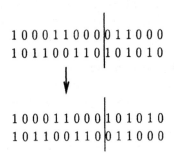

Fig. 2. Crossover operation

```
repeat
{
    Select members from the current population using roulette-wheel
    selection or tournament selection to create the mating pool;
    repeat
    {
    Choose two parents at random from the current generation;
    Create two offspring using the crossover operator;
    Bring about a random localized change in each offspring using a
    mutation operator;
    Add the offspring to the next generation;
    } until the next generation has been completely generated;
    Replace current generation by the next generation;
    } until the convergence criterion is met;
```

Fig. 3. Outline of the canonical genetic algorithm

3.2   The GA and Figure-Ground Separation

In order to apply the GA to the figure-ground separation problem, the edgel map is modeled as a chromosomal bit string where the ith bit position represents the classification of the ith edgel in the edgel map; if the ith edgel is classified as a figure (noise) edgel then the ith bit in the bit string is 1 (0) and conversely. For

```
repeat
{
  repeat
  {
    Select two members from the current population using
    roulette-wheel selection or tournament selection;
    Create two offspring using the crossover operator;
    Bring about a random localized change in each offspring
    using a mutation operator;
    If neither offspring exists in the population already then
        replace the weakest member in the current population by
        the stronger of the two offspring;
    Else
        replace the weakest member in the current population by
        the offspring that does not exist in the population already;
  } until a certain predefined percentage of the weakest members in
      the current generation have been replaced;
} until the convergence criterion is met;
```

Fig. 4. Outline of the steady state genetic algorithm

an edgel map with N edgels, there are 2^N possible bit strings. The ideal edge map is one in which all the edgels have been correctly classified. The problem of determining this ideal string is NP-complete since the only algorithm that ensures an optimal solution is one that does an exhaustive search of the space of all the possible 2^N bit strings, resulting in an algorithm with exponential complexity.

The raw fitness value F for a chromosome is defined as $F = -E$ where E is the energy associated with the corresponding edgel map (equation (9)). The fitness values are normalized to circumvent the problem of negative fitness values. The normalized fitness value F_n is given by:

$$F_n = F - F_{min} + \beta(F_{max} - F_{min}) \tag{14}$$

where F_{min} and F_{max} are the minimum and maximum F values respectively in the current population. If $\beta \geq 0$ the value of F_n is positive for all chromosomes in the population.

4   Experimental Results

The CGA and SSGA were tested on synthetic edgel maps as well as on edgel maps derived from grayscale images. One of the synthetic edgel maps is shown in Figure 5 and is referred to as *Synthetic-1*. *Synthetic-1* contains 96 figure edgels and 160 noise edgels. The noise edgels have lengths that are uniformly distributed in the range [0, 40] pixels, intensities uniformly distributed in the range [0, 255],

383

orientations uniformly distributed in the range $[0, \pi]$, and x and y coordinates of
the edgel center that are uniformly distributed in the range $[0, 511]$ for an image
of size 512×512 pixels.

One of the grayscale images *Spaceship* is shown in Figure 6 and the corresponding edgel map in Figure 7. The edgel maps for the grayscale images were
generated using a Canny edge detector[3] and a simple edgel following algorithm
that tracks edge points in the direction of the local gradient.

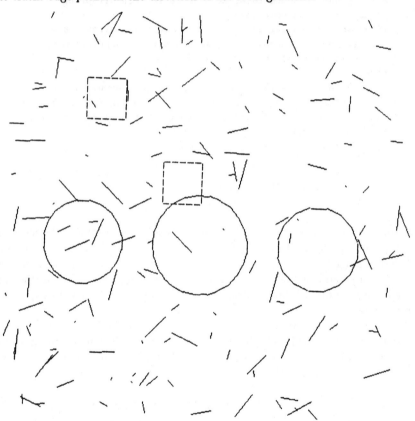

Fig. 5. Synthetic edgel map *Synthetic-1*

4.1 Performance of the CGA and SSGA

The performance of the CGA and that of the SSGA were compared using several
synthetic edgel maps. The population size was chosen to be 100, the crossover
probability to be 0.7, the mutation probability to be 0.05 and the halting criteria
to be the fact that the best member in the population has not changed over the
past 5 consecutive generations. For the purpose of comparison a figure of merit

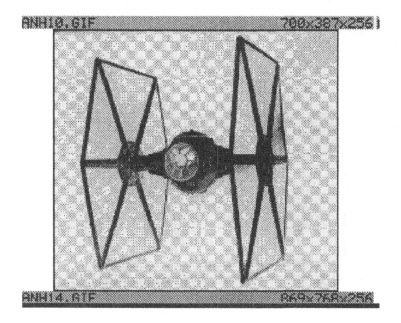

Fig. 6. Grayscale image *Spaceship*

M was defined as

$$M = \frac{1}{1 + \gamma \frac{F_d}{F} + \delta \frac{N_r}{N}} \qquad (15)$$

where F is the total number of figure edgels, F_d is the number of figure edgels deleted in the final edgel map, N is total number of noise edgels, N_r is the number of noise edgels retained in the final edgel map, and γ and δ are penalty factors. For comparison between the algorithms, the following criteria were used:
(i) Figure of merit associated with the final edgel map.
(ii) The number of generations needed for convergence.
(iii) The execution time needed for convergence.
(iv) Sensitivity to the chromosome encoding scheme.

Table 1 tabulates the performance of the CGA on three of the synthetic edgel maps used in our experiments: *Synthetic-1* (shown in Figure 5) and two other synthetic edgel maps termed as *Synthetic-2* and *Synthetic-3*. The performance of the CGA is tabulated for both cases; where the edgels have been generated and encoded in the chromosome in a raster-scan manner and where the edgels occupy random bit positions on the chromosome. Our experiments have shown that the CGA is sensitive to the value of α, in that very low values of α drive the

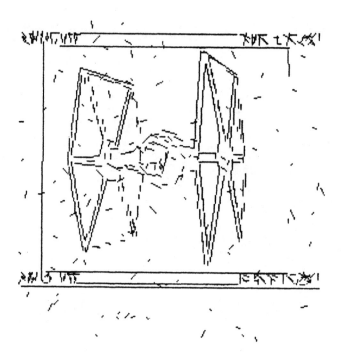

Fig. 7. Edgel map of *Spaceship*

algorithm towards premature convergence to a suboptimal solution where most of the noise edgels persist in the resulting image. Conversely, a high value of α removes a larger number of noise edgels but simultaneously removes some of the figure pixels as well. Recall that α is a threshold for the interaction coefficient $c_{i,j}$; values of $c_{i,j} > \alpha$ are deemed to denote strongly interacting (i.e., mutually reinforcing) edgels whereas values of $c_{i,j} < \alpha$ denote weakly interacting edgels. CGA_{ras} where the edgels are encoded in the chromosome in raster scan order exhibits superior performance compared to CGA_{ran} in which the edgels are encoded in the chromosome in random order. The former exhibits a higher value of M over a large range of α values thereby implying a greater degree of noise removal while retaining a greater number of figure edgels. This goes to show that the CGA is sensitive to the chromosome encoding scheme employed.

Table 2 tabulates the performance of the SSGA on the same three synthetic edgel maps *Synthetic-1* (Figure 5), *Synthetic-2* and *Synthetic-3* for both, raster-scan and random encoding of edgels in the chromosome. The SSGA replaced 10% of its weakest chromosomes in each generation. The other parameters were chosen to be identical to the ones for the CGA. The SSGA showed greater insensitivity to the encoding technique used and the value of α as far as the figure

Table 1. Performance of CGA on the synthetic edgel maps. CGA$_{ras}$: edgels encoded in chromosome in raster scan order, CGA$_{ran}$: edgels encoded in chromosome in random order, NG: no. of generations, T: execution time in ms, $\gamma = \delta = 1$.

Edgel Map	α	CGA$_{ras}$					CGA$_{ran}$				
		F_d	N_r	M	NG	T	F_d	N_r	M	NG	T
Synthetic-1	$\frac{1}{N}$	0	111	0.59	151	1277	0	119	0.57	173	1465
$F = 96, N = 160$	$\frac{5}{N}$	0	53	0.75	156	1315	0	70	0.70	177	1498
	$\frac{10}{N}$	4	14	0.89	155	1307	8	28	0.79	174	1472
	$\frac{15}{N}$	8	12	0.86	159	1340	11	32	0.76	174	1473
	$\frac{20}{N}$	14	10	0.83	157	1325	13	38	0.73	178	1510
Synthetic-2	$\frac{1}{N}$	0	42	0.70	143	1211	0	57	0.63	158	1337
$F = 96, N = 96$	$\frac{5}{N}$	0	30	0.76	147	1245	0	41	0.70	161	1363
	$\frac{10}{N}$	0	22	0.81	143	1210	3	29	0.75	163	1379
	$\frac{15}{N}$	0	20	0.83	145	1225	7	25	0.75	162	1370
	$\frac{20}{N}$	11	10	0.82	144	1220	17	17	0.74	159	1346
Synthetic-3	$\frac{1}{N}$	0	93	0.56	138	1165	0	98	0.55	153	1295
$F = 100, N = 120$	$\frac{5}{N}$	0	62	0.66	138	1170	0	74	0.62	151	1275
	$\frac{10}{N}$	0	28	0.81	140	1184	3	37	0.75	155	1310
	$\frac{15}{N}$	5	24	0.80	141	1190	10	32	0.73	153	1293
	$\frac{20}{N}$	8	21	0.80	140	1185	13	25	0.75	152	1285

of merit of the final result was concerned. The encoding scheme however, did affect the performance of the SSGA in terms of the number of generations needed to arrive at the final result. Although the SSGA needed a greater number of generations to converge to a solution than did the CGA, the number of crossover and mutation operations for each generation of the SSGA are a fraction of those needed per generation of the CGA resulting thereby in a lower overall execution time for the SSGA. Figure 8 shows the result of applying the SSGA with random encoding of edgels in the chromosome on the synthetic edgel map *Synthetic-1*. Figure 9 shows the result of applying the SSGA to the edgel map of the grayscale image *Spaceship*.

4.2 Discussion of Results

Based on our experimental results, the CGA-based and the SSGA-based figure-ground separation algorithms are seen to have the following advantages:

(a) The selection and crossover operators enables useful subsolutions, referred to as *building blocks* or *schema* in the GA literature, to be propagated and combined to construct better and more global solutions with every succeeding generation.

(b) The CGA and SSGA are naturally parallel. In fact it has been shown that the CGA and the SSGA exhibit both *explicit* and *implicit* parallelism[11]. Implicit parallelism arises from the fact that by evaluating a certain chromosome, the GA simultaneously and implicitly evaluates all the schema of which the chromo-

Table 2. Performance of SSGA on the synthetic edgel maps. SSGA$_{ras}$: edgels encoded in chromosome in raster scan order, SSGA$_{ran}$: edgels encoded in chromosome in random order, NG: no. of generations, T: execution time in ms, $\gamma = \delta = 1$.

Edgel Map	α	SSGA$_{ras}$					SSGA$_{ran}$				
		F_d	N_r	M	NG	T	F_d	N_r	M	NG	T
Synthetic-1	$\frac{1}{N}$	0	94	0.63	1235	1043	0	99	0.62	1422	1211
$F = 96,\ N = 160$	$\frac{5}{N}$	0	23	0.87	1242	1050	0	28	0.85	1437	1218
	$\frac{10}{N}$	3	18	0.87	1222	1035	4	20	0.87	1417	1197
	$\frac{15}{N}$	5	8	0.90	1225	1033	7	12	0.87	1420	1201
	$\frac{20}{N}$	7	8	0.89	1220	1032	9	12	0.86	1418	1198
Synthetic-2	$\frac{1}{N}$	0	38	0.72	1213	1020	0	42	0.70	1395	1180
$F = 96,\ N = 96$	$\frac{5}{N}$	0	15	0.86	1170	987	0	18	0.84	1332	1127
	$\frac{10}{N}$	3	8	0.90	1188	1005	3	10	0.88	1370	1156
	$\frac{15}{N}$	4	5	0.91	1173	990	5	6	0.90	1345	1138
	$\frac{20}{N}$	5	4	0.91	1180	998	7	5	0.89	1353	1145
Synthetic-3	$\frac{1}{N}$	0	39	0.75	999	845	0	45	0.73	1153	973
$F = 100,\ N = 120$	$\frac{5}{N}$	0	15	0.89	1015	860	0	19	0.86	1165	988
	$\frac{10}{N}$	0	12	0.91	1025	867	2	14	0.88	1180	997
	$\frac{15}{N}$	2	8	0.92	1005	851	3	10	0.90	1155	975
	$\frac{20}{N}$	4	5	0.92	1010	852	5	8	0.90	1160	980

some is an instance. Explicit parallelism can be attributed to the fact that the selection, crossover and mutation operators can be performed in parallel over all the chromosomes in the population.

(c) The population of candidate solutions enables one to explore a diversity of solutions and hence a larger fraction of the search space. The Schema Theorem [8, 11] enables the GA to sample a large fraction of the search space even with a relatively small population size. This increases the chances of the GA being able to arrive at a globally optimal solution.

However, the CGA- and SSGA-based figure-ground separation techniques are seen to have the following shortcomings :

(a) The performance (especially that of the CGA) is extremely sensitive to the manner in which the chromosome is encoded. It is crucial that strongly interacting edgels have their corresponding bits positioned very close to each other on the chromosome and vice versa.

(b) The results are sensitive to the value of α especially when the encoding order is random. The value of α corresponding to the best observed result changes with the encoding scheme used.

(c) In the absence of a hill-climbing mechanism, the number of generations (and hence the execution time) needed for convergence is fairly large.

(d) With the incorporation of a deterministic hill-climbing mechanism the CGA and SSGA exhibit premature convergence to a suboptimal solution[2].

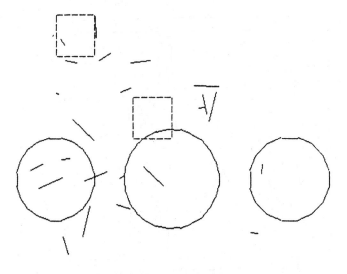

Fig. 8. SSGA results on edgel map of *Synthetic-1*

5 Conclusions and Future Directions

In this paper, the problem of figure–ground separation was tackled from the viewpoint of combinatorial optimization. A mathematical model encoding the figure–ground separation problem that makes explicit the definition of shape in terms of attributes such as cocircularity, smoothness, proximity and contrast was described. The model was based on the formulation of an energy function that incorporates pairwise interactions between local image features in the form of edgels and was shown to be isomorphic to the interacting spin (Ising) system from quantum physics. The desired edgel map was deemed to be the one that corresponded to the global minimum of the energy function.

Previous attempts at figure–ground separation via energy minimization have used deterministic optimization techniques based on relaxation and gradient descent-based search, and stochastic optimization techniques based on simulated annealing (SA) and microcanonical annealing (MCA). This paper explored the use of evolutionary algorithms, in particular, the canonical genetic algorithm (CGA) and the steady-state genetic algorithm (SSGA), in the context of figure–ground separation.

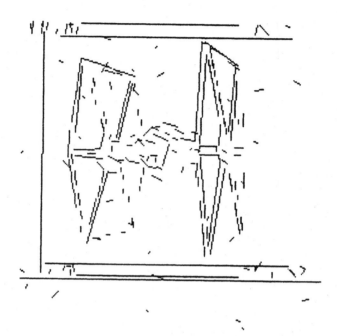

Fig. 9. SSGA results on edgel map of *Spaceship*

In spite of the computational advantage derived from the *Schema Theorem* and their inherent parallelism, evolutionary algorithms like the CGA and the SSGA were seen to suffer from certain inherent drawbacks in the context of the figure–ground separation problem. The CGA and SSGA showed a great degree of sensitivity to the value of the threshold α as well as to the manner in which the edgel map was encoded in the form of a chromosome. The absence of a hill climbing mechanism resulted in a large number of generations (and a correspondingly high execution time) for the convergence of the CGA and SSGA whereas the incorporation of a deterministic hill-climbing mechanism drove the CGA and SSGA towards premature convergence to a local minimum (i.e., a suboptimal solution).

In our future work we propose to design hybrid evolutionary algorithms that combine the stochastic hill-climbing and asymptotic convergence properties of SA and MCA algorithms with the *building blocks* property of the GA. We envisage that the hybrid evolutionary algorithms will combine the advantages and alleviate the shortcomings of both evolutionary algorithms and stochastic hill-climbing-based approaches.

References

1. S.T. Acton and A.C. Bovik, Anisotropic Edge Detection Using Mean Field Annealing, *Proc. IEEE Intl. Conf. Acoustics, Speech and Signal Processing*, Vol. II, pp. 393 – 396, 1992.

2. S.M. Bhandarkar, Y. Zhang and W.D. Potter, Edge Detection Using Genetic Algorithm-based Optimization, *Pattern Recognition*, Vol. 27, No. 9, pp. 1159 – 1180, Sept. 1994.

3. J. Canny, A Computational Approach to Edge Detection, *IEEE Trans. Pattern Analysis and Machine Intelligence*, Vol. 8, No. 6, pp. 679–698, Nov. 1986.

4. P. Carnevali, L. Coletti and S. Patarnello, Image Processing by Simulated Annealing, *IBM Jour. Res. and Dev.*, Vol. 29, No. 6, pp. 569–579, Nov. 1985.

5. L. Davis, *Handbook of Genetic Algorithms*, Van Nostrand Reinhold, New York, NY.

6. D.B. Fogel, An Introduction to Simulated Evolutionary Computation, *IEEE Trans. Neural Networks*, Vol. 5, No. 1, pp. 3–14, 1994.

7. S. Geman and D. Geman, Stochastic Relaxation, Gibbs Distribution and the Bayesian Restoration of Images, *IEEE Trans. Pattern Analysis and Machine Intelligence*, Vol. 6, pp. 721–741, 1984.

8. D. Goldberg, *Genetic Algorithms in Search, Optimization and Machine Learning*, Addison-Wesley Pub. Co., Reading, MA, 1988.

9. D. Gutfinger and J. Sklansky, Robust Classifiers by Mixed Adaptation, *IEEE Trans. Pattern Analysis and Machine Intelligence*, Vol. 13, No. 6, pp. 552–567, June 1991.

10. L. Herault and R. Horaud, Figure-Ground Discrimination: A Combinatorial Optimization Approach, *IEEE Trans. Pattern Analysis and Machine Intelligence*, Vol. 15, No. 9, pp. 899–914, Sept. 1993.

11. J.H. Holland, *Adaptation in Natural and Artificial Systems*, University of Michigan Press, Ann Arbor, MI, 1975.

12. S. Kirkpatrick, C. Gelatt Jr. and M. Vecchi, Optimization by Simulated Annealing, *Science*, Vol. 220, No. 4598, pp. 671–680, May 1983.

13. W. Kohler, *Gestalt Psychology*, Meridian Press, New York, NY, 1980.

14. P. Parent and S.W. Zucker, Trace Inference, Curvature Consistency and Curve Detection, *IEEE Trans. Pattern Analysis and Machine Intelligence*, Vol. 11, No. 8, pp. 823–839, Aug. 1989.

15. F. Romeo and A. Sangiovanni-Vincentelli, A Theoretical Framework for Simulated Annealing, *Algorithmica*, Vol. 6, pp. 302–345, 1991.

16. G. Roth and M.D. Levine, Geometric Primitive Extraction Using a Genetic Algorithm, *Proc. IEEE Intl. Conf. Comp. Vis. Patt. Recog.*, pp. 640–643, 1992.

17. T.J. Sejnowski and G.E. Hinton, Separating Figure from Ground with a Boltzmann Machine, in *Vision, Brain, and Cooperative Computation* (M. Arbib and A. Hanson, Eds.), MIT Press, Cambridge, MA, pp. 703–724, 1988.

18. A. Sha'ashua and S. Ullman, Structural Saliency: The Detection of Globally Salient Features Using a Locally Connected Network, *Proc. IEEE Intl. Conf. Computer Vision*, Tampa, FL, pp. 321–327, Dec. 1988.

Structural Models

Probabilistic Relaxation: Potential, Relationships and Open Problems

Josef Kittler

Centre for Vision, Speech and Signal Processing,
School of Electronic Engineering, Information Technology and Mathematics,
University of Surrey, Guildford GU2 5XH, United Kingdom

Abstract. We discuss the recent developments in probabilistic relaxation techniques which are used as a tool for contextual sensory data interpretation. The successes of a range of applications of probabilistic relaxation reported in the literature are briefly reviewed. We show that the implementation of a probabilistic relaxation process by means of multilayer perceptron computation has implications on the neural net design methodology. Further, the relationship of probabilistic relaxation to the Hough transform is exposed.

1 Introduction

Probabilistic relaxation refers to a family of techniques designed to achieve a global consistency when interpreting a network of interacting objects. Its origins go back to the seminal paper of Rosenfeld, Hummel and Zucker [10] which in turn was inspired by the work of Waltz [18] concerned with discrete relaxation. Waltz studied the problem of how to impose a global consistency on the labelling of idealised line drawings where the objects or object primitives are assumed to be given and therefore can be labelled unambiguously. Rosenfeld, Hummel and Zucker extended this work to a more realistic scenario where the objects to be labelled have to be extracted from noisy data and therefore their identity could be genuinely ambiguous. Their endeavour resulted in the replacement of the hard labels used by Waltz by label probabilities. This softening of labels appeared to have also computational benefits as the labelling process could be accomplished by a local iterative updating of each label probability, instead of the exhaustive search required by discrete relaxation.

The potential and promise of probabilistic relaxation as demonstrated in [10] spured a lot of interest in the approach which has been sustained over the last two decades. The effectiveness of probabilistic relaxation has been demonstrated on numerous applications including line and edge detection [20,21,15,25]. For a comprehensive list of applications the reader is referred to the review article of Kittler and Illingworth [12].

Notwithstanding its practical potential, the early applications of probabilistic relaxation unveiled many theoretical problems, including inherent bias of the updating process which was exhibited in no information experiments, questions relating to convergence, interpretation of the computed probabilities, and the specification of the compatibility coefficients and support functions [22], [23], [24]. A detailed account of the attempts to overcome these problems can be found in [12]. Most of these problems were overcome in two key papers published in the nineteen eighties [13], [14]. In [13] Hummel and Zucker laid down the theoretical foundations of probabilistic relaxation by formally defining the notion of consistency and by showing that under certain assumptions the optimization of a simple functional was synonymous with improving the consistency of object labelling. They also developed a constrained optimization procedure to optimize the functional by extending the work of Faugeras and Berthod [11].

In spite of this progress the relaxation process design methodology remained very heuristic until the publication of the work of Kittler and Hancock [14] which was aimed at providing theoretical underpinning of probabilistic relaxation using the Bayesian framework. It led to the development of an evidence combining formula which fuses observations and a priori contextual information in a theoretically sound manner. The polynomial combinatorial complexity of the approach has been avoided by means of introducing and developing the concept of label configuration dictionary. The methodology has been validated on problems of edge and line postprocessing [15], [25].

Two important criticisms of probabilistic relaxation, namely that

1. the process does not utilise measurement information with the exception of the initialisation stage where observations are used to compute the initial, noncontextual probabilities for the candidate labels at each object, and
2. the richest source of contextual observational information contained in object relations (binary relations) is never tapped,

have been overcome most recently [17], [16]. In this newly developed form the probabilistic relaxation has been demonstrated to have wide applicability from relaxation problems on a lattice [27] to graph matching problems [26].

The approach contrasts with discrete relaxation techniques exemplified by the iterative conditional modes algorithm (ICM) of Besag [2] and the works of Blake [6], Blake and Zisserman [7], Koch, Marroquin and Yuille [8], and Witkin, Terzopoulos and Kass [9]. Their stochastic optimization counterpart represented by the method developed by Geman and Geman [3] is based on the simulated annealing technique introduced in [5]. More recent are the attempts to use the mean field theory [4] to simplify and speed up the discrete optimization process. An alternative to stochastic optimisation is offered by the idea of a label error process which has been introduced by Hancock and Kittler [19] to cope with the two fundamental problems of the original Waltz's algorithm [18]: i) inadmissible label configurations introduced by initial object labelling and ii) the optimization process deadlock. The idea has been extended from lattice structures to general object arrangements in [46,47].

The paper concentrates on the recent developments in probabilistic relaxation. First, mathematical preliminaries are introduced in Section 2. Section 3 contains a review of the recent results in probabilistic relaxation which incorporate observations on relational information about the interacting objects.

Section 4 relates probabilistic relaxation to other well known object recognition approaches, i.e. neural networks and the Hough transform. These relationships can be exploited by importing the positive features of one technique to benefit another method. For instance, the computational efficiency of the Hough transform could suggest how to reduce the computational complexity of probabilistic relaxation. Outstanding problems which include label probability amplification for weakly supported objects, and label probability dilution for objects with multiple interpretations are briefly discussed in Section 5. Finally, Section 6 concludes with a summary of the paper.

2 Preliminaries

Probabilistic relaxation addresses one of the most important aspects of machine perception, namely object recognition. The term object is understood here in a very general sense and covers not only 2D and 3D geometric entities but also physical phenomena and events. Moreover, as objects are often represented as composites of object primitives we shall view the problem of object recognition in machine perception as one of labelling object primitives. Effectively, the same type of primitive can be labelled in different ways depending on the object it is a part of. The set of admissible labels for each object primitive will then depend on the goal of interpretation, which should specify the hypothesised objects either by means of external input from the user of the sensory system, or by object invocation from bottom up processing.

Naturally, the complexity of objects may be such that a single level representation may be inadequate for capturing the details of the object description. It will then be necessary to adopt a hierarchical representation whereby object primitives at one level become objects at a lower level of representation. Bearing this fluidity of terminology in mind, in the future discussion, rather than referring to object primitives and their identity, we shall simply talk about object labelling where a collection of objects defines some perceptually significant whole.

Let us consider a set of measurement vectors $\mathbf{x}_j$, representing respectively objects $a_j, j = 1, ..., N$ arranged in a network with a particular neighbourhood system. Each component of vector $\mathbf{x}_j$ denotes one of three types of measurements:

1. Binary relation measurements A_{ji}^k, $k = 1, 2, ..., m$ between the jth and i^{th} objects.
2. Unary relation measurements y_j^l, $l = 1, 2, ..., r$ from which the binary relations are derived.
3. Unary relation measurements v_j^i, $i = 1, 2, ..., n$ which augment the observational evidence about node j but do not serve as a basis for deriving binary relation measurements A_{ji}^k.

Let us arrange these measurements into vectors as follows:

$$\mathbf{A}_j = \begin{bmatrix} \mathcal{A}_{j1} \\ \cdot \\ \cdot \\ \mathcal{A}_{j(j-1)} \\ \mathcal{A}_{j(j+1)} \\ \cdot \\ \cdot \\ \mathcal{A}_{jN} \end{bmatrix} \tag{1}$$

where

$$\mathcal{A}_{ji} = [A_{ji}^1, ..., A_{ji}^m]^T. \tag{2}$$

For the unary relations we have

$$\mathbf{y}_j = [y_j^1, ..., y_j^r]^T \tag{3}$$

and

$$\mathbf{v}_j = [v_j^1, ..., v_j^n]^T \tag{4}$$

Thus $\mathbf{x}_j$ is an $[m(N-1) + r + n]$ dimensional vector which can be written as

$$\mathbf{x}_j = \begin{bmatrix} \mathbf{v}_j \\ \mathbf{y}_j \\ \mathbf{A}_j \end{bmatrix} \tag{5}$$

We wish to assign each object a_j a label θ_j. We shall consider the problem of object labelling in the framework of the Bayesian decision theory. The theoretical result underpinning the design of any object classification system is the Bayes decision rule (e.g. Devijver and Kittler, 1982 [1]). In its general form it specifies how best decisions about class membership of objects can be made taking into account the probability distribution of the measurements providing observational evidence about the objects.

Following the conventional Bayesian approach object a_i would be assigned to class ω_r based on the information conveyed by measurement vectors $\mathbf{v}_i$ and $\mathbf{y}_i$ according to the minimum error decision rule [1]. However, objects by definition do not exist in isolation. Thus the distinguishing feature of object labelling problems in machine perception is that we deal with a large network of objects which interact with each other. The a priori world knowledge or context can be used to help to disambiguate decisions based simply on noisy features of individual objects. For instance in text recognition individual characters are an integral part of larger objects such as words or sentences formed by character groups. Word dictionary and rules of grammar dictate which combinations of characters and implicitly which individual characters are possible. In contextual labelling we effectively associate with each object a decision making process which attempts to combine evidence from observations made on the object together with the contextual information conveyed by the other objects in the network to deduce which label assignment is most appropriate from the point of view of the available measurement information, local constraints and global labelling consistency.

Thus in contrast here we wish to decide about label θ_i using not only the information contained in unary relation measurements relating to object a_i but also any context conveyed by the network. In other words we wish to utilise also the binary relation measurements, i.e. the full measurement vector $\mathbf{x}_i$ plus all the information about the other objects in the network contained in $\mathbf{x}_j$, $\forall j \neq i$. This is a general statement of the problem but in order to develop contextual labelling schemes our formulation will have to be somewhat more precise.

The contextual labelling problem can be formulated either as the *object centered* or *message centered* interpretation. In object centered interpretation the emphasis is on one node at a time. Contextual information is used to reduce the ambiguity of labelling a single object. Note that object centered interpretation does not guarantee that the global interpretation makes sense. For example, individually most likely object categories in a character recognition problem will not necessarily combine into valid words. The use of context merely reduces the chance of the global labelling being inconsistent.

In contrast, message centered interpretation is concerned with getting the message conveyed by sensory data right. In our text recognition problem the main objective of message centered labelling would be to label characters so that each line of text gives a sequence of valid words. Generally speaking, in message centered interpretation we search for a joint labelling $\theta_1 = \omega_{\theta_1}, \theta_2 = \omega_{\theta_2}, ..., \theta_N = \omega_{\theta_N}$ which explains observations $\mathbf{x}_1, \mathbf{x}_2, ..., \mathbf{x}_N$ made on the objects in the network. The most appropriate measure of fit between data and interpretation (but by no means the only one) is the aposteriori probability $P(\theta_1 = \omega_{\theta_1}, ..., \theta_N = \omega_{\theta_N} | \mathbf{x}_1, ..., \mathbf{x}_N)$.

The object centered counterpart computes, instead $P(\theta_i = \omega_{\theta_i} | \mathbf{x}_1, \mathbf{x}_2, .., \mathbf{x}_N)$, the aposteriori probability of label θ_i given all the observations which can be rewritten as

$$P(\theta_i = \omega | \mathbf{x}_1, ..., \mathbf{x}_N) = \frac{p(\mathbf{x}_1, ..., \mathbf{x}_N | \theta_i = \omega)\hat{p}(\theta_j = \omega)}{p(\mathbf{x}_1, ..., \mathbf{x}_N)} \qquad (6)$$

where $\hat{p}(\theta_j = \omega)$ is the a priori probability of label θ_i taking value ω. Note that the denominator in (6) can be dismissed. We can expand the first term of the numerator over all possible labellings in the usual fashion, i.e.

$$p(\mathbf{x}_1, .., \mathbf{x}_N | \theta_i = \omega) = \sum_{\Omega_1} .. \sum_{\Omega_j} .. \sum_{\Omega_N} p(\mathbf{x}_1, .., \mathbf{x}_N, \theta_1, ..\theta_j.., \theta_N | \theta_i = \omega) =$$

$$= \sum_{\Omega_1} .. \sum_{\Omega_j} .. \sum_{\Omega_N} p(\mathbf{x}_1, .., \mathbf{x}_N | \theta_1, ..\theta_i = \omega.., \theta_N) P(\theta_1, ..\theta_j.., \theta_N | \theta_i = \omega) \quad \forall j \neq i (7)$$

where Ω_i is the set of labels admitted by object a_i. For simplicity we shall assume that

$$\Omega_i = \{\omega_0, \omega_1, ..., \omega_M\} = \Omega \qquad \forall i$$

where ω_0 is the null label used to label objects for which no other label is appropriate. Thus we finally find

$$P(\theta_i = \omega | \mathbf{x}_1, \ldots, \mathbf{x}_N) =$$
$$= \frac{\sum_{\Omega_1} \cdots \sum_{\Omega_j} \cdots \sum_{\Omega_N} p(\mathbf{x}_1, \ldots, \mathbf{x}_N | \theta_1, \ldots \theta_i = \omega \ldots, \theta_N) P(\theta_1, \ldots \theta_i = \omega \ldots, \theta_N)}{p(\mathbf{x}_1, \ldots, \mathbf{x}_N)} \quad (8)$$

where the first term of the product in the numerator, the conditional joint probability density function $p(\mathbf{x}_1, \ldots, \mathbf{x}_N | \theta_1, \ldots, \theta_N)$ of measurement vectors $\mathbf{x}_1, \ldots, \mathbf{x}_N$ models the measurement process. The second term embodies our a priori knowledge of the likelihood of various combinations of labels occurring. It is our global, world model.

Thus computing the probability of a particular label ω on a single object a_i amounts to scanning through all the possible combinations of labels $\theta_1, \ldots, \theta_N$ with label θ_i set to ω and summing up the corresponding products of the respective joint measurement and label probabilities.

Finally, an important and physically realistic assumption regarding the unary measurement process distribution is that the outcomes of measurements are conditionally independent.

$$p(\mathbf{v}_1, \mathbf{y}_1 \ldots, \mathbf{v}_N, \mathbf{y}_N | \theta_1, \ldots \theta_i, \ldots, \theta_N) = \Pi_{i=1}^{N} p(\mathbf{v}_i, \mathbf{y}_i | \theta_i = \omega_{\theta_i}) \quad (9)$$

For binary relations, on the other hand, we assume that

$$p(\mathcal{A}_{i1}, \ldots, \mathcal{A}_{iN} | \theta_1, \ldots \theta_i, \ldots, \theta_N) = \prod_{j \neq i} p(\mathcal{A}_{ij} | \theta_i, \theta_j) \quad (10)$$

3 Probabilistic Relaxation

Under some mild conditional independence assumptions concerning measurements $\mathbf{v}_j$, $\mathbf{y}_j$ and $\mathcal{A}_{ij}$, $\forall j$ the object centered labelling formulation (8) leads to an iterative probability updating formula [16]

$$P^{(n+1)}(\theta_i = \omega_{\theta_i}) = \frac{P^{(n)}(\theta_i = \omega_{\theta_i}) Q^{(n)}(\theta_i = \omega_{\theta_i})}{\sum_{\omega_\lambda \in \Omega} P^{(n)}(\theta_i = \omega_\lambda) Q^{(n)}(\theta_i = \omega_\lambda)} \quad (11)$$

where $P^{(n)}(\theta_i = \omega_{\theta_i})$ denotes the probability of label ω_{θ_i} at object a_i at the nth iteration of the updating process and the quantity $Q^{(n)}(\theta_i = \omega_\alpha)$ expresses the support the label $\theta_i = \omega_\alpha$ receives at the nth iteration step from the other objects in the scene, taking into consideration the binary relations that exist between them and object a_i. (11) represents a generic probabilistic relaxation process. After the first iteration (n=1) the computed entity is the contextual aposteriori class probability $P(\theta_i = \omega_{\theta_i} | \mathbf{x}_1, \mathbf{x}_2, \ldots, \mathbf{x}_N)$. With the increasing value of n the updating scheme drives the probabilistic labelling into a hard labelling.

The support $Q^{(n)}(\theta_i = \omega_{\theta_i})$ is defined as

$$Q^{(n)}(\theta_i = \omega_{\theta_i}) = \quad (12)$$

$$\sum_{\omega_{\theta_j}, j \in N_i} \frac{P\left(\theta_j = \omega_{\theta_j}, \forall j \in N_i\right)}{\hat{p}\left(\theta_i = \omega_{\theta_i}\right)} \left\{ \prod_{j \in N_i} \frac{P^{(n)}\left(\theta_j = \omega_{\theta_j}\right) p\left(A_{ij} | \theta_i = \omega_{\theta_i}, \theta_j = \omega_{\theta_j}\right)}{\hat{p}\left(\theta_j = \omega_{\theta_j}\right)} \right\}$$

where $p\left(A_{ij} | \theta_i = \omega_{\theta_i}, \theta_j = \omega_{\theta_j}\right)$ is the compatibility coefficient quantifying the mutual support of the labelling $(\theta_i = \omega_{\theta_i}, \theta_j = \omega_{\theta_j})$. N_i denotes the index set of all nodes exluding the node i, i.e.

$$N_i = \{1, 2, ...i - 1, i + 1, ..., N\} \tag{13}$$

It is worth noting that when binary relations are not used the support function (12) becomes the standard evidence combining formula developed in [14], i.e.

$$Q^{(n)}(\theta_i = \omega_{\theta_i}) = \tag{14}$$

$$\sum_{\omega_{\theta_j}, j \in N_i} \frac{1}{\hat{p}\left(\theta_i = \omega_{\theta_i}\right)} \left\{ \prod_{j \in N_i} \frac{P^{(n)}\left(\theta_j = \omega_{\theta_j}\right)}{\hat{p}\left(\theta_j = \omega_{\theta_j}\right)} \right\} \times P\left(\theta_j = \omega_{\theta_j}, \forall j \in N_i\right)$$

On the other hand, when no additional unary relation measurements are available apart from the set used for generating the binary measurements, the support reduces to

$$Q^{(n)}(\theta_i = \omega_{\theta_i}) = \tag{15}$$

$$\sum_{\omega_{\theta_j}, j \in N_i} \frac{1}{\hat{p}\left(\theta_i = \omega_{\theta_i}\right)} \left\{ \prod_{j \in N_i} p\left(A_{ij} | \theta_i = \omega_{\theta_i}, \theta_j = \omega_{\theta_j}\right) \right\} \times P\left(\theta_j = \omega_{\theta_j}, \forall j \in N_i\right)$$

The probability updating rule (15) in this particular case will act as an inefficient maximum value selection operator. Thus the updating process can be terminated after the first iteration, the maximum contextual aposteriori label probability selected and set to unity while the probability of all the other labels to zero.

The support function (12) exhibits exponential complexity. In practice its use, depending on application, could be limited only to a contextual neighbourhood in the vicinity of the object being interpreted. Such a measure is appropriate for instance in the case of edge and line postprocessing where the objects to be labelled are pixel sites. A small neighbourhood, say a 3 by 3 window may be sufficient to provide the necessary contextual information. In any case by iteratively updating the pixel label probabilities using formula (11) contextual information would be drawn from increasingly larger neighbourhoods of each pixel.

A more dramatic, complementary reduction in the computational complexity is achieved by noting that in practice many potential label configurations in the contextual neighbourhood of an object are physically inadmissible. By listing the admissible labellings in a dictionary, the above support function can be evaluated by summing up only over the entries $\left(\theta_j = \omega_{\theta_j}^k, \forall j \in N_i\right)$, $\forall k$ in the dictionary [15], i.e.

$$Q^{(n)}(\theta_i = \omega_{\theta_i}) = \tag{16}$$

$$\sum_{k=1}^{Z(\omega_{\theta_i})} \frac{P\left(\theta_j = \omega_{\theta_j}, \forall j \in N_i\right)}{\hat{p}\left(\theta_i = \omega_{\theta_i}\right)} \left\{ \prod_{j \in N_i} \frac{P^{(n)}\left(\theta_j = \omega_{\theta_j}^k\right) p\left(A_{ij} | \theta_i = \omega_{\theta_i}, \theta_j = \omega_{\theta_j}^k\right)}{\hat{p}\left(\theta_j = \omega_{\theta_j}^k\right)} \right\}$$

where $Z(\omega_{\theta_i})$ denotes the number of dictionary entries with label θ_i set to ω_{θ_i}.

In many labelling problems neither of the above simplifications of the support function is appropriate. For instance, in correspondence matching tasks or object recognition all features of an object interact directly with each other. Moreover, without measurements, no labelling configuration is a priori more likely than any other. Then it is reasonable to assume that the prior probability of a joint labelling configuration can be expressed as

$$P\left(\theta_j = \omega_{\theta_j}, \forall j \in N_i\right) = \prod_{j \in N_i} \hat{p}\left(\theta_j = \omega_{\theta_j}\right) \tag{17}$$

Substituting (17) into (12) and noting that each factor in the product in the above expression depends on the label of only one other object apart from the object a_i under consideration, we can simplify the support computation as

$$Q^{(n)}(\theta_i = \omega_\alpha) = \prod_{j \in N_i} \sum_{\omega_\beta \in \Omega} P^{(n)}(\theta_j = \omega_\beta) p(A_{ij} | \theta_i = \omega_\alpha, \theta_j = \omega_\beta) \tag{18}$$

It is interesting to note that through this simplification the exponential complexity of the problem is eliminated.

A further simplification can be made under the assumption that the contextual support provided by the neighbouring objects is weak, i.e. it differs only marginally from some nominal value p_o representing indifference. In such situations the product evidence combination rule can be approximated by a sum rule

$$Q^{(n)}(\theta_i = \omega_\alpha) = \sum_{j \in N_i} \sum_{\omega_\beta \in \Omega} P^{(n)}(\theta_j = \omega_\beta) [p(A_{ij} | \theta_i = \omega_\alpha, \theta_j = \omega_\beta) - p_o] \tag{19}$$

which resembles the original support function suggested in [10]. The updating rule in (19) represents a benevolent information fusion operator, in contrast to the severe fusion operator constituted by the product rule.

The iteration scheme can be initialised by considering as $P^{(0)}(\theta_i = \omega_{\theta_i})$ the probabilities computed by using the unary attributes only, i.e.

$$P^{(0)}(\theta_i = \omega_{\theta_i}) = P(\theta_i = \omega_{\theta_i} | \mathbf{v}_i, \mathbf{y}_i) \tag{20}$$

We discuss this initialisation process in detail elsewhere [16]. The problem of estimating the binary relation distributions is addressed in [33,34]. The computational complexity of the iterative process can be reduced by pruning the binary relations taking into account auxilary information about the problem being solved [35].

4 Potential and Relationships

The probabilistic relaxation has been used successfully in a number of application domains. It has been applied to object recognition based on colour using a colour adjacency graph representation [40]. The technique has been used to solve the correspondence problem in stereo matching [26]. It has been found useful in 2D shape recognition [45] and is applicable also to 3D object recognition [43]. It has been demonstrated to have the potential to establish an accurate registration between infrared image data obtained by an airborne sensor and a digital map for the purposes of autonomous navigation [26], and in vision based docking [44].

In the following subsections we discuss the relationship of the probabilistic relaxation with other approaches.

4.1 Multilayer Perceptron

The aim of this section is to demonstrate how the probabilistic relaxation processes discussed in Section 3 can be mapped on neural net architectures. The purpose of the mapping is at least twofold. First of all, neural net computation has inspired and motivated a considerable activity in specialist hardware and software architecture design and implementation. Software, and hardware systems, including VLSI chips, have been developed to implement various families of neural networks. A successful mapping of contextual decision making processes on such systems would facilitate their wide applicability.

The second, and perhaps more significant purpose is to argue that the mapping process could offer a route to neural network design which is not plagued by the typical problems associated with the development of neural network solutions to pattern classification tasks: lack of guidelines for the choice of architecture and node connectivity, lack of data, unacceptably long training phase, and the last but not the least, the lack of criteria for the selection of the node activation functions and for the weight initialization.

Rather than attempting a comprehensive coverage of all the updating formulae discussed in the paper, we shall illustrate the basic ideas for a relaxation labelling process. In particular, we shall consider the probabilistic ralaxation scheme in (11) with the support function given in formula (18). A neural network performing the same computation is presented in Figure 1 [38,37]. It is basically a multilayer perceptron with two main layers and an auxilary layer which performs a normalisation computation to maintain the network outputs in the zero - one range and ensuring that the outputs representing label excitation for each object primitive sum up to a unity. There are only N such auxilary units as there are N object primitives to be labelled. The inputs P_{ij} to the multilayer perceptron are computed by a noncontextual artificial neural network which at its input is stimulated by unary relation measurements observed for each object primitive. We shall not dwell on the methodology that can be used for designing such a neural network as the number of unary measurements one deals with is normally relatively small and therefore the neural net design problems identified earlier are not applicable. The outputs P_{ij} of this initializing

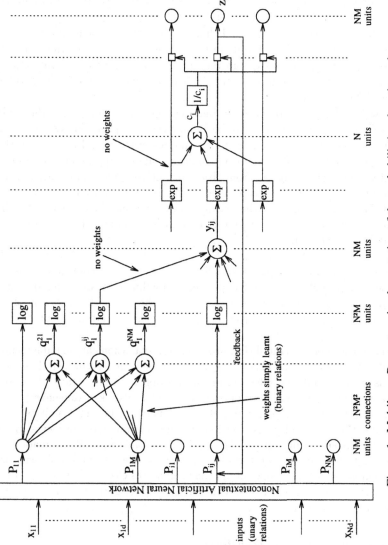

Figure 1: Multilayer Perceptron implementation of the probabilistic relaxation scheme with support function (18)

network correspond to the aposteriori (noncontextual) label probabilities for the object primitives based on the unary relations.

The main network has the normal characteristics of a typical multilayer perceptron design. The number of units in the second layer expands wheras for the final layer it contracts. In our design the number of output units is the same as the number of input units to the network with a separate unit for each object primitive/label combination.

The weights applied to the links between the input nodes and the nodes of the second layer are defined by the binary relation probabilities which can be easily estimated during training by techniques of statistical inference rather than weight adaption [33]. The output of each node q_i^{jk} represents the support for label k on object primitive j from object primitive i. Note that the activation function of the units in the second layer is the *log* function and not the usual sigmoid. The connections from the second layer to the third layer have no weights associated with them. The activation function of the units in this third layer is the exponential function.

A distinguishing characteristic of the network is the feedback link from the normalised output to the input. If this link is broken, the output units generate the contextual probabilities of object primitive labelling corresponding to a single iteration of the label updating process in (11). The feedback forces one of the outputs associated with each object primitive to a unity and all the others to a zero.

We have thus demonstrated that probabilistic relaxation can be implemented as a multilayer perceptron. This relationship can be exploited in neural network design as it can guide the selection of an appropriate architecture, the choice of the activation functions, inteconnectivity, and feedback arrangements. But even more importantly, the training of such a network becomes a simple task of inferring the probability distributions of the relevant measurements in low dimensional spaces. A first guess of these distributions can easily be made from the presentation of very few prototypical patterns to the system. In this sense the training capability of the proposed approach emulates closely that of the human central nervous system which also can learn complex patterns very efficiently from just a few experiences.

4.2 Generalised Hough Transform

The Generalised Hough Transform (**GTH**) devised by [28] an applied to many problems [29,30] can be briefly described in terms of graph terminology as follows. An object model is represented in terms of a look-up table. An entry of the look-up table represents a binary relation between a virtual reference node and an object primitive node. The unary properties of the object node are used as an index into the look-up table. An accumulator array is set up over the domain of parameters which characterise the reference node and the array is initialised. During the recognition process the unary relations on a node are used to index into the precomputed object look-up table and the corresponding binary relations are used to calculate the parameters of the reference node which would be consistent with the evidence furnished by the node. The corresponding cell of the accumulator has its counter incremented by one. When all the evidence is mapped into the parameter space via the look-up table, local peaks are searched for in the accumulator array. Each such peak of sufficient height indicates an instance of a hypothesised object.

The original **GTH** scheme is very inefficient in terms of storage requirements as any multidimensional parameter space requires a huge accumulator array associated with it. The storage space grows exponentially with the number of parameters characterising the unknown reference point. This shortcoming motivated Lee et al [31] to propose a method whereby the object reference point is confined to be coincident with one of the object primitives which should be present in the image. Each image feature (object primitive) has a counter associated with it. Image evidence for a given hypothesis is accumulated by indetifying, via the binary relations stored in the look-up table, the corresponding candidate reference node and verifying, whether this node exists in the image. Provided the reference node is contained in the image, the available image evidence should coherently vote for the object reference node. A vote exceeding a prespecified threshold would be indicative of an instance of the hypothesised object in the image. In order to make the approach resilient to occlusion which could cause the object reference node to be missing from the image, and consequently the proposed **GTH** process would fail to detect the instantiated object, one can use several reference points, each associated with a distinct feature of the model.

Suppose that an object is represented by a set Ω of M primitives, $\Omega = \{\omega_k|\ k = 1, ..., M\}$ and each primitive is treated as a reference node. It is interesting to note that the Hough transform can be viewed to compute evidencial support for the hypothesis that observed image primitive a_i, $i = 1, ...N$ corresponds to a reference node ω, i.e. $\theta_i = \omega$ as

$$H(\theta_i = \omega) = \sum_{j=1}^{N} \sum_{\omega_{\theta_j} \epsilon \Omega} P(\theta_j = \omega_{\theta_j}) q(\mathcal{A}_{ij}|\theta_i = \omega, \theta_j = \omega_{\theta_j}) \qquad (21)$$

where $q(\mathcal{A}_{ij}|\theta_i, \theta_j)$ represents the compatibility of the binary relation $\mathcal{A}_{ij}$ of nodes a_i and a_j interpreted as $\theta_i = \omega$ and $\theta_j = \omega_{\theta_j}$, with the entry in the look-up table. The probability $P(\theta_j = \omega_{\theta_j})$ reflects the information content of the unary measurement associated with object a_j. If the measurement identifies precisely the appropriate entry in the look-up table, the probability value will be one. When, from the point of view of indexing into the look-up table, the information content of the unary measurement is minimal, the probability will have a uniform distribution, i.e. $P(\theta_j = \omega_{\theta_j}) = \frac{1}{M}$.

Conventionally, the voting kernel would be a top hat function but recently it has been recognised that in order to ensure robustness to contamination the kernel shape should be smooth. It has been shown in [41,42,39] that a parabolic kernel smoothly approaching zero at the boundaries of a window defining the width of the feature error distribution has such properties but a number of other robust kernels have been suggested in the literature.

Now the voting function in (21) has a close similarity with the sum updating formula (19). In principle the two computational processes are the same. However, their implementation in practice would differ. The Hough transform tends to look simultaneously for an instance of an object and its pose (transformation between the model and its instance in the data). Thus for every candidate transformation the probability $P(\theta_j = \omega_{\theta_j})$ would pick a unique correspondence between nodes and the formula (21) simply performs a hypothesis verification. The probabilistic relaxation scheme in (19), on the orther hand, compounds all the pose hypotheses by allowing $P(\theta_j = \omega_{\theta_j})$ to be distributed over all the possible correspondences. From the point of view of the Hough transform this process is based on the premise that all the incorrect pose hypotheses will contribute as supporting evidence in an incoherent way and therefore they will not obscure the true solution to the data interpretation problem. However, as a result of iteration the distribution of the label probabilities sharpens and eventually the relaxation algorithm will be performing the verification process in exactly the same way as the Hough transform.

5 Outstanding Problems

The partition function in the probability updating formulas, which normalises the updated values so that they satisfy the axiomatic properties of probabilities, may cause some problems. The normalisation function is a consequence of the assumption that two conflicting interpetations of the same object are mutually exclusive outcomes of one event. This assumption does not hold when one deals with objects which for one reason or another have multiple interpretations. In such situations, rather than accepting all valid interpretations, probabilistic relaxation process will tend to distribute the probability mass over all admissible labellings. This may result in a *dilution of label probabilities* even below the level of noise.

Second, even when the observational evidence does not support any valid interpretation, the partition function will normalise the weak contextual support to sum up to one. The effect of the normalisation process will be *label probability amplification*. This problem is traditionally handled by means of a null attractor but its design so that it is neither over competitive nor over modest is quite difficult, requiring a careful tuning. In a recent paper [32] these two problems were overcome by adopting an evidence combination framework based on the fuzzy set theory. However, within the probabilistic framework no solution to these problems has been found to date.

Another open issue is whether unary measurements should be brought to bare their influence on the probability updating process. Conventionally, the process is deemed to start from noncontextual label probabilities which are then refined using contextual support from the neighbouring objects. The formula (12) and those derived from it incorporate the binary relation information throughout the updating process but not the unary measurement information. Although one can develop, via the Baum Eagon theorem, a probability updating formula which includes unary relations during iteration, any positive benefit of this information source on the final interpretation result is far from evident as demonstrated in [36].

There is also some argument whether one should be updating the noncontextual posterior probabilities or the noncontextual priors. The latter would have implications on the claim that formula (15) is noniterative. Hopefully, these issues will be resolved in the future. However, the successes achieved with and attributed to probabilistic relaxation algorithms in their current form moderate any sense of urgency one might otherwise feel about these problems.

6 Conclusions

The recent developments in probabilistic relaxation techniques which are commonly used as a tool for contextual sensory data interpretation have been discussed. The successes of a range of practical applications of probabilistic relaxation reported in the literature have been reviewed. We then showed that the implementation of a probabilistic relaxation process by means of multilayer perceptron computation had implications on the neural net design methodology. In particular, the computational structure suggests what architecture, node connectivity, activation function and feedback a multilayer perceptron should have to be able to solve complex contextual decision making problems. Further, the relationship of probabilistic relaxation to the Hough transform has been exposed. It has been shown that probabilistic relaxation, in the first iterations, can be viewed as a hypothesis generation process. As the iterations proceed, the nature of the computation changes into a hypothesis verification process.

7 Acknowledgements

This work was supported by the Science and Engineering Research Council, UK (GR/J89255).

References

1. P A Devijver and J Kittler, Pattern recognition: A statistical approach, Prentice-Hall, Englewood Cliffs, NJ, 1982.
2. J Besag, On the satatistical analysis of dirty pictures, *Journal Royal Statist. Society*, **48**, Series B, 259-302, 1986.
3. S Geman and D Geman, Stochastic relaxation, Gibbs distributions and the Bayesian restoration of images, *IEEE Trans. Pattern Analysis and Machine Intelligence*, **PAMI-6**, 721-741, 1984.
4. D Geiger and F Girosi, Parallel and deterministic algorithms from MRF's: Surface reconstruction, *IEEE Trans. Pattern Analysis and Machine Intelligence*, **PAMI-13**, 181-188, 1991.
5. S Kirkpatrick, C D Gellatt and M P Vecchi, Optimization by simulated annealing, *Science*, **220**, 671-680, 1983.

6. A Blake, The least disturbance principle and weak constraints, *Pattern Recognition Letters*, **1**, 393-399, 1983.

7. A Blake and A Zisserman, Visual reconstruction, MIT Press, Cambridge MA, 1987.

8. C Koch, J Marroquin and A Yuille, Analog neuronal networks in early vision, *Proc Nat. Academic Science*, **83**, 4263-4267, 1986.

9. A Witkin, D Terzopoulos and M Kass, Signal matching through scale space, *Intern. Journal Computer Vision*, 133-144, 1987.

10. A Rosenfeld, R Hummel and S Zucker, Scene labeling by relaxation operations, *IEEE Trans System Man and Cybernetics*, **SMC-6**, 420-433, 1976.

11. O Faugeras and M Berthod, Improving consistency and reducing ambiguity in stochastic labeling, *IEEE Trans. Pattern Analysis and Machine Intelligence*, **PAMI-3**, 412-423, 1981.

12. J Kittler and J Illingworth, A review of relaxation labelling algorithms, *Image and Vision Computing*, **3**, 206,216, 1985.

13. R Hummel and S Zucker, On the foundations of relaxation labeling process, *IEEE Trans. Pattern Analysis and Machine Intelligence*, **PAMI-5**, 267-286, 1983.

14. J Kittler and E R Hancock, Combining evidence in probabilistic relaxation, *Intern. Journal of Pattern Recognition and Artificial Intelligence*, **3**, 29-51, 1989.

15. E R Hancock and J Kittler, Edge labeling using dictionary-based relaxation, *IEEE Trans. Pattern Analysis and Machine Intelligence*, **PAMI-12**, 165-181, 1990.

16. J Kittler, W J Christmas and M Petrou, Probabilistic relaxation for matching problems in computer vision, *Proc 4th Intern. Conference on Computer Vision*, Berlin, 1993.

17. J Kittler, P Papachristou and M Petrou, Combining evidence in dictionary based probabilistic relaxation *Proc 8th Scandinavian Conference on Image Analysis*, Tromso, 1993.

18. D L Waltz, Understanding line drawings of scenes with shadows, in *The Psychology of Computer Vision*, P H Winston, ed., McGraw-Hill, New York, 1975.

19. E R Hancock and J Kittler, Discrete relaxation, *Pattern Recognition*, **23**, 711-733, 1990.

20. S Peleg and A Rosenfeld, Determining compatibility coefficients for curve enhancement relaxation processes, *IEEE Trans Systems, Man and Cybernetics*, **SMC-8**, 548-555, 1978.

21. S Zucker, R Hummel and A Rosenfeld, An application of relaxation labelling to line and curve enhancement, *IEEE Tranc Computers*, **C-26**, 394-404, 1977.

22. R M Haralick, An interpretation of probabilistic relaxation, *Computer Vision, Graphics and Image Processing*, **22**, 388-395, 1983.

23. R L Kirby, A product rule relaxation method, *Computer Graphics and Image Processing*, **13**, 158-189, 1985.

24. S Peleg, A new probabilistic relaxation scheme, *IEEE Trans. Pattern Analysis and Machine Intelligence*, **PAMI-2**, 362-369, 1980.

25. E R Hancock and J Kittler, Relaxation refinement of intensity ridges, *Proc 11th Internat. Conference on Pattern Recognition*, 459-463, 1992.

26. W J Christmas, J Kittler and M Petrou, Structural matching in computer vision using probabilistic relaxation, *IEEE Trans Pattern Analysis and Machine Intelligence*, **PAMI-17**, 749-764, 1995.

27. J Kittler, P Papachristou and M Petrou, Probabilistic relaxation in line postprocessing, *Proc Workshop on Statistical Methods in Pattern Recognition*, Tromso, 1993.

28. D H Ballard, Generalising the Hough Transform to detect arbitrary shapes, *Pattern Recognition*, **13**, 111-122, 1981.

29. J Illingworth and J Kittler, A survey of the Hough Transform, *Computer Vision, Graphics and Image Processing*, **44**, 87-116, 1988.
30. A Califano and R Mohan, Multidimensional indexing for recognising visual shapes, *Proc. IEEE Conf. Computer Vision and Pattern Recognition*, 28-34, 1991.
31. H M Lee, J Kittler and K C Wong, Generalised Hough Transform in object recognition, *Proc. 11th International Conference on Pattern Recognition*, 285-289, 1992.
32. Z Shao and J Kittler, Fuzzy non-iterative ARG labelling with multiple interpretations, *Proc 13th Internat. Conf. on Pattern Recognition*, **II-B**, 181-185, 1996.
33. W J Christmas, J Kittler and M Petrou, Probabilistic feature-labelling schemes: modelling compatibility coefficient distributions, *Image and Vision Computing*, **14**, 617-625, 1996.
34. M Pelillo and M Refice, Learning compatibility coefficients for relaxation labelling, *IEEE Trans Pattern Analysis and Machine Intelligence*, **PAMI-16**, 933-945, 1994.
35. W J Christmas, J Kittler and M Petrou, Labelling 2-D geometric primitives using probabilistic relaxation: reducing the computational requirements, *Electronic Letters*, **32**, 312-314, 1996.
36. A J Stoddart, M Petrou and J Kittler, A new algorithm for probabilistic relaxation based on the Baum Eagon theorem, *Proceedings of the 6th International Conference on Computer Analysis of Images and Patterns*, V Hlavac and R Sara eds., 647-679, Springer-Verlag, Berlin, 1995.
37. W J Christmas, J Kittler and M Petrou, Analytical approaches to the neural network architecture design, *in Pattern Recognition in Practice IV: Multiple Paradigms, Comparative Studies and Hybrid Systems*, E S Gelsema and L Kanal Eds., 325-335, North Holland, Amsterdam 1994.
38. J Kittler, relaxation methods and their neural net implementation, *From Statistics to Neural Networks*, V Cherkasky and H Wechsler, Eds., Springer Verlag, Berlin, 1994.
39. P L Palmer, J Kittler and M Petrou, A Hough transform algorithm with a 2D hypothesis testing kernel, *Proceedings of the 11th IAPR International Conference on Pattern Recognition*, 1992.
40. J. Matas, R Marik and J Kittler, Colour-based object recognition under spectrally non-uniform illumination, *Image and Vision Computing*, **13**, 663-669, 1995.
41. J Princen, J Illingworth and J Kittler, Hypothesis testing: a framework for analysing and optimising Hough transform performance, *IEEE Transactions on Pattern Analysis and Machine Intelligence*, **16**, 329-341, 1994.
42. J Illingworth, G Jones, J Kittler, M Petrou and J Princen, Robust statistical methods of 2D and 3D image description, *Annals of Mathematics and Artificial Intelligence*, **10**, 125-148, 1994.
43. Z Shao and J Kittler, Shape Recognition Using Invariant Unary and Binary Relations, Workshop on Visual Form, Capri, 1997 (submitted).
44. W J Christmas, J Kittler and M Petrou, Error propagation for 2D-to-3D matching with application to underwater navigation, *Proceedings of the Seventh British Machine Vision Conference*, 555-564, 1996.
45. W J Christmas, J Kittler and M Petrou, Location of objects in a cluttered scene using probabilistic relaxation, *In: Arcelli C, Cordella LP, Sanniti di Baja G ed. Aspects of Visual Form Processing*, 119-128, Singapore: World Scientific, 1994.
46. R C Wilson, A N Evans and E R Hancock, Relational matching by discrete relaxation, *Image and Vision Computing*, **13**, 411-422, 1995.
47. R C Wilson and E R Hancock, Relational matching with dynamic graph structures, *Proceedings 5th Intern. Conf. Computer Vision*, 450-456, Cambridge, 1995.

A Region-Level Motion-Based Graph Representation and Labeling for Tracking a Spatial Image Partition[*]

Marc Gelgon and Patrick Bouthemy

IRISA/INRIA
Campus de Beaulieu, F-35042 Rennes cedex, France.

tel:(+33) 2.99.84.74.32
fax:(+33) 2.99.84.71.71

e-mail : mgelgon@irisa.fr, bouthemy@irisa.fr

Abstract. This paper addresses the problem of tracking an image partition along a sequence. We consider the case in which the regions composing such a partition display texture homogeneity properties. Several issues in dynamic scene analysis or in image sequence coding can motivate this kind of development. A general-purpose methodology involving a region-level motion-based graph representation of the partition is presented. This graph is built from both the topology of the spatial segmentation map and from spatial and temporal features related to the regions. The motion-based graph labeling is formalized within a Markovian approach. This framework is applied to the tracking of texture-based segmentation maps which are obtained at a pixel level using also a MRF-based method. Results on synthetic and real-world image sequences are shown, and provide a first validation of the proposed approach.

1 Introduction

Image segmentation, regardless of the segmentation criterion, is among the most fundamental tasks faced in image analysis. The problem of performing this segmentation on a whole set of successive frames is also frequently met.

In this paper, we tackle the problem of tracking of spatial image partitions over time. By spatial image partition, we mean a set of disjoint regions, the union of which forms the image, resulting from a spatial image segmentation stage, regardless of the considered criterion, which could be intensity-based, colour-based or texture-based. Such a tracking scheme requires the construction of a relevant structure exploiting the motion information which relates two successive image partitions. This paper mainly focuses on this stage consisting in a region-level motion-based graph representation and labeling. We aim at putting forth some first steps

---

[*] This study is supported in part by DRET Agency (Direction de la Recherche Et de la Technologie - French Ministry of Defense) through a student grant.

towards a general-purpose methodology for tracking a partition *as a whole*. This will result in a far more efficient and complete tracking scheme than if regions were considered independently. Region-level contextual information has to be formalized and exploited. The introduction of a region-level motion-based valued graph is then proposed. The application presented here is concerned with texture-based segmentation in infra-red image sequences as well as grey-level segmentation in the visible domain, with motion as inter-frame transformation.

Several issues can motivate this kind of development. For instance, in a surveillance task, extracting small moving objects within spatially homogeneous tracked regions is easier than detecting them directly from the image. Object-based coding applications can also benefit from such an achievement. Besides, such a tracking scheme can facilitate the determination itself of the partition map at each instant in terms of quality of results and saving of computational time by providing an appropriate prediction step.

The handling over time of image segmentation maps has already received some attention. Short-term approaches were chosen for motion-based segmentation in [5], and in [9] for grey-level segmentation. A longer-term view is introduced in [12] by temporally integrating frames. Occlusions and crossings have been coped with in [14], but considering only a small number of regions, and by tracking them independently. Spatial and motion information were combined at the same level in [4], in contrast with [1] and [8], in which regions from a spatial segmentation stage are first extracted, and then merged if they share the same motion. An explicit region-level merging procedure has been embedded in a Markovian framework in [11], [20] for a motion criterion, and in [2] for a spatial criterion, whereas respectively adaptive $k-means$ and $k-medoid$ clustering algorithms were used in [18] and [8]. However, no tracking stage was introduced in these works. In [19], motion-based merging of spatially homogeneous regions is included in a object-oriented coding scheme, also handling occlusions. A 2D mesh model of an object of interest was employed in [17] to track its motion, intensity and boundary. Finally, addressing thoroughly the data-track correspondence issue through multiple hypothesis testing, for instance, as it was recently proposed in [7], could make a valuable extension to most tracking schemes.

This paper is organized as follows. Section 2 introduces the proposed tracking algorithm and its advantages over an elementary tracking method. The texture segmentation scheme is described in Section 3. Section 4 details the central point of the approach, i.e., how a motion-based graph representation of the image can be built. The use of this graph for tracking is the scope of Section 5. Results obtained both on a patch of natural textures undergoing synthetic motions, and on real-world sequences are presented in Section 6. Finally, Section 7 contains concluding remarks.

2 Principles of the approach for image partition tracking

We present in this section the main features of our original partition tracking method outlined in Fig.1. The updating at each instant of the image partition, obtained according to a spatial criterion, is one of the desired output of the algorithm.

The tracking process is carried out using a "tracking graph" associated to this partition. Building this "tracking graph" requires several intermediate steps to be performed. A "spatial region graph" is first derived from the spatial partition $\mathcal{P}$ (Fig. 1b). Then, the nodes of this graph are considered as sites of a region-level Markov Random Field, and are assigned motion labels using a statistical regularization scheme. Motion is estimated within each region. A region-level label configuration is sought for using an energy minimization approach, such that regions undergoing similar (resp. different) motions are given the same (resp. different) labels. This label map is considered in turn as a region-level and motion-based partition $\mathcal{P}m$, from which a second graph is derived. In doing this derivation, it is possible to make n disconnected subsets of nodes with identical labels give rise to either one or n nodes on tracking graph. This graph, valued by motion information measured on the resulting regions (Fig. 1e) is the one used for tracking. Then, a prediction of the motion-based graph can be built for the next instant, from which in turn, a predicted spatial partition is inferred. The following, also introduced in [1],[8], [10]

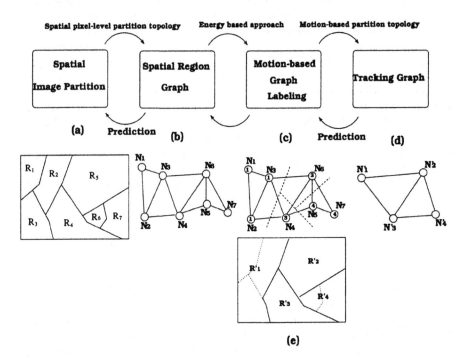

Fig. 1. *The various structures involved in the method and how they are related to one another.*

is exploited : motion boundaries are supposed to coincide with spatial boundaries.

The comparison between our algorithm and an elementary (or short-term) tracking scheme (sketched in Fig.2) highlights its advantages. The latter method, as the one we have defined in [5], relies on alternate image partition prediction and updating phases. Given a partition determined at time t, motion is estimated within each region, a predicted segmentation map is projected at $t+1$ using the estimated motion sub-field in each region or motion model (depending on the techniques), then updated.

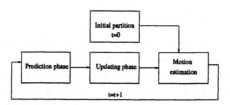

Fig. 2. *Diagram of an elementary short-term tracking scheme, relying on alternate partition prediction and updating phases*

With this simple short-term tracking scheme, the initial label configuration used for the energy minimization process delivering the image segmentation, and supplied by means of the described prediction technique, is generally close to the optimal one. It enables the deterministic relaxation step to converge quickly to an adequate local minimum, i.e. to update the partition in a satisfactory way. Moreover, provided no special event (like occlusion or crossing) occurs, the label associated to each region remains identical from t to $t+1$ in a straightforward manner. Yet, occlusions are not handled, i.e, temporarily occluded label information is lost. Furthermore, this method considers the region-level features (i.e. motion parameters) individually, regardless of region-level contextual information. This last point causes the algorithm to under-perform, for instance, in the case of a region where motion cannot be accurately measured. In addition, the global evolution of the partition structure is not accounted for. While keeping the advantages of the simple tracking scheme, our approach brings in new benefits. Firstly, in poorly textured areas, little intensity gradient is available, for the differential motion estimation method used [16] , to supply accurate estimates. We recall that this was not such a critical issue in [5], since the pixel-level segmentation criterion was not texture but directly motion. In this case as in general, if several regions can be jointly considered for motion estimation, they are likely to provide more intensity gradient information that helps to deliver more accurate estimates. The use of higher degree polynomial motion models than affine models may also be correctly achievable in that case. Secondly, as far as long-term tracking is concerned, involving recursive filtering and an explicit formalized temporal evolution model, the tracking graph structure is obviously much simpler than the spatial region graph, while involving all the useful information.

In contrast with approaches that operate a progressive and irreversible simplification of the partition topology through merging, the labeling approach presented here keeps track of the spatial regions composing a motion-based grouping, so that nodes that are identically labeled at a given iteration or at a given instant can subsequently be labeled differently along the energy minimization. Also, region-level contextual information can be taken into account through a contribution to the energy function.

We now examine in more details the various image representations mentioned at the beginning of this section and the way they are derived from one another.

3 Texture segmentation scheme

For the spatial image segmentation stage, we will consider a texture-based segmentation of the image. The unsupervised texture segmentation method described in [13] is employed. During the partition updating phase, the number of regions is adapted on-line. No prior information is required about the nature of the textures. We recall here the main features of the segmentation algorithm.

It operates within a Bayesian estimation framework. Let $E = \{E_s, s \in s\}$ be the label field defined on the set S of sites s corresponding to the image discrete grid, i.e. sites are pixels. Let $O = \{O_s, s \in s\}$ be the observation field. Let $e = \{e_s, s \in s\}$ (resp. $o = \{o_s, s \in s\}$) be a realization of E (resp. O). Given a neighbourhood system, (E, O) is modeled as a Markov Random Field. The optimal label field $\hat{e}$ is derived according to the *Maximum a posteriori (MAP)* criterion. Thanks to the equivalence between Gibbs distributions and Markov Random Fields, this optimal label configuration in fact results from : $\hat{e} = \arg\min_{e \in \Omega_e} U(e, o)$, where Ω_e is the set of all possible realizations of E and $U(e, o)$ is the so-called energy function encompassing the interactions between labels and observations and a prior information on the label field.

In order to make a texture feature selection to build the observation vectors $\{o_s = [o_s^1, \ldots, o_s^m], s \in S\}$, two classes of images are considered. In the case of poorly textured images (eg. Fig. 5), a grey-level and a variance feature were found sufficient to discriminate between regions ($m = 2$), whereas for significantly textured images (infra red images (Fig. 7) or Brodatz texture patchwork (Fig. 4)), second order statistical features extracted from co-occurency matrices were added.

Let C be the set of all cliques c (a clique is a subset of sites which are mutual neighbours). We use a second-order neighbourhood, but only two-site cliques will be considered. The energy function $U(e, o)$ is expressed as a sum of two terms, which both break into the sum of local potentials defined on cliques :

$$U(e, o) = U_1(e, o) + U_2(e)$$

- $U_1(e, o)$ expresses the relation between the observations at hand and the labels to be determined. It is given by:

$$U_1(e, o) = \sum_s V_1(o(B_s), o(R_{e_s})) \tag{1}$$

where $V_1(o(B_s), o(R_{e_s}))$ conveys the likelihood of a particular label being assigned to site s, given the observations o. $o(B_s)$ is the set of observation vectors in a local window centered at s, and $o(R_{e_s})$ is the set of all observation vectors corresponding to sites currently labeled e_s and forming region R_{e_s}. The potential V_1 is defined as follows :

$$V_1(o(B_s), o(R_{e_s})) = \sum_{i=1}^{m} \begin{cases} +1 \text{ if } d(o^{(i)}(R_{e_s}), o^{(i)}(B_s)) > \alpha^{(i)} \\ -1 \text{ if } d(o^{(i)}(R_{e_s}), o^{(i)}(B_s)) < \alpha^{(i)} \end{cases} \quad (2)$$

where $d(.,.)$ stands for the Kolmogorov-Smirnov distance between the distributions estimated on the local window and on the entire current region R_{e_s}. Thresholds $\alpha(i)$ are predetermined constants.

- $U_2(e)$ reflects the *a priori* constraint on the label map (regularisation term). We have:

$$U_2(e) = \sum_{(s,t) \in C} V_2(s, t)$$

where $V_2(s, t) = \mu(1 - 2\delta(e_s - e_t))$ \hfill (3)

μ is a predetermined positive constant, and $\delta(e_s - e_t) = 1$, if $e_s = e_t$, 0 otherwise. By penalizing local configurations where two neighbouring labels are different, homogeneous regions are globally favored.

Energy minimization is performed using a modified ICM algorithm [6]. A binary stability label is attached to each site, all of which are initially unstable. A site is randomly selected among the unstable sites. The set Λ_s of candidate labels (that may be assigned to site s) include labels currently assigned in the neighbourhood $\nu(s)$ of site s, the current label e_s and an outlier label ρ. This last label enables the creation of new regions [5],[13]. Let $\hat{r}$ be the label, among those labels, which minimizes the 'local' energy function ΔU_s. ΔU_s is given by :

- For $r \neq \rho$,

$$\Delta U_s(r) = \sum_{i=1}^{m} \begin{cases} +1 \text{ if } d(o^{(i)}(R(e_s = r)), o^{(i)}(B_s)) > \alpha^{(i)} \\ -1 \text{ if } d(o^{(i)}(R(e_s = r)), o^{(i)}(B_s)) < \alpha^{(i)} \end{cases} + \sum_{c_s} V_2(c) \quad (4)$$

where c_s designates the subset of cliques c containing s.
- For $r = \rho$, we extend the definition of $\Delta U_s(r)$ as follows :

$$\Delta U_s(\rho) = \sum_{\nu(s)} \mu[1 - 2\delta(\rho - e_t)] + \phi \quad (5)$$

Then, $\hat{r} = \arg\min_{r \in \Lambda_s} \Delta U_s(r)$

The value of ϕ is set to 4 for well-textured images and 2 for poorly-textured images. Once the relaxation process is completed, new labels are attributed to the connected subsets of sites with the ρ-label, which size exceeds a pre-set threshold.

4 Building of a region-level motion-based graph

The central point of the algorithm is now introduced. Given the spatial partition $\mathcal{P} = \{R_k, k = 1 \ldots p\}$, containing p regions, an irregular graph is derived from its topology. We denote it $\mathcal{G}$, the nodes N_k of which correspond to the regions R_k of the spatial partition. Let arcs A_j joint in $\mathcal{G}$ the nodes associated to neighbouring regions in the spatial partition.

$$\mathcal{G} = \{\{N_1, \ldots, N_p\}, \{A_1, \ldots, A_q\}\} \tag{6}$$

We aim at assigning a motion label to every node in the graph, with a view to partitioning this graph into node subsets corresponding to groupings of regions of coherent motion. Each grouping is hence numbered by its label. The labeling of the graph is formalized within a Markovian framework. To this purpose, we identify the nodes of the graph to the sites of a region-level MRF. The cliques are deduced in a straightforward manner from the arcs of the graph. Let $\nu = \{\nu_1, \ldots, \nu_p\}$ be the set of sites and $\Gamma = \{\gamma_1, \ldots, \gamma_q\}$ be the set of binary cliques. We now focus on the definition of a suitable energy function for our region grouping objective.

4.1 Energy function definition and minimization

As in the case of the pixel-level energy function for the texture-based segmentation stage, the region-level energy function U' can be split up into a observation/label interaction term and a regularization term. However, the interaction term is here defined over a binary clique. The energy function is expressed as

$$U'(e', o') = \sum_{\gamma_j \in \Gamma} V_1'(e'(\gamma_j), o'(\gamma_j)) + \sum_{\gamma_j \in \Gamma} V_2'(e'(\gamma_j)) \tag{7}$$

where $e'(\gamma_j)$ stands for the pair of labels attached to the clique γ_j ($\gamma_j = \{\nu_k, \nu_{k'}\}$) and o' for the region-level observations, which we will examine below. This is an elegant and flexible way to formalize the merging of regions of similar motions. Potential $V'1$ will express a discrepancy measure between the two motion model fields attached to the sites ν_k and $\nu_{k'}$ composing clique γ_j. The motion estimation technique and the chosen discrepancy measure are now presented.

Parametric motion estimation

The inter-frame transformation between frame I_t at time t and frame I_{t+1} at time $t + 1$ is modeled by a set of 2D affine motion models, one per region. The displacement vector at site $s = (x, y)$ in region R_k which gravity center $g_k = (x_g^k, y_g^k)$, is expressed as :

$$\mathbf{d}_{(\Theta_k)_t^{t+1}}(s) = \begin{pmatrix} a_0^k + a_2^k(x - x_g^k) + a_3^k(y - y_g^k) \\ a_1^k + a_4^k(x - x_g^k) + a_5^k(y - y_g^k) \end{pmatrix}$$

$$\tag{8}$$

in which the motion parameter vector $(\widehat{\Theta_k})_t^{t+1} = [a_0^k \ldots a_5^k]$ is estimated on each region $R_k, k = 1 \ldots p$, using the robust multi-resolution estimator described in [16]. A M-estimation criterion is minimized by means of an incremental technique based on the Gauss-Newton method :

$$(\widehat{\Theta_k})_t^{t+1} = \arg\min_{\Theta_k} \sum_{s \in R_k(t)} \rho\left(\text{DFD}(s, \Theta_k)\right) \tag{9}$$

where $DFD(s, \Theta_k) = I_{t+1}(s + \mathbf{d}_{(\Theta_k)_t^{t+1}}(s)) - I_t(s)$ and $\rho()$ is Tukey's function. This method in fact only involves the computation of the spatio-temporal derivatives of the intensity function.

Construction of a motion-based distance between regions

An estimation of the covariance matrix associated to the motion parameter vector is also provided. Owing to the robustness of the estimator, the motion measurement is rather insensitive to minor errors in region border determination and to minor motions due to small mobile objects, if any within the region.

In order to characterize the difference between the estimated motions within two neighbouring regions R_k and $R_{k'}$, we consider the two motion fields issued from the motion models estimated within each region. We extend these fields over the support corresponding to the union of the two regions. The discrepancy between these two fields, denoted $D(\gamma_j)$, is expressed as the average, over the union of the two regions, of a weighed distance ϵ between the velocity vectors that form these fields :

$$D(\gamma_j) = \frac{1}{card(R_k \cup R_{k'})} \sum_{s \in (R_k \cup R_{k'})} \epsilon(\overrightarrow{d\Theta_k}(s), \overrightarrow{d\Theta_{k'}}(s)) \tag{10}$$

We wish to define a distance between motion vectors taking into account the covariance information. The diagonal elements of the covariance matrix associated to the motion vector $\overrightarrow{d\Theta_k}(s) = (d_{x,k}, d_{y,k})(s)$ estimated on region R_k are expressed as

$$\sigma_{d_{x,k}}^2 = \sigma_{a_0^k}^2 + \sigma_{a_2^k}^2(x - x_g^k)^2 + \sigma_{a_3^k}^2(y - y_g^k)^2 \tag{11}$$

$$\sigma_{d_{y,k}}^2 = \sigma_{a_1^k}^2 + \sigma_{a_4^k}^2(x - x_g^k)^2 + \sigma_{a_5^k}^2(y - y_g^k)^2 \tag{12}$$

Much investigation has been devoted to the definition of distances between two Gaussian vectors [3]. Although measures such as Bhattacharya or Malahanobis distance, or Kullback divergence, are well suited to measure separability between two distributions, a log-type weighing function was preferred to the $\frac{1}{\sigma^2}$-type laws, because the dynamic range of the variances would too strongly influence the distance. Such a weighing function was empirically determined, as follows :

$$\epsilon(\overrightarrow{d\Theta_k}, \overrightarrow{d\Theta_{k'}}) = |d_{x,k} - d_{x,k'}|.f(\sigma_{d_{x,k}}^2 + \sigma_{d_{x,k'}}^2) + |d_{y,k} - d_{y,k'}|.f(\sigma_{d_{y,k}}^2 + \sigma_{d_{y,k'}}^2) \tag{13}$$

in which $f(x) = -0.15.\log_{10}(x) - 0.2$. The constants were set according to the motion vector variance dynamic range experimentally observed, so that for $(\sigma_{d_{y,k}}^2 + \sigma_{d_{y,k'}}^2) = 10^{-8}$, $f(x) = 1$ and for $(\sigma_{d_{y,k}}^2 + \sigma_{d_{y,k'}}^2) = 10^{-2}$, $f(x) = 0.1$.

V_1' (Fig. 3) aims at favouring identical neighbouring labels when the attached motions are similar, and different labels when motions are strongly different. In contrast with the progressive transition introduced here, a binary penalty value resulting from a test on the hypothesis that two estimated motions really correspond to two really identical underlying motions is defined in [20]. In our case, the potential is defined as in (14). Only one parameter (τ) sets both the threshold and the slope of the function.

$$V_1'(e'(\gamma_j), o'(\gamma_j)) = \begin{cases} \dfrac{1}{1+e^{\frac{3}{\tau}(D(\gamma_j)-\tau)}} & \text{if } e_k' = e_{k'}' \\ 1 - \dfrac{1}{1+e^{\frac{3}{\tau}(D(\gamma_j)-\tau)}} & \text{if } e_k' \neq e_{k'}' \end{cases} \quad (14)$$

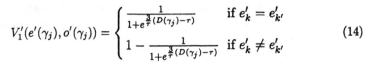

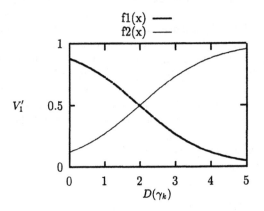

Fig. 3. V_1' *potential as a function of the difference* $D(\gamma_j)$ *between two motion fields, for identical labels (curve f2) and different labels (curve f1). Parameter value :* $\tau = 2$.

V_2' corresponds to the regularization term. To take into account the "degree" of adjacency between two regions, two geometrical features are computed per region pair (k, k') : the length of the common border (denoted as $\xi_{k,k'}$) and the distance between the region gravity centers. They are combined into a geometrical "compacity factor" $\eta_{k,k'}$ of the pair which takes part in the definition of the potential:

$$\eta_{k,k'} = \frac{\xi_{k,k'}}{\xi_{k,k'}+\|g_k-g_{k'}\|_2}$$

$$(15)$$

$$V_2'(e'(\gamma_j)) = \begin{cases} -\beta.\eta_{k,k'}, & \beta > 0 \text{ if } e_k' = e_{k'}' \\ 0 & \text{if } e_k' \neq e_{k'}' \end{cases} \quad (16)$$

The relative small number of regions allows us to utilize an energy minimization technique based on the HCF method [6]. For the first frame of the sequence, all regions are initially given different motion labels. Sites are visited according to their rank in an unstability stack [6]. Candidate labels at a given site include the current label at this site and the labels currently assigned to the neighbour sites. A new label is also proposed. For each candidate label, the local energy involved is computed. For the new label, the potentials defined in (14) and (16) are calculated considering $e'_k \neq e'_{k'}$. The label giving rise to the smallest local energy is then selected. The addition of the new label to the list of candidate labels makes possible a correct on-line determination of the number of relevant motion entities. We chose, arbitrarily, to label disconnected site subsets with different labels. If necessary, this choice can easily be set on or off.

According to the final estimated label values, the label map is partitioned into subsets of identically labeled nodes. A second graph $\mathcal{G}_m$, called "tracking graph" can be deduced from this partition : a node in $\mathcal{G}_m$ is associated to each subset and if at least one arc in $\mathcal{G}$ joins the two subsets, then the two corresponding nodes in $\mathcal{G}_m$ are linked by an arc. The next section describes how partition tracking can exploit the graph $\mathcal{G}_m$.

5 Partition tracking using the graph $\mathcal{G}_m$

Tracking of spatial regions aims first at establishing a correspondence between these regions in successive frames. It can also increase reliability, efficiency and consistency of features attached to the regions to be tracked, such as geometry and motion. To this end, the tracking graph is introduced. Its purpose, in the occlusion-free case, which the scope of this paper is limited to, is first to maintain label consistency over time, both for pixel-level and region-level labeling, secondly to provide initial label configurations, also at both levels, that are close to the optimal configurations, to ensure a fast energy minimization phase, and thirdly to improve reliability of motion estimates through temporal filtering.

5.1 Region-level label map prediction

We first examine how $\mathcal{G}$ can be predicted at $t+1$. We seek to build a relevant label configuration to initialize the motion-based region-level relaxation at $t+1$. Given a spatial partition $\mathcal{P}_t$ at time t, the spatial partition $\mathcal{P}_{t+1}$ at $t+1$ can be split into two subsets : Let $\mathcal{P}_{t+1/t}$ include the regions that already existed in $\mathcal{P}_t$ and $\overline{\mathcal{P}_{t+1/t}}$ include the regions that emerged at $t+1$. We have : $\mathcal{P}_{t+1} = \mathcal{P}_{t+1/t} \cup \overline{\mathcal{P}_{t+1/t}}$.

Prior to motion estimation at $t+1$, no information is available to favor any particular labeling for regions created at $t+1$. We hence attach a new initial label to the corresponding nodes. On the other hand, the prior belief that the motion-based region grouping should be maintained from t to $t+1$ suggests that for regions that survive from t to $t+1$, node labels have to be initialized at $t+1$ with the label obtained at t. If we denote $\tilde{e}'_{k,t+1}$ the predicted label attached to the node corresponding to region R_k,

$$\tilde{e}'_{k,t+1} = \begin{cases} \bar{e}_{k,t} & \text{if } R_k \in \mathcal{P}_{t+1/t} \\ \text{a new label} & \text{if } R_k \in \overline{\mathcal{P}_{t+1/t}} \end{cases}$$

Thanks to the scheme defined in Section 4, with which spatial regions are not irreversibily merged, the groupings determined for a given frame can be called into question and label distribution appropriately updated during the energy minimization phase, an update of the number of motion-based regions being jointly performed.

5.2 Pixel-level label map prediction

The spatial partition prediction technique is now explained. Motion parameter vectors are estimated on coherent region subsets (Fig 1e) as follows :

$$(\widehat{\Theta_n})_t^{t+1} = \arg\min_{\Theta_n} \sum_{s \in (\bigcup R_k | e'_k = n)} \rho\left(\mathrm{DFD}(s, \Theta_n)\right) \tag{17}$$

For each region grouping R'_n, the six motion parameters are considered as non correlated and account for measurements supplied to six independent Kalman filters. A constant second order derivative evolution model, also found suitable for a similar usage in [14], is selected here. Equal and constant process and measurement noise variances for all motion parameters of all regions were set. Each filter outputs two values : the predicted and the filtered motion parameter. The filtered and the predicted outputs of the recursive filter at a given node of $\mathcal{G}_m$ can be identically attributed to all nodes of $\mathcal{G}$ in the corresponding node subset. Thus, the predicted measurement can hold as an initial value for the motion estimator at $t+1$. On the other hand, the filtered parameter vectors are passed on to their respective regions in the spatial partition, in order to provide a prediction for this spatial partition at $t+1$.

In the occlusion-free case, we take the filtered motion parameter as the most reliable available measurement from t to $t+1$. Let $\widehat{\Theta^{t/t}}$ stand for this filtered value. Given the estimated spatial label $\hat{e}_t$ at time t, the predicted spatial label field $\tilde{e}_{t+1}$ is derived from a motion-oriented propagation of labels [5]:

$$\tilde{e}_{t+1}(s) = e_t\left(s + \mathbf{d}\,\widehat{(\Theta'_{e_s})_t^{t+1}(s)}\right) \tag{18}$$

Since $s + \mathbf{d}_\Theta(s)$ usually points to a place of non integer coordinates, the label is assigned to the four nearest sites on the image grid. Sites that receive no label or multiple labels are respectively assigned "uncovered" and "occlusion" labels. Both labels are considered neutral when it comes to the relaxation algorithm.

6 Results

The proposed scheme was validated on both synthetic and real-world sequences. For all experiments, the texture-based segmentation and motion-based region-level regularization constants μ and β are respectively set to 0.4 and 0.1. The evolution model parameters for temporal filtering, i.e., measurement and process noise variances, were taken constant and both equal to 0.01.

The method was first validated using synthetic sequences. The different regions of a 256x256 image *texture Patchwork* made up of natural textures taken from the Brodatz album are imparted different and time-varying affine motions. The statistics extracted from co-occurence matrices of quantized grey-level values calculated on 7x7 pixel local windows are : mean, variance and correlation [13]. τ was set to 0.2. The true region labels are given on Fig. 4(a). Regions 1 and 2, in the foreground, undergo horizontal motion, first accelerating then slowing down. Region 3 is imparted combined translation, rotation, divergence, while region 4 undergoes combined divergence and translation. A first increasing, then decreasing divergence is applied to region 5. The determined motion contours and the estimated motion model fields, superimposed on the original images, are shown on Fig. 4 for various frames. Three groupings are initially formed : (1),(2),(3,4,5) (Fig. 4(b)). The region-level label configuration then varies along the sequence. As the motion in region 3 gets strongly different from the motion imparted to regions 4 and 5, region 3 becomes a separate motion entity (Fig. 4(c)), in accordance with the ground truth. A new motion-based region is further created (Fig. 4(d)), because of the increasing strength of the divergence applied to region 5. Close to the end of the sequence, regions 2 and 5 become almost static, and thus form a grouping with very slowly moving region 4. In this example, regions undergoing similar motions are correctly grouped and region-level labeling is consistent over the sequence. The number of groupings being also updated in agreement with the ground truth.

In the *Interview sequence* (337x268), the woman on the right is getting up, while slowly twisting her body and bringing her left arm forward. This gives rise to a complex articulated motion. Meanwhile, the camera is tilting upwards, more slowly than the woman's motion, causing a downwards apparent motion for the rest of the scene. The spatial and motion-based segmentation contours and the spatial contours with the superimposed estimated motion fields are shown on Fig. 6 for several frames. The woman is extracted from the background, first the upper part of her body (b_1) then her whole body (b_2), finally split into two parts (b_3). The node labels are stable over time. Motion contours are either accurately determined, or poorer in cases where such motion contours were not identified as spatial contours. In Fig. 5(b_3), two such cases can be noticed on the hair and left elbow areas, those spatial contours exist but are not clearly perceptible. In order to reveal such contour parts, a motion-uniformity test could be applied into each spatial region to split sub-regions that do not conform to the estimated motion model. This sequence illustrates the benefits of the proposed scheme : it can be seen on Fig. 5(a_1) that the regions composing the spatial partition are numerous and rather small and hence may be difficult to track at that level. The motion-based regions (Fig. 5 (b_1)) are generally much larger and thus their motion can be much better estimated. Moreover, they represent more meaningful regions of the image. Finally, the small number of motion-based regions also implies that the tracking graph has a much simpler topology than the spatial region graph, which would be particularly attractive for interpretation purposes, or if the motion region descriptors were to be enriched, for instance by a geometrical description of motion-based regions. Processing each pair of frames takes around 80 seconds using non-optimized code on an UltraSparc, 4 seconds of which are devoted to the motion estimation and 4 seconds to the region-level computations (distance calculations and energy minimization), the rest of the time is in fact spent by the updating of the spatial segmentation.

In Fig. 6, we show some results of a comparison of motion-based partitions between the approach proposed in this paper and a motion-only pixel-level segmentation method [15]. Fig. 6(a) is to be compared with Fig. 5(b_2) and Fig. 6(b) with Fig. 6(c). At $t = 15$, the accuracy of the detected motion boundaries of our method is illustrated. At $t = 62$, the direct dependency of the motion-based partition on the quality of the spatial partition is shown to be a limitation of our method (a single motion descriptor is assigned to the hair and the dark background).

In the *Power Station* infra-red sequence (500x236), only camera motion is present. Then, motion discontinuities are only due to differences in depth relatively to the camera, or to different surface orientations. Texture is taken as the segmentation criterion, all parameters being as for the *Patchwork* sequence. Results are shown of Fig. 7 for two frames. Motion grouping can be observed between regions that are located at similar depths. Labels and boundaries are consistently maintained through the sequence.

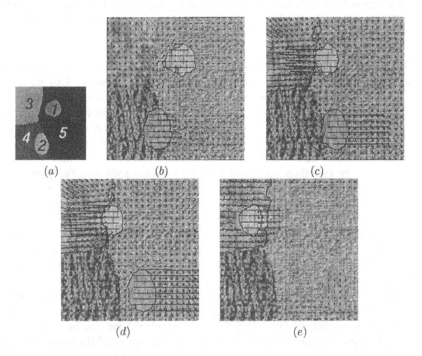

(a) (b) (c)

(d) (e)

Fig. 4. *Patchwork sequence : true region numbering (a), and original image with estimated motion model fields and motion contours at time $t = 4$ (b), $t = 16$ (c), $t = 20$ (d) and $t = 38$ (e).*

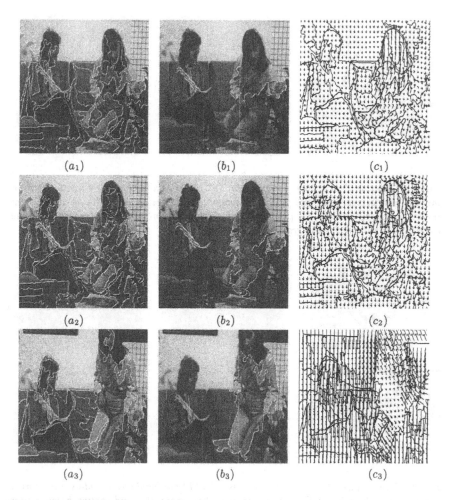

Fig. 5. *"Interview" sequence : spatial segmentation superimposed on the original images* $(a_i, i = 1, 2, 3)$, *contours of the motion-based region groupings* $(b_i, i = 1, 2, 3)$ *and spatial contours with estimated motion fields* $(c_i, i = 1, 2, 3)$ *at times* $t = 7$, $t = 15$ *and* $t = 49$.

7 Conclusion

First steps towards a global method for spatial image partition tracking have been presented, through the definition of a motion-based graph representation of the spatial partition as the key-tool to tracking, and of several intermediate representations. Thereby, introducing region-level context, motion estimation accuracy and map prediction coherence and quality are improved. Promising results have been obtained on image sequences of relative complexity. We are currently dealing, within this framework, with occlusions and crossings. We intend to extend the tracking graph $\mathcal{G}_m$ with some geometrical features of the regions, so that it contains a comprehensive and compact representation of the partition. Should some regions be occluded, tracking could then rely only on the predicted motion and predicted

423

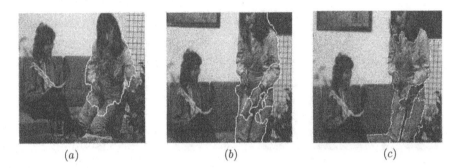

(a)   (b)   (c)

Fig. 6. *"Interview" sequence : comparison of the region-level motion-based partition method with a pixel-level motion-based segmentation technique [15]. Motion contours at time t = 15 (a) and t = 62 (b) for the pixel-level motion-based technique and at time t = 62 (c) for the technique presented in this paper.*

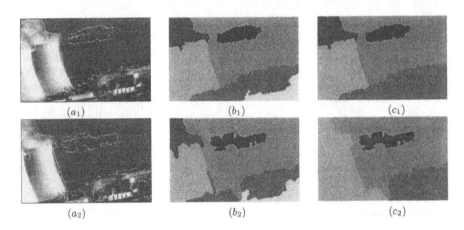

(a_1) (b_1) (c_1)

(a_2) (b_2) (c_2)

Fig. 7. *"Power station" sequence (by courtesy of SAT) : original images with superimposed spatial region boundaries (a), spatial segmentation maps (b), and motion-based region groupings (c) at times t = 1 and t = 15 .*

geometry of these regions, and benefit further from the simplicity of structure of the motion-based graph $\mathcal{G}_m$ relatively to the spatial-based graph $\mathcal{G}$, as demonstrated in the *Interview* sequence, for instance. This also provides a high-level representation and interpretation of the dynamic content of the image sequence.

References

1. S. Ayer, P. Schroeter, and J. Bigün. Segmentation of moving objets by robust motion parameter estimation over multiple frames. In *Proc. of Third European Conference on Computer Vision*, pages 316–327, Stockholm, Sweden, May 1994.
2. R. Azencott and C. Graffigne. Non supervised segmentation using multi-level Markov random fields. In *Proc. of the 11th Int. Conf. on Pattern Recognition*, pages 201–204, The Hague, August 1992.

3. M. Basseville. Distance measures for signal processing and pattern recognition. *Signal Processing*, 18(4):349–369, December 1989.
4. M.J. Black. Combining intensity and motion for incremental segmentation and tracking over long image sequences. In *Proc. of Second European Conference on Computer Vision*, pages 485–493, Santa Margherita Ligure, Italy, May 1992.
5. P. Bouthemy and E. François. Motion segmentation and qualitative dynamic scene analysis from an image sequence. *International Journal of Computer Vision*, 10(2):1578–182, April 1993.
6. P.B. Chou and C.M. Brown. The theory and practise of Bayesian image modelling. *International Journal of Computer Vision*, 4:185–210, 1990.
7. I.J. Cox and S.L. Hingorani. An efficient implementation of Reid's multiple hypothesis tracking algorithm and its evaluation for the purpose of visual tracking. *IEEE Trans. on Pattern Analysis and Machine Intelligence*, 18(2):138–150, February 1996.
8. F. Dufaux, F. Moscheni, and A. Lippman. Spatio-temporal segmentation based on motion and static segmentation. In *Proc of Second Int. Conf. of Image Processing*, pages 306–309, Washington, October 1995.
9. V. Garcia-Garduño and C. Labit. On the tracking of regions over time for very low bit rate image sequence coding. In *Proc. of PCS'94*, pages 257–260, Sacramento, CA, USA, September 1994.
10. F. Heitz and P. Bouthemy. Multimodal estimation of discontinuous optical flow using Markov random fields. *IEEE Trans. on Pattern Analysis and Machine Intelligence*, 15(12):1217–1232, December 1993.
11. C. Hennebert, V. Rebuffel, and P. Bouthemy. A hierarchical approach for scene segmentation based on 2d motion. In *Proc. of the 13th Int. Conf. on Pattern Recognition*, pages 218–222, Vienna, August 1996.
12. M. Irani, B. Rousso, and S. Peleg. Detecting and tracking multiple moving objects using temporal integration. In *Proc. of Second European Conference on Computer Vision*, pages 282–287, Santa Margherita Ligure, Italy, May 1992.
13. C. Kervrann and F. Heitz. A Markov random field model-based approach to unsupervised texture segmentation using local and global spatial statistics. *IEEE Trans. on Image Processing*, 4(6):856–862, June 1995.
14. F. Meyer and P. Bouthemy. Region-based tracking using affine motion models in long image sequences. *CVGIP : Image Understanding*, 60(2):119–140, September 1994.
15. J.M Odobez and P. Bouthemy. MRF-based motion segmentation exploiting a 2D motion model robust estimation. In *Proc of Second Int. Conf. of Image Processing*, pages 628–631, Washington, October 1995.
16. J.M Odobez and P. Bouthemy. Robust multiresolution estimation of parametric motion models. *Journal of Visual Communication and Image Representation*, 6(4):348–365, December 1995.
17. C. Toklu, A.T. Erdem, M.I Sezan, and A.M. Tekalp. Tracking motion and intensity variations using hierarchical 2-d mesh modeling for synthetic object transfiguration. *Graphical Models and Image Processing*, 58(6):553–573, November 1996.
18. J.Y.A Wang and E.H Adelson. Representing moving images with layers. *IEEE Trans. on Image Processing*, 3(5):625–638, September 1994.
19. L. Wu, J. Benois-Pineau, Ph. Delagnes, and D. Barba. Spatio-temporal segmentation of image sequences for object-oriented low bit-rate image coding. *Signal Processing : Image Communication*, 8:513–543, September 1996.
20. W. Xiong and C. Graffigne. A hierarchical method for detection of moving objects. In *Proc of First Int. Conf. of Image Processing*, pages 795–799, Austin, November 1994.

An Expectation-Maximisation Approach to Graph Matching

Andrew M. Finch, Richard C. Wilson and Edwin R. Hancock

Department of Computer Science
University of York
York, Y01 5DD, UK.

Abstract. This paper describes how relational graph matching can be effected using the EM algorithm. The matching process is realised as a two-step iterative process. Firstly, updated symbolic matches are located so as to minimise a Kullback-Leibler divergence between the model and data graphs. Secondly, with the updated matches to hand probabilities describing the affinity between nodes in the model and data graphs may be computed. The probability distributions underpinning this study are computed using a simple model of uniform matching errors. As a result the Kullback-Leibler divergence is defined over a family of exponential distributions of Hamming distance. We evaluate the noise sensitivity of our matching method on synthetically generated graphs. Finally, we offer comparison with both mean-field annealing and quadratic assignment.

1 Introduction

Graph matching [25,18,17,29,8,9,38,37] has been a topic of central importance in pattern perception since Barrow and Popplestone [3] first demonstrated that relational descriptions could be used to represent and recognize pictorial information. It was the classical work on structural pattern recognition of the 1980's that first identified the main practical difficulties associated with relational graph matching [29,30]. The main issues are how to compute the distance between inexact relational descriptions [31,29] and how to search efficiently for the best match [30]. These two issues have recently stimulated renewed interest in the connectionist literature [32,25,18,17,33]. For instance Simic [32], Mjolsness *et al* [25], Suganathan *et al* [33] and Gold *et al* [18,17] have addressed the issue to how to expressively measure relational distance. Both Gold and Rangarajan [18] and Suganathan *et al* [33] have shown how non-linear optimisation techniques such as mean-field annealing [33,40,28] and graduated assignment [5,18] can be applied to find optimal matches.

In a recent series of papers we have developed a Bayesian framework for relational graph matching [8,9,14,15,37,38]. The novelty resides in the fact that relational consistency is gauged by an exponential probability distribution that uses Hamming distance to measure structural differences between the graphs under match. This new framework has not only been used to match complex infra-red [9] and radar imagery [37], it has also been used to successfully control a graph-edit process [38] of the sort originally proposed by Sanfeliu and Fu [29]. The optimisation of this relational consistency measure has been studied using both discrete [19,37,8,9] and continuation methods [14,15]. Specifically, we have investigated discrete relaxation [37], simulated annealing [9], genetic search [8], mean-field annealing [14] and soft-assign [15] as alternative optimisation strategies. Our aim in this paper is to consider how the search for optimal matches can be realised by using the EM algorithm.This offers an interesting compromise between discrete and continuous methods of optimisation. In fact, we draw on our recent work to construct a mixture distribution defined over the discrete state-space of matching assignments. By applying the apparatus of the EM algorithm to the mixture distribution we seek matches in a two-stage iterative process. In the maximisation step we find discrete matching assignments which minimise the Kullback-Leibler divergence between the graphs. The Hamming distances for the updated matching assignments are used to estimate *a posteriori* probabilities in the expectation step. These probabilities are themselves used to compute the divergence in the succeeding maximisation step. This process is iterated to convergence.

The outline of this paper is as follows. We commence by motivating our use of the EM approach in Section 2. In Section 3 we present details of our mixture model for the graph-matching problem. Section 4 details how the EM algorithm can be used to locate optimal matches. In Section 5 we briefly review two mean-field algorithms which we use for the purposes of experimental comparison. Section 6 presents an experimental evaluation of the method. This compares the method with both mean-field annealing and gradient ascent. Finally, Section 7 offers some conclusions.

2 Motivation

Relational graph matching is intrinsically symbolic in nature. In consequence, the most straightforward search strategy is to exploit some form of discrete configurational optimisation process. Unfortunately, because the underlying relational consistency measure is defined over a set of discrete states it is prone to develop local optima. There are two principle ways which can be exploited to overcome the difficulties associated with local convergence. The first of these is to retain the discrete representation of the matching process and incorporate a stochastic element into the update process. Examples of this form of global configurational optimisation process include simulated annealing [1,22,8] and genetic search [9]. The alternative is to adopt a continuation method. Here the discrete matching variables are replaced by softened assignment variables. Examples include mean-field annealing [39,33,14] and soft-assign [18,6,15].

Although continuation methods offer the advantage of being deterministic, they have the shortcoming of decoupling the state-space of the optimisation process from the physical representation of the matching problem. The reason for this is that the true probability distribution representing the problem in-hand must be parameterised by mean-field variables according to an appropriate softening ansatz. The mean-field update formulae are obtained by solving the set of saddle-point equations which minimise the Kullback-Leibler divergence between the true distribution and its parameterised form [4,10]. This has two consequences. In the first-instance, while the mean field approach effectively smoothes the cost-function of the original discrete optimisation problem, it may also have the undesirable effect of degrading the fidelity of representation. In other words, the mean-field distribution may poorly parameterise the distance measure underpinning the original probability distribution. Secondly, if the mean-field parameterisation is inappropriate then the hard solutions of the mean-field equations may bear little relationship with the true state-space of the original discrete optimisation problem. In other words, the mean-field representation may admit infeasible solutions.

One way of circumventing these difficulties is to seek a compromise between retaining the original distance measure and permitting soft assignment variables. This is exactly the optimisation process underpinning the expectation-maximisation idea of Dempster Laird and Rubin [11]. In the maximisation stage parameters are extracted so as to minimise the Kullback-Leibler divergence between distributions. However, rather than adopting a mean-field parameterisation of the appropriate distance-measure it is the physical distance between model and data that is used. If the data is described by a mixture distribution defined over a family of exponential probability density functions, then the Kullback-Leibler divergence is simply a weighted distance between model and data. The weighting terms are *a posteriori* probabilities of the model-datum affinity. In the expectation step of the algorithm these probabilities are iteratively recomputed by applying the Bayes rule to the appropriate components of the mixture probability distribution.

Our basic interest in the EM algorithm lies in the possibilities that if offers for graph-matching. In a recent series of papers we have constructed a simple Bayesian model of the relational graph matching process [37,38]. This model commences from the assumption that matching errors are uniform and memoryless. As a result the discrete state of symbolic match is represented by an exponential function of the Hamming distance between data and model graphs. We have extensively explored the optimisation of the implied relational distance measure by both discrete and continuation methods. Here our aim if to explore the symbiosis of representation provided by the EM algorithm.

3 A Mixture Model for Graph Matching

Our overall goal in this paper is to formulate relational graph matching as an expectation-maximisation process. To commence we must define some notation. We use the notation $G = (V, E)$ to denote the graphs under match, where V is the set of nodes and E is the set of edges. Our aim in matching is to associate nodes in a graph $G_D = (V_D, E_D)$ representing data to be matched against those in a graph $G_M = (V_M, E_M)$ representing an available relational model. Formally, the matching is represented by a function from the nodes in the data graph G_D

to those in the model graph G_M. In developing our EM algorithm, we will need to distinguish between the state of match at various iterative epochs. Suppose that the state of match between the two graphs at iteration n is represented by the function $f^{(n)} : V_D \to V_M$. In others words the statement $f^{(n)}(a) = \alpha$ means that the node $a \in V_D$ is matched to the node $\alpha \in V_M$.

The basic goals of the matching process are twofold. In the first instance, the discrete matching configuration is updated to maximise a weighted likelihood function. The second goal is to update the *a posteriori* matching probabilities which weight the individual contributions to the likelihood function. The probability distributions required as the building blocks of this expectation-maximisation framework have been developed in a recent series of papers by Wilson and Hancock [37,38]. The basic idea is to construct a probability distribution which models the effect of memoryless matching errors in generating departures from consistency between the data and model graphs. Suppose that $S_\alpha = \alpha \cup \{\beta | (\alpha, \beta) \in E_M\}$ represents the set of nodes that form the immediate contextual neighbourhood of the node α in the model graph. The aim in gauging relational consistency is to measure the structural differences between the set of model-graph neighbourhoods and their matched counterparts in the data-graph. Furthermore, suppose that $\Gamma_a^{(n)} = f^{(n)}(a) \cup \{f^{(n)}(b) | (a, b) \in E_D\}$ represents the set of matches assigned to the contextual neighbourhood of the node $a \in V_D$ of the data graph at iteration n of the update process. Basic to Wilson and Hancock's modelling of relational consistency is to regard the complete set of model-graph relations as mutually exclusive causes from which the potentially corrupt matched model-graph relations arise. In other words, the probability of the matched configuration $\Gamma_a^{(n)}$ can be represented by the mixture distribution

$$P(\Gamma_a^{(n)}) = \sum_{\alpha \in V_M} P(\Gamma_a^{(n)} | S_\alpha) P(S_\alpha) \tag{1}$$

The component densities appearing in this mixture distribution are modelled under the assumption that discrete matching errors are uniform and memoryless. Accordingly the confusion probability $P(\Gamma_a^{(n)} | S_\alpha)$ can be factorised over the component matches

$$P(\Gamma_a^{(n)} | S_\alpha) = \prod_{b \in C_a} P(f^{(n)}(b) | \beta) \tag{2}$$

The confusion probabilities are modelled by distinguishing between two classes of matching error. The first of these are misassignments. These errors can be rectified by re-configuring the match. Individual misassignment errors are assumed to occur with a uniform probability P_e. The second class of errors are associated with unmatchable nodes. These nodes may represent noise or clutter in the data graph. We aim to assign these nodes to a null category ϕ which augments the set of model-graph nodes as an additional matching category. Null matches are again assumed to be uniformly distributed and to occur with probability P_ϕ. With these two ingredients, the single node match probabilities are distributed as follows

$$P(f^{(n)}(b)|\beta) = \begin{cases} P_\phi & \text{if } f^{(n)}(b) = \phi \\ (1 - P_\phi)(1 - P_e) & \text{if } f^{(n)}(b) = \beta \\ (1 - P_\phi)P_e & \text{if } f^{(n)}(b) \neq \beta \text{ and } f^{(n)}(b) \neq \phi \end{cases} \tag{3}$$

Under this distribution rule the mixture components acquire an exponential form. There are two physical quantities appearing in the distribution. The first of these is the Hamming-distance $H(\Gamma_a^{(n)}, S_\alpha)$ between the non-null matched nodes. The second quantity is the number of null-matches appearing on the data-graph neighbourhood $\Phi(\Gamma_a^{(n)})$. The exponential distribution for the probability of match between the data-graph neighbourhood centred on the node a and the model graph neighbourhood centred on the node α is

$$P(\Gamma_a^{(n)}|S_\alpha) = K_a \exp\left[-\left(\mu_e H(\Gamma_a^{(n)}, S_\alpha) + \mu_\phi \Phi(\Gamma_a^{(n)})\right)\right] \tag{4}$$

The two exponential constants are related to the uniform error probabilities as follows

$$\mu_\phi = \ln \frac{(1 - P_e)(1 - P_\phi)}{P_\phi} \tag{5}$$

and

$$\mu_e = \ln \frac{1 - P_e}{P_e} \tag{6}$$

The distribution of misassignment errors is measured by the Hamming distance $H(\Gamma_a^{(n)}, S_\alpha)$ between the current matching configuration $\Gamma_a^{(n)}$ residing on the data graph and the configuration S_α from the model graph. In terms of our discrete representation of the matching process, the Hamming distance is computed using a series of Kronecker delta functions defined over the data-graph node-matches and the assignments demanded by the model-graph configurations

$$H(\Gamma_a^{(n)}, S_\alpha) = \sum_{b \in C_a} (1 - \delta_{f^{(n)}(b),\beta}) \tag{7}$$

The number of clutter or noise nodes is similarly obtained by counting the occurrence of the null-label, i.e.

$$\Phi(\Gamma_a^{(n)}) = \sum_{b \in C_a} \delta_{f^{(n)}(b),\phi} \tag{8}$$

Finally, the constant of normalisation appearing in the distribution is given by

$$K_a = [(1 - P_\phi)(1 - P_e)]^{|C_a|} \tag{9}$$

As a result of our assumed model, the components of the mixture density are simply exponential functions of the two physically meaningful error measures. In the next section of this paper we show how this mixture model can be used to construct a log-likelihood function over the space of discrete matching assignments.

4 Updating matches using the EM Algorithm

The EM algorithm was first introduced by Dempster, Laird and Rubin as a means of fitting incomplete data [11]. The algorithm has two stages. The expectation step involves estimating a mixture distribution using current parameter values. The maximisation step involves computing new parameter values that optimise the expected value of the weighted data likelihood. This two-stage process is iterated to convergence. Despite its relatively poor convergence properties, the algorithm provides a powerful statistical framework for fitting sparse data that has many features in common with robust parameter estimation [24]. Recently, the methodological basis of the EM algorithm has attracted renewed interest in the domain of artificial neural networks where it has not only been shown to have an intimate relationship with mean-field annealing [4], but also to provide a convenient framework for hierarchical data processing [21]. Yuille *et al* [39] have established the relationship between the EM algorithm and the elastic net of Durbin and Willshaw [12,13]. Novovicova *et al* have utilised the algorithm for feature selection; rather than applying the EM algorithm to the expected likelihood, they use as their utility measure the Kullback J-divergence [27].

In the domain of machine vision, the EM algorithm has been exploited for estimating multiple motion parameters [23,?] and for face recognition [26]. Several authors have considered how the problem of point pattern matching can be addressed using the EM framework. Utans recovers translation parameters [34], while Gold *et al* are more ambitious in matching under affine transformation [18]. Recently, the EM algorithm has been exploited in the recovery of object pose by both Wells [36], and, by Hornegger and Nieman [20]. In contrast to these approaches, the main contribution of this paper is to demonstrate the effectiveness of the algorithm in matching symbolic relational graphs without recourse to an explicit transformational model.

4.1 Expectation

The utility measure underpinning the EM algorithm is the Kullback-Leibler divergence between the estimated probability distributions at successive iterations. At each iterative epoch the aim is to find the updated parameter values which minimise the divergence. Formally, the divergence is intimately related to the expected likelihood function. In fact Dempster, Laird and Rubin [11] used Jensen's inequality to demonstrate that minimising the J-divergence was equivalent to maximising the expected log-likelihood function.

To commence our development we need to construct a Kullback-Leibler divergence measure for the graph matching process. This divergence must gauge the differences in the mixture components given in equation (4) at iterations n and $n + 1$ of the matching process. The justification for our choice of divergence measure is outside the scope of this paper. In a recent study we have used the apparatus of statistical physics to compute the Gibbs potentials for a Boltzmann machine which can used to find matching configurations that maximise the likelihood for the mixture distribution given in equation (1) [14]. Moreover, we have also demonstrated that the resulting Gibbs distribution minimises a certain Kullback-Leibler divergence between the data and model graphs [7]. Building on this previous work, the divergence quantity which lends itself to our purposes is

$$Q(f^{(n+1)}|f^{(n)}) = \sum_{a \in V_D} \sum_{\alpha \in V_M \cup \phi} P(f^{(n)}(a) = \alpha|\Gamma_a^{(n)}) \ln \frac{P(\Gamma_a^{(n)}|S_\alpha)}{P(\Gamma_a^{(n+1)}|S_\alpha)} \qquad (10)$$

The structure of this expression deserves further comment. In our graph-matching example, the parameters are discrete matching assignments between the graphs at successive epochs of the matching process. The divergence effectively compares the distribution of matching errors over the contextual neighbourhoods of the data and model graphs. The quantity $P(f^{(n)} = \alpha|\Gamma_a^{(n)})$ fulfils the role of an *a posteriori* matching probability. By applying the Bayes-rule, we can compute these *a posteriori* probabilities from the conditional densities given in equation (4)

$$P(f^{(n+1)}(a) = \alpha|\Gamma^{(n)}) = \frac{P(\Gamma_a^{(n)}|S_\alpha)P(S_\alpha)}{\sum_{\beta \in V_M \cup \phi} P(\Gamma_a^{(n)}|S_\beta)P(S_\beta)} \qquad (11)$$

We develop the divergence further by explicitly substituting for the exponential Hamming-distance distributions described appearing in equation (4). Under this substitution the divergence takes on the following simple form

$$Q(f^{(n+1)}|f^{(n)}) = \sum_{a \in V_D} \sum_{\alpha \in V_M \cup \phi} P(f^{(n)}(a) = \alpha|\Gamma_a^{(n)})$$
$$\times \left[\mu_e \left(H(\Gamma_a^{(n+1)}, S_\alpha) - H(\Gamma_a^{(n)}, S_\alpha) \right) + \mu_\phi \left(\Phi(\Gamma_a^{(n+1)}) - \Phi(\Gamma_a^{(n)}) \right) \right] (12)$$

There are two distinct terms appearing in the divergence. The first of these measures the change in Hamming distance due to the modification of potential misassignment errors. The second term measures the change in the number of null matches. The relative importance of these two terms is controlled by the coupling constants μ_e and μ_ϕ. In the maximisation step we regulate the two classes of error by exerting control over the coupling constants. We take the view that although misassignment errors are acceptable in the early iterative epochs, in the final match they should be consigned to the null category. This behaviour is regulated by gradually increasing the misassignment constant μ_e while keeping the null-constant μ_ϕ fixed. Initially, $\mu_e < \mu_\phi$ and in consequence null matches are energetically unfavourable. At later epochs $\mu_e \gg \mu_\phi$ and it is the misassignment errors which become unfavourable. In other words, null-matches do not enter the matching process until $\mu_e \simeq \mu_\phi$.

4.2 Maximisation

The maximisation step involves locating parameters which optimise the expected-likelihood function. In our graph-matching problem these parameters are the discrete matching assignments between the model and data graphs. Formally, the minimum-divergence matching configuration is the one which satisfies the condition

$$f^{(n+1)} = \arg\min_{\hat{f}} Q(\hat{f}|f^{(n)}) \tag{13}$$

We realise the update process by parallel iterative computations. In computing the most likely label updates we need confine our attention only to the contributions to the divergence which originate from the immediate contextual neighbours of the node under consideration. The updated matching configuration generated in this way modifies the Hamming-distance between the data and model-graph contextual neighbourhoods. These updated Hamming distance can be used to re-estimate the *a posteriori* matching probabilities in the following manner

$$P(f^{(n+1)}(a) = \alpha|\Gamma_a^{(n+1)})$$

$$= \frac{\exp\left[-\mu_e H(\Gamma_a^{(n+1)}, S_\alpha)\right]}{\sum_{\beta \in V_M} \exp\left[-\mu_e H(\Gamma_a^{(n+1)}, S_\beta)\right] + \exp\left[-\mu_\phi \Phi(\Gamma_a^{(n+1)})\right]} \tag{14}$$

While the null-match probabilities are updated as follows

$$P(f^{(n+1)}(a) = \phi|\Gamma_a^{(n+1)})$$

$$= \frac{\exp\left[-\mu_\phi \Phi(\Gamma_a^{(n+1)})\right]}{\sum_{\beta \in V_M} \exp\left[-\mu_e H(\Gamma_a^{(n+1)}, S_\beta)\right] + \exp\left[-\mu_\phi \Phi(\Gamma_a^{(n+1)})\right]} \tag{15}$$

The coupling constants μ_e and μ_ϕ are regulated in the manner suggested in the previous subsection.

5 Relational Matching with Mean-field Updates

In Section 6 we describe an experimental comparison between the EM update process and mean-field annealing. In this Section we briefly review the algorithms used in this comparison. There are two variants used in this study. The first aims to optimise a mean-field approximation to the mixture distribution given in equation (1). The derivation of this approximation is outside the scope of this paper and can be found in the recent account of Finch, Wilson and Hancock [14]. The second algorithm is based on the well-known quadratic assignment potential [15].

To develop the mean-field framework we represent the structure of the two graphs using a pair of connection matrices. The connection matrix for the data graph consists of the binary array

$$D_{ab} = \begin{cases} 1 & \text{if } (a,b) \in E_D \\ 0 & \text{otherwise} \end{cases} \tag{16}$$

while that for the model graph is

$$M_{\alpha\beta} = \begin{cases} 1 & \text{if } (\alpha,\beta) \in E_M \\ 0 & \text{otherwise} \end{cases} \tag{17}$$

The current state of match between the two graphs is represented by a set of assignment variables which convey the following meaning

$$s_{a\alpha} = \begin{cases} 1 & \text{if } f(a) = \alpha \\ 0 & \text{otherwise} \end{cases} \tag{18}$$

With these ingredients, the mean field energy function associated with the match is [14]

$$\mathcal{E}_{MFT} = \sum_{a \in V_D} \sum_{\alpha \in V_M} \sum_{b \in V_D} \sum_{\beta \in V_M} \left[(1 - s_{a\alpha}) + D_{ab}M_{\alpha\beta}(1 - s_{b\beta}) \right] s_{a\alpha} \tag{19}$$

This energy-function is a more elaborate form of the familiar quadratic assignment energy. It contains additional terms that both facilitate node self-amplification [18] and inhibit multiple matches [14]. By contrast, the standard quadratic formulation of the matching problem investigated by Simic [32], Suganathan et al [33] and Gold and Rangarajan [18] aims to optimise the cost function

$$\mathcal{E}_H = -\frac{1}{2} \sum_{a \in V_D} \sum_{\alpha \in V_M} \sum_{b \in V_D} \sum_{\beta \in V_M} D_{ab}M_{\alpha\beta}s_{a\alpha}s_{b\beta} \tag{20}$$

In the case of both energy functions, the mean-field update equations for the assignment variables are as follows

$$s_{a\alpha} \leftarrow \frac{\exp\left[-\frac{1}{T}\frac{\partial \mathcal{E}}{\partial s_{a\alpha}}\right]}{\sum_{\alpha' \in V_M} \exp\left[-\frac{1}{T}\frac{\partial \mathcal{E}}{\partial s_{a\alpha'}}\right]} \tag{21}$$

This update process is iterated while annealing the temperature T [18,33].

6 Experiments

In this Section we compare the EM matching process with some alternatives. In particular we offer comparison with both quadratic assignment and mean-field annealing. This Monte-Carlo study is aimed at evaluating relative algorithm performance and is confined to synthetic graphs.

6.1 Experimental Data

The data for our Monte-Carlo study is provided by synthetic Delaunay graphs. These graphs are constructed by generating random dot patterns. Each random dot is used to seed a Voronoi cell. The Delaunay triangulation is the region adjacency graph for the Voronoi cells. The average connectivity of the nodes in the Delaunay triangulation is six edges. Moreover, the graphs are planar.

In order to pose demanding tests of our matching technique, we have added controlled amounts of corruption to the synthetic graphs. This is effected by deleting and adding a specified fraction of the dots from the initial random patterns. The associated Delaunay graph is therefore subject to structural corruption. We measure the degree of corruption by the fraction of surviving nodes in the corrupted Delaunay graph.

Our experimental protocol has been as follows. For a series of different corruption levels, we have generated a sample of 100 random graphs. The graphs contain 30 nodes each. According to the specified corruption level, we have both added and deleted a predefined fraction of nodes at random locations in the initial graphs so as to maintain their overall size. For each graph we measure the quality of match by computing the fraction of the surviving nodes which are correctly matched. In each of our experiments we commence from an initial configuration in which 50% of the matches are erroneously assigned.

6.2 Performance Comparison

We have compared the results obtained with three alternative matching algorithms. The first of these involves performing mean-field annealing on the cost-function given in equation (9). We have reviewed this algorithm in Section 5 and more details can be found in the recent paper of Finch, Wilson and Hancock [14]. The second mean-field algorithm is based on the more familiar quadratic assignment cost function [18,33]. Brief algorithm details are again reviewed in Section 5. The final algorithm is a deterministic gradient ascent method which aims to optimise the configurational probability specified in equation (1). The update process is as follows

$$f^{(n+1)}(a) = \arg \max_{\alpha \in V_M \cup \phi} \sum_{b \in C_a} K_b \sum_{\beta \in S_\alpha} \exp\left[-\left(\mu_e H(\Gamma_b^{(n)}, S_\beta) + \mu_\phi \Phi(\Gamma_b^{(n)})\right)\right]$$

(22)

Figure 1 shows the final fraction of correct matches for each of the algorithms in turn. The data curves show the correct matching fraction averaged over the graph samples as a function of the corruption fraction. The main conclusion that can be drawn from these plots is that the EM matching technique described in this paper significantly outperforms both the gradient ascent and mean-field methods at low corruption levels. However, when the level of added corruption exceeds 30%, then the mean-field optimisation of the cost-function of equation (10) outperforms the EM optimisation of the same quantity. This observation can be reconciled in the following way. In order to obtain mean-field

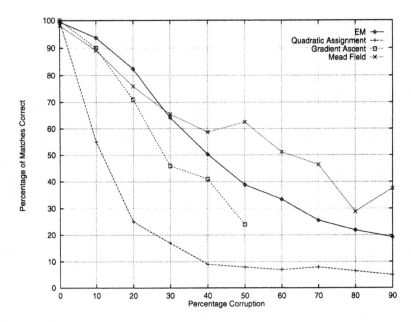

Fig. 1. Experimental comparison: EM (bold solid curve); mean-field annealing (faint solid curve); gradient ascent(dotted curve); quadratic assignment (dashed curve).

equations we have approximated the Hamming distance computation with a softened representation of the matching problem. This has inevitably compromised the ability of the cost-function to distinguish relatively small differences in the structure of the graphs under match. This insensitivity is most pronounced at small corruption levels. When corruption is high, then the mean-field method is most effective because of its global optimisation capabilities.

The quadratic cost-function delivers very poor results at all corruption levels. This is due to the fact that it uses a relatively unsophisticated measure of matching similarity. The deterministic gradient ascent procedure produces results which are slightly poorer than the EM approach. In other words, we appear to have gained performance as a result of using the two-step update procedure.

Finally, some illustrative examples of the graphs used in our comparative study are shown in Figures 2, 3 and 4. Figure 2 shows the model graph. Figures 3 and 4 show the initial and final matches of the data graph. These nodes are labelled and colour coded according to match. Light-grey circles are correctly matched while dark-grey circles indicate matching errors. The grey-shaded circles are null-matches; the light-grey–circled ones are correctly null-matched while the dark-grey-circled ones are incorrectly null-matched. The numbers beside the mismatched nodes indicate the identity of the erroneous match.

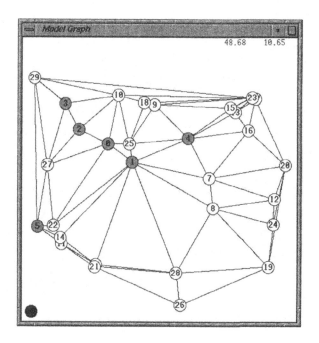

Fig. 2. Model graph.

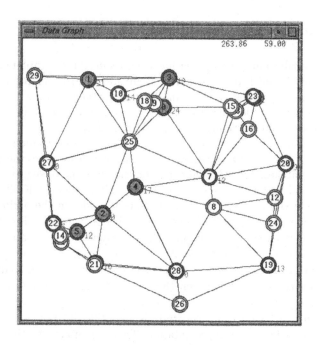

Fig. 3. Initial match of the data graph.

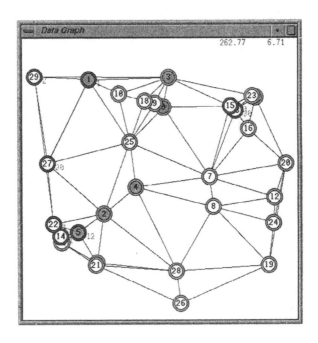

Fig. 4. Final match of the data graph.

7 Conclusions

The main contribution of this paper has been to show how graph matching can be realised using the EM algorithm of Dempster, Laird and Rubin [11]. Our interest in this process is twofold. In the first instance, we have recently developed a mixture model which describes the graph-matching process using a family of exponential distributions of the Hamming distance between subgraphs [37,38]. Hitherto, our search from graph-matches has been confined to locating matches which maximise a consistency measure which averages the probability of subgraph-matches. The EM algorithm, on the other hand, suggests that maximum likelihood matches should be located by minimising the Kullback-Leibler divergence between graphs. Our second interest resides in the optimisation architecture underpinning the EM algorithm. This is two-stage. Firstly, discrete matches are located so as to minimise the divergence. These matches are then used to compute *a posteriori* probabilities for weighting the Hamming distances which appear in the divergence. This mixture of soft and hard ingredients offers an interesting compromise between the use of discrete [8,9] and continuation methods [14,15] of optimisation.

The main conclusion from our study is that the EM process offers advantages in terms of fidelity of representation. This is exhibited by the its superior performance over mean-field optimisation at levels of structural corruption not exceeding 30%. However, at higher levels of corruption the method is limited by the local optimisation strategy adopted in the maximisation step. We are currently working at overcoming this shortcoming by incorporating a stochastic optimisation process into the maximisation step of the algorithm [8,9].

References

1. Aarts E. and Korst J., "Simulated Annealing and Boltzmann Machines", *John Wiley and Sons, New York*, 1989.
2. Adelson E.H. and Weiss Y., "A Unified Mixture Framework for Motion Segmentation: Incorporating Spatial Coherence and Estimating the Number of Models" *Proceedings IEEE CVPR Conference*, pp. 321–326, 1996.
3. Barrow H.G. and R.J. Popplestone, "Relational Descriptions in Picture Processing", *Machine Intelligence*, **6**, 1971.
4. Becker S. and Hinton G.E, "Learning Mixture Models of Spatial Coherence", Neural Computation, **5**, pp 267–277, 1992.
5. Blake A. and Zisserman A., "Visual Reconstruction", *MIT Press*, 1987.
6. Bridle J.S. "Training stochastic model recognition algorithms can lead to maximum mutual information estimation of parameters" *NIPS2*, pp. 211-217, 1990.
7. Cross A.D.J., R.C. Wilson and E.R. Hancock, "Discrete Relaxation on a Boltzmann Machine", *Proceedings ICANN 95*, pp. 491–496,1995.
8. Cross A.D.J., R.C.Wilson and E.R. Hancock, "Genetic Search for structural matching", *Proceedings ECCV96*, Lecture Notes in Computer Science 1064, pp. 514–525, 1996.
9. Cross A.D.J. and E.R.Hancock, "Relational Matching with stochastic optimisation" *IEEE Computer Society International Symposium on Computer Vision*, pp. 365–370, 1995.
10. Dayan P., Hinton G.E., Neal R.M., Zemel R.S., "The Helmholtz Machine", *Neural Computation*, **7**, pp. 889–904, 1995.
11. Dempster A.P., Rubin N.M. and Rubin D.B., "Maximum-likelihood from incomplete data via the EM algorithm", J. Royal Statistical Soc. Ser. B (methodological),**39**, pp 1-38, 1977.
12. Durbin R. and Willshaw D., "An analogue approach to the travelling salesman problem", *Nature*, **326**, pp. 689–691, 1987.
13. Durbin R., Szeliski R. and Yuille A.L., "An analysis of the elastic net approach to the travelling salesman problem", *Neural Computation*, **1**, 348–358, 1989.
14. Finch A.M., Wilson R.C. and Hancock E.R., "Relational Matching with Mean-Field Annealing", *Proceedings of the 13th International Confererence on Pattern Recognition*, Volume II, pp. 359–363, 1996.
15. Finch A.M., Wilson R.C. and Hancock E.R., "Softening Discrete Relaxation", *to appear in Advances in Neural Information Processing Systems 9*, MIT Press 1997.
16. Geman S. and D. Geman, "Stochastic relaxation, Gibbs distributions and Bayesian restoration of images," *IEEE PAMI*, **PAMI-6** , pp.721–741, 1984.
17. Gold S., A. Rangarajan and E. Mjolsness, "Learning with pre-knowledge: Clustering with point and graph-matching distance measures", *Neural Computation*, **8**, pp. 787–804, 1996.
18. Gold S. and A. Rangarajan, "A Graduated Assignment Algorithm for Graph Matching", *IEEE PAMI*, **18**, pp. 377–388, 1996.
19. Hancock, E.R. and J. Kittler, "Discrete Relaxation," *Pattern Recognition*, **23**, pp.711–733, 1990.

20. Hornegger J. and H. Niemann, "Statistical Learning Localisation and Identification of Objects" *Proceedings Fifth International Conference on Computer Vision*, pp. 914–919, 1995.

21. Jordan M.I. and Jacobs R.A, "Hierarchical Mixtures of Experts and the EM Algorithm", *Neural Computation*, **6**, pp. 181-214, 1994.

22. Kirkpatrick S., C.D. Gelatt and M.P. Vecchi, "Optimisation by Simulated Annealing", *Science*, **220**, pp. 671–680, 1983.

23. Maclean J. and Jepson A,, "Recovery of Ego-motion and Segmentation of Independent Object Motion using the EM Algorithm", *Proceedings BMVC*, pp. 175–184, 1994.

24. Meer P., Mintz D., Rosenfeld A. and Kim D.Y., "Robust Regression Methods for Computer Vision - A Review", *International Journal of Computer vision*, **6**, pp. 59–70, 1991.

25. Mjolsness E., G.Gindi and P. Anandan, "Optimisation in model matching and perceptual organisation", *Neural Computation*, **1**, pp. 218–219, 1989.

26. Moghaddam B. and Pentland A., "Probabilistic Visual Learning for Object Detection", *Proceedings of the Fifth International Conference on Computer Vision*, pp. 786–793, 1995.

27. Novovicova J., Pudil P. and Kittler J., "Divergence Based Feature Selection for Multi-modal Class Densities", *IEEE PAMI*, **18**, pp. 218–223, 1996.

28. Peterson C. and Soderberg B., "A New Method for Mapping Optimisation Problems", *International Journal of Neural Systems*, **1**, pp 2-33, 1989.

29. Sanfeliu A. and Fu K.S., "A Distance Measure Between Attributed Relational Graphs for Pattern Recognition", *IEEE SMC*, **13**, pp 353–362, 1983.

30. Shapiro L. and R.M.Haralick, "Structural Description and Inexact Matching", *IEEE PAMI*, **3**, pp 504–519, 1981.

31. Shapiro L. and R.M.Haralick, "A Metric for Comparing Relational Descriptions", *IEEE PAMI*, **7**, pp 90-94, 1985.

32. Simic P., "Constrained nets for graph matching and other quadratic assignment problems", *Neural Computation*, **3** , pp. 268–281, 1991.

33. Suganathan P.N., E.K. Teoh and D.P. Mital, "Pattern Recognition by Graph Matching using Potts MFT Networks", *Pattern Recognition*, **28**, pp. 997–1009, 1995.

34. Utans J., "Mixture Models and the EM Algorithms for Object Recognition within Compositional Hierarchies", *ICSI Berkeley Technical Report*, TR-93-004, 1993.

35. P. Viola and W. Wells, "Alignment by Maximisation of Mutual Information", *Proceedings of the Fifth International Conference on computer Vision*, pp. 16–23, 1995.

36. Wells W.M., "MAP Model Matching", *IEEE Computer Society Computer Vision and Pattern Recognition Conference*, pp. 486–492, 1991.

37. Wilson R.C., Evans A.N. and Hancock E.R., "Relational Matching by Discrete Relaxation", *Image and Vision Computing*, **13**, pp. 411–421, 1995.

38. Wilson R.C and Hancock E.R., "Relational Matching with Dynamic Graph Structures", *Proceedings of the Fifth International Conference on Computer Vision*, pp. 450-456, 1995.

39. Yuille A.L., Stolorz P. and Utans J., "Statistical Physics, Mixtures of Distributions, and the EM Algorithm" *Neural Computation*, **6**, pp. 334–340, 1994.

40. Yuille A., "Generalised Deformable Models, Statistical Physics and Matching Problems", *Neural Computation*, **2**, pp. 1-24, 1990.

An Energy Minimization Method for Matching and Comparing Structured Object Representations[*]

Robert Azencott and Laurent Younes

Sudimage Research Laboratory
and
CMLA, ENS Cachan, CNRS URA 1611
61 av. du Président Wilson, 94235 Cachan CEDEX, France
email: younes@cmla.ens-cachan.fr

Abstract. We present a general method for matching segmented parts of objects by energy minimization. The energy is designed in order to cope with possible imperfections of the compared segmentations (merged, or missing regions), and relies on the comparison of shape and positional descriptors. The minimization of the energy is performed by a simulated annealing procedure

1 Introduction

Structural representations describe objects by a list of elementary parts (or components, or primitives) and relations between them. Such representations may be used for a large range of objects. One-dimensional representations describe curves as objects outlines ; it may be a polygonal approximation of the curve, a list of feature points, the sequence of its concave/convex parts ([11]). Many segmentation procedures have been designed to provide 2D and 3D decomposition. Representation by line segments or feature points are also commonly used. Recognition is then performed by comparing these representations, and graph-matching paradigms and algorithms have been designed by many authors.

In any case, when comparing two objects, at least one representation is directly extracted from observed data. In fact, most of the methods dedicated to object recognition assume the existence of of prototypes, for which a presumably perfect representation is computed once and for all, and consider that an instance of one of them is observed and must be recognized. The protype which provides the best match to the observation is selected. However, the extraction of the structural representation from real data is a difficult task. It is, for example, hardly possible to design a perfectly reliable image segmentation procedure, because of the inherent ambiguities of 2-D images (shadows, specularities, occlusions...). Thus, at least one of the compared structures will be imperfect, and

---

[*] This work partially comes from a project on object recognition, supported by the D.R.E.T, helded at SUDIMAGE research laboratory. Publication is courtesy of the D.R.E.T.

sometimes both, since an exact description of the prototypes need not be always available. Matching (and comparison) has to cope with these imprecisions. A general approach for inexact graph matching has been presented in [9]. In this reference, trangressions of relational constraints between the matched primitives are allowed up to a certain amount. However, for many representations, typical variations may strongly affect the structures. The case of segmented images is illustrative : one of the most frequent perturbations is oversegmentation, in which case the graph structure may be drastically changed. This corresponds to a union of nodes in the graph, which cannot be ignored by the matching process. In [12], a solution is provided by the use of augmented association graphs. Our approach in the present work aims at the same objective, that is comparing structured representations in which similar objects may yield significant differences in the structures, albeit with substantial differences.

A first difference with the most frequent approaches is that our primary goal is not explicitly recognition, but merely comparison. We want to design a method to decide whether two representations are similar or not, and incidentally quantify this similarity (of course, recognition would be the goal of a second stage). In addition, we do not assume that one of the representation is perfect, so that both objects will be treated in a symmetric way.

So, our matching paradigm is not one-to-one but many-to-many, in order to handle possible unions of components in one representation before matching the other. Aggregating primitives yields a new, simpler, but less informative, representation of the object. It is always possible to simplify in that way the original representations so that they become similar, or at least comparable. This provides the principles of our method : object views will be considered as similar if slight simplifications of their representation can be matched so that they have a similar structure.

A large part of the paper deals with the problem with a more or less general formulation. We assume a decomposition into components, but we do not explicitly place a graph structure on the representation, the relationships being described by a family of descriptors, which are real valued functions of several components. A simplification of this structure is formalized as an operation which permits to agglomerate parts, or to discard them. In such a context, we design a method for matching, then comparing representations. Our approach is variational and we design a cost function which is small for a correct matching. The construction of the cost function is based a general framework, in which we include unspecified features which depend on the application.

In the second part of the paper, we complete the cost function in order to deal with the particular case of comparing segmented views of objects.This application is a part of a global project on multi-view object recognition.

2   General formulation

Let an object representation, $\mathcal{R}$, be composed with a certain number, N, of parts (N depending on the object), which we shall write $\mathcal{R} = (R_1, \ldots, R_N)$. The representation $\mathcal{R}$ is characterized by a family of *relational descriptors*, which describes the relationship between the elements of $\mathcal{R}$: let q be a positive integer, the order of the description, and $\mathcal{P}_q$ be the collection of all the subsets of $\{1, \ldots, N\}$ with less than q elements : for each $C \in \mathcal{P}_q$, denote by $\mathcal{R}_C$ the collection $(R_i, i \in C)$, and the descriptor associated to C is a feature $\lambda_C(\mathcal{R})$ computed from $\mathcal{R}_C$. Note that λ_C can be multi-dimensional (even infinite dimensional : for example the regions boundaries in the case of segmented images of objects). In our experiments, the order q is limited to $q = 2$. One basic principle is that two representations $\mathcal{R}$ and $\mathcal{R}'$ will be considered to be similar if their descriptors are close.

When given two object representations, one must determine compatible orderings before comparing, that is, the parts in each representation have to be matched one to another. Moreover, since the number of components in the representations of two different objects need not be equal, some parts in one representation may not find any related parts in the other one. Finally, we may also be in a situation in which a component R_k is divided into several parts in the other representation. This is likely to happen when the representation is extracted from observed data (as in our study, in which we use image segmentation algorithms), but this can also correspond to a case in which the second object is similar, but simpler than the first one. Thus, some transformations of the representations must be allowed before the matching: a) discarding components from any of the two representations; b) grouping several parts together. For the last one, we assume that some aggregation operation is available, which associates to two components R_1 and R_2 their union which will be denoted $R_1 \cup R_2$. We furthermore assume that this operation is commutative and associative. In our application, components are regions in the image plane, and aggregation simply is set union. These operations have the effect to simplify a representation ; we do not allow for the possibility to divide a component into several ones, which would induce a complexification of the representation, and would require some extraneous information which is not necessarily available. Thus, the matching problem is to determine compatible simplified representations of the objects from the original representations. To summarize, its solution requires to

a– Discard some components from each representation (those which cannot be correctly matched)

b– Aggregate some components in each representation

c– Find compatible orderings of the aggregated components

It is clear that there is no reason for which any of these three steps could be performed before the other two : it is impossible to decide whether a component in the first representation should rather be discarded or aggregated to others unless one has tried to match the aggregated group to some other group in the second representation. These operations must in fact be performed simultaneously. For this reason, we minimize a single criterion combining several cost functions, each of which being concerned with one step (a– to c–) of the procedure.

3 Notation for the matching problem

We fix some notation. Let $\mathcal{R} = (R_1, \ldots, R_N)$ ans $\mathcal{R}' = (R'_1, \ldots, R'_M)$ be the two representations to match. In order to indicate that two groups of components are matched, it suffices to mark each element of these groups with a common label. Denote by $\{1, \ldots, L\}$ a set of labels, to be used to mark matched components, and add to it a new label, 0, to mark the components which have not been matched. Specifying a common labelling of the representations boils down to defining two mappings, ϕ and ψ, which respectively provide the labels of the components R_i and R'_i:

$$\phi : \{1, \ldots, N\} \longrightarrow \{0, \ldots, L\} , \; \psi : \{1, \ldots, M\} \longrightarrow \{0, \ldots, L\} .$$

We do not know the exact number of labels in the matching, that is L is unknown, but it can be bounded (for example, $L \leq L_0 = \min(N, M))$). Labels in $\{1, \ldots, L\}$ being reserved for matched components, introduce the notation (for $k \in \{0, \ldots, L\}$) $\Sigma_k = \cup_{\phi(i)=k} R_i$ and $\Sigma'_k = \cup_{\psi(i')=k} R'_{i'}$. The discarded parts, Σ_0 and Σ'_0 may be empty, but, for $k = 1, \ldots, L$, we impose that Σ_k and $\Sigma'_k \neq \emptyset$.

Thus, another way to formulate the problem is that we are looking for two simplified representations $\mathcal{S} = (\Sigma_0, \ldots, \Sigma_L)$, $\mathcal{S}' = (\Sigma'_0, \ldots, \Sigma'_L)$, with the convention that Σ_0 and Σ'_0 are the (possibly empty) aggregation of discarded components, and that the components Σ_k and Σ'_k are matched together, for $k \in \{1, \ldots, L\}$. The representations $\mathcal{S}$ and $\mathcal{S}'$ are called *simplifications* of the original representations $\mathcal{R}$ and $\mathcal{R}'$.

We assume that, for any object representation $\mathcal{R} = (R_1, \ldots, R_N)$, one can compute relational descriptors $\lambda_C(\mathcal{R})$, where C are subsets of $\{1, \ldots, N\}$, which describes some relationship between the R_i, $i \in C$. We assume that λ_C only depends on $R_i, i \in C$ and on $\mathcal{U}(\mathcal{R}) = \cup_{k=1}^N R_k$ (this last dependence holding to allow global normalisation of the descriptors). Note that if $\mathcal{S}$ is a simplification of $\mathcal{R}$, we set $\mathcal{U}(\mathcal{S}) = \mathcal{U}(\mathcal{R})$ (that is we include the discarded regions to compute the global properties of $\mathcal{S}$), so that $\mathcal{U}(\mathcal{R})$ and $\mathcal{U}(\mathcal{R}')$ are invariant of the matching process. Thus, our problem is to determine $\mathcal{S}$ and $\mathcal{S}'$ so that $\lambda_C(\mathcal{S}) \simeq \lambda_C(\mathcal{S}')$.

Together with the similarity of the simplifications of $\mathcal{R}$ and $\mathcal{R}'$, we add, in order to evaluate the matching, a parcimony constraint to ensure that the representations are not over-simplified : there should not be too many discarded regions (otherwise, there will be nothing left to compare) and the aggregation process should be limited, in order to keep as much as possible of the information contained in the original representations. The cost function we built takes into account the previous constraints as a sum of penalty terms.

4 Quantitative evaluation of the quality of the matching

4.1 General principle

We follow a variational approach and define a cost function which will be small when the matching is adequate (according to the previous qualitative criteria).

The cost function will be the sum of several terms, each of which being designed in order to constrain a particular behaviour. Since we have selected three criteria, there will be three terms, each of them respectively aiming at

1- Similarity of the descriptors λ_C computed on the simplifications $\mathcal{S}$ and $\mathcal{S}'$
2- Restriction of the sizes of the sets Σ_0 and Σ'_0 (unmatched regions)
3- Limitation of the aggregation process : Σ_k and Σ'_k should not be composed with too many regions of the original segmentations

In some applications, one can imagine some hard constraints imposed on the aggregation process. For example, connectivity of the aggregates may be enforced, or aggregation of some uncompatible components may be forbidden.

4.2 Cost function

In this section, we only give the general form of the cost function, leaving the detailed description to the next sections. This function is of the kind

$$E(\phi, \psi) = E_1(\phi, \psi) + E_2(\phi, \psi) + E_3(\phi, \psi)$$

each of these terms corresponding to one of the criteria 1 to 3 above.

In order to estimate the importance of the components (for example to quantify the second criterion), we assume that we can compute, for each part R of a representation, a measure of size, which we shall denote by $\mathcal{A}(R)$. In addition, to compare the descriptors, we assume that, for all $k \leq q$ (q being the order of the description), we have designed a measure of the difference between two descriptors λ_C and λ'_C for $|C| = k$, which will be denoted $\Delta_k(\lambda_C, \lambda'_C)$. We shall put, writing, for short, $\lambda_C = \lambda_C(\mathcal{S})$ and $\lambda'_C = \lambda_C(\mathcal{S}')$ for subsets C of $\{1, \ldots, L\}$,

$$E_1(\phi, \psi) = \sum_{p=1}^{q} \sum_{C, |C|=p} \Delta_p(\lambda_C, \lambda'_C) \mu_p(C),$$

where μ_p is a weight which depends on the sizes of the sets Σ_k and Σ'_k for $k \in C$.

For the second criterion, we simply set $E_2(\phi, \psi) = \mathcal{A}(\Sigma_0) + \mathcal{A}(\Sigma'_0)$.

Finally, to define the cost associated to point 3, we assume a dispersion measure for the representation $\mathcal{R}$, denoted Γ, which can be computed on any family $R_i, i \in V$ (with $V \subset \{1, \ldots, N\}$), which is large when the sets R_i are (in a sense to be defined) far apart one from each other. Similarly, a dispersion measure Γ' in $\mathcal{R}'$ is defined. Let us put, for short, $\Gamma_k = \Gamma(R_i, i \in \phi^{-1}(k))$ and $\Gamma'_k = \Gamma'(R'_i, i \in \psi^{-1}(k))$

$$E_3(\phi, \psi) = \sum_{k=1}^{L} \nu(\Sigma_k) \Gamma_k + \sum_{k=1}^{L} \nu(\Sigma'_k) \Gamma'_k.$$

There again, ν is a weight, depending on the sizes of the components Σ_k and Σ'_k.

A good choice of the weights μ_k and ν is decisive for the success of the method. They can be calibrated by analyzing the variations of the cost function under simple transformations of the matching. This is a general method (cf [1]) which ensures that the weights are calibrated in order to provide a correct matching at least for particular cases. In order to carry on the analysis, we make some additional assumptions which will be satisfied in the application below.

The first one is that the comparators Δ_k and the dispersion measures Γ and Γ' are normalized so that their typical values are near the unity. The second one is that the size measure is additive, that is $\mathcal{A}(R_1 \cup R_2) = \mathcal{A}(R_1) + \mathcal{A}(R_2)$. Under these hypothesis, let us consider the following case. Start with simplifications $\mathcal{S}$ and $\mathcal{S}'$ with L labels, and consider the variation in which all the components which form Σ_L and Σ'_L are discarded and added to Σ_0 and Σ'_0. Because of the additivity assumption, the variation of E_2 would be $\Delta E_2 = \mathcal{A}(\Sigma_L) + \mathcal{A}(\Sigma'_L)$.

The variation of E_3 is $\Delta E_3 = -\nu(\Sigma_L)\Gamma_L - \nu(\Sigma'_L)\Gamma'_L$, and for E_1, it is

$$\Delta E_1 = -\sum_{p=1}^{q} \sum_{C, |C|=p, L \in C} \Delta_p(\lambda_C, \lambda'_C)\mu_p(\Sigma_i, i \in C).$$

Without any knowledge about the regions which have been discarded, there is no reason to priviledge any of the terms of the cost function. Thus, the weights should be tuned in order that each of the terms have comparable size for "average" values of Δ_p, Γ_k (according to our hypothesis, these average values are 1). The analysis will also provide "average values" for the weights (this is why we speak of "calibration" of the weights). It appears however that the weights which are provided by such rough computations are sufficiently well fitted to yield good results, and that slight variations around these values provide matchings of comparable quality. If needed, further variations of the same analysis can provide additional constraints which would induce some more acute information on the weights.

Thus, $\mathcal{A}(\Sigma_L) + \mathcal{A}(\Sigma'_L)$ should have the same size as $\nu(\Sigma_L) + \nu(\Sigma'_L)$ which naturally leads to set $\nu(\Sigma) = \mathcal{A}(\Sigma)$. This should also be the size of

$$\sum_{p=1}^{q} \sum_{C, |C|=p, L \in C} \mu_p(\Sigma_i, i \in C),$$

and we assume that each term of this sum has the same size, so that relationships of all orders have the same influence. The first term (for $p = 1$) is $\mu_1(L)$, and it is natural to set $\mu_1(L) = \mathcal{A}(\Sigma_L) + \mathcal{A}(\Sigma'_L)$.

Now, for $p = 2$, the term is $\sum_{k \neq L} \mu_2(k, L)$ which should have the same size as $\mu_1(L)$. One possibility is to put $\mu_2(k, L) = \mu_1(k)\mu_1(L)/\sum_l \mu_1(l)$, with the assumption that $\mu_1(L)$ is small compared to $\sum_{k \neq L} \mu_1(k)$. Terms of order larger than 2 can be handled similarly.

5 Minimization Procedure

The discrete minimization problem, in its full generality is a hard problem. It requires to find partitions of the sets $\{1, \ldots, N\}$ and $\{1, \ldots, M\}$, and the best matching between them. The size of all acceptable matchings is quite large (about 10^{12} for $M = N = 10$, 10^{31} for $M = N = 15$) so that the optimal matching cannot be determined by systematic exploration. In some cases, for example, when dealing with curves or acyclic graphs, global optimization algorithms, such as dynamic programming, may be devised. In all cases, simulated annealing is a good general procedure for massive discrete optimization. This is the one we have used in our application. In order to determine the labels ϕ and ψ, the algorithm works as follows. At each stage, it proposes a small modification of the current ϕ and ψ, which induces some variation ΔE of the cost function. The modification may be refused, and this is done with probability $\max(0, 1 - \exp(-\Delta E/T))$, T being a factor which slowly decreases to 0 during the procedure. If the elementary modifications are suitably designed, and the decreasing of T is slow enough, the algorithm provides the global minima of E.

Besides the theoretical slow decreasing rate of T (which is practically unachievable, and replaced by an exponentially fast decreasing rate — cf. [4] for a justification of this choice in the case of finite horizon annealing processes), the other condition for a good behaviour of this minimization algorithm holds on the choice of the elementary transition at each time. Assume that, when the current state is (ϕ, ψ), the new proposal is taken at random in a set $A(\phi, \psi)$ (which may vary with time). Then, sufficient conditions for convergence are :

if $(\phi', \psi') \in A(\phi, \psi)$, then $(\phi, \psi) \in A(\phi', \psi')$ and both sets have the same cardinality.

there exists a fixed integer n such that, a transition between any (ϕ, ψ) and (ϕ', ψ') is possible, with positive probability, in n steps.

Note that, when modifying ϕ and ψ, we must take care that the constraint that no label can be used for a representation and not for the other, is satisfied. To simplify the implementation, we fix the number L_0 of labels and allow for the possibility of unused labels. If $L_0 = \min(M, N)$, this does not affect the generality of the search. The constraint is then : for all $k \in \{1, \ldots, L_0\}$, $\phi^{-1}(k) = \emptyset \Leftrightarrow \psi^{-1}(k) = \emptyset$.

The sets $A(\phi, \psi)$ that we propose may be of two kinds. The first one contains transformations which simultaneously modify the values of $\phi(i)$ and $\psi(i')$ among the family of all admissible new labels. The second one contains transformations which exchange the values of $\phi(i)$ and $\phi(j)$ (or $\psi(i')$ and $\psi(j')$) if these values are different, and different from 0. Both types satisfy the conditions above, and they are alternated during the procedure.

Remark : The updating phase may become computationaly costly when the order of the description increases. For $q > 2$, it becomes necessary to define λ_C only for a restricted family of sets C with cardinality q, so that, for any i, the number of C with cardinality q for which λ_C is modified remains bounded independently of q. For example, the restriction may be to sets C for which all components are large enough, or close enough one to each other. But, this notion of size, or nearness, depend on the components whose labels are in C, and maybe also on other global properties of the representations : one consequence of it is that, under such a framework, when comparing two segmentations, some

λ_C could be defined in one case, and not in the other. This may be bypassed by letting $\lambda_C = K$, a constant, if C is not admissible, so that, effective computation of λ_C still is restricted to admissible C. Choosing K large enough is a way to forbid matching in which admissible C are matched to non admissible C.

6 Application : comparison of segmentations

6.1 Introduction

We now particularize the above approach to the problem of comparing segmentations. Given an image of an object, trying to separate it into functional parts is attractive, but a genuine functional decomposition is hardly feasible without high-level information on the observed object. A less ambitious program is to use the decomposition given by low-level image segmentation algorithms which separate the picture into homogeneous parts, based on features related to gray-level or color distribution. This representation often provides substantial information on the object, each homogeneous region in the image being most of the time associated to a single functional part of the object. However, starting at low-level, one has to cope with the usual drawbacks of image acquisition. Light variations, shadows, specularities, are elements which may cause errors and biase the results, and it is hopeless to expect that any segmentation procedure would provide outcomes bypassing these problems. Some enhancement, more robustness may be obtained by carefully selecting the algorithm, and it is an important, still largely open, issue in image processing to design efficient, robust, using minimal a priori information, low-level segmentation methods. However, when passing to comparison, the possibility of having to deal with over-segmentations, or strong variations in the shapes of regions, must be kept in mind, and this is precisely what is handled by our matching method.

Thus from now on, our representation is a family $\mathcal{R} = (R_1, \ldots, R_N)$ of regions of the image plane. Simplifications are obtained by discarding regions and aggregation by set union. Before completing the concepts presented in the previous paragraphs, we start with a brief discussion of the segmentation algorithm.

6.2 Segmentation algorithm

We just say a few words about the way we segment images. It is not in our intent to give a precise description of the method, which would be too long and out of the scope of the paper. The aim is, given a 2-D view of an object, to provide a partition of the image into regions $R_1, \ldots, R_N$ which corresponds to homogeneous parts of the picture relatively to a chosen criterium. In the present study, segmentation is based on colour. Once this characteristic is fixed, the procedure is entirely unsupervised, with respect to the number of regions, which is unknown, or to the various parameters (α, λ_1 and λ_2 below) which are estimated on line. The final segmentation is obtained by minimizing a discrete cost function, the general form of which being

$$E = \sum_i V(R_i) + \sum_{i \neq j} \sum_{(s,t) \in \partial_{ij}} [\lambda_1 - \lambda_2 \Delta_{st}].$$

where : $V(R_i)$ measures how much colour varies in region R_i; for $i \neq j$, ∂_{ij} is the (possibly empty) common boundary of regions R_i and R_j, composed with couples of pixels (s,t) such that $s \in R_i$, $t \in R_j$, and s and t are nearest neighbours on the image grid; Δ_{st} is an indicator function, equal to 1 if the difference of the colours at pixels s and t is larger than a threshold α and 0 if not.

We assume that the object is completely included in the picture, and we discard from the segmentation all the regions which meet the image frame. Assuming that the background is more or less homogeneous, this will discard most of the parts of the picture which do not belong to the object. Some piece of background may however be still present in the final segmentation, which provide a new kind of perturbation which must be handled by the matching procedure.

6.3 Descriptors

Generalities There are some desireable properties which may be expected from the descriptors. A first property is that they are rich enough to characterize the view of the object with satisfying accuracy. A second one comes from the fact that the object characterization must hold up to some parasit rigid transformation, since the relative positions of the compared objects are unknown, but should not influence the matching. The minimal rigid invariance which should be imposed are scale invariance and rotation invariance in the image plane. These are the invariance which will be explicitly addressed in this work. Affine invariance can also be required, to cope with variations in the angle of view of the objects. This seems too be less important than rotation and scaling, especially for complex objects, since variations of the angle of view are likely to yield appearance of occluded parts which cannot be modeled by affine transformation and would rather require a multi-view approach. Affine invariance however brings more robustness, and we will give some indication on how this can be achieved. Note that the use of relational descriptors gives much more latitude for the construction of invariant features, since there are much more invariant functions of several variables than of only one.

A last property which has to be aimed at by the descriptors is computational. Indeed, during the matching, the compared descriptors depend on the simplifications S and S' which are unknown. Given the combinatorial structure of the matching algorithm, it is essential that the calculation of the descriptors could be simple enough to avoid prohibitive computer time. At least, their updating after the changes which are proposed in the annealing algorithm of section 5 should not consume too much time. This is a strong limitation to the range of acceptable descriptors, and comes somewhat in contradiction with the first requirement on the accuracy of the description, but this is essential for practical use. It seems, however, that the constraints imposed by relational descriptors of several variables (even simple ones) are restrictive enough to yield good performance of the matching without harming too much the computation time.

We now pass to the explicit presentation of the descriptors which are used. They are of two kinds : a) positional, which depend on the centers of gravity of the regions, and b) relative to shape, which will be based on (rough) descriptions of the outline of the regions. The order of the representation is $q = 2$, so that we only have unary and binary descriptors. We thus assume that we have two segmentations $\mathcal{R} = (R_1, \ldots, R_N)$ and $\mathcal{R}' = (R'_1, \ldots, R'_M)$ and try to find two matched simplifications $\mathcal{S} = (\Sigma_0, \Sigma_1, \ldots, \Sigma_L)$ and $\mathcal{S}' = (\Sigma'_0, \Sigma'_1, \ldots, \Sigma'_L)$.

Importance evaluation To measure the size of a region Σ in a simplification $\mathcal{S}$, we simply use its relative area:

$$A(\Sigma) = \frac{\text{area}(\Sigma)}{\text{area}[\mathcal{U}(\mathcal{S})]}$$

where $\mathcal{U}(\mathcal{S})$ is the aggregate of all the components in $\mathcal{S}$.

This measure is used for the weights μ_k and ν, and also for the shape descriptors below. It is translation, rotation and scale invariant (in fact, it is affine invariant).

Positional descriptors The position of a region in the image plane is represented by its center of gravity, ie the mean position of the pixels which are contained in the region. In order to obtain translation invariance for unary descriptors, we use their relative position to the center of gravity of the complete object. Thus, we denote by G (resp. G') the center of gravity of $\mathcal{U} = \mathcal{U}(\mathcal{S}) = \Sigma_0 \cup \cdots \cup \Sigma_L$ (resp. $\mathcal{U}' = \Sigma'_0 \cup \cdots \cup \Sigma'_L$), which are constant during the matching. We let G_k (resp. G'_k) be the center of gravity of Σ_k (resp. Σ'_k). To induce rotation invariance, we only use the Euclidean distances between these points, letting our unary descriptors be the distance between G and G_k, denoted GG_k, and the binary descriptors be the collection of all $G_k G_l$, for $k \neq l$ larger than 1. Finally, in order to also obtain scale invariance, we use a unit length which depends on the total area of the segmentation : letting $A_{tot} = \sum_k \text{area}(R_k)$, we measure the lengths in terms of multiples of $1/\sqrt{A_{tot}}$.

Thus we have obtained unary and binary positional descriptors which are translation, rotation and scale invariant. If affine invariance were required, unary positional descriptors of the previous kind have to be dropped. Concerning binary descriptors, the area of the triangle (G, G_k, G_l) is an example of an affine invariant descriptor.

Shape descriptors To shorten notation, we let $A_k = A(\Sigma_k)$ be the relative area of Σ_k in $\mathcal{S}$ (and $A'_k = A(\Sigma'_k)$): this forms our first shape descriptor. The second one is the ellipse of inertia of the region Σ_k, which we denote by $\mathcal{E}_k$. If I_k is the matrix of inertia of Σ_k, ie

$$I_k = \int_{\Sigma_k} \overrightarrow{G_k X} \overrightarrow{G_k X}^t \, dX \, ,$$

the ellipse of inertia (up to scaling) is defined by $\overrightarrow{G_k X}^t I^{-1} \overrightarrow{G_k X} = $ cte. On the computational level, A_k, G_k and I_k can be very efficiently obtained by incremental formulae when S varies.

Similarly, we denote by A'_k and $\mathcal{E}'_k$ the area and ellipse of inertia of Σ'_k.

Since they are centered at G_k, the ellipses of inertia are translation invariant, but they are not rotation nor scale invariant. Therefore, the unary descriptors can only depend on the excentricities of the ellipses. The binary descriptors will be based on the comparison of the relative positions of two ellipses.

We shall in fact use two distances in order to compare two ellipses $\mathcal{E}$, $\mathcal{E}'$; we denote them by $d_0(\mathcal{E}, \mathcal{E}')$ and $d_1(\mathcal{E}, \mathcal{E}')$. The first one is invariant by scaling and rotation of any of the ellipses $\mathcal{E}$ and $\mathcal{E}'$, so that it only depends on the excentricities of the ellipses and will be used for unary descriptors. The second one is scale invariant, and invariant by simultaneous rotation of the ellipses (with a common angle), it thus depends on the relative positions of the ellipses. If we are only interested in comparing ellipses, there are many ways to define such distances. However once the matching will be computed, we want to use, for comparison, richer information than the ellipses of inertia, and use distances which have been designed to compare arbitrary plane curves (cf. [13]). They are computed (once the curves have been rescaled to have length 1), on the basis of the functions which give the orientations of the tangent vectors to the curves in function of the arc-length. An optimal matching is computed between these functions (denoted by θ and $\tilde{\theta}$), letting

$$d_1 = \inf_g \left\{ \arccos \int_0^1 \sqrt{\dot{g}_s} \left| \cos \left(\frac{\tilde{\theta} \circ g(s) - \theta(s)}{2} \right) \right| ds \right\}$$

g being a diffeomorphism of $[0, 1]$, and

$$d_0 = \inf_{g,c} \left\{ \arccos \int_0^1 \sqrt{\dot{g}_s} \left| \cos \left(\frac{\tilde{\theta} \circ g(s) - \theta(s) - c}{2} \right) \right| ds \right\}$$

g being a diffeomorphism of $[0, 1]$, and c being a number in $[0, 2\pi]$.

We have also used these distances to compare the ellipses. In order to reduce computation time, their values have been discretized off-line and stored in a look-up table.

We use two binary descriptors : first, the relative areas of Σ_k and Σ_l, $\frac{A_k}{A_l}$, and second, the distance $d_1(\mathcal{E}_k, \mathcal{E}_l)$. We compute in fact a single number, which is

$$B_{kl} = \frac{1}{2} \left| \log \frac{A_k}{A_l} \right| + d_1(\mathcal{E}_k, \mathcal{E}_l)$$

and, similarly for $\mathcal{S}'$, $B'_{kl} = \dfrac{1}{2} \left| \log \dfrac{A'_k}{A'_l} \right| + d_1(\mathcal{E}'_k, \mathcal{E}'_l)$.

Once again, these descriptors are not affine invariant. An affine invariant matching could de based on higher order moment-based invariant of the shape (the area of the ellipse of inertia being the only moment invariant of order 2).

6.4 Comparison of the descriptors

We now define the functions Δ_1 and Δ_2 which are used to compare unary and binary descriptors. Note that, in order that our discussion on the calibration of the weights be valid, their values much be properly normalized to have a typical range arount the unity. We set

$$\Delta_1(k) = \max \left\{ \frac{1}{2} \left| \log \frac{A_k}{A'_k} \right| + d_0(\mathcal{E}_k, \mathcal{E}'_k), 2 \frac{|GG_k - G'G'_k|}{GG_k + G'G'_k} \right\}. \tag{1}$$

and

$$\Delta_2(k,l) = \max \left\{ 2 \frac{|B_{kl} - B'_{kl}|}{B_{kl} + B'_{kl}}, 2 \frac{|G_k G_l - G'_k G'_l|}{G_k G_l + G'_k G'_l} \right\} \tag{2}$$

6.5 Measure of dispersion

The last point to describe is the measure of dispersion used in the cost term E_3, which has been denoted $\Gamma_k = \Gamma(R_i, i \in \phi^{-1}(k))$ and $\Gamma'_k = \Gamma'(R'_i, i \in \psi^{-1}(k))$. Note that this is the only term which refers to the original segmentation, the other ones depending only on the matched simplifications $\mathcal{S}$ and $\mathcal{S}'$. Assume that a distance D_{ij} is defined between regions R_i and R_j. We let

$$\Gamma_k = \frac{1}{A_k^2} \sum_{i,j \in \phi^{-1}(k)} D_{ij} \operatorname{area}(R_i) \operatorname{area}(R_j),$$

The term Γ'_k being similarly defined for the segmentation $\mathcal{R}'$.

To define the internal distance D_{ij} we take into account the topological structure of the segmentation $\mathcal{R}$. For each pair of regions R_i and R_j, we let ∂_{ij} be the possibly empty common boundary of R_i and R_j. Let a path from i to j in the set $\{1, \ldots, N\}$ be a sequence $i_0 = i, i_1, \ldots, i_p, i_{p+1} = j$. We define the length of such a path by a formula of the kind

$$L = \sum_{q=0}^{p} F(R_{i_q}, R_{i_{q+1}}) + \sum_{q=1}^{p} G(R_{i_{q-1}}, R_{i_q} R_{i_{q+1}})$$

where $F(R_i, R_j)$ is a cost associated to the transition between regions R_i and R_j. It is equal to a constant plus the minimum distance between all non empty boundaries ∂_{ik} and ∂_{jl}, for all $k, l \in \{1, \ldots, N\}$, which is 0 if $\partial_{ij} \neq \emptyset$; $G(R_i, R_j, R_k)$ is the distance between the closest boundary of R_i to R_j and the closest boundary of R_j to R_k. Thus the length of path is large when two successive regions are not adjacent, and it crosses some large region. The distance between two boundaries ∂ and ∂' is the mean value of $d(i, \partial')$ for $i \in \partial$ plus the mean value of $d(i', \partial)$ for $i' \in \partial'$.

7   Comparison after matching

Once the combinatorial part of the comparison (ie. the maching procedure) has been achieved, it is possible to use richer descriptors to quantify the differences between the objects. We adopt a hierarchical approach, and use successive criteria of increasing complexity to decide whether the viewed objects are similar or not.

The first criterion is based on the sizes of the discarded components Σ_0 and Σ_0' after the matching. Indeed, if the matching algorithm couldn't do better, while minimizing the cost function, than discarding a large proportion of the original components, this means that the representations were very different and there is no need to push the comparison further. So, we have a stopping crtiterion after matching which is based on

$$\rho = \max(\mathcal{A}(\Sigma_0), \mathcal{A}(\Sigma_0')) .$$

If ρ ou ρ' is larger than a threshold (we used 0.4) comparison is stopped.

The second criterion compares the centers of gravity G_k and G_k' of Σ_k and Σ_k'. Denote by z_k and z_k' the complex numbers representing the 2D vectors $\overrightarrow{GG_k}$ and $\overrightarrow{G'G_k'}$, where G and G' are the centers of gravity of the aggregation of the components of $\mathcal{R}$ and $\mathcal{R}'$. We let τ be a number in $[0, 2\pi[$ and set

$$d_{pos}(\tau) = 2 \arccos \frac{\text{real part}(\sum_{k=1}^{L} z_k \overline{z_k'} e^{-i\tau})}{\sqrt{\sum_{k=1}^{L} |z_k|^2} \sqrt{\sum_{k=1}^{L} |z_k'|^2}}$$

which, for each τ, is a distance comparing the z_k and $e^{i\tau}.z_k'$ up to scaling. This distance is small if, after a rotation of angle τ, the configurations of complex numbers, (z_k) and (z_k') are close enough. We compute this value for a discrete family of angles τ, and select those which are below a fixed threshold (we used 0.5). These τ are retained for the last stage, and if one could not find any, the procedure stops, and we conclude to high dissimilarity of the objects. In our experiments, we always found at least one correct τ, sometimes (but quite rarely) two.

The last criterion compares the outlines of the regions Σ_k and Σ_k'. Note that these regions can be very complex, since we have imposed no constraint on the aggregation process : Σ_k need not be convex, can contain holes. In order to obtain a reasonable candidate for the outline, we adopt the following procedure. For all $\theta \in [0, 2\pi[$, we compute the length $r_k(\theta)$ between G_k (the center of gravity of Σ_k) and the furthest point of Σ_k which belongs to the half-line of angle θ starting from G_k. The curve, parametrized in polar coordinates by $\theta \to r_k(\theta)$ will be denoted C_k and is our definition of the outline of Σ_k.

Given this, we let, for one of the τ selected at the previous stage, r_τ be a rotation of angle τ. We then compute the distance

$$d_{shape}(\tau) = 2 \arccos \frac{\sum_k \sqrt{A_k A_k'} \cos d_1(C_k, r_\tau C_k')}{\sqrt{\sum_k A_k} \sqrt{\sum_k A_k'}}$$

That this is a distance between the families of matched curves $(C_1, \ldots, C_L)$ and $(C'_1, \ldots, C'_L)$ can be deduced from the results of [13]. We finally select the τ for which $d_{shape}(\tau)$ is minimal, and this forms our final evaluation of the similarity of the views.

8 Experiments

Our experiments use a small database of video color images of toy vehicles. The matching algorithm performs well in finding a good matching when such a matching exists. If the objects differ too much, this is detected by one of our three criteria above.

Each figure describes a matching and is organized as follows. The upper left and upper right pictures provide the contours of the original segmentations $\mathcal{R}$ and $\mathcal{R}'$ which are compared : they provide all the information which is used for comparison and matching. The lower left and lower right pictures provide the obtained matching : the associated regions have the same gey colour and are patched with the same number.

In figures 1 to 3, we compare different views of a truck. In figure 1, d_{shape} is quite large (about 0.4). This is due to the fact that regions labeled 3 includes the lower part of the truck in one segmentation, and not in the other.

Figures 4 and 5 compare different objects, and the difference is well detected.

Finally, figures 6 to 8 provide comparisons of views of a truck, with various degrees of segmentation.

Fig. 1. Comparison of segmentations: truck 1 under different angles ; percentage of matched regions : 89.7% and 80.2%; $d_{pos} = 0.15$ radian (4 regions); $d_{shape} = 0.42$ radian

Fig. 2. Comparison of segmentations: truck 1 under different angles ; percentage of matched regions : 65.8% and 64%; $d_{pos} = 0.1$ radian (2 regions); $d_{shape} = 0.35$ radian

Fig. 3. Comparison of segmentations: truck 1 under different angles ; percentage of matched regions : 78% and 77.3%; $d_{pos} = 0.27$ radian (5 regions); $d_{shape} = 0.32$ radian

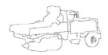

Fig. 4. Comparison of segmentations: plane and truck 2 ; percentage of matched regions : 75.3% and 57.9%; no computed distances

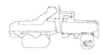

Fig. 5. Comparison of segmentations: truck 1 and truck 2 ; percentage of matched regions : 75.2% and 79.5%; $d_{pos} = 0.1$ radian (4 regions); $d_{shape} = 0.53$ radian

Fig. 6. Comparison of segmentations: truck 2 under different angles ; percentage of matched regions : 92% and 80.9%; $d_{pos} = 0.12$ radian (5 regions); $d_{shape} = 0.31$ radian

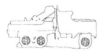

Fig. 7. Comparison of segmentations: truck 2 under different angles ; percentage of matched regions : 96.2% and 81.7%; $d_{pos} = 0.24$ radian (5 regions); $d_{shape} = 0.37$ radian

Fig. 8. Comparison of segmentations: truck 2 under the same angle (different segmentation) ; percentage of matched regions : 80% and 78.2%; $d_{pos} = 0.06$ radian (5 regions); $d_{shape} = 0.27$ radian

References

1. R. Azencott (1987): Image analysis and Markov random fields. Proc. of the int. Conf. on Ind. and Appl. Math. SIAM, Paris.
2. J. Ben-Arie and A. Z. Meiri (1987) : 3D Object recognition by optimal search of multinary relation graphs *Comp. Vis. Graph. Im. Proc.* 37, 345-361
3. R. Bergerin and M. Levine (1993) : Generic object recognition: building and matching coarse descriptions from line drawings *IEEE Trans. Pat. Anal. Mach. Intel.* Vol. 15, no 1, 19-36
4. O. Catoni (1990) Rough Large deviation estimates for simulated annealing. Application to exponential cooling schedules *Ann. of Proba.*, 20,1109-1146
5. W. E. L. Grimson and D. P. Huttenlocher (1991) : On the verification of hypothetized matches in model-based recognition *IEEE Trans. Pat. Anal. Mach. Intel.*Vol 13, no 12, 1201-1213
6. A. R. Pope (1994) : Model-based object recognition A survey of recent research Tech. Report 94- 04
7. E. Rivlin, S. J. Dickinson, A. Rosenfeld (1994) Recognition by functional parts. (preprint Center for automation research).
8. L. G. Shapiro (1980) A structural model of shape *IEEE Trans. Pat. Anal. Mach. Intel.* vol 2 no 2 111-126
9. L. G. Shapiro and R. M. Haralik (1981) : Structural description and inexact matching *IEEE Trans. Pat. Anal. Mach. Intel.* vol 3, no 5, 504-519
10. L. G. Shapiro and R. M. Haralik (1985) : A metric for comparing relational descriptors *IEEE Trans. Pat. Anal. Mach. Intel.* vol 7 no 1 90-98
11. N. Ueda and S. Suzuki (1993) : Learning visual models from shape contours using multi-scale convex/concave structure matching *IEEE Trans. Pat. Anal. Mach. Intel.* vol 15 no 4 337-351
12. B. Yang, W. E. Snyder and G. L. Bilbro (1989) : Matching over-segmented 3D images to models using association graphs *Image and vision comp.* Vol 7 no 2 135-143
13. L. Younes (1996) : Computable elastic distances between shapes (preprint).
14. S. Zhang, G. D. Sullivan, K. D. Baker (1993) : The automatic construction of a view independent relational model for 3-D object recognition *IEEE Trans. Pat. Anal. Mach. Intel.* Vol 15 no 6 531-544

Applications

Consistent Modeling of Terrain and Drainage Using Deformable Models

P. Fua (fua@ai.sri.com)*

Computer Graphics Lab (LIG)
EPFL
Ecublens
CH-1015 Lausanne
Switzerland

Abstract. We propose an automated approach to modeling drainage channels—and, more generally, linear features that lie on the terrain—from multiple images, which results not only in high-resolution, accurate and consistent models of the features, but also of the surrounding terrain. In our specific case, we have chosen to exploit the fact that rivers flow downhill and lie at the bottom of local depressions in the terrain, valley floors tend to be "U" shaped, and the drainage pattern appears as a network of linear features that can be visually detected in single gray-level images.

Different approaches have explored individual facets of this problem. Ours unifies these elements in a common framework. We accurately model terrain and features as 3–dimensional objects from several information sources that may be in error and inconsistent with one another. This approach allows us to generate models that are faithful to sensor data, internally consistent and consistent with physical constraints. We have proposed generic models that have been applied to the specific task at hand—river delineation and data elevation model (DEM) refinement—and show that the constraints can be expressed in a computationally effective way and, therefore, enforced while initializing the models and then fitting them to the data. We will also argue that the same techniques are robust enough to work on other features that are constrained by predictable forces.

1 Introduction

We propose an automated approach to modeling drainage channels—and, more generally, linear features that lie on the terrain—from multiple images, which results not only in high-resolution, accurate and consistent models of the features, but also of the surrounding terrain.

This is an important problem from both a practical point of view—drainage modeling is an essential component of map making—and a theoretical point of

---

* This work was conducted at SRI International, Menlo Park, CA and supported in part by contracts from the Defense Advanced Research Projects Agency.

view: We must address two key generic problems. The first is the obvious requirement to replace reliance on generally unavailable prior knowledge of explicit shape with more general ways of recognizing and describing natural objects. The second is the necessity to merge several sources of information that may not be consistent with one another.

In our specific case, we have chosen to exploit the fact that

- Rivers flow downhill and lie at the bottom of local depressions in the terrain.
- Valley floors tend to be "U" shaped and locally horizontal in the direction perpendicular to the main valley at the river locations.
- The drainage pattern appears as a network of linear features that can be visually detected in single gray-level images.

Different approaches have explored individual facets of this problem. There is extensive literature on the extraction of valleys from terrain models, for example see [17, 1, 3] among many others. The terrain model, however, is almost always assumed to be error-free, which, in practice, only rarely is the case. Furthermore, Koenderink and Van Doorn have shown [12] that the local differential criteria many of these systems use to detect valleys have inherent problems. Much work has also been devoted to the extraction of linear patterns from single images using techniques such as dynamic programming [5, 14] or graph-based techniques [4]. These techniques typically do not use the terrain information or guarantee that the recovered drainage pattern satisfies the physical constraints discussed above. Furthermore they do not take advantage of the fact that multiple images of the same site may be available.

Our approach unifies these elements in a common framework. Because the features and the physical constraints we deal with are fundamentally 3–D and because we want to be able to deal with an arbitrary number of images, there are very significant advantages in using an object-centered 3–D representation of the terrain surface and features that allows us to effectively enforce consistency constraints.

We have chosen to concentrate on the extraction and the refinement of drainage patterns because they are potentially complex but obey well-understood physical constraints and therefore constitute a very good test case for our research. However, we will show that, the same techniques are robust enough to work on other linear features that are constrained by predictable forces such as roads and ridelines.

We view the contribution of this paper as proposing a general approach to what is essentially a difficult data-fusion problem: Accurately modeling terrain and features from several information sources that may be in error and inconsistent with one another. This approach allows us to generate models that are faithful to sensor data, internally consistent and consistent with physical constraints. We have proposed generic models that have been applied to the specific task at hand—river delineation and data elevation model (DEM) refinement—and shown that the constraints can be expressed in a computationally effective way and, therefore, enforced while initializing the models and then fitting them to the data.

We first introduce our overall framework. We then review our approach to modeling the terrain and estimating its curvature and present the techniques we use to quickly sketch the drainage pattern and to automatically enforce the consistency constraints.

2 Approach

We model the terrain as a triangulated mesh that can be refined by minimizing an objective function, and we model the rivers' locations as polygonal paths

- that lie on the terrain surface,
- that are located where the curvature of the terrain surface is locally maximal,
- whose tangent vectors are the directions of maximal elevation decrease,
- whose altitude decreases monotonically.

We start by recovering the approximate shape of a terrain mesh by minimizing a multi-image stereo score [8] and computing a curvature map. From this map, we extract paths of maximal curvature using dynamic programming. This simple approach would be sufficient if the recovered terrain surface was perfect and if the terrain was steep enough for all streams to flow at the bottom of the sort of "V" shaped valleys that erosion produces. In practice, this is not always the case. There may not be enough relief to tell the real but shallow valleys from spurious valleys that may be present in the recovered terrain surface. Furthermore, even if there are deep and easy-to-detect "V" shaped valleys, vegetation tends to be taller on river banks, thus making the elevations computed by our surface-reconstruction algorithm unreliable. As a result, the recovered path may not follow the true valley bottom and may not exhibit monotonically decreasing elevations.

To solve these problems, we have developed a more sophisticated approach:

- We use both the terrain model and the actual gray-level images to extract a rough estimate of the features' locations, thus preventing the estimate from being too far off if there are errors in the terrain model.
- We simultaneously refine the models of the terrain and features under consistency constraints that ensure that they fit the image data as well as possible while conforming to the physical constraints known to apply.

We will show that this technique allows the quick generation of accurate and consistent 3-D models of the drainage channels and the surrounding terrain with minimal manual intervention.

3 Terrain Modeling and Curvature Estimation

Many object-centered surface representations could be used to represent the terrain. However, practical issues are important in choosing an appropriate one. First, it should be relatively straightforward to generate an instance of a surface from standard data sets such as depth maps or data elevation models. Second, there should be a computationally simple correspondence between the parameters specifying the surface and the actual 3-D shape of the surface, so that images of the surface can be easily generated, thereby allowing the integration of information from multiple images. Finally, it should be natural to express the geometric constraints inherent to the problem we are attempting to solve.

A regular 3-D triangulated mesh is an example of a surface representation that meets the criteria stated above, and is the one we have chosen for our previous work [8] and use here. We will refer to it as $\mathcal{S}$.

3.1 Recovering the Shape of the Terrain

The shape of a mesh $\mathcal{S}$ is defined by the position of its vertices. It can be refined by minimizing a regularized objective function that accounts for the stereo information present in multiple images of a cartographic site to produce models such as the one shown in Figure 1(c).

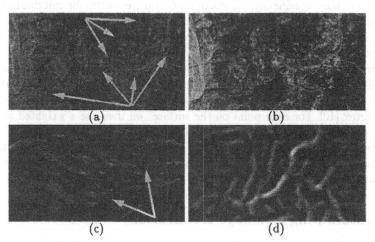

Fig. 1. Terrain modeling at the National Training Center (NTC), Ft. Irwin. (a,b) A stereo pair of a hilly site. The linear structure that runs horizontally in the middle of the images is a streambed and is indicated by the cluster of arrows in (a). The other cluster of arrows denotes a second streambed that runs vertically. (c) A shaded view of the terrain mesh recovered by our system after optimization. The two arrows point at the valley of the horizontal streambed shown in (a). The second streambed is hidden behind one of the hills. (d) The curvature image registered to the image shown in (a). Regions of high positive curvature—that is, candidate valley regions—are shown in white.

The objective function $\mathcal{E}(\mathcal{S})$ is taken to be

$$\mathcal{E}(\mathcal{S}) = \mathcal{E}_D(\mathcal{S}) + \mathcal{E}_{St}(\mathcal{S}) \; , \tag{1}$$

where $\mathcal{E}_D(\mathcal{S})$ is a regularization term that is quadratic in terms of the vertices' coordinates and $\mathcal{E}_{St}(\mathcal{S})$ is a multiple-image correlation term. It is derived by comparing the gray levels of the points in all the images for which the projection of a given point on the surface is visible. This comparison is done for a uniform sampling of the surface [8]. $\mathcal{E}_{St}$ is closely related to the terms used by Wrobel [19] and Heipke [10] in their least-squares approaches. This method allows us to deal with arbitrarily slanted regions and to discount occluded areas of the surface.

In our application, we fix the x and y coordinates of the vertices of $\mathcal{S}$, and the free variables are the z coordinates. The process is started with an initial estimate of the elevations typically derived from a coarse DEM. In the course of the optimization, we progressively refine the mesh by iteratively sub dividing the facets into four smaller ones whose sides are still of roughly equal length, thus preserving its regularity.

3.2 Differential Properties of the Terrain Surface

In Section 4, we will show that we can combine the differential properties of the terrain surface—specifically, its maximal curvature—with the information present in the gray-level images to automate the delineation of the drainage pattern. It is therefore important to be able to represent both kinds of information in a common frame of reference. In our application, we deal with near-vertical aerial imagery and we either use an ortho photo or the vertical-most available image.

Following Sander and Zucker [18], we estimate the maximal curvature at each vertex of the surface by fitting a quadric to the vertices in the neighborhood of that vertex [13]. For each point on the surface, we then use a weighted average of the curvatures of the three vertices of the facet to which it belongs.

Using this method and given a surface triangulation, we can compute, for each original gray-level image, a "curvature image" that is registered with it such as the ones shown in Figure 1(d).

4 Automating Drainage Delineation

We outline our approach to sketching the drainage pattern with a minimum of user intervention. We distinguish between steep terrain where the geometry of the terrain surface is usually sufficient to detect the drainage channels and less steep terrain where geometry becomes less relevant and the information present in the original images must be used more directly.

4.1 Steep Terrain

In high-relief areas, rivers create valleys by eroding the surrounding terrain and over time carve channels that typically are not completely filled. As a result they tend to appear as local depressions and their center lines closely match maxima of curvature in the terrain surface.

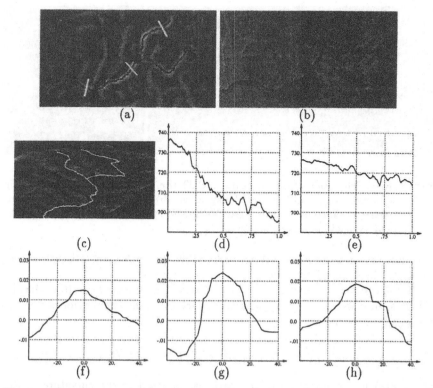

Fig. 2. Sketching the rivers at the NTC site. (a) The maximal curvature paths overlaid on the curvature image of Figure 1(f). For one of the paths, we specified two endpoints and one intermediate point denoted by the black circles; for the other we specified only the two endpoints denoted by the black rectangles. (b) The paths overlaid on the original image. (c) The paths overlaid on a shaded view of the terrain mesh of Figure 1(e). (d,e) Elevations along the paths. Note that because of imprecisions in the reconstruction, they are not monotonic. (f,g,h) Curvature of the surface along the three perpendicular cross sections shown as yellow segments in (a). Note that the paths lie at local maxima of curvature.

It is therefore natural to look for paths of maximum curvature in the "curvature images" introduced in Section 3.2 and computed using the terrain mesh. As shown in Figure 2 and 3, this can be achieved by simply specifying endpoints and using a dynamic programming algorithm [4] to find a path $\mathcal{C}$ that minimizes

$$\mathcal{E}_{Curv}(\mathcal{C}) = \int (C_{max}(\mathbf{f}(s)) - C_{max}^1)^2 \, ds \;, \qquad (2)$$

where $\mathbf{f}(s)$ is a vector function mapping the arc length s to points (u, v) along the curve, $C_{max}(u, v)$ is the terrain's surface maximal curvature at image location (u, v), and C_{max}^1 is the largest value of $C_{max}(u, v)$ in the curvature image. Using recent dynamic programming implementations [16, 2], this can be done in near

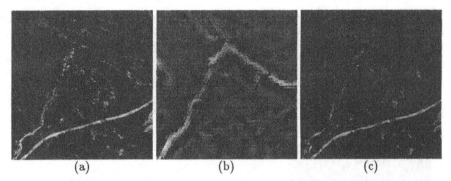

Fig. 3. River delineation at the McKenna, MOUT site, Ft. Benning. (a) One of a pair
of stereo images with a meandering ditch. (b) The corresponding curvature
image. (c) Maximal curvature path computed by specifying only the endpoints
and overlaid on the original image.

real time on a regular workstation, making this approach a very attractive way
to sketch the drainage pattern.

In the companion report [6], we prove that if $\mathcal{C}$ minimizes $\mathcal{E}_{Curv}(\mathcal{C})$—that is,
if it is a local minimum of $\mathcal{E}_{Curv}$ with respect to infinitesimal deformations of
the curve—it verifies:

$$\frac{\partial C_{max}(s)}{\partial n} = 1/2\kappa(s)(C_{max}(s) - C_{max}^1) \ \forall s \ , \qquad (3)$$

where $\kappa(s)$ is the curvature of the path—as opposed to the curvature of the
surface $C_{max}(s)$—and $\partial/\partial n$ denotes the derivative in the direction normal to
the curve. It follows that, wherever $\kappa(s)$ is small,

$$\frac{\partial C_{max}}{\partial n} \ll (C_{max}(s) - C_{max}^1) \ . \qquad (4)$$

Therefore $\mathcal{C}$ is close to being the locus of points that are maxima of curvature in
the direction normal to the curve. We therefore refer to these paths as "maximal
curvature" paths.

In practice, because $\mathcal{C}$ is computed using dynamic programming, it is discretized and made of points with integer coordinate values. Therefore, Equation 4
does not hold strictly. But, as illustrated by Figure 2, we have verified experimentally that the points of $\mathcal{C}$ are fairly close to actual maxima of curvature of
the terrain surface.

4.2 Flat Terrain

As the terrain's relief becomes less pronounced, the channels become increasingly
difficult to detect from the geometry of the surface mesh alone. In the limit, a
river meandering through an almost flat flood plain could not be sketched using
the technique described above.

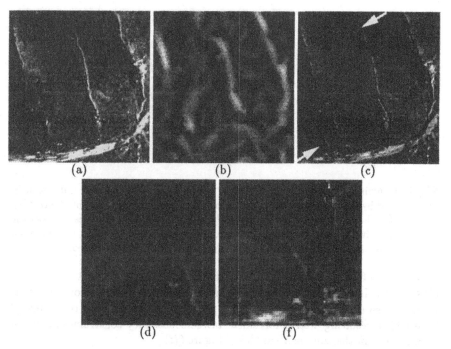

Fig. 4. Drainage delineation in flatter terrain. (a) One of three images of an area where the terrain is close to being a slanted plane with the highest elevations at the top of the image. Note the three gullies running from top to bottom of the image. (b) The corresponding curvature image. (c) The maximal curvature paths computed by specifying two endpoints for each gully. (d) Detail of the upper part of the middle path—denoted by the topmost white arrow in (c)—that meanders away from the clearly visible linear structure that marks the actual location of the gully. (e) Similar problem in the lower part of the leftmost path, denoted by the other white arrow in (c).

Figure 4 illustrates this problem in an area where the terrain's shape is close to that of a slanted plane. In such cases the clues to the river's presence are to be found in the original gray-level images where they appear as elongated linear structures that can be detected using a low-resolution linear delineation (LRLD) system.

Because it has demonstrated excellent performance, we use the LRLD system developed by Fischler and Wolf [5]. It yields results such as those shown in Figure 5(a). These linear features can then be chamfered and used to mask the curvature image. This operation produces the image of Figure 5(b) in which the curvature of all points but those that are close to one of the linear structures is set to C^0_{max}, the smallest value in the original curvature image, and will therefore tend to be avoided by the dynamic programming algorithm. Using the same endpoints as previously, we obtain the paths shown in Figure 5(c) that are much closer to those that a human analyst would delineate using a stereoscope.

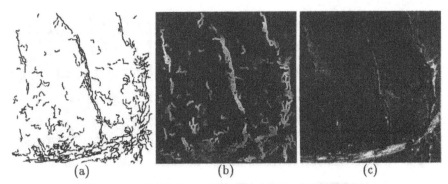

Fig. 5. Combining gray-level and curvature information. (a) The linear features detected by the low-resolution linear delineation system in the image of Figure 4(a).
(b) The potential image computed by using those linear features to mask the
curvature image. (c) The linear structures delineated by using the potential
image (b) and supplying two endpoints for each of the three linear structures.

In Figure 6, we use a second site at the National Training Center to further
illustrate the importance of combining gray-level and 3–D information. Note that
we have also used dynamic programming to outline the roads in the image of
Figure 6(a), resulting after enforcement of the consistency constraints discussed
in Section 5, in the composite model of Figure 6(f).

To highlight the generality of the approach, in Figure 7, we show that it can
also be used to delineate ridgelines. They are characterized by extremal *negative*
curvatures. They can therefore be delineated using the same technique after
replacing the curvature potential of Equation 2 by

$$\mathcal{E}_{Curv}(\mathcal{C}) = \int \left(C_{max}(\mathbf{f}(s)) - C^0_{max}\right)^2 ds \ , \tag{5}$$

where C^0_{max} is the smallest value in the curvature image.

5 Enforcing the Physical Constraints

We now turn to the physical constraints that the drainage pattern and surrounding terrain must fulfill. As illustrated by Figures 2, there is no guarantee that
the features sketched using the techniques of Section 4 will be consistent with
the laws of physics because the terrain model may be in error.

Our goal is therefore to enforce these constrains while deviating as little as
possible from what the image data predicts; otherwise we might be "hallucina-
ting" river valleys where there are none. Constrained optimization [9, 15] is an
effective way to achieve this goal because it allows the use of arbitrarily large
numbers of constraints while retaining good convergence properties. In fact, the
more constraints there are, the smaller the search space and the better the convergence becomes. In previous work [7], we have developed a constrained optimization algorithm that exploits the specificities of the models we use to reduce

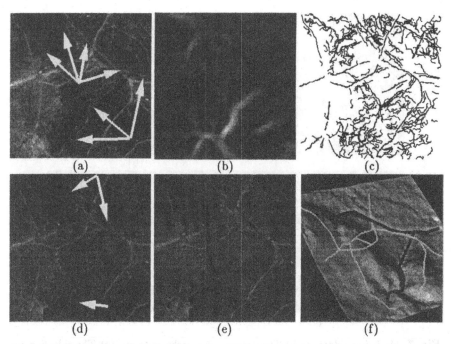

(a)   (b)   (c)

(d)   (e)   (f)

Fig. 6. Rivers and road delineation. (a) One of four aerial images with two stream-beds denoted by the two clusters of white arrows. (b) The curvature image. Regions of high positive curvature are shown in white. Because the relief is not as pronounced as in the case of Figure 1, the valleys do not appear as clearly. (c) The linear features detected by the low-resolution linear delineation system. (d) The paths delineated by using only the curvature image shown in (b). For the path at the top, we specified two endpoints and one intermediate point denoted by the black circles. For the path at the bottom, we specified only the two endpoints denoted by the black rectangles. Because there is not enough relief, the paths wander away from their apparent location at the places indicated by the white arrows. (e) The paths delineated by specifying the same endpoints and using a potential image that combines the curvature image and the output of the linear delineation program shown in (c). (f) The paths, shown in blue, overlaid on a shaded view of the terrain mesh after constrained optimization using all four images. We have also used dynamic programming to outline the roads, shown in yellow, in the gray-level images and have refined them by treating them as 3–D snakes that are attracted by maxima on intensity.

the required amount of computation and to allow us to impose the constraints at a very low computational cost.

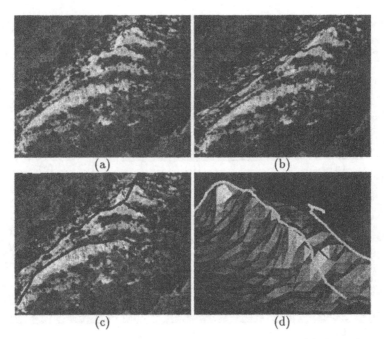

Fig. 7. Modeling ridges. (a,b) Two images of a rocky outcrop. (c) The ridgeline recovered by the dynamic programming algorithm. (d) A shaded view of the terrain mesh recovered by our algorithm.

5.1 Constrained Optimization

Formally, a constrained optimization problem can be described as follows. Given a function f of n variables $S = \{s_1, s_2, .., s_n\}$, we want to minimize it under a set of m constraints $C(S) = \{c_1, c_2, .., c_m\} = 0$. That is, minimize $f(S)$ subject to $C(S) = 0$.

It can be generalized to handle inequality constraints by replacing the constraints of the form $c_i(S) = 0$ by constraints of the form $c_i(S) \leq 0$.

In our application, we model the terrain as a triangulated mesh S and linear features as a set of l polygonal curves $C_{j,1 \leq j \leq l}$. We associate to each an energy term $\mathcal{E}(S)$ and $\mathcal{E}(C_j)$—$\mathcal{E}(S)$ is discussed in Section 3 and $\mathcal{E}(C_j)$ is introduced below. S is therefore the vector of all the x, y and z coordinates of the vertices of S and of the C_js. $f(S)$ is taken to be

$$f(S) = \{\mathcal{E}(S), \mathcal{E}(C_1), ..., \mathcal{E}(C_l)\} \ ,$$

and our algorithm minimizes each component of f while attempting to satisfy the constraints.

We must now express the fact that rivers flow downhill and lie at the bottom of local depressions in the terrain and that valley floors tend to be "U" shaped and locally horizontal in the direction transverse to the river's direction in terms of a set of constraints of the form $c_i(S) = 0$ or $c_i(S) \leq 0$:

- **Rivers lie at the bottom of valleys:** We treat a river as smooth 3–D curve $\mathcal{C}$. We refine its position by minimizing an energy $\mathcal{E}(\mathcal{C})$ that is the weighted sum of a regularization term $\mathcal{E}_D(\mathcal{C})$—the integral of the square curvatures along the curve—and a potential term $\mathcal{E}_P(\mathcal{C})$—minus the integral of the elevations along the curve. In practice, following standard snake practices [11], we model $\mathcal{C}$ as a list of regularly spaced 3–D vertices S_3 of the form

$$S_3 = \{(x_i\ y_i\ z_i),\ i = 1,\ldots,n\}\ , \tag{6}$$

$$\mathcal{E}_D(\mathcal{C}) = \frac{1}{2}\sum (2x_i - x_{i-1} - x_{i+1})^2 + (2y_i - y_{i-1} - y_{i+1})^2 + (2z_i - z_{i-1} - z_{i+1})^2$$

$$\mathcal{E}_P(\mathcal{C}) = \sum z_i\ .$$

As discussed below, during the optimization the curve $\mathcal{C}$ is constrained to remain on the terrain and while the vertices are moved to minimize $\mathcal{E}_P(\mathcal{C})$ and therefore the elevations of the individual vertices. As a result, at the end of the optimization, the curve has to lie at the bottom of a valley.

- **Rivers flow downhill:** The z coordinates of the curve's list of n 3–D vertices S_3 decrease monotonically, which is expressed as a set of $n - 1$ inequality constraints

$$z_{i+1} \leq z_i\ , \tag{7}$$

that we refer to as "downhill" constraints.

- **Rivers lie on the terrain:** For each edge $((x_1, y_1, z_1), (x_2, y_2, z_2))$ of the terrain mesh and each segment $((x_3, y_3, z_3), (x_4, y_4, z_4))$ of the polygonal curve representing the river that intersect when projected in the (x, y) plane, the four endpoints must be coplanar so that the segments also intersect in 3–D space. This is written as

$$\begin{vmatrix} x_1 & x_2 & x_3 & x_4 \\ y_1 & y_2 & y_3 & y_4 \\ z_1 & z_2 & z_3 & z_4 \\ 1 & 1 & 1 & 1 \end{vmatrix} = 0\ , \tag{8}$$

which yields a set of constraints that we refer to as "on-terrain" constraints.

- **The valley is horizontal in the direction transverse to the river's direction:** Each edge $((x_1, y_1, z_1), (x_2, y_2, z_2))$ of the terrain mesh that intersects, in the (x, y) plane, a segment $((x_3, y_3, z_3), (x_4, y_4, z_4))$ of the polygonal curve representing the river must have the following property: the component of the vector $\overrightarrow{e_{12}} = (x_2 - x_1, y_2 - y_1, z_2 - z_1)$ that is perpendicular to the vector $\overrightarrow{e_{34}} = (x_4 - x_3, y_4 - y_3, z_4 - z_3)$ must be horizontal. This can be written as

$$\begin{vmatrix} x_2 - x_1 & x_4 - x_3 & y_3 - y_4 \\ y_2 - y_1 & y_4 - y_3 & x_4 - x_3 \\ z_2 - z_1 & z_4 - z_3 & 0 \end{vmatrix} = 0\ , \tag{9}$$

because it implies that $\overrightarrow{e_{12}}$ is a linear combination of $\overrightarrow{e_{34}}$ and of the vector $(y_3 - y_4, x_4 - x_3, 0)$ which is both horizontal and perpendicular to $\overrightarrow{e_{34}}$. This yields another set of constraints, the "valley-bottom" constraints.

In practice, the downhill constraints are inequality constraints that are turned on and off during the optimization as required, following an active set strategy [7]. Before the start of the constrained optimization, we compute the intersections in the x, y plane between the edges of the mesh and the polygonal curves to instantiate the required number of on-terrain and valley-bottom constraints. Optionally, we could reiterate this procedure during the optimization. This would be necessary if the polygonal curves deformed a lot. However, because the delineation method of Section 4 is robust, the initial location of the curves is accurate enough so that, in practice, they do not deform very much.

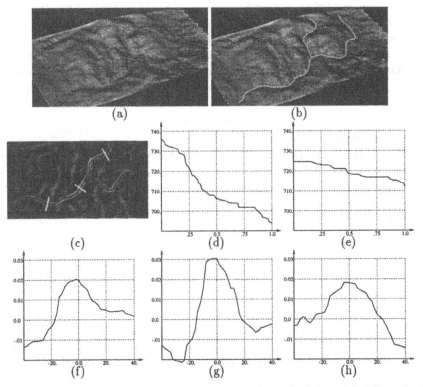

Fig. 8. NTC model after constrained optimization. (a) A shaded model of the refined and constrained surface mesh of Figure 2 (c). Note the flat-bottomed valleys. (b) The two optimized streambeds overlaid on the mesh. (c) The optimized streambeds overlaid on a recomputed curvature image. (d,e) Their elevations are now monotonically decreasing, unlike those of Figures 2. (f,g,h) Curvature of the surface along the three perpendicular cross sections shown as yellow segments in (c).

Figures 8 and 9 demonstrate the improvement in consistency brought about by constrained optimization: The channels now have monotonically decreasing

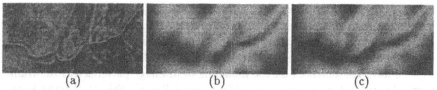

Fig. 9. Comparing the elevations before and after reoptimization under constraints. (a) A window of the image of Figure 1(a) centered on a section of the horizontal valley. (b) A pseudo-color depiction of the corresponding elevations computed using the terrain mesh of Figure 1(e), that is, before constrained optimization. The lowest elevations appear in black. (c) A pseudo-color depiction of the elevations using the terrain mesh of Figure 8(a), that is, after reoptimization under constraints. Note that the valley is now much better defined.

elevations and the rivers lie at their bottoms, which also is close to being a maximum of curvature in the direction normal to the feature. In Figure 9, we compare the elevations computed before and after constrained optimization and show that imposing the constraints improves the definition of the valley.

5.2 Quantitative Evaluating of the Results

Having refined the terrain model using the technique of Section 3 and enforced physical constraints as described in Section 5, we are now confronted with the perennial Computer Vision question: How close are we to ground truth? In our specific case, we also want to know if we have paid any price—in terms of accuracy, for instance—to enforce consistency. For example, how often have we mistakenly constrained the slope of the terrain to be in a certain direction to satisfy the constraints?

In the companion report [6], we use two methods to generate "ground truth." The first is to use a good algorithm and to consider its results only in areas where it is known to be particularly reliable and accurate. The second method is to do it manually to the best of the ability of a human operator. In the report, by comparing the outputs of both these methods on the scenes of Figures 1 and 4 against the results produced by our system, we show that our approach to surface modeling yields excellent accuracy whether or not we impose our physical constraints—in the order of 0.2 to 0.3 RMS error in disparity—and that imposing the constraints does not detract from the accuracy.

6 Conclusion

We have presented an approach to terrain modeling and 3–D linear delineation that allows us to generate site models including terrain drainage channels and roads that are accurate and consistent with minimal human intervention.

We have shown that, by refining an object-centered representation of the terrain and features under a set of well-designed constraints, we can generate, with a high level of automation, models that are faithful to sensor data, internally consistent and consistent with physical constraints. We have also shown that we can achieve this result in a highly automated fashion: the operator is only required to specify a few endpoints, and the system handles everything else.

We have concentrated on the modeling of drainage patterns but the framework described here extends naturally to modeling all objects obeying known physical constraints. For example, man-made objects such as roads, railroad tracks, or buildings are built according to well-understood engineering practices. Similarly, silhouette edges can be extracted from ground-level views of mountain ridges and used to constrain the terrain modeling from aerial views.

We believe that the capabilities described here will prove indispensable to automating the generation of complex object databases from imagery, such as the ones required for realistic simulations or intelligence analysis. In such databases, the models must not only be as accurate—that is, true to the data—as possible but also consistent with each other. Otherwise, the simulation will exhibit "glitches" and the image analyst will have difficulty interpreting the models.

Acknowledgments

We wish to thank Martin Fischler and Yvan Leclerc for the invaluable advice they provided during the development of the techniques described here. We also would like to thank Lee Iverson for providing us with a real-time implementation of the dynamic programming algorithm; it has proved to be a powerful tool for experimenting with different approaches to generating the cost arrays of Section 4.

References

1. L.E. Band. Topographic Partition of Watersheds with Digital Elevation Models. *Water Resources Research*, 22:15–24, 1986.
2. L. Cohen and R. Kimmel. Global Minimum for Active Contour Models: A Minimal Path Approach. In *Conference on Computer Vision and Pattern Recognition*, pages 666–673, San Franciso, CA, June 1996.
3. J. Fairfield and P. Leymarie. Drainage Networks from Grid Digital Evaluation Models. *Water Resources Research*, 27(5):709–717, May 1991.
4. M.A Fischler, J.M. Tenenbaum, and H.C. Wolf. Detection of Roads and Linear Structures in Low-resolution Aerial Imagery Using a Multisource Knowledge Integration Technique. *Computer Vision, Graphics, and Image Processing*, 15(3):201–223, March 1981.
5. M.A. Fischler and H.C. Wolf. Linear Delineation. In *Conference on Computer Vision and Pattern Recognition*, pages 351–356, June 1983.
6. P. Fua. Fast, Accurate and Consistent Modeling of Drainage and Surrounding Terrain. *International Journal of Computer Vision*, 1997. Accepted for publication, available as Tech Note 555, Artificial Intelligence Center, SRI International.
7. P. Fua and C. Brechbuhler. Imposing Hard Constraints on Soft Snakes. In *European Conference on Computer Vision*, pages 495–506, Cambridge, England, April 1996. Available as Tech Note 553, Artificial Intelligence Center, SRI International.

8. P. Fua and Y. G. Leclerc. Object-Centered Surface Reconstruction: Combining Multi-Image Stereo and Shading. *International Journal of Computer Vision*, 16:35–56, September 1995.

9. P.E. Gill, W. Murray, and M.H. Wright. *Practical Optimization*. Academic Press, London a.o., 1981.

10. C. Heipke. Integration of Digital Image Matching and Multi Image Shape From Shading. In *International Society for Photogrammetry and Remote Sensing*, pages 832–841, Washington, D.C., 1992.

11. M. Kass, A. Witkin, and D. Terzopoulos. Snakes: Active Contour Models. *International Journal of Computer Vision*, 1(4):321–331, 1988.

12. J.J. Koenderink and J. van Doorn. Local Features of Smooth Shapes: Ridges and Courses. In *SPIE*, volume 2031, 1993.

13. R. Lengagne, P. Fua, and O. Monga. Using Crest Line to Guide Surface Reconstruction from Stereo. In *International Conference on Pattern Recognition*, Lausanne, Switzerland, September 1996.

14. N. Merlet and J. Zerubia. New Prospects in Line Detection by Dynamic Programming. *IEEE Transactions on Pattern Analysis and Machine Intelligence*, 18(4), April 1995.

15. D. Metaxas and D. Terzopoulos. Shape and Nonrigid Motion Estimation through Physics-Based Synthesis. *IEEE Transactions on Pattern Analysis and Machine Intelligence*, 15(6):580–591, 1991.

16. E.N. Mortensen and W.A. Barrett. Intelligent Scissors for Image Composition. In *Computer Graphics, SIGGRAPH Proceedings*, pages 191–198, Los Angeles, CA, August 1995.

17. J. O'Callaghan and D.M. Mark. The Extraction of Networks from Digital Elevation Data. *Computer Vision, Graphics, and Image Processing: Image Understanding*, 28:323–344, 1984.

18. P.T. Sander and S.W. Zucker. Inferring Surface Trace and Differential Structure from 3-D Images. *IEEE Transactions on Pattern Analysis and Machine Intelligence*, 12(9):833–854, September 1990.

19. B.P. Wrobel. The evolution of Digital Photogrammetry from Analytical Photogrammetry. *Photogrammetric Record*, 13(77):765–776, April 1991.

Integration of Confidence Information by Markov Random Fields for Reconstruction of Underwater 3D Acoustic Images

Vittorio Murino

Dept. of Mathematics and Computer Science (DIMI), University of Udine
Via delle Scienze 206, I - 33100 Udine, Italy

Abstract. This paper describes a technique for the integration of confidence information using a Markov Random Fields approach to improve the reconstruction process of 3D acoustical images. Beam-forming, a method widely applied in acoustic imaging, is used to arrange backscattered echoes received by a two-dimensional array antenna in order to generate two images where each pixel represents the distance (range) from the sensor plane and the related confidence of the measure, respectively. Unfortunately, this kind of images are plagued by several problems due to the nature of the signal and to the related sensing system, thus heavily affecting data quality. In the proposed algorithm, range and confidence images are modelled as Markov Random Fields and several energy formulations are devised to exploit both types of data, leading to the reconstruction and segmentation of acoustic images. Results show the better performances of the proposed method as compared with classical methods disregarding reliability information.

1 Introduction

Object recognition and, in general, image interpretation [1,2] are far better improved if preceded by efficient and accurate low-level processes like restoration, reconstruction, and segmentation tasks. Typically, all real sensorial systems of whatever nature (e.g., optical, acoustical, etc.) acquire data that do not represent the actual information gained from the real world, but cluttered data in which the correct properties of the considered scene are altered by the sensing system. In the specific case, acoustic systems used to "understand" underwater environments have an important and useful implicit property, missing in simple optical systems, that is, they allow to directly recover range information about the scene considered. Unfortunately, in underwater environments, three-dimensional (3D) information extraction and processing are complex tasks due to bad quality of acoustic data. For this reason, there is an absolute need of efficient techniques useful to recover precise 3D information and to facilitate the understanding of acoustic images, useful for specific underwater applications, like sea bed inspection, off-shore inspection, Remotely Operated Vehicle (ROV) navigation, bathymetry, submerged object detection and recognition, etc..

Beamforming (BF) is the most widely used technique to form 3D acoustic images as a high frame rate can be obtained, light sensorial devices can be used and images present a good visual quality (as compared with the other acoustic acquisition systems) [3,4]. In this paper, BF is also used to derive, associated with a dense range image, a reliability measure for each depth estimate, namely the "confidence" of each 3D measure [5]. Unfortunately, this approach exhibits two critical problems, speckle noise due to the coherence of the acoustical signal [6], and side lobes due to the non-ideal sensor characteristics (beam pattern, see Fig. 1(b)) [3]. Typically, confidence information is not recovered in such kind of systems, and, although the use of confidence information is highlighted in many vision processes, actually, only a small part of them addresses this issue using it as a goodness index of the final result [2].

The goal and one of the main contribution of this paper is to show how reconstruction of acoustic 3D images can be improved by actively integrating confidence information. To this end, range and confidence maps are modelled as Markov Random Fields (MRFs) [7,8], whose associated single energy function has been devised to include confidence estimates in the reconstruction process and, at the same time, to reduce the physical effects due to speckle and side lobe so as to obtain a good restored image, too.

Generally, acoustic data are on-line visualized in real sonar systems by simply thresholding the acquired rough signals, i.e., by considering only sampled signal values above a certain threshold [4]. Although this method is very fast, it produces results of poor quality, as compared with *ad hoc* methods. Moreover, even though there exists a considerable literature on the reconstruction and segmentation of range images, a very few works deal with the same processes for underwater acoustic images and none of them addresses these tasks in a cooperative way making explicit use of confidence information. The MRF approach was previously addressed in the literature for range image segmentation. In [9], range and intensity (optical) images were separately segmented by fusing boundary information at multiple scales by using a nonlinear MRF algorithm. The proposed energy functional embedded classical smoothness and observation closeness constraints, a line process and a coupling term between adjacent scales. In [10], the "gradient limit effects" [11] were reduced by fusing registered range and intensity images by an extended weak membrane model enforcing the line process. The fusion occurred by means of a coupled term in the energy function that penalized different edge configurations in the two kinds of images. Considering specific literature on acoustical images, restoration of side scan sonar images by using Simulated Annealing and Iterative Conditional Modes was addressed in [12]. Here, restoration was intended as the process of reducing the speckle noise modelled as having a Rayleigh or Gaussian probability density function. Error evaluation in the context of the reconstruction of sea bed bathymetric data was addressed in [13] by using the Graduated Non-Convexity [11] minimization method. Here, to reconstruct correct bathymetric data acquired with a multibeam sonar, either a weak membrane or a thin-plate model [2] was used, and a line process was included to remove the smoothness constraint at surface boundaries. Segmentation of images acquired by a multibeam echosounder by MRFs is also addressed in [14]. By arranging the acoustical map on the basis of the acquisition parameters, they devise a classical MRF process modeling the prior energy as weighting coefficients depending on its geometrical location and the observation energy term as a χ^2 distribution.

These works show several ways of approaching the problem of reconstruction and restoration of acoustical images as well as the fusion of range and (visual) intensity maps, but none of them deals with coupled segmentation and reconstruction based on MRF and capable to exploit restored reliability measures.

The problem of reconstruction of acoustic data extracted by an acoustical multibeam system was already addressed by the author in [15,16]. In [15], it is proposed an energy functional jointly considering the dual information in such a way that, only those pixels belonging to the 3D image showing high confidence are retained, whereas the 3D values were assumed unreliable in those pixels showing low confidence. In [16], this mechanism is evolved in the definition of a different functional which takes into account the physical significance of the coupling term between 3D and confidence images.

In the present work, we investigate and compare reconstruction and segmentation processes performed by MRFs using different energy functionals, each one actively embedding confidence data. The energy functionals include prior and observation (sensor) knowledge for the confidence and range fields adequately devised to account for the problem at hand. The energy terms related to segmentation aim at enhancing those points whose value shows the presence of an echo backscattered from an object, while weakening those points derived by clutters. The energy terms related to reconstruction consist in different formulations that make it possible to integrate, in an intelligent way, the restored reliability information largely improving final reconstruction results. In general, the estimated confidence values operate to both reinforce the closeness to observation constraint and to prevent smoothing at the object boundaries. Since clique potentials [8] for the line process are not included owing to the coupled process, this functional allows to avoid the determination of regularization parameters which is one of the main problems when the weak membrane model is adopted for visual surface reconstruction and boundary detection [10]. The presented results are also compared with classical MRF-based methods showing the better performances obtained by using confidence in an active way. It should be also noted here that, although the visual quality of the estimated images might seem poor, they represent very good results as compared with those obtained by other methods for the same kind of images. In fact, the quality of acoustic images is very poor with respect to the quality of images acquired by a laser range finder for instance.

The paper is organized as follows. In Section 2, the process of image formation is described and modelled, analyzing the significance of the confidence map and the nature of the degrading effects (speckle and side lobes). In Section 3, the MRF approach is presented, with special emphasis on the energy functional formulations. In Section 4, results are presented and discussed and, finally, conclusions and future work are addressed in Section 5.

2 The Acoustic Imaging System

Beamforming (BF) is a technique aimed at estimating signals coming from a fixed steering direction, while attenuating those coming from other directions [3]. It is a spatial filter that combines linearly temporal signals spatially sampled by a discrete antenna made up of sensors located in space according to a known geometry. When a scene is insonified by a pulse, BF processes the backscattered signals in order to form the so-called beam signals, $bs_{\mathbf{u}}(t)$, each steered in a different direction $\mathbf{u}$. In general, a beam signal is equal to the product of the wave measured (by an omnidirectional sensor) in the reference system origin and a complex beam pattern dependent on the geometry of the array and the wave frequency. The beam pattern presents a main lobe in the direction $\mathbf{u}$, in which the antenna is steered, and side lobes of minor, but not negligible, magnitudes that cause the generation of artefacts degrading useful information (see Fig. 1(b)). In the ideal case, the envelope of a beam signal, $b_{\mathbf{u}}(t)$, should present a replica of the insonification pulse backscattered by an object present in the steering direction.

A common method to detect the distance of a scattering object is to look for the maximum peak of the beam signal envelope [4]. Denoting by t^* the time instant at which the maximum peak occurs (see Fig. 1(a)), the related distance, $R^*=ct^*/2$ (being c the sound velocity in water), can be computed. A suitable and simple measure of confidence, s^*, can be the amplitude of the maximum peak, that is, $s^* = b_{\mathbf{u}}(t^*)$. Therefore, a triplet $(\mathbf{u}, R^*, s^*)$ can be extracted for each steering direction in the field of view of the sensor, thus generating a range and a confidence image.

Unfortunately, in real situations, the replica of the pulse is very deformed and its detection is generally difficult [3]. Moreover, it is typically assumed that the amplitude of a signal does not depend on the distance of the source since, during the acquisition phase, Time Varying Gains (TVGs) [3] are applied to the signals received by each sensor to recover the spreading and absorption due to water, thus compensating for the attenuation due to the propagation distance. Owing to the TVGs, objects located at different distances from the array have the same response signals (i.e., confidence), whereas if no objects are located along certain directions, the related signals do not present significative response, but only low amplitude clutters.

As shown in Fig. 1(a), the above mentioned triplets can be projected on two orthoscopic images parallel to the plane of the array and characterized by a regular grid of pixels whose resolution is finer than the better lateral resolution of the imaging system. Using a conventional polar-Cartesian coordinate transformation, points defined in polar coordinates by $\mathbf{u}$ and R^* are converted into Cartesian coordinates (x^*, y^*, z^*), so allowing the generation of a range image $z^* = f(x^*,y^*)$ and a confidence image $s^* = g(x^*,y^*)$. A linear relation between z^* values and grey-level scale is utilized, so that the smaller the z^* value the darker the pixel and vice versa (see Fig. 2(a)). The confidence information is normalized between 0 and 1 (denoting 1 as maximum confidence); however, we map such information in an image by linearly transforming confidence values between 0 and 255, and visualize this image in a negative way. As an example, Fig. 2(b) shows a confidence image where black pixels correspond to the maximum confidence.

Speckle and side lobes are two sharp sources of noise affecting the imaging system: speckle effects cause a non-deterministic magnitude of backscattered echoes, whereas side lobes do not allow a correct detection of echoes coming from the steering direction. As a consequence, every beam signal is a sum of echoes with stochastic magnitudes, generated from different parts of the scene and attenuated on the basis of the corresponding main-lobe and side-lobe elevations.

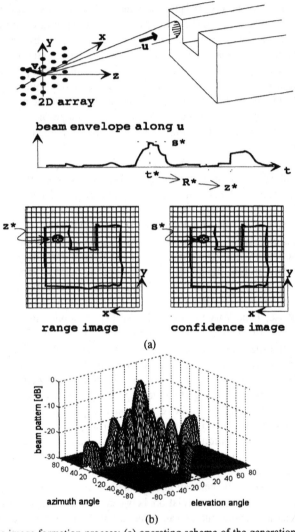

Fig. 1. Acoustic image formation process: (a) operating scheme of the generation of range and confidence images; (b) directivity characteristic (beam pattern) for a 9×9 array.

These disturbing factors give rise to images of the type shown in Fig. 2(b), where one can notice a non-null response where no objects are present (due to side lobes), and null or very low responses inside objects (due to speckle). Therefore, the peak of a beam signal does not always indicate the right distance between the array and the object (if any) placed in the steering direction. However, the criterion stating that the larger the peak amplitude over the mean of beam signals, the higher the probability of correct estimation, and vice versa, seems to be a reasonable statement in accordance with both the above discussion and the experience in short-range 3D acoustic imaging.

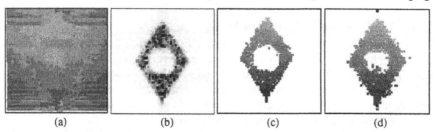

(a)   (b)   (c)   (d)

Fig. 2. Images resulting from the beamforming process and peak detection: (a) noisy range image Z; (b) noisy confidence image S; (c) noisy range image retaining z points whose associated confidence value s is over an arbitrary threshold TH = 40; (d) the same as (c) with TH = 20.

Confidence data derived from the maximum peak amplitudes can be used in several ways. The simplest and, probably, most common way is to consider as valid only the z^* points whose related confidence values s^* are above a fixed threshold. Typically, in real acoustic systems, this threshold, TH, is variable and manually set by an operator, in order to allow the display of a scene for different settings, so that its interpretation can be easier. However, a physically justified threshold, T_c, can be fixed on the basis of the level of the highest side lobe, calculable from the sensor geometry and the signal frequency. For instance, when unitary weighting is adopted for the sensors, the highest side lobe measures -13 dB (see Fig. 2(c)). Therefore, in many systems, s^* values lower than 22% of the amplitude of the maximum peak are not considered valid, as they are produced by side lobes or are simply noise. Unfortunately, this simple and fast procedure, even by using the suitable threshold, removes side lobe effects together with many correct points whose confidence values are low due to speckle noise. This fact suggests that a punctual analysis of the depth and confidence maps does not seem sufficient.

Speckle [7] can be modelled in different ways depending on the surface roughness of the considered target objects. In this paper, a Gaussian distribution will be adopted as a probability density function for the peak values of the beam envelopes, due to the roughness of typical man-made submerged objects considered [4,16]. However, owing to the MRF framework, a different noise modeling can be devised and straightforwardly included in the proposed methodologies. Considering a Gaussian distribution for the peak values, it is assumed that the desired (constant) amplitude of the peak related to a beam signal steered toward an object is the mean value of a Gaussian distribution and then, overall, to consider the speckle noise involved in this kind of situations as additive white Gaussian noise (AWGN). To complete the noise model for the acoustic imaging process, a measure of the noise variance is also necessary. This parameter is related to the roughness characteristics of the surface and is difficult to compute *a priori* [6]. However, an estimation of the variance on the basis of the peak values is possible by taking into account only the peaks exceeding a fixed threshold based on the highest side lobe level used to detect reliable target objects' echoes in conventional systems. As will be shown in the section devoted to results, this method, despite its simplicity, gives not too inaccurate estimates of the variance. Concerning the map Z, an additive Gaussian noise model has been considered as well, like typically assumed for range images [2].

3 The MRF-based Integration Methods

MRFs constitute a probabilistic regularization methodology capable to handle nonlinear physical processes, i.e., whenever the observation model that relates an actual physical signal to the one observed and sampled by a sensor is not linear. In addition, such properties as smoothness and continuity can be embedded using only dependencies among local neighbours, thus making it possible to exploit local characteristics instead of punctual or global properties.

In short, an MRF is defined on a lattice field of random variables in which the probability of a specific realization is given by a Gibbs distribution (Hammersley-Clifford theorem [7]). The energy function associated with such distribution can be computed by summing only *local* contributions with respect to a neighbourhood system defined on the lattice. Therefore, the energy minimization, correspondent to the maximization of the a-posteriori probability distribution, leads to the best estimate. For a complete formal definition of an MRF the reader can refer to [7].

The formulation of the energy functions to perform the reconstruction process integrating confidence has followed two main routes. Denoting as Z(x,y) and S(x,y) the range and confidence images, respectively, the coupled reconstruction (of the Z image) and restoration (of the S image) processes by using a single energy function is addressed in two cases. The third case consists in two separate processes in cascade, first, the restoration of the confidence image S and then, the reconstruction of the range image Z by using the final estimation of the map S. It should be noted that the restoration of the image S gives rise to a binary segmentation of the scene, so, either the term restoration or segmentation will be used.

3.1 First Case

Let us consider $Y = (Y_s, Y_z)$ as the observable random field pair, where Y_s is related to the M×M confidence image S and Y_z is related to the M×M range image Z to be estimated, respectively. We regard both Z and S as sample realizations of an MRF for a given neighbourhood system; then, the process of coupled restoration and reconstruction lies in estimating the true fields S and Z, given the noisy input image pair Y. Therefore, we formulate the reconstruction and restoration problems in terms of maximization of the a-posteriori probability associated with the prior and sensor models by devising a unique joint energy functional.

As prior models, a weak membrane energy term for reconstruction (as previously proposed in [11,7,8]) has been assumed and, for restoration, a function based on the physical acquisition process has been devised, enforcing those points associated to an object and penalizing the others. As sensor models, a Gaussian modelling is used for restoration, whereas, for reconstruction, the usual data compatibility term is utilized [2,7]. Moreover, we include in the global energy function two modulating terms weighting the a-priori and sensor models of the field Z.

Therefore, under the assumption of additive i.i.d. (independent, identically-distributed) Gaussian noise for the two maps and using the Hammerslay-Clifford equivalence and the Bayes criterion, we can write the a-posteriori joint energy function (related to the a-posteriori probability [7]) as a sum of several terms:

$$E(Z,S/Y_z,Y_s) = E_p(Z,S) + E_{obs}(Y_z,Y_s / Z,S) = E_p(Z/S) + E_p(S) + E_{obs}(Y_z/Z,S) + E_{obs}(Y_s/Z,S) \quad (1)$$

where E_p are functions related to a-priori modelling and E_{obs} are functions related to observation models. Thus, Eq. (1) represents the global energy function composed of the a-priori and observation models of the coupled field (Z,S). Due to the specific process involved, the coupled models can be divided into energy terms as a function of only one field. The a-priori coupled model has been divided into an energy term for S plus another energy term for Z given S that results in an a-priori energy term of Z (weak membrane [7,2]) modulated by a function of S:

$$E_p(Z/S) = \sum_{i \in Z} \sum_{j \in N_i} E_p(z_i, z_j) \cdot V_a(s_i, s_j) = \sum_{i \in Z} \sum_{j \in N_i} (z_i - z_j)^2 \cdot V_a(s_i, s_j) \quad (2)$$

where i is a generic pixel site, z_i is the value of the pixel i of the depth field Z, s_i is the value of the pixel i of the confidence field S, N_i is the neighbourhood of the pixel i (on both fields S and Z) and V_a is a modulating function of S that reinforces or weakens the a-priori contribution of Z. We consider the same first-order neighbourhood system on both fields S and Z.

The coupled observation model in Eq. (1) has been divided into two separate terms, given the conditional independence of the Y_z and Y_s fields given (Z,S). Therefore, like the prior energy, the term $E_{obs}(Y_z/Z,S)$ is modelled as the product of data compatibility constraint (derived by the Gaussian noise assumption) and a modulating function dependent on the confidence:

$$E_{obs}(Y_z / Z,S) = \sum_{i \in Z} E_{obs}(y_{z_i} / z_i) \cdot V_b(s_i) = \frac{1}{2\sigma_z^2} \sum_{i \in Z} (z_i - y_{z_i})^2 \cdot V_b(s_i) \quad (3)$$

where y_{z_i} is the value of the pixel i of the observation Y_z and V_b is a modulating function of S that reinforces or weakens the observation contribution of Z.

The function V_a, modulating the a-priori function of Z is:

$$V_a(s_i, s_j) = 1 - s_i \cdot s_j \quad \forall i \in S, \forall j \in N_i \quad (4)$$

This function stresses the weak membrane constraint for Z if a generic pixel z_i or its neighbours z_j are little confident. Practically, the observed image can be more or less reliable and, on this basis, the prior model of Z can be more or less emphasized. Note that, like the weak membrane constraint, V_a does not only consider the selected pixel but also the local neighbourhood system, so it carries out a local analysis of the confidence information. The function result will be in the range [0,1], as, in this case, we assume that the values of the pixels of S are normalized between 0 and 1.

The second function V_b modulating the sensor model of Z, $E_{obs}(Y_z / Z)$, is:

$$V_b(s_i) = \sqrt{s_i} \quad \forall i \in S \quad (5)$$

This function reaches the maximum value, equal to 1, if the confidence of the pixel z_i is 1, stressing the data compatibility constraint. The square root operation is used to weight, in a different manner, low- and high-confidence points enhancing the observation constraint also for pixels having weak confidence levels.

The functions V_a and V_b take into account the physical significance of the map Z (derived from S) which is built by detecting the maximum peak for each beam signal. In other words, they allow to actively integrate confidence information to bias the contributions of the prior and sensor models of Z in order to get a more accurate final estimation. The particular profiles of the modulating functions (linear for V_a and quadratic for V_b) have been chosen after a set of trials and the related error calculation, realizing that boundary conditions should be satisfied and that the observation constraint should be considered even if the confidence is low. However, small variations in these profiles do not considerably affect the final results.

Concerning the restoration of the field S, it should be noted that the Z estimates would not have to affect the prior and sensor models of confidence, then $E_{obs}(Y_s / Z,S) = E_{obs}(Y_s / S)$. In fact, the map S represents a true confidence associated pixel by pixel with the map Z, in that low S values do not imply an incorrect Z value but only less reliability in the correctness of that value. As a consequence, the prior knowledge on the field S should force the observed confidence map to become binary, i.e., 1 (maximum confidence) where an object is present, and 0 otherwise. The function related to the prior model is:

$$E_p(S) = \sum_{i \in S} E_p(s_i) = \sum_{i \in S} (s_i - s_{i,t})^2 \tag{6}$$

where the value $s_{i,t}$ can be 0 or 1 on the basis of the number of neighbourhood pixels whose value is larger than a fixed threshold T_c. This threshold is set considering the side lobe level of the beam pattern characteristic of the sensor. On the basis of this level, it is possible to calculate the attenuation of the beam signals due to the side lobes, likely allowing to separate confident from non-confident pixels. In practice, the term $s_{i,t}$ is equal to 1 if most of the pixels in the neighbourhood (of the first order) of s_i are above the threshold T_c, and is equal to 0 otherwise.

For the sensor model of S, a Gaussian model is adopted, as previously described in Section 2:

$$E_{obs}(Y_s / S) = \sum_{i \in S} E_{obs}(y_{s_i} / s_i) = \frac{1}{2\sigma_s^2} \sum_{i \in S} (s_i - y_{s_i})^2 \tag{7}$$

where y_{s_i} is the value of the pixel i of the observation Y_s.

3.2 Second Case

In this case, a coupled reconstruction and segmentation process is performed as in the first case. The difference lies in using we use a sort of region process (dual of a line process [8]) to prevent smoothing at the boundaries between objects and background. Actually, instead of using the modulating function V_a enforcing the prior model when local confidence was low, a nonlinear term r_i is inserted to separate zones where local confidence was very likely low or high and zones where local confidence is uncertain. In this way, the term $E_p(Z/S)$ is changed in:

$$E_p(Z/S) = \sum_{i \in Z} \sum_{j \in N_i} E_p(z_i, z_j) \cdot r_i(N_i) = \sum_{i \in Z} \sum_{j \in N_i} (z_i - z_j)^2 \cdot r_i(N_i) \tag{8}$$

where $r_i(N_i)$ is defined as:

$$r_i(N_i) = \begin{cases} 1 & \text{if } high(s_i) > low(s_i) \text{ OR } low(s_i) > high(s_i) \\ 0 & \text{otherwise} \end{cases} \tag{9}$$

The variables $high(s_i)$ and $low(s_i)$ are two counters containing the number (for each site s_i) of pixels belonging to the neighbourhood of s_i, s_j, having a value larger or less than a threshold T_c, respectively. This threshold is set considering the side lobe level of the sensor used, like in the 1st case. In other words, the term r_i related to the generic site i is function of the confidence values of the neighbourhood N_i, and is set to unity if the most number of pixels is over or below a fixed threshold T_c, and is set to zero, otherwise. In this way, when a generic point z_i has a clear local (related to the associated neighbourhood system of s_i) high or low confidence, the smoothness term is applied as such point is likely derived by an object surface or background. Otherwise, if local confidence is not clearly high or low, no smoothness is performed as such point likely belongs to a boundary.

The other energy terms remain unchanged: the prior and sensor model for the map S are the same as in the first case and the observation model related to the Z map is still weighted by the modulating function V_b enforcing the closeness to observation if the point has high confidence.

3.3 Third Case
In this case, two different energy functionals have devised for the *separate* reconstruction and restoration problems has been formulated. Specifically, the global energy function of the 1st case has been split, considering only the terms related to the S field for segmentation, and the terms related to the Z field utilizing the final estimated field, S^*, for reconstruction.

Therefore, under the assumption of additive i.i.d. (independent, identically-distributed) Gaussian noise for the two maps and using the Hammerslay-Clifford equivalence and the Bayes criterion, we can write the a-posteriori energy function for S as follows (the apex 1 denotes the energy related to the field S) :

$$E^1(S/Y_s) = E_p^1(S) + E_{obs}^1(Y_s / S) \tag{10}$$

while, for the field Z, those realization depends from the final confidence estimates, S^*, we have (the apex 2 denotes the energy related to the field Z):

$$E^2(Z/Y_z, S^*) = E_{obs}^2(Y_z / Z, S^*) + E_p^2(Z / S^*) \tag{11}$$

where E_p and E_{obs} are referred to the prior and observation models, respectively.

A good segmentation of the map S is fundamental for information retrieval. In fact, it allows 1) to recover 3D data by simply matching the Z map with the segmented one, retaining only the Z value of those pixels having high confidence, 2) to perform a more accurate reconstruction of the map Z exploiting the restored reliability, 3) to easily perform shape analysis on the segmented S image. The functional E^1 includes the two terms related to the S field described for the 1st case. It should be noticed from the results that, despite its simplicity, this functional works quite well for the restoration of the map S as it implicitly takes into account local cliques to set the value $s_{i,t}$.

For the reconstruction process related to the Z map, the same functions used for the 1st case are utilized, i.e., prior and observation models of Z are weighted by two modulating terms V_a and V_b, this time function of the restored S field, S^*, previously estimated.

3.4 The Optimization Algorithm
The minimization of the global energy function leads to the optimal (in the MAP sense) reconstructed and restored estimates. To this end, we adopted a simulated

annealing [17] procedure in which the fields Z and S evolve iteratively in a set of sample configurations in order to achieve the optimal ones.

In the first two cases, the fields are changed according to a process similar to the dual process of restoration and edge-extraction (grey-level and line fields) performed in [8]. For the image Z, a Gibbs sampler is used [7]. First, the Z field is updated taking fixed the S field, then, after a complete scan of the image Z, the S field is updated taking fixed the Z image. The new states of the fields' variables are randomly chosen among a set of allowable states. The new change is accepted if leading to minimize the energy, otherwise is accepted in probability [17,7] in order to avoid local minima. The current temperature (related to the Gibbs distribution formulation [7]) is lowered following a logarithmic scheduling after a complete scan of the two fields.

The third case, being two separate processes, follows the classical procedure of updating like the previous cases, considering only a single field at a time: the map S is first segmented and the map Z is reconstructed by using the final S estimation, S^*.

For the first and third cases, a reconstructed range map and a restored image are obtained at the end of the processes. The restored image S^* resulting in a quasi-binary segmentation is used to select confident range points belonging to an object and disregarding the background. The second case, having included a region process, directly produces a segmented S image and a reconstructed Z image without the need of performing the final match between the reconstructed S and Z.

4 Results and Discussion

The proposed algorithm was tested on acoustic 3D images provided by a simulator of active imaging systems whose output signals were processed by a beamformer. Generally, the acoustic scattering from a surface can be simulated by adding the effects produced by many punctiform ideal scatterers placed on the surface [18]. To achieve real effects, we simulated object surfaces by a random distribution of points placed on a given smooth surface and having an average density higher than 25 scatterers per λ^2, as typically used in underwater experiments [18]. After the distribution of the points and the scene insonification, the signal received by a given array sensor was computed on the basis of the sum of the spherical waves emitted from the scatterers composing the objects. This kind of simulation is widely accepted as the correct mode of generation of (synthetic) acoustic images, as it makes it possible to generate very realistic images of slightly rough objects affected by speckle noise.

The synthetic example consists of a single but quite complicated object for an acoustic imaging process: it is an inclined rhomb with a circular inside hole. The geometric model of the scene is shown in Fig. 3(a). The distance of the rhomb from the array ranges from 4.5 m to 4.7 m, in accordance with the equation $z = 4.6 + 0.1818y$, with $y \in (-0.55, 0.55)$. Inside the rhomb, a circular hole with a radius of 0.2 m is present, increasing the difficulty of the segmentation and reconstruction operations. The proposed algorithms aim at obtaining object representations that are as equal as possible to the ideal ones shown in Figs. 3(b) and 3(c), starting from (1st and 3rd case) the noisy images in Fig. 2(a) and Fig. 2(b) for range and confidence data, respectively. Figures 3(b) and 3(c) represent the ideal 2D projections of the inclined rhomb in terms of range and confidence. One can notice that the ideal confidence is high inside the object and null outside it.

The 2nd case assumes as initial Z map a range image containing as valid points z^* only those associated with confidence values s^* above a fixed threshold arbitrarily chosen (see Fig. 2(c) and (d)). In other words, the initial Z configuration is obtained by preprocessing the very rough data (Fig. 2(a)) as usually made in acoustic acquisition systems. I would like to stress that the value of such a manually set threshold does not affect the goodness of the final estimations, but only the convergence period of the algorithm. Actually, the proposed algorithm can achieve good reconstruction and segmentation results also starting with a Z image very degraded similar to that used in the first and third case (where a null threshold has been considered) and avoiding the final match operation between the two estimated images.

The proposed MRF algorithm uses the following parameters for the restoration process: 128×128 pixel images, 256 grey levels, a first-order neighbourhood system, a variance $\sigma_z^2 = 846$, initial temperature equal to 4000 lowered by a logarithmic scheduling. The side of each 128×128 image is fixed equal to 1.4 m and the bottom of the scene, represented by white pixels, is 4.9 m far from the antenna. The confidence threshold $T_c = 40$ was fixed in accordance with the highest side lobe level equal to -13 dB, corresponding to the 22% of the average of the 100 highest values of confidence. This threshold was also used to select the samples used for the variance computation related to the noise model of the confidence map.

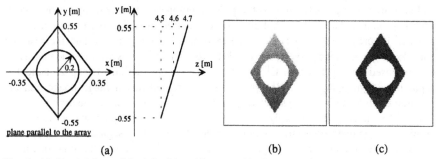

(a)　　　　　　　　(b)　　　　　　　　(c)

Fig. 3. (a) Geometric model of the "rhomb" scene; (b) ideal range image; (c) ideal confidence image.

Figures 4(a) and 4(b) show the reconstructed range image and the restored confidence image, respectively, for the 1st case. Fig. 4(a) was obtained after the match between the restored confidence image and the reconstructed range image at the output of the MRF process. The result is twofold: first, the algorithm removes holes and side-lobe effects from inside and outside objects, respectively; secondly, the final confidence map is a binary image that separates confident points (black) from non-confident ones (white). These results represent good approximations of the ideal map and images shown in Fig. 3. Figures 4(c) and 4(d) show the reconstructed range image and the restored confidence image, respectively, for the 2nd case, starting from a Z map shown in Fig. 2(c).

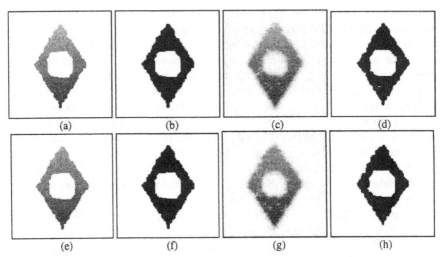

Fig. 4. (a) Final reconstructed range image and (b) segmented confidence image for the 1st case; (c) final reconstructed range image and (d) segmented confidence image for the 2nd case; (e) final reconstructed range image and (f) segmented confidence image for the 3rd case. Segmented and reconstructed images (2nd case) by using a degraded initial Z image: (g) final reconstructed range image; (h) segmented confidence image.

One can notice that the segmentation is quite good while the reconstruction of the map Z presents a poor visual quality. However, the mean square error is lower and the bad appearance is probably due to the poor smoothness performed inside the object. This is probably due to the simplicity of the function modeling the proposed region process. Figures 4(e) and 4(f) show the reconstructed range image and the restored confidence image, respectively, for the 3rd case. The map S is well segmented using the proposed energy function E^1 as well as the reconstruction of map Z using E^2, separately. Figures 4(g) and 4(h) show the final reconstructed range image and the restored confidence image, respectively, in the second case, but considering an initial Z map very degraded (Fig. 2(d)), i.e., considering all the points z whose associated confidence s is over an arbitrary low threshold (TH = 20), in such a way that speckle and side lobes effects were strongly retained. One can notice that the final quality is comparable with that of the other algorithms and also the error is of the same order. Therefore, also using very degraded initial images the proposed algorithm succeeds to recover original information.

To verify the improvement of the proposed algorithms over other techniques suitable for this type of reconstruction, the mean square error (*MSE*), the relative percentage *MSE* (*RMSE*) between the actual and estimated z data, and over- and under-segmentation errors have been considered. Table A provides the results of a comparative analysis performed by applying to the above-considered scene three types of different algorithms: one based on a simple threshold and the other based on the classical MRF approach. Row A reports the results obtained by the match of the range and confidence image, retaining those range points showing confidence larger than the threshold T_c. This approach gives the worst result, as it performs only a punctual analysis of the images, presenting a lot of holes in the reconstructed image, so increasing the error. Row B reports the results obtained by a technique consisting in the application of a reconstruction MRF algorithm to the range map obtained in the previous case (Row A). This technique adopts a dual process, one for reconstruction and the other for edge detection (line process [8]) and does not exploit the confidence information. This result is the best obtained using alternative MRF-based methods starting from adequately thresholded maps to decrease as much as possible the initial error. Row C, D and E shows the results of the proposed techniques, for the 1st, 2nd and 3rd cases, respectively. Row F presents a complementary case related to the 3rd algorithm proposed; it consists in using the ideal confidence map (see Fig. 3(c)) for the reconstruction. It can be noticed a very precise recovery of the 3D information, proving that the better the S estimate, the more precise the reconstructed Z map.

Row	Method	*MSE*	*RMSE*	Segment. error
A	simple threshold	93.1 cm^2	0.041 %	591 pixels
B	MRF process on Z after match with S	78.0 cm^2	0.036 %	N.A.
C	prop. alg. 1st case	22.0 cm^2	0.0092 %	413 pixels
D	prop. alg. 2nd case	19.34 cm^2	0.0082 %	415 pixels
E	prop. alg. 3rd case	26.3 cm^2	0.011 %	403 pixels
F	prop. alg. 3rd case using ideal S	0.15 cm^2	0.000073 %	0 pixels

Table A. Comparative results in terms of *MSE*, *RMSE*, and segmentation errors for the proposed techniques and other algorithms suitable for the problem (N.A. = not applicable). See text.

To evaluate the correct retrieval of the object shapes, another kind of error was considered, related to the number of pixels different from that of the ideal confidence image, i.e., we assessed the segmentation error (see Table A). Also in this case, our approach provided the smallest errors, concerning both over- and under-segmentation.

Finally, we consider a real example of a scene composed of two anchor chains and a little round object (8 cm in diameter) placed from 3 to 7 m far from the array. The images were acquired with an acoustic camera Echoscope 1600, i.e., a real-time 3D camera with the following characteristics: array of 40×40 sensors, carrier frequency: 600 KHz, lateral resolution: 6.25 cm (at a distance of 5 m), range accuracy: ±3.5 cm. In Figs. 5(a) and 5(b), one can see the actual range and confidence images composed of 128×128 pixels covering an area of 3.2×3.2 m^2. The two anchor chains appears like two narrow rectangles with different orientations and distances with respect to the array plane and the round object is placed between them and closer to the array. One can notice that these real images are similar to those synthetically generated, thus proving the goodness of the simulation algorithm used. Figures 5(c) and 5(d) show the final reconstructed and restored images using the energy related to the 1st case, while Figs. 5(e), 5(f) and 5(g), 5(h) those related to the 2nd and 3rd cases, for reconstruction and restoration, respectively. One can notice that, in the 3rd case, a spurious small object is present in the images, which is probably related to inaccurate threshold used during the restoration of the image S. As expected, our algorithm works quite well with real data: the chains are well identified, like the little round object located between them. Apart the 3rd case, cluttering data inserted by side lobe effects above the round object location are correctly removed and the 3D scene structure seems well determined.

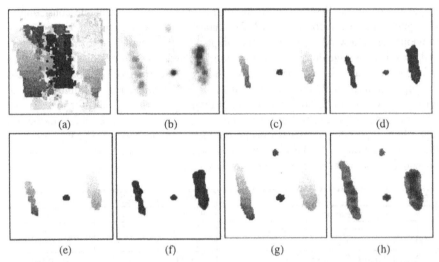

Fig. 5. Results related to the real scene: (a) input noisy range image, (b) input noisy confidence image; (c) final reconstructed range image (1st case); (d) restored confidence image (1st case); (e) final reconstructed range image (2nd case); (f) restored confidence image (2nd case); (g) final reconstructed range image (3rd case); (h) restored confidence image (3rd case).

5 Conclusions

In this paper, we have presented probabilistic methodologies for the integration of confidence information (directly extracted by an acquisition system) aimed at the reconstruction of underwater 3D acoustic images. Confidence represents a measure of reliability associated point by point to the range measures

Three MRF-based processes are proposed. Two consider a coupled segmentation (of the confidence image S) and reconstruction (of the range image Z) performed at the same time. The third case considers the segmentation of the confidence first and the successive use of the final segmented S to reconstruct range data, performing two separate MRF processes in series.

Both images have been represented as a random field pair affected by noise modelled as AWGN. Energy functionals for restoration and reconstruction were devised incorporating physical constraints allowing a more accurate estimation. The optimal estimates (in the MAP sense) have been found by minimizing these functionals. Owing to the MRF approach, confidence information is actively used in the reconstruction phase leading to a better reconstruction. The final segmentation of the confidence image allows to discriminate between object(s) and background making it possible a easy recovering of the shape for subsequent higher level tasks (e.g., recognition).

Finally, a lot of operations can be carried out, thanks to the double nature of the data provided (e.g., a different merging of the confidence information). Future investigations will specifically deal with 3D segmentation and reconstruction problems to get an improved image representation together with a precise reconstruction estimate.

Acknowledgments

The author would like to thank Dr. Rolf K. Hansen and Roger Jakobsen of Omnitech A/S who kindly provided real data acquired with their real-time 3D acoustic camera.

References

[1] A.K. Jain, P.J. Flynn, (Eds.), *Three-Dimensional Object Recognition Systems*, Elsevier, Amsterdam (1993).

[2] R. Szelinsky, *Bayesian Modeling of Uncertainty in Low-Level Vision*, Kluver Academic Publ., Boston (1989).

[3] R.O. Nielsen, *Sonar Signal Processing*, Artech House, Boston (1991).

[4] M. Okino, Y. Higashi, "Measurement of Seabed Topography by Multibeam Sonar Using CFFT", *IEEE Jour. Oceanic Engineering*, Vol. OE-11, pp. 474-479, October 1986.

[5] V. Murino, A. Trucco, "Acoustic Image Improvement by Confidence Levels", *Proc. IEEE Ultrasonics Symposium*, Cannes (France), pp. 1367-1370, November 1994.

[6] E. Jakeman, R.J. Tough, "Generalized *K* distribution: a statistical model for weak scattering", *Jour. Optical Society of America*, Vol. 4, pp.1764-1772, September 1987.

[7] J.L. Marroquin, *Probabilistic Solution of Inverse Problems*, Ph.D. Thesis, MIT, Boston, 1985.

[8] S. Geman, D. Geman, "Stochastic relaxation, Gibbs distribution, and Bayesian restoration of images", *IEEE Trans. on Pattern Analysis & Machine Intelligence*, Vol. PAMI-6, pp. 721-741, November 1984.

[9] B.Günsel, A.K.Jain, E.Panayirci, "Reconstruction and Boundary Detection of Range and Intensity Images using Multiscale MRF Representations", *Computer Vision and Image Understanding*, Vol. 63, No. 2, pp. 353-366, March 1996.

[10] B. Günsel, A.K. Jain, "Visual Surface Reconstruction and Boundary Detection using Stochastic Models", *Proc. 11th Int. Conf. on Pattern Recognition (ICPR)*, The Hague (The Netherlands), pp. 343-346, 1994.

[11] A. Blake, A. Zisserman, *Visual Reconstruction*, MIT Press, Cambridge (1987).

[12] R.S.Beattie, S.C.Elder, "Side Scan Sonar Image Restoration using Simulated Annealing and Iterative Conditional Modes", *Proc. Int. Conf. on Sonar Signal Processing*, Loughborough (UK), pp. 161-167, Dec. 1995.

[13] S. Show, J. Arnold, "Automated Error Detection in Multibeam Bathymetry Data", *Proc. IEEE OCEANS '93*, Victoria (Canada), Vol. II, pp. 89-94, 1993.

[14] S.Dugelay, J.M.Augustin, C.Graffigne, "Segmentation of multibeam acoustic imagery in the exploration of the deep sea bottom", *13th Int. Conf. onn Pattern Recognition*, Vienna, pp. 437-445, August 1996.

[15] V.Murino, "Acoustic Image Reconstruction by Markov Random Fields", *Electronics Letters*, Vol. 32, N. 7, pp. 697-698, March 1996.

[16] V.Murino, E.Frumento, F.Gabino, "Restoration of noisy underwater acoustic images using Markov Random Fields", in *Lecture Notes in Computer Science n. 974*, Springer Verlag, Berlin, pp. 355-360, 1995.

[17] S. Kirkpatrick, C.D. Gellatt Jr., M.P. Vecchi., "Optimization by simulated annealing", *Science*, Vol. 220, No. 4598, pp. 671-680, 1983.

[18] T.L. Henderson, S.G. Lacker, "Seafloor Profiling by a Wideband Sonar: Simulaton, Frequency-Response, Optimization, and Results of a Brief Sea Test", *IEEE Jour. Ocean. Engin.*, Vol. 14, pp. 94-107, January 1989.

Unsupervised Segmentation Applied on Sonar Images

M. Mignotte[‡] *C.Collet* [‡] *P.Pérez* [•] *P.Bouthemy* [•]

[‡] Groupe de Traitement du Signal, Ecole Navale, Lanvéoc-Poulmic,
29240 Brest-Naval, France.
email : name@ecole-navale.fr
[•] IRISA/INRIA, Campus Universitaire de Beaulieu, 35042 Rennes cedex, France.
email : name@irisa.fr

Abstract. This work deals with unsupervised sonar image segmentation. We present a new estimation segmentation procedure using the recent iterative method of estimation called Iterative Conditional Estimation (**ICE**) [1]. This method takes into account the variety of the laws in the distribution mixture of a sonar image and the estimation of the parameters of the label field (modeled by a Markov Random Field (**MRF**)). For the estimation step, we use a maximum likelihood technique to estimate the noise model parameters, and the least squares method proposed by Derin *et al.* [2] to estimate the **MRF** prior model. Then, in order to obtain an accurate segmentation map and to speed up the convergence rate, we use a multigrid strategy exploiting the previously estimated parameters. This technique has been successfully applied to real sonar images [1], and is compatible with an automatic processing of massive amounts of data.

1   Introduction

Due to its high-resolution performance a high frequency sonar allows to visualize all kinds of objects located on the sea-bottom. The detection of these objects and their classification (as wrecks, rocks, man-made objects, and so on...) are based on the extraction and the identification of their associated cast shadows in sonar pictures [3]. Before any classification step, one must segment the sonar image between *shadow* areas and *sea-bottom reverberation* areas. Nevertheless, segmenting an image into different classes without *a priori* information is not an easy task in computer vision: the main difficulty is that the estimation of the model parameters introduced is required for the segmentation, while the

---

[1] Acknowledgements : The authors thank the **GESMA** (Groupe d'Etude Sous-Marine de l'Atlantique) for having provided us with numerous real SONAR pictures and the **DRET** (Direction des Recherches Etudes et Techniques de la DGA) for partial financial support of this work.

segmentation is needed for the parameter estimation. For example a supervised Markovian segmentation [4] [5] gives good results; nevertheless, a substantial number of estimated parameters is usually required in order to solve the difficult problem of unsupervised sonar images segmentation.

To circumvent this difficulty, a scheme was proposed in [6] in which the estimation and the segmentation are implemented recursively. Although the method proved to converge in the case of independent Gaussian model, it is not clear that it can be extended to **MRF** model. Also, the method requires very complicated computations. An alternate approach to solve the unsupervised **MRF** segmentation problem consists in having a two steps process. First, a parameter *estimation step* in which we have to estimate the noise model parameters and the **MRF** model parameters. Then, a second step in which we apply the segmentation algorithm with the estimated parameters.

First, let us consider the estimation of the noise model parameters. There are a number of methods that use the image histogram. Most of them (Fourier, polynomials and cumulate histogram methods) are inefficient in the case of an important distribution mixture and without mathematical justification to estimate a mixture of different laws [7]. Several techniques have been proposed to determine a Maximum Likelihood estimate of the noise model parameters from a given image. **EM** (*Expectation Maximization*) or **SEM** algorithms (*Stochastic Expectation Maximization*) can be used in the case of Gaussian distribution mixtures [8] [9]. In a specific application to sonar imagery, we have taken into account the variety of laws in the distribution mixture [3]. Nevertheless, these algorithms do not account for the properties of the label field defined in a **MRF** segmentation as a Gibbs distribution. As we will show in this paper, another way to estimate these parameters consists in using the **ICE** procedure [1].

Let us consider now the estimation of the **MRF** model parameters. The **MRF** model provides a powerful tool for incorporating the knowledge about the spatial dependence of the labels of the segmented image. The knowledge about the scene is incorporated into an energy function that consists of appropriate clique functions. In most of the previous work using **MRF** models, the parameters of the prior model are assumed to be known and determined in an *ad hoc* fashion. Howewer, the values of these parameters determine the distribution over the configuration space to which the system converges. Besides, in our application, it is difficult to find appropriate values for the clique parameters since the real scenes are different for each picture (sea floor with pebbles, dunes, ridges, sand, ...). Thus, estimating these parameters is very crucial in practice for successful labelling. One way to estimate them from a given image is to use a gradient descent algorithm [10] but this method is slow and very sensitive to the initial value given to initialize the procedure. In [11], the **EM** algorithm is used but this iterative scheme also requires a lot of computing time [12]. Besides these two iterative methods may run into a local maximum without reaching the proper solution. In [13], the authors propose to implement the estimation of the parameters associated with clique functions as a neural network whose weights are learned from examples by the error backpropagation algorithm. This method is interesting but requires a learning step from a sample training data. Let us mention also the use of Metropolis algorithm in [14].

In this paper, we adopt for the *Estimation Step* the **ICE** procedure [1] to estimate simultaneously the **MRF** prior model parameters (with the Least Square estimator **LSQR** described by Derin *et al* [2]) and the noise model parameters (with a Maximum Likelihood estimator). For the *Segmentation Step*, we use a multigrid segmentation with the previously estimated parameters. This paper is organized as follows : In sections 2 and 3, we define the notation and we give a brief description of the **ICE** procedure and the used estimators. Sections 4 and 5 detail the *Estimation Step* and the initialization of the procedure. The experimental results on real scenes are presented in section 6.

2 Iterative Conditional Estimation

We consider a couple of random fields $Z = (X, Y)$, with $Y = \{Y_s, s \in S\}$ the field of observations located on a lattice S of N sites s, and $X = \{X_s, s \in S\}$ the associated label field. Each of the Y_s takes its value in $\Lambda_{obs} = \{0, \ldots, 255\}$ and each X_s in $\{e_0 = shadow,\ e_1 = sea\ bottom\ reverberation\}$. The distribution of (X, Y) is defined by, firstly, $P_X(x)$, the distribution of X which is supposed stationary and Markovian and, secondly, the site-wise likelihoods $P_{Y_s/X_s}(y_s/x_s)$. In this work, these likelihoods depend on the class label x_s. The observable Y is called the *incomplete data* and Z the *complete data*.

In the unsupervised segmentation case, we have to estimate in a first step (*Estimation Step*), parameter vectors Φ_x and Φ_y which define $P_X(x)$ and $P_{Y/X}(y/x)$ respectively. We estimate them using the iterative method of estimation called Iterated Conditional Estimation (**ICE**) [1]. This method requires to find two estimators, namely $\hat{\Phi}_x = \Phi_x(X)$ and $\hat{\Phi}_y = \Phi_y(X, Y)$ for completely observed data. When X is unobservable, the iterative **ICE** procedure defines $\Phi_x^{[k+1]}$ and $\Phi_y^{[k+1]}$ as conditional expectations of $\hat{\Phi}_x$ and $\hat{\Phi}_y$ given $Y = y$, computed according to the current values $\Phi_x^{[k]}$ and $\Phi_y^{[k]}$. These are the best approximations of Φ_x and Φ_y in terms of the mean squares error. By denoting E_k, the conditional expectation using $\Phi^{[k]} = [\Phi_x^{[k]}, \Phi_y^{[k]}]$, this iterative procedure is defined as follows:

- One takes an initial value $\Phi^{[0]} = [\Phi_x^{[0]}, \Phi_y^{[0]}]$.

- $\Phi^{[k+1]}$ is computed from $\Phi^{[k]}$ and $Y = y$ by :

$$\Phi_x^{[k+1]} = E_k[\hat{\Phi}_x | Y = y] \tag{1}$$
$$\Phi_y^{[k+1]} = E_k[\hat{\Phi}_y | Y = y] \tag{2}$$

The computation of these expectations is impossible in practice, but we can approach (1) and (2), thanks to the law of large numbers by:

$$\Phi_x^{[k+1]} = \frac{1}{n} \cdot [\Phi_x(x_{(1)}) + \cdots + \Phi_x(x_{(n)})] \tag{3}$$

$$\Phi_y^{[k+1]} = \frac{1}{n} \cdot [\Phi_y(x_{(1)}, y) + \cdots + \Phi_y(x_{(n)}, y)] \qquad (4)$$

where $x_{(i)}$, $i = 1, \ldots, n$ are realizations of X according to the posterior distribution $P_{X/Y, \Phi^{[k]}}(x/y, \Phi^{[k]})$. Finally, we can use the **ICE** procedure for our application because we get:

- An estimator $\Phi_y(X, Y)$ of the *complete data* : we use a Maximum Likelihood (**ML**) estimator for the noise model parameter estimation. In order to estimate $\hat{\Phi}_x = \Phi_x(X)$, given a realization x of X, we use the **LSQR** estimator [2] described by Derin *et al.* which will be summarized in subsection 3.2.

- An initial value $\Phi^{[0]}$ not *too far* from the optimal parameters (see section 4).

- A way of simulating realizations of X according to the posterior distribution $P_{X/Y}(x/y)$ by using the Gibbs sampler [15].

The **ICE** procedure is not limited by the form of the conditional distribution of the noise. This algorithm is well adapted for our application where the speckle distribution in the sonar images is not exactly known and varies according to experimental conditions. Besides, let us recall that this method does not assume the independence of the random variables X_i such as the **SEM** or the **EM** algorithm [8][9] and takes into account the Markovian characteristics of the *a priori* label field.

3 Estimation of the Model Parameters for the complete data

3.1 Noise Model Parameters

The Gaussian law, $\mathcal{N}(\mu, \sigma^2)$, is an appropriate degradation model to describe the luminance y within *shadow* regions (essentially due to the electronical noise). The most natural choice of the estimator $\hat{\Phi}_y = \Phi_y(x = e_0, y)$ is the empirical mean and the empirical variance. If N_0 pixels are located in the shadow areas, we have:

$$\hat{\mu}_{ML} = \frac{1}{N_0} \cdot \sum_{s : x_s = e_0} y_s \qquad (5)$$

$$\hat{\sigma}_{ML}^2 = \frac{1}{N_0 - 1} \cdot \sum_{s : x_s = e_0} (y_s - \hat{\mu}_{ML})^2 \qquad (6)$$

In order to take into account the speckle noise phenomenon [16], we model the conditional density function of the *sea bottom* class by a shifted Rayleigh law $\mathcal{R}(min, \alpha^2)$ [3] :

$$P(y_s/x_s = e_1) = \frac{y_s - min}{\alpha^2} \cdot \exp\left[-\frac{(y_s - min)^2}{2\alpha^2}\right]$$

The maximum value of the log-likelihood function is used to determine a Maximum Likelihood estimator of the *complete data*. If $\hat{y}_{min}$ is the minimum grey level in the *sea bottom* areas and N_1 the number of pixels located within the *sea bottom* regions, we obtain the following results:

$$\hat{\alpha}_{ML}^2 = \frac{1}{2N_1} \cdot \sum_{s:x_s=e_1} (y_s - \widehat{min}_{ML})^2 \tag{7}$$

$$\widehat{min}_{ML} \approx \hat{y}_{min} - 1 \tag{8}$$

In the two cases, π_k (the proportion of the kth class) is given by the empirical frequency:

$$\hat{\pi}_k = \frac{N_k}{N_o + N_1} \qquad k \in \{0,1\}$$

3.2 A Priori Model Parameters

A **MRF** prior model is specified in terms of parameters, called the clique parameters. These parameters correspond to the clique potential values of an equivalent Gibbs Random Field representation. Several schemes have been proposed in the computer vision literature for the estimation of the **MRF** parameters. We can cite the coding and the maximum pseudo likelihood method proposed by Besag in [4]. Let us also mention the stochastic gradient method converging to the maximum of the likelihood developped in [17]. These methods offer a rigorous mathematical justification, but they are iterative and have to solve a set of non-linear equations. This means that they require an initial guess for the solution and may run into a local maximum without reaching the proper solution.

The **MRF** parameter estimation method described in this section has been proposed by Derin *et al.* This scheme is not iterative and parameters estimated are close to the optimal parameters [2]. We briefly describe this estimator in terms of our model, *i.e.*, with respect to the 2nd order neighborhood system. Let X_{ν_s} represent the set of labels assigned to the neighbors of site s and $\Phi_x = [\beta_1, \beta_2, \beta_3, \beta_4]$ be the *a priori* parameter vector corresponding to two-site clique potentials (see **Fig. 1**).

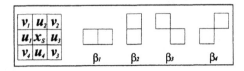

Fig. 1. 2nd *order neighborhood and two-site associated cliques.*

We define:

$$\Theta^t(x_s, \eta_s) = [\mathcal{I}(x_s, u_1) + \mathcal{I}(x_s, u_3), \mathcal{I}(x_s, u_2) +$$
$$\mathcal{I}(x_s, u_4), \mathcal{I}(x_s, v_1) + \mathcal{I}(x_s, v_3), \mathcal{I}(x_s, v_2) + \mathcal{I}(x_s, v_4)]$$

Where $\quad \mathcal{I}(z_1, z_2) = \begin{cases} 0 \text{ if } z_1 = z_2, \\ 1 \text{ otherwise.} \end{cases}$

The local energy function U_s can be expressed as:

$$U_s(x_s, \eta_s, \Phi_x) = \Theta^t(x_s, \eta_s)\Phi_x \tag{9}$$

The prior local conditional probability at site s can be written as:

$$P_{X_s/X_{\nu_s}}(x_s/\eta_s) = \frac{P_{X_s, X_{\nu_s}}(x_s, \eta_s)}{P_{X_{\nu_s}}(\eta_s)} = Z_s^{-1} \cdot \exp^{-U_s(x_s, \eta_s, \Phi_x)}$$

Where Z_s is the local partition function and $P(e_1, \eta_s)$ is the joint distribution of the label e_1 with the neighborhood η_s. We obtain the following expression for the two different values of x_s ($x_s = e_0$ and $x_s = e_1$) with identical neighborhood η_i:

$$\exp[-U(e_1, \eta_i, \Phi_x) + U(e_0, \eta_i, \Phi_x)] = \frac{P_{X_s, X_{\nu_s}}(e_1, \eta_i)}{P_{X_s, X_{\nu_s}}(e_0, \eta_i)}$$

Taking logarithms on both sides and substituting for U from (9), we have:

$$[\Theta(e_0, \eta_i) - \Theta(e_1, \eta_i)]^t \Phi_x = \ln\left[\frac{P_{X_s, X_{\nu_s}}(e_1, \eta_i)}{P_{X_s, X_{\nu_s}}(e_0, \eta_i)}\right] \tag{10}$$

Φ_x is the unknown parameter vector to be estimated and the ratio of the right hand side of (10) may be estimated using simple histogramming (by counting the number of 3×3 blocks of type (e_1, η_i) and dividing by the number of blocks of type (e_0, η_i) over the image). By substituting for each value of η_i in (10), we obtain 256 equations (2^8 possible neighborhood configurations) in four unknowns. A specific combination (e_j, η_i) may not exist. In this case we cannot obtain a linear equation because of the logarithm in (10). Moreover $\Theta(e_0, \eta_i) = \Theta(e_1, \eta_i)$ implies equations of type $0 = C^{st}$, therefore we ignore those types of equations too. This overdetermined linear system of equations is solved with the least squares method.

We present some examples of the parameters estimation of a Gibbs Distribution (**GD**) using realizations that are generated with specified values. The estimates are compared to the specified values of the parameters in Table 1. Realizations of **GD** are presented in Figure 2.

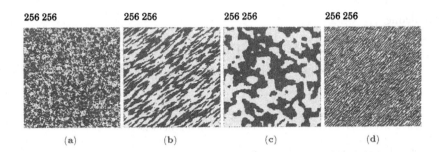

Fig. 2. *Realizations of* **GD** *with specified parameters (see* **Table 1** *for parameters values).*

Fig	Φ_x	β_1	β_2	β_3	β_4
(a)	Φ_x	0.3	0.3	0.3	0.3
	$\hat{\Phi}_x$	0.3	0.29	0.31	0.31
(b)	Φ_x	2	1	−1	1
	$\hat{\Phi}_x$	1.77	0.94	−0.86	0.98
(c)	Φ_x	2	2	0	0
	$\hat{\Phi}$	1.93	1.94	−0.05	0.01
(d)	Φ_x	1	1	−1	1
	$\hat{\Phi}$	0.95	0.93	−0.96	1.03

Table 1. *Specified* (Φ_x) *and estimated parameters* $(\hat{\Phi}_x)$. $\beta_1, \beta_2, \beta_3, \beta_4$ *designate the potentials associated with the horizontal, vertical, right diagonal, left diagonal cliques.*

Synthetic textures created in Figure 2 show that the Gibbs Random Field representation is an appropriate spatial distribution to model the *a priori* label field distribution. Figure 2.*a* shows inhomogeneous shapes such as segmented pebbly sea bottom. Figure 2.*b* and 2.*c* depict homogeneous shapes respectively with a dominant orientation representative of segmented dunes (2.*b*) or with geometric shapes as for the shadows of manufactured objects (2.*c*). Figure 2.*d* looks like segmented real scenes containing ridges of sand.

Parameter variation for a **GD** class gives a wide range of texture realizations. Those presented are only a few samples. These experiments demonstrate that estimated parameters are close to the true parameters.

4   Initialization

The initial parameter values have a significant impact on the rapidity of the convergence of the **ICE** procedure and on the quality of the final estimates. In our application, we use the following method: The initial parameter of the noise model $\Phi_y^{[0]}$ are determined by applying a small non overlapping sliding window over the image and calculating the sample mean, variance and minimum grey level estimates. Each estimation calculated over the sliding window thus gives a sample x_i, (*i.e* a three component vector). These samples $\{x_1, \ldots, x_M\}$ are then clustered into two classes $\{e_0, e_1\}$ using the **K-means** clustering procedure. This algorithm uses a similarity measure that is the Euclidean distance of the samples and a criterion J defined by:

$$J = \sum_{i=1}^{K} \sum_{x_l \in C_i} \mid x_l - c_i \mid^2$$

where the second sum is over all samples in the ith cluster and c_i is the *center* of the cluster. It is easily seen that for a given set of samples and class assignements, J is minimized by choosing c_i to be the *sample mean* of the ith cluster. Moreover, when c_i is the sample mean, J is minimized by assigning x_j to the class of the cluster with the nearest mean. A number of other criteria are given in [18]. The complete algorithm is outlined below:

1. Choose K initial cluster centres $c_1^{[1]}, \ldots, c_K^{[1]}$. These could be arbitrarily, but are usually defined by:

$$c_i^{[1]} = x_i \qquad 1 \leq i \leq K$$

2. At the kth step, assign the sample x_l, $1 \leq l \leq M$ to cluster i if

$$\parallel x_l - c_i^{[k]} \parallel < \parallel x_l - c_j^{[k]} \parallel \qquad \forall \ j \neq i$$

In fact, we reassign every sample to the cluster with the nearest mean. In our application, the measure of similarity between two samples is the Euclidean distance. In the case of equality, we assign x_l arbitrarily to i or j.

3. Let $C_i^{[k]}$ denote the ith cluster after Step 2. Determine new cluster centres by:

$$c_i^{[k+1]} = \frac{1}{N_i} \cdot \sum_{x \in C_i^{[k]}} x$$

where N_i = number of samples in $C_i^{[k]}$. Thus, the new cluster centre is the mean of the samples in the old cluster.

4. Repeat until convergence is achieved $(c_i^{[k+1]} = c_i^{[k]} \ \forall i)$.

Although it is possible to find pathological cases where convergence never occurs [18], the algorithm does converge in all tested examples. The rapidity of convergence depends on the number K, of cluster centers chosen, the choice of initial cluster centers and the order in which the samples are considered. In our application $K = 2$.

Figure 3.a represents a sonar image and the result of the K-means clustering algorithm is reported in Figure 3.b. Figure 3.c shows the representation of the

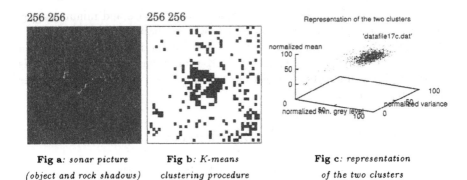

| **Fig a:** *sonar picture* | **Fig b:** *K-means* | **Fig c:** *representation* |
| (object and rock shadows) | clustering procedure | of the two clusters |

Fig. 3.

two clusters associated to the *shadow* class and *sea bottom reverberation* class. Each sample $\mathbf{x}_l$ is represented by a point.

ML estimation is then used over the K-means segmentation to find $\Phi_y^{[0]}$. On one hand, a small size window can increase the accuracy of the segmentation and then the precision of the distribution mixture estimation. On the other hand, it decreases the number of pixels with which $\mathbf{x}_l$'s are computed and can increase the misclassification error. In our application, good results are obtained with a $6 * 6$ pixels window.

The initial parameters of the Gibbs distribution are obtained by using the **LSQR** method from the **ML** segmentation $\hat{x}^{[0]}$.

$$\Phi_x^{[0]} = \Phi_{\mathrm{LSQR}}(\hat{x}^{[0]}) \quad \text{with} \quad \hat{x}_s^{[0]} = \arg\max_{x_s} P_{Y_s/X_s, \Phi_y^{[0]}}(y_s/x_s, \Phi_y^{[0]}) \quad (\forall s \in S)$$

5   Parameters Estimation Procedure for the incomplete data

We can use the following algorithm to solve the unsupervised sonar image segmentation problem. Let us remind that this method takes into account the diversity of the laws in the distribution mixture estimation as well as the problem of the estimation of the label field parameters.

- **Parameter Initialization**: K-mean algorithm (see section 4). Let us denote $\Phi^{[0]} = [\Phi_x^{[0]}, \Phi_y^{[0]}]$, the obtained result.

- **ICE procedure**:
  $\Phi^{[k+1]}$ is computed from $\Phi^{[k]}$ in the following way:
  ▷ Using the Gibbs sampler, n realizations $x_{(1)}, \ldots, x_{(n)}$ are simulated according to the posterior distribution with parameter vector $\Phi^{[k]}$, with:

  $$P_{Y_s/X_s}(y_s/x_s = e_0) \qquad \text{a Gaussian law (shadow area)}$$
  $$P_{Y_s/X_s}(y_s/x_s = e_1) \quad \text{a shifted Rayleigh law (sea bottom area)}$$

▷ For each $x_{(i)}$ $(i = 1, \ldots, n)$, the parameter vector Φ_x is estimated by the Derin *et al.* algorithm and Φ_y with the **ML** estimator of each class.

▷ $\Phi^{[k+1]}$ is obtained from $(\Phi_x(x_{(i)}), \Phi_y(x_{(i)}, y))$ $1 \leq i \leq n$ by (3) and (4).

If the sequence $\Phi^{[k]}$ becomes steady, the **ICE** procedure is ended and one proceeds to the segmentation using the estimated parameters.

In order to estimate the *min* parameter of the *sea bottom reverberation* class during the **ICE** procedure, we can associate a very low probability for the pixels in the sonar image with a grey level equal to *min* [12].

We can regulate the importance of the "*stochastic*" aspect of the **ICE** by choosing n. When n increases, the "*stochastic*" side of the algorithm decreases. The intentional choice of a small value for n ($n = 1$ in our application) can increase its efficiency [19]. In [12], we have shown the superiority of the **ICE** procedure over the **EM** or **SEM** algorithm in case of different distributions mixture estimation or Rayleigh law mixture estimation. We have shown also that the estimation of the noise model parameters Φ_y was better according to the Kolmogorov distance or χ^2 error [12], when Φ_x and Φ_y are jointly estimated.

The Figure 4 represents the mixture of distributions of the sonar image shown in section 4, and the convergence of the estimation of the *a priori* parameters can be seen in Figure 4.b. The obtained results are given in Table 2.

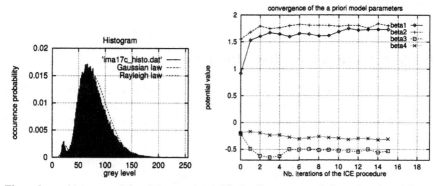

Fig a: *Image histogram of the picture reported in Figure 3.a and estimated mixture*

Fig b: *Convergence of the estimation of the a priori parameters*

Fig. 4.

The quality of the estimations is difficult to appreciate in absence of the real values. We can roughly perform such an evaluation by comparing the image histogram with the probability densities mixture corresponding to the estimated parameters. Figure 4.a shows the resulting mixture solution in graphical

	Initialization : **K-means**		
$\hat{\Phi}^{[0]}_{y_{(shadow)}}$	$0.16_{(\pi)}$ $\quad 55_{(\mu)}$	$286_{(\sigma^2)}$	
$\hat{\Phi}^{[0]}_{y_{(sea-bottom)}}$	$0.84_{(\pi)}$ $\quad 37_{(min)}$	$952_{(\alpha^2)}$	
$\hat{\Phi}^{[0]}_{x}$	$0.9_{(\beta_1)}$ $\quad 1.6_{(\beta_2)}$ $\quad -0.2_{(\beta_3)}$ $\quad -0.2_{(\beta_4)}$		
	ICE procedure		
$\hat{\Phi}_{y_{(shadow)}}$	$0.03_{(\pi)}$ $\quad 25_{(\mu)}$	$32_{(\sigma^2)}$	
$\hat{\Phi}_{y_{(sea-bottom)}}$	$0.97_{(\pi)}$ $\quad 35_{(min)}$	$1424_{(\alpha^2)}$	
$\hat{\Phi}_{x}$	$1.7_{(\beta_1)}$ $\quad 1.8_{(\beta_2)}$ $\quad -0.6_{(\beta_3)}$ $\quad -0.3_{(\beta_4)}$		

Estimated parameters on the picture reported in Figure 3.a. π stands for the proportion of the two classes within the sonar image. μ and σ^2 are the Gaussian parameters (shadow area). min and α are the Rayleigh law parameters (sea floor reverberation). β_i 's are the a priori parameters of the Markovian modeling. $\Phi^{[0]}$ represents the initial parameter estimates and the final estimates are denoted $\hat{\Phi}$.

Table 2.

form. The two dashed curves in the figures represent the individual components $P_{Y/X_s}(y/e_m)(0 \le m < K)$. The histogram is quite close to the mixture densities based on the estimated parameters, and a segmentation with these estimates (see section 6) gives good results.

6 Segmentation on Real Pictures

The segmentation of sonar images in two classes is stated as a statistical labelling problem according to a global Bayesian formulation in which the posterior distribution $P_{X/Y,\Phi}(x/y,\phi) \propto \exp -U(x,y)$ has to be maximized. The corresponding energy function to be minimized is of the form:

$$U(x,y) = \underbrace{\sum_{s \in S} \Psi_s(x_s, y_s)}_{U_1(x,y)} + \underbrace{\sum_{<s,t>} \beta_{s,t}\, \mathcal{I}(x_s, x_t)}_{U_2(x)}$$

where U_1 expresses the adequacy between observations and labels ($\Psi_s(x_s, y_s) = -\ln P(y_s/x_s)$), and U_2 the energy of the *a priori* model ($\beta_{s,t} = \beta_1, \beta_2, \beta_3$, or β_4 according to the type of neighboring pair $< s,t >$). The energy function is complex and the **MAP** (Maximum a Posteriori) solution is difficult to estimate. In order to avoid local minima and to speed up the convergence rate, we use a multigrid strategy [20]. The observation field remains at the finest resolution, only the **MRF** model will be hierarchically defined. The energy function is rewritten at each scale as a coarser **MRF** model.

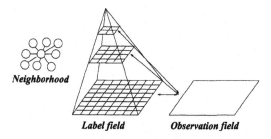

Fig. 5. *Neighborhood system and the multiscale relaxation structure.*

To generate the multigrid **MRF** model, the grid S is hierarchically partitioned into N_i sets b_k^l (with $k \in \{1 \ldots N_i\}$) of size $2^l \times 2^l$. We consider that the label x_k^l assigned to a block b_k^l is constant over all the pixels of the block. Given this constraint, an energy $U^l(x^l, y)$ can be easily derived from the original one by rewritting and properly grouping terms of $U(x, y)$ when x is actually block-wise constant relative to the partition ($\forall p \in b_k^l, x_p = x_k^l$) [5][20] :

$$U^l(x^l, y) = U_1^l(x^l, y) + U_2^l(x^l)$$

$$\text{with} \quad U_1^l(x^l, y) \triangleq \sum_{s \in S^l} \Psi_s^l(x_s^l, y_{b_s^l}) = \sum_{k=1}^{N^l} \sum_{p \in b_k^l} \Psi_s^l(x_k^l, y_p)$$

$$\text{and} \quad U_2^l(x^l) = \sum_{<k,m>} \beta_{k,m}^l \, \mathcal{I}(x_k^l, x_m^l)$$

where $y_{b_k^l}$ stands for the set of all the observations of the cell b_k^l and $\beta_{k,m}^l$ are deduced from the β_i's [20]. For propagating information through scale, we use a *coarse to fine* minimization strategy: in order to minimize the energy function associated with the **MRF** model at each scale, we use the **ICM** algorithm [4]; The final estimate obtained at a given level is interpolated to be used as an initialization for the relaxation process at the next finer level.

The segmentation result obtained for the image shown in Figure 6.a is reported in Figure 6.b.

We have presented in Figure 7 and 8 the different steps of two other unsupervised segmentation on real sonar images. Figures 7.a and 8.a represent two original observations. Figures 7.b and 8.b show the result of the K-means clustering algorithm and Figures 7.c and 8.c, the representation of the two clusters associated to the *shadow* class and *sea-bottom* class. The mixture of distributions is represented by Figures 7.d and 8.d and the final result of the segmented image is reported in Figures 7.e and 8.e. The obtained results are given in Table 3 and Table 4.

One can see that this approach gives convincing results and allows to converge toward a good image segmentation in spite of speckle noise. The rocks and manufactured object shadows are well segmented and close to the result we expected. The cast shadow of a manufactured object (reported in Figure 6.b) has a

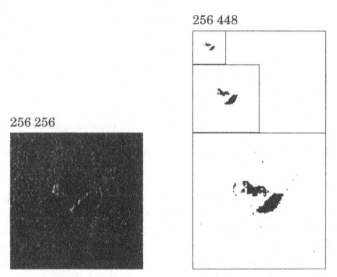

Fig a: *sonar picture*   **Fig b**: *Multigrid* **MAP** *segmentation results*
(object and rock shadows)   *with parameters obtained with the* **ICE** *procedure*

Fig. 6.

geometric shape easily identifiable for the classification step. This method allows to detect the little rocks (see Figure 7.e) and to preserve their shadow shapes at the finest resolution. Nevertheless, we can see in Figure 8.e that the proposed algorithm do not permit to eliminate totally the speckle noise effect which induces false small shadow areas. In order to still improve the results, we are now working on unsupervised hierarchical approach with inter-level connections.

7 Conclusion

We have described an unsupervised iterative estimation procedure based on the **ICE** algorithm [1] which offers an appropriate estimation of the noise model and Gibbs distribution parameters. The *Estimation Step* takes into account the diversity of the laws in the distribution mixture of a sonar image and can be used in a global estimation-segmentation procedure in order to solve the hard problem of unsupervised sonar image segmentation. This scheme is computationally simple, exhibits rapid convergence properties and well suited to automatic extraction of information from a large variety of sonar images. This method has been validated on a number of real sonar images demonstrating the efficiency and robustness of this scheme. The extension of the method to unsupervised hierarchical segmentation (with inter-level connections) will be the topic of our next research.

256 256 256 256

 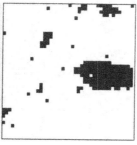 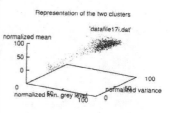

Fig 7.a: *sonar picture*   **Fig 7.b**: *K-means*   **Fig 7.c**: *representation*
(object and rock shadows)   *clustering procedure*   *of the two clusters*

	Initialization : **K-means**		
$\Phi_{y_{(shadow)}}^{[0]}$	$0.11_{(\pi)}$	$34_{(\mu)}$	$149_{(\sigma^2)}$
$\Phi_{y_{(sea-bottom)}}^{[0]}$	$0.89_{(\pi)}$	$39_{(min)}$	$2830_{(\alpha^2)}$
$\Phi_x^{[0]}$	$1.2_{(\beta_1)}$ $1.7_{(\beta_2)}$	$-0.3_{(\beta_3)}$	$-0.2_{(\beta_4)}$

	ICE procedure		
$\hat{\Phi}_{y_{(shadow)}}$	$0.10_{(\pi)}$	$28_{(\mu)}$	$34_{(\sigma^2)}$
$\hat{\Phi}_{y_{(sea-bottom)}}$	$0.90_{(\pi)}$	$39_{(min)}$	$4960_{(\alpha^2)}$
$\hat{\Phi}_x$	$1.2_{(\beta_1)}$ $1.7_{(\beta_2)}$	$-0.2_{(\beta_3)}$	$-0.2_{(\beta_4)}$

Table 3: *estimated parameters on the picture reported in Figure 7.a. π stands for the proportion of the two classes within the sonar image. μ and σ^2 are the Gaussian parameters (shadow area). min and α are the Rayleigh law parameters (sea floor reverberation). β_i's are the a priori parameters of the Markovian modeling. $\Phi^{[0]}$ represents the initial parameter estimates and the final estimates are denoted $\hat{\Phi}$.*

256 448

256 256

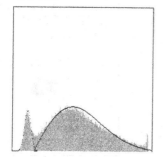

Fig 7.d: *Image histogram of the picture reported in*   **Fig 7.e**: *Multigrid MAP segmentation estimates*
Figure 7.a and estimated mixture   *with parameters obtained with the ICE procedure*

Fig 8.a: *sonar picture*
(sandy sea floor and a tyre)

Fig 8.b: *K-means*
clustering procedure

Fig 8.c: *representation*
of the two clusters

Initialization : **K-means**			
$\hat{\Phi}^{[0]}_{y_{(shadow)}}$	$0.35_{(\pi)}$	$78_{(\mu)}$	$406_{(\sigma^2)}$
$\hat{\Phi}^{[0]}_{y_{(sea-bottom)}}$	$0.65_{(\pi)}$	$46_{(min)}$	$1640_{(\alpha^2)}$
$\hat{\Phi}^{[0]}_x$	$1.0_{(\beta_1)}$ $\quad 1.5_{(\beta_2)}$	$-0.16_{(\beta_3)}$	$-0.2_{(\beta_4)}$

ICE procedure			
$\hat{\Phi}_{y_{(shadow)}}$	$0.03_{(\pi)}$	$36_{(\mu)}$	$84_{(\sigma^2)}$
$\hat{\Phi}_{y_{(sea-bottom)}}$	$0.97_{(\pi)}$	$46_{(min)}$	$1879_{(\alpha^2)}$
$\hat{\Phi}_x$	$1.5_{(\beta_1)}$ $\quad 1.7_{(\beta_2)}$	$-0.3_{(\beta_3)}$	$-0.6_{(\beta_4)}$

Table 4: *estimated parameters on the picture reported in Figure 8.a. π stands for the proportion of the two classes within the sonar image. μ and σ^2 are the Gaussian parameters (shadow area). min and α are the Rayleigh law parameters (sea floor reverberation). β_i's are the a priori parameters of the Markovian modeling. $\Phi^{[0]}$ represents the initial parameter estimates and the final estimates are denoted $\hat{\Phi}$.*

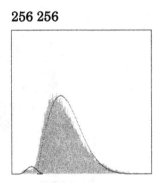

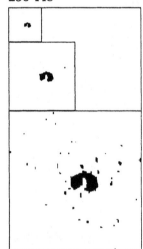

Fig 8.d: *Image histogram of the picture reported in Figure 8.a and estimated mixture*

Fig 8.e: *Multigrid* **MAP** *segmentation results with parameters obtained with the ICE procedure*

References

1. F. Salzenstein and W.Pieczinsky. Unsupervised bayesian segmentation using hidden markovian fields. *In proc. ICASSP'95*, pages 2411-2414, May 1995.
2. H. Derin and H. Elliot. Modeling and segmentation of noisy and textured images using Gibbs random fields. *IEEE Trans. Pattern Anal. and Machine Intell.*, PAMI-9(1):39-55, January 1987.
3. F. Schmitt, M. Mignotte, C. Collet, and P. Thourel. Estimation of noise parameters on sonar images. In *Signal and Image Processing, SPIE'96*, volume 2823, pages 1-12, Denver, Colorado, USA, August 1996.
4. J. Besag. On the statistical analysis of dirty pictures. *Journal of the Royal Statistical Society*, B-48:259-302, 1986.
5. C. Collet, P. Thourel, P. Pérez, and P. Bouthemy. Hierarchical MRF modeling for sonar picture segmentation. In *proc. ICIP'96*, Lausanne, September 1996.
6. S. Lakshmanan and H. Derin. Simultaneous parameter estimation and segmentation of Gibbs random fields using simulated annealing. *IEEE Trans. on PAMI*, 11(8):799-813, August 1989.
7. J.G. Postaire and P.A. Vasseur. An approximate solution to normal mixture identification with application to unsupervised pattern classification. *IEEE Trans. on PAMI*, (2):163-179, 1981.
8. G. Celleux and J. Diebolt. A random imputation principle : the stochastic EM algorithm. Technical Report 901, INRIA, September 1988.
9. A.P. Dempster, N.M. Laird, and D.B. Rubin. Maximum likelihood from incomplete data via the EM algorithm. *Royal Statistical Society*, pages 1-38, 1976.
10. Z. Kato, J. Zerubia, and M. Berthod. Unsupervised parallel image classification using a hierarchical Markovian model. In *Proc. ICCV'95*, volume 1, pages 169-174, Cambridge, Massachusetts, 20-23 June 1995.
11. B. Chalmond. An iterative gibbsian technique for reconstruction of m-ary images. *Pattern Recognition*, 22(6):747-761, 1989.
12. M. Mignotte. Modèle markovien: estimation des paramètres. Technical Report 7, Ecole Navale, March 1996.
13. Y. Kim and H.S Yang. Efficient image labelling based on Markov random field and error backpropagation network. *Pattern Recognition*, 26(11):1695-1707, 1993.
14. P. A. Kelly, H. Derin, and K. D. Hart. Adaptative segmentation of speckled images using a hierarchical random field model. *IEEE Transactions on Acoustic Speech and Signal Processing*, 36(10):1628-1641, October 1988.
15. S. Geman and D. Geman. Stochastic relaxation, Gibbs distributions and the Bayesian restoration of images. *IEEE Trans. Pattern Anal. and Machine Intell.*, PAMI-6(6):721-741, November 1984.
16. J. W. Goodman. Some fundamental properties of speckle. *Journal of Optical Society of America*, 66(11):1145-1150, November 1976.
17. L. Younes. Parametric inference for imperfectly observed Gibbsian fields. *Springer-Verlag Prob. Th. Rel. Fields 82*, pages 625-645, 1989.
18. S. Banks. Signal processing image processing and pattern recognition, 1990.
19. B. Braathen, P. Masson, and W. Pieczynski. Global and local methods of unsupervised Bayesian segmentation of images. *GRAPHICS and VISION*, (1):39-52, 1993.
20. F. Heitz, P. Pérez, and P. Bouthemy. Multiscale minimisation of global energy functions in some visual recovery problems. In *Computer Vision Graph. and Image Proces. : Image Understanding*, volume 59, january 1994.

SAR Image Registration and Segmentation Using an Estimated DEM

C.A. Glasbey

Biomathematics and Statistics Scotland
JCMB, King's Buildings, Edinburgh EH9 3JZ, Scotland

Abstract. Synthetic aperture radar (SAR) images are notoriously difficult to interpret. Segmentation is simplified if a digital map is available, to which the image can be registered. Also, registration is simplified if a digital elevation model (DEM) is available. In this paper it is shown that, if a DEM is unavailable, it can be estimated by minimising an energy functional consisting of a measure of agreement between the SAR image and a digital map together with a thin-plate bending-energy term. A computationally-efficient, finite-element algorithm is proposed to solve the optimisation problem. The method is applied to automatically align an airborne SAR image with a digital map of field boundaries, producing an image which is simultaneously registered and segmented.

1 Introduction

Synthetic aperture radar (SAR) is an active remote-sensing system: microwave radiation is beamed down to the earth's surface from a plane or satellite, a sensor detects the reflected signal, and from this an image is constructed. SAR images are notoriously difficult to interpret, even by eye. For example, Fig 1 shows a log-transformed SAR image of an area near Feltwell, England. A pattern of fields can be discerned, and there is a waterway in the top-right of the image. The small, bright features in the top-right, bottom-left and bottom-right of the image are the result of farm buildings acting as *corner reflectors* to the radar. Many ambiguities remain in the image, such as the positions of some field boundaries.

Pixel values in SAR images are highly variable, a phenomenon termed *speckle*, which makes it desirable to segment the images into homogeneous regions as a first step in their interpretation. Segmentation is often performed manually, an approach which is both tedious and subjective. Glasbey and Horgan [17] used Fig 1 to explore several generic methods for automatic image segmentation, including iterated conditioned modes (ICM) classification [4], thresholding combined with post-classification smoothing by majority filter [30] and Horowitz and Pavlidis's [22] split-and-merge algorithm. These methods were able to distinguish between light and dark fields, but did little more. For other attempts to segment SAR images, see [1, 28], and see [13] for criteria for success.

Domain-specific knowledge, such as constraining boundaries to be straight, and techniques such as the Hough transform [27] and the fitting of snakes [25], could be used to improve the segmentation. However, SAR images are not usually analysed in isolation: a more specific form of domain knowledge is often

Fig. 1. *Log-transformed C-band, HH-polarization, SAR image, obtained by plane in August 1989 during Maestro-1 campaign (Joint Research Centre, Ispra, report IRSA/MWT/4.90).*

available in the form of either a digital map or other remotely sensed images. For example, Fig 2 shows a line drawing of field, road and other boundaries for a region approximately corresponding to, but slightly larger than, that imaged by the SAR sensor. By registering the SAR image with this digital map, as a by-product the image is automatically segmented.

Registration of SAR images is important in its own right, irrespective of whether or not we also wish to segment the images, because outputs from SAR interpretation cannot be put to practical use unless their geographical locations are known. SAR image registration is often performed manually (for example, see [12, 14, 36, 11]). Li [29] reviewed automatic methods, distinguishing between

Fig. 2. *Digital line drawing of field, road, and other boundaries for approximately the same region as Fig 1, extracted from a map of an area to the north of the village of Feltwell in East Anglia.*

area- and feature-based ones. The former approach typically involves maximising correlations between small windows in two images, whereas in the latter approach contours or distinctive features are matched between images. Caves et al [10] used linear filters, whereas Kher and Mitra [26] used morphological methods, to locate features in SAR images. Li [29] extracted contours from an optical, remotely-sensed image, and then used elastic warping methods to align them with a SAR image.

Warping is common to many image analysis problems: it may be needed to remove optical distortions introduced by a camera or viewing perspective, to register an image with a reference grid, or to align two or more images. There is a potential conflict between insisting the distortion is smooth and achieving a good match. This can be resolved by an appropriate choice of energy functional. Smoothness can be ensured by assuming a parametric form for the warp, such as a bilinear transformation, or by insisting that the warp satisfies partial differential equations such as Navier's equilibrium equations for elastic bodies [3]. Dependent on the application, matching might be specified by points to be brought into alignment [6], by local measures of correlation between images, or by the coincidence of edges [9].

Digital elevation models (DEMs), when available, greatly simplify SAR image registration, because the warping can be constrained to be a projective transformation of the DEM [16, 21, 24, 34]. In this paper we show that, if a DEM is unavailable, it can be estimated by minimising an energy functional. This approach is distinct from previous attempts to estimate DEMs using either stereo SAR [15, 33] or interferometric SAR [31]. In § 2, we assume that the ground being imaged is planar, and apply an affine transformation to register the SAR image to the digital map. Then, in § 3 we generalise this approach, by estimating a DEM using a thin-plate spline, to improve the registration. Finally, in § 4 the approach is critically discussed and areas of further work are identified.

2 Affine Transformation

We seek a transformation which maps a position (u, v) on the digital map, where u denotes row number and v denotes column number, to (x, y) in the SAR image. The appropriate transformation is a *projection*. This simplifies to an affine transformation if the ground being imaged can be assumed to be planar and the viewing position is sufficiently distant that foreshortening effects can be ignored. Mathematically, based on Euler's angles [23], we have:

$$x = \alpha + u\gamma \cos\theta + v\gamma \sin\phi \sin\theta$$

$$y = \beta + u\gamma \sin\theta \sin\psi + v\gamma(\cos\phi \cos\psi - \sin\phi \cos\theta \sin\psi),$$

involving six unknown parameters $(\alpha, \beta, \gamma, \phi, \theta, \psi)$. This is the most general linear transformation, permitting translation, rotation, different stretching along rows and columns, and shearing. One characterisation is that there is an orthogonal pair of directions in the u-v image which are also orthogonal in the x-y image, and the transformation either stretches or shrinks in these two directions [5]. The inverse transformation $(u, v) \leftarrow (x, y)$ has the same functional form. Therefore, the transformation is guaranteed to be bijective, i.e. it is impossible for folding to occur where two points in the u-v image map to the same point in the x-y image. The affine transformation can be generalised by using a perspective transformation, or by including higher-order polynomials of u and v. See [7, 8, 35] for reviews of geometric transformations.

In order to choose the parameters in the transformation, a measure of agreement between the SAR image and the digital map is required [29]. As a first step, we applied an edge filter to the SAR image. Because of the low signal-to-noise ratio it was desirable to use a large window for the filter. Most edges appear to be step edges, therefore a template matching approach was taken, with the filter output defined to be

$$g_{x,y} = \max_{0 \le \omega < \pi} \left| \sum_{(x',y') \in S_\omega} f_{x+x',y+y'} - \sum_{(x',y') \in S_{\omega+\pi}} f_{x+x',y+y'} \right| ,$$

for $x, y = 1 \ldots n$. Here $f_{x,y}$ denotes the log-transformed SAR value at (x, y), and S_ω is a semi-circular set of pixel locations specified by

$$S_\omega = \{(x,y) \; : \; 0 < x^2 + y^2 \le r^2 \; , \; \omega \le \tan^{-1} y/x < \omega + \pi \; (\text{mod } 2\pi)\},$$

with $\tan^{-1}$ assumed to produce output over the range 0 to 2π (using, for example, the function ATAN2 in Fortran77). Fig 3 illustrates the filter, showing pixels with positive and negative weights, for a window of radius $r = 4.5$ pixels and a particular choice of ω. This size of window appeared to be most effective in locating edges in the SAR image. For efficient computation, at each (x, y)-location, output can be computed recursively as ω is increased. Fig 4 shows the result of applying the edge filter to Fig 1. Output has been scaled so the largest values appear black and zero values appear white.

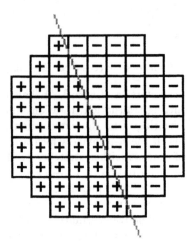

Fig. 3. *An illustration of the edge filter: pixels with positive and negative weights are shown, for a window of radius $r = 4.5$ pixels, and a particular choice of ω corresponding to an edge shown by the grey line.*

The measure of agreement between Fig 4 and a warped version of Fig 2 was defined by the energy functional:

$$E = \frac{1}{N_S} \sum_{(u,v) \in S} (\bar{g} - g_{x,y}) ,$$

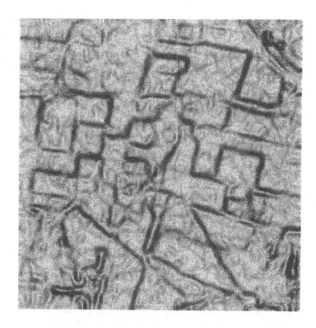

Fig. 4. *Result of applying edge filter to Fig 1.*

where $S = \{(u,v) \, : \, M_{u,v} = 1 \, , \, 1 \leq x,y \leq n\}$ is the set of all black points in the digital map (indicated by $M_{u,v} = 1$) which transform to points (x,y) within the region of Fig 4, N_S denotes the number of points in S (which will depend on the parameters in the affine transformation) and $\bar{g}$ is the mean pixel value in Fig 4. Thus, the energy functional is an inner product between Figs 2 and 4, after mean correction.

The matching problem becomes one of finding the values of the affine parameters which minimise E. Unfortunately, the function to be minimised has many local minima. Therefore, it is necessary to conduct a grid search to determine good starting values for the parameters, before using an iterative optimisation algorithm to locate the minimum. We proceeded in two stages:

1. Initially we limited ourselves to a four-parameter family of rectangular transformations, by setting $\phi = \psi = 0$. E was evaluated for a range of values of the parameters, and the best value was used as a starting value for the Nelder-Mead simplex algorithm, implemented as NAG routine E04CCF [32].
2. We then considered the six-parameter affine transformation, starting the Nelder-Mead algorithm from the best fitting rectangular transformation.

Fig 5 shows the final result: the outline of the map boundaries is displayed rather than the boundaries themselves, in order to show the alignment more clearly. Agreement appears to be close between the edges in the SAR image and the map, except that a few field boundaries are absent from the map. Detailed examination also reveals some places where the boundaries are slightly displaced, for example at the bottom-centre and bottom-right of Fig 5, suggesting that the assumption of level ground is not quite appropriate. Therefore, in § 3 we generalise the approach to include estimation of a DEM is the registration procedure.

Fig. 5. *Map aligned with edge-filtered SAR image using an affine transformation (the outline of the map boundaries is displayed rather than the boundaries themselves).*

3   Thin-plate Spline DEM

Parametric transformations do not perform well in the presence of local distortions. Splines offer one alternative, either piecewise linear [18] or cubic [19]. Equating warping with the distortions achievable on an elastic sheet is one way of introducing smoothness constraints. Bajcsy and Kovacic [3] invoked Navier's equilibrium equations for elastic bodies, which they insisted on being satisfied at all points except those where a match between images had been identified. Solution requires the use of finite element methods. Burr [9] used sums of Gaussian weight functions to interpolate between matched points, justifying them as an elastic Green's function in an appropriate medium. Tang and Suen [35] found transformations which minimised a harmonic function. Again finite element methods are required. Note that Kass et al [25] used similar methods to constrain *snakes* to be smooth.

Another approach is to regard a warping as two two-dimensional surfaces, corresponding to x as a function of u and v, and similarly y as a function of u and v. Arad et al [2] used a sum of radial basis functions plus affine transforms to represent the x-transformation:

$$x = \sum_{i=1}^{m} \eta_i \, F\left(\sqrt{(u - u_i)^2 + (v - v_i)^2}\right) + \xi_0 + \xi_1 u + \xi_2 v,$$

where $(u_1, v_1) \ldots (u_m, v_m)$ are a set of m labelled points and F is a radial basis function, and similarly for the y-transformation. Many choices of F correspond to the minimisation of some energy functional. In particular, the thin-plate spline, $F(z) = z^2 \log z$, leads to a surface which minimises

$$\sum_{i=1}^{m} \{x_i - x(u_i, v_i)\}^2 \ + \ \lambda J(x),$$

with respect to the function x, where the m labelled points are warped to x-coordinates $x_1 \ldots x_m$,

$$J(x) = \int\int_{-\infty}^{\infty} \left\{ \left(\frac{\partial^2 x}{\partial u^2}\right)^2 + 2\left(\frac{\partial^2 x}{\partial u \partial v}\right)^2 + \left(\frac{\partial^2 x}{\partial v^2}\right)^2 \right\} du \, dv$$

denotes the bending energy of a thin plate and λ is a non-negative constant which controls the smoothness of the warping. Larger values of λ produce smoother results, but with poorer alignment of the labelled points. Coefficients $\eta_1 \ldots \eta_m, \xi_0, \xi_1$ and ξ_2 can be obtained as the solution of $(m + 3)$ simultaneous linear equations [20].

Pairs of thin-plate splines have no physical interpretation in the context of image warping; there use is entirely ad hoc. However, in applications such as ours, which consists of a projective view of a surface, a single thin-plate spline can be used with physical motivation, although it will not permit any step changes in elevation. We assume that the elevation $h_{u,v}$ at map location (u, v) is specified by a thin-plate spline. The energy functional from § 2 is generalised to include a bending energy term:

$$E = \frac{1}{N_S} \sum_{(u,v) \in S} (\bar{g} - g_{x,y}) \ + \ \lambda J(h),$$

and the projective transformation [23] generalises the affine transformation:

$$x = \alpha + u\gamma \cos\theta + v\gamma \sin\phi \sin\theta + h_{u,v}\gamma \cos\phi \sin\theta$$

$$y = \beta + u\gamma \sin\theta \sin\psi + v\gamma(\cos\phi \cos\psi - \sin\phi \cos\theta \sin\psi)$$
$$- h_{u,v}\gamma(\sin\phi \cos\psi + \cos\phi \cos\theta \sin\psi).$$

This problem lacks an analytic solution, but can be solved numerically using finite element methods. We divide the map into a $(p + 1)$ by $(p + 1)$ grid, and specify the elevations of the $(p + 1)^2$ points

$$(k\Delta_u, l\Delta_v) \qquad \text{for } k, l = 0, \ldots, p,$$

by $H_{k,l}$, where $\Delta_u = n_u/p$, $\Delta_v = n_v/m$ and the digital map is $n_u \times n_v$ pixels in size. Then we use bilinear interpolation for the elevation of intermediate points. If

$$k\Delta_u \leq u \leq (k+1)\Delta_u \quad \text{and} \quad l\Delta_v \leq v \leq (l+1)\Delta_v,$$

then

$$h_{u,v} = H_{k,l} + (H_{k+1,l} - H_{k,l})\left(\frac{u}{\Delta_u} - k\right) + (H_{k,l+1} - H_{k,l})\left(\frac{v}{\Delta_v} - l\right)$$

$$+ (H_{k+1,l+1} - H_{k+1,l} - H_{k,l+1} + H_{k,l})\left(\frac{u}{\Delta_u} - k\right)\left(\frac{v}{\Delta_v} - l\right).$$

It follows from the projective transformation that x and y are also piecewise bilinear. $J(h)$ can be approximated, to within a scaling term, by

$$\sum_{k=1}^{p-1}\sum_{l=0}^{p}\left(\frac{H_{k+1,l} + H_{k-1,l} - 2H_{k,l}}{\Delta_u^2}\right)^2$$

$$+ 2\sum_{k=0}^{p-1}\sum_{l=0}^{p-1}\left(\frac{H_{k+1,l+1} + H_{k,l} - H_{k,l+1} - H_{k+1,l}}{\Delta_u\Delta_v}\right)^2$$

$$+ \sum_{k=0}^{p}\sum_{l=1}^{p-1}\left(\frac{H_{k,l+1} + H_{k,l-1} - 2H_{k,l}}{\Delta_v^2}\right)^2 .$$

The parameters $H_{k,l}$ can be estimated to minimise the energy functional. This was done by perturbing each elevation in turn to minimise E, while keeping the projective transform parameters fixed at the values estimated in § 2. Note that the speed of computation can be improved significantly by only computing local terms in E after each adjustment in $H_{k,l}$, and at each iteration only perturbing elevations one of whose neighbours was changed at the previous iteration. The optimisation was started with $H_{k,l}$ set to zero in a 17×17 grid and $\lambda = 1000$, a value established by trial-and-error to allow sufficient changes in elevation to align the image with the map, but without producing a very rough DEM. The elevations estimated by the algorithm are shown in perspective in Fig 6.

Fig 7 shows an outline of the map boundaries aligned with the edge-filtered SAR image. The result is very similar to Fig 5 but, in particular, note the improved fit at several positions, including the bottom of the map. The average strength of the aligned edges is increased by 40%. However, there is some evidence that the warping is too severe in the top-right of the image, where the waterway has been distorted to align with a bright feature which is probably a building, and as a consequence the waterway does not appear to be horizontal in Fig 6. Fig 8 shows the SAR image registered with the digital map, obtained by inverting the projective transformation. The alignment can be seen to be very good, and automatically yields an almost complete segmentation of the image. It is a relatively straightforward task to identify, and further partition, the few heterogeneous segments.

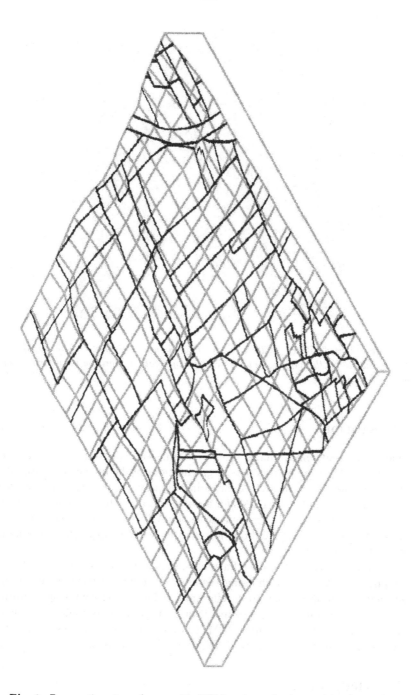

Fig. 6. *Perspective view of map with DEM estimated using a thin-plate spline.*

Fig. 7. *Map aligned with edge-filtered SAR image using a thin-plate spline transformation (the outline of the map boundaries is displayed rather than the boundaries themselves).*

4 Discussion

We have shown how SAR images can be automatically registered with digitised maps while yielding, as by-products, segmentations of the images and estimated DEMs. Much work remains to be done, primarily to validate the method by comparing estimated and known DEMs for a range of images. Results also need to be compared with those from other approaches to SAR registration, such as [10, 29]. However, the new method should perform better because of the physically-based constraint on the warping.

The method is open to many refinements, such as the use of other edge filters, development of criteria for choosing the smoothing parameter λ in the energy functional, and improvements to the efficiency and robustness of the optimisation algorithm. For example, the projective transform parameters could be adjusted to take account of the estimated DEM. It would also be of interest to use the method to register SAR and optical, remotely-sensed images.

Acknowledgements

The work was supported by funds from the Scottish Office Agriculture, Environment and Fisheries Department.

518

Fig. 8. *Superposition of aligned SAR image with map.*

References

1. Ali, S.M., Burge, R.E.: New automatic techniques for smoothing and segmenting SAR images. Signal Processing **14** (1988) 335–346
2. Arad, N., Dyn, N., Reisfeld, D., Yeshurun, Y.: Image warping by radial basis functions: applications to facial expressions. CVGIP: Graphical Models and Image Processing **56** (1994) 161–172
3. Bajcsy, R., Kovacic, S.: Multiresolution elastic matching. Computer Vision, Graphics and Image Processing **46** (1989) 1–21

4. Besag, J.: On the statistical analysis of dirty pictures (with discussion). Journal of the Royal Statistical Society, Series B **48** (1986) 259–302

5. Bookstein, F.L.: The Measurement of Biological Shape and Shape Change. Springer-Verlag, Berlin (1978)

6. Bookstein, F.L.: Principal Warps: thin plate splines and the decomposition of deformations. IEEE Transactions on Pattern Analysis and Machine Intelligence **11** (1989) 567–585

7. Bookstein, F.L.: Morphometric Tools for Landmark Data : Geometry and Biology. Cambridge University Press, Cambridge (1991)

8. Brown, L.G.: A survey of image registration techniques. ACM Computing Surveys **24** (1992) 325–376

9. Burr, D.J.: A dynamic model for image registration. Computer Graphics and Image Processing **15** (1981) 102–112

10. Caves, R.G., Harley, P.J., Quegan, S.: Matching map features to synthetic aperture radar (SAR) images using template matching. IEEE Transactions on Geoscience and Remote Sensing **30** (1992) 680–685

11. Cihlar, J., Pultz, T.J., Gray, A.L.: Change detection with synthetic aperture radar. International Journal of Remote Sensing **13** (1992) 401–414

12. Collins, M.J., Livingstone, C.E.: On the dimensionality of multiparameter microwave image data from thin sea-ice in the Labrador-sea. IEEE Transactions on Geoscience and Remote Sensing **34** (1996) 114–136

13. Delves, L.M., Wilkinson, R., Oliver, C.J., White, R.G.: Comparing the performance of SAR image segmentation algorithms. International Journal of Remote Sensing **13** (1992) 2121–2149

14. Dobson, M.C., Pierce, L.E., Ulaby, F.T.: Knowledge-based land-cover classification using ERS-1/JERS-1 SAR composites. IEEE Transactions on Geoscience and Remote Sensing **34** (1996) 83–99

15. Fernandes, D., Waller, G., Moreira, J.R.: Registration of SAR images using the chirp scaling algorithm. IGARSS'96 – International Geoscience and Remote Sensing Symposium (1996) 799–801

16. Frankot, R.T., Hensley, S., Shafer, S,: Noise resistant estimation techniques for SAR image registration and stereo matching. IGARSS'94 – International Geoscience and Remote Sensing Symposium (1994) 1151–1153

17. Glasbey, C.A., Horgan, G.W.: Image Analysis for the Biological Sciences. Wiley, Chichester (1995)

18. Goshtasby, A.: Piecewise linear mapping functions for image registration. Pattern Recognition **19** (1986) 459–466

19. Goshtasby, A.: Piecewise cubic mapping functions for image registration. Pattern Recognition **20** (1987) 525–533

20. Green, P.J., Silverman, B.W.: Nonparametric Regression and Generalised Linear Models: a roughness penalty approach. Chapman and Hall, London (1994)

21. Guneriussen, T., Johnsen, H., Sand, K.: DEM corrected ERS-1 SAR data for snow monitoring. International Journal of Remote Sensing **17** (1996) 181–195

22. Horowitz, S.L., Pavlidis, T.: Picture segmentation by a tree traversal algorithm. Journal of the Association for Computing Machinery **23** (1976) 368–388

23. Ito, K. (ed.): Encyclopedic Dictionary of Mathematics (2nd edition). MIT Press, Massachusetts (1987) 1729

24. Johnsen, H., Lauknes, L., Guneriussen, T.: Geocoding of fast-delivery ERS-1 SAR image mode product using DEM data. International Journal of Remote Sensing **16** (1995) 1957–1968

25. Kass, M., Witkin, A., Terzopoulos, D.: Snakes: active contour models. International Journal of Computer Vision **1** (1988) 321–331
26. Kher, A., Mitra, S.: Registration of noisy SAR imagery using morphological feature extractor and 2-D cepstrum. Applications of Digital Image Processing **XV** (1993) 281–291
27. Leavers, V.F.: Shape Detection in Computer Vision Using the Hough Transform. Springer-Verlag, London (1992)
28. Lee, J.S., Jurkevich, I.: Segmentation of SAR images. IEEE Transactions on Geoscience and Remote Sensing **27** (1989) 674–680
29. Li, H., Manjunath, B.S., Mitra, S.K.: A contour-based approach to multisensor image registration. IEEE Transactions on Image Processing **4** (1995) 320–334
30. Mardia, K.V., Hainsworth, T.J.: A spatial thresholding method for image segmentation. IEEE Transactions on Pattern Analysis and Machine Intelligence **10** (1988) 919–927
31. Marechal, N.: Tomographic formulation of interferometric SAR for terrain elevation mapping. IEEE Transactions on Geoscience and Remote Sensing, 1995 **33** (1995) 726–739
32. Numerical Algorithms Group: Library Manual Mark 16. NAG Central Office, 256 Banbury Road, Oxford OX2 7DE, UK (1993)
33. Prati, C., Rocca, F.: Limits to the resolution of elevation maps from stereo SAR images. International Journal of Remote Sensing **11** (1990) 2215–2235
34. Takeuchi, S.: Image registration between SAR and TM data using DEM and slant range information. IGARSS'93 – International Geoscience and Remote Sensing Symposium (1993) 1351–1353
35. Tang, Y.Y., Suen, C.Y.: Image transformation approach to nonlinear shape restoration. IEEE Transactions on Systems, Man and Cybernetics **23** (1993) 155–172
36. Vornberger, P.L., Bindschadler, R.A.: Multispectral analysis of ice sheets using co-registered SAR and TM imagery. International Journal of Remote Sensing **13** (1992) 637–645

Deformable Templates for Tracking and Analysis of Intravascular Ultrasound Sequences

Francisco Escolano, Miguel Cazorla, Domingo Gallardo and Ramón Rizo

Grupo i3a: Informática Industrial e Inteligencia Artificial
Departamento de Tecnología Informática y Computación
Universidad de Alicante
E-03690, San Vicente, Spain
Fax/Phone: 346-5903681
e-mail: sco@i3a.dtic.ua.es

Abstract. Deformable Template models are first applied to track the inner wall of coronary arteries in intravascular ultrasound sequences, mainly in the assistance to angioplasty surgery. A circular template is used for initializing an elliptical deformable model to track wall deformation when inflating a balloon placed at the tip of the catheter. We define a new energy function for driving the behavior of the template and we test its robustness both in real and synthetic images. Finally we introduce a framework for learning and recognizing spatio-temporal geometric constraints based on Principal Component Analysis (*eigenconstraints*).

1 Introduction

1.1 Intravascular Ultrasound Sequences

Intravascular Ultrasound is a recent technique which provides a source of high quality medical imaginery for precisely quantifying arterial obstruction and in consequence for the assessment of coronary interventions (bypass, balloon angioplasty, stent deployment or atherectomy) [27], [9]. A catheter with a transducer mounted on its tip is placed inside the artery and rotated to generate, by emitting pulses of ultrasound and receiving echoes, planar cross-sections corresponding to the traversed arterial structure. In the output obtained (see Fig. 1) the center of the catheter is taken as origin of the new reference system and the image typically reveals three types of echo: *vessel lumen* (dark echoes), *plaque* (soft grey echoes) and *vessel wall* (white echoes). The analysis of the type of plaque helps specialists to choose the best interventional modality.

1.2 Previous Approaches for Representation and Analysis

The problem of automatically obtaining suitable representations of the intravascular structure from two dimensional slices has been adressed in the past. These models must be suitable for extracting and analyzing quantitative features, in order to help both in diagnosis and intervention control. The most significant approaches developed to date are the following:

1. *Rendering Stacked Slices* [25], [17], [13], [23].

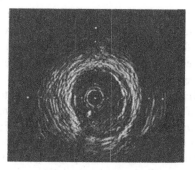

Fig. 1. Slice obtained by intravascular ultrasound

(a) Static geometry and non-curved vascular structure are assumed. Visualizations are based on slice stacking. The problem of this approach is that the obtained geometry is usually unrealistic and distorted.

(b) Extended approaches [19] introduce curved, but still static, structure.

2. *Introducing Snakes:* [12]

(a) Spatio-temporal structure extraction by application of deformable models is addressed in the context of angiography (tracking of the 2D projections of the lumen).

(b) Deformable models allow to obtain the actual dynamic geometry.

3. *Integration with Angiography:* [18]

(a) First step consists of obtaining, by variational stereo-matching based on snakes, the three-dimensional angiographic structure.

(b) This information is integrated, using the spatio-temporal synchronization of the transducer and the angiography, with the transversal slices for generating the visualization by volume rendering based on interpolation.

(c) In this sense slice positioning is guided by *landmarks* corresponding to branching points located at the arterial tree.

In our opinion future approaches must address the problem of analyze the internal structure of the slices in order to detect plaque (texture analysis) or to improve clinical procedures (e.g. angioplasty).

1.3 The Proposed Approach: Outline of the Paper

The approach presented in this paper is based on *Deformable Templates* [1], [10], [11], [15], [6], [28], [29], [30], [31], [20], [26]. In the context of intravascular ultrasound imaging we introduce improvements mainly in two directions:

1. *Wall Tracking:* given the morphology of the vessel walls (typically circular or elliptical), the problem of wall tracking can be addressed by using deformable templates. Wall tracking is interesting in, at least, two cases:

(a) *Locating plaque:* once the wall is identified the zone where the plaque can be located is bounded . In consequence a texture driven local search, from the wall to the center of the vessel, can extract the actual boundary of the plaque in order to obtain the thickness of the lession. Tracking experiments with circular templates are presented in Section 2.2.

(b) *Control of medical procedures:* In this context one of the medical procedures in which the use of non-rigid tracking can introduce some level of automation is the *Coronary Angioplasty.* Such procedure consists of placing a small baloon at the catheter end in order to dilate the plaque that obstructs the artery (see Figs. 2, 3 and 4). Balloon inflating induces a pressure that compresses and slashes the plaque and reduces or eliminates the arterial stenosis. In Section 2.3. we present several tracking experiments in angioplasty defining and using elliptical templates.

2. *Sequence Analysis:* given the spatio-temporal geometrical information derived from the application of the templates to the slices, it can be *learnt* and used for *recognizing* correct evolution paths in the angioplasty process (e.g. uniform expansion, unitary excentricity, etc.). We propose the use of *Principal Component Analysis* in the temporal dimension for defining *compact spatio-temporal constraints.* In Section 3 we introduce this approach presenting several synthetic experiments.

Fig. 2. Introduction of the catheter with a balloon.

Fig. 3. Balloon deployment to compress and fracture the plaque.

Fig. 4. Plaque extinction, stenosis clearing and flow normalization.

2 Tracking Based on Deformable Templates

A *single deformable template model* is defined by a *geometrical structure* $g_{\mathcal{D}}(\Theta)$ (circle, parabola, ellipse, segment, etc.), where Θ is a vector of relevant parameters and $\mathcal{D}$ is the spatial domain. This structure reacts to an specific *image model* or *potential field*

$\Psi(u, v)$. Reaction behavior (dynamics) is established by an *energy function* $\mathcal{E}(\Theta)$. In this way optimal positioning of the structure over the potential is characterized by a minimum of $\mathcal{E}(\Theta)$ which is usually found by gradient descent. In this section we present the application of two types of templates (circular and elliptical) to track the inner wall of the artery.

2.1 Image Model: Potential Fields

As we need to bound the zone where the plaque can be we apply first grey thresholding. This is followed by a morphological closing which clears local structures that can introduce distortions, and, finally, we apply a Gaussian filter to smooth the geometry of the gradient. The result is showed in Fig. 5 whereas Fig. 6 contains the filtered gradient. Both images will be used as potential fields in our experiments.

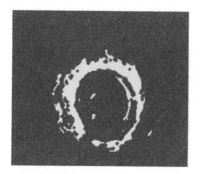

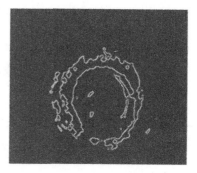

Fig. 5. Binary potential field after filtering.

Fig. 6. Gradient potential after Gaussian filtering.

This procedure gives us an ad-hoc *basic potential field* which contains the vessel wall. More robust fields can be obtained by applying a region based strategy [14], [24]. Moreover *speckle noise* or high correlated noise, due to the acquisition process and caused by tissue microstructures, can be modeled by a Rayleigh distribution [5].

2.2 Circular Templates: Wall Tracking and Initial Position

Circular Templates (CT) were first proposed in [32] as a part of a method to find the skeleton of a binary shape[1] with certain levels of noise tolerance. Let be (x, y) the center position, r the radius and $\mathcal{D}$ the circular domain bounded by the CT. We consider a binary image as potential: the function $I(x, y)$ returns 1 if the pixel is inside the template domain, and otherwise returns 0. The dynamic of the CT is defined by the function $\mathcal{E}(x, y, r)$, and its optimum is obtained by gradient descent. The original equations are showed at Table 1 and explained below:

---

[1] This model was originally named The Free-Travelling Circle.

Table 1. Circular Template Equations

Global Energy		
$\mathcal{E}(x, y, r)$	$\int\int_{\mathcal{D}} \mathcal{E}_{shape}(u, v, r) * \mathcal{E}_{image}(x + u, y + v)dudv + \mathcal{E}_{noise}(r)$	
$\mathcal{E}_{noise}(r)$	$\mathcal{E}_{image}(x, y)$	$\mathcal{E}_{shape}(x, y, r)$
$-\frac{\alpha}{a}r^a$	$\mathcal{I}(x, y)$	$(r - \sqrt{x^2 + y^2})$
CT Dynamics		
Center Dynamics	$\begin{pmatrix} \frac{dx}{dt} \\ \frac{dy}{dt} \end{pmatrix} = - \begin{pmatrix} \frac{\partial \mathcal{E}}{\partial x} \\ \frac{\partial \mathcal{E}}{\partial y} \end{pmatrix} = \int_{\Gamma \cap \mathcal{D}}(r - \sqrt{u^2 + v^2})(-\nabla \mathcal{I})ds$	
Radius Dynamics	$\frac{dr}{dt} = -\frac{\partial \mathcal{E}}{\partial r} = -\int\int_{\mathcal{D}} \mathcal{I}(x + u, y + v)dudv + \alpha r^{a-1}$	

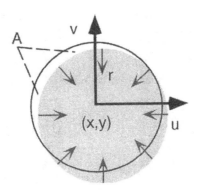

Fig. 7. CT: Noise (A) and gradient forces

1. *Dynamics of the center:* Let be Γ the shape contour and $\nabla \mathcal{I}$ the gradient. Then $-\nabla \mathcal{I}$ can be considered as a force of opposite direction which is weighted by $r - \sqrt{u^2 + v^2}$. The CT motion will converge when all the forces inside the CT are balanced (See Fig. 7).

2. *Dynamics of the radius:* The first term is the white pixels area inside the CT domain (See area A in Fig. 7) and represents a force which makes the radius decrease. The second term is the expansion force of the CT. The CT will converge when the area A will be equal to αr^{a-1}. The α and a parameters determine the tolerated noise level. Tipical values used are: $1 < a < 3$ and $0 < \alpha < 20$.

We have applied this basic model to locate an estimate of the inner wall. The spatio-temporal structure obtained is showed, by rendering and interpolation, in Fig. 8. Arterial tightness can be observed at the bottom example. As we will see later, this approach is also useful to initialize other templates (like elliptical ones).

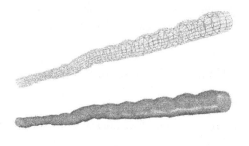

Fig. 8. Rendered sequeces of inner radius.

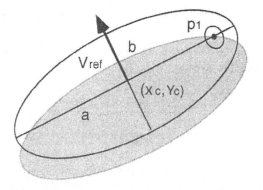

Fig. 9. Elliptical Deformable Template.

2.3 Elliptical Templates: Tracking in Angioplasty

As we said in the first section the shape geometry induced by inflating the balloon can be elliptical. In consequence we have extended the circular model to an elliptical one. Elliptical template formulation is given by the following terms (see Fig. 9):

1. *Geometrical structure, potential and global energy:* template elliptical structure is formulated by $g_{\mathcal{D}}(\Theta) = (x_c, y_c, a, b, \mathbf{V}_{ref})$ where: $\mathcal{D}$ is the elliptical domain, centered at (x_c, y_c), with major and minor axes a, b and with a reference vector $\mathbf{V}_{ref} =$

$(\cos\theta, \sin\theta)$ being θ the orientation of the secondary axe (b). Using the potentials previously extracted, we derive the global energy:

$$\mathcal{E}(x_c, y_c, a, b, \mathbf{V}_{ref}) = \mathcal{E}_{shape}(x_c, y_c, a, b) + \mathcal{E}_{rot}(x_c, y_c, \mathbf{V}_{ref}) + \mathcal{E}_{noise}(a, b) \quad (1)$$

with the following terms:

(a) *Shape energy:* position, curvature and scale parameters are driven by:

$$\mathcal{E}_{shape}(x_c, y_c, a, b) = \int\int_{\mathcal{D}}(1 - (\frac{u^2}{a^2} + \frac{v^2}{b^2}))\,\mathcal{I}(x_c + u, y_c + v)\,du\,dv \quad (2)$$

(b) *Rotation energy:* reference vector adapting behavior is based on:

$$\mathcal{E}_{rot}(x_c, y_c, \mathbf{V}_{ref}) = (\mathcal{N}(\mathbf{V}_{ref}) \cdot \mathcal{N}(\nabla\mathcal{I}(p_1)))^2 \quad (3)$$

where $\mathcal{N}$ gives the unitary vector (in the direction of the argument), $\cdot$ represents the scalar product and p_1 is the first point of the positive semi-axe of a with nonzero gradient, that is:

$$p_1 = (x_c + i\cos(\theta - \frac{\pi}{2}), y_c + i\sin(\theta - \frac{\pi}{2}))\ |\ 0 < i < a, \nabla\mathcal{I}(p_1) \neq 0 \quad (4)$$

(c) *Noise Energy:* the noise term allows to specify a different noise tolerance for each axe, and it is given by

$$\mathcal{E}_{noise}(a, b) = -\frac{\alpha_a}{\lambda_a}a^{\lambda_a} - \frac{\alpha_b}{\lambda_b}b^{\lambda_b} \quad (5)$$

2. *Dynamics of the ellipse:* the parameters that minimize $\mathcal{E}(x_c, y_c, a, b, \mathbf{V}_{ref})$ are obtained by gradient descent:

(a) *Dynamics of the center :* similarly to the circular template, the dynamics of the center is given by the contact between the elliptical primitive and the gradient of the shape (vascular boundary):

$$\begin{pmatrix} \frac{\partial x_c}{\partial t} \\ \frac{\partial y_c}{\partial t} \end{pmatrix} = -\begin{pmatrix} \frac{\partial \mathcal{E}}{\partial x_c} \\ \frac{\partial \mathcal{E}}{\partial y_c} \end{pmatrix} = \int_{\mathcal{D}}(1 - (\frac{u^2}{a^2} + \frac{v^2}{b^2}))(-\nabla\mathcal{I})ds -$$

$$2(\mathcal{N}(\mathbf{V}_{ref}) \cdot \mathcal{N}(\nabla\mathcal{I}(p_1)))(\mathcal{N}(\mathbf{V}_{ref})\mathcal{N}(\nabla^2\mathcal{I}(p_1))) \quad (6)$$

The effect of the gradient is used to center the primitive (first term) and the point p_1 (second term). The second term has a secondary effect while the reference vector is not orthogonal to the gradient in p_1 or to its variation around this point (Laplacian), which is the equilibrium condition.

(b) *Rotation Dynamics:* since the primitive could not be correctly oriented, a term to induce a rotation, when needed, must be introduced. For that reason we use the square of the dot product between the reference vector and the gradient vector at p_1. This gives us an estimate of the deviation with respect to the ideal orientation (orthogonal):

$$\begin{pmatrix} \frac{\partial \mathbf{V}_{ref_x}}{\partial t} \\ \frac{\partial \mathbf{V}_{ref_y}}{\partial t} \end{pmatrix} = - \begin{pmatrix} \frac{\partial \mathcal{E}}{\partial \mathbf{V}_{ref_x}} \\ \frac{\partial \mathcal{E}}{\partial \mathbf{V}_{ref_y}} \end{pmatrix} = -2(\mathcal{N}(\mathbf{V}_{ref}) \cdot \mathcal{N}(\nabla \mathcal{I}(p_1))) \mathcal{N}(\nabla \mathcal{I}(p_1)))$$

(7)

(c) *Dynamics of the axes:* the variation of the axes follows the same formulation that the circular model, and in each case is considered the noise factor associated to each axe:

$$\frac{da}{dt} = -\frac{\partial \mathcal{E}}{\partial a} = - \int \int_{\mathcal{D}} 2 \frac{u^2}{a^3} \mathcal{I}(x_c + u, y_c + v) \, du \, dv + \alpha_a a^{\lambda_a - 1} \quad (8)$$

$$\frac{db}{dt} = -\frac{\partial \mathcal{E}}{\partial b} = - \int \int_{\mathcal{D}} 2 \frac{v^2}{b^3} \mathcal{I}(x_c + u, y_c + v) \, du \, dv + \alpha_b b^{\lambda_b - 1} \quad (9)$$

the convergence will arrive when both noise levels be balanced by the number of included pixels.

Two examples of adaptation of the template are shown in Fig. 10. The left ellipse is one with a no elliptical shape. We fix the noise levels parameters in: $\alpha_a = 15$, $\alpha_b = 15$, $\lambda_a = 1$ and $\lambda_b = 1$. In the first case the adaptation deficiency is due to the discrete nature of the rotation and to the no-elliptical shape, and in the second it is only due to discretitation errors.

Fig. 10. Examples of Elliptical Templates.

We have found that, when using elliptical templates in a noisy environment, circular initialization improves the final result: the circular template is expanded in order to find the elliptical border and its radius and center position are used as the initial parameters for the elliptical template. This effect is showed in Fig. 11 and in Fig. 12. In Fig. 11, we present two sequences of experiments with increasing noise rate: in the upper sequence we have used elliptical initialization whereas at the bottom one we have used circles.

The final results are better in the second case as we can corroborate in Fig. 12 where we represent, for each initialization policy, the Euclidean distance between the result and the actual shape for different levels of noise.

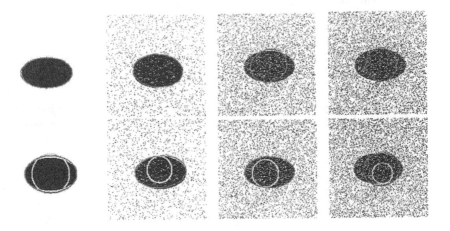

Fig. 11. Analysis of noise tolerance. Effect of circle vs. elliptical initialization.

Final results of the aplication of the proposed model to an inflating sequence are shown in Fig. 13 where we can see some evolution steps. We have empirical selected the noise levels parameters as follows $\alpha_a = 4$, $\alpha_b = 5$, $\lambda_a = 2$ and $\lambda_b = 2$.

3   Spatio-Temporal Analysis: EigenConstraints

3.1   Motivation and Principal Component Analysis

Tracking of angioplasty based on deformable templates allows us to recover spatio-temporal data which can be very useful for experts (wall thickness, blood flow, etc.). In the Fig. 14 we can see the evolution of the inner radius. We can distinguish three stages. In the first one the radius decreases to reach a valley (frame number 11). This implies the existence of a lession. In the second stage (frames 14 to 30) we apply the balloon and the radius increases. Finally (third stage) at frame 30 we recover the normal behavior (oscillating peaks are related to cardiac pulse).

This fact motivates the development of representations for analyzing the evolution of the geometry along the sequence. In this sense we can design compact (low-dimensional) geometric constraints over interesting features or parameters obtained in the tracking process in order to define evolution cathegories. We address this question by using Principal Component Analysis (PCA) [8]. This method has been successfully applied to design deformable models [3], [4], [2] to learn and matching image models [21] and sequences [16], [22] and, finally, to represent primitive shapes [32].

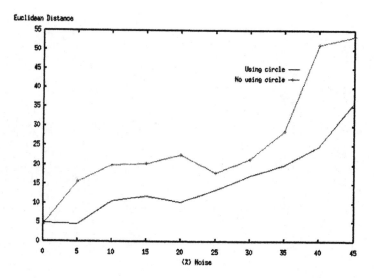

Fig. 12. Initialisation behavior vs. increasing Gaussian noise levels.

3.2 Designing EigenConstraints

Given an spatio-temporal geometrical structure $\Theta(t)$ obtained by tracking we can define a set of constraints $C(t)$ which express *evolving geometric relations* (e.g. relative curvature between several parameters of $\Theta(t)$). The main purpose of using PCA in this context is to obtain a low-dimensional representation of the evolution of each relation over time.

As an illustrative example we have established three *ideal constraints* that must be satisfied by a correct inflating process: $r_a/r_0(t)$, $r_b/r_0(t)$, $r_a/r_b(t)$ (see Fig. 15). The two first relations express the local averaged evolution of each axe (local average is applied to filter cardiac pulses) normalized by the initial inner radius r_0, whereas the third express the relative evolution of the axes (i.e. an estimate of the excentricity) also locally averaged. Then it is preferred moderated (medium slope) and uniform (excentricity near the unit) balloon inflating. We have learnt these constraints and have expressed them with a reduced number of parameters (those corresponding to greater eigenvalues associated to the covariance matrix of the training set) to capture 90% of the variability. In Fig. 16 we represent acceptance results (by applying Mahalanobis distance [7]) for $r_a(t)/r_0$ given a prototype set of lines generated by varying their slope.

4 Conclusions and Future Developments

This paper first introduces the use of deformable templates for tracking the inner wall of vessels in intravascular ultrasound sequences. Tracking is applied in two cases: a simple circular template is used to recover the inner wall along the transducer path and is also used for initializating an elliptical template for extracting wall shape evolution when inflating the balloon. In both cases exhaustive experiments where performed in order to

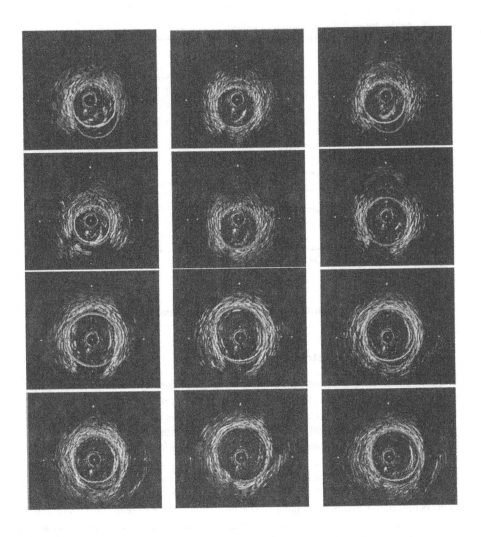

Fig. 13. Tracking results in angioplasty.

find the ideal parameters of noise and to test the adequacy of each template to the problem. Finally a new framework based on eigenconstraints is presented for evolution recognition. The purpose of the later experiments is to show its potential application to the geometric analysis of the sequences. Future work includes: automatic learning of noise parameters, the improvement of the quality of the fields (e.g. solving boundary discontinuities) and, finally, extensive application of PCA to extract constraints to accurately define clinical quality criteria of the angioplasty process.

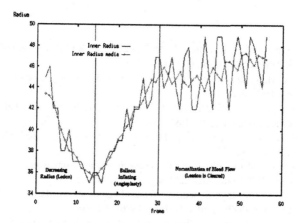

Fig. 14. Evolution path of the inner radius.

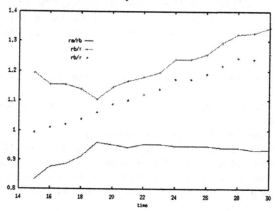

Fig. 15. Ideal constraints for recognition.

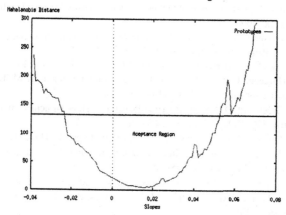

Fig. 16. Experimental results for the $r_a/r_0(t)$ constraint. Prototype recognition.

References

1. Amit, Y., Grenander, U., Piccioni, M.: Structural Image Restoration through Deformable Templates. J. Amer. Stat. Ass. **86** (1991) 376-387.
2. Baumberg, A., Hogg, D.: Learning Flexible Models in Image Sequences. European Conference on Computer Vision. (1994)
3. Cootes,T.F., Taylor, C.J., Cooper, D.H., Graham J.: Trainable Method of Parametric Shape. Image and Vision Computing. **10** (1992) 289-294
4. Cootes, T.F., Taylor, C.J.: Active Shape Models. Smart Snakes. Proc. British Machine Vision Conference. (1992) 266-275
5. Dias, J., Leytão, J.: Wall Position and Thickness Estimation from Sequences of Echocardiographic Images. IEEE Trans. Medical Imaging. **15** (1996) 25-38.
6. Dubuisson, M., Lakshmanan, S., Jain, A.: Vehicle Segmentation and Classification Using Deformable Templates. IEEE Trans. PAMI. **18** (1996) 293-308
7. Duda, R.O., Hart, P.E.: Pattern Classification and Scene Analysis. John Wiley and Sons. (1973)
8. Fukunaga, K.: Introduction to Statistical Pattern Recognition. New York: Academic (1972)
9. Goar, F. ST., Pinto, F.J., Alderman, E.L., Fitzgerald, P.J., Stadius, M.L., Popp, R.L.: Intracoronary Ultrasound Imaging of Angiographically Normal Coronary Arteries: An In Vivo Comparison with Quantitative Angiography. Journal of the American College of Cardiology. **18** (1992) 979-987
10. Grenander, U.: General Pattern Theory: A Mathematical Study of Regular Structures. Oxford University Press. (1993)
11. Grenander, U., Miller, M.: Representation of Knowledge in Complex Systems. J. Royal Stat. Soc. **56** (1994) 1-33
12. Hyche, M., Ezquerra, N., Mullick, R.: Spatiotemporal Detection of Arterial Structure Using Active Contours. Proc. Visualization in Biomedical Computing. (1992) 52-62
13. Isner, J.M., Rosenfield, K., Losordo, D.W., Krishnaswamy, C.",: Clinical Experience with Intravascular Ultrasound as an Adjunct to Percutaneous Revascularization. Intravascular Ultrasound Imaging. Ed. J.M. Tobis ,P.G. Yock. Churchill Livingstone Inc.,New York (1992) 186-197
14. Ivins, J., Porril, J.: Active Region Models for Segmenting Medical Images. Proc. ICIP94 (1994) 227-231
15. Jain, A., Zhong, Y., Lakshmanan, S.: Object Matching Using Deformable Templates. IEEE Trans. PAMI. **18** (1996) 267-277
16. Kirby, M., Weisser, F., Dangelmayr, G.: A model problem in the representation of digital image sequences. Patter Recognition. **26** (1993) 63-73
17. Krishnaswamy, C., D'Adamo, A.J., Sehgal, C.M.: Three Dimensional Reconstruction of Intravascular Ultrasound Images. Intravascular Ultrasound Imaging. Ed. J.M. Tobis ,P.G. Yock. Churchill Livingstone Inc.,New York. (1992) 141-147
18. Lengyel, J., Greenberg, D.P., Popp, R.: Time-Dependent Three Dimensional Intravascular Ultrasound. Proc. SIGGRAPH'95. (1995) 457-464
19. Lengyel, J., Greenberg, D.P., Yeung, A., Alderman, E., Popp, R.: Three Dimensional Reconstruction and Volume Rendering of Intravascular Ultrasound Slices Imaged on a Curved Arterial Path. Proc. CVRMed'95. (1995)
20. Lipson, P., Yuille, A.L., OKeefe, D., Cavanaugh, J., Taafle, J., Rosenthal, D.: Deformable Templates for Feature Extraction from Medical Images. Proc. 1st European Conference on Computer Vision. (1990)
21. Moghaddam, B., Pentland, A.: Face Recognition using View-Based and Modular Eigenspaces. M.I.T. Technical Report No. 301. (1994)

22. Murase, H., Sakai, R.: Moving object recognition in eigenspace representation: gait analysis and lip reading. Patter Recognition Letters. **17** (1996) 155-162
23. Roedlandt, J.R., Di Mario, C., Pandian, N.G., Wenguang, L., Keane, L., Slager, C.J., De Feyter, P.J., Serrius, P.W.: Three Dimensional Reconstruction of Intracoronary Ultrasound Images. Circulation. **90** (1994) 1044-1055
24. Ronfard, R.: Region-Based Strategies for Active Contour Models. Int. Journal of Computer Vision. **13** (1994) 229-251
25. Rosenfield, K., Losordo, D.W., Ramaswamy, K., Pastore, J.O., Langevin, E., Razvi, S., Kosowski, B.D., Isner, J.M.: Three Dimensional Reconstruction of Human Coronary and Peripheral Arteries from Images Recorded During Two-Dimensional Intravascular Ultrasound Examination. Circulation. **84** (1991) 1938-1956
26. Xie, X., Sudhakar, R., Zhuang, H.: On Improving Eye Feature Extraction Using Deformable Templates. Pattern Recognition. **27** (1994) 791-799
27. Yock, P., Linker, D., Angelson, A.: Intravascular Ultrasound: Technical Development and Initial Clinical Experience. Journal of the American Society of Echocardiography. **2** (1989) 296-304
28. Yuille, A.L., Cohen, D.S., Halliman, P.W.: Feature Extraction from Faces Using Deformable Templates. Proc. CVPR. (1989) 104-109
29. Yuille, A.L.: Generalized Deformable Models, Statistical Physics and Matching Problems. Neural Computation. **2** (1990) 1-24
30. Yuille, A.L. Honda, K., Peterson, C.: Particle Tracking by Deformable Templates. Proc. International Joint Conference on Neural Networks. (1990)
31. Yuille, A.L., Halliman, P.W.: Active Vision. Ed. A.L. Yuille ,A. Blake. MIT Press. (1992) 21-38
32. Zhu, S.C., Yuille, A.L.: FORMS: A Flexible Object Recognition and Modelling System. Harvard Robotics Laboratory, TR No.94-1 (1994)

Motion Correspondence Through Energy Minimization

A.Branca, E.Stella, A.Distante

Istituto Elaborazione Segnali ed Immagini - C.N.R.
Via Amendola 166/5, 70126 Bari - ITALY
e-mail:[branca,stella,distante]@iesi.ba.cnr.it

Abstract. The main aim of this work is to define a general algorithm to solve the well-known motion correspondence problem by minimizing an energy function where constraints leading to solution are defined. Starting from some approximated correspondences, estimated for features with high directional variance using radiometric similarity, optimal correspondence are obtained through an optimization technique. The new contribution of this work consists in the matching process based on refinement of raw measurements, in the energy function minimization technique converging to an optimal solution by taking advantage from some good initial guess, and in the applicability in a lot of contexts requiring motion correspondence just combining appropriate constraints functions. The approach has been tested in two common contexts: **tracking of 3D coplanar points** and **passive navigation**.

1 Introduction

Motion correspondence is a fundamental problem in computer vision and many other disciplines. Recently there has been significant interest in the analysis of image sequences for purpose of estimating camera motion, 3D scene geometry, and 3D motion. Such analysis usually requires knowledge of frame-to-frame correspondences between measurements taken at different times but originated from the same geometric feature [1, 3, 4, 2, 5]. There are a number of reasons why motion correspondence is hard. Not all feature points in one image are visible in the other image. Occlusion or shading caused by the light source may hide or displace some of the feature points in the second image. Only a number of points in the first image may find a correct match in the second image. However, the best solution should satisfy the uniqueness constraints. Resolving these ambiguities is the essence of motion correspondence. Correspondence problem occur in a variety of diverse domains, for example, in psychology, where it is called perceptual grouping, in biological and computer vision, robotics, particle physics, molecular dynamics and target tracking where it is referred to as the data association problem.

In literature, two frameworks seem to approach the correspondence problem: direct and optimization methods. Both frameworks consider a low level stage in which 2D sparse robust features like edge pixels [41],[42], line segments [44], or curves [43] are extracted from images. Direct methods find correspondences

[46, 9, 45, 6, 7] using local constraints on features, often based on correlation of grey levels of patches centered on features extracted from considered images, assuming to be radiometric similarities.

Direct methods are fast, but more sensitive to noise; in contrast, the optimization based techniques are more reliable but have the drawback to require a burdensome processing.

The optimization methods [12, 11, 8, 13, 22, 23, 24, 10] use global constraints on features determined considering feature characteristics, such as uniqueness, ordering, disparity continuity, or using a-priori known properties about acquired scene (ex.: planar objects) or a-priori knowledge about the typology of the TV camera motion (ex.: predominant translational motion) to formulate an energy function to be minimized in order to estimate correspondences.

One approach to obtaining an optimal solution is to use parallel matching techniques such as graph matching [14] or relaxation techniques [16, 17, 15], where compatibility measures between matched features are used to find the best solution. One major problem with conventional graph matching techniques is the computational complexity involved in finding all possible configurations. In the case of relaxation technique the uniqueness constraint or any other constraint on the solution cannot be explicitly included in the algorithm. However, the matching problem can be formalized as minimization of a cost function (constrained optimization) where all the constraints on the solution can explicitly be included in a cost function. Minimization of cost function can then be performed by a distributed network such as a Hopfield network [25, 26, 12, 13, 18] or by stochastic optimization techniques such as a simulated anelling [12, 19].

The main problem of all such approaches is to require all features to be extracted a-priori from each image of the sequence independently. Optimal correspondences must be computed between the available features, consequently, due to errors in the selection of features, a lot of time is consumed in solving the combinatorial optimization problem. Moreover, techniques to eliminate all mismatches should be successively applied: only a subset of features are matched.

A more simple and general approach to solve the motion correspondence is proposed in the present work. Previous described problems are overcome by considering a fixed set of features only in the first frame of the sequence. Features in the second frame are selected as measurements satisfying some imposed constraints included in an appropriate energy functional. In other words, extraction of features in the second frame and match computation are considered a whole process consisting in an energy function minimization.

Synthetically, the approach consists in selection of high variance features in the first frame using the Moravec's interest operator [9] and computation of corresponding features in the second frame by correcting raw matches estimated through radiometric similarity minimizing a cost function.

In the following the approach with the minimization technique are first presented as a general tool (section 2), after the application in two different contexts (**tracking of 3D coplanar points** (section 3) and **passive navigation** (section 4)) is proposed by describing as the corresponding appropriate cost functions can be minimized with our method.

2 The Motion Correspondence Approach

Our aim is to describe a general approach to solve the motion correspondence problem through minimization of an energy functional combining appropriate constraint functions depending to the particular context to estimate optimal matches for features extracted only in the first frame of a sequence.

Displacement vectors are estimated only for features of "high" interest which are salient points that can be more easily matched than other points. These points generally occur at the corners and edges.

We propose to use the interest operator introduced by Moravec to isolate points with high directional variance [9]. The variance between neighboring pixels in *four* directions (vertical, horizontal and two diagonal) is computed over a window (the smallest value is called the interest operator value). Features are chosen where the interest measure has local maxima in windows of variable size.

Raw matches are computed maximizing the radiometric similarity between windows centered on first image high variance features and second image candidate features. Actually, since we compute correspondences between regions, false matches are unavoidable: the correct match point can mismatch the center of highest correlated window or several windows can have the same correlation. Matches computed through correlation can represent only an initial guess to improve through an optimization approach. Appropriate constraints must be imposed in order to verify the goodness of these matches and correct them.

2.1 Match Optimization

Optimization approaches are based on satisfaction of global constraints requiring given equations to be solved by N-dimensional variables representing subsets of N unknown measurements. Actually, we are dealing with a combinatorial optimization, requiring appropriate constraints to be satisfied by all N-dimensional combinations of the unknown measurements.

Solving combinatorial optimization problems is a difficult task due to the large number of involved variables, making the solution of an exponential complexity.

Combinatorial problems often are solved by combining corresponding constraint functions into an energy function consisting of the sum of all constraint function values obtained on all possible combinations of the unknown measurements.

In our context, unknown measurements are represented by features in the second image which are best matched to features extracted in the first image of the sequence, and the energy function to be minimized consists of the sum of the quadratic norm of constraint function estimated on feature subsets:

$$E = \sum_{n=0}^{N_S} \|C(S_n)\|^2 \tag{1}$$

where

- C is the considered constraint function;
- S_n is a subset of matches represented by pair of features extracted in the first image (p_i) through the interest operator of Moravec and the second image (q_i) initialized with the radiometric similarity;
- N_S is the number of considered subsets of matches;

We propose to perform the energy minimization by relaxation using the well known Steepset Descent Gradient (SDG).

Since the energy function E could not be convex, depending of the constraint function, the SDG could stop the minimization process in a local minimum. This problem could be resolved using alternative minimization technique, like Graduate Non Convexity algorithm proposed in [21]. However the result of minimization strongly depends from reliability of input data [20]. In fact, if some of initial matches estimated by the correlation are correct enough, the SDG is able to determine the global minimum of E.

In our case, some correct matches, a priori estimated through correlation in the match initialization step, satisfying the imposed constraint, will improve the optimization process. Once matches are initialized, they are refined by minimizing the norm (1). The norm E will be minimized only when its partial derivatives with respect to all features in the second image equal zero:

$$\frac{\partial E}{\partial q_i} = \sum_{n=0}^{N_S} \delta_{in} C(S_n) \frac{\partial C(S_n)}{\partial q_i} = 0 \tag{2}$$

where δ_{in} is a binary function assuming value 1 if the i-th feature is involved in a match of the n-th subset.

Satisfying the condition in (2) for each of the q_i then a system on $NFeat$ simultaneous equation in $NFeat$ unknowns is generated. Thus, the solution which minimize the squared norm of a difference-vector (1) amounts to find the set of points $\{q_i\}$ such that the equation (2) is solved. Since the system (2) is nonlinear we must use an iterative approach to compute optimal solution. Starting from some approximate matches, the algorithm improve the solution until a predetermined convergence criterion is satisfied. Due to the nonlinearity of the system more than one solution can exist. The success to reach a global minimum, and not be trapped in local minimum, depends on having a good first-guess for the solution. The algorithm will converge to an optimal solution if a number of input matches are quite correct. The goal is to reject the noise introduced by the correlation measurements.

The approach we propose converges through iteration upon the desired correspondence points $\{q_i\}$ by implementing gradient descent along the $E(q_i)$ surface, which expresses the quadratic cost function's dependency on all of the $\{q_i\}$ points.

Optimal correspondences are estimated by updating iteratively the initial corresponding second image features using the following updating rule:

$$q_i+ = \frac{\partial E}{\partial q_i}(1 - R_i) \tag{3}$$

where the $R_i \in [0,1]$ term, representing the radiometric similarity, has been introduced to avoid, in the cooperative process, bad matches to influence the correct ones. Correct measurements are not influenced from erroneous estimates, because the computed adapting signal control is zero due to the satisfaction of the imposed constraints. On the other hand, mismatches are influenced by correct matches determining the noise rejection.

3 Tracking of 3D Coplanar Points

A lot of applications of computer vision involve tracking of 3D coplanar points: video-based motion, medical image sequences, planar motion.

Tracking 3D coplanar points is a 2D-3D problem involving a 2D-2D tracking of image coordinates followed by a planar reconstruction requiring the computation of the perspectivity linking the 3D plane and the image plane as well as the computation of the projectivity maps points of two transformed images [27, 28].

In contexts where features to be matched are coplanar, the correspondence problem can be solved by minimizing the energy function (1) where the constraint function C is a projective geometric invariance function of coplanar points [29, 30, 31].

Five coplanar points $Q = (p_1, p_2, p_3, p_4, p_5)$ have the familiar **cross ratio** $CR(Q)$ as their projective invariant:

$$CR(Q) = \frac{sin(\alpha_{13}) * sin(\alpha_{24})}{sin(\alpha_{23}) * sin(\alpha_{14})} \tag{4}$$

where $sin(\alpha_{ij})$ is the sin of the angle $\widehat{p_i p_5 p_j}$.

Supposing all features are coplanar, for each subset of five coplanar points P_n in the first image the corresponding points in the second image Q_n should have the same cross ratio. The matches can be computed imposing the cross-ratio similarity should be satisfied for all subsets.

The global **cross ratio constraint** to be satisfied to solve the correspondence problem consists of the sum of all differences between the cross ratio computed for each subset of five features of the first image and the cross ratio computed for the corresponding points in the second image.

The energy function to be minimized to solve the correspondence problem is:

$$E = \sum_{n=1}^{N_S} ||CR(P_n) - CR(Q_n)||^2 \tag{5}$$

where $CR(P_n)$ is the cross ratio function defined in eq. 4 estimated in the first image, while $CR(Q_n)$ is the cross ratio estimated for the same points in the second image.

The corresponding partial derivative with respect to a feature q_i, which is used in the updating rule, is:

$$\forall i, \qquad \frac{\partial E}{\partial q_i} = \sum_{n=0}^{N_s} \delta_{in} \tag{6}$$
$$((CR(P_n) - CR(Q_n))\frac{\partial CR(Q_n)}{\partial q_i}$$
$$(1 - R_i))$$

where P_n and Q_n are respectively the nth subsets of five points from the first a second image, δi is a binary function assuming value 0 if the ith feature is in the subset P_n (or Q_n), N_S is the number of subsets which are considered, it is computed as:

$$N_S = \binom{Nfeat}{5} \tag{7}$$

3.1 Experimental Results

The approach has been tested on a number of image sequences with the aim to verify the ability of the algorithm to correct bad matches. Moreover, the algorithm is able to recover matches also for new features without initialization through correlation. The tests there reported are relative to two sequences (fig.(1) and fig.(2)). Other obtained experimental results and more accurate comments can be found in [29, 31]).

Figs. (1b) and (2b) show the energy function minimization.

4 Passive Navigation

Passive navigation [34] is the ability of an autonomous agent to determine its motion with respect to the environment.

In the context of vehicle navigation the most important goal is to recover the relative motion between the observer and the scene [35], in order to avoid collisions or to make on-line adjustments to the current navigational path. That the two main egomotion parameters, that allow to perform the above tasks, are the *Heading Direction* (FOE) and the *Time To Collision* (TTC).

In our application context the viewer can translate on a flat ground and rotate only around an axis orthogonal to the ground. The resulting 2D visual motion field has a radial topology: on the image plane all 2D velocity vectors radiate from a singular point (that is the point where the flow vanishes) named focus of expansion (FOE) that is a fixed point of the 2D motion field, which is geometrically defined as the intersection of the heading direction of the TV camera with the image plane.

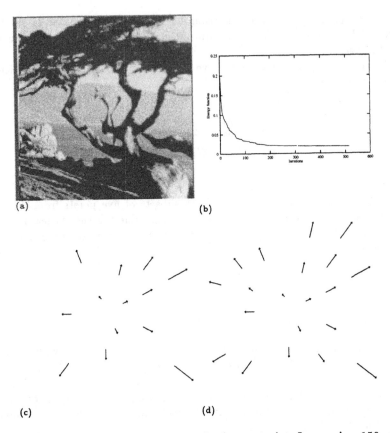

Fig. 1. Results obtained with the Cross-Ratio constraint. Image size: 150 × 150 pixels. (c) Flow estimated through correlation. Initial matched points: 13. (d) Flow estimated after minimization. Sparse points: 20.

In literature several methods have been proposed for FOE estimation, [33],[36], [37], [38],[39], [40]. Actually an accurate computation of FOE location from 2D motion field seems to be an hard problem, mainly due to digitization errors, unreliable flow vectors and image noise.

2D motion field computation and and FOE estimation can be considered as a whole optimization process solved by minimizing an appropriate cost function where constraints about flow radial shape are defined [32].

A radial flow is a map whose flow vector directions seems to radiate from a common center (FOE).

Let **i** and **j** be two flow vectors of the map and $\mathbf{P}_{ij}$ the image coordinates of the intersection point between the two straight lines representing the directions of each flow vector.

The **radial shape constraint** imposes the standard deviation of intersection points of all 2D displacement vector direction pairs from their average is zero.

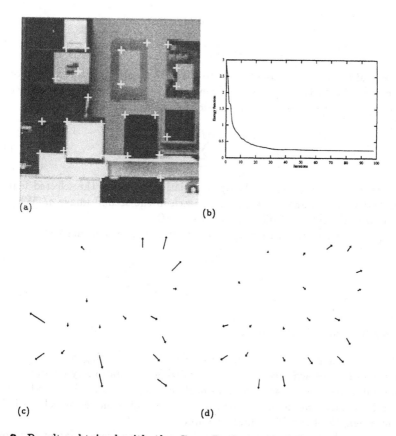

(a)

(b)

(c)

(d)

Fig. 2. Results obtained with the Cross-Ratio constraint. Image size: 120 × 120 pixels. (c)Flow estimated through correlation. Initial matched points: 18. (d)Flow obtained after minimization. Sparse points: 25.

The average of such intersection points represents the FOE when this constraint is satisfied.

Second image feature locations must be moved in order to minimize the distance between all intersection points by preserving always the radiometric similarity between matched features.

Supposing all intersection points P_{ij} have uniform probability distribution with mean

$$\mu = \sum_{i=1}^{Nfeat} \sum_{j=i+1}^{Nfeat} \frac{P_{ij}}{N_P} \tag{8}$$

where $N_P = \binom{Nfeat}{2}$ is the number of intersections generated by the directions of the $Nfeat$ available displacement vectors, and variance

$$\sigma^2 = \sum_{i=1}^{Nfeat} \sum_{j=i+1}^{Nfeat} (\mathbf{P_{ij}} - \mu)^2 \qquad (9)$$

The goal to obtain a radial map is to vary the displacement vectors in order to minimize the variance σ^2 of their generated intersections. So, the matching process can be formulated as minimization of the following cost function:

$$E = \sum_{i=1}^{Nfeat} \sum_{j=i+1}^{Nfeat} (\mathbf{P_{ij}} - \mu)^2 \qquad (10)$$

where S_i represents the similarity (correlation) between the selected feature in the first image p_i and the candidate match in the second image q_i. When E is minimized the mean μ will represent the FOE.

Its partial derivative with respect to points in the second image is

$$\frac{\partial E}{\partial q_i} = (1 - S_i) \sum_{j=1}^{Nfeat} (\mathbf{P_{ij}} - \mu)\frac{\partial \mathbf{P_{ij}}}{\partial q_i} = 0 \qquad (11)$$

4.1 Experimental Results

This application provides a method to estimate the heading direction from a sequence of images acquired by a vehicle moving in a stationary environment.

A set of experiments has been performed on images acquired in our laboratory with a TV camera mounted on a pan-tilt head installed on our vehicle SAURO. The focal length of the TV camera is 6mm.

In proposed experiments it is shown that even in the case of larger rotations, which shift the FOE location far away from the image plane, correct estimates can be recovered anywhere.

In figs. (3a-b) (4a-b) (5a-b) images of sequences acquired during a forward translational motion of SAURO are shown, and in figs. (3c) (4c) (5c) the corresponding optical are shown.

Figs. (3d) (4d) show the energy function minimization.

5 Conclusions

The paper proposes a novel technique to estimate a robust sparse correspondence map between features extracted from images acquired at different times. The approach is based on iterative refinements of matches initialized through correlation, by minimizing a cost function combining constraint functions leading to the solution in any particular motion correspondence context. The method is context-independent, it only requires to set appropriate constraint functions depending to the goals to be reached. Moreover, in this work two application contexts have been presented: tracking of coplanar points and passive navigation.

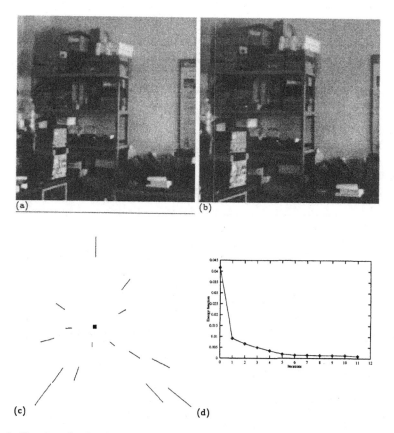

Fig. 3. Results obtained with the radial shape constraint. The images have been acquired while the vehicle is translating on a rectilinear path, the distance between the two frames is of 500mm. Estimated FOE: x=-10, y=15

References

1. L.Dreschler, H.Nagel "Volumetric model and 3D trajectory of a moving car derived from monocular TV frame sequences of a street scene" *Comput. Graphics Image Processing* Vol 20 pp 199-228(1982).
2. F.Glazer, G.Reynolds, P.Anandan "Scene matching by hierarchical correlation" *Proc. IEEE Conf. Comput. Vision Patt. Recogn.* (1983).
3. E.C.Hildreth *The measurement of visual motion* Cambridge MA:MIT Press (1983).
4. W.Hoff, N. Ahuja "Surfaces from stereo: Integrating feature matching, disparity estimation, and contour detection" *IEEE Transactions PAMI* Vol 11 No 2 (1989).
5. J.Weng, N.Ahuja, T.S.Huang "Matching two perspective views" *IEEE Transaction PAMI* Vol 14 No 8 (1992).
6. P.Fua, "Combining Stereo and Monocular Information to Compute Dense Depth Maps that Preserve Depth Discontinuities". In Proc. IJCAI91.
7. J.Martin and J.L.Crowley "Comparison of Correlation techniques" *Intelligent Autonomous Systems* U.Rembold et al. (Eds.), IOS Press, 1995.

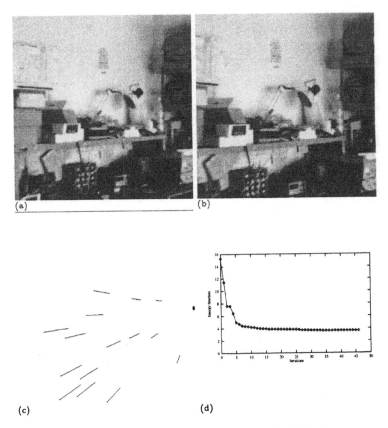

Fig. 4. Results obtained with the radial shape constraint. The images have been acquired while the vehicle is moving on a curvilinear path, the distance between the two frames is of 500mm, the rotation angle of 1 degree. Estimated FOE: x=126, y=-1

8. J.P.Pascual Starink, E. Backer *Finding point correspondences using simulated annealing*, Pattern Recognition, Vol.28,No.2,1995.

9. H.P.Moravec *The Stanford Cart and the CMU Rover*,Proc. IEEE,1983.

10. S. Ullman *The Interpretation of Visual Motion*, MIT Press,1979.

11. J. Clark and A. Yuille, *Data Fusion for sensory information processing systems*, Kluwer Academic Publishers, 1990

12. J.J.Lee,J.Chang,Y.Ho Ha, *Stereo Correspondence using the Hopfield Neural Network of a new energy function*, Pattern Recognition, Vol.27,No.11, 1994.

13. N. M. Nasrabadi, C.Y. Choo, *Hopfield Network for Stereo Vision Correspondence*, IEEE Trans. Neural Networks, Vol. 3, No. 1, pp. 5-13, 1992.

14. N.M. Nasrabadi and Y.Liu, "Stereo vision correspondence using a multichannel graph matching technique" *Image and Vision Computing* vol. 7, no.4, pp. 237-245, Nov. 1989

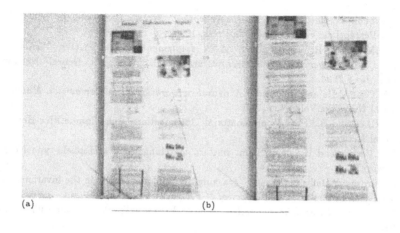

(a)   (b)

(c)

Fig. 5. Results obtained with the radial shape constraint. The images have been acquired while the vehicle is moving on a curvilinear path, the distance between the two frames is of 500mm, the rotation angle of 2 degrees. Estimated FOE: x=150, y=-2

15. N.M.Nasrabadi "A stereo vision technique using curve-segments and relaxiation matching" *IEEE Trans PAMI* vol. 13, Nov. 1991.

16. A.Rosenfeld, R.Hummel, and S.Zucker "Scene labeling by relaxtion operations" *IEEE Trans. Syst., Man, Cybern.* vol. SMC-6, pp 420-453, June 1976.

17. S.Barnard and W.Thompson "Disparity analysis of images" *IEEE trans. PAMI* vol.2, pp 333-340, July 1980.

18. J.Hopfield and D.W.Tank, " Neural computation of decisions in the optimization problems" *Biol. Cybern.* vol.52, pp 141-152, 1985.

19. S.Krikpatrick, C.D.Gellatt, Jr., and M.P.Vecchi, "Optimization by simulated anealling" *Science* vol. 220, no.4598, pp.671-680, May 1983.

20. O.Axelsson and V.A.Barker *Finite Element Solution of Boundary Value Problems: Theory and Computation*, Academic Press, 1984.

21. A.Blake and A.Zisserman *Visual Reconstruction*, MIT Press, 1987.

22. Y.T.Zhou, R. Chellappa, *A Neural Network for Motion Processing*, In Neural Network Perception, Vol. 1, Academic Press, 1992.

23. M.S.Mousavi, R. J. Schalkoff, *ANN Implementation od Stereo Vision Using a Multi-layer Feedback Architecture*, IEEE trans. on Neural Network, Vol.24,No.8,1994.

24. J.M.Cruz,G.Pajares,J.Aranda, *A neural network Model in stereovision Matching*, Neural Networks,Vol.8,No.5,1995.

25. B.W.Lee and B.J.Sheu "Combinatorial Optimization Using Competitive-Hopfield Neural Network"

26. D.R.Uecker and H.Sakou "Point pattern matching using a Hopfield-type Neural Network"

27. P.Gurdjos, P.Dalle, S.Castane "Tracking 3D Coplanar Points in the Invariant Perspective Coordinates Plane" *Proc. of ICPR'96* Vienna 1996.

28. O.Faugeras *Three Dimensional Computer Vision* MIT Press, Cambridge, MA, 1992.

29. A.Branca, E.Stella, A.Distante "Feature Matching by Optimization using Environmental Constraints " *Proc. of Time Varying Image Processing and Object Recognition* Firenze 1996.

30. A.Branca, E.Stella, G.Attolico, A.Distante "Stereo Matching by optimization using weak environmental constraints" *Proc. of SPIE96* Boston 1996.

31. A.Branca, E.Stella, A.Distante "Passive Navigation using Focus of Expansion" *Proc. of Workshop on applications of computer vision* Sarasota 1996.

32. A.Branca, G.Cicirelli, E.Stella, A.Distante "Mobile Vehicle's Egomotion Estimation from Time Varying Image Sequences " *Proc. of ICRA97* New Mexico 1996 (submitted).

33. R.C.Nelson, J.Aloimonos, *Obstacle Avoidance Using Flow Field Divergence*, IEEE Trans. on Patt. Anal. and Mach. Intell., VOL.11, NO. 10. Oct. '89.

34. C.Fermuller *Passive Navigation* Int. Journal of Computer Vision, 14(2):147-158, March 1995.

35. C.Fermuller *Qualitative egomotion* Int. Journal of Computer Vision, 15(1/2):7-29, 1995.

36. W. Burger, B. Bhanu, *Estimating 3D Egomotion from Perspective Image Sequences*, IEEE Trans. on PAMI, Vol. 12, No. 18,pp. 1040-1058, Nov. 1990.

37. E.De Micheli, V.Torre, S.Uras, *The accuracy of the computation of optical flow and of the recovery of motion parameters*, III Trans. on Patt. Anal. and Mach. Intell.,vol.15, n.5, May '93.

38. R.Hummel, V.Sundareswaran *Motion Parameter Estimation from Global Flow Field Data*, IEEE Trans. on Patt. Anal. and Mach. Intell., vol.15, no.5, May '93.

39. F.G.Meyer, *Time to collision from first-order models of the motion field*, IEEE Trans. on Rob. and Autom., VOL.10, NO. 6, Dec. '94

40. K. Prazdny, *Determining the Instantaneous Direction of Mo tion from Optical Flow Generated by a Curvilinearly Moving Observer*, CGIP, Vol. 17, pp. 238-248, 1981.

41. Y.Ohta and T.Kanade, "Stereo by Intr- and Inter-Scanline Search. *IEEE Trans. on Pat. Anal, and Mach. Intell.*,7,No.2:139-154,1985.

42. A.Meygret, M.Thonnat, and M.Berthold, "A pyramidal Stereovision Algorithm Based on Contour Chain points". In *Proc. European Conf. on Comp. Vision* Antibes, France, April 1990. Springer-Verlag.

43. L.Robert and O.D.Faugeras "Curve-based Stereo: Figural Continuity and Curvature" In CVPR91, 57-62.

548

44. N.Ayache and B.Faverjon, "Efficient Registration of Stereo Images by Matching Graph Descriptions of Edges Segments" *The Int. Journal of Comp. Vision* 1(2):107-131, April 1987.
45. D.Marr, T.Poggio, "A computational theory of human stereo vision", Proc. of Royal Society of London B, Vol.204.
46. N.Ayache, "Artificial Vision for Mobile Robots",MIT Press, 1991

Author Index

Lecture Notes in Computer Science

For information about Vols. 1–1147

please contact your bookseller or Springer-Verlag

Lecture Notes in Computer Science

This series reports new developments in computer science research and teaching, quickly, informally, and at a high level. The timeliness of a manuscript is more important than its form, which may be unfinished or tentative. The type of material considered for publication includes

– drafts of original papers or monographs,

– technical reports of high quality and broad interest,

– advanced-level lectures,

– reports of meetings, provided they are of exceptional interest and focused on a single topic.

Publication of Lecture Notes is intended as a service to the computer science community in that the publisher Springer-Verlag offers global distribution of documents which would otherwise have a restricted readership. Once published and copyrighted they can be cited in the scientific literature.

Manuscripts

Lecture Notes are printed by photo-offset from the master copy delivered in camera-ready form. Manuscripts should be no less than 100 and preferably no more than 500 pages of text. Authors of monographs and editors of proceedings volumes receive 50 free copies of their book. Manuscripts should be printed with a laser or other high-resolution printer onto white paper of reasonable quality. To ensure that the final photo-reduced pages are easily readable, please use one of the following formats:

Font size (points)	Printing area (cm)	(inches)	Final size (%)
10	12.2 x 19.3	4.8 x 7.6	100
12	15.3 x 24.2	6.0 x 9.5	80

On request the publisher will supply a leaflet with more detailed technical instructions or a T$_E$X macro package for the preparation of manuscripts.

Manuscripts should be sent to one of the series editors or directly to:

Springer-Verlag, Computer Science Editorial III, Tiergartenstr. 17, D-69121 Heidelberg, Germany

ISSN 0302-9743